D0881373

The Dominican Crisis

The Dominican Crisis
The 1965 Constitutionalist Revolt and American Intervention

Piero Gleijeses

translated by Lawrence Lipson

The Johns Hopkins University Press ● Baltimore and London

Originally published as *La Crise Dominicaine, 1965,* thesis no. 240 of the
University of Geneva, University Institute of Advanced International Studies,
by A.G. Battaia, Milan, 1973.

Manufactured in the United States of America

The Johns Hopkins University Press, Baltimore, Maryland 21218
The Johns Hopkins Press Ltd., London

Library of Congress Catalog Number 77-29253
ISBN 0-8018-2025-1

Library of Congress Cataloging in Publication data will be found
on the last printed page of this book.

To Letterina Gleijeses and Setsuko Ono

Contents

Acronyms

AP1J4 Agrupación Política 14 de Junio (Political Group 14th of June)

ASD Alianza Social Demócrata (Social Democratic Alliance)

BRUC Bloque Revolucionario Universitario Cristiano (Revolutionary Christian University Bloc)

CASC Confederación Autónoma de Sindicatos Cristianos (Federation of Christian Labor)

CEC Comité Ejecutivo Central (Central Executive Committee)

CECP Comité Ejecutivo Central Provisional (Provisional Central Executive Committee)

CEFA Centro de Entrenamiento de las Fuerzas Armadas (Armed Forces Training Center)

CONATRAL Confederación Nacional de Trabajadores Libres (National Federation of Free Workers)

FED Federación de Estudiantes Dominicanos (Federation of Dominican Students)

FOUPSA Frente Obrero Unido Pro-Sindicatos Autónomos (United Labor Front for Autonomous Unions)

GRN Gobierno de Reconstrucción Nacional (Government of National Reconstruction)

IAPF Inter-American Peace Force

ISZ International Security Zone

MAAG Military Advisory and Assistance Group

MPD Movimiento Popular Dominicano (The Dominican People's Movement)

MR1J4 Movimiento Revolucionario 14 de Junio (14th of June Revolutionary Group)

PAR Partido de Acción Revolucionaria (Revolutionary Action Party)

PDC Partido Demócrata Cristiano (Christian Democratic Party)

PLE Partido Liberal Evolucionista (Liberal Evolutionist Party)

PNRD Partido Nacionalista Revolucionario Democrático (National Revolutionary Democratic Party)

PPDC Partido Progresista Demócrata Cristiano (Progressive Christian Democratic Party)

PRD Partido Revolucionario Dominicano (Dominican Revolutionary Party)

PRDA Partido Revolucionario Dominicano Auténtico (Authentic Dominican Revolutionary Party)

PRSC Partido Revolucionario Social Cristiano (Social Christian Revolutionary Party)

PSP Partido Socialista Popular (Popular Socialist Party)

SIM Servicio de Inteligencia Militar (Military Intelligence Service)

UCN Unión Civica Nacional (National Civic Union)

VRD Vanguardia Revolucionaria Dominicana (Dominican Revolutionary Vanguard)

1J4 14 de Junio (14th of June)

Preface

On 24 April 1965, a military revolt shattered the uneasy peace of the Dominican Republic. This coup, however, was markedly different from those habitually plaguing Latin America.

The increasingly bitter civil conflict that ensued pitted Dominican "rebels" against their "loyalist" enemies, the putative defenders of "democracy." To Washington's relief, by the afternoon of the twenty-seventh the revolt seemed on the verge of collapse, and the following morning Dominican and American newspapers announced the rebels' defeat. Their judgment was premature, for in Santo Domingo—national capital and rebel stronghold—a "miracle" had already occurred: an armed populace had braved the tanks of the "loyalist" generals, throwing the adversary back toward his camp across the Ozama River. By the afternoon of the twenty-eighth it was clear that a rebel victory was inevitable, perhaps only hours away. At San Isidro, "loyalist" bastion, an American military attaché found the commanding officers in tears, panicky, urging "retreat." But tears and "retreat" were unnecessary. In response to the embassy's frantic cables, early in the evening of 28 April President Lyndon B. Johnson ordered the landing of marines in the Dominican Republic. Thus commenced the first overt American military intervention in the Western Hemisphere since Franklin D. Roosevelt's proclamation of the "Good Neighbor Policy" more than three decades before.

The American intervention marked the close of the first phase of the crisis, the "five glorious days" of 24-28 April during which the Dominican actors were largely left free to determine their destiny. The second phase—which did not end until the inauguration of a government of "conciliation" on 3 September—saw the oppressive presence of thousands of American troops and the confinement of the insurgents to a few square miles of downtown Santo Domingo. Throughout these long months the forlorn rebels stubbornly refused to acknowledge their defeat—a refusal both shocking and grating to the Johnson administration. But the administration's discomfiture did not endure for long. The "compromise" formula of a Provisional Government of conciliation was soon transformed into a quite definitive solution—the election of Joaquín Balaguer in June 1966. Balaguer has ruled the Republic ever since.

This intervention suddenly thrust a small, little-noticed Caribbean nation into the international spotlight. Abundant literature on the crisis has subsequently emerged, largely by American authors and primarily treating the

American side of events. Much of this literature is flawed, however, and led me to conclude that both the Dominican policy of the United States as well as internal Dominican events have been inadequately studied.

This inadequacy and my fascination with the crisis spurred the writing of this book, a substantially expanded and revised version of my Ph.D. dissertation. The end product is the result of close scrutiny of previous writings and the fruits of eighteen months of research conducted in the Dominican Republic between 1969 and 1975, where I was able to examine countless unpublished documents and to hold numerous lengthy interviews with key participants in the crisis. Wherever possible I have let the actors and documents speak for themselves; and when another author has lucidly stated that which I wish to express, I have quoted rather than paraphrased him. I believe this to be fairer to both that writer and the reader.

Since what happened in 1965 can be understood only in light of a larger historical background, the first part of this volume is devoted to the period before 24 April 1965, with special emphasis on the years between the death of Trujillo (30 May 1961) and the outbreak of the revolt nearly four years later. The first two appendixes—one covering the American role in Trujillo's assassination and the other tracing the evolution of the Dominican far left parties until early 1962—are best read following Chapters 1 and 2, respectively. The anatomy of the initial days of revolt—the first phase noted above—is the core of the second part of this study. One long chapter is then devoted to the revolt's other phase and to the inevitable outcome, the establishment of a government of "conciliation" that led to Balaguer's election in 1966.

I hope that this analysis and reconstruction of events will not only illumine the political evolution, in a particularly critical period (1961-65), of the Dominican Republic, but will also provide a useful case study of American foreign policy set against the broader background of the Latin American policy of the United States.

It is indeed a pleasant task to thank those who have supported me throughout the writing of this volume. Setsuko Ono, to whom it is fondly dedicated, spent long hours on each of the several drafts of the manuscript. A severe and brilliant critic, she has shared her scholarly skills and intelligence. Robert W. Tucker, my former professor and now colleague, merits an acknowledgment of gratitude as warm as our deep friendship. Ivelisse Prats-Ramírez de Pérez, Antonio Abreu Flores, Frank Moya Pons, "Chino," and Hugo Tolentino Dipp were at first simply persons I wanted to interview; they soon became good acquaintances, and then still more, dear and close friends. I cannot list all the other Dominicans who have helped me, as the list would be too long, but I can at least single out a few: Emilio Cordero Michel, María Elena Muñóz Marte, Emilio Rodríguez Demorizi, and Colonel Pedro Bartolomé Benoit.

Other individuals have assisted me, both in Washington and Geneva, where I studied for many happy years. Among my friends in Geneva, Carol Witzig,

Thierry Hentsch, Jacques Freymond, and Miklós Molnar occupy a special place. In Washington, Brewster C. Chamberlin went over the drafts of the English manuscript with characteristic skill and intelligence. Larman C. Wilson generously shared his deep knowledge and clear insights of the Dominican Republic. Herbert Dinerstein read the final draft of the manuscript, and his comments were always welcome and perceptive. Mary Ann Likar, my former research assistant, was a very valuable collaborator, performing difficult tasks with great ability and usually gracious forbearance. I am also indebted to Philip Geyelin of the *Washington Post* for a considerable number of previously unpublished documents relating to Johnson's Dominican policy.

Other friends and colleagues at The Johns Hopkins University have helped in different but always useful ways, among them Len Ackland, Frederico Canuto, Linda Carlson, Enzo Grilli, George Lawton, Edward Luttwak, William Stivers, and Edward Wiener. Dean Robert E. Osgood, warm and generous when I was a hungry student, has so remained now that I am an adequately fed professor.

When thanking other persons, it is customary for the author of a book to conclude that he alone bears responsibility for its mistakes. This I must do in regard to the translation of this book. Not only have I added directly in English considerable portions of this revised edition of a French manuscript, but I have, throughout the manuscript, introduced an important number of stylistical changes for which the translator, Mr. Lipson, has not been consulted. Therefore, while I thank him for his contribution, I consider it to be fair to both of us that I assume, on this matter too, full responsibility for the final product.

PIERO GLEIJESES

Washington, D.C.
October, 1977

The Dominican Crisis

Chapter 1

An Outline of Dominican History from "Discovery" to the Death of Trujillo (30 May 1961)

Hispaniola is an island in the middle of the Greater Antilles, between Cuba and Puerto Rico, too close to the United States, too far from the protective landmass of South America. On her northern shores break the waves of the Atlantic; to the south stretches the Caribbean Sea. It is a small island, yet two states divide the land: one of these, the Dominican Republic, occupies the eastern two-thirds of the territory—19,129 out of a total 29,979 square miles.

Hispaniola, "the island Columbus loved," was the first Spanish colony in the New World. On this land, the new lords built their first city, their first church, their first school. From this island Spanish power and influence spread over the Americas. But these were fleeting moments of greatness in a past that betrayed its promise. The natives were enslaved, massacred, and soon became extinct. Less than thirty years after the coming of the white man, the genocide was complete.[1] The African replaced the Indian and proved a tougher animal, surviving in pain in an alien land.

The Spanish had come searching for gold, conquest, easy riches, and glory; soon they moved on toward Mexico and Peru. Bereft of precious metals, Hispaniola was left to languish in the backwaters of Spanish America. She was, however, rich in livestock, fat from the lush vegetation of the island. But Spain's trade monopoly stifled the export of cowhides, driving the remaining colonists to massive smuggling. On 4 August 1603, Philip II, opposed to any relaxation of Spain's monopoly of the colony's trade and determined to halt the flourishing traffic in contraband, ordered the depopulation of the "guilty" regions. The towns in the north and the west were to be destroyed and the people removed to the southeast. The evacuation would be total: animals, slaves, everything that could be moved. The people resisted, but Governor Antonio de Osorio carried out the king's orders. He hanged insurgents, demolished property, tore up and burned the towns. All the inhabitants were removed from the "guilty" regions and forbidden ever to return under penalty of death. Thus Spain abandoned half the island, and dealt a death blow to the economy of Hispaniola.

The seventeenth century witnessed the decline of Spanish power, both in Europe and the New World. In the Caribbean, Spanish control weakened under the onslaught of its European rivals. Coming from the neighboring island of Tortuga, the French slowly infiltrated the western part of Hispaniola, now depopulated, but still rich in wild livestock. The first intruders were buccaneers,

1

but close behind them loomed the shadow of French power: the France of Richelieu and of Colbert.

The French established the colony of Saint-Domingue on the western coast of Hispaniola. Spain proved too weak and too indifferent to the value of the island to halt the steady advance of the French. A century of border skirmishes followed, intermingled with periods of peace. In 1777 by the Treaty of Aranjuez, Spain officially acknowledged the French conquest. The division of the island was now final.

Thus, on the eve of the French Revolution, two strikingly different economic systems coexisted in Hispaniola. In the western third of the island was Saint-Domingue, the richest colony in the world. Massive capital investments and a vast concentration of slave labor had made it the world's leading producer of coffee and sugar and a major exporter of cotton and indigo. Comprising more than 40 percent of the foreign trade of France, the colony's exports gave life to the economies of such ports as Bordeaux, Nantes, Marseille, La Rochelle, Rouen, and Le Havre, and provided the chief economic base for the French maritime bourgeoisie.

In 1789 about 520,000 persons lived in an area of less than ten thousand square miles: 40,000 whites, 28,000 freedmen (mostly mulattoes), and 452,000 slaves.[2] Ruthlessly exploited for the greater profit of their masters and the French maritime bourgeoisie, the slaves died by the thousands—but more were imported, 30,000 in 1788 alone.

This then was Saint-Domingue, jewel and pride of France, which had overshadowed Jamaica and the other British Antilles in the sugar markets of the world and in the misery of its slaves.

On the other side of the island lay Spanish Santo Domingo. For this colony, the century that followed the *despoblaciones* was one of poignant misery. Neglected by Spain, it cowered under the constant threat of French intruders and the pirates who infested the Caribbean Sea. It was a rare ship that braved the dangerous waters to reach such a modest colony. The inhabitants were thus deprived of an outlet for their potential exports—cowhides above all. It became a vicious circle, for failure to export meant inability to import, further reducing the number of ships that ventured to Santo Domingo.[3]

There was autarchy, then, and abject poverty. Historian Frank Moya Pons has described how many inhabitants fled to the countryside, hoping to escape hunger. Others, impoverished members of the colonial "elite," also chose a lonely life, away from the towns, to hide the opprobrium of their ragged clothes.[4]

Finally, in the second half of the eighteenth century, the colony experienced a period of revival. This prosperity was relative, however, and paled before the astonishing growth of Saint-Domingue. The economy and the social order continued to be based on cattle, as had been the case for over two hundred years. But now at least there was a market for these cattle, thanks not to Spain, but to the historical enemy, the French colonists. Border skirmishes increasingly gave way to an illegal but tolerated trade. Saint-Domingue produced the great commercial staples for world markets (sugar, coffee, cotton, indigo); Santo Domingo helped to satisfy the increasing needs of its great neighbor through exports of cattle, horses, some tobacco, and wood.

The diverse economies of the two colonies resulted in dissimilar population patterns. Twice the size of its neighbor, by 1789 Santo Domingo had only one-fifth the population, about 103,000 inhabitants. The Spanish colony had 35,000 whites and 28,000 freedmen as against the 40,000 whites and 38,000 freedmen in Saint-Domingue. But in the number of slaves, the contrast was dramatic: in 1789 there were at most 30,000 slaves in Santo Domingo compared with 452,000 in the neighboring colony.[5]

The modest prosperity of Santo Domingo did not last. In Europe the French Revolution shook the pillars of a tottering civilization. Sparks from the conflagration soon reached Hispaniola. Saint-Domingue was the first to explode. The free mulattoes demanded political and social equality with the whites. The latter refused, and a rebellion led by Vincent Ogé and Jean-Baptiste Chavanne broke out. The uprising was ruthlessly crushed. On 9 March 1790, in the town of Le Cap, Ogé and Chavanne had their arms, legs, and elbows broken on a scaffold, then they were bound on wheels, "their faces turned to the sky, to remain thus while it pleased God to keep them alive."[6] Even in death the racial division was maintained. They were tortured and died on the side of the square opposite to where whites were executed.

But the white terror failed to stifle hopes nourished by the rhetoric of the French Revolution. Other mulattoes—Beauvais, Rigaud, Pinchinat—took up the standard of revolt. While whites and mulattoes fought, below them—in the pit of hell—the mass of black slaves began to stir, rising up and breaking out in fury:

> On the night of 14 August 1791, a crowd of blacks, delegates from the neighboring plantations, gathered in a clearing in the Bois Caïman. . . . During a ceremony only vaguely preserved in memory, a slave named Bouckman got the assembly to swear in blood to fight to the death for their freedom and the freedom of their brothers. . . . On the night of 16 August, a revolt erupted, with the slaves setting fire to the Chabaud plantation and murdering their white masters. . . . By 30 September, a thousand whites had been massacred, twelve hundred coffee plantations destroyed, and two hundred sugar plantations burned down.[7]

The masters met the violence of the slaves with ruthless terror. A merciless war had begun that would rage for twelve years. It was at once a social war, slave against slaveholder; a racial war, black against white;[8] and a war of national liberation. To achieve their freedom the former slaves had to defeat in turn the French, the Spanish, and the British armies. This they did, and in 1804 the first independent republic of Latin America was born: Haiti.

The Spanish colony could not escape the chaos that engulfed Saint-Domingue. "Dominican history was about to undergo a period of rapid change, a victim

of the events unleashed in Europe by the French revolution and in the island by
the revolution in Haiti . . . and from this period of change the people emerged
exhausted and on the verge of extinction."[9]

Even before 1801, when war reached Santo Domingo, the economy had
started to decline. Dominican prosperity rested on exports to the French colony,
but the chaos in Saint-Domingue disrupted this vital commerce. Cut off from its
most important market, the Dominican economy was doomed.

And before war reached Santo Domingo, the whites had begun to abandon
a territory that was too close to the Haitian inferno. This exodus had started
during the last months of 1795, when news of the Peace of Basel reached Santo
Domingo. By the terms of the treaty, the colonists, who were slaveholders, came
under the dominion of France, which on 4 February 1794 had abolished slavery
in all its colonies. But the French, threatened by the European monarchs, were
not in a position to occupy the new colony. Thus ensued a bizarre entr'acte in
the Dominican drama: Santo Domingo was French de jure, Spanish de facto—
and committed to slavery. Suddenly on 4 January 1801 the entr'acte was cut
short. Coming from Haiti, Toussaint L'Ouverture, a black and a former slave, invaded Dominican territory with an army of men who, like him, had been slaves.
In panic, thousands of colonists fled to the nearest points of the Spanish empire:
Puerto Rico, Maracaibo, Caracas.

Beginning in 1802, and for seven long years, French, Spanish, and Haitian
troops fought each other on Dominican soil in intermittent but destructive wars.
Meanwhile, the British fleet bombarded the colony's ports and thousands of
colonists fled the country, many with their slaves. Slavery was abolished during
the brief Haitian occupations (Toussaint in 1801, Dessalines in 1804-5), only to
be immediately restored with the return of "European civilization"—be it
French or Spanish. In this squalid drama Napoleon Bonaparte made his mark by
restoring slavery throughout the French empire, bringing havoc to Haiti.

In 1808 the "Dominicans"[10] revolted against the French, the uneasy masters of the colony since 1804. Napoleon had invaded Spain and placed his
brother on the throne of the Bourbons—a betrayal that exasperated many in
Santo Domingo. But equally grave was the decision of General Louis Ferrand,
the colony's governor, to stop the newly reopened trade with Haiti. This decision damaged too many powerful interests, and the *hateros* (cattle owners)
rose in revolt.

For a year war raged anew, devastating Santo Domingo, where the British
fleet and a few hundred Spanish soldiers from Puerto Rico supported the rebels.
Once again chaos reigned, and once again many fled the colony. Finally, by August 1809, with the defeat of the French and the departure of the British, the
Dominicans seemed at last in control of their own country. Winds of revolt were
stirring in South America, but the oldest colony of the New World had lost the
pulse of history. No Dominican cried for independence—Santo Domingo placed
itself once again under Spanish rule.

And so the Spanish returned, to find a country devastated by years of war, its agriculture in shambles and its cattle decimated. The Dominicans now expected that a grateful mother country would shoulder the burden of economic recovery. They forgot that Spain had never been more than a stepmother and was now nearly as destitute as Santo Domingo, fighting on her own soil a desperate war against French invaders.

Bitterly, Dominican historians have called the next twelve years of Spanish rule (1809-21) the period of "Stupid Spain" (*España Boba*). They have accused the governors that Spain sent to the island, first Carlos Urrutia and then Sebastián Kindelán y Oregón, of gross incompetence and corruption. Urrutia and Kindelán y Oregón were not bad administrators, but their task was hopeless.[11] After the defeat of Napoleon, Spain exhausted its limited resources in a vain effort to subjugate its rebel colonies in South America. Thus it was unable to provide the vast sums of money necessary for the economic recovery of Santo Domingo; it was unwilling, moreover, to allocate even the smaller sums that were necessary to cover the administrative expenses. Deaf to the constant pleas of Urrutia and Kindelán y Oregón, the Spanish government considered Santo Domingo too modest and too faithful a colony to warrant any attention.

So Santo Domingo continued in abject misery. By 1821, it was, in the words of Juan Bosch, "the seat of poverty, the image of a backward country. There were no schools . . . no funds for public spending. . . . Towns fell in ruin, roads were overgrown with brush, and . . . the population eked out an existence in the mountains and valleys."[12] In 1789 the colony had 120,000 inhabitants; now only 60,000 remained—the others had either emigrated or died.

Not only was Spain bankrupt and discredited, but her military weakness became increasingly obvious. Since the battle of Boyacá in Colombia (1819), the tide in northern South America had turned against the Spaniards, and Bolívar scored success upon success. In the summer of 1821, Spanish rule in Mexico collapsed without resistance; the few troops in Santo Domingo, unpaid and in rags, constituted one more proof of Spain's poverty. The outcome was inevitable: no one stepped forward in the name of Spain when a group of *hateros* and government officials, led by José Núñez de Cáceres, arrested the governor and proclaimed the independence of the colony on 1 December 1821.

The new republic was stillborn. The *hateros* refused social change. Theirs was a world of master and slave and racial inequality. The blacks and mulattoes received this vision of society with indifference, at best, while many looked westward toward Haiti. In January 1822, the Haitian president Jean-Pierre Boyer led his troops across the border; on 9 February they entered Santo Domingo unopposed.

The *hateros* and their friends recognized Haiti's military might and the unpopularity of their own cause. "Núñez de Cáceres knew that the majority of the Dominican population was colored and favored annexation to Haiti."[13] Thus, the whites chose not to fight. Many fled the country; those who remained submitted. The majority of the population welcomed the invaders with "demonstrations of support. Wherever he went, Boyer was met by throngs of sympathizers."[14] For the slaves, the invasion meant freedom; for the freedmen, whose color made them outcasts, it brought the promise of equality.

The Haitian occupation of Santo Domingo had begun; it would last twenty-two years.

Many scholars in the United States have lashed out against what they have called "Haiti's cruel and barbarous" rule,[15] seeing in it "the fundamental cause for the conditions of anarchy, unrest, and civil disturbance which have existed almost continuously from the liberation of the Dominican Republic from Haiti in 1844 until the American Military Occupation in 1916. . . . [It was] a tyranny which had for its chief object not only the eradication of the Caucasian race but also the obliteration of all the foundations of European culture and civilization upon which the institutions of the American world have been builded [sic]."[16] Victims of their own prejudices or of intellectual sloth, too many writers have refused to see that in Hispaniola "European culture and civilization" were responsible for the death of a people, slavery, racism, a hateful caste system, a contempt for work, a debilitating parasitism, the ruin of a once-rich land: in short, all that turns "culture and civilization" into a farce.[17] These same writers forget that it was the Haitian Boyer who ended slavery on Dominican soil once and for all—the slavery that another Haitian, Toussaint, had previously abolished, but that France had reestablished and Spain had kept in force; slavery, the sacred institution unchanged by Núñez de Cáceres, the "hero" of 1821. Some authors have even indignantly accused the Haitians of disrupting the economy of Santo Domingo. They forget, of course, that the *relative* prosperity of the second half of the eighteenth century had collapsed well before Boyer's invasion, and that it was a destitute country the Haitians found in 1822. And they forget the drama of Haiti, ravaged by constant wars in the 1790s. Only in 1798 did the British depart in defeat. A few months later Toussaint L'Ouverture, the great Haitian liberator, crushed André Rigaud, leader of the mulattoes, and launched his country on a valiant and successful effort at economic recovery. Then came the French invasion in February 1802.

Again it was war, and again the French spread ruin, chaos, and horror, until they departed in shame, defeated, in November 1803.

France had failed to enslave Haiti, but French "honor" demanded that its former slaves pay a large indemnity and give heavy trade concessions in order to be granted the independence they had won on the battlefields.

Twice, in 1815 and 1816, Haiti offered refuge to Simón Bolívar, *El Libertador,* who was then an impoverished exile. At a time when the cause of independence in Spanish America seemed lost, when the Spaniards scored success upon success, Haiti alone offered help and the means to start the struggle anew. A grateful Simón Bolívar wrote to his benefactor, Alexandre Pétion: "Haiti will not remain isolated among her sisters. Haitian ideals will influence all the countries of the New World."[18] This was, however, in 1816. In 1825, Bolívar was no longer a refugee, but a great hero at the peak of his glory. He betrayed his debt to Haiti and joined the *criollo* elites who shunned the only country of Latin America that had fought for something more than a shallow independence. Faced with the constant threat of French invasion, of blockade, of bombardment of its ports, Haiti stood alone, the pariah of the hemisphere. It had no choice but to submit to French extortion. In July 1825, it agreed to pay the indemnity and to grant the trade concessions. This was a crushing burden which Santo Domingo, by then a part of Haiti, would have to share. It aggravated the economic life of the island and created resentment among the people of Santo Domingo. Yet this resentment was not directed at those who were guilty, the French, but at their victims, the Haitians.

For many years, Dominican historians joined ignorant and biased foreigners in presenting a distorted picture of the period. Breaking with this unjust tradition, a new and more serious trend has appeared in recent years in Dominican historiography.[19] While much research remains to be done, it is now evident that Santo Domingo experienced under Haitian rule a period of relative economic recovery in spite of the crushing financial burden imposed on the island by French rapacity and the many mistakes made by the Haitian government. A certain level of prosperity was reached, and this in turn fostered the growth of a middle class—a petty bourgeoisie of merchants, professionals, sawmill owners (in the south, Banda del Sur), and tobacco growers (in the central region, Cibao).

But for Santo Domingo, the Haitian occupation meant more than an incipient economic recovery. In 1820, when the colony still belonged to Spain, its governor, Sebastián Kindelán y Oregón, made a point of addressing the "Most Loyal Natives and Inhabitants of Hispaniola." He wanted to dissipate the "dangerous ideas" which certain "troubled and rebellious spirits spread among the gullible" through an "erroneous interpretation" of the restored constitution of 1812. "You know full well," declared His Excellency, "that our people is made up of a variety of colors and conditions—whites, mulattoes, blacks—and in these last two classes there are both freedmen and slaves." Although "the benefits of the Constitution are many . . . *this does not mean that the slave can become free, nor that the freedman can suddenly become equal to the white man.*"[20]

This was the message of a spokesman for the new Spain, which, "liberal and thirsting for liberty," had just ended the absolute rule of Ferdinand VII. Yet nineteen months later the Haitians invaded Dominican soil, and under their "cruel and barbarous" administration the slave became free, and the colored suddenly became the equal of the white man. Hence the cry of pain from Sumner Welles over the "eradication of the Caucasian race" and the "obliteration of all the foundations of European culture and civilization."

By 1844, when the territory seceded from Haiti and became the Dominican Republic, a point of no return had been reached. The whites who had stayed and those who returned once the Haitians were gone still clung to the notion of belonging to a superior caste. But they had to learn to live with former slaves and freedmen. Most of the men who were to shape Dominican history were colored. Francisco del Rosario Sánchez—a "father of the Republic"—was a mulatto, as was Buenaventura Báez, a slave's son who served five terms as president. Gregorio Luperón and Ulises Heureaux were blacks. And Rafael Trujillo Molina was a mulatto, despite all his attempts to "whiten" himself.[21]

The nascent middle class led the struggle against Haitian domination. On 16 July 1838, young Juan Pablo Duarte founded La Trinitaria, a secret society that had as its primary objective the establishment of an independent state—the "Dominican Republic." On 27 February 1844, a revolt broke out, led by Duarte's friends, Francisco del Rosario Sánchez and Ramón Mella (Duarte was in exile). Within a few days the entire country had rallied to the cause, while the Haitian regime crumbled without resistance. But the petty bourgeoisie of Duarte and his friends was too weak to assume the direction of the country they had brought to independence. This weakness became painfully apparent when, in mid-March, the Haitian army of President Charles Hérard invaded the territory of the new Republic.

Forced to ally with the traditional powerholders—the *hateros*—the petty bourgeoisie sealed its own fate. The *hateros* and their associates soon held a majority in the Junta Central Gubernativa, the provisional government of the new state. Pedro Santana, an *hatero*, was named commander of the troops mustered to halt the Haitians, and Tomás Bobadilla, his confederate, became the Junta's president.[22] Collaboration between the two groups quickly dissolved. The "fathers of the Republic"—Duarte, Sánchez, and Mella—were branded "traitors to the Republic" and driven into exile. Meanwhile, the Dominican Congress was forced to grant Pedro Santana not only the presidency of the Republic but also the dictatorial powers he demanded.

The petty bourgeoisie had lost. Conservative by today's standards, it nevertheless stood for the forces of progress at the time. The *hateros* prevailed, and the Dominican people were about to be engulfed in a new period of troubles.

From 1844 to 1916, the country was torn by a series of internal struggles. There were many contenders for power, all claiming to be "generals." Each had his wretched army of tattered and starving peasants who followed their leader, fought, and died. At times a strong man emerged and laid his rivals low. Peace was restored "his" way: by dictatorship. Sooner or later "liberators" appeared and eliminated the tyrant, then fought among themselves to take his place. War or peace, anarchy or tyranny, for the Dominican people it was a tragedy without end.

This was an anguished history, but hardly uncommon. Civil wars, ambitious and corrupt *caudillos*, exploitation, and misery: such seemed to be the destiny that no Latin American country could escape. Two factors intervened, however, to break this "monotony," as if to exalt the agonizing originality of "the land Columbus loved."

First was the Haitian threat. For twelve years, from 1844 to 1855, Haitian armies repeatedly violated Dominican boundaries they refused to acknowledge: the island had to be "one and indivisible." At stake were not a few acres of land, but the sovereign right of a people to determine its own destiny. Again and again the Dominicans showed their determination to defend that right. Again and again they drove back the invaders in heady but costly victories. In a country scant of men, the cost in human life was high. The nation paid a further price in the effort expended and the sacrifices exacted for survival. During those years, every Dominican of military age joined in the struggle against the Haitian invader, and the economy suffered in all areas, particularly in agriculture.

So the Haitian threat met with Dominican resistance, and suffering and loss resulted. Why, then, did the Dominicans give up their hard-won independence, especially since, by 1859, the threat from Haiti was already on the wane?

The Haitian threat developed alongside an even greater menace from within. Two men—Buenaventura Báez and Pedro Santana—dominated the life of the Republic during its first seventeen years (1844-61). They vied for power and succeeded each other in office with monotonous regularity.[23] They shared the same program: satisfying their own greed and the needs of their cronies. For this, they were ready to despoil the country of its few remaining riches. They called themselves Dominicans, but for them "the Dominicans were objects, not people: cattle to be auctioned off, not a society of human beings with aspirations—however vague—as a nation."[24]

Santana and Báez realized how insecure their power was. They knew that a pack of ambitious aspirants was only too ready to contest their property rights. Rather than risk being "expropriated," they chose to sell. They undertook an extensive search for a buyer, "offering the nation to the highest bidder . . . to any buyer interested, and even . . . to parties not in the market to buy."[25] They wanted a "good price," but above all they wanted a new master who would retain them as "administrators." In this way they could reap the benefits of power while escaping its responsibilities.

Báez, president of the Republic five times, "engaged in a lifelong business—the securing of a foreign protectorate which would insure his own perpetuation close to the moneybags."[26] Santana, president three times, "devoted his life to the cause of annexation. All his energies worked to that end, and he never faltered. . . . He constantly denied all national values and undermined the Dominican people as an independent, enduring society."[27]

Under such conditions, it is remarkable that the country was able to retain its independence for seventeen years. This was possible only because of the indifference, or at times the rivalry, of the countries solicited by the two *caudillos*: France, Spain, England, and the United States.

Spurred by a rebellion that threatened his power, in 1861 Santana finally succeeded in selling the country to Spain. Civil war in the United States and the dreams of grandeur of the O'Donnell government in Madrid had rekindled Spanish ambitions. Santana had reason to believe that he had made a good deal. He was named captain-general and civil governor of the new colony, and his long-time friends Antonio Abad Alfau, Tomás Bobadilla, and Jacinto de Castro received high positions: Abad Alfau became field marshal, Bobadilla and de Castro, justices of the Royal Court. The case is unique in Latin American history: an independent country voluntarily renouncing independence to subject itself to the former colonial metropolis.[28]

The Dominican people had returned to Spanish rule only because they had been forced to do so. Spain was as incompetent as ever. In 1863 a revolt against the Spanish erupted and two years later this war of *restauración* ended with the definitive departure of the Spanish.

The Dominican Republic was independent again. Its economy was even more wretched than in 1861, for the violence of the war had been severe, but the country was "richer" by several dozen new "patriotic" and "enlightened" generals. During the revolt they had squabbled over the division of spoils—the Republic itself—even though the country was not yet in their clutches. They fought and on occasion killed each other.[29] With the Spanish gone and everything back "in the family," the generals fought with a vengeance: General Pedro Pimentel, named president on 25 March 1865, was toppled a few weeks later by General José María Cabral. Then General Pedro Guillermo ousted Cabral and on 8 December installed Báez, the man "who in the fateful hour of annexation had accepted the sash of field marshal from Spain and pledged to do his utmost 'to pacify the Colony.' "[30] Next General Gregorio Luperón, a relentless foe of the new strong man, entered the fray at Puerto Plata. The uprising failed, but others followed: in Azua, in San Cristóbal, in Santiago, in the south. Báez had had enough. He left the country on 28 May 1866. Before his departure, however, he indulged his favorite pastime: the sale of a piece of Dominican territory—in this case, the strategic peninsula of Samaná. The United States showed interest, but was too slow to keep pace with the dynamic Dominican generals. Báez was gone before he had time to conclude the deal.

Thus, within a year three presidents had come and gone: Pimentel, Cabral, and Báez. The sad procession marched on, as generals solemnly ascended the steps of the Presidential Palace, only to descend them a few months later in haste. Some coups succeeded, others failed. Riots, mutinies, uprisings, and revolts, a jumble of juntas, triumvirates, and rigged elections filled these years. While the *caudillos* struggled for the same aim—control of the nation's revenues—the nation itself presented a sorry spectacle of infinite desolation. Commerce was in ruin and agriculture in shambles. The country's fledgling industries lay prostrate, the courts were in disarray, and the schools were neglected.

In December 1879, in the wake of a successful revolt, General Luperón became the provisional president of the Republic. After introducing several needed reforms, he bowed out in September 1880 before a constitutionally elected president, Father Fernando A. de Meriño, in the first peaceful transfer of power since the overthrow of Spanish rule in 1865. Meriño pursued and broadened

Luperón's program of reforms, while Luperón's most brilliant lieutenant, the black general Ulises Heureaux, swiftly neutralized the opposition by putting a tight rein on any general eager for a fling at power. When Meriño's term expired in 1882, Heureaux was chosen as his successor. "A man of the people, bursting with talent and energy,"[31] Heureaux rose to power on a wave of social and economic progress, but by the mid-1880s he had succumbed to the temptations of dictatorship. His rule proved brutal and corrupt. He used the state's money to enrich his friends and buy off potential rivals. At the same time, however, he assured the country of a period of relative political stability. Indeed, this stability was the keynote of the last two decades of the century, in dramatic contrast to the first period of independence. In turn, it permitted economic growth. The absence of anarchy made the Republic attractive to numerous Cuban sugar planters, who fled their country during its first war of independence (the "Ten Years War," 1868-78). They brought with them the skills and money the Dominican Republic lacked and gave impetus to the cultivation of sugar cane. Some were extremely successful. Their success, the political stability of the country, and the favorable attitude of the Heureaux government attracted other foreigners, especially North American entrepreneurs, Europeans, and Puerto Ricans. Supported by favorable international prices, a sugar boom began, although it was modest in comparison to that of the first quarter of the next century. The profits made in sugar were used to develop other activities, such as coffee, cacao, tropical fruit (chiefly banana) cultivation, and, in the 1890s, modern cattle farming. In turn, the economic development of this period provided the conditions for the emergence of a powerful socioeconomic elite. This *gente de primera* combined a small number of socially prominent Dominican families (whose prestige had been based more on their Spanish colonial origin than on their economic position or political influence) with a group of recent immigrants who were both economically successful and socially acceptable. For both groups, a decisive requisite for social status was whiteness of skin.

Heureaux's assassination on 26 July 1899 marked the beginning of a new series of political convulsions. In 1906 it looked as if President Ramón Cáceres might succeed in bringing a bit of calm and prosperity to the land, yet five years later another assassin's hand opened the gates to anarchy.

The Republic was in its death throes. During the first seventeen years of its existence it had struggled to survive the near-fatal blows of Báez and Santana. Betrayed in 1861, the country recovered its independence four years later. Santana had died in 1864, but Báez remained, still attempting to sell or rent Samaná Bay to the United States. He failed in 1866, but his successor, General José María Cabral, renewed the project. Two years later Báez was back in power, and this time he attempted a masterstroke, an exploit even Santana would have been proud of. He tried to negotiate the annexation of the Republic to the United States. In exchange the latter would "advance" the sum of $1,500,000 "to liquidate the Dominican public debt" and "remit forthwith to the Dominican government the sum of . . . $150,000, one hundred thousand dollars to be in cash, and fifty thousand in arms, for the purpose of defraying the unavoidable expenses of the State."[32] Only the opposition of the U.S. Senate thwarted the deal and prevented an annexation for which Báez, with his persuasive methods, had already won the "enthusiastic" support of the Dominican people in a rigged referendum (sixteen thousand votes to eleven). Undaunted by Báez's failure, other Dominican leaders would follow his example. Heureaux, for one, strove with almost pathetic insistence throughout his presidency to revive the Samaná deal.

Beginning in 1869, however, Dominican presidents devised a new system for enriching themselves. Since the resources of the country were inadequate, they would borrow from abroad. Loans were negotiated at exorbitant discounts, but the harsh conditions mattered little to the borrowers. Their motto might well have been: Money today, *mañana* we pay—and "in the long run we are all dead."

Again, Báez set the precedent. In 1869, during his fourth presidency, he borrowed £420,000 from the British company Hartmont, on extremely onerous terms.[33] Later, in 1888, Heureaux negotiated a loan with the Dutch company Westendorp that was equally exacting. Two years later he arranged for another loan from the same company. The country was crushed by these debts. Nevertheless, for unscrupulous men, the Republic offered easy pickings. The vultures—and there were many—flocked to the feast. In 1892, the Santo Domingo Improvement Company of New York joined the crowd, buying out Westendorp. Five years later, despite clear evidence that the government of Heureaux was a poor risk, the company floated a new issue. There was a reason:

> When it floated bond issues, the company seems to have paid the Dominican government from 30 to 43 percent of the face value of the securities. It then sold the bonds to investors, mostly in Belgium and France, at such prices as it could obtain. A considerable proportion of the proceeds was always mysteriously absorbed in the expense of the operation. . . . The success of such operations depended, of course, on finding gullible investors.[34]

Financial collapse ensued. The Republic was bankrupt, and political chaos was imminent. With Heureaux gone, coup followed upon coup in rapid succession. It was as if the *caudillos*, sensing the Republic's impending demise, became frenzied in their attempts to seize power. There was still profit to be had, and they wanted it before it was too late, before an inevitable foreign occupation put an end to their exciting and lucrative game.

It is true that the large concerns that made deals with the Dominican government—Hartmont, Westendorp, Santo Domingo Improvement Company—had acted like a pack of highwaymen. But the loans had never been forced on the Republic by foreign warships; they had been contracted freely by Dominican presidents, often the same men who had done their best to sell off a piece—if not all—of the country. The Dominican people cannot be blamed for the actions of their unscrupulous leaders. The Dominicans were victims of those leaders, just as the small investors who bought the bonds were victims of the large concerns. But before attacking foreign imperialism, today's Dominican historian ought to vent his anger at the men who opened the way to imperialism by selling out their country. No one individual, but a whole group—the nation's leaders—must be indicted. The leaders, driven by a blind and irresponsible ambition, brought the country to the edge of ruin. Their corrupt, mindless mismanagement of finances led to an inevitable takeover by creditors, who were all too aware of the nation's bankruptcy.

Eventually the foreign creditors grew restless. The threat of intervention by their governments loomed ever greater. Their sole recourse in dealing with irresponsible *caudillos* seemed to be the use of force. For the Dominican Republic, the end was near. In January 1903, the United States government and General Horacio Vásquez, president of the Republic, signed a protocol. It stated that the Dominican government would have to pay the Santo Domingo Improvement Company the sum of $4,500,000. The terms and method of payment were to be set by a commission of arbitration. On 14 July 1904, the commission decreed that the Dominicans pay the Company $37,500 a month for two years and $41,666 a month thereafter. A financial agent named by the United States would take control of the Puerto Plata customhouse if the monthly payment was not met. The remaining customhouses would follow should the first one not produce the required amount.[35]

In August 1904 the U.S. government named John T. Abbott of the Santo Domingo Improvement Company as financial agent.[36] On 21 September, when the Dominican government failed to make its first payment, Abbott demanded that the Puerto Plata customhouse be turned over to him. The new Dominican president, General Carlos Morales, refused, but the insistent pressure of the American minister, Thomas C. Dawson, forced him to yield. On 20 October, Abbott's representative took charge of the customhouse.

Other foreign powers—"the European Governments whose rights were disregarded"[37]—threatened to follow suit. "The French and Belgian representatives at Santo Domingo indicated that their governments were considering the seizure of the customhouses at that city and San Pedro de Macorís to collect revenues that had been specifically promised them as security. The Italian Embassy at Washington took up the matter . . . emphatically with the Department of State on December 24."[38]

The United States had come to regard Latin America as its back yard, over which it claimed special and exclusive rights. As Secretary of State Richard Olney boasted in 1895: "Today the United States is practically sovereign on this continent, and its fiat is law upon the subjects to which it confines its interposition."[39] Within the broad sphere of influence that Washington had staked out, the Caribbean was of unique importance at the turn of the century. The Panama Canal was about to elevate the region "to a commanding position among the trade routes of the world,"[40] and the Caribbean was destined to be the *mare nostrum* of a country still heady from its easy victory over Spain. Thus, the

United States would not tolerate a repetition of the Venezuelan affair of 1902-1903, when European powers had used force to compel Venezuela to pay its debts.[41] President Theodore Roosevelt "determined to act, and, as always, to act swiftly."[42] Hence the "Roosevelt Corollary" to the Monroe Doctrine:

> Certain foreign countries have long felt themselves aggrieved because of the non payment of debts due their citizens. The only way by which foreign creditors could ever obtain from the Dominican Republic itself any guarantee of payment would be either by the acquisition of territory outright or temporarily, or else by taking possession of the custom-houses, which would of course in itself, in effect, be taking possession of a certain amount of territory.
>
> The United States then becomes a party in interest, because under the Monroe Doctrine it cannot see any European Power seize and permanently occupy the territory of one of these republics; and yet such seizure of territory, disguised or undisguised, may eventually offer the only way in which the Power in question can collect debts, unless there is interference on the part of the United States.[43]

Such "interference" was already a reality. On 30 December 1904, Secretary of State John Hay contacted the American minister in Santo Domingo, Thomas C. Dawson. Hay asked Dawson to sound out President Morales "discreetly but earnestly" so as to "ascertain whether the Government of Santo Domingo would be disposed to request the United States to take charge of the collection of duties and effect an equitable distribution of the assigned quotas among the Dominican Government and the several claimants." In this way, Hay hoped to resolve "the disquieting situation which [was] developing owing to the pressure of other governments having arbitral awards in their favor and who regard our award as conflicting with their rights."[44] Morales agreed to the proposal. This was not a free and spontaneous decision, but a bid for bondage to a single country as the alternative to dismemberment. For their part, "the European Claimants would evidently accept whatever line of action we [the United States] decided upon. They merely wanted their money, while we wanted both our money and our Monroe Doctrine."[45]

A protocol signed in February 1905 put the United States in control of the Dominican customhouses. Santo Domingo was to receive 45 percent of the revenues, and her creditors 55 percent, less the cost of collection. The receivership was to have a free hand in the customhouses.[46]

Even at the negotiations, "what was really in the minds of the two American negotiators was to copy British rule in Egypt."[47] Their scheme was to achieve "a real superintendence of all administrative matters, which in wise hands can be used to great advantage."[48] During Ramón Cáceres' term as president (1905-11), the American government was content to abide by the protocol, which in 1907 was replaced by a formal treaty. Cáceres proved adept at guaranteeing the internal stability that Washington now required of the countries in its sphere of influence. Above all, he showed a healthy "understanding" of American economic interests.[49]

From Washington's point of view, the situation in the Dominican Republic was particularly gratifying to the extent that "in defending his dollar diplomacy in Central America, [Taft's Secretary of State Philander] Knox repeatedly pointed to the Dominican Republic as an example of the benefits conferred by an American customs receivership."[50] Here was a model to apply elsewhere.

In November 1911, however, Cáceres was assassinated. Anarchy again plunged the country into financial chaos. Knox's "splendid model" was shattered. The United States reacted to this sudden regression to past sins with increasingly brutal interference in the internal affairs of the Republic. Faced with this heightened pressure, a weak, impermanent president could only point to the treaty of 1907, which set the limits on United States involvement. But "might lends extraordinary advantages in the interpretation of legal phrases."[51] Thus the U.S. government could pretend to respect Dominican sovereignty while ordering a Dominican president (General Eladio Victoria) to dismiss the head of the army and a ranking minister. And it could maintain a comforting sense of self-righteousness while telling that same president to resign. The necessary support for so much "friendly advice" was provided by a series of measures in open contravention of the 1907 treaty: ominous "visits" by U.S. warships to Dominican ports, threatened and actual Marine landings, and threats to withhold the Dominican share of customs revenues.[52] The latter was a dire threat indeed, since these revenues were virtually the only source of government income.

Woodrow Wilson assumed the American presidency in March 1913. His liberalism and repudiation of "Dollar Diplomacy" seemed a welcome change from the cynicism of his predecessors. A breath of hope stirred Latin America, but the illusion was short-lived. While Wilson's respect for small nations may have applied to Europe, for Belgium or Czechoslovakia, in Central America and in the Caribbean he trampled the rights of the small countries. Constitution, law, and democracy were words he loved, but in the "American Mediterranean" he respected them only insofar as they proved useful to the United States.[53]

Presidents Roosevelt, Taft, and Wilson shared the same aim: to control the political lives of the countries in the region and to bar any possibility, however remote or absurd, of European "interference," all in the name of that special "right to security" the United States has always claimed for itself and denied to others. Security and economic expansion were intimately linked in the minds and deeds of these three presidents.

To this reality Wilson added a new dimension: his intolerant dogmatism. The only justice he recognized was that which fit into his rigidly preconceived schemes; any objection to his "advice" by his Latin American wards was for him proof of bad faith, or, at best, irresponsibility. He always saw the faults of those who dissented, but he never seemed aware of the dramatic contradiction between his rhetoric and the reality of his Latin American policy.

It is therefore not surprising that Wilson's policy differed from that of Roosevelt and Taft in only one way: U.S. interference in the internal affairs of the Central American and Caribbean countries sharply increased.

In 1913, Wilson's Secretary of State William Jennings Bryan—the "great Commoner"—had opened the doors of the State Department to reward "deserving Democrats" who knew nothing of diplomacy but needed a sinecure. Shut out from the more important diplomatic posts, for which a minimum of qualifications was required, the gang descended on Central America and the Caribbean. "Nearly all were incompetent and some had personal failings that soon made their removal necessary."[54] The incompetence, the "personal failings," and the dubious past of one man stood out from the crowd. This was James M. Sullivan, an adventurer whom the new administration named minister at Santo Domingo.[55]

Sullivan proved a disaster, slipping from one blunder to the next. He meddled continuously but erratically in Dominican politics, supporting first one faction, then another. He used his official position to secure financial gain for his friends and relatives. The State Department soon realized that its minister was incompetent, less than honest, and extremely unpopular in Santo Domingo, but it waited until May 1915 before forcing him to resign because "the removal of a political appointee was always a difficult matter."[56] The man who replaced him, William W. Russell, while more honest, shared Sullivan's contempt for Dominican sovereignty.[57]

Ever since Cáceres' death in 1911, the situation in the Dominican Republic had been chaotic: crippled governments, rebellions, anarchy. To this sad situation, Wilson knew only one solution: the United States would have to increase its control over the country. And since the 1907 treaty did not go far enough to provide the necessary legal basis for the protectorate he had in mind, other more sweeping agreements would have to be forced on the Dominican leaders. This was to be the goal of American diplomacy toward the Dominican Republic.

But the Dominicans, usually at odds with one another, showed a vexing unanimity in rejecting Washington's propositions. This "ill will" sorely tried the president's patience. On 19 November 1915, Washington made its position clear in a harsh note to the Dominican government. The United States demanded the immediate appointment of a financial adviser of its choice to the Dominican Republic, as well as the creation of a constabulary organized and commanded by an American nominated by the U.S. president. This officer, in turn, would be able to appoint other American and Dominican officers.[58]

President Juan Isidro Jimenes, one of the Americans' few friends in the country, refused to accept Washington's demands; his own supporters would have abandoned him had he yielded. The pretensions of the United States and the arrogant way in which they were expressed succeeded once again in bringing the Dominican people together.

As always, unanimity was fleeting. Hence no true union could be forged to save the country. If the *caudillos* had been momentarily distracted by the threats from outside, they soon returned to their old ways, squabbling as before. Civil war broke out again in April 1916. But this was the last one. American troops occupied the capital in early May, under the pretext of protecting foreign lives and properties. Their occupation soon spread to the rest of the country.[59]

Jimenes chose to resign rather than remain in office under the "protection" of American bayonets. His successor, Francisco Henríquez y Carvajal, took the same route, his compromise proposal—acceptance of a financial adviser but not of U.S. control over the armed forces—having been rejected by the State Department. In a country that produced so many Báezes and Santanas, a paradoxical situation arose wherein no collaborator could be found to join in forming even the semblance of a government. On 29 November 1916, Captain Harry S. Knapp issued from his flagship in the harbor of Santo Domingo a proclamation announcing the U.S. military occupation of the Dominican Republic.[60] The United States had no other choice. Through its own intransigence it had backed itself into a blind alley. For the second time since 1844, the Dominican Republic had lost its independence. This time, however, it perished with dignity.

The military occupation lasted eight years, from 1916 to 1924. Melvin Knight, an authority on the subject, said in 1928: "So much propaganda was written about . . . [the occupation] and so little that was not propaganda that any sane estimate is very difficult to make. Even the Dominican official publications were used by the Americans to sing their own praise."[61] And today, fifty years later, the situation has changed very little. Most U.S. scholars still shy away from any realistic evaluation of the occupation; instead, they prefer to repeat a litany of stereotypes, in keeping with the image Americans have of themselves. Thus, the noted specialist on Latin America, Edwin Lieuwen, has written:

> Political stability was maintained by use of force, finances were put back in order, roads were constructed into the interior, the school system was reorganized, and a sanitation program was inaugurated. In addition, the United States Marines overhauled and trained the hitherto undisciplined army, reorganized it along up-to-date professional lines. Despite such well-intentioned reforms, the Dominican people remained hostile toward their Yankee conquerors.[62]

On the positive side, three major roads were built, largely for military purposes, connecting for the first time the capital with Santiago in the Cibao, Azua in the West, and San Pedro de Macorís in the East; and one must admit that the system of forced labor used by the Americans in Haiti was, for the most part, absent in the Dominican Republic.[63] Building construction for primary education was noticeable between 1917 and 1920, but, on the whole, school reform was hardly successful. Lack of money and particularly the well-known American incapacity to understand and work with foreign cultures—especially those of "inferior" people—hampered progress. The best results were obtained in the field of public health although, as Dana Munro acknowledges, "not always in a tactful way."[64]

These material achievements were accomplished with Dominican money. Indeed, the military government began with an overriding financial advantage. In the months before the occupation the customs receivership had refused to disburse to the Dominican government the latter's share of the customs receipts—an economic blackmail in flagrant violation of the 1907 treaty. This money, several hundred thousand dollars, became the property of the U.S. Military Government. Then, in 1917, the final payment on a loan from the National City Bank freed Dominican finances from a heavy burden, leaving over $300,000 available annually for other purposes; but this repayment would have taken place in any case, and the intervention was not responsible for it. Finally, and this was crucial, World War I brought a steep rise in the price of Dominican exports, notably sugar. Melvin Knight aptly concludes: "If ever a governing group had a chance to make a showing, it was the American Military Government of Santo Domingo."[65] But the end of the war brought a plunge in the price of Dominican exports and only added to the unstable financial situation already created by the Americans. When the money ran out, the Military Government solved its financial troubles by floating two loans for over $8 million on the American market—debts the 1924 evacuation treaty obliged the Dominicans to assume.

Above all, the military occupation upset the entire economic structure of the country. The economy was wrenched in order to serve U.S. interests. Knight writes that "in 1905 there was hardly more than the beginning of the vast web of American business that was to grow up later in the shadow of the customs receivership, with its tariff readjustments, and especially under the protection of the Military Government."[66] By 1924 the situation had changed drastically. A prime example of American inroads was the sugar industry. The land registration law promulgated by the military government in 1920 was just what the sugar interests had wanted for years. Its purpose was to permit U.S. sugar concerns to get legal title to huge tracts of land. It was enforced with great zeal: Dominican peasants were driven off their lands and Dominican villages burned for the benefit of foreign—mostly American—sugar companies.

When United States troops finally withdrew in 1924, sugar companies owned nearly a quarter of the agricultural area of the Dominican Republic— 438,132 acres. Of this total, 9,568 belonged to Dominican and 355,854 to American companies.[67] Among the latter was the Central Romana, a subsidiary of the South Puerto Rico Sugar Company. Established in 1912, the Central Romana already owned 144,418 acres by 1924. Henceforth, as in Cuba and Puerto Rico, sugar would dominate the Dominican economy. By 1925, exports in sugar and sugar derivatives reached 63 percent of the total exports. Dominican sugar earned millions of dollars, but the country profited very little from that money. Since nearly all the companies belonged to foreigners, the profits went to fatten foreign bank accounts. The representatives of the companies in the Dominican Republic were mostly Americans. Those who worked in the sugar fields were mostly Haitians, since the Dominican peasants shunned the extremely low pay and inhuman working conditions. All too often, the companies prevented the workers from spending their wages outside the company stores. As a result Dominican small businesses dried up.

The tariff structure of the country, already "improved" in 1910 (see n. 49) also attracted the attention of the military government. By the end of the occupation 245 articles had been placed on the duty-free list and 700 more subjected to low duties. Nearly all of the favored goods were American. Protection of Dominican industries such as leather, tobacco, coffee, and cocoa was reduced or abolished. Unable to compete, many local crafts and industries were ruined. The only Dominican product favored by the American-made tariff of 1919 was sugar—an American-owned industry.[68]

From a political viewpoint, the record of the occupation is even more bleak. If the Americans intended to bring the benefits of democracy to the Dominican people—as Wilson claimed—they certainly chose the oddest routes. They set up a military government with a marine captain as president and other American officers in cabinet posts. Congress was suspended, elections postponed indefinitely, and local governments kept under tight control. Executive Order No. 44, published in the *Gaceta Oficial* of 24 March 1917, revealed the extent of this control: "The continuance in office of the present personnel of the Ayuntamientos [local governments] is at the pleasure of the Military Government." The very documents of the occupation held out little hope for Dominican dignity. The words "government" and "constitution" began with small letters when modified by "Dominican," but "government" was capitalized when modified by "American" and "military."[69]

And where were the benefits of democracy when the newspapers were forbidden to comment on any act of the military government, or to use such terms as "national," "freedom of thought," or "freedom of speech"?[70] A censorship that was "humiliating and arrogant . . . ridiculous and childish"[71] stifled a press that had been free. Under the American occupation, the suppression of newspapers occurred innumerable times. In their cells, journalists and writers had time to contemplate the merits of democracy "Made in USA." They had been convicted by military courts where in place of Dominican judges sat U.S. officers ignorant of both the law of the country and the Spanish language. Established to judge "offenses against the military government," these courts were "unjust and cruel."[72] They soon overextended their authority, and it became a crime to make "any remark, verbally or in print, regarded by the Military Government as uncomplimentary to itself—sufficiently so that it 'tended' to incite 'unrest, disorder and revolt'. This 'tendency' being purely a matter for the military court to decide, it did not need to be very strong."[73]

An inevitable consequence of any occupation is the problem of collaboration. For the Americans, a patriotic Dominican was a man who rushed forward to serve the U.S. invader. Those who protested were treated as agitators and duly punished. Any man who took up arms to resist was considered a bandit. Gregorio Gilbert was such a bandit, for he had shot down an American officer invading Dominican soil. And so was Cayo Báez, "in whose breast American bayonets, heated until they were red hot, left their cruel marks."[74] The rebels in the eastern provinces, whom the marines "hunted down . . . mercilessly,"[75] were bandits, too. American repression was brutal. Monseigneur Nouel, the very moderate archbishop of Santo Domingo, was moved to write in 1920:

> It is true that more than once in the course of their political upheavals the Dominican people have witnessed unjust persecutions, trampling of individual rights, summary executions, etc., but never did they hear of the water torture, the cremation of women and children, the torture of the noose, or the hunting of men on the plains as if they were wild animals, nor of tying an old man in his seventies to the tail of a horse in full daylight in the plaza of Hato Mayor.[76]

The Military Government was led by officers who could not speak the language of the people, who felt contempt for their color, and who had no idea of their history or national psychology.[77] If the occupation brought a degree of peace and stability, it was the crushing peace and stability of dictatorship. In the end, the occupation made the possibility of democracy on Dominican soil even more remote.

With the departure of the marines in September 1924, the country recovered its independence, and the painful legacy of a past that recent events had only aggravated.[78] During the occupation the people had been disarmed, the bands of the *caudillos* dispersed, and a unified military force had sprung up in their place: the Constabulary, armed and staffed by American officers. Now one of two roads lay open: either the Constabulary would break up into hostile factions, which would breed future civil wars, or, if it held together, the man who dominated it would become a dictator. Given the reality of Dominican history, a third road was blocked from the start: the Constabulary serving as champion of the constitution and guarantor of democracy in an ordered society. Which road would history take? It would be dictatorship: the Constabulary became the private instrument of one man, General Rafael Leonidas Trujillo Molina.

Rafael Trujillo was the fourth of eleven children of José Trujillo Valdez, a postal clerk and small businessman in the village of San Cristóbal. The family was mulatto and *de segunda*, that is, above the plebs (the *infelices*), but well below the golden circle of the elite (the *gente de primera*). At first Rafael Trujillo held modest posts: telegraph operator and member of a private police force on a sugar plantation. The U.S. occupation gave him a chance to move up through the ranks of society. The Military Government was in dire need of native-born officers for the Constabulary, but upper-class youths refused to serve the invader. Thus when the twenty-seven-year-old Trujillo asked in December 1918 to be admitted as an officer, he was immediately accepted. In January 1919 he became a second lieutenant.

As an officer, Trujillo won the esteem of his American superiors, who described him as "calm, even-tempered, forceful, active, bold and painstaking . . . one of the best in the service."[79] By September 1924—when the last marines were leaving—he was already a major. A year later, at age thirty-three, he was made a colonel and chief of the National Police, the old Constabulary. Then in 1927, a law transformed the police into the National Army. Its brilliant chief was promoted to general and put in charge of the new force.

The ambition of politicians hastened the day of Trujillo's triumph. In February 1930, a revolt broke out against the president of the Republic, Horacio Vásquez, an aging *caudillo*. Trujillo, the "loyalist" general, joined forces with Rafael Estrella Ureña, the rebel leader. The same ambition that brought them together would soon force them to part. Only too late did Estrella Ureña, the brilliant *de primera* politician, realize that instead of using Trujillo, he had been the latter's tool. In the presidential elections that followed the "resignation" of Vásquez, Estrella Ureña was forced to take second place as Trujillo's running mate. Soon he was relegated to obscurity. Trujillo's time had come. On 16 May 1930, the young general was elected president—after such a "persuasive" campaign that he had become the only candidate.

The "Era of Trujillo" had begun. At first nothing distinguished his dictatorship from the many the country and the hemisphere had known. He rose to power when the crisis of 1929 was spawning dictators throughout the world. Thus there was nothing extraordinary in Trujillo's success. On the contrary, it would have been surprising if democracy had survived in such a hostile environment. Trujillo's reign was astonishing, however, for its longevity. His dictatorship broke all national and many international records. Above all, it was astonishing for the unprecedented grip which the new master held over all aspects of Dominican life.

The armed forces were his foremost instrument of control. Even before 1930, Trujillo had surrounded himself with a select group of soldiers and officers ready to do his bidding. These he welded into a machine of terror which he refined over the years. To maintain his grip over the military, Trujillo combined lavish rewards with a constant distrust. He never allowed any general, even the most trusted, to remain for long in any command that might have enabled him to build an independent power base. The changes in the highest commands were repeated throughout the hierarchy. The military was the institution upon which the regime was based, but no single chief could dream of controlling the armed forces at any time.

In numbers and materiel, the Dominican armed forces had become one of the largest and most powerful military institutions in the Central American and Caribbean area. But the effectiveness of the military was undermined by the endless, arbitrary shifting of officers, the brazen nepotism, the downgrading of "professionalism" for blind obedience to the regime. This weakness, however, hardly mattered. The Dominican military was not intended to fight wars. "It [was] an army of internal occupation, an instrument of political tyranny. . . . It was a police force."[80]

But Trujillo's control stretched far beyond the military. He dominated not only the political system, the press, the radio, and the fledgling trade unions, but also the masonic lodges, exclusive clubs, chambers of commerce, and professional associations—in short, every group able to exert even limited influence on public life. He met little opposition. Already during his campaign for the presidency in 1930, Trujillo had managed to rid himself of most of his rivals. Some were found riddled with bullets; others, more fortunate, escaped into exile.

Although their power had been sapped, some of the old *caudillos* did at first challenge the new dictator. General Cipriano Bencosme rose in revolt, but was killed in November 1930, battling the army in the fields around Puerto Plata. General Desiderio Arias also rebelled and failed, falling in battle in June of the following year. His death marked the end of the era of *pronunciamientos*. The *caudillos* had learned their lesson.

Who, then, could hope to curb an omnipotent leader in control of the military? Perhaps the United States, the "big brother." But Washington had no intention of moving against a dictator of such virtues. Trujillo was a trusty ally: he had been the foremost antifascist in Latin America when the United States went to war with the Axis,[81] and the most vehement anticommunist in the hemisphere during the cold war. And Trujillo was an honorable man. In the words of U.S. Acting Secretary of State William Phillips, he made the Dominican Republic "an example worthy of emulation" by maintaining interest payments on foreign debts during the depression years.[82] On 21 July 1947, he paid the balance in full, anticipating the maturity date of the bonds by more than twenty years. Cordell Hull led those who praised this action. Finally, Trujillo was a champion of order: the man who replaced the chronic anarchy with the pro-American stability so prized in Washington by politicians and businessmen alike.

Because he was determined to build his own economic empire, Trujillo compelled certain American companies to sell back their properties. In this way, he became the largest sugar plantation owner in the country. Of course, he was careful always to pay a good price, and he never put undue pressure on those companies with strong support in Washington. Furthermore, he offered lucrative investment opportunities to American firms whose interests did not conflict with his own. The Dominican Republic was big enough to satisfy a number of appetites: the Aluminum Corporation of America (Alcoa) and the Granada Company, a subsidiary of United Fruit, among others. The *pax trujillista* assured a docile, uncomplaining work force: only two strikes in thirty years, one of which (in 1942) was immediately quashed. For too many Americans, Trujillo became the "man responsible for the great work of Dominican progress, the man who brought trade between the Republic and the other American nations to a peak."[83]

So many virtues! And Trujillo had a talent for using them to his own advantage. He did so at times through small, but significant, gestures. Thus in the Dominican capital, the boulevard running along the seafront bore the name "George Washington," while another street was named "Marine Corps Boulevard." A replica of the Washington Monument stood conspicuously in the city. Sometimes his gestures could be spectacular: for example, the grandiose offer his representatives made at Winterthur on 12 August 1938. The Dominican Republic, they claimed, would accept immediately up to one hundred thousand European refugees.[84] Such a promise—no matter how unrealistic—had an impact on international opinion, especially on the influential American Jewish community, since it was directed mainly at European Jewry.

Year after year, Trujillo invited U.S. legislators and other prominent Americans to come to the Dominican Republic with their families to inspect the "Trujilloist miracle." While the Dominican people starved, tens of thousands of dollars were spent to entertain the noble guests lavishly, paying all their expenses. This was a costly but effective maneuver. The courtly receptions bedazzled the Americans. They were conquered and returned home to sing the praises of the Jefe.

Meanwhile, respected American public relations firms and lobbyists willingly sold their services to Trujillo in order to enhance his image in the United States. Full-page advertisements in the press constantly reminded the American people that Rafael Trujillo was their friend and best ally in the fight against communism. The dictator contributed large sums of money to the Democratic and Republican parties. No one knows to this day how much Trujillo spent to buy American politicians and journalists.[85]

For more than a quarter of a century, Trujillo's efforts and alleged loyalty paid off. In the government and the Congress of the United States, the foes of his regime were rare, his friends, many and powerful.

If the United States was unwilling to check Trujillo's excesses, what about the Dominican Catholic Church? Though economically weak and lacking able men,[86] the Church still wielded real power over a broad segment of the population, especially the peasants. And it maintained important links with the outside world: with Rome, of course, but also with the influential Catholic community in the United States. Therefore, the Church could not be dismissed. It could have prevailed upon the dictatorship to temper its violence and to respect certain limits, but it rejected this role. As it had done so often throughout its troubled history, the Church abandoned the weak and needy for communion with the powerful. It prostituted itself, placing its moral authority at the service of the regime. The Church remained "the only organization in the country over which Trujillo did not have complete control, since an attempt to establish such control would likely have involved the regime in a struggle which it realized could not be won." But "there was little reason for Trujillo to hold absolute authority over the Church as he did over other groups and institutions. Trujillo and the Church assisted each other in fostering the distinct interests of each, and both benefited from their close association."[87]

The *caudillos* had been crushed and independent political parties abolished.[88] The army was loyal, the Church was an accomplice, and the United States was friendly. Who dared to challenge the great Trujillo?

Not the Dominican Senate. Its last independent act had been in 1931, when it declared three days of mourning for Desiderio Arias, the late general and senator. The Senate, as well as the Chamber of Deputies and the Judiciary, were reduced to tragic parodies of the institutions they were meant to be. Trujillo turned the government into a circus of puppets and clowns bouncing and turning to the ringmaster's whip.[89]

"The Jefe is just even when he punishes."[90] And Trujillo punished ruthlessly—no one could forget that he was the master. He broke down resistance by systematic terror; the Dominican Republic became a vast concentration camp, haunted by a secret police that seemed, with its informers and hidden microphones, to be everywhere. An atmosphere of mistrust prevailed, even between members of the same family; terror and opportunism led to betrayal and denunciation.

Fear went hand in hand with indoctrination. In the schools, in the university, in the "intellectual" life, the cult of Trujillo was foremost. Self-respect became a rare and costly virtue. No one could remain neutral; indifference toward the regime was considered to be opposition. Abject adulation became a civic virtue, with Congress setting the example. A law of 1936 changed the name of the capital—the oldest Spanish city of the New World—from Santo Domingo de Guzmán to Ciudad Trujillo. Thereafter a spate of edicts spread the name of the dictator and his family throughout the country's cities and provinces. At the same time, the press, professional associations, and private citizens competed with each other in a sycophantic frenzy. Trujillo was proclaimed the country's first lawyer, first doctor, first engineer, first intellectual. He was compared to Napoleon, to Caesar, to the greatest figures of the past and the present. "God and Trujillo" became a common expression. It would have been more appropriate to say "Trujillo and God."

Trujillo answered the unbounded adulation of his subjects with the constant humiliation of those citizens most in the public eye. The arrogant *gente de primera*—the country's old elite—chose to submit, joining in the chorus of praises, and accepting insults and humiliation from the master.[91]

But it was not enough for Trujillo to dominate the political and social life of the Dominican Republic, or to be the richest man in the country. He strove for something that few Latin American dictators have attempted and even fewer have achieved: the absolute control of the economic life of the nation. And he largely succeeded.

Exact figures are still lacking, but even a summary listing of the dictator's properties would fill pages. In 1960, the personal fortune of Trujillo amounted to at least $800 million. This fact becomes truly significant when set against the poverty of the country from which it was exacted in the short span of thirty years. It is well known that Trujillo was the largest landowner and cattlerancher in the Dominican Republic; it only remains to be determined whether he and his family owned 30, 40, or 50 percent of the best farming and grazing lands in the country. And there was sugar, the largest export of the Dominican Republic: the Trujillos owned 63 percent of total production.

In addition, one could mention his salt monopoly, his state tobacco concession, his monopoly on meat exports, that on the natural resources of the country, his ownership of the only two Dominican airlines, and his share in the manufacture of cigarettes (72 percent), cement (63 percent), paper (73 percent), and more and more . . . the list runs on ad nauseam.

Under Trujillo, state and ruling family were one and the same, and the state afforded its master a decisive protection: it bought back at a high price whichever enterprises Trujillo wanted to unload; it then resold them to Trujillo at a much lower price when they seemed about to make money. Moreover, because the businesses (all monopolies) faced no competitors, inefficiency was rampant. "No one bothered to increase productivity. With a guaranteed market and virtually frozen wages, the businesses practically ran themselves. Demand stayed relatively stable, and the family reaped huge profits."[92]

Trujillo transformed the Dominican Republic into an immense personal empire. "The Dominican armed forces guarded his vast agricultural, industrial, and commercial holdings; the national territory was his field of operations; the government was his legal servant, the populace his labor force, producer and consumer." A better name for the Dominican Republic would have been "Trujillo, Inc."[93]

By the mid-1950s, El Jefe appeared to be at the peak of his power. The Feria Internacional de la Paz, organized to celebrate the twenty-fifth anniversary of the Era, seemed a tribute to the stability of the regime. At the same time, however, forces emerged that would eventually destroy him. A wave of sentiment for democratic government swept across Latin America. At first it was only the rumble of distant thunder. In Argentina, Trujillo's friend Juan Perón was overthrown on 19 September 1955. Julio Lozano Díaz in Honduras (21 October 1956) and Gustavo Rojas Pinilla in Colombia (10 May 1957) suffered the same fate, while in Cuba, Fulgencio Batista was unable to eliminate Fidel Castro's guerrillas. And in the United States, following the Galíndez-Murphy affair, public pressure forced a reluctant government to slacken its ties with the Dominican Republic.[94] Yet despite occasional discomfort, the regime seemed in remarkably good health. But the first symptoms of a deadly disease had appeared.

By 1958, the condition had worsened. In January, Venezuela's powerful dictator Marcos Pérez Jiménez was overthrown and replaced by a provisional government that called for free elections. Trujillo's southern flank was now threatened. To the east, Batista's troubles mounted. Although Trujillo felt no great love for Batista, he could sympathize with a dictator at bay. The United

States, meanwhile, became increasingly aware of new realities dramatically expressed by the "spit and stone" reception of Vice-President Nixon in Lima and Caracas in May 1958. Suddenly struck by the extent of anti-Americanism in the hemisphere, it realized that one cause of such hostility was U.S. support for Latin American dictators. Of these dictators, Trujillo was a glaring symbol. Thus, relations between the United States and the Dominican Republic grew increasingly distant. The United States refused to grant new licenses for arms and munitions and recalled its Air Force mission from the country.

A year later, the malady erupted with force. On New Year's Day, 1959, Batista fled from Cuba before a triumphant Castro. "The flight of the Batista entourage to the Dominican Republic in the first hours of 1959, their arrival just as dawn was breaking . . . marked the end of an era, not only in the Caribbean, but in the entire Hemisphere."[95]

A few weeks later, Rómulo Betancourt, victor in the elections of 20 December 1958, was sworn in as president of Venezuela. He had already demonstrated his bitter hostility toward Trujillo and his support for Dominican exiles between 1945 and 1948, when his party, Acción Democrática, ruled in Caracas.[96] In Washington, meanwhile, the Eisenhower administration had come to view Trujillo with increasing distaste, "an embarrassment, an awkward inheritance from an earlier time, now lingering too long and imperilling the future and unwittingly preparing the way for Castroism."[97]

With enemies in power in Caracas and Havana, sentiment for democratic government sweeping Latin America, and a growing chill from the United States, Trujillo would have been wise to make himself as inconspicuous as possible and ride out the storm, as he had done in 1946-47. Instead, he compounded his mistakes and forged the very instruments of his downfall.

To the surprise of many, Betancourt showed a desire early in his presidency to maintain correct relations with the Dominican Republic. It was a golden opportunity for Trujillo, already threatened by Castro, but he failed to seize it. With the tide of hemispheric affairs running against him, he should have summoned all of his diplomatic skill and unscrupulous cunning to survive. Instead, the courtly statesman fell prey to his baser nature. "Instinct and emotion had come to rule Trujillo . . . and among his emotions none was stronger than the blind dislike he felt for Rómulo Betancourt. . . . The press and La Voz Dominicana were mobilized, and the air became heavy with verbal assault beamed to Venezuela."[98] Trujillo had taken on a formidable rival. The contest was unequal, even pitiful, except that the aggressor inspired such disgust. The Dominican Republic, small and poor, challenged oil-rich Venezuela, giant among the Caribbean nations. Trujillo, a man of sullied reputation and a growing blot on Latin America's self-image, stood against Betancourt, the "champion of liberty," *Wunderkind* of the "democratic left," whose increasing influence was felt even in Washington.

The fall of the dictators—especially of Pérez Jiménez and Batista—demoralized Trujillo's supporters and gave heart to his enemies. On 14 and 20 June

1959, with Castro's help and Betancourt's moral backing, Dominican exiles launched an invasion of their homeland. The attacks failed, but they had disastrous repercussions for the regime. The martyrdom of the "heroes of June" stirred large sectors of a middle-class youth that had already been aroused by the shock waves of the Cuban revolution. A vast underground movement sprang up. Alerted by an informer, the police easily crushed it in January 1960.[99] But for the regime, this was only a fleeting victory. For the second time in just seven months, the peace of the cemetery that had so long reigned in the Dominican Republic had been shattered. At the very moment that Trujillo should have tried to appear as "democratic" as possible, the regime unleashed a wave of terror that could not pass unnoticed in the hemisphere since its victims were numerous and "respectable"—they belonged mostly to the middle and upper middle classes.

Even the Church, which had been the regime's accomplice for thirty years, broke its silence for the first time. A pastoral letter of 25 January 1960 expressed "paternal sympathy . . . profound sorrow and . . . a common feeling of grief . . . at the deep suffering that has struck so many Dominican families." Addressed "to the supreme Authority in the land," the letter called for "understanding on both sides to prevent excesses that, in the long run, can only hurt the perpetrators: and so may the tears soon be dried, the wounds healed, and peace be again in the land."[100] This timid challenge questioned neither the regime as such nor the principle of violence upon which it rested. Only this particular wave of terror came in for censure. The Church could hardly ignore these new outrages: the international condemnation of Trujillo was too severe; moreover, the regime had struck at "respected citizens"—not at the rabble, the infelices.

Yet Trujillo felt betrayed. Now protesting a few hundred arrests was the same Church that in 1937 had shut its eyes to the massacre of more than fifteen thousand Haitians.[101] Trujillo answered this breach of faith with a storm of violence against the Church. To onlookers in the hemisphere, the regime appeared to be in its final agony.

Trujillo's enemies now saw their chance. Eager to exploit the opportunity presented by the wave of repression and the resulting quarrel with the Church, Venezuela asked for an immediate meeting of the OAS Council to consider Dominican developments. On 7 June 1960, the Inter-American Peace Committee, charged by the Council with the investigation, made its report, accusing the Dominican government of "flagrant and widespread violations of human rights."[102] This was the first official condemnation dealt the regime by the "American family." Soon Trujillo laid himself open to a second, fatal condemnation. Since the beginning of 1959, he had hatched, or encouraged, various plots to overthrow President Betancourt. They all had failed. Undaunted, Trujillo concluded that stronger means were necessary: he decided to have Betancourt assassinated. The solution, Robert Crassweller writes, "was instinctual, not rational. It was, indeed, quite irrational, for the act, whether successful or unsuccessful, would bring down upon his head every retaliation that an indignant community of Caribbean nations could contrive. . . . But none of this . . . mattered. Trujillo's instincts told him to kill."[103]

On 24 June 1960, hired assassins made an unsuccessful attempt on the life of President Betancourt. Trujillo had gone too far. In August 1960, the OAS took action at the Sixth Meeting of Consultation of Ministers of Foreign Affairs in San José, Costa Rica. For the first time in its history, the OAS decreed sanctions against a member state. It called for:

> (a) Interruption of diplomatic relations between all the member states and the Dominican Republic;
> (b) Partial interruption of economic relations between all the member states and the Dominican Republic, beginning with an immediate embargo on all arms shipments and war material of any kind. The Council of the Organization of American States shall study—in accordance with the circumstances and in consideration of the constitutional and legal restrictions of each and every member state—*the possibility and appropriateness of extending to other articles the interruption of commerce with the Dominican Republic.*[104]

Even before the San José declaration, Trujillo, feeling the heat of inter-American hostility, had turned to a familiar ruse: "democratization." On 2 August, his brother Héctor, puppet president of the Republic, resigned in favor of yet another puppet, Joaquín Balaguer, an able servant of the reigning family. Balaguer promised free elections and invited opposition parties to organize. But these efforts were in vain. In September the Eisenhower administration imposed a special fee on American purchases of Dominican sugar. And on 4 January 1961 the OAS Council voted to broaden its sanctions.[105] Trujillo's farce had failed. The players had performed with their usual skill, but this time the audience was more exacting.

The OAS sanctions and the American special fee flayed an already ailing Dominican economy. Fearing that Dominican exiles might launch a new invasion with the support of his enemies in the hemisphere, Trujillo had embarked on a staggering program of arms purchases abroad, one that his country's economy could ill afford. In 1959 the regime announced an extra appropriation of $50 million for weapons, in addition to the $38 million already budgeted that year for the armed forces. And the total national budget in 1959 was approximately $130 million![106]

At the same time, the regime had seen its sources of foreign exchange decrease. An unfavorable international image led to a sharp decline of the Dominican tourist trade, while lower international prices reduced the earnings of the major Dominican exports (sugar, cacao, and tobacco).

Afraid that the dictatorship might not survive, the Trujillo family had stopped reinvesting the profit they derived from their economic empire in the Dominican Republic. From 1959 on, the flight of capital was the result of deliberate government policy, as the Trujillos sent millions of dollars into foreign, mostly European, banks. The Dominican upper class tried to follow the example, and the Dominican peso, for years one of the most stable currencies of the hemisphere, lost its strength.

The regime had to finance a bloodletting of such magnitude; it also wanted to maintain a balanced budget. It succeeded on both accounts, paralyzing the country's economy and exacerbating social tensions.

Having exhausted almost all its international reserves, the government imposed a strict control on imports and froze all investments. Public employees at every level saw their nominal salaries reduced, while inflation, minimal throughout the early and mid-fifties, rose sharply.

Private enterprise, which had enjoyed government protection, was dragged into the crisis. Strict controls resulted in a drop in imports, bringing the regime into conflict with the importers, who watched their revenues dwindle. The reduction in public and private spending caused a drastic decline in the construction industry, a source of important profits for the private sector. Political insecurity and economic retrenchment created a climate utterly unpropitious for business.[107]

Government policies thus resulted in staggering unemployment, high inflation, new indirect taxes and salaries even more miserable than in the past, and heightened the suffering of the Dominican lower classes. Of course, their suffering was not that important: they were the *infelices*, born to endure. But the economic crisis also increased the disaffection of the leisure classes. From then on, for many middle- and upper-class *trujillistas*, the regime's continuance signified disaster. For years they had accepted incredible humiliation, giving up the last shreds of human dignity, all for the glorification of El Jefe. The dictatorship was all-powerful; it could make a man at one moment and break him the next. But now Trujillo's power was crumbling. Outlawed by the OAS, a pariah in the "family" of Latin American states, faced with the growing hostility of the United States, the regime lashed out in blind and increasingly self-destructive rage. Repression fell not only on the "guilty ones" of January 1960 and their families, but also on those who might be or might become "guilty." No one was safe any longer. No one, no matter how well prepared to endure humiliation or to betray his family, knew what the next day would bring. At the same time the deteriorating economic situation threatened sacred interests. At the end of the road loomed yet another danger: the regime might suddenly collapse. The invaders of 1959 were dead. But what if a new attack, abetted by those states that had sworn to destroy Trujillo, should succeed? What, then, would be the fate of the men who had enriched themselves in the shadow of Trujillo?

At that moment a band of servants of the regime resolved to kill the tyrant. On the night of 30 May 1961, on a lonely road, Rafael Leonidas Trujillo was cut down like a dog.[108]

Chapter 2

"Nicaraguization" or Democratization? From the Death of Trujillo (30 May 1961) to the Establishment of the Second Council of State (18 January 1962)

Caesar was dead. The conspirators had succeeded in eliminating the tyrant, but they were unable to seize power.[1] They went into hiding and were hunted like animals. Of the fourteen men who formed the hard core of the conspiracy, twelve perished, many after being brutally tortured. Two escaped; the Dominican people would have many occasions to regret their survival.[2]

The assassins' disarray was met with a swift and violent reaction from the Trujilloist machine. Although the Jefe was dead, the machine he had built over thirty years continued to function. Acting in self-defense, the generals, Trujillo's creatures, linked their own fate to that of the ruling family. Joaquín Balaguer, the puppet president, continued to play his role as servant of the regime with his usual cunning. The press, radio, and television printed or broadcast only official propaganda.

The power vacuum lasted but a few hours. Ramfis, the dictator's eldest son and heir to the Trujillo empire, was summoned at once from Paris by his family. He returned on 31 May by chartered plane to assume command of the armed forces. Balaguer lost no time in naming the new master "Head of the Joint Chiefs of Staff," a position Congress had just created for him.[3]

Ramfis had inherited the vices of his father, but none of his talents. The overprotected child of an all-powerful ruler, he was a colonel at age four, a general at six, the "best" student at a university he rarely attended, chief of staff, and ambassador. In May 1961, at age thirty-one, Ramfis was a playboy corrupted by too much flattery and the large amounts of money he received through no effort of his own.

He was the caricature of a dictator, yet even a caricature will do when there is no opposition. There were no celebrations and no threats of revolt at Trujillo's death. "The populace reacted . . . with a stunned and fearful silence";[4] the "always quiet capital appeared quieter than ever."[5] The silence was shattered only by the bursts of machine-gun fire in the center of town as the secret police went efficiently about their work, hunting down the assassins,[6] and by "scenes of hysterical weeping" at Trujillo's funeral. "Both the Presidential Palace and the church were surrounded by throngs of people, many of them weeping and clearly grief-stricken."[7]

Amid the shock and hysteria, those who rejoiced at the murder kept silent. What horrors would the stricken hydra inflict in its convulsive death throes? "No one knew just what would happen, and people feared the worst. . . . Trujillo's death . . . pushed the anti-Trujilloists' fears to a pitch. At any minute they expected a wave of vengeance to sweep over them, making Trujillo's worst crimes look like trifles."[8]

Only one force in the land could still make its voice heard: the Catholic Church. But once again the Church sided with the dictatorship, and again its betrayal was not limited to mere silence. In a public letter, Bishop Francisco Panal proposed that requiem masses be held for the "Generalissimo." He explained: "The faithful, the clergy, and the bishops acknowledge their debt of charity to General Trujillo as a fellow Catholic. . . . We have profited abundantly from the innumerable benefits which he has brought to the nation and the Holy Church."[9]

"Tyranny . . . will perish the day Rafael Leonidas Trujillo falls from power or yields up his life," one eminent opponent of the regime had predicted.[10] Nevertheless, in early June 1961, the realities of power in the Dominican Republic seemed to render an irrevocable verdict. In the absence of any overt opposition, the Trujilloist machine prevailed despite the sudden disappearance of its creator.

A process of "Nicaraguization" had apparently begun. In 1956 the Nicaraguan dictator "Tacho" Somoza was assassinated after twenty years of rule. But his regime survived. "His tame legislature elected his son Luis president of the republic, and his other son, Anastasio Jr., continued as commander of the armed forces." The word "democratization" was heard, but the loosening of the regime's grip "was so slight that for all practical purposes there might have been none. . . . The Somozas continued to dominate the country. They still owned all the property their father had amassed, they still had the armed forces under their command, and they still had the constitution that made the president a legal dictator."[11]

Nicaragua, September 1956; the Dominican Republic, June 1961. Would events in Santo Domingo follow the Nicaraguan precedent?

"Tacho" Somoza, an unrepentant despot, was, at the time of his death, a member in good standing of the "free world," a champion of the "Christian and democratic" West. Washington valued such a leader and welcomed the continuance of his regime.

Five years had gone by. New forces were shaking Latin America. These forces, which Washington could not ignore, took Rafael Trujillo, the dean of dictators, as a symbol, the hideous emblem of a past that had to be erased. With the imposition of the OAS sanctions, the Dominican Republic became legally what it already was morally—the pariah of the hemisphere. At the time of Trujillo's death, four consulates (including that of the United States) and two consulates general were all that remained of the ties between the Dominican Republic and the other OAS countries.

The sanctions dealt the regime only a light blow, but the measures the Eisenhower administration adopted in September 1960 against Dominican sugar deprived the country of a potential windfall in the wake of the elimination of the Cuban sugar quota.[12] The lack of diplomatic relations, moreover, gave President Kennedy a pretext to cut off the Dominican Republic from the benefits of the Alliance for Progress.

Only Rafael Leonidas Trujillo could dare to defy his neighbors in the hemisphere and still maintain his rule despite the sanctions and the hostility of the United States. The Dominican Republic was his fief, and he was the lord: "Through his energy he degraded and made slaves of the people. Through his sense of authority and his capacity for rule he instituted a system of terror. Through his talent for organization he created a despotic state. Through his unflagging mental and physical activity he succeeded in establishing a system of economic exploitation and political submission which the world has rarely seen."[13] But Ramfis—the playboy, the callow young heir to an empire built without his hand—could not afford to defy the hemisphere. To consolidate his victory he had to do more than pursue a helpless foe. It was imperative that he secure his country's reintegration into the inter-American "family." He had to shake off the yoke that only a man of his father's stature could bear—and make bearable. In short, he had to see that the sanctions were lifted, and the key to that end was to be found in Washington.

Enshrined in the charter of the OAS is the principle of nonintervention. The United States had vigorously supported it, at times: between 1947 and 1950, for instance, when Caribbean and Central American exiles (the mythical Caribbean Legion) assisted by Guatemala, Cuba, and, until November 1948, Venezuela,[14] tried to overthrow the dictatorships of Somoza and Trujillo. At other times the United States had brutally violated this same principle—as it did in 1954 at the expense of Jacobo Arbenz, probably the most democratic and certainly the best president Guatemala has ever had.

Once again, in 1959, dictators in the Central American-Caribbean area were threatened—but this time, in the wake of Castro's victory, by exiles far more radical than those of the Caribbean Legion. At the Fifth Meeting of Consultation of OAS Foreign Ministers, held at Santiago de Chile, 12 to 18 August 1959, to consider the problem of Caribbean tensions, Venezuela and, above all, Cuba called in vain for a relaxation of the principle of nonintervention, so that the people of the Americas might live under representative governments and be accorded respect for their individual rights. A "narrow and captious interpretation" of the principle of nonintervention, affirmed Cuban Foreign Minister Raúl Roa, only served to shield dictators—the scourge of Latin America. Nonintervention, asserted the Venezuelan delegate, should protect only popular and legitimate states, not dictatorships.[15]

The United States, however, rose in defense of the principle of nonintervention, the "foundation stone for the relations between our countries."[16] Secretary of State Christian Herter argued that "to weaken the principle of non-intervention and of collective security in an effort to promote democracy is . . . a self-defeating activity."[17] In truth, the United States was defending that precious anti-Communist stability it now saw threatened by antidictatorial exile expeditions largely inspired and certainly supported by Cuba.

And yet, less than a year later, Washington "dropped its ardent support of the doctrine of non-intervention. . . . The shift in United States policy was foreshadowed in two reports of the United States chaired Inter-American Peace Committee, released in April and June of 1960."[18] For the first time in the history of the inter-American system, these reports established a link between violations of human rights or the nonexercise of representative democracy, on the one hand, and the political tensions affecting the peace of the hemisphere, on the other.[19]

Thus, despite scrupulous adherence to the principle of nonintervention, any regime could now be cited as a threat to the peace of the hemisphere simply because of the nature of its government. Any regime could legally be accused and subjected to the sanctions laid down by the inter-American system. The June 1960 report of the Inter-American Peace Committee was explicit: "International tensions in the Caribbean have been aggravated by flagrant and widespread violations of human rights which have been committed and continue to be committed in the Dominican Republic."[20]

This shift in United States policy expressed itself even more clearly a few weeks later at the Sixth Meeting of Consultation of OAS Foreign Ministers in San José, Costa Rica (16 to 21 August 1960). When the Venezuelan delegate demanded that sanctions be adopted against the Dominican government for its complicity in the attempted assassination of President Betancourt, Secretary of State Herter replied that evil must be attacked at its roots: "Quoting approvingly the Peace Committee's conclusion that international tensions in the Caribbean were directly related to the 'flagrant and widespread violations of human rights in the Dominican Republic,' Herter argued that the Dominican Republic would be bound to continue its 'aggressive and interventionist policy' as long as it was ruled by a dictatorship."[21] The OAS should therefore use the threat of sanctions to impose a change on the regime in power in the Dominican Republic: in short, it should intervene directly in the internal affairs of a sovereign state.

In its quest for anti-Communist stability, the U.S. was merely following an old, familiar policy, one that only recently had led it to accept—and even to favor—a whole gang of dictators. But the means were changing spectacularly.

Cuba was the immediate cause of the new methods. In 1959-60 the old structure collapsed; Fidel Castro triumphed and proclaimed his intention to spread his message to all the disinherited in the Western Hemisphere. In the face of such a challenge, the best allies of which were poverty, injustice, and a justly bitter nationalism, the United States was forced into an agonizing search for a policy that would prevent a repetition of the Cuban disaster. Despite its own resistance and prejudices, Washington had to acknowledge a new possibility: that these dictators, who for so long had seemed the surest guarantors of anti-Communist stability, might instead be Communism's unwitting allies. Their blind refusal to undertake indispensable political and social reforms promoted the most dangerous agents of their own destruction, future recruits for Castro's cause. In the particular case of the Dominican Republic, where opposition to the dictatorship had begun to stir in 1959, the U.S. could not longer discount this proposition: "Batista is to Castro as Trujillo is to X." But who would "X" be? A Castro or a Betancourt?

Along with the goal of preventing the spread of Castroism throughout Latin America went still another aim: to destroy this new disease in its Cuban stronghold. But in order to strike at Castro, the doctrine of nonintervention would have to be violated. It was Castro, not Trujillo, who was Washington's primary target. It was Castro, not Trujillo, whom the United States had foremost in mind when it withdrew its "ardent support of the doctrine of non-intervention" and proclaimed that the Dominican Republic "would be bound to continue its 'aggressive policy' as long as it was ruled by a dictatorship."

But Castro's prestige was too great, the memory of the Sierra Maestra too fresh, for enough Latin American countries to follow Washington in sanctioning the man who had toppled Batista. Their refusal was usually made in the name of the doctrine of nonintervention. Thus it was important that the United States set a precedent: by striking at the most discredited, hated regime in Latin America, Washington would open a breach in the principle of nonintervention in preparation for the moment when it would be possible to strike at the real foe, the archenemy: Fidel Castro. Arthur Schlesinger writes: "As for a hemisphere policy towards Castro, Betancourt argued that if the OAS first took action against Trujillo it would be easier to unite the American republics against Castro."[22] This was Eisenhower's policy, which Kennedy was to prolong, cloaking it in new rhetoric.

In the period between Kennedy's inauguration on 20 January 1961 and Trujillo's death on 30 May, two crucial events set the tone of the Latin American policy of the new administration: the announcement of the Alliance for Progress on 13 March and the attempted invasion of Cuba at the Bay of Pigs on 17 April. As Secretary of State Dean Rusk made abundantly clear, these events were in fact two facets of the same policy: "The Alliance for Progress is the best way of attacking the long-run sources of the Communist appeal—poverty, hunger and ignorance. But the Alliance cannot by itself provide a means of warding off the short-run Communist tactics of disruption and subversion. . . . Vitamin tablets will not save a man set upon by hoodlums in an alley."[23] The Communist "hoodlums" would have to face the policeman's big stick. The United States was ready to act—in concert with the "sister republics" if possible, without them if necessary. Said President Kennedy: "Let the record show that our restraint is not inexhaustible. Should it ever appear that the inter-American doctrine of non-interference merely conceals or excuses a policy of nonaction—if the nations of this hemisphere should fail to meet their commitments against outside Communist penetration—then I want it clearly understood that this Government will not hesitate in meeting its primary obligations, which are to the security of our Nation."[24]

At a moment when the lustrous rhetoric of the Alliance for Progress was tarnished by the U.S. aggression against Cuba, Trujillo's death suddenly presented Washington with a situation that called for immediate decisions and tested the sincerity of its "new policy." "The Kennedy Administration's avowed declaration of support for democrats and opposition to dictators throughout the hemisphere thus meets another test," observed the *New York Times*. "Little has been done in Washington so far to develop techniques of such support and opposition, and they will now have to be improvised in the Dominican situation, under the stress of rapidly changing and potentially explosive events."[25]

Trujillo dead, the United States justified its massive intervention in Dominican internal affairs by freely interpreting the resolution by which the OAS had condemned the Dominican Republic. The resolution charged the OAS Council to lift the sanctions "as soon as the Dominican Government ceases to constitute a threat to the peace and security of the Continent."[26] A certain ingenuity was required to argue that Trujillo's heirs, busy maintaining their grip on the country and aware of the hemisphere's hostility, had the means or the desire to be a continental threat, or indeed to meddle in any way in the internal affairs of the "sister republics"; to do so risked repeating an experience which, for the Jefe, had ended unhappily. But had the Inter-American Peace Committee's reports not concluded that a link existed between "violations of human rights or the non-exercise of political democracy" on the one hand, and "the political tensions that affect the peace of the hemisphere" on the other? In particular, the June report noted that "international tensions in the Caribbean region have been aggravated by flagrant and widespread violations of human rights which have been committed and continue to be committed in the Dominican Republic." Thus, the very nature of the regime had to be changed before the Dominican Republic would cease to be a "threat to the peace and security of the Continent," and the regime would have to undertake a real process of democratization before the yoke of the sanctions could be lifted. This logic was tenuous at best, but the United States, with the firm support of a number of Latin American nations,[27] was able to exact agreement from the other OAS members.

On 2 June, the United States proposed to send an OAS committee to the Dominican Republic "to observe, on the spot, the situation in that country, particularly the nature of the Government and its policies."[28] In fact, the committee was meant to oversee and encourage the process of democratization. When the committee left Santo Domingo after only a brief stay, the United States expressed disappointment. "I personally believe," said Secretary of State

Rusk, that "the OAS committee left the Dominican Republic somewhat too soon."[29] The United States position dominated the report filed by the committee on its return to Washington (12 June): despite promises of democratization from President Balaguer, the report observed, it was still "too early to determine the degree of change that has occurred in the character and policies of the Dominican Government. . . . The Committee deems it necessary to continue watching the progress of events in this regard."[30] Meanwhile, the sanctions would be maintained, despite the protestations and appeals of the new regime.

The U.S. government had not yet found a long-term solution to the Dominican problem. For Washington's policy makers, the Dominican Republic was "a sick, destroyed nation, to be viewed as one ravaged by a thirty years war, even one to be occupied and reconstituted. . . . Not only did we have no democratic traditions or institutions to build on, worse, we confronted deep-rooted traditions of authoritarianism and anarchy."[31] Was it possible, given these conditions, for a political democracy to take root and function in a country where "potential political leadership had been suppressed, murdered or exiled for more than a generation?"[32] In President Kennedy's opinion, there were "only three possibilities, in descending order of preference: a decent democratic regime, a continuation of the Trujillo regime or a Castro regime. We ought to aim at the first, but we really can't renounce the second until we are sure that we can avoid the third."[33] Desiring a democratic regime, but apprehensive that democracy would fail; hostile to the Trujillos, but wary lest their departure plunge the country into chaos; "sensitive to the charge of supporting dictatorships," but afraid that out of the ashes of dictatorship would arise a triumphant Castroism, "the Kennedy administration . . . appeared caught in the middle."[34] A prisoner of its own contradictions, it was doomed to pursue a tentative and unsure policy that seemed to change daily.

In fact, the American administration was divided. On one side was the "Puerto Rico Group," men such as Arturo Morales-Carrión, Teodoro Moscoso, and Luis Muñoz Marín.[35] In large measure their sensitivity toward the Dominican drama can be explained by common language, geographic proximity, and the legacy of a common culture. Though recognizing the need to proceed with great prudence and the weakness and inexperience of the Dominican democratic opposition, this group believed that the opposition had a chance of success as a third alternative to Trujillo and Castro that should not be denied.[36] At the other extreme were the conservatives, particularly the old hands at the State Department. They did not believe that democracy could survive in the Dominican Republic, nor did they forget that the United States had refused Batista the support he needed to defend his dictatorship . . . and Castro had replaced Batista. The plight of three million Dominicans scarcely moved them, and the Dominican "democratic opposition" often evoked only a "certain scorn."[37]

Between these two groups were the pure "Kennedyites": the president himself, his brother Robert, always there "if the matter was one in which the president took a deep interest,"[38] Stephen Smith and Sargent Shriver, Kennedy's brothers-in-law, and presidential aides such as Arthur Schlesinger Jr., Richard Goodwin, and McGeorge Bundy. The Kennedyites, who considered themselves idealists with a sense of reality, wavered between the theories of the State Department conservatives and the arguments of the Puerto Rican "ultraliberals." The situation in the Dominican Republic was unpredictable and Washington knew so little.[39] Now persuaded by the viewpoints of some, then attracted by the "sober eloquence"[40] of others, they tried to gain time, to devise a policy that would leave their options open. They hoped to avoid any sudden development that might push the Dominican situation to a point of no return. Any change in the status quo had to be "smooth, very smooth, step by step."[41] The *New York Times* observed that "the U.S. government appears to be split as to what policy should be followed toward the Dominican Republic. The result is a virtual absence of policy."[42]

Owing to the lack of open opposition in the Dominican Republic, the Kennedy administration at first dealt only with the Ramfis-Balaguer duo. Ramfis tried to play along following the only rules he knew. If the United States wanted him to be a democrat, he would comply. Beginning in early June, a series of decrees, declarations, and resounding promises appeared, all heralding the birth of a new era in the Dominican Republic, the era of "democracy." The minister of foreign affairs was dispatched to Washington with the surprising announcement that "his Government would gladly receive the proposed visit"[43] of an OAS committee (5 June). At San Isidro, the country's chief military installation, Ramfis held a press conference at which he proclaimed that he was a democrat— and thus openly pro-American and fiercely anti-Communist. As for the elections scheduled for May 1962, they were to be "democratic in fact as well as in name."[44]

The armed forces and the police were kept under tight control, and the press, radio, and television printed or broadcast only official propaganda. But these were trifles. The regime was "transformed." True, the Trujillo clan maintained its position: under Commander-in-Chief Ramfis were the family's several generals, one of whom even had his own private army.[45] Yet who would dare to assert that the regime had not embarked on a vigorous purge? True, the masters remained, but some especially unsavory underlings were sent into exile. One such exile was José Martí Otero, "who had been director of *El Caribe*, the newspaper which had followed an anti-American and pro-Communist line during the last year of the reign of Trujillo."[46] Obviously there was no place for his kind in a Dominican Republic that had become "democratic" and "anti-Communist." Also exiled was Lieutenant Colonel Johnny Abbes García, the redoubtable chief of the infamous Servicio de Inteligencia Militar (SIM), "the man whose ferocious reputation gave credence to the reports of brutal repression."[47] Before he left the country, he was dismissed from the army.[48] The purge went ahead at full strength. Even the name of the SIM was changed to Agencia Central de Información.[49] Where would the wave of democratization stop?

If Ramfis could be a democrat, so could Balaguer. Balaguer wanted all Dominicans to vote in the upcoming elections, so he invited the exiles to return, pledging full amnesty. And he went even further. Wishing "to normalize the civic life of the Dominican nation,"[50] he made an eloquent appeal to the "democratic" opposition to show itself. These and other moves did influence the American press:

> The successors to . . . Trujillo . . . have surprisingly been doing all the right things, and are not yet giving their many and powerful enemies any valid reasons for attacking them.[51]
> Their adept policy of reforming the worst features of Trujilloism and welcoming the OAS ha[s] gained them some favour with the United States and other American republics, which feared above all the rise of a Dominican Fidel Castro phoenix-like from the ashes of a country torn asunder in chaos. The Dominican Government's promise of amnesty for political exiles and its program of allowing them political freedom ha[s] also been praised.[52]
> The world must wait. It would be ironical to complain about the new Dominican regime because it has not lived up to expectations of brutality, strife and political extremism.[53]

Alas, the sweet harmony was to be short-lived. Timid at first but bolder in time, a new actor entered the scene: the Dominican opposition. The concessions forced on Ramfis and Balaguer played a role in its revival. This revival was a victory for the United States, since there could be no real "democratization" without an opposition. But it was a dangerous success. A third interlocutor was introduced into the dialogue between Ramfis and the Americans, one that, by its presence alone, broadened and complicated the issues. In spite of its weakness and the regime's strength, the Dominican opposition too often proved to be "unreasonable"; it refused to be led or advised. In short, it would not be coerced by Washington. By its "excessive" demands, the opposition triggered an acceleration of events, upsetting the smooth evolution the United States desired.

On 5 July 1961, in response to Balaguer's appeals, three exiles—Angel Miolán, Ramón Castillo, and Nicolás Silfa—returned to the Dominican Republic. These three men were the delegates—the vanguard—of the "anti-Communist"[54] Dominican Revolutionary Party (Partido Revolucionario Dominicano or PRD), "a moderate Leftist group" that claimed "a membership of 3,000 exiles and 3,000 persons in the Dominican underground."[55] Founded in 1939 in Havana by a group of political exiles, at the time of Trujillo's death the PRD had several branches—"wherever membership was large enough to warrant one"[56]—in Caracas, Mexico City, Aruba, San Juan de Puerto Rico, and New York. The party was substantially smaller than its leaders claimed. In numbers, the PRD was no different from all the other anti-Trujilloist organizations in exile; it was a mere skeleton.[57]

But the PRD had two members who set the organization apart from others in the chaotic, shifting world of Dominican exile. One was Angel Miolán, secretary general of the party; the other was Juan Bosch, its president. "Stocky, swarthy and Indian-featured,"[58] Miolán had developed his remarkable gifts for organization during twenty-seven years of exile. A skilled politician, he "talked little and gave an air of knowing exactly what he was about."[59] His professionalism set him apart from the rhetorical dilettantism of many leaders of the Dominican opposition.

Juan Bosch, one of the party's founders, was at the time of Trujillo's death far more than the obscure leader of a tiny group of refugees. In twenty-four years of exile he had been in close association with such leaders as Rómulo Betancourt, "Pepe" Figueres, and Luis Muñoz Marín. These were the men recognized by Washington in the spring of 1961 as the hope of Latin America, as "a symbol," as Kennedy described Betancourt, "of what we wish for our own country and for our sister republics."[60] Their friendship and esteem added to Bosch's prestige. His hostility to Castroism reinforced the confidence he inspired. "Bosch was strongly in the progressive, democratic tradition," wrote Arthur Schlesinger, Jr.[61] His talent as a writer, known throughout the hemisphere, completed the portrait of this man, "one of the great figures of the democratic-left movement in Latin America."[62] His name gave luster to his party.

In July the pace of events began to quicken. On the fifth the PRD delegates arrived in Santo Domingo. After a rally on the seventh in which thousands took part—it was the party's first public meeting—a crowd of some eight thousand, "carried away by the excitement, . . . proceeded through the streets with torches and burned down Radio Caribe. . . . It was the first such popular demonstration in the 31 years of the Trujillo dynasty."[63] Ten days later an open letter to President Balaguer and the nation announced the birth of a new movement, the National Civic Union (Unión Cívica Nacional or UCN). Rejecting the label "political party," the UCN described itself as a "civic-patriotic movement" with a single mission: the struggle for democracy against the Trujillos.[64]

On 30 July a new party was born, the Political Group 14th of June (Agrupación Política 14 de Junio or 1J4).[65] Its social concepts were vague and unclear, but there were no doubts about the vehemence of its anti-Trujilloism. The name was in itself a challenge. It honored the martyrs of 14 June 1959, the anti-Trujillo exiles who had invaded the Dominican Republic at Constanza. It also recalled the 14th of June Revolutionary Movement (Movimiento Revolucionario 14 de Junio or MR1J4), the underground anti-Trujillo organization brutally crushed by the dictator in January 1960, of which the new party considered itself an outgrowth.[66] Thus, in less than a month, the three groups that would eventually be the leading Dominican political parties had appeared on the

scene. Soon they would be engaged in an inexorable struggle. The 1J4 would become the Castroite party of the Dominican Republic, ready to sacrifice political
democracy for social justice. On the other extreme, the UCN would be eager to
do away with political democracy so as to prevent social reforms, while in the
middle the PRD would follow the illusions of a leader who believed that both
political and social democracy were possible in the Dominican Republic.

But for the moment, in the summer of 1961, the three groups were united
by a common goal: to rid the country of the Trujillos. Yet the Trujillos were
entrenched, holding in their hands the essence of political, military, and economic power. The reforms of the regime were merely a facade. If freed from outside pressure, Ramfis could quickly re-establish "order" and "discipline": his
tanks and soldiers stood ready to crush defenseless crowds, civilians who were
just emerging from a past permeated with terror. But Ramfis' hands were tied.
He, who had known only adulation, had to be a "democrat," had to seem
tolerant.

As late as July, "a month and a half after Trujillo's death, thousands of
Dominicans . . . still pledged their loyalty to the family of the deceased. . . . The
newspapers were filled with hundreds of telegrams expressing condolences to
the former dictator's widow and sons."[67] Little by little, however, the opposition gained confidence. Its first newspapers appeared, and committees sprang up
in the provincial towns, bringing the message of liberty. But the deathly silence
of the *pax trujillista* still reigned in the rural areas. The university, which for
thirty years had been totally subservient to Trujillo,[68] emerged—finally!—as a
center of "subversion." On 13 July the Federation of Dominican Students (Federación de Estudiantes Dominicanos or FED) was created. At first the federation limited itself to modest, corporative requests: "the right to university autonomy and inviolability."[69] Soon, however, the students became the spearhead
of the anti-Trujilloist movement.

Violence mounted. In vain the regime, obsessed with escaping the sanctions,
granted concessions. But the reforms, though painful, were futile, as were the
terrorist tactics used against the most vocal dissidents. This bloody, savage violence lacked that systematic character which alone could have subdued a nation
heady with a dream of liberty.

Caught in the middle between Ramfis and the opposition was the United
States, still searching for a viable Dominican policy. The reforms of the regime
were superficial, and the "democratic" opposition could not be abandoned to its
fate. But for the United States this opposition was "divided, its leaders childlike and politically naive, patriotic, but of doubtful ability to govern."[70] The
American government found it increasingly difficult to navigate safely through
the Dominican Republic's storm-tossed politics. On the right, Charybdis: the
peril continually invoked by Ramfis and Balaguer of a coup d'etat by powerful
military groups dissatisfied with a democratization that threatened their privileges and yet failed to obtain a lifting of the sanctions. "The great danger,"
said John Kennedy, "is a take-over by the army which could lead straight to

Castro."[71] And on the left, Scylla: in Balaguer's words, "a potentially explosive situation among the masses and a lack of political leadership, as well as economic difficulties were creating a serious danger of disintegration [which] . . . could be used by the Communists to their advantage."[72] In the eyes of the United States, the hazards were many: a coup by the right, "Castro-Communist" infiltration, a weak and divided opposition, and sanctions that deepened the economic crisis of the country. This crisis in turn only heightened the risk of a coup by the right and thus increased the Communist threat. The main question was: "Should we urge the OAS to lift its sanctions against the Dominican Republic?"[73] Without the sanctions, "democratization" would come to an end. It was a vicious circle, an impasse from which the United States had to escape. Finally, near the end of August, the State Department believed that it had found a solution: it would "try to induce the army, Balaguer, Ramfis Trujillo, and the moderate opposition to stick together in order to lay the foundations for movement toward self-government."[74] And Kennedy agreed. "Balaguer is our only tool. The anti-Communist liberals aren't strong enough. We must use our influence to take Balaguer along the road to democracy."[75]

"To take Balaguer along the road to democracy" was an impossible dream. His rhetoric was agile. Earlier Balaguer had extolled the policies of Rafael Trujillo "to whom the country owes its greatest era of progress and the noblest conquests of its history."[76] He had sworn over the body of his "Beloved Chief" to "defend his memory and remain faithful to his principles."[77] Now, with the same ardor and sincerity, Balaguer proclaimed his zeal as a democrat, his passion for democracy reborn at last, as he put it, "after thirty-one years of political obscurantism," under the sway of "one of the harshest dictatorships of the modern era."[78] Ramfis as well had to be shown "the road to democracy." Like Balaguer, he was a great talker. He had already declared himself a democrat—and of the left. "If I were a politician in this country," he explained, "I would be a leftist."[79]

The United States adopted a "flexible" policy. It made its first concession on 5 September by raising its consulate in the Dominican Republic to the level of consulate general. This action, the State Department emphasized, "reflects the continuing United States interest in the progress of President Balaguer's program to democratize his country."[80] And deLesseps Morrison, the U.S. ambassador to the OAS, foresaw the day, already close at hand, when the sanctions would be lifted.[81]

But the Dominican opposition refused to cooperate; it demonstrated its lack of "maturity" by refusing "to stick together" with Balaguer the "democrat" and Ramfis the "leftist." On 12 September, with the arrival of an OAS subcommittee to verify the progress of "democratization," riots broke out, "the worst since the assassination . . . of . . . Trujillo."[82] "It was different from what I had expected," wrote ambassador Morrison, a member of the subcommittee. "I had expected the Trujillos to be highly unpopular in many quarters, but I was unprepared for the almost universal wave of hatred. . . . I had come hoping that

we could lift sanctions, thus stabilizing the country so it would not fall to
Castro, or be taken over in a rightist coup. I could not recommend this now. To
lift sanctions while the Trujillos remained would make it appear that the United
States supported them and wanted a return to dictatorial rule."[83] And so, with
the opposition unanimous in its demand that the sanctions be maintained,[84]
Washington had to retreat. On 14 September, the *New York Times* reported:
"The United States is urgently reviewing its policies toward the Dominican Re-
public in the light of the violent developments of the last two days."[85]

Because of the strength of its reaction, the anti-Trujilloist opposition effectively thwarted the American policy of "flexibility." Although aware of the
need for further concessions from the Trujillo heirs before the sanctions could
be lifted, in part or in full, Washington continued to believe that only one solution could ensure the indispensable anti-Communist stability. That solution was
"to induce the army, Balaguer, Ramfis Trujillo and the moderate opposition to
stick together." This "happy reunion" would be accomplished by setting up a
coalition government, which in turn would be rewarded by a lifting of the sanctions. In a more relaxed political climate, the Dominican Republic would move
toward the elections of May 1962.

On 21-22 September, Balaguer asked the leaders of the 1J4, the PRD, and
the UCN to join in a coalition government with members of the Partido Dominicano, the official Trujilloist party. Each group would hold three of the twelve
cabinet seats.[86] Negotiations dragged on for weeks, amid increasingly violent
demonstrations. Meanwhile, "savage attacks on members of the opposition continued unabated. One incident of violence after another was reported throughout the month as the toll of dead and wounded mounted. For the first time
President Balaguer was forced to admit that atrocities were continuing under his
regime" when, answering a plea by the country's bishops for an end of the repression, he commented: "The chiefs of police have received instructions to
avoid any unlawful act, [but] it cannot be denied that on several occasions
during the process of democratization savage acts have occurred."[87]

Between crackdowns, Balaguer tried as best he could to go on with the
charade of democratization. On 11 October he announced that "the matter of
exile for . . . eleven military leaders, including Héctor and José Arismendi Trujillo—uncles of Ramfis—was under consideration."[88] This was one of a number
of conditions laid down by the UCN, the leading opposition group, for its participation in a coalition government.[89] But then Balaguer hastened to take the
substance out of the concession by declaring Ramfis, the most undesirable of the
military chiefs in the eyes of the opposition, to be "indispensable as Chief of the
Armed Forces." Without him, "anarchy will take hold of the Military, and the
Government cannot function without the support of the Military."[90] Ramfis
himself, worn out perhaps by the nervous strain of too many weeks of "democracy," was increasingly unable to keep up the charade. Indeed he even provided
additional proof of the hollowness of Trujilloist "democratization." Faced
with Balaguer's statements, "the successor to the dynasty spoke up":[91] during

a press conference he publicly reminded the puppet president of the limits to the power granted him by the Trujillos. Reported *El Caribe*: "The Head of the Joint Chiefs of Staff, General Rafael L. Trujillo, Jr., declared yesterday that, in the case of the supposed statements concerning the establishment of a Coalition Government, the position of the military has been made plain to the President of the Republic; that is to say, the role of the Armed Forces will henceforth be excluded from such discussions. As for the possibility that 'officers in active service might be sent into exile', that would be 'contrary to the position of the Armed Forces and unacceptable to the same.' "[92]

Thus the United States had little success in "bringing the army, Balaguer, Ramfis Trujillo and the moderate opposition together." It had better luck on the anti-Communist front, where it fought with equal, if not superior, energy. True, in the Dominican Republic "there weren't many Communists,"[93] but that hardly mattered. By that time, and especially since Castro's takeover in Cuba, paranoia over Communism had gripped Washington. Consciously or unconsciously, U.S. officials made any Latin American Communist into a superman capable of routing whole armies of "democrats." Latin American democrats were so weak, so inexperienced, so disorganized! After all, the argument went, Castro had started with only eleven men and found himself, twenty-five months later, the master of Cuba. And the Dominican Republic had only a third the population of Cuba![94]

It is not surprising, therefore, that Ambassador Morrison wrote of a 28 August meeting at the White House: "High on our memo . . . was an all-important question, what to do about Communist activity in the country." The CIA's deputy director for plans, General Richard Bissell, "gave us a list of twelve Moscow-trained Communists whom the CIA felt strongly the Dominican Government should deport." A tragicomedy then unfolded in Santo Dominigo. On one side, Ambassador Morrison, representative of democracy,[95] pressed the Dominican president with a list of Communists—Dominican citizens—whom President Kennedy "would very much like to see him expel at once." But Balaguer, the servant of a dictatorship, refused in the name of democracy to deport the Communists. "I allowed them to return," he explained, "as a part of my pledge to permit complete political freedom." Finally, "Balaguer sighed and . . . nodded. Yes, he would take action against them." Balaguer, concluded Morrison, "had no need to prove his anti-Communism."[96]

Deporting Communists and preventing others from returning were, in Washington's view, decisive and indispensable steps in a healthy drive for Dominican democratization.[97] But these steps could not break the deadlock facing the country, for the "childlike" opposition still refused to accept conditions that the future U.S. Ambassador Martin later admitted were tantamount to "political suicide."[98] Determined to cut through this Gordian knot, the United States forced the issue. There was still no coalition government, and judging from the state of the negotiations it would be a long time before a coalition could be formed.[99] But Washington would wait no longer and decided that the latest concessions from Ramfis and Balaguer, especially the forced departure of Héctor and José Arismendi Trujillo, two hated brothers of the deceased dictator, deserved a reward. On 14 November 1961, at a meeting of the OAS committee investigating the Dominican case, Robert F. Woodward, assistant secretary of state of inter-American affairs, expressed the United States view:

> The Committee should recommend that action be taken by the Council at this time which would give recognition to the constructive efforts of the Government of the Dominican Republic—sufficient recognition to encourage that Government to continue the further progress which is so deeply desired. . . . Fortunately there is a ready and convenient method of providing this encouragement. This would be the withdrawal by the Council of the OAS of the formal indication which it made to the member states in the resolution approved on January 4, 1961. This resolution stated that it was "feasible and desirable" to extend the suspension of trade with the Dominican Republic so that the suspension would apply to trade in petroleum and petroleum products and in trucks and spare parts for trucks.
>
> My Government proposes that the Special Committee recommend that the Council withdraw the action taken in the resolution of January 4, 1961, as a gesture of encouragement to further progress by the Government of the Dominican Republic.[100]

The United States asked only for a partial lifting of the sanctions—yet for the Dominican opposition even this was excessive. The Ramfis-Balaguer brand of democratization was a farce; the violations of human rights perpetrated by the regime were the only reality. The bloody image of the massacre of the calle Espaillat (20 October 1961, Santo Domingo) was still vivid, and repression continued. Power remained in the hands of the Trujillos. The departure of two brothers of the late dictator and of a few minor figures could in no way change this fact.[101]

In a joint communiqué issued on 27 October, the UCN, the 1J4, and the PRD unanimously demanded that the sanctions be maintained. "In spite of their fighting spirit," the Dominican people were impotent against the violence of the regime. In recent weeks they had won a few "highly limited and circumscribed liberties"—at a price high in blood and suffering. But even these victories would have been impossible "without the effective pressure for civil rights exerted by the sister republics of Latin America." This pressure had materialized because of the sanctions. To lift the sanctions, even partially, under the pretext of rewarding the "constructive efforts" toward democracy by the regime meant in effect to encourage this regime in its chosen path—not a path of "democratization," but one of continued repression.[102] Such action would deal a "terrific psychological blow"[103] to those struggling to transform "highly limited and circumscribed liberties" into an irreversible reality.[104]

Partisans of the regime clearly understood the significance of the U.S. action. The lifting—"albeit partial"—of the sanctions was "a gratifying result of the efforts made by the Government of President Balaguer";[105] it was an event "most pleasing to the Dominican people,"[106] one "that positively mark[ed] the beginning of the end of an unjust discrimination."[107] Thus both partisans and adversaries of the regime agreed in their analysis of the U.S. move, the partisans rejoicing that the "official Dominican position ha[d] triumphed,"[108] and the adversaries vowing that the "Dominican people would never forgive those responsible for lifting the sanctions."[109] But at the very moment victory was in sight, Ramfis Trujillo's nerves gave way.

Poor Ramfis.[110] For weeks on end that coddled child had been under extreme tension. He was not used to being insulted or attacked. He longed for order: order Trujillo style. "I want no disorder," he declared. "Disorder upsets me. . . . And let no man offend the memory of my father."[111] The opposition, still respectful in July, had lost its deference by November. The Trujillo name was vilified; busts of the "Benefactor" were smashed; unruly, threatening crowds gathered in the streets. Ramfis had to keep silent and endure. If now and then the police were unleashed as in the old days, it was only a passing indulgence, for it was necessary to be "democratic." The opposition grew bolder, and the insults grew louder; instead of reprisals, concessions had to be made—insignificant ones, of course, but how painful to a wounded pride!

Yet it was neither the Dominican opposition nor the United States (which he hated) that caused Ramfis his greatest agony. His own family misunderstood him, failed to appreciate his wisdom, his courageous efforts to save the empire by making a few sacrifices. His mother María, his brother Radhames, his uncles all considered him a traitor, a coward. "Your father always thought you were a coward," wrote Doña María from Paris: a "coward" who let the name of the Trujillos—the dead and the living—be defiled, a "coward" who said nothing when Balaguer, a mere servant, openly maligned the dead master before the United Nations. "And you stand idly by," his mother continued. "You dishonor your family name."[112] Then toward the end of October the last straw was added when Héctor and José Arismendi Trujillo—the "Wicked Uncles"—were compelled to leave with Ramfis' consent. "You are a coward, a traitor, you allow your father's brothers to be driven from the country," fumed Doña María. Under severe nervous strain, Ramfis needed a quick, sweeping victory, but not to prove his hold over his officers, whose thoughts were far from rebellion. Rather, he had to demonstrate to himself and to his family that his "tolerance" sprang not from weakness but from an overriding political motive, that, far from having besmirched the family name, he had actually saved the Trujillo empire.

But the time was not ripe. The United States demand for a partial lifting of the sanctions had opened a breach, which Balaguer would patiently try to exploit. Now it was best to wait. Ramfis, however, had been waiting too long. The gap between the public smile and the secret burning to strike grew too wide, and the corrupt and feckless playboy cracked. Ramfis gave up a role for which he was ill suited, a game he found too painful, too complex. The alternative was alluring: the peace of a gilded exile with millions stolen by his father, the millions already in foreign banks and those he would take with him.

On 14 November 1961, Ramfis "withdrew from the contest."[113] In a letter dated that day he announced to a stunned Balaguer his intention to resign as head of the joint chiefs of staff. He then retired to his seaside villa at Boca Chica, where he spent three days "drinking and living it up,"[114] free at last of the "burdens of state." At noon on 17 November, Ramfis left the Dominican Republic "and headed for the bright lights of Paris on the family yacht, the 'Angelita,' "[115] taking with him his father's body and, reportedly, $90 million. Before leaving—and "this was his last act in the Dominican Republic"[116]— he personally executed the six surviving imprisoned assassins of Rafael Trujillo.[117] It was a macabre gesture, intended perhaps to convince his family that he was not a "coward," unworthy of his father. Just a few weeks earlier the *New York Times* had written: Ramfis "is not the awesome figure his father was. It is doubtful that he would personally countenance ruthless repression. He inclines toward a liberalization of the Government."[118]

Ramfis had given up, but the era of the Trujillos was far from ended. That same 14 November, before abandoning his high military rank, Ramfis phoned uncles Héctor and José Arismendi Trujillo in Jamaica. The "flexible" policy he had tried to follow had collapsed. He had forced this path on his family, and the family held him responsible. Now it was their turn to try their hand, if they were so inclined. Ramfis' message to Héctor and José Arismendi was "come at once,"[119] and they lost no time. They were back on Dominican soil the evening of 15 November. The following morning, *El Caribe* announced briefly that "prominent travelers" had returned to the country.[120] Their arrival caught Balaguer off guard, for Ramfis had not informed him of his message to his uncles. The United States and the Dominican opposition were also taken by surprise.[121] The very presence of the "Wicked Uncles" at that moment constituted a challenge. The minuet of "democratization" was abruptly halted as the orchestra fell silent and a pall settled over the dancers. The "Wicked Uncles" had come back with machine guns in their hands to claim their inheritance: the succession to the Trujillo throne that their nephew had been unable to defend. If they prevailed, a return to the worst aspects of Trujilloism was inevitable. The "Wicked Uncles" had no taste for subtleties, and they turned to the instrument their brother had used thirty-one years earlier to seize power: the army.

This turn of events was unacceptable to the United States. The U.S. was too committed to the process of democratization, however illusory it might be, to tolerate its flagrant failure. Washington would not allow a brusque reversal that would tarnish U.S. prestige and undermine the fragile rhetoric of the Alliance for Progress. The failure of democratization, moreover, could have disastrous consequences in the Dominican Republic itself; blind, mindless brutality from a new Trujillo dictatorship could be the spark that, sooner or later, would ignite an equally blind and mindless explosion among the people, to the advantage of the Castro-Communists. On a global scale such a failure would reduce Washington's chances of persuading enough Latin American countries to join in a common front against Castro. How could one take a stand against Castroist Cuba while the hated Trujillos triumphed in the Dominican Republic?[122]

A test of strength between the "Wicked Uncles" and the United States began. Balaguer's choice was obvious: both his wish to be on the winning side and a reflex of self-defense drove him into Washington's camp. The "hardliners," champions of old-style Trujilloism, thought Balaguer had in recent months given in too often, permitted too much. He had let his master's name be sullied; worse, he himself had sullied it. Balaguer became an anti-Trujilloist, and for the next four days he was to play that role with dignity and courage. If he lost, his life would be endangered, but if he won, there was the promise of power, not as a servant of the Trujillos, but for himself.

Yet in his refusal to leave office and make way for the new pretenders, Balaguer played a passive role. The United States was in command. Washington's strategy was to persuade, or to pressure, if necessary, important sectors of the Dominican armed forces to oppose the schemes of the "Wicked Uncles." This was to be the task of the American diplomats in the Dominican Republic, and of Consul General John C. Hill in particular, whom later accounts described as having played an "extraordinarily skillful"[123] role. It was a role made all the more difficult by shifts of policy in Washington: at first a determined reaction— a halt in U.S. efforts for a partial lifting of the sanctions[124]—then forty-eight hours of silence.

During that uncertain interval the "Wicked Uncles" had their one chance to act. But they failed to do so. Entrenched in the powerful military base at San Isidro, which their partisans controlled, the uncles tried in vain to obtain Balaguer's submission and to rally the support of the military units stationed in the interior. Time was running short. On 18 November the United States finally launched its counteroffensive. In an "unusual statement"[125] that evening, Secretary of State Rusk announced that "in view of the possibility of political disintegration and the dangerous situation which could ensue, the Government of the United States is considering the further measures that unpredictable events might warrant."[126] The terseness of the phrase "further measures" seemed to harbor a threat. In fact, "Department officials would not exclude the possibility that troops might be sent if the Dominican Government [that is, Balaguer] requested them."[127] The threat seemed to materialize when "on orders from Washington the cruiser Little Rock, flagship of Admiral John N. Taylor, commander of the United States second fleet, and a screen of three destroyers, steamed during the night toward the Dominican coast." In their wake came the "60,000-ton aircraft carrier Franklin D. Roosevelt and a group of other warships." On the morning of the nineteenth, "the ships halted off Ciudad Trujillo at the three-mile limit of territorial waters." A landing force of 1,800 marines waited on board, while "United States naval jet planes flew past the shore line twice."[128]

Faced with this imposing show of will by the United States, the relations among the forces vying for power shifted. Planes out of Santiago, the country's second largest air base, swept over the capital dropping tracts signed by the commander of the air base, General Pedro Rafael Rodríguez Echavarría, and by officers of the Dominican Air Force. The tracts alerted the Dominican people that the air force, "with the support of a large part of other branches of the armed forces" and "conscious of its patriotic responsibilities of the moment, backs the civil Government and will not tolerate any attempt to reinstitute in the country a regime of tyranny and reaction."[129] The Santiago air base demanded the "immediate"[130] departure of the "Wicked Uncles."

Now there could be no looking back. Major General Fernando Sánchez, Jr., commander of the San Isidro air base and air force chief of staff, wanted to act, even, apparently, to the point of sending tanks to crush the dissidents at Santiago. But it was too late. At San Isidro the Trujilloists lost heart; the American fleet lay off the coast with nearly two thousand marines aboard. Perhaps the United States would not go so far as to give the order to land, but Consul General Hill succeeded in conveying another impression.[131]

And so the Trujillos yielded. Exile beckoned once again. At 11:45 that evening, 19 November 1961, Héctor and José Arismendi fled the Dominican Republic accompanied by twenty-seven friends and relatives, including General José García Trujillo, the army chief of staff, and Major General Fernando Sánchez, Jr., of the air force. The Trujillo empire had crumbled, and the people celebrated their victory. In a matter of days, "the capital and almost all other areas . . . [were] stripped of the statues, busts, likenesses and other symbols evocative and laudatory of the late dictator and his family. Mobs in the streets display[ed] huge portraits of the once-deified tyrant covered with epithets like Crook, Thief, Murderer."[132]

Thus ended the gravest crisis to shake the country since Trujillo's death. The United States had been forced to abandon its vacillating Dominican policy and to take a clear, straightforward stand. "Down with the Trujillos!": Washington had adopted—had had to adopt—the battle cry of the Dominican opposition. With the Trujillos gone, U.S. prestige in the Dominican Republic was greater than ever. "The extraordinary sight of hundreds of Dominicans standing on their shore and cheering the American Navy," marveled the *New York Times*, "may symbolize a new era in Latin American history."[133]

The U.S. government seemed to have won on all fronts. Not only had Washington thwarted the "Wicked Uncles," but also, "aware of the possible negative impact in highly sensitive Latin America,"[134] it had achieved its goal without openly saying those fateful words: "military intervention." U.S. warships had not penetrated Dominican territorial waters; Dominican sovereignty had been respected. True, U.S. planes had violated Dominican airspace, but who, amid the euphoria of the Trujillos' departure, was thinking about that? Certainly not Balaguer. While he felt the need to emphasize that the "Dominican Government had not solicited the presence of United States warships," he stressed that

that pressure had been "salutary";[135] after all, it had saved his power and even his life.

As always, what seemed a "local" crisis actually encompassed a broader issue. For the United States there was a "prophylactic" aspect to this Dominican crisis: the struggle against Castro's Cuba loomed in the background. Just a few days earlier, on 9 November, the Colombian government had asked the OAS Council to call a meeting of foreign ministers on 2 January "to consider measures for the defense of the hemisphere from any threat posed by 'the intervention of extra-continental powers.' "[136] But the four major Latin American countries (Brazil, Argentina, Chile, Mexico) as well as Ecuador and El Salvador showed little enthusiasm for a proposal that, though couched in general terms, was nevertheless aimed at a member state: Cuba.[137] The proposal was yet another step in the drive to establish collective sanctions against that country, and was therefore a challenge to the principle of nonintervention. At their 14 November meeting, the OAS Council stalled for time, putting off a decision until 14 December. The delay was interpreted by many in Washington as a defeat, evidence of the bad faith of the Latin American "allies."

Meanwhile, the crisis of the "Wicked Uncles" had erupted on 15 November, and the United States had acted boldly. Applauding the "first clear-cut and tough-minded United States diplomatic victory in this hemisphere in a very long time," the columnist William S. White echoed the feelings of a great number of his fellow Americans when, with brutal frankness, he drew a lesson from the recent crisis that went far beyond the immediate turmoil:

> Mexico, Brazil and Chile, among others, raise no moans to the heavens now about the American gunboats that prevented the Dominican Republic from falling into extremist chaos. But only a little while ago they were not willing even to go along with the United States to the point of calling a Pan American meeting even to discuss the menace which Castro poses to us all. The lesson for the United States is plain. In the Dominican Republic we rightly accepted the responsibility laid upon us as the greatest power in this hemisphere to end a danger to the common peace. The hour must soon come, however—unless, hopefully Castro himself brings Castro down—when we accept the same responsibility as to Cuba, even if it means more than gunboats. Evil is evil. And danger to the common peace is danger to the common peace, whether from a Trujillo or a Castro. The United States Government cannot shirk its duty because other powers prefer not to see that threats from Castros are at least as real as threats from Trujillos.[138]

On 16 November, having approved the Woodward proposal to delay decision on the sanctions, the OAS Council had "gone on vacation." Only after the crisis in the Dominican Republic had passed—three days later—did the Council vote to send a subcommittee to the country, thus resuming a pretense of OAS participation in Dominican events. During the crisis the United States had acted on its own. "There . . . [had been] no time," explained the *New York Times*, "to do anything more than hastily consult other members of the Organization of American States, and then take the very grave risk of acting alone."[139] Perhaps. At any rate, Washington had acted "to defend democracy." Yet three years and five months later—April 1965—a second crisis was to shake the Dominican Republic, and again there would be "no time." Once again the United States would act on its own, but this time with thousands of marines invading Dominican soil.

These events were still distant. On 19 November, with the flight of the "Wicked Uncles," the United States believed that its troubles in the Dominican Republic were over. The Trujillos and some of their chief military men were gone; the opposition's primary condition for collaboration with the government had been met. Thus for Washington, nothing stood in the way of an agreement between President Balaguer and the "democratic" opposition led by the UCN. According to a *New York Times* editorial, "a coalition government under President Balaguer can at last be formed, and a transition to relative democracy is a hopeful possibility."[140] The transition, of course, would be calm, orderly, and free from violence.

Balaguer, for his part, was eager to fill the political void. For over a year he had been president of the Republic in name only; now he wanted to rule: "From this moment I assume, in my capacity as President of the Republic, . . . supreme command of the Armed Forces. As such, I hereby order the Chiefs of Staff of the Air Force, the Army and the Navy, as well as the Chief of the National Police, to obey no orders except those emanating directly from the President of the Republic."[141] "The Era of Trujillo has ended,"[142] he announced. But amid the wreckage, Balaguer was determined to cling to power. Denying responsibility for the past—"this is the first time that I address the nation in the full exercise of my constitutional powers"—the president asked for "a vote of confidence from . . . [his] fellow Dominicans."[143] Had he not, since 15 November, blocked the bid for power of Héctor and José Arismendi Trujillo? Had he not, for four interminable days, defended the hopes of Dominican democracy against the Trujillo menace?

Balaguer appealed "to the patriotism of all Dominicans, military and civilians alike, . . . whatever their political persuasion." He invited them all to unite behind him: "at stake is the ideal I have taken it upon myself to realize." This union, however, was to be built around his own person, for he embodied "the legitimate power of the nation."[144] In his obsession with power, Balaguer forgot—or seemed to forget—that he owed his authority to the whim of a Trujillo. But the Era of Trujillo had ended.

While Balaguer was appealing for unity, four political movements vied for the favor of the Dominican people: (1) the Dominican party; (2) the National Civic Union (UCN); (3) the 14th of June Political Group (1J4); (4) the Dominican Revolutionary Party (PRD).[145]

The Dominican Party, the official party of the Era, had from its inception existed only to serve the master. The Jefe's death and the subsequent disruptions shook its power. Although greatly weakened in the cities, it remained strong in the rural areas, where the opposition had not yet penetrated. But the defeat of the "Wicked Uncles" signaled the end of the Era: the Dominican Party was on the verge of collapse. Determined to survive, it offered itself to Balaguer, who alone could assure its existence. But for Balaguer, this moribund party was much more a burden than a boon. The times were anti-Trujilloist. Early in December the Dominican Party ceased to exist, and its assets reverted to the state.

The National Civic Union continued to deny it was a political party, claiming to be "apolitical and patriotic," a "refuge for all those Dominicans yearning for the real advent of democracy."[146] In fact, it was merely the tool of its founders, members of the Dominican upper class, and the instrument they would use to seize power. This reality, however, went largely unnoticed by most Dominicans. Everything was subordinated to the struggle against the Trujillos. In that struggle the UCN showed a resolve that won it the admiration of leaders such as those of the 1J4, who were politically naive and beclouded by political passions. The image of the UCN was enhanced by its wise choice of a standard-bearer, Dr. Viriato Fiallo, a man of prestige who had never served the regime. In the comforting shadow of that standard, however, stood many former Trujilloists, men who were now leaders in the new movement.

At the close of the Trujillo Era, the UCN was without a doubt the dominant force of the Dominican opposition. "A movement . . . based on principles of non-violence and anti-communism,"[147] and "with respectable middle-aged leaders,"[148] the UCN enjoyed the favor of the United States as well. Everything pointed to a privileged role for the *cívicos** in the forthcoming talks with Balaguer about the establishment of a coalition government. But the *cívicos* opposed any concession. The departure of the Trujillos was only a first step; now it was Balaguer's turn to leave.

Like the UCN, the 14th of June Political Group (1J4)[149] knew what it did not want: a Trujillo or a Balaguer. But what it wanted was not clear. Many longings stirred within the minds of the *catorcistas*,† ardent youths seduced by the image, however cloudy, of Fidel Castro. They felt a desire for social justice and defense of human dignity, and a fierce love for the humiliated homeland. The 1J4 appealed to many young middle-class Dominicans, students in particular, for it offered "a mystique, martyrs and heroic leaders—assets no other Dominican group had."[150] Mystique and sincere feelings, however, hardly compensated for the lack of a concrete program. Suddenly emerging from the long night of the Trujillo Era, the leaders of the 1J4 concealed their confusion about the future in vague formulas. For the present, they spent themselves in the fight against the regime and followed the lead of the UCN, which they naively mistook for an "apolitical and patriotic movement." In fact, the young *catorcistas* were to become the *cívicos'* shock troops when the UCN took to the streets.

---

*Members of the UCN were called *cívicos,* from Unión Cívica Nacional.

†Members of the 1J4 were called *catorcistas*, from *catorce*, "fourteen," a reference to the 14th of June in the party's name and history.

In Washington, meanwhile, the American government observed with growing suspicion a party tainted by the Castroite disease. Even its name—1J4—
seemed to hurl a challenge. Thus an American journalist warned: "In a manner
reminiscent of the Castro 26th of July movement, the group takes its name from
an abortive 1959 invasion attempt to oust the dictator Trujillo."[151] John B.
Martin, then a special envoy of President Kennedy, concluded that the 1J4 was
deeply split between moderates and extremists, some of the latter "Communists
trained in Havana or Moscow." After talking to the *catorcista* leader Alfredo
Manzano Bonilla, Martin "left convinced" that he had "finally met one of the
new breed of Moscow-directed Dominicans." In brief, the 1J4 was, at best,
"unreliable."[152] From "unreliable" to "guilty as charged" was a short step,
given the jury.

The Dominican Revolutionary Party (PRD) was the "party of exiles."
Founded not in Santo Domingo, but in Havana, it was led by men who had just
returned to the country after long years of exile. Against the homegrown UCN
and 1J4, the PRD was only a fledgling group. Its leaders, however, knew what
they wanted and how to get it. Juan Bosch, president of the PRD, had cut
through the rhetoric and realized the real aims of the *cívico* leaders: "to seize
the Trujillo legacy."[153] Unlike the 1J4, the PRD's vision extended beyond the
immediate task of dismantling the Trujillo empire.

Bosch's analysis of the national and international scene after the fall of the
Trujillos can be sketched as follows:[154]

1. Because of the intense international pressure, no Dominican government
henceforth could avoid free elections in 1962.

2. The National Civic Union, neither civic-minded nor patriotic, sought
power. "Once the Trujillo regime had been liquidated, . . . I knew that . . . the
cívicos would inevitably form a party, which given the social position of its
leaders would become a party of the right; not exactly of the democratic right,
but rather of a right disposed to seize power by whatever means it could." The
cívicos "needed power to provide their caste with what it lacked: economic
wealth."

3. The UCN was bitterly opposed to social reform; the PRD, a member of
the Latin American democratic left, fought for social change. Between the two
groups there could be no understanding.

4. "Free at last of the Trujillos," Balaguer, who in his origins was closer to
the people than to the *gente de primera*, "was in a position to take steps that
would transform, however slightly, the economic and social plight of the
masses."

5. The PRD was still too weak to take Balaguer's place in the near future.
Nor did the party intend to participate in a coalition government. As an ally of
the *cívicos*, it would be powerless to undertake real social reforms. As an ally of
Balaguer, it would become a choice target for *cívico-catorcista* propaganda.
Day after day, the people would be told that the PRD had betrayed the cause of
anti-Trujilloism by prostituting itself to the Jefe's old servant. In either case,

participation in a coalition government would be a grave mistake. Later, at the polls, the Dominican people would exact a heavy retribution from a party too eager to get a share of the political pie.

From this analysis, Bosch drew the following conclusions:

1. Balaguer in no way threatened Dominican democracy; to a certain extent, his role might even prove beneficial.

2. The PRD, therefore, had no wish "to conspire to overthrow Balaguer," especially since he would be replaced by the UCN, a movement "that in the end would reveal its rightist aspect."

3. For the time being, "our aim could not be the conquest of power, but rather the mobilization of the people, and we realized that this would take time—a long time."[155]

Now that the Trujillos had fled, the common goal that had tied the PRD to the other opposition forces was gone. Certain of its objectives and how to achieve them, the PRD set out on a "highly independent political course." The United States, despite the special favor accorded the powerful and "safe" UCN, showed a degree of sympathy toward the PRD. The latter, although weak, was "well organized and anti-Communist,"[156] and its program, though rigid, seemed reasonable.

Because of his party's weakness, Bosch's analysis could, at the time, have had only a limited impact on the course of events. For this reason an in-depth examination of his conclusions would be superfluous. Instead, a few brief remarks will suffice.

Bosch's conclusions on the nature and the goals of the UCN are accurate. It is also true that, for the reasons noted earlier, the PRD was in no position to take power, but had to devote itself to laying the groundwork among the Dominican masses. But Bosch was wrong about Balaguer. Throughout a long career Balaguer never evinced the slightest sensitivity toward social problems. To see such a sensitivity in November 1961 was wishful thinking. Bosch, furthermore, was wrong about the threat of prolonged dictatorship following Trujillo's death. The threat was real, embodied in Balaguer and his new armed forces minister, Rodríguez Echavarría. If the threat never materialized, it was because the UCN and the 1J4, regardless of their motives, took up the struggle against Balaguer and thus forced the United States to admit that the case was still open, despite an over-hasty willingness to see it closed. The events that followed the crisis of the "Wicked Uncles" would seem to support this view. To strengthen his own analysis, Bosch had to paint an idealized and distorted portrait of Rodríguez Echavarría.[157]

On 23 November, Balaguer was optimistic about the negotiations that had just opened with the opposition parties: "I can assure the nation that in the coming days, perhaps even in the coming hours, the agreement we are all longing for will be reached."[158] Four days later everything fell apart. Balaguer made the perpetuation of his own power the sine qua non of any coalition. The UCN and the 1J4, however, rejected any plan that did not include Balaguer's removal. Agreement was impossible. On 27 November the talks were broken off, and on the same day a general strike against Balaguer broke out in Santo Domingo. Triggered by a number of pro-*cívico* professional associations[159] and ardently supported by the UCN and the 1J4, the strike spread rapidly to the cities of the interior. The test of strength had begun.

The UCN and the 1J4 enjoyed massive support in the urban centers, but Balaguer had the backing of the armed forces.[160] Out of the crisis of the "Wicked Uncles" a new strong man had emerged, General Pedro Rafael Rodríguez Echavarría, commander of the air base at Santiago. On 19 November, Rodríguez Echavarría had taken charge of the forces opposing the Trujillos. He had become a popular hero, the embodiment of the "new officer" the Dominican people dreamed of. Most important, he had become minister of the armed forces on 22 November. On the same day his brother, Colonel Santiago Rodríguez Echavarría, became air force chief of staff and was two days later promoted to general. The Rodríguez Echavarrías' power over the Dominican armed forces—and thus over the country—was very rapidly taking hold.[161]

Pedro Rodríguez Echavarría threw his support behind Balaguer, denouncing the "false prophets"[162] of the opposition. The general was ambitious. He "seemed both to be backing Balaguer . . . and . . . to be reaching out for the reins of power himself."[163] The Ramfis-Balaguer team had seen its day, and a new one, that of Rodríguez Echavarría and Balaguer, was about to make its bid.

Directed by the middle class, the general strike continued; the lower classes followed enthusiastically, and the students, mostly *catorcistas*, furnished the shock troops that battled in the streets. The *New York Times* called it "one of the most impressive popular demonstrations in recent Latin-American history."[164] And the bourgeoisie did much more than simply close down their handful of factories and numerous shops. "Orders went out to the movement's [UCN] headquarters and members throughout the country to help provide meals for poor people who might go back to work for food or money."[165] Indeed, "many companies paid their employees two weeks' wages before the strike to ensure its success, while others provided food money to the strike committee."[166] In vain Balaguer, hoping to dissociate the masses from the strike, indulged in frenzied demogoguery. "There seemed to be an element of frantic haste"[167] in the daily issuance of laws and decrees that cut the cost of living, conferred favors on well-organized pressure groups, and furthered the process of "de-Trujilloization" begun by the people on 20 November.[168] "The trouble with all this was that the concessions were in large part badly timed, coming always a little late, and that much of what was being done was so obviously a mercenary and even reckless campaign to bribe public opinion. So far as the public was concerned, nothing that Balaguer and those behind him could do was honestly motivated and sufficent. Only the armed forces could keep him in office even for one day."[169] The strike went on. Rodríguez Echavarría's violent efforts to break the middle-class support of the general strike were equally futile. The capital witnessed "policemen . . . leading gangs of hoodlums in smashing open stores that had been closed by the strike," "armed uniformed air force officers in sound trucks" rousing the population "to mob action" and ordering the "armed patrols on the streets to refrain from action against any crowds demanding that the stores be opened." But the Dominican people gave the armed forces a lesson in civic pride, for although it "stirred some excitement," the call to looting "met with a basically hostile reaction from the crowds that heard the harangues." "Crowds of up to 1,000 people stoned the store-smashers . . . and pelted them with pieces of metal." And the strike—massive, its disparate elements tightly bound—continued, bringing "nearly all economic activity to a standstill."[170] This was true not only of Santo Domingo. "Travelers returning from Santiago and the Cibao Valley in the north central area said the strike . . . was even more effective there than in the capital."[171] Throughout the country, the cry "Echavarría—assassin!" rose up with mounting fury. Balaguer was even worse off than Rodríguez Echavarría, for he aroused not only hate but scorn. He was the first to admit that he had never been anything more than Trujillo's puppet. And now he seemed destined to play the same role with Rodríguez Echavarría. "Balaguer, Balaguer: little dolly on a string!" chanted the crowds in Santo Domingo.

In Washington the Dominican events were viewed with growing alarm as the crisis that had seemed headed for solution flared up anew. Already on 24 November, the deputy assistant secretary of state for Latin American affairs, Arturo Morales-Carrión, had joined Consul General Hill in Santo Domingo. Together they tried to persuade the UCN to be "reasonable" and join in an interim government, under Balaguer, that would lead the nation to free elections. A few days later they tried to persuade the *cívicos* to stay out of the general strike.[172] But once again the pygmy dared to defy the giant, well aware that the latter could ill afford to abandon him. The UCN refused to collaborate with Balaguer and supported the strike. And so the United States "found itself caught in a power struggle."[173] Appeals to moderation fell on deaf ears. In vain the State Department exhorted "responsible elements in the Dominican Republic, both within and outside the Government, to continue to strive . . . to reach a prompt resolution of the present situation."[174] The strike aggravated an atmosphere in which passions ran high, deepening the chasm between the parties that Washington had hoped to make partners.

In the Dominican Republic itself, the U.S. position was deteriorating. The prestige won during the crisis of the "Wicked Uncles" began to fade. U.S. warships still lay at anchor off the Dominican coast. Applauded only a week earlier, they were now seen as a hostile presence. The United States, it was said, backed Balaguer, and its ships were there—"visible offshore"—as proof of that support.[175] The initiative for the attacks came most often from elements of the far left. But the seeds of hostility found fertile soil among a population that had known eight years of American military occupation (1916-24), that had witnessed three decades of American friendship toward Trujillo, and that now was aroused by Balaguer's repression. The anti-Americanism was echoed even among such moderate leaders as Viriato Fiallo.[176]

But for Washington more than prestige was at stake. The clash between an impotent Balaguer—still in office thanks to the armed forces—and an exasperated population could lead to "a military dictatorship led by General Rodríguez Echavarría, using . . . Balaguer as a helpless figurehead." This in turn would leave the country open to the inevitable "Castro-Communist" threat. The *New York Times* concluded: "As the State Department said yesterday, the Opposition is responsible and moderate. However, if it is thwarted by military reaction, extremist elements could get the upper hand."[177] It was no longer enough for Washington to appeal in all directions for "moderation." With renewed determination to settle things once and for all, the United States resumed its massive intervention in the internal affairs of the Dominican Republic. And the OAS watched in silence.[178]

Hill and Morales-Carrión led the diplomatic maneuvering. They had two objectives: first, to convince the two antagonists—the Dominican government and the UCN—to renew the talks they had broken off on 27 November; and then to steer the discussions in the right direction. But this time the Americans had "second thoughts about the success of the power play that had committed Washington to Balaguer."[179] Henceforth, the major concessions would be exacted from Balaguer and Rodríguez Echavarría. Pressure could be applied in various ways: the sanctions, whose maintenance the UCN and the 1J4 demanded, still weighed heavily on the country; the memory of the quasi-military intervention of 19 November was still vivid; finally, Rodríguez Echavarría's position was weak. For five months following Trujillo's death, Ramfis had been the master of the armed forces. Some of his numerous generals had been expected to challenge his power. Ramfis himself, as a political maneuver, had encouraged such speculations. But the military had remained docile; the Trujillo name, fear, and common interest had sufficed. Now things had changed. For one, Rodríguez Echavarría was a mere parvenu. He had been a colonel until the previous June; his control over the armed forces was too recent to have taken root, his rise too swift not to have stirred jealousy.[180] On the other hand, Rodríguez Echavarría's policies were leading to a dangerous confrontation with an opposition that now was much stronger. Out of conviction, envy, or mere opportunism, many officers began to challenge Rodríguez Echavarría's authority.[181]

The negotiations resumed on 2 December. Three parties were involved: the Dominican government, the UCN, and—in the middle—the United States. Hill and Morales-Carrión took an "active" part in the discussions, leaning toward the *cívicos* without actually endorsing them.[182] And the strike went on. A week passed. Finally, on 9 December, an "agreement was . . . reached, about 2:30 a.m., after John Calvin Hill . . . and Arturo Morales Carrión . . . kept an all night

vigil on the negotiations."[183] Balaguer was forced to make the biggest concessions: Congress was to be dissolved and legislative and executive powers were to
be invested in a seven-member Council of State (Consejo de Estado). Balaguer
was to be a member of the Council and its president, but only until the end of
the year, when he would have to resign.

The UCN seemed to have triumphed. The general strike, a dangerous weapon for a party devoted to the social status quo, had served its purpose; the
UCN now urged the population to return to work. The middle class, *cívicos* in
the great majority, abandoned the strike. The masses, weary from the ordeal,
followed suit. The 1J4 cried treason, but no one listened. On 9 December, the
general strike collapsed just as suddenly as it had begun. It had lasted thirteen
days.

Balaguer, however, refused to accept his defeat. Encouraged, perhaps, by
the end of the strike and no doubt prodded by the ambitious Rodríguez Echavarría, Balaguer broke his word. Using the pretext that "the Armed Forces refused to consider his resignation as part of a political settlement," he declared
that "he would not resign before the end of his term, next August."[184] "We
are on the verge of a disaster," cried one of the leaders of the UCN, announcing the collapse of the negotiations.[185] The strike was not renewed, but violent
demonstrations supported by both the UCN and the 1J4 took place daily in the
capital. Mounting tensions gripped the city.

With the breakdown of "diplomacy," the Dominican crisis seemed to be
headed toward a violent conclusion: a coup by Balaguer backed by Rodríguez
Echavarría or a popular explosion led by the 1J4. Both possibilities were unacceptable to the United States, hence the need for a rapid diplomatic solution.
Pressure from the Americans intensified once again. Rodríguez Echavarría,
"openly critical of Mr. Hill and Mr. Morales Carrión," expressed his indignation
in a press conference: "If you and your wife have a fight, I say that you should
fix it up by yourselves."[186] But the two American representatives "intervened
and virtually took command of the negotiations."[187] Washington lent them
valuable support, henceforth its exasperation would be expressed in unusually
firm language reminiscent of that used against the "Wicked Uncles" on 18
November. The State Department expressed its concern about "reports that certain elements of the Dominican military opposed final action on the decisions
reached by President Balaguer and responsible civilian elements in his Government and in the moderate opposition."[188] Lincoln White, the State Department spokesman, "did not identify the military elements, but it was known that
the Administration had in mind Gen. Pedro Rafael Rodríguez Echavarría."[189]

Rodríguez Echavarría yielded. On 17 December, in a message to the nation,
Balaguer dropped his demand to hold onto power until the next August, when
his term would end. He adopted, almost word for word, the terms of the agreement rejected a week earlier. But he insisted on one change, whose significance
only the future could determine: he would not leave office at the end of the
month, but rather when the Republic was free of the yoke of the sanctions.

Once "the process of democratization . . . is complete and the nation again part of the Latin American family . . . 'I will consider my mission accomplished and I shall willingly surrender the Presidency of the Republic.' " Aware of the suspicions this new delay would stir, Balaguer sought to calm fears by stressing that he hoped to resign on "27 February, at the latest."[190] After a few hours, Rodríguez Echavarría announced his "full support of Dr. Balaguer's plan."[191]

Weary of the struggle, two days later, on 19 December, the UCN also acquiesced. The *cívicos* nevertheless chose to emphasize their "grave concern over Dr. Joaquín Balaguer's continued tenure in the presidency of the Republic, and the danger it entails for the security and well-being of the aggrieved motherland."[192] They also stressed their "well-founded fears"[193] as to the attitude of the armed forces and of General Rodríguez Echavarría in particular. The time for celebration was still far off. Vigilance was the watchword.

Only Washington reacted with enthusiasm. In the warmest terms, President Kennedy hastened to express satisfaction with an agreement that left everyone in the Dominican Republic unsatisfied. For him, the poorly patched agreement was "an impressive demonstration of statesmanship and responsibility by all concerned." Praises for good behavior were followed by promises of reward:

> I understand that the Council of the OAS is now considering the lifting of the sanctions. . . . If the Council of the OAS takes such action—and our representatives are supporting that step—we will resume diplomatic relations with the Dominican Republic promptly. When this takes place, the Department of Agriculture will authorize purchases under the Dominican allocation of nonquota sugar for the first six months of 1962.
>
> In addition I propose to send, upon the installation of the new Council of State, a United States economic assistance mission . . . to visit the Dominican Republic. . . . I expect that this mission will arrive in the Dominican Republic late this month or very early in January.
>
> I understand that Mr. Felipe Herrera, President of the Inter-American Development Bank, will head a high-level mission to the Dominican Republic in the near future to begin discussions and inquire into economic and social development projects.[194]

By alternating praise and threats, promises and sanctions, the United States believed once again that the Dominican crisis had been resolved. But the solution had left out a key party: the 1J4.

After the flight of the "Wicked Uncles," the 1J4 haughtily refused to take part "in any kind of negotiations involving remnants of the Trujillo regime."[195] Balaguer was on the verge of defeat and only one solution could satisfy "the sacred interests of the Dominican people: . . . the ABSOLUTE AND UNCONDITIONAL SURRENDER OF THE CRIMINAL GOVERNMENT OF PRESIDENT BALAGUER AND THE CREATION OF A NEW PROVISIONAL GOVERNMENT OF NATIONAL UNITY."[196] To defeat Balaguer, the people had no need for ambiguous and humiliating negotiations: they had found their weapon, the general strike that was spreading throughout the country. Instead of negotiations, there would be a glorious struggle with "the masses in the streets to defend it and carry it on."[197] This struggle would lead to the "nationalist democratic revolution of the Dominican people, historically inevitable."[198] Nor was the 1J4 alone, for it could count on the support of its "loyal ally," the UCN, which "by its nature, its pledges, and the actions of its leaders neither is nor ever will be a political party."[199]

On 2 December, the *catorcistas* suffered a first shock: the UCN renewed the negotiations with Balaguer and accepted the "interference . . . of foreign officials . . . in the role of arbiters."[200] The 1J4 refused to join in the talks—to everyone's satisfaction. The Americans rejoiced over the absence of a party tainted with "Castro-Communism," while Balaguer was spared a most intransigent opponent. And the UCN? The *cívicos* had no intention of sharing the sweet fruits of victory with the "radicals" of the 1J4—nor, for that matter, with anyone else. As a leader of the 1J4 bitterly complained: "We spent ourselves in the struggle in the streets, and it is the *cívicos* who profited from our struggle."[201] This in fact was the strategy of the UCN: let the *catorcistas* battle in the streets with the police and in support of the general strike, thus providing an excellent and inexpensive means of pressure on Balaguer and on the United States.

Then, on 9 December, the *cívicos* abandoned the general strike, and ten days later they reached a final agreement on the Council of State with Balaguer. Cries of rage and indignation went up in the *catorcista* camp. Rejecting "in toto" the "neo-Trujilloist Council of State" created "behind the people's backs,"[202] the 1J4 broke with the UCN. Now the *catorcistas* saw the UCN as an organization "controlled by reactionaries and neo-Trujilloists, and servile to U.S. imperialism."[203] Theirs was an impotent rage, a frustrated indignation. To the starving Dominican people, exhausted after months of struggle, the 1J4 could only offer more struggle and more suffering, with rewards both distant and vague. As a former *catorcista* leader admits: "We ourselves didn't know what we wanted . . . we were simply fighting in the streets . . . we had no achievable, feasible goals."[204] To the reality of the Council of State, the *catorcistas* opposed grandiose and ill-defined schemes. An abundance of words and slogans could not mask their great confusion.

The UCN, on the other hand, offered the Dominican people the mirage of democratic government (the Council of State), the illusion of social reforms, of bread, of work. All this would begin at once, in peace and with the generous support of the United States.

The people were tired—they followed the lead of the UCN and welcomed the Council of State. In late 1961 and early 1962 the UCN was without doubt the strongest political force in the Dominican Republic, while the 1J4 lost droves of supporters alienated by its intransigence. On 6 January 1962 the UCN officially became a political party, thus completing an "evolution" that Juan Bosch had predicted from the outset. Again the *catorcistas* cried treason—and again in vain.

While the 1J4 vented its fury against one and all, the party of Juan Bosch appeared as a model of moderation. Soon after the flight of the "Wicked Uncles," the PRD for the first time broke the opposition's united front. To Bosch, "the people had nothing to gain by the overthrow of Balaguer,"[205] and the PRD refused to support the general strike.[206] At the same time, however, it rejected Balaguer's and Rodríguez Echavarría's invitations to enter the government. "I told Echavarría that it was not in my interest, nor in his, nor in the interest of Dr. Balaguer to continue discussions on that topic," Juan Bosch later wrote.[207] In fact, the PRD chose an independent course and preached moderation to the opposing forces. It condemned violence, urged the Catholic Church to act as a mediator, and exhorted the antagonists to renew the negotiations, while itself refusing to participate in the talks. When at last the UCN and Balaguer agreed on the establishment of the Council of State, the PRD gave further proof of its "moderation": while the 1J4 attacked the "remnants of Trujilloism," the UCN, the United States, and the PRD, and while the *cívicos* continued to stress their mistrust of Balaguer, Bosch briefly announced that the PRD was not opposed to the Council.[208] Still, the PRD refused the few cabinet posts that the UCN offered the party. According to Bosch, this refusal "no doubt made the *cívicos* sigh with relief, for it meant more spoils for them."[209]

The "moderation" of the PRD during this period was welcomed as "constructive" by Consul General Hill and Arturo Morales-Carrión, the U.S. negotiators in Santo Domingo,[210] but it provoked the hatred of the 1J4. The refusal of the PRD to participate in the general strike was, for the *catorcistas*, the first in a series of betrayals. And thus began the myth of the "Trujilloism" of the PRD, the party of the anti-Trujilloist exiles. It was a myth that the UCN would try in vain to revive and exploit a year later, in the final weeks of the electoral campaign.

Bosch's analysis of the situation explains the moderation of the PRD. This moderation, however, was not passive, for it concealed both long-range goals and, at the moment, feverish activity. Said Bosch:

> While the *cívicos* were moving into positions of power—without our opposition, let me add—throughout the country, in villages, towns, and cities, PRD activists devoted themselves to establishing party committees. They worked around the clock, with a crusader's zeal, winning converts, handing out leaflets, rounding up furniture—desks, chairs, typewriters—everything needed to set up Party offices. . . . They went on the air and organized rallies; they scouted around for medicine and old clothes and distributed them to the poor in the slums; they went wherever a community needed them and applied themselves to alleviating the problem; they served as mediators between workers and their bosses, between the authorities and the people.[211]

On 1 January 1962 the Council of State was installed. Confronting Balaguer, Trujillo's last president, were the six "colleagues" forced on him by the UCN and the Americans. They all belonged to the "democratic opposition"; all had fought for the end of the Trujillo regime. With three members on the

Council, the UCN dominated the new government. The three—Rafael Bonnelly, Nicolás Pichardo, Eduardo Read Barreras—were prominent *cívicos* and representatives of the *gente de primera*.[212] A fourth councilman, Monsignor Eliseo Pérez Sánchez, "described as a critic of the Trujillo family and an open opponent of Dr. Balaguer's Government,"[213] brought the prestige of the church and the desired political orientation: he was "a follower of the UCN."[214] The other two members of the Council—Antonio Imbert Barrera and Luis Amiama Tió—were "independents." As the sole survivors of the group that had planned Trujillo's murder, they were chosen, at the suggestion of the Americans, because of their status as "national heroes."[215]

And yet there was something unsettling about this anti-Trujilloist Council: perhaps it was the Trujilloist past of all the members. Imbert Barrera and Amiama Tió had killed the tyrant, but only after they had served him.[216] Had their act been the result of a suddenly awakened "democratic spirit,"[217] or the vile plot of underlings who, seeing their master on the verge of disaster, looked to the future and betrayed him? Were these men Judases or "national heroes"? Judases, given their Trujilloist past; Judases, judging by what they would do in the coming years. Monsignor Pérez Sánchez—that "critic of the Trujillo family"—had served Trujillo as a senator since 1956. The master's death did not shake his "fidelity" to the regime. Only after Ramfis' flight and the debacle of the "Wicked Uncles" did that "courageous" priest decide to switch camps.[218] Pichardo? Read Barreras? They, too, made the ignominious transition from servants of Trujillo to opposition leaders.[219]

But the epitome of opportunism was Rafael Bonnelly, standard-bearer of a greedy, unscrupulous minority that fed on the misery of the people; Rafael Bonnelly, prominent *cívico*, first vice-president of the Council of State, and president-designate after Balaguer. During the long night of the Trujillo regime, Bonnelly had been cabinet minister, ambassador, and government prosecutor at the trials of the anti-Trujillo "criminals." If because of his past Balaguer deserved to be exiled, then Bonnelly was a fit traveling companion. "From head to foot, from one end to the other, inside and out, Bonnelly was as stanch a *trujillista* as Balaguer, and more blameworthy than Balaguer for the vilest aspects of Trujilloism."[220] Bonnelly fell from favor in 1960, when his son, a member of the clandestine 1J4, was arrested by the SIM. To his son's "mistakes," and to them alone, Bonnelly owed his good fortune of having been cut off from the high-ranking posts he coveted. As Bosch wrote: "A great many fathers of . . . [*catorcista*] youths found in their sons' revolt against the Trujillo regime—in the jailings, torture, and exile of their offspring—the necessary justification to go on enjoying the fruits of power after Trujillo's fall. Strong evidence in support of this assertion: Rafael F. Bonnelly."[221]

These were the men who the UCN had picked to lead the country toward "democracy." One might react to the choices with surprise, but surprise could only betray ignorance. For the UCN was far from being the party of Viriato and Antinoe Fiallo, men who had been genuinely anti-Trujilloist.[222] The UCN was the party of a particular sector of Dominican society, the *gente de primera*. This sector had submitted to Trujillo, collaborating with him, not out of inclination or conviction, but out of inherent opportunism. Rather than a Viriato Fiallo, the Bonnellys and the Pichardos were the true representatives of their caste and hence their party. It was only logical, then, that Bonnelly take over the power that he never would cease to covet.[223] Still, the UCN's victory was incomplete and would be so as long as Balaguer and Rodríguez Echavarría remained. Even before the new government began to function, the party newspaper ominously predicted that "the [*cívicos*] on the Council will have serious obstacles to overcome."[224]

On 4 January 1962 the OAS lifted the sanctions. The move was intended to reward the "resolution" of the Dominican crisis, but in fact only added to it. Since Balaguer had agreed to quit once the sanctions were gone, the UCN now vehemently took him at his word. True, Balaguer had left himself room to maneuver: he would leave by "27 February, at the latest." But the *cívicos* would not wait. Crowds demonstrated again in the streets. Economic chaos aggravated the political crisis: "We are hungry," cried the masses gathered around the Presidential Palace.[225] Once again the 1J4 threw itself into the struggle. Balaguer and Rodríguez Echavarría were still the targets, but as usual the *catorcistas* lacked clear objectives, and once again they played into the hands of the UCN, a party the 1J4 had learned to despise.

It was a crisis without heroes. Bonnelly, Rodríguez Echavarría, Balaguer, and the UCN played out their roles as eternal protagonists in an inglorious battle. The only ones worthy of admiration—or at least sympathy blended with compassion—were those who were fighting in the streets for a cause not their own: the starving Dominican people and the young *catorcistas*, middle-class youths expiating the crimes of their fathers.

"The situation deteriorated daily," until finally, on 16 January at 4 P.M., the powder keg exploded. At UCN headquarters in Independence Park in the heart of Santo Domingo a pair of loudspeakers demanded "the resignation of Balaguer and the immediate dismissal of Rodríguez Echavarría."[226] The crowd that was gathered around the building shouted its approval. Suddenly half a dozen tanks rumbled into the area, accompanied by a detachment of infantry. The air was heavy with tension. Colonel Manuel Antonio Cuervo Gómez, commander of the detachment of troops, demanded that the loudspeakers be silenced and the radio equipment turned over to him. The *cívicos* refused. The crowd was edgy, agitated, aroused against the soldiers. Tensions were at a peak. Then, "without warning, the soldiers fired on the unarmed crowd, . . . killing and wounding."[227]

Who gave the order to fire? Neither Balaguer nor Rodríguez Echavarría, and not Colonel Cuervo either, it seems. But it does not really matter. Events that no "compromise" could stop had been set in motion—once again there would be a test of strength. Rodríguez Echavarría struck first. Balaguer cleared the way for him by resigning from the Council. His resignation, which the UCN had long strived to impose, was rich with irony, for Balaguer's successor would not be the *cívicos'* candidate, Rafael Bonnelly. Bonnelly was arrested along with Pichardo and Read Barreras, the other *cívico* councilmen. "Out of respect to the Church,"[228] Rodríguez Echavarría chose not to arrest Monsignor Pérez Sánchez. The choice was easy, since in or out of jail Pérez Sánchez was too great a coward to represent a threat.

A "civil-military" junta was set up under the puppet presidency of Huberto Bogaert, a personal friend of Balaguer. Power, however, was in the hands of Rodríguez Echavarría. Balaguer swore in the members of the junta, including the "national heroes" and former councilmen Imbert Barrera and Amiama Tió. The "heroes" chose to escape the fate of their colleagues Bonnelly, Pichardo, and Read Barreras, and remained at the Presidential Palace, making the switch from Council to junta.[229] Was this a manifestation of the "democratic ideal" that had stirred them at the time of Trujillo's death? Here was a first clue to the question: Judases or patriots?[230]

But the junta survived for only two days. First came the popular reaction: beginning on 17 January, a general strike once again paralyzed the country; massive walkouts by government personnel brought the machinery of state to a standstill; in the streets crowds boldly confronted the "forces of order" defying the curfew, and at least ten more victims were added to the four killed at Independence Park.[231] Then came the reaction of the United States. John Hill, chargé d'affaires ad interim since the renewal of diplomatic ties between Washington and Santo Domingo, refused all contact with a government he did not recognize.[232] At the same time the State Department warned that "the United States is obliged to restudy its policies towards the Dominican Republic, since those policies have been based on the assumption of continued constitutional rule and an uninterrupted transition to a fully democratic government."[233] In effect, the statement threatened a return to the status quo ante: absence of diplomatic relations and an abrupt end to the indispensable economic aid that had begun since the establishment of the Council of State.

By 17 January, the rats had begun to flee the sinking ship: the two "national heroes" sought asylum in the U.S. embassy.[234] A day later at San Isidro, Dominican officers arrested the unresisting General Rodríguez Echavarría, together with the rest of the junta. Balaguer had already taken refuge at the Nunciature.

So the crisis was over. It never approached the severity of the one set off two months earlier by the return of the "Wicked Uncles." This time the Dominican opposition was stronger, and the position of the "would-be dictator" weaker. Rodríguez Echavarría's dismissal of a number of officers had not sufficed to ensure his control over the armed forces.[235] There was a widespread conviction, moreover, that the enterprise was doomed to failure from the start, for how could a parvenu like Rodríguez Echavarría, already defeated a month earlier, succeed where the Trujillos themselves had failed? This time, for many opportunists the choice had been obvious, hence the flood of resignations within the government and the sudden revival of "civic" spirit among many high-level officials.

And this time the United States had not played the decisive role. Rather, the Dominican people had wrecked the plans of General Rodríguez Echavarría, who was now in jail; Balaguer had taken refuge at the Nunciature. On 7 March they were both allowed to leave the country.[236] Bonnelly replaced Balaguer at the head of the government; Imbert Barrera and Amiama Tió continued to sit unperturbed in the Council. Donald Reid Cabral, important member of the UCN and illustrious representative of the *gente de primera*, was named the seventh member of that august body. A phase in Dominican history—"Nicaraguization or democratization"—seemed at an end. The second Council of State was born.

Chapter 3

The Provisional Government of the Council of State (18 January 1962-27 February 1963) and the Constitutional Government of Juan Bosch (27 February 1963-25 September 1963)

When the second Council of State took power, the Dominican Republic was struggling with extremely serious economic and social problems.

The country was agricultural. In August 1960, 69.7 percent of the population was rural—2,124,980 out of a total of 3,047,070 Dominicans.[1] Dominican agriculture always had been characterized by the unequal distribution of land, and the inequality had intensified during the last years of the Trujillo Era. In the ten years from 1950 to 1960, the total area under cultivation had increased by only 13 percent, yet the number of farms rose by 62 percent, from 276,848 to 450,335 (table 3.1).[2] This increase in the number of units was achieved by breaking up medium-sized estates and even *minifundia*. Clearly, "the [Trujillo] regime's highly touted land reform program . . . only increased the number of *minifundia*."[3] "Nearly two million people [were] living . . . in subhuman condition."[4] Landed property was concentrated in a few hands (table 3.2).

All too often the peasants did not even own the scraps of land they tilled. In 1968, a team of Dominican investigators reported: "Of the farms in the survey, 43.7% are worked under *contratos de arriendo, colonato* or some such system. The rents exacted in these cases amount to more than 50% of the harvest."[5] The absence of modern agricultural methods and techniques and the unhealthy division between *latifundia* and *minifundia* meant that, despite the country's favorable climate and soil, the yield from Dominican agriculture was "notoriously low."[6]

The standard of living on the farms was even lower. "Many . . . live little or no better than the next-door Haitians, who are proverbially cited as the poorest of the hemisphere. Those dependent on subsistence farming are the worst off, but even the rural employed work for a pittance. In the area around Cotuí cane cutters were earning 55 cents per ton in 1962 with an entire family, including the women, able to cut around two tons per day. These wages occur in a country where prices, including those for such basics as rice and beans, were higher by far than in the U.S."[7]

65

Table 3.1. Number and Size of Farms in the Dominican Republic: 1950-60

Area (in hectares)	1950		1960	
	Number	%	Number	%
less than 1	92,854	33.5	225,817	50.1
1-5	116,553	42.1	162,766	36.1
6-10	32,864	11.9	34,071	7.6
11-20	17,289	6.2	15,548	3.5
21-50	9,778	3.5	7,872	1.7
51-100	3,249	1.2	2,630	0.6
101-200	1,213	0.4	954	0.2
201 or more	920	0.3	677	0.2
undeclared	2,128	0.8	--	--
Total	276,848	99.9	450,335	100

SOURCE: Inter-American Development Bank, *Progreso Socio-económico en América Latina. Cuarto Informe Anual–1964,* p. 513. Because of the dearth of statistics on the Dominican Republic, most of these figures must be regarded with reservation and accepted only as indicative.

In a few areas of the country, in particular the Cibao, the highly fertile soil eased the misery: "Most of the campesinos in these areas wear Western clothes (however raggy) and shoes (however full of holes). Their houses are made out of wood, and may even have a floor. They may own a chicken or two and have a small plot of land on which they grow a few beans and some yucca for home consumption."[8] Above all, they could eat two meals a day!

Such "luxuries," however, were unknown in other parts of the country. Wiarda observed: "Most [peasants] have inadequate clothes, food or housing, no readily available water[9] and no electricity. Their shanties are patched together with leaves and mud and their clothes with hardly more substantial materials. Little malformed children run naked wallowing in the same grime and filth as the pigs. . . . Many have bloated bellies due to malnutrition, while scars

Table 3.2. Concentration of Property

Area (in tareas)*	Percent of total number of farms	Occupied area	Percent of total area
80 or less	86.2	8,484,700	19
81-800	12.8	11,989,000	27
801 or more	1	23,701,200	54

SOURCE: Gifford E. Rogers, *Agrarian Reform Defined and Analyzed with Special Emphasis on the Dominican Republic* (Santo Domingo: International Development Services, March 1964), p. 103.

*A hectare=15.901 *tareas.*

and marks frequently cover their bodies as a result of the bites and diseases which they accumulate."[10]

This grim picture is supported by statistics. As late as 1968, the average daily income of a peasant family was $1.21, and the per capita income, $0.22. Of the latter, $0.18, or 80 percent, went for food.[11] And "only 0.5% of rural housing [was] made of permanent materials. With an average of six persons per family, which would require dwellings of at least three rooms, only 5% of the 407,000 rural housing units ha[d] three rooms or more; 75% of those units had only one room."[12]

Even Trujillo was unable to stem the flow of peasants leaving the farms to seek their fortunes in the cities. From 1950 to 1960, the urban population swelled by 81.3 percent—from 508,408 to 922,090. The population of the capital more than doubled—from 181,533 to 369,980.[13] The *barrios altos*, a succession of squalid slums to the north and northwest of Santo Domingo, were proof that the peasants had traded the misery of the countryside for even more wretched conditions in the city. Former ambassador John Martin's picture of the slums of Moca—"fetid, hot, squalid, hideous—pigs, children, and nursing mothers penned up in six-by-six dirt-floored huts jammed almost wall to wall, only narrow urine-muddied dirt pathways between them"—was a familiar Dominican, and Latin American, scene.[14]

Under Trujillo, between 1950 and 1958, the GNP increased at an annual rate of 7 percent. Dominican "industrialization" had begun, but to what effect? "Industrialization began under conditions of woeful inefficiency. . . . From 1950 to 1958, the nation's industry was characterized by lack of coordination, technological and organizational inefficiency, dependence on imported raw materials and very costly native fertilizers, and an extreme concentration of industry ownership. Industrial growth, therefore, had little impact on the development of the national market."[15]

At the same time, the government followed a "deliberate policy of keeping the people in ignorance and of barring the young from the institutions of higher learning and the technical schools. Illiteracy and the dispersal of the vast majority of the population in the rural areas shielded [the regime] from the threat of the social pressures born of dire poverty, political awareness and contact between different income groups. Most of our urban population had never seen, let alone held, a passport."[16]

Futhermore, "the reading material, both technical and nontechnical, available to the young was extremely limited, and selected in strict accordance with the regime's security norms. In short, isolation was virtually complete. The lack of trained administrators and of a skilled work force that afflicts our country today—and undermines rapid technological advances in agriculture, industry and public services—is the offshoot of this isolation and the deliberate policy of under-education."[17] Such a policy was, however, "the only way of keeping the young pacified and of forcibly reconciling the poverty of the people with social tranquillity." At the same time, it made possible "a low level of social services, especially health care, housing and urbanization, provision of drinking water, and such, all of which matched the rampant poverty, the subsistence wages, the high rate of unemployment and the inability of the people to realize their plight and press for change."[18]

"If one suspends judgment as to the Government's ends, then the economic means it applied were coherent and compatible with the goal of achieving rapid growth in the national product in order to increase the incomes of a small minority." Using any other criteria, "it would be difficult to find a more defective model for growth anywhere on the continent."[19]

Despite these problems, the 1950s were the "golden age" of the Dominican economy under the Trujillo regime. In 1959, however, economic crisis gripped the nation. A poor country slipped even deeper into poverty; its wretched people became even more miserable. Table 3.3 tells the story.

Table 3.3. Rates of Growth of the Leading Economic Variables (Base Year Prices: 1962)

Economic Variables	Years	
	1950-58	1958-61
	(in percentages)	
Gross national product	7.0	-0.3
Gross domestic product	6.5	-0.3
Gross investment	12.5	-26.0
Public investment	10.7	-18.4
Private investment	14.0	-32.0
Exports	5.4	3.8
Imports	9.8	-15.5
Private consumption	5.9	-0.2

SOURCE: Dominican Republic, *Plataforma para el desarrollo*, p. 8, table 1.

Thirty weeks of chaos followed Trujillo's assassination. First Ramfis and Balaguer, then Balaguer and Rodríguez Echavarría, clung tenaciously to power. The political chaos exacerbated the economic crisis. In 1961, the GNP plunged by 8 percent compared with the 1960 figure and exports were down by 19 percent. Unemployment was estimated at between 33 and 56 percent of the total labor force.[20] Such reality demanded dramatic measures that the "do-nothing Consejo"[21] was neither able nor willing to take, partly since its nature doomed it to inefficacy: "Because it owed its very existence to American intervention, and because its stated purpose was to phase itself out of being, the Council lacked genuine sources of authority."[22] Added to this was the shortage of trained personnel, a scourge common to underdeveloped countries, indeed a main characteristic of underdevelopment. The shortage was particularly acute in the Dominican Republic—one more unhappy legacy of the Trujillo years. "There were only three Dominicans with bachelor degrees in business administration. There were no economists and no planners to direct the change toward . . . all the sorely needed economic and social reforms which the country urgently required."

Incompetence and inefficiency were rife at all levels. "Such was the lack of administrative experience in the Dominican government that the Council of State members were forced to spend precious hours on simple matters like the authorization of licences for carrying weapons or the addition of a few employees to the Santo Domingo Sanitation Department—all matters that should have been handled at a much lower level."[23]

With the end of the Trujillo Era, the family's holdings passed into the hands of the state, but the men who had managed those holdings were gone. Most of the key managers and technicians in Trujillo's various enterprises were foreigners, and when the regime collapsed, nearly all naturally left the country. Since Dominicans qualified to fill the vacated posts were scarce, under the Council "the majority of these industries were being operated by men totally inexperienced and incapable of successfully conducting business."[24]

Despite an abundance of attenuating circumstances, one fact should not be forgotten: the *civicos* had not seized power with the intention of pursuing a "social revolution," democratic or otherwise. The Council was the tool of those sectors that had dominated Dominican society until Trujillo appeared and made them all his lackeys. With Trujillo gone, the *civicos* hoped for "a new government in which their privileges and prerogatives would not be usurped." Some, perhaps, recognized the bitter necessity of initiating nominal reforms, but even then, their outlook continued to be limited to a world "in which their lofty position would be maintained."[25]

Corruption was rampant. Power in the Dominican Republic had always been "a means of gaining personal advantage, usually economic, for oneself. If a member of the government failed to enrich himself through peculation, he was considered either stupid or a fool." Though not quite the "wholesale plundering" of the Trujillo era, under the *civicos* "this style of peculation was particularly pronounced: . . . awarding government contracts to friends and relatives, . . . receiving favors and goods in return for some service, . . . self-aggrandizement by virtue of one's inside knowledge of a pending government program."[26] At times—indeed often—this meant outright robbery. Staff members told Ambassador Martin that "some four million dollars disappeared from the sugar mill in Haina during 1962 and 1.5 million dollars from the Foreign Office petty cash fund." But, as usual, there was not sufficient evidence to apprehend the thieves even though there were plenty of clues. Antonio Imbert Barrera, for one, "was deeply involved in Haina." The "national hero" who "treated the poor as a feudal lord might have, . . . carried large rolls of ten dollar bills" around the country "and distributed them to the crowds."[27] And what was the source of his new-found wealth?

Only the economic assistance of the United States in the amount of $50 million permitted the Council to survive.[28] And American pressure pushed the Council to enact on 14 June 1962 the law of agrarian reform. But to get this "poorly drafted law"[29] through the Council, the U.S. embassy had to overcome the resistance of the unwilling councilors. The embassy encountered particularly fierce opposition from Donald Reid Cabral, one of the most influential of the *Consejeros*. Reid Cabral was "adamant against agrarian reform. . . . 'I will fight it in the Consejo and if it passes anyway, I will fight it outside,' " he stormed.[30]

Halfhearted in the field of social reform, the Council was fired with enthusiasm in the face of the "red threat." It waged war not only on the "national front"—against the Dominican "Communists"—but on the international front as well: against Castroist Cuba, outpost of "Soviet imperialism" in the western hemisphere. Only recently reintegrated into the inter-American family, the Council proved vehemently combative. At the OAS Foreign Ministers Meeting at Punta del Este (22-31 January 1962), José Antonio Bonilla Atiles, the Council's foreign minister, voted "correctly" all along the line, adding his voice to those clamoring for harsh measures against Castro's Cuba. Stressing "the parallels between the Trujillo tyranny and the regime of Premier Fidel Castro," he urged the conference "to apply against Cuba the kind of sanctions that helped destroy the Trujillo dictatorship."[31] Two months later, Bonilla Atiles renewed his appeal. "Just as the OAS had helped the cause of Dominican liberation, so it should now assist the Cuban people to achieve their liberty."[32] This was the theory of the "precedent," so dear to the U.S. government (see above, Chapter 2).

In September, at Caracas, Bonilla Atiles declared that the Dominican Republic "favored the recognition of the Cuban government-in-exile and the invocation of the Rio de Janeiro Treaty of 1947 in an effort to solve the Cuban question."[33] A month later, when the Cuban missile crisis erupted, the Council rallied to the cause. "No government in Latin America cooperated more wholeheartedly." The Council went beyond mere declarations of unconditional support for the U.S. naval blockade of Cuba. "Two Dominican ships became the first to join the U.S. on the quarantine line."[34] Ambassador Martin later wrote that these ships

> soon developed trouble and limped into Puerto Rico, where we [the U.S.] spent about a hundred thousand dollars repairing them and paying the crews—Dominican officers had pocketed the subsistence money sent by the Dominican government. We installed some three hundred light bulbs in the ships; the crew promptly stole them. And, returning to Santo Domingo, the quarantiners smuggled in eighty-two refrigerators duty-free. Despite all this I thought a show of Hemispheric solidarity worth the price.[35]

Tireless defender of "democracy" abroad, the Council fulfilled its obligations at home as well. At first, it is true, there was some rather disconcerting wavering. To underscore its break with the "Trujilloism" of Balaguer, in the chaos of those initial days the Council sanctioned—or was helpless to prevent—the return of a certain number of exiles, "reds" of various shades who had been barred from the Republic. Hugo Tolentino Dipp, a bright young Dominican historian, returned on 21 January 1962. With him came Rafael Calventi Gaviño, Chito Henríquez Vásquez, and Diego Bordas Hernández. A second group included the leader of the MPD, Máximo López Molina, and also the first members of the PSP, Tulio Hostilio Arvelo Delgado, Juan Ducoudray Mansfield, and a few others.

But the Council quickly recovered. Although the MPD and the PSP were still outlawed, the new authorities were not yet content. As foreign minister Bonilla Atiles told Ambassador Martin, "Deportations were essential—public trials created martyrs."[36] Thus, on 20 February 1962, Law 5819 was promulgated, declaring a state of national emergency: "Any person or group of persons whose conduct or actions may be thought to constitute a threat to the nation's peace because of subversive activities or agitation aimed at obstructing the electoral process may be banished by the Council of State from Dominican soil until the state of emergency is over."[37] A few days later, Hugo Tolentino, Rafael Calventi, Chito Henríquez, and Diego Bordas were again driven into exile, soon followed by others. The Council, which alone could decide who would be deported, was very broad-minded in its choice of victims. By the end of the year, the United States alone had received some 125 deportees.[38]

But an exasperated and disappointed population confronted the "do-nothing Council" with a wave of violent demonstrations in the country's major cities, demonstrations that at times flared into riots. "Deportations were no real solution to the riots," Martin later observed, since "the Consejo, fearing the parties' wrath, did not deport many."[39] Martin successfully urged other measures—

> methods once used by the police in Chicago. There, if a policeman saw an ex-convict or a known hoodlum on the street, he picked him up 'on suspicion,' took him to the station, held him the legal limit, then released him— only to raid his flat that night, rout him out of bed, and start all over; time after time harassing him, hoping finally to drive him out of town. It was illegal detention, and often worse—prisoners were sometimes beaten. It is one of the gravest abuses of a citizen's constitutional rights. Frequently as a writer I had inveighed against it, and my wife had been a member of the Illinois board of the American Civil Liberties Union.
>
> Now, trying to support a faltering Caribbean government that the Castro/Communists sought to overthrow, I favored such methods. The alternatives simply seemed unacceptable—a leftist takeover, a military takeover in reaction, or slaughter in the streets. Just the same, I knew that bad means tend to corrupt good ends. And I remembered Adlai Stevenson's denouncing Senator McCarthy's methods of attacking communism: "We begin to resemble the thing we hate."[40]

Yet the Dominican far left was weak.[41] The PSP was returning to the country after twelve years of exile, [42] its members full of hope. Their past was glorious and even in exile they had never stopped fighting. The *catorcistas* received them with respect and admiration; they were the "AltKommunisten," the "sabios," the real Marxists. Why shouldn't the PSP nourish hopes of winning the nation's ardent youth to communism, of making the 1J4 more like the

PSP, of ultimately building a mass party? At the university, important student leaders, such as Asdrúbal Domínguez Guerra, were already moving toward the PSP. The return from exile of Quirico Valdez and Justino José del Orbe, former labor leaders of rank, members of the party's Central Committee, and the "conquest" of Mario Sánchez Cordoba, legal affairs secretary of the United Labor Front for Autonomous Unions (Frente Obrero Unido Pro-Sindicatos Autónomos or FOUPSA)[43] fed all too many illusions within the PSP.

Little came of these hopes. By February the PSP cell of the 1J4 had been destroyed, and the *catorcistas'* respect quickly turned to reserve, reserve soon hardened to distrust, and distrust led inexorably to hostility. At the University, even Asdrúbal Domínguez's influence could not erase the bitter fact that the 1J4 "attract[ed] the young"[44] and the PSP was doomed to remain a minority party. Disappointments within the worker movement took their toll. In May 1962, Mario Sánchez Cordoba was forced out of FOUPSA. Despite scattered gains throughout the year, the PSP's influence was limited to a few secondary labor unions, and even there the party was largely a minority.[45]

In February 1963, as the term of the Council of State came to an end, the PSP was a mere *grupito* of some two hundred, most of them in the capital. Only a few cells existed in the cities of the interior, and the party was nonexistent in the rural areas.[46] Yet even two hundred Communists can seem impressive to those who, in the Latin American context, see all Communists as supermen. The party, however, was bereft of supermen; the members of the PSP were youths—bold, able, willing, but inexperienced. They were led by a small core of older members—the *viejos*—who seemed ill-adapted to Dominican reality. To make matters worse, the repression unleashed by the Council of State hampered efforts at organization and propaganda. "If only the party cadres had been steeled in their clandestine struggle."[47] Unfortunately, they had not.

Equally despondent was the MPD, whose inglorious route in October 1961 we have seen (see Appendix II). It had learned nothing from its failures. Under the Council of State, the party's "methods of struggle and . . . style of operating were vague and wayward, rather than definite and clear." But it was no longer a matter of right-wing opportunism: "Our Party, with only a rudimentary cellular organization and a feeble ideological training, plunged into ultraleftist deviations, leading to the creation of the Movimiento Revolucionario 20 de Octubre [Revolutionary Movement of 20 October] or MR 20-10."[48] "Enough politicking, let's act!"[49] The MR 20-10 was born out of the "fierce contempt for politics" of Andrés Ramos Peguero, who, together with Máximo López Molina, headed the MPD. Since February 1962, Ramos Peguero had been selecting "activists in different parts of the capital, individuals who were generally politically unsophisticated, but had a good military training."[50] These he welded into the MR 20-10, the military arm of the party, which was designed to trigger "the REVOLUTIONARY struggle à outrance, using whatever means were necessary to defeat the Trujilloist murderers and hatchet men in the service of the Council of State,"[51] in effect, "an attempt to make the revolution by killing off the police force one by one."[52]

This absurd undertaking involved a few dozen ill-equipped men fired by the "opportunistic, adventurous idea of armed action in the cities without the participation of the urban and rural masses."[53] The scheme was doomed from the start. Indeed, the "epic" of the MR 20-10 amounted to the murder of a single policeman on 31 March 1962. Soon thereafter, Ramos Peguero was arrested with a number of his associates and later sentenced to twenty years hard labor.[54] Deprived of its leader, poorly organized, and unable to survive underground, the MR 20-10 collapsed.

Thus the MPD lost its "military arm." Not until the civil war of 1965—three years later—did the party "reestablish its military apparatus,"[55] and then on a very limited basis. Weakened by the repression and bereft of its two historical leaders (López Molina was arrested on 14 November 1962 and deported a few days later), by early 1963 the MPD had as few members as the PSP. Even weaker than the PSP within the university and among the workers, the MPD drew its strength from "its" sector of Dominican society, a sector the PSP could never touch—the *chiriperos*, the unemployed.

From December 1961 to January 1962, the 1J4 had lost much of its influence, but in the months that followed, the party recouped at least part of its losses. Disappointed in the Council of State—"white, oligarchical and remote"[56]—large segments of the population turned to the two main opposition parties: the PRD and the 1J4.[57] At the same time that it "move[d] . . . upward,"[58] in early spring the 1J4 became involved in a "growing trend toward guerrilla warfare,"[59] that, once again, would isolate it from the masses.

In March 1962 a handful of former members of the MR1J4—led by Hipólito ("Polo") Rodríguez Sánchez—returned to the Dominican Republic from Cuba, where they had spent a few months. Completely identified with Castro's Movimiento Revolucionario 26 de Julio, they talked with the authority of men who had seen the "promised land." There was no doubt in their minds: the 1J4 must never become an "electoral" party; it must seize power through armed struggle, following the Cuban example.

Within the 1J4's Central Committee (Comité Ejecutivo Central or CEC), a group of "hard-liners"—the *duros*—emerged, men particularly susceptible to the "ultra-Castroist" influence of Polo Rodríguez and his friends. At the heart of the group stood Manolo Tavárez and the four men later mocked as the "smart boys"—the *supersabios*—of the party: Fidelio Despradel Roque, Roberto Duvergé Mejía, Luis Genao Espaillat, Juan Miguel Román. Opposed to this group were the "softies"—the *flojos*—who, although they called themselves "Castroites" and accepted the principle of guerrilla warfare, believed victory by force to be impossible. A third group, clearly in the minority, was headed by Félix M. Germán, a Central Committee member, and Carlos A. Grisanty. They staunchly opposed the principle of guerrilla warfare and all Marxist influence.

Torn by these internal divisions, the party's Central Committee was impotent. It was "outside the Central Committee"[60] that the *duros*, deriving strength from Manolo's influence, plotted their course of action that "converted the Party into a band of conspirators."[61] As the electoral campaign gathered momentum throughout the land, the *duros* inaugurated their "training program."[62] In each city, those *catorcistas* most inclined to armed struggle were selected, while the *flojos* were alienated from the party, or at least from certain key posts.[63] Thus was born, in June 1962, the Infrastructure, which as the 1J4's military arm would trigger the insurrection before 20 December, the date of the elections. The "electoral farce" would not take place; instead, the 1J4 would seize power by force. The *duros* were so convinced of the ease of the enterprise that they did not even consider collaborating with the other far-left parties.

Summer came. Then autumn. December—and the elections—were approaching rapidly. The time had come for the 1J4 to begin its armed struggle. But the *duros* were forced to admit their impotence. The Infrastructure existed only as a fragile skeleton. Arms—and popular support—were sorely lacking. Badly weakened in the cities, the 1J4 was virtually nonexistent in the rural areas, where the population was often openly hostile. "If we had launched guerrilla warfare, the peasants themselves would have driven us down from the hills with clubs."[64] The *duros* wavered—what was to be done? The *flojos* "did them the favor of persuading them . . . to put up their guns and . . . wait till tomorrow."[65]

The elections would proceed as expected. But, particularly since June, the 1J4 had followed an "adventurous path" that "cut [the party] off completely . . . from the masses."[66] Both the *duros* and the *flojos* recognized that participation in the elections would have dramatically exposed the party's weakness, but they could not concur on an alternative strategy. The *flojos* were convinced that the 1J4 had to face reality: the Dominican people wanted elections— the first free elections since 1924—and would go to the polls unless barred by the kind of force the party lacked. While agreeing that the 1J4 should not present candidates, they thought that this refusal had to be tempered so as to mollify "the masses." Thus, the party should urge its partisans to vote for Bosch, "the least reactionary" of the candidates; they were going to vote for him anyway. The *duros*, however, made no distinction between Bosch and his adversaries, who were all "pawns" of American imperialism, hence equally deserving of scorn.[67] The *duros*—Manolo and the *supersabios*—imposed their will: the people were urged to boycott the elections.[68]

Once again "the 1J4 abused the masses, dictating a policy the masses could not accept." The massive turnout of the Dominican people at the polls on 20 December 1962 was a fresh and cruel defeat for the young middle-class revolutionaries. "Everybody voted: even 1J4 militants, even party cadres."[69]

The Council of State faced only a feeble threat from the far left; it faced a much graver one from the armed forces. To provoke the military, wrote Ambassador Martin, would be "quite probably the most dangerous thing the Consejo could do."[70]

Trujillo was dead; the empire had crumbled. Along with Ramfis and the "Wicked Uncles," some of the officers most associated with the Trujillo dynasty had chosen exile. Others, scapegoats, had been dismissed in recent weeks—sacrifices on the altar of "democratization." But those were mere trifles. If the Dominican Republic was indeed "a sick, destroyed nation, to be viewed as one ravaged by a thirty-years war,"[71] then what of the armed forces? For over thirty years the military had been the blind tool of the Trujillo dictatorship—hired assassins in uniform, their hands bloodied by countless crimes. Trujillo's armed forces had been a hotbed of corruption, an occupation force in their own country, a greedy parasite devouring as much as a third of the national budget.[72] Given such conditions, how important could the departure of a few officers be? To introduce political democracy—and a degree of prosperity—into the Dominican Republic, the Augean stables would first have to be cleaned. This meant a drastic reduction of the military budget and in the size of the armed forces,[73] the dismissal of hundreds of hopelessly corrupt officers, including most of the senior commanders. In short: "provoke the military."

Such an immense undertaking involved a number of risks. The threat of a military takeover was a recurring nightmare. Yet at times the Council, which was dominated by the UCN, showed a desire to act against the military chiefs who posed a threat to the monopoly of power and national wealth coveted by the *cívicos*.[74] Action was possible if the United States was willing. According to Ambassador Martin, the Americans "had several advantages. Fresh in their [the Dominican military's] memory was the appearance of the U.S. fleet on the horizon in November 1961. Fresh, too, was General Rodríguez Echavarría's unsuccessful two-day coup in January 1962." But Washington preached moderation. "We decided," wrote Martin, "I should tell president Bonnelly that, while we were in complete sympathy with his desire to purge the Armed Forces of Trujillistas, he could not count on United States help at this time in this matter."[75]

Washington's prudence was motivated in part by fear that an untimely action would push the military to revolt. But more important was the feeling that it was not only possible but necessary to reach a "working arrangement" with the armed forces. In Washington's view, as expressed by Ambassador Martin, "the military did not want to govern." They wanted only to be protected from the people's vengeance and to go on lining their pockets: "some hoped to become rich and were becoming so as they rotated the lucrative graft posts." In short, they were willing to accept the Council, as long as it kept its nose out of "military affairs." Above all "they hated and feared the Communists. Batista and his officers, fleeing Castro, had told the Dominican officers how Castro had shot their confreres at the wall; they never forgot."[76]

Washington was obsessed by the specter of another Cuba. Certainly, in the long run, the wonders wrought by the Alliance for Progress would wipe out Communism's "natural allies": poverty and illiteracy. In the long run . . . but "vitamin tablets will not save a man set upon by hoodlums in an alley." In the meantime, how could that indispensable anti-Communist stability be guaranteed in the Dominican Republic? Ramfis was gone, Balaguer was in exile, and the

Council, in the words of its friend, the U.S. ambassador, was a "tottering, un-popular, do-nothing government," on the verge of collapse. To counter the Castro-Communist threat, a single bastion remained: the armed forces, ready to step in and defend "Dios, Patria, Libertad." It was "their God, their country, and their kind of liberty," of course, but at least they were rabidly anti-Com-munist.[77]

The United States faced the same problem in the Dominican Republic that it faced in most of the hemisphere. The "Castro-Communist" threat had led the Kennedy administration to launch the Alliance for Progress and to pledge its support for social reform and political democracy in Latin America. This same threat prompted the administration to increase its support of the Latin American armed forces, the bitter enemy of political democracy and social change.

Washington dreamed of resolving this dilemma. It was decided that the American military would regenerate and democratize Dominican officers. Am-bassador Martin writes: "My attachés . . . saw [the Dominican officers] . . . daily. They made friends among them. Assiduously they worked at convincing them that democracy was here, and in a democracy the military is subordinate to the civilian power."[78] The forty-four-man Military Assistance and Advisory Group (MAAG), under the command of Lieutenant Colonel David C. Wolfe of the U.S. Marine Corps, was given the task of easing the transition of the Domini-can military from dictatorship to democracy. "Democratization" took predict-able shape: "The indoctrination of the armed forces, under the direction of Colonel Elías Wessin y Wessin, . . . concentrated primarily on simple anti-com-munism to the exclusion of almost all else. The materials used for this instruc-tion were comparable to the Birchite literature employed by General Edwin Walker."[79] Like "democratization," the civic action program aimed at cleaning up the public image of the armed forces also failed.

The United States wanted more than just "democratization." The death of Trujillo occurred when a new United States president was redirecting the major thrust of the military assistance program in Latin America from hemispheric de-fense to internal security. In a conversation with senior Dominican officers, Ambassador Martin indicated that the purpose of the Dominican armed forces was not to fight Cuban MIGs—the U.S. would do that if necessary. "In the [Dominican] Republic we wanted Dominican troops trained in counter-insur-gency in case Castro-Communist guerrilla activity began." The MAAG set to work: "By the end of the year, despite Castro/Communist outcry, we had trained three companies of counter-insurgency troops." These soldiers had to be "carefully selected—they would become the crack troops of the Republic, and we didn't want them shooting in the wrong direction."[80]

Other measures—always with the aim of buttressing the "defense capability" of the Dominican "democracy"—were undertaken. The national police force was increased from three thousand to ten thousand members at the insistence of the U.S. military mission. The hope "that the Police could be kept under civilian control and remain apolitical . . . was naive." Under its new chief, General Belisario Peguero Guerrero, the police became "the most oppressive, most corrupt, and most Trujillista of all the armed forces." Nevertheless, it proved uncommonly efficient at maintaining order against defenseless crowds, which it did until the moment of truth on 25 April 1965.[81]

The United States thus secured "peace" and "harmony" throughout 1962 by "re-educating" the Dominican armed forces. The military was reminded again and again that "Bonnelly was the President and Commander in Chief" and that the United States supported him. At the same time, the Americans repeatedly told Bonnelly that he should in no way "provoke the military."[82] The Council was thus a model of prudence, and the military, "democratic."

Neither the armed forces nor the far left posed a serious threat to the Council of State. The real danger, at least in Ambassador Martin's view, came from within: from the *Consejeros* themselves, or more accurately, from certain members of the Council, who undermined its stability by their ambition, their will to perpetuate their power, and their rivalries. This threat was embodied primarily in two men: Antonio Imbert Barrera and Luis Amiama Tió, sole survivors of the conspiracy against Trujillo. "I probably spent more time in 1962 on them and their plots than on any other single problem," wrote Martin. Imbert Barrera, convinced that "democracy would never work" and that "anyone could be bought," spent hours shut up in his office "shuffling stacks of telegrams and stacks of money, handing out jobs, ordering people arrested, firing policemen, hiring others": in short, "usurping the Presidency." Imbert Barrera and Amiama Tió, the inseparable duo, set about "running the country," "quietly collecting power, . . . pushing their relatives and friends deeper and deeper into the Government's power centers," and "trying to put together a third-power coalition of their own, hoping, no doubt, to use gangs of thugs, leftists, and police to win or steal the election." Already in control of the "machinery of criminal justice—police, secret police, immigration and Attorney General"— they strove incessantly "to get hold of the Army." "They never stopped trying to get their own man in as Army Commander," while simultaneously hoping "to put a relative of Amiama in command of the Navy."[83]

Imbert Barrera and Amiama Tió failed in this attempt to seize power in 1962. But Antonio Imbert Barrera was given a second chance three years later, in May 1965. Martin—the "liberal," the "democrat"—picked "Tony," an aspiring dictator but henceforth "a necessary bulwark against anarchy,"[84] to head a nonexistent third force that would represent only the most corrupt sectors of Dominican society (see Chapter 10). It was the last poisonous gift to the Dominican people from John B. Martin, the man who pretended to be their friend.

Thus in 1962, between two plots and two crises, the Council staggered forward, sustained, guided, and rebuked by the United States embassy. Slowly and painfully, the fateful election day approached. The first real elections in thirty-eight years—such an unexpected chance, such an exciting opportunity! Many "men of rank" were convinced that their hour had come, that they had a special message for the Dominican people. Above all, they saw a chance to steal the spotlight and enhance their prestige. For many, of course, the thought of playing a secondary role in parties that already had leaders meant humiliation, an insult to their past, to their name, but especially to their ambitions! To become president of a party and candidate for the presidency of the Republic was a far more attractive and exalting role.

Political parties were springing up like mushrooms. At one point during the height of the election struggle some twenty-nine parties could be counted. First there were the mass parties: the UCN and the PRD. The 1J4 was a case apart. There followed the little parties and the miniparties. Finally, there were the "one-man operations, existing one day and merging, dividing or disappearing the next." These latter groups "were based largely on family ties; in one of them the father was president of the party, his wife was secretary general, and his two daughters typists. Usually some friends or relatives would consent to have their names included in the party's membership rolls, but few others."[85]

If these family enterprises are excluded, the picture comes into focus. The miniparties were numerous and vexing; their programs, submerged in floods of rhetoric, were a mystery. Their leaders counted on their prestige and at times on powerful connections to garner the few thousand votes needed to elect one or two deputies—perhaps a senator—and to allow them to engage in a pleasant, profitable game: selling their votes and their influence, getting their names in the papers, going on the radio. Their goal was to be important and sought after.

"General" Virgilio Vilomar was such an aspirant. In the 1920s, he had been a pillar of the now-defunct Partido Nacional, Horacio Vásquez's party. In December 1962, he hoped to revive the party, making it his "colossus." Vilomar was a *caudillo* in search of the past.

A second contender was Horacio Ornes Coiscou, head of the Dominican Revolutionary Vanguard (Vanguardia Revolucionaria Dominicana or VRD). Ornes Coiscou boasted an impressive past. He had been one of the leaders of the anti-Trujilloist invasion at Luperón in 1949. Later, in exile, he founded the VRD. Now that Trujillo was dead, and everyone had his own party, why should he give up his? Why, indeed, would he renounce his party, when he had the friendship and support of his brother, Germán, the owner-publisher of *El Caribe*, the most widely read newspaper in the country?

General Miguel Angel Ramírez Alcantara also joined the parade. His past was honorably anti-Trujilloist, and in "his" city of San Juan de la Maguana he was the "boss," the *caudillo*. He thought of himself as "the patron of San Juan"; the townspeople and the whole province were inclined to agree. He headed the Nationalist Revolutionary Democratic Party (Partido Nacionalista Revolucionario Democrático or PNRD).

Still others tossed their hats into the ring. Nicolás Silfa and Ramón Castillo, renegade PRDistas, yielded to the lure of great adventure and founded their own miniparty. Silfa, expelled from the PRD for having violated party discipline, became founder and president of the Authentic Dominican Revolutionary Party (Partido Revolucionario Dominicano Auténtico or PRDA). Castillo, who quit the PRD because of its overly "leftist" stance, became founder and president of the Progressive Christian Democratic Party (Partido Progresista Demócrata Cristiano or PPDC). Both parties were to fail.

The UCN as well saw one of its members break off to form his own party. Claiming that it was too rightist, on 2 April 1962 Juan Isidro Jimenes Grullón broke dramatically with the UCN. The scion of an illustrious family, ennobled by over twenty years of exile, a man of uncommon culture and integrity, Jimenes Grullón would have been an eminent addition—if he could bear the discipline—to the party of his choice. He was too proud, too sure of his destiny, however, to accept any spot but the first. With a handful of partisans, he chose instead to found his own Social Democratic Alliance (Alianza Social Demócrata or ASD), which he insisted would be the party of the "democratic left." But Jimenes Grullón had forgotten that all he knew of politics was theory and that theory is no substitute for experience.

Finally, there was Mario Read Vittini. Vice-president of the Social Christian Revolutionary Party (Partido Revolucionario Social Cristiano or PRSC), Read Vittini strove to become top man. He failed, was expelled from the PRSC in October 1962, and at once founded the Christian Democratic Party (Partido Demócrata Cristiano or PDC), with himself, of course, as president.

The PRSC deserves special mention. For the Dominican Republic, it seemed to represent a modern party. In 1960 young exiles like Mario Read Vittini, Guido d'Alessandro Tavárez, and Alfonso Moreno Martínez came into contact with the Christian Democratic parties of Western Europe and Latin America. Out of this contact grew the Dominican Internal Front Assistance Group (Grupo de Ayuda al Frente Interno Dominicano or GAFID). After Trujillo's death, these same men met in Venezuela, where for three months they studied political organization under the auspices of the Venezuelan Social Christian Party, COPEI. In Caracas the PRSC's "Steering Committee" was formed, and from Caracas the party's leaders returned to the Dominican Republic in the latter half of November 1961. On 2 December, a communiqué in *El Caribe*[86] announced the creation of the new party and its statement of principles. The PRSC pretended to replace *caudillismo* with a concrete program and claimed membership in the Christian Democratic family, which was predominant in a number of Western European countries and making headway in such Latin American nations as Chile and Venezuela. It professed to be "revolutionary" but "democratic." Virulently anti-Castro, the PRSC seemed genuinely committed to political democracy.

At the time, the party was little more than a small band of "young, dedicated anti-Communist activists."[87] At no point during the election year of 1962 did the Social Christians appear to be close to victory at the polls. But what the present denied, the future, perhaps, would grant. There were a number of reasons for optimism. "Social Christian doctrine, though little known, attract[ed] workers and students alike."[88] The powerful Federation of Christian Labor (Confederación Autónoma de Sindicatos Cristianos, or CASC) established close ties with the PRSC. At the University, Social Christian students, regrouped in the Revolutionary Christian University Bloc (Bloque Revolucionario Universitario Cristiano or BRUC), were the only ones capable of stemming the tide of the "extremist" *Fragueros*.[89]

A number of priests also rallied to the new party. These "militant" priests, mostly Jesuits, were not afraid of certain social reforms. But all objectives, all reforms, had to be subordinated to a supreme task: the struggle against Communism *in all its guises*. It was not a crusade but an obsession which led the zealots to detect the "red virus" even among sincere anti-Communists and ultimately drove them into an unholy alliance with those opposed to any kind of reform.[90]

When Balaguer took refuge at the Nunciate in January 1962, the UCN was the country's dominant political force. The following months would witness its decline. The increasingly unpopular Consejo had the UCN as its chief base of support. In the eyes of the people, the UCN *was* the Consejo. In vain Viriato Fiallo did his utmost to show that "only three of the seven members of the Council could claim affiliation with the UCN."[91] In an equally futile maneuver to escape disrepute, the party decided, in its 16 April assembly, that all members who held political posts in the government should resign within ten days.

The *Consejeros*, however, clung to their posts. Of the fourteen cabinet ministers, nearly all of them *cívicos*, only two resigned: Severo Cabral y Ortíz, minister of agriculture, and Federico Alvarez, minister of the presidency. "The danger from the UCN pullout had passed," wrote Ambassador Martin.[92] As a matter of fact, no such danger ever existed.

The UCN was confident of victory at the polls. Its candidate for the presidency of the Republic, Viriato Fiallo, was a hero of anti-Trujilloism; the *cívicos* "emphasized Fiallo's nobility."[93] He was "the most honest, the most responsible, the man who most loved and loves the noble and long-suffering Dominican people."[94] But, of course, all the *cívicos* were "noble." An august assembly of distinguished names, meeting place of the cream of Dominican society, the UCN was led by men blessed from birth, whose forebears had won a place in the unhappy history of the nation, superior beings who had money, education, and white skin; they were the *gente de primera*, born to govern.

After thirty years of nearly total eclipse and abstention, their time had come. The Bermúdez, León, Cabral, Vicini, and other families launched the attack. They were vigorous leaders, braced for the rigors of an electoral campaign. They traveled "in cavalcades of big cars, wearing business suits." They were white, but they loved the blacks: "Fiallo went into a *barrio* and referred to 'my little Negritos,' a patronizing phrase that could scarcely have been better calculated to cost him their votes."[95] Their love of the people was demonstrated by a refusal to stir up class hatreds, to pit the lowly against the mighty.

The *cívicos* refused to exacerbate the sufferings of a downtrodden people by reminding them of the excessive wealth of others—wealth that, should the UCN win at the polls, those suffering masses would never see. On the contrary, their theme was nobility: "Fiallo's nobility, the people's nobility, freedom's nobility."[96] They understood the people's needs. The peasants' major ambition was not for two meals a day, a pair of shoes, school for their children. Why should peasants learn to read? No, they understood that the dream of the Dominican people was to struggle against the Communists and the Trujilloists.

Trujillo was dead and his family exiled, but for the *cívicos* the country was still thick with Trujilloists. They had to be stamped out, but with justice, not blindly. President Bonnelly himself had held important cabinet posts in the Trujillo government. Bonnelly, however, was no Trujilloist; he was the president of the anti-Trujilloist Council of State. Yet had Bonnelly not been an accomplice to Trujillo's crimes? Had he not been the powerful, feared secretary of interior and police? What a trifling, irrelevant question! For those crimes—in which he did indeed have a hand—Bonnelly, of course, felt, as his friend Ambassador Martin explained, "the contempt . . . that so many Santiago oligarchs feel; . . . he was connected, by marriage and friendship, with the Santiago oligarchy."[97]

The blame, then, lay not on Bonnelly but on those who by Trujillo's favor had risen to positions—in government, the military, business—from which their humble origins should have barred them. Balaguer, for instance, who, as a boy in Santiago, "sold soap for pennies to the poor of his neighborhood."[98] Those were the guilty ones, who had robbed what others had the right to rob, who, profiting shamelessly from the tyrant's bounties, had time and again during thirty endless years humiliated their betters, the *gente de primera*. These men were the targets of the *cívicos*' wrath. A holy crusade—a purge of the government and the military—was being mounted, and the "noble, long-suffering Dominican people" were invited to join in.[99]

On the twin war horses of anti-Communism and anti-Trujilloism, the UCN galloped toward victory, intoxicated by a triumph it already tasted. The *cívicos* dreamed of a democracy, pure and sturdy, able to refuse debilitating compromise and materialistic, demagogic reforms. Theirs would be a Christian democracy, exalting spiritual values and crowned by an atheneum of distinguished names, men of culture and refinement—a parliament in the image of the UCN. At times, however, the crusaders were plagued by doubts. Would the people fall victim to demagogues weaving secret plots? Would matter triumph over spirit? The reactionary UCN awoke with a start, promised the public the moon, and even stooped to radical proclamations.

But the attempt was halfhearted. No matter how it tried, the UCN would never lose its image as the party of the rich, indifferent to the plight of the people. Indeed, "it was difficult for a laboring man to see how he could benefit from a party led by the same elements who had traditionally kept him subjugated. It was likewise difficult for a campesino to comprehend how he would gain from an agrarian reform when some UCN leaders urged that the government-owned lands earmarked for the agrarian reform be returned to private ownership."[100] But for the *cívicos* these were trifles. With or without enthusiasm, "the campesinos would vote the way Don Juan, or Don Eduardo, told them to"[101]—that is, the UCN ticket. Besides, the party was counting on Fiallo's "heroism" and the support of large sectors of the clergy and the middle class. The outcome was never in doubt. "To hear Fiallo, the elections were a rather tiresome formality to be completed before his inauguration."[102] Perhaps that is why the UCN was slow to begin its campaign in the countryside.

Rivals in the race for power seemed insignificant. The PRD spared no effort, but its funds were scarce and its means limited. It was the party of "mediocrities": no illustrious names—no Espaillat, no Cabral.[103] It hoped to make up for these shortcomings by the organizational genius of its secretary general Angel Miolán, by the efforts of its militants, by the clarity of its message and most of all by the charisma of Juan Bosch, party president and candidate for the presidency of the Republic.

Realizing the importance of the peasant vote, the PRD set out to win the rural areas while the other parties exhausted themselves in verbal skirmishes. Although they lacked big cars and business suits, the PRD lieutenants ranged throughout the countryside gathering information on the local needs of each community. Then they created the Federación Nacional de Hermandades Campesinas (FENHERCA), the peasant arm of the PRD. Before long the party had "representatives and a functioning office at almost every widening of the road where half a dozen shacks were gathered together."[104] By contrast, the rich, powerful—but overconfident—UCN had offices only in the fifteen most important Dominican towns. Meanwhile, Bosch traveled "quietly" up and down the country in a Jeep, "his activities unreported in the press."[105] In a country lacking good roads and comfortable hotels, Bosch waged a "highly unorthodox electoral campaign of unannounced visits to virtually every slatternly settlement in the Dominican countryside."[106] He talked to the peasants "with simple, powerful eloquence."[107] Upon leaving, he never said "adios" but always "hasta la vista." His radio broadcasts, primarily aimed at rural communities, "were heard twice a day in the countryside on cheap Japanese transistor radios."[108]

Who was this Juan Bosch, this unknown at the head of a band of exiles[109] who dared to challenge the right of the "honorable men"—the *cívicos*—to recapture the levers of power? No Bosch had ever figured in Dominican history—nor in the history of any other nation. No Bosch had ever been close to the *gente de primera*, frequented their clubs, shared their way of life, their ambitions, their interests. Juan Bosch was the son of immigrants. His mother, Angela Gaviño, was Puerto Rican; his father, José ("Don Pepe"), was Spanish, a simple artisan whose dream of a better future drove him to emigrate, and who, in the Dominican Republic, never became more than a shopkeeper.

Juan Bosch was self-taught. He had no university degree to offset his lowly origins.[110] Elsewhere in Latin America, many considered him a great writer, but his books had been banned by Trujillo and were practically unknown in his own country. Few Dominicans *de primera* felt any need to explore Bosch's literary work; his lack of culture was all too obvious to them. One had only to listen to his campaign speeches, delivered in everyday language very different from that of the *gente de primera*. His language was so common that even a peasant could understand him when he said:

> In general the farmer doesn't have the means to store, for example, his beans, and he doesn't have the money to wait for a better price even if he can keep them preserved. Now, if the government bought the farmer's product from him, and if the government preserved that product, stored it or somehow kept it, then the merchant would have to buy from the government and at the price fixed by the government; or he would buy from the farmer directly, but at the fixed government price . . . .
>
> Thanks to scientific progress, we can store for up to several months not only beans and rice but also bananas, tomatoes, avocados, mangos, oranges, papayas. Suppose that you sell avocados at one cent each; a thousand rotten avocados means a loss of ten dollars—and a loss of ten dollars means a loss of meals for at least five Dominicans, . . . and this is not to mention rotten eggs, rotten pineapples, overripe tomatoes. Every year in this country we lose millions of dollars in rotten produce, and that means, for most Dominicans, several days' meals. To grow, to store and to obtain a fair price for the farmer: this is one of the country's most important needs.

And this was, "so far as we are able,"[111] what the PRD pledged. What poverty of style, what ordinary language! "Beans" and "papayas," compared with Fiallo's concern over the "noble and long-suffering Dominican people" and Jimenes Grullón's outrage at the "betrayal of the revolutionary ethic."[112]

To the *cívicos*, Bosch was a demagogue, a sower of discord and division; his message was one of hate. Calling for a "clean slate" (*borrón y cuenta nueva*), he refused to acknowledge that in the Dominican Republic the dividing line was between the "Trujilloists" and the "anti-Trujilloists." He refused to participate in a witch hunt aimed at affirming the interclass unity of the Dominican people, the Christian harmony between rich and poor, the unshakable community of interests between the *gente de primera* and the wretched masses. Instead, he emphasized the divisions in Dominican society, stressing that even without Trujillo, "the people were and always have been ruled by a minority,"[113] and, with or without Trujillo, cruelly exploited by it.

Bosch's battle was directed against this minority. To imprint vividly on the people the image of "its habitual exploiters," he resurrected an old word, *tutumpote*: the all-powerful man, the one with money and might. The word was extremely effective with the poor; it swept the country and became part of the language as a mark of infamy. Bosch wanted to teach the people to distinguish between "a miserable *calié* [police informer] and the mighty gentleman who amassed huge fortunes from the regime supported by the *caliés*." The masses had to realize that "between the *calié* and the *tutumpote*, their real enemy was the *tutumpote*."[114]

To the *cívicos'* accusation that he had brought class struggle to the Dominican Republic Bosch replied: "Class struggle, and class hatred, have always existed in Santo Domingo, but they were only used to the advantage of the *gente de primera*, while the people, who were the victims, were unaware of the injustice or saw no choice but to endure." In the eyes of the *cívicos* the argument only strengthened the accusation. In Bosch's own words, in calling attention to the exploitation that existed—and had always existed—in the Dominican Republic, he was guilty of showing the poor that "the social structure . . . was unjust and a source of injustice," and of trying to "convince them that they had the right to be given the chance to get what they had always been deprived of." This was the first time that "somebody had treated the 'children of Machepa' as if they mattered, and that somebody was the PRD. It was only logical that the 'children of Machepa' became PRDistas."[115]

A few weeks before the elections, the UCN finally realized that the PRD "demagogues" stood a good chance of stealing the victory that belonged to the *cívicos*. Their righteous anger was formidable. "We are going to use some psychological tricks," explained Luis M. Baquero, the UCN's secretary general, to Ambassador Martin. He was specific: "The Church priests are saying quietly, Bosch is bad."[116] "Bad," of course, meant "Communist." And so, in the last days of the campaign, the church raised the Communist issue.

Quietly at first, then with drums beating, elements of the clergy unleashed the offensive. Time was short and subtlety would not longer suffice. It was the moment to strike, and the heaviest blow was delivered by the Spanish Jesuit Láutico García, in an article entitled "Juan Bosch, Marxist-Leninist?" that was more a statement than a question.[117] And there were "threats of excommunication for PRD supporters, launched from pulpits . . . and in the Catholic newspaper El Amigo del Hogar."[118] Using two Catholic radio stations—Radio Santa María del Santo Cerro in La Vega and Radio Sol in Higüey—clergymen urged the people to vote against the "Marxist-Leninist" Bosch, whom they likened to "the most infamous dictators, men like Hitler, Mussolini, Himmler [!] and Castro." "If Bosch is elected," broadcast Father Faustino García over Radio Santa María del Santo Cerro, "he will be able to trample any citizen, any peasant, any worker, any woman, any child, like Fidel Castro who has shot even children."[119] The cynical Dominican episcopate refused to disavow the authors of these attacks, smugly claiming that it was up to Bosch to clear himself of these charges—with less than a week till the elections and before an electorate unaware that "only the Bishops had the authority to broadcast the official opinions of the Church."[120] Bosch's accusers, of course, failed to mention this little-known fact at the end of their diatribes. In Bosch's irrefutable words: "The hierarchy of the Dominican Church washed its hands of the matter like Pontius Pilate while a group of Pharisees shouted: 'Release Barabbas, we want Barabbas.' "[121]

Naturally, the UCN picked up and developed the Marxist-Leninist charge that the most fanatical clergymen flung at Bosch and his party. There was no longer any doubt; the case against Bosch was overwhelming:

> The Fraud is Unmasked. . . .
>
> Because all their attempts to seize power by violence have failed, the Communists have now played their last card, held in reserve for the ultimate trick. Juan Bosch was the tool of international communism, the man that the Supreme Soviet Command intended to use in case organized subversion failed. For years Bosch had been hiding his communism under the guise of democracy. At the last moment, thirteen days before the elections, Bosch has dropped his mask, showing himself as he always has been: a true Communist.[122]

New "revelations" piled up: "According to unimpeachable sources, in the last few days the supreme command of the Dominican Communists held a meeting with the PRD leader in the hope of reaching an agreement over dividing up the spoils of the Public Administration. As far as it can be determined, the PRD leaders have agreed to name three prominent red leaders to cabinet positions; from there they intend to launch a well-planned Communist invasion of the Government."[123] The UCN was not satisfied with accusing Bosch of being a Marxist-Leninist or with describing his party as "the last resort of the Communists in their bid to take over the country." The Trujilloists were dragged into the picture. The UCN press reported that "the *trujillistas* as well are giving full support—both money and manpower—to the PRD candidates, and are ready to support the PRD in a desperate and vain effort to take over the county in league with the Communists." Headlines proclaimed: "COMMUNISTS AND TRUJILLOISTS UNITE IN THE PARTY OF THE DEMAGOGUES."[124]

Even this was not enough. Blinded by its obsession to "unmask" Bosch and completely overestimating the gullibility of the Dominican people, the UCN pushed calumny to new heights: Bosch, the Trujilloist-Marxist-Leninist, was also a *latifundista* and a millionaire; in short, a *tutumpote* who owned "five hundred thousand acres in Costa Rica and . . . [had] two million dollars in Venenzuelan banks."[125] The PRD, then, was the party of Communists, Trujilloists, and millionaires!

Even Ambassador Martin, friend of the *cívicos*, admitted that, for the UCN, these attacks proved to be "dreadful mistakes."[126] It was so easy to refute the charges. Bosch the *trujillista*? He had only to point to his twenty-five years of exile and the torrents of hate that fell on him during the Era. Bosch the *tutumpote*? He had often lived in conditions of penury unknown to the "heroic" Fiallo; moreover, he "scornfully offered to sell his land for twelve cents an acre and his money for a nickel on the dollar."[127] Bosch the *comunista*? He met this charge head-on, challenging Father Láutico García, whose article had done the most harm, to a public debat. The night of 17 December, the entire country was engrossed in the debate between Bosch and the Spanish Jesuit broadcast on radio and TV. Láutico García retracted little, but he failed to prove his charges. To hundreds of thousands of Dominicans, Bosch emerged the winner of a contest "in which no benefit, and much discredit, befell the Church."[128]

Finally, on 20 December 1962, the "crime" was consummated. In an election free of violence, the people—"the humble and ignorant class"[129]—swept Bosch, the "demogogue," into the presidency of the Republic (table 3.4). The PRD triumph was complete.

Table 3.4. Election Returns: 20 December 1962

	National Office		Others		Senate	Chamber	City Council	Mayor
					Candidates for			
PRD	619,491	58.7%	592,088	56.5%	22	49	265	62
UCN	317,327	30.1%	315,371	30.1%	4	20	120	11
PRSC	54,638	5.2%	56,794	5.4%	— —	1	11	— —
PNRD	35,764	3.4%	36,972	3.5%	1	4	19	4
ASD	17,898	1.7%	18,726	1.8%	— —	— —	3	— —
VRD	6,886	.7%	18,586	1.8%	— —	— —	— —	— —
PN	1,667	.2%	4,161	.4%	— —	— —	— —	— —
PRDA	1,273	.1%	5,306	.5%	— —	— —	— —	— —

SOURCE: *Gaceta Oficial* 8749, 31 March 1963, pp. 3-116. Two of the miniparties discussed above are not listed in the table: the PPDC of Ramón Castillo and the PDC of Mario Read Vittini. The PPDC put up no candidates, while Read Vittini led the PDC into a coalition with the PNRD and became the vice-presidential nominee on the PNRD ticket. Two other miniparties, the PN and the VRD, put up their own candidates for the parliamentary and the municipal elections, but supported the PRD candidates in the presidential election. The PRDA's nominee for president was Joaquín Balaguer, in exile in New York. But the candidacy was rejected, and the party put up no candidates for the presidential election.

Two months later, on 27 February 1963, Juan Bosch was sworn in as president of the Republic. Around the cradle of this new-born democracy hovered the guardian angels, the leaders of the Latin American "democratic left": Rómulo Betancourt, president of Venezuela, Francisco Orlich, president of Costa Rica, Ramón Villeda Morales, president of Honduras, Luis Muñoz Marín, governor of Puerto Rico, who had come to wish a fellow member well. Blessings from Washington were transmitted by Vice-President Lyndon Johnson, who arrived with a gift of U.S. support.

Seven months later, Bosch was a prisoner in the Presidential Palace. A communiqué issued by the armed forces and the police informed the Dominican people that the government they had freely elected on 20 December 1962 was defunct. The democratic interlude had ended. At dawn the leaders of six "democratic" parties rushed through the deserted streets of the capital toward the Palace, there to feed, like jackals, on the carcass of the government they had so valiantly helped to liquidate. The date was 25 September 1963.

In the United States journalists and scholars were soon hard at work explaining the significance of Bosch's downfall. For conservative writers it was an easy job: Bosch was a Communist, or "soft on Communism," and his disgrace was the salvation of Dominican democracy. For the "liberals" the task was harder. Too sophisticated to take up the "Communist" tune and too "civiliz-ed" not to condemn the coup, they tried to evaluate the events more subtly and thereby reassure themselves: of course, the coup was a step backward, but poli-tical democracy in the Dominican Republic was still possible. Bosch had dug his own grave by making too many mistakes. He was too conservative—liberals like to think of themselves as progressives—and failed to carry out the sweeping social reforms he had promised. He was an inept administrator, unable to direct the machinery of government. Moreover, he was intransigent. Wiarda called him a "poet, writer and intellectual who had no experience in the give-and-take that is politics." For the liberals, Bosch proved unable to make the compromises nec-essary to placate his non-Communist opponents. Above all, he failed to persecute the far leftists, and this, they claimed, "was among the principal rea-sons for his overthrow."[130]

In truth, the regime had agonized for seven months. The new president was under constant attack from the very day he took office. His was the victory of a segment of the Dominican population that previously had never played a role in the political life of the nation: the peasants, the urban unemployed, the work-ing-class poor. Much of the lower middle class and the overwhelming majority of the "middle" middle class had opposed him, particularly the youth. At the university, the PRDistas of FURR were crushed under the massive onslaught of the far leftists of FRAGUA and the Social Christians of BURR.

To be faithful to his word, Bosch would have to undertake real social re-forms. He was willing to recognize the role of private property and of free en-terprise.[131] But social reforms are never "revolutionary" in themselves; they are revolutionary only in terms of the society to which they apply. To the "tradi-tional" elements of Dominican society, any real change would have seemed re-volutionary. It hardly mattered that Bosch intended to carry out his reforms while respecting liberties, for, as Bonnelly told his friend Martin, "Interests are interests, and they are powerful."[132]

The constitution of 29 April 1963—the Magna Carta of the regime—em-bodied Bosch's dreams for the nation. Modern and democratic, it resembled the constitutions of the Western European countries. For the Dominican Re-public, it was a "revolutionary" document that struck at some of the most deep-ly rooted inequities of Dominican life. Recognizing the need for land reform, the constitution condemned the twin evils of Latin America: the *minifundio*—"un-economical and antisocial"— and the *latifundio*—"the ownership or possession of excessive amounts of land by individuals or private concerns." While acknow-ledging and guaranteeing the right of private ownership, the constitution af-firmed the right of expropriation. Indeed it went further, stating that "In order to set the proper indemnity, [two factors] will be taken into account: on the one hand, and most importantly, the interest of the collective; on the other hand, the interest of the proprietors concerned."[133] This principle—particular-ly bold in a country accustomed to injustice—alone made it possible for an im-poverished state to carry out expropriations.

The propertied classes saw their worst fears confirmed. And the constitution was too vague, explains Ambassador Martin, a "liberal" too frequently open to the arguments of the right. The constitution, for example, condemned the *latifundio*, but left its definition to future laws. This is the usual procedure, but what was normal elsewhere could not be tolerated in the case of Bosch.

Recognizing the importance of democratic ideals, the constitution affirmed that "no Dominican will suffer expulsion from his country."[134] This provision also violated national "traditions" and upset all the "democrats" who, under the Council of State, had heartily indulged in the practice of deportations.[135] Finally, the constitution confronted the problem of cohabitation, a widespread practice among the poorer classes. It provided that "the law will determine under which conditions cohabitation between persons capable of legal matrimony might, for reasons of equity and social welfare, be considered from a *purely* [italics added] economic standpoint to be similar to wedlock." In the same spirit, the constitution forbade "public officials from drawing up birth certificates indicating whether the birth was legitimate or illegitimate, or mentioning in any way whatsoever the nature and character of the filiation, except in those exceptional cases provided for by the law." It further guaranteed that "all children, without distinction, shall enjoy the same chance for social, physical and spiritual growth."[136]

Of course, the constitution recognized "marriage as the legal basis of the family" and emphasized that "the State shall grant special protection to matrimony and the family."[137] Such "concessions," however, failed to satisfy the Dominican clergy, which regarded the constitution as an attack on "the stability of the family."[138] The constitution, moreover, contained no mention of the Concordat concluded by Trujillo in 1954,[139] nor did it grant any privileges to religious education. In short, for the church, "the New Constitution . . . [lacked] the universality necessary to be fair; . . . it [lacked] any spiritual sense whatever; . . . it [regressed] to a period when demogogic influence ignored concrete historical situations, or stifled them by means of erroneous and fanatical ideas."[140]

The constitution of 29 April 1963 was Bosch's legacy to his countrymen. With it went two other bequests: the fight against corruption and the defense of civil liberties.

Power in the Dominican Republic had always been a means of gaining for oneself pecuniary advantage, a practice that remained under the Council of State. Bosch had hoped to shatter this sorry inheritance of the past, this bitter fact of the present. Although he failed to uproot the evil—seven months could not wipe out the rot of centuries—it was not for lack of drive. Bosch waged a tireless, dramatic, almost self-destructive war on corruption that led him into the preserve of the armed forces, where he threatened what the officers held most dear: their economic base, fed by theft and peculation; the institutionalized system whereby "the intendants were regularly rotated, to make sure that everyone had a chance at the graft and that no one was dissatisfied."[141]

Bosch waged his war on all fronts: inside the armed forces, inside the civil administration, inside his own party. His goal was to create a sense of civic spirit, an elementary honesty that could have sparked a true renaissance of Dominican society. In his obsession to raise the moral standards of public life, Bosch took steps the significance of which went beyond mere economic considerations. "A country our size, confronting immense problems, has no right to indulge in the luxurious salaries I found in the public payroll,"[142] he declared, whereupon the monthly salaries of his ministers were slashed in half—from $2,000 to $1,000. The chief justice of the Supreme Court and the attorney general suffered the same cut. Altogether, by reducing the salaries of high officials and eliminating "soft jobs," the Bosch government effected total savings of $2,658,600 a year—a considerable sum for the Dominican Republic.[143] For once the example came from the top. Having cut his own salary from $2,400 to $1,500 a month, Bosch "took the step, unprecedented in Dominican history, of declaring that he and his family would live on his salary without perquisites."[144] Bosch departed for exile as he had come, "penniless, reportedly leaving $101.04 in a bank to pay his creditors."[145] He also left the Dominican people a memory to cherish, as even Ambassador Martin, certainly no friend of Bosch, had to acknowledge: "The indisputable fact that his brief Administration may well have been the most honest in Dominican history, if not in Latin America."[146]

Bosch—the "poet, writer and intellectual who had no experience in the give-and-take that is politics"—furnished to his American critics even more flagrant proof of his "political naiveté" when he refused to violate the constitution and reduce political democracy to a farce. Under the pretext that "a democratic government cannot be democratic for some and dictatorial for others, just as a dictatorship cannot be tyrannical for some and democratic for others,"[147] Bosch refused to find the Castro/Communists guilty a priori, simply because of their political convictions. He refused to deport them, just as he had rejected the Chicago police tactics advocated by Ambassador Martin for the Dominican Republic—Martin, who had bitterly opposed such tactics in the United States. Under Bosch, the Dominican police for once exercised restraint. Moreover, in the name of "freedom of movement," under which "all citizens of the Republic ha[d] the right to leave and to enter the country,"[148] Bosch let the men deported by the Council return. Pushing freedom to the point of license, Bosch even lifted the ban on travel to Cuba. And he granted the parties on the far left—not only the 1J4 but the PSP and the MPD—the same rights as the "democratic" parties. More acutely aware than John Martin of how "we begin to resemble the thing we hate," the man whose opposition to dictatorship had cost him twenty-five years of exile refused "to head a dictatorship—total or partial—in the Dominican Republic." Bosch stressed: "We have not come back to persecute. We want to be positive, not negative."[149]

Bosch's political considerations coincided with his moral philosophy. To crack down on the "Communists," especially when the real threat to freedom was posed by the "democratic" opposition, would have made martyrs of them. Such action might momentarily have deprived the right of a pretext in its slanderous attacks against Bosch and enabled him to cling a little longer to an increasingly meaningless power. But Bosch would have antagonized not only the "Communists" but also a part of the Dominican youth who were loath to build a pretense of democracy on the persecution of a minority. First to protest would be the young *catorcistas*. The PRD youth and the mass of adolescents still searching for a "truth" to believe in would follow. And the man who had come to power to build a political *and* social democracy would find himself a prisoner of forces that, in typical Latin American fashion, accepted political democracy only when it was divorced from social democracy.

Bosch, however, proved he could react decisively when the far left broke the law. Even Martin acknowledged that "Bosch, unlike the Consejo the previous year, had broken the leftist-led strikes"[150] —notably those by the electrical and telephone workers, whose unions (Sindicato de la Corporación Dominicana de Electricidad; Sindicato de la Compañía de Teléfonos) had been deeply infiltrated by the 1J4. The exceedingly militant and very powerful National Federation of Public Employees and Autonomous Institutions (Federación Nacional de Empleados Públicos e Instituciones Autónomas or FENEPIA), also under *catorcista* influence, was likewise "unexpectedly demolished."[151] Bosch "had destroyed FENEPIA."[152]

Bosch's brief presidency did not realize the "sweeping social reforms" the Dominican people expected. When he was driven from office in September 1963, land reform was just beginning, unemployment was still rife,[153] and the administration was disorganized and inefficient. But irresponsible critics ignore the realities of Bosch's presidency: its brevity, the constant threat of a coup, the meager economic help from the United States of about $8 million (that is, six times less than the Council had received; see also note 202 below).

Bosch was not a brilliant administrator. Some of his own lieutenants, moreover, grouped around Angel Miolán and Thelma Frías de González, engaged in familiar practices of party nepotism: "Before long, a series of dismissals began within the administration. The vacancies, which ranged from the so-called political posts to less important jobs in the villages of the interior, were filled with men recommended by the PRD,"[154] though the PRD was short of able administrators. But Bosch's struggle to combat this practice met with increasing success. Indeed, this was one of the reasons for his clash with the Miolán clique. The new government was also faced with the crushing legacy of the Council of State in the field of public administration. This legacy the Council had inherited from the Era, and it could not be easily overturned. Bosch's task was made especially difficult by the resistance—at times passive, at times openly hostile— that his fight against corruption, his austerity program, and his reformist policies provoked in large segments of the Dominican bureaucracy. Howard Wiarda has aptly commented: "One reason why Bosch became unpopular with the government employees is that now they had to get their little rake-off or work their shady deals not in the open, as was the accustomed norm, but when the President wasn't looking. Discovery meant dismissal, a new and short-lived method in the Dominican bureaucracy." For instance, "at the Housing Bank the traditional five-hour work day was replaced by the U.S.-model eight-hour day with only a short lunch break instead of the accustomed two hour *siestas* that usually stretched into three by the time the work began again."[155] Examples could be piled up monotonously.

To be sure, the government made mistakes in the crucial area of agrarian reform. A "web of overlapping and conflicting authorities" added to the confusion and slowed all chance for action.[156] But there were other reasons for the failure of Bosch's land reform program. The courts became flooded with former landowners attempting to recover the lands that Trujillo had appropriated, and much time was lost in complex litigations in the notoriously slow Dominican judicial system. Indeed, until the end of July, only forty peasant families had received land, though much effort had been spent in collecting social and economic data from applicants.

For all its mistakes and weaknesses, in September 1963 the Bosch government seemed at last to have found its way. Not only did the public administration show signs of improvement, but in August agrarian reform began in earnest. In less than two months—from early August until the *golpe*—fourteen hundred families were settled on state-owned lands. At the same time the "sugar price ceilings" law sharply limited the profits of the sugar companies, and gave hope to the subproletariat on the sugar plantations.[157] Other projects were underway. Bosch was keenly aware that his country needed assistance in the administrative and managerial field, so he brought in technicians, mainly from Latin America. A training school was set up to teach peasant leaders to organize and run cooperatives, and the government wanted to extend such instruction to rural schools: "The hope was that these youths would carry the methods back to their home communities and that more cooperatives would thus be begun. But like many of the government's projects to organize the campesinos, this one was just beginning when the Bosch administration was ousted."[158]

Finally there was the Inter-American Center of Social Studies (Centro Interamericano de Estudios Sociales or CIDES), "one of the most fascinating semi-autonomous agencies set up during the period," that included among its aims the "intensive mass education of key sectors of the Dominican population—notably labor and the peasants—in the ways of democratic government." After the overthrow of Bosch, the *golpistas* dismantled CIDES; "nothing comparable to this brain trust, kitchen cabinet, educational center, administrative clearing house, planning board, and bill-drafting center was organized to replace it."[159]

The *Listín Diario*—hardly a Boschist newspaper—concluded its editorial on 25 September 1963 on an optimistic note: "The financial situation of the country cannot yet be considered optimal, nor even normal, yet it is clear that the arduous process of recovery is being carried out successfully."[160] The editorial appeared on the day of the coup d'état.

Whatever the assessment of the economic and social policies of the Bosch administration, however, the fact remains that Bosch's popularity was in decline. The masses were disillusioned. They had expected a dramatic—and immediate—change in their circumstances. When it was slow in coming, the opposition demagogically stoked the fire of discontent. Yet the masses did not topple Bosch or applaud the coup. Bosch did not fall because his reforms were too timid or too late; he fell precisely because he made, or initiated, some reforms. He fell because a certain element feared that he might keep his pledges. As Bonnelly said, "Interests are interests."

"What the Republic will need," predicted Martin even before the elections, "will be not a good winner, but several good losers."[161] There were no "good losers" in the Dominican Republic. Bosch, the "divider,"[162] asked the UCN and four other parties to join his government in a national unity front, offering cabinet posts and other important government positions as inducement. With the lonely exception of the tiny Partido Nacional (PN), the vanquished parties refused.[163] This was their prerogative, but they transformed what they had pledged would be a loyal and constructive opposition into a pack of ravenous wolves. At the head of the pack stood the *cívicos* with their jaded hero, the "good" and "valiant" Fiallo. The rest of the "democratic" parties, with the exception of the PRSC and of the PN, followed their lead. They were determined to overthrow the government and never considered forming a democratic opposition and enduring four years of Bosch in hopes of winning the next elections.

It was inevitable: along with economic interests—the fear of reforms and the need to regain lost power (with all the opportunities this presented to corrupt men)—went a "moral" interest. The *gente de primera* could not forgive a *de segunda* for having usurped what they believed was their right to power. Bosch owed his triumph to the "humble and ignorant class," and such a victory was an unacceptable blow to men for whom the masses—the *infelices* born to serve their masters—counted for nothing. Hatred for the man himself also ran deep, rooted in a vitriolic electoral campaign.[164]

The parties were agreed that the Bosch government had to be destroyed. To this end, the "democratic" opposition revived the battle cry that the UCN had adoped during the elections: "constant, dirty attacks, accusations that Bosch was in cahoots with the Communists or was a Communist himself."[165] But the parties, already falling apart,[166] lacked the power to topple the government on their own. The numerous professional associations that joined the crusade were equally impotent. Only the armed forces could strike the fatal blow. Thus began the stream of politicos to the army barracks.

The military chiefs were also uneasy. In his campaign against corruption, Bosch intended to force the military to live solely on their salaries.[167] This was a dire threat, and others would follow. For the time being, at least, Bosch did not dare to cut back either the military force or its budget. Still, his ambitious program of social reform and economic development could be realized only by substantially reducing those funds traditionally reserved for the armed forces. Bosch, moreover, was determined to subordinate the military to civilian power. As a result, a growing number of high-ranking officers paid increasing heed to the appeals of the "democratic" parties. The nation's salvation was at stake: the "Communist" threat had to be thwarted!

The Church's voice was added to the chorus of Pharisees. To be sure, the Episcopate never openly accused the new president of being a Communist; such attacks were left to individual priests. In the vanguard were a number of militantly anti-Communist Spanish Jesuits who stressed the Communist issue, picturing Bosch as the agent of Communist penetration. These charges were preached not only in the pulpits of the churches, but in the parochial schools and by army chaplains. The aim was to encourage the military to intervene. Meanwhile, as in December 1962, "the Church hierarchy washed its hands of the matter, like Pontius Pilate." The bishops issued no reprimand against these "latter-day Torquemadas."[168] Their reproaches were reserved for those who "seek to deceive by insisting that the problem is not that of Christianity against Communism, but the struggle between the rich and the poor."[169] The Church warned against "the forces of evil spreading in the land, wolves in sheep's clothing."[170] The "bitter reality presently afflicting Dominican society"[171] called for vigilance. "Our armed forces must neither fall asleep nor be deceived by the sirens' song; they must keep on the alert in defense of the Republic."[172] The mob wanted Barabbas again.[173]

In the face of the rising tide threatening to sweep over the government, the "constitutionalist" forces could erect only the feeblest of barriers. Weakness, irresolution, and bad faith combined to undermine their defenses. From a tiny band of exiles in May 1961, the PRD grew in only a few months into a mass party, sweeping the national elections, a miracle due in large measure to the charisma of Juan Bosch. But the PRD inevitably suffered when the leader's popularity slipped in 1963. Moreover, its earlier hypertrophic growth created a severe imbalance: it was a party without cadres, a giant with the head of a dwarf.

Nineteen sixty-three should have been the year of organization; instead it was the year of disaster. The team of Bosch, the charismatic leader, and Miolán, the organizational genius had led the party to victory at the polls. In 1963, the team fell apart. "Serious differences"[174] divided the chief and his principal lieutenant. The source of these differences was unclear, but the consequences were fatal. While Miolán enjoyed only a modest prestige with the people, he had the support of the party machinery, a group of "notables" eager for lucre and in revolt against the "puritanism"[175] and personalism[176] of Bosch. Meanwhile, in the midst of chaos, a group of young PRDistas struggled to organize and to breathe some life into a party incapable of facing its responsibilities. The group was quickly denounced as "factionalist"—even "Communistic." Many party notables, jealous of their own prerogatives and influence, felt threatened by the enthusiasm—too pure, too "revolutionary"—of these young PRDistas. Bosch, oddly passive, failed to intervene in behalf of the group, his staunchest supporters. By September 1963, then, the PRD—an amorphous mass on the decline and racked by internal strife—was a shadow of its former self. The party appeared easy prey for the wolves poised to strike.

The PRSC also underwent a crisis. Conservative "democrats," the Social Christian leaders were prisoners of their own contradictions. Although hostile to a coup d'etat, they were equally antagonistic to the regime because of its "demagogic" policies, its "tolerance" of the Communists, and its "contempt" for the "rights" of the church. Their opposition was virulent. The party's "revolutionary" minority, however, demanded "absolute support"[177] for the government, believing that the threat to Dominican democracy was too grave for anything less. They found PRSC policy sterile—"mired in a deadly passivity that threatened the party's survival."[178]

The battle between *flojos* and *duros* was joined, and for three years it dominated the life of the PRSC. On 1 September 1963, the party's Third National Convention ended with the victory of the *flojos*. It was a Pyrrhic victory, for communication between the warring factions became impossible. The "rebels" were subjected to disciplinary actions and sanctions.[179] But they enjoyed the support of the sectors that in 1962 had been the party's hope: BRUC and the Social-Christian Revolutionary Youth (Juventud Revolucionaria Social Cristiana or JRSC). The powerful CASC, however, spurned the PRSC. The rhetoric of the Social Christians had once seduced the labor federation, but henceforth the party's timid reformism and lack of "revolutionary" drive exposed another purpose. Both the PRSC's internal rupture and the estrangement of the CASC would worsen in the months ahead.

What of the role of the United States? On 20 December 1962, despite the call by the far left for a boycott, the Dominican people turned out en masse at the polls. No incidents marred the day: the voters showed "an almost Scandinavian phlegm" and the police "kept a respectful distance from the urns."[180] In the United States, a wave of naive enthusiasm swept the "liberals," who hailed the events as "the first free and honest elections in the experience of the majority of the [Dominican] electorate."[181] The elections represented not only an immediate victory for democracy, but, more important, a promise for the future: "After thirty years the Dominican Republic had returned to the democratic fold, and now it was to be a showcase for the . . . Alliance for Progress."[182] The liberals welcomed Bosch's success, for they saw in the elected president a man they could trust, a Dominican copy of Betancourt or Víctor Paz Estenssoro. "Here is the chance to demonstrate freedom's alternative to the police state reforms in Cuba," heralded the *Washington Post*, "but if the Alliance fails in this critical country, it is hard to see how it could succeed anywhere else."[183]

The United States seemed determined to seize this chance. "Beginning even before Bosch's accession, when the newly-elected Dominican President was cordially received at the White House, the Kennedy administration repeatedly made clear its support for Bosch." But "the glow was to fade quickly."[184] Bosch proved to be a worrisome problem for Washington. His "exasperating" nationalism shocked the framers of the Alliance for Progress. He was haunted by a memory:

> As a boy I had seen the Dominican flag hauled down from public buildings and the North American flag hoisted in its place, and no one can ever imagine what effect this had on my little seven-year-old soul. Surely I cannot say by what route the Mexican songs telling of Pancho Villa battling the North American soldiers who had invaded Mexico reached La Vega, the little town where I was born and raised. But I can say in all truthfulness that Pancho Villa became my idol. . . . At night I prayed that a Dominican Pancho Villa might appear, someone who would do what he did in Mexico and what Martí, Gómez and Maceo had done in Cuba.
>
> The man I am today was prefigured in the boy I was then. Maybe I love my little Antillean homeland with such a passion because I first became conscious of it for the very reason that it was no longer a homeland but rather a dominion, and this so pained me—I cannot tell how much—that often I lay awake long after I had been sent to bed, and lying awake is difficult for a child. . . . With the years that pain and that shame turned to passion for my Dominican homeland; . . . and when it fell to me to be the head of a political party and the President of my country, I took care to conduct myself at all times like a Dominican who took pride in his nationality.[185]

Gone was the time when a Bonnelly would see "the Consejo's only salvation in close identification with the United States."[186] Nor could Ambassador Martin regard himself any longer as a member of the Dominican government. Bonnelly and the other councilmen "seemed to feel that I was one of them," he writes,[187] the wisest, of course. For a man like Martin, it was an exalting and necessary feeling.

Bosch began to reassert the nation's sovereignty. Many foreigners—Morales-Carrión, Moscoso, Muñoz Marín, and especially Martin—were ready to guide the new president. But Bosch refused to be led. "Ungrateful," "obstinate," unwilling to share his power with foreigners, Bosch desired cordial relations with the U.S., but still intended to remain independent. In an "aberration" that "baffled people in Washington," Bosch dared to invite Juan José Arévalo, "the anti-American former president of Guatemala,"[188] to the swearing-in ceremony. In his inaugural address "he angered U.S. officials by failing to mention the Alliance."[189] Throughout his presidency, Bosch never praised the benefits of the Alliance for Progress warmly or frequently enough to satisfy the Americans.[190] His desire to secure aid from sources other than the United States led him to travel to Europe where he negotiated a $150 million line of credit with a Zurich-based consortium to finance his larger development projects.[191] He denounced the contract that the Balaguer administration had concluded in September 1961 with Thomas A. Pappas and Associates, an American firm, claiming that Dominican interests had been grossly flouted.[192] On the same grounds he tried to annul various agreements reached between the Council of State and American sugar firms, but he was forced to desist on pressure from the State Department, which threatened to apply the Hickenlooper amendment.[193] Bosch's plans for social reforms, moreover, earned him the enmity of American business interests in Santo Domingo.[194] The "sugar price ceilings" law was a particularly direct threat to the interests of the South Puerto Rico Sugar Company, which controlled 30 percent of Dominican sugar production.

In the OAS, the United States could no longer take the Dominican vote for granted. When the United States demanded drastic measures against Castroist Cuba, the Bosch government sided with those recalcitrant nations that asserted the principle of nonintervention and refused to join the holy war against Castro. Martin regarded Bosch as "isolat[ing] himself in the Hemisphere from the United States, the OAS and the Alianza,"[195] but he forgot that the recalcitrant nations accounted for more than half the population of Latin America.

"We did not think Bosch was a Communist. We did not think he was the Communists' creature," Martin admitted. How then does one explain Bosch's "surprising" tolerance, his astonishing "passivity" vis-à-vis the Dominican Communists? This cardinal sin more than any other alienated American sympathies and roused the worry and distrust of Bosch's potential supporters. "I believe," Martin concluded, "that during the campaign, before he was sure of victory, Bosch had reached an understanding with certain Communists . . . ; that, as President, he overestimated their strength and so feared them unreasonably; and that, possibly, he lived quite literally in terror that one or another of the Castro/Communists would kill him if he double-crossed them." This same Bosch was "a reckless political plunger, willing to risk everything, including the democratic system itself, to gain a personal political objective."[196]

Martin's conclusions were widely held among members of the American mission in Santo Domingo. "People in AID and MAAG," relates Martin, "were talking at cocktail parties about the danger of communism in the Republic. This was most serious." Colonel Wolfe, head of MAAG in the Dominican Republic, "had reservations about Bosch." And Lieutenant Colonel Bevan Cass, "probably our most influential attaché," had "misgivings about Bosch's attitude toward the Castro/Communists" and "was not altogether sure Bosch's critics were wrong."[197]

A cold wind rose on the banks of the Potomac. The "Puerto Rico group," their trust betrayed, left Bosch to his fate.[198] Kennedy was "extremely disappointed."[199] And the State Department "quickly soured on the first democratically elected Dominican President in over thirty years."[200] "We feel a stiffening toward the Dominican Republic in Washington," observed Newell Williams, the chief of AID in Santo Domingo and one of the few members of the American mission favorable to Bosch. "Ever since Bosch has been in, we've been turned down. The fact is, we're no longer the fair-haired boys up there."[201]

Martin recognized that he was largely responsible for Bosch's precarious status:

> Upon reflection, I realized that I too had thought I detected a certain reserve, or skepticism, in Washington about Bosch. It was not surprising. I myself, by my detailed reporting, had probably disabused Washington of any notion that Bosch was an ideal President. And the CIA's reporting on the Castro/Communists had hurt him. . . . Several times recently I had noticed routine CIA reports on the Castro/Communists that gave rumors a credibility far higher than I would have . . . . In reporting a Castro/Communist plot, however wildly implausible, it is obviously safer to evaluate it as 'could be true' than as nonsense. Moreover, such Dominicans as last year's Foreign Minister Bonilla Atiles . . . preferred not to stay here and help but to poison Washington against Bosch. It showed up in little things—the casual way the Department informed me that Juan Isidro Jimenes Grullón had made a trip to Washington to propose a coup against Bosch. . . . It showed up in big things—we had committed something over fifty million dollars to last year's Consejo but not a cent to Bosch.[202]

Must one then conclude that the U.S. government was in part responsible for the fall of Juan Bosch? If so, in what way? Were its sins those of commission or of omission? How can we explain that from February to September 1963 the United States officially supported Bosch and reacted to the coup with suspension of diplomatic relations and interruption of economic aid?

Lack of documentation and the absence of a coherent policy in Washington confuse the picture. If it hoped to salvage any of the rhetoric of the Alliance for Progress, the Kennedy administration had to take a public position in support of the Bosch regime. The same considerations dictated the official U.S. reaction to the coup.

Martin has provided revealing evidence of the contradictions in the U.S. position:

> [On 24 September] I . . . sent a top-priority cable. Now, after dozens of false alarms stretching over a year and a half, now, this time, the golpe was for real. I relayed Bosch's request for a carrier,[203] recommended that a carrier at least be alerted, inquired how far away one was, and outlined the course of legislative action I had proposed and he had rejected.[204] . . . And then the cable we had been waiting for came in. It said that the Department could do little more to save Bosch in view of his past performance despite all my efforts to persuade him to govern effectively. The forces arrayed against him were largely of his own creation. Now he must save himself. The Department did not oppose the moves I had already recommended to him but warned me not to tie such moves to any commitment by the United States. It suggested that perhaps he should also take some 'positive' steps. (I wondered how.) As for the aircraft carrier, the Department refused to intervene militarily unless a Communist takeover were threatened. A show of force that we were not prepared to back up would only be a meaningless gesture, ineffective in a situation which had gone so far.[205]

Martin maintains that he always opposed a coup, and he may be telling the truth. Still, one must question the degree of energy and resolution he brought to his defense of constitutional government in the Dominican Republic. According to Martin, his resolve was unshakable. And yet he regarded Bosch as a man made prisoner of the Dominican far left by obscure agreements and fear for his own person, as "a divider, a splitter, a schemer, a destroyer"; "like Lenin," his tactics were "always to split, never to unite." Even before Bosch took office, Martin expressed his contempt: "I am frankly heartsick. That after thirty-one years the people got stuck with him. I said last summer, Bosch won't do. He won't, either."[206]

There is no proof that MAAG or the American military attachés—either on their own or on orders from the Pentagon—ever incited Dominican officers to overthrow Bosch, although such a thesis is not impossible. Nevertheless, even if we take the official American position at face value—that the U.S. military tried to prevent Bosch's overthrow—another consideration arises. The American military personnel were not diplomats. It is doubtful that they could defend with the necessary conviction a government in which they had no confidence. According to Martin, Bevan Cass, for one, "was having problems of conscience about Bosch." Cass wondered "how much longer I can go on supporting him." Martin wondered whether Cass "could keep a straight face while doing it. Cass was, in a sense, too honest." And yet the "slightest sign of hesitancy on his part could bring Bosch down."[207] Dominican officers needed no prodding to perpetrate a coup. On the contrary, they needed strong pressure to check their urge to strike, and this pressure was missing.

At least one American diplomat worked overtly to overthrow Bosch: Fred Somerford, a labor attaché with the American embassy in Santo Domingo and boss of the powerful labor federation CONATRAL, which was created, supported, and financed by the United States. Somerford regarded Bosch as "a thief and a hoodlum,"[208] and CONATRAL became his weapon against the president. At the same time that the *golpistas* were plotting their coup, CONATRAL refused to join the constitutionalist front and bitterly attacked Bosch.

The federation "criticized the President openly for not suppressing the Communists and at one time placed an advertisement in the newspapers urging the people to put their faith in the armed forces to defend the country against what it thought was a growing Communist menace. Robinson Ruiz López, former secretary general of CONATRAL, came right out and publicly asked the military to oust the President."[209] The day Bosch fell, two of the country's three leading labor federations—FOUPSA-CESITRADO and CASC—harshly condemned the coup. But "CONATRAL . . . praised the 'patriotic gesture' of the Armed Forces, warmly hailed the new civilian junta, and applauded the 'exemplary conduct' of the workers in not more strongly rising up to defend the PRD government."[210]

Somerford triumphed. And the question arises: how could an influential member of the American embassy pursue for seven long months a policy that openly contradicted that of the American ambassador? Was Martin an accomplice? Or was the matter simply one of gross negligence on the part of a man utterly incapable of running an embassy? The reader may weigh the facts as he will. It is still too early to make a final judgment, yet two tentative conclusions are inescapable: that those in the highest echelons of the Kennedy administration abandoned Bosch to his fate, while some members of the American embassy in Santo Domingo actively conspired for his overthrow. Somerford certainly did; for the others there is no proof.

Bosch's fall dealt an added blow to the rhetoric of the Alliance for Progress, a rhetoric that for a long time had been moribund. The hopes Kennedy had raised when first he proclaimed an Alliance for Progress, hopes apparently confirmed by the first meeting at Punta del Este, proved to be out of touch with reality. Did the pot of gold at the end of the rainbow turn out to hold nothing but lead? Or was there never any rainbow to begin with, only a mirage that vanished under the test of time?

"Buenos días, Señor Presidente."[211] Oddly mild after months of invective against Bosch, the 1 March editorial of *El 1J4* signaled an abrupt change. The *catorcistas* had turned constitutionalist, and they were joined by the PSP and the MPD. Suddenly, the entire far left had discovered that there was a difference between "the oligarchs of the UCN" and "the demagogues of the PRD."[212] The lesson of the elections was clear: at present any systematic opposition to the government was unwise, for it would not be understood by the masses. In their public statements the MPDistas, the *catorcistas*, the PSPistas all advocated a "loyal" opposition: support for the regime's "democratic" measures and attacks on its "weaknesses." The December election, so often decried in the past as an "anti-democratic farce,"[213] was now lauded as "the result of the people's desperate will to wrest control over the means of production from the hands of the few and to end once and for all corruption and crime in government."[214] The far left claimed to be the guardian of that will, while stressing the limits imposed by reality: "Everybody in our country recognizes the nature of the present government. We are all aware of its vacillations and of the conservative make-up of its Cabinet. This is not a revolutionary government. This is not an anti-imperialist government."[215] "More royalist than the King," the far left rebuked the president for his passivity in the face of rightist plots, urging him to crack down and pledging their full support.

Such was the facade. The truth was quite different. Aware of its own weakness and that of the other parties of the far left, the PSP "did not contemplate Bosch's overthrow,"[216] but its extreme distrust of him remained undiminished. *El Popular*, the PSP organ, warned that American imperialism "wants to achieve a complete Betancourtization of the Dominican government, that is, reactionary violence and lackey-like servility at their worst."[217] It failed to note, however, the foregone conclusion of the party leaders that Bosch, the unscrupulous opportunist, would inevitably bend to Washington's demands. This conviction explains the PSP's extreme timidity between February and September 1963. Not until June did the party reluctantly come out of hiding.[218] It had neither a headquarters nor a radio program. Expecting the police to move in to crush the far left, the PSP decided to lie low even to the point of inaction. "The Bosch government lasted seven months and the PSP made no use of that time. It was in effect a seven-month vacation for the revolutionaries."[219] When the vacation ended on 25 September 1963, the party was practically as weak as before, counting barely over two hundred members.

During that same period, the leaders of the MPD were preparing for guerrilla action, but only over coffee on El Conde Street. The party had no military force. This cold truth could never have stopped Andrés Ramos Peguero, but he was in jail, a victim of the very reality he held in such contempt. The MPD profited from the climate of freedom guaranteed by Bosch: "With the rise to political power of the liberal bourgeoisie, our deported leaders were allowed to return."[220] First to arrive was Máximo López Molina, the party's *caudillo*. Like the PSP with *El Popular*, the MPD was free to publish its organ, *Libertad*. But the party went further by opening offices on Caracas Street and broadcasting a radio program.

The MPD attempted to reorganize. Its goals were ambitious: to build a "solid cellular organization," to reinforce its support "within the working class," and "to establish the Frente Unido de Liberación Nacional (FULN),"[221] under the joint control of MPDistas and *catorcistas*. This last aim reflected a long-standing claim of the tiny MPD: to be accepted as a full partner by the 1J4, the leader of the Dominican left. But the party's gains were modest: no FULN, no "equal rights" with the 1J4, no appreciable progress in the unions, and a weak cellular organization.[222] Having just "discovered" Mao Tse-tung, the MPD directed its greatest energies against the "revisionism" of the PSP. Meanwhile, on 20 July, a group of MPD leaders, among them Cayetano Rodríguez del Prado, left for Cuba, depriving the party of its best men at the very moment that the threat of a *golpe* was growing. They were still in Cuba when Bosch was overthrown.

The 1J4, a mass party in the months following Trujillo's death, suffered its first serious crisis between December 1961 and January 1962. It recovered during the spring, only to "isolate itself from the masses again"[223] until the following December.

After Bosch's victory, the 1J4 was on the rise again. Its partisans rejoined the fold, and the party was "moving . . . up, more and more every day."[224] The people were disillusioned by the new regime, whose social reforms appeared too timid. Bosch's "shortcomings" were countered by the 1J4's bold but "constructive" criticism, which was now free of the violence and the sectarianism that had marked the party's actions and roused fears in the preceding months.

But some of the party's leaders, the *duros* in particular, again fell victim to "delusions of grandeur."[225] They believed that all the malcontents were flocking to their party, "and the crowd seemed immense."[226] On 14 June, commemorations organized by the 1J4 to honor the martyrs of Constanza, Maimón, and Estero Hondo drew large popular participation. For the *duros*, this was added proof of the party's power and a turning point. They forcefully posed the question of guerrilla action to the Central Committee.

They argued that the 1J4 had recovered its strength. Let the right strike, if it dared; let it overthrow the Bosch government: the party would not oppose such a move, since a "reactionary coup would deepen the contradictions"[227] and create conditions especially conducive to armed struggle. Yet, should the right falter, the 1J4 would be ready to act, since it could never "tolerate four years of Boschist rule."[228]

In the Central Committee, the *flojos* and the *duros* clashed: the former rejected the idea that violence should be used "on every occasion and at every moment," while the latter "let themselves be guided solely by the Cuban revolution and by the guerrilla experience of Fidel, without taking into account that the struggle of the Cuban people was not a product of improvisation."[229] In vain, the *flojos* argued that despite its gains the party was still too weak. The climate of freedom created by Bosch gave the 1J4 the chance to develop its propaganda at the very time that disappointment with the reforms ensured fertile ground for the party's growth. A "reactionary coup," however, would force the 1J4 to go underground, a move for which it was unprepared. Nor would a coup prove conducive to armed struggle, since the power relationships in the country did not favor the 1J4. The party should therefore oppose any "reactionary coup" and, if need be, resign itself to four years of Boschist rule. For, should the *catorcistas* launch guerrilla activity, the bourgeoisie—Bosch and the *cívicos*—would join a holy alliance to crush them.

Of course, the *flojos* did not reject the principle of armed struggle, for the 1J4 was a guerrilla party. The party would fight if the right were to overthrow Bosch, but in alliance with the *Boschistas*. They would even consider the possibility of a *catorcista* uprising against Bosch, if particularly favorable—but ill-defined—conditions were to appear. The latter possibility was remote and theoretical, but necessary, for the *flojos* knew that otherwise they would be branded as *electoreros*.[230]

The logic of the *flojos* clashed with the passion of the *duros*. For the *duros*, guerrilla action was a must because Bosch was a "Betancourt in disguise," a "pawn of Yankee imperialism," who would soon drop his mask and take the 1J4 for his first victim. Bosch was a "liberal," and a "liberal" government could "lull the masses to sleep"[231] with a few pacifying reforms. Therefore, the party had to strike.

Such were the arguments of the *duros*. The passion that inspired them was like a drug, inducing "mountain madness"—the obsessive dream of "coming down from the mountains and seizing power."[232] Fidel had done it. Fidel—a magical name with an irresistible attraction. Cuba was the new Mecca, but it was also a fortress besieged by the dark forces of American imperialism. For many *duros*, both under the Council and under Bosch, "one of the reasons to revolt was to relieve the pressure on Cuba."[233] At the same time, the Cubans pushed the *catorcistas* in the direction of armed revolt.[234] Polo Rodríguez, undoubtedly the heart of the *duro* faction, had the support of the four *super-sabios*.[235] Manolo Tavárez, the party president, fell victim to the "mountain madness," and Leandro Guzmán, the secretary general, once again followed Manolo's lead. Thus within the Central Committee, the *duros* were sure of seven out of fourteen votes. The *flojos* could count on five: those of Jimmy Durán, Fafa Taveras, Norge Botello, Hugo Toyos, and Daniel Ozuna. The remaining two members, Emilio Cordero Michel and Juan B. Mejía, while sympathetic to the *flojos*, wavered between the two factions.

The disproportion between *duros* and *flojos* was far greater than the division of votes within the Central Committee indicates. Manolo Tavárez, the party's *caudillo*, as well as Polo Rodríguez, Fidelio Despradel, and Juan Miguel Román, the most influential leaders after Manolo, were all *duros*. And the power of the *duros* was all the greater since, without openly speaking of "guerrilla action," they undermined the influence of the *flojos* throughout the spring of 1963 by "destroying and rebuilding"[236] the provincial committees. Incessantly they prepared for the moment when they would again raise the question of armed insurrection.

That day came in June 1963. Within the Central Committee, the two factions met head-on. Both agreed that the party needed a military organization—the famous Infrastructure, which should have overthrown the Council in 1962. But the *flojos* demanded that the organization be put under the collective control of the Central Committee. This was their only hope of exercising some leverage over the party's military arm. As the violence of the debate grew, a vote was taken, resulting in a seven to seven stalemate. Finally, thanks to an abstention, the *duros* triumphed. This meant that the Infrastructure would be headed by one man, Manolo Tavárez. Manolo, and not the Central Committee, would choose the members of a Comisión Política, "charged with planning the tactics and strategy to be followed in order to thwart a *golpe* from the right."[237] Manolo would also select the members of a Comité Militar to oversee the development of the Infrastructure. With Manolo's consent, the Comité Militar rather than the Central Committee held true power within the party. Its role was both military and political. Made up entirely of *duros*, the Comité prepared for armed struggle, but with the aim of overthrowing Bosch. The *flojos*, meanwhile, suffered yet another defeat when Marco Rodríguez—a *duro*—was brought into the Central Committee by a vote of seven to six. That left the *flojos* with, at best, seven votes against eight. Henceforth, the Central Committee would be little more than a rubber stamp.

On 13 September 1963, four men left for Cuba: Jimmy Durán, Fafa Taveras, Hugo Toyos, and Norge Botello. All were *flojo* leaders who chose—or agreed—"to sever themselves temporarily from the leadership of the party."[238] Their departure was an admission of defeat. Powerless to challenge the "mountain madness" within the Central Committee and aware that henceforth all important party decisions would be made without them, the *flojo* leaders refused to carry the debate down to the party rank and file. Such a move would have exposed the party's preparations for guerrilla warfare to the public, an action tantamount to denouncing the 1J4 in the eyes of the reactionaries. In Cuba, however, they would take courses in guerrilla tactics and meet with Cuban leaders. Upon returning to Santo Domingo, they would be able to speak with greater authority and enjoy the respect automatically accorded every faithful pilgrim back from Mecca. The *duro* leaders viewed the departure of the four *flojos* with pleasure. In fact, they had suggested the trip, fully aware that coexistence within the 1J4 had become impossible. Rather than expel them from the party and thus create a public display of internal divisions, the *duros* urged upon their rivals a gilded exile that they hoped would last several months. Thus they believed that Jimmy Durán and his friends would be surprised in Cuba by the outbreak of the *catorcista* guerrilla action. The *duros* thought the Infrastructure was growing rapidly. Contacts were made with "revolutionaries" within the armed forces, and arms were procured, some from the government armory at San Cristóbal.

As yet, no date had been set for the attack, though some were considering January 1964. But the *duro* leaders were much given to dreams, and the date set for the uprising and the estimates of the actual strength of the Infrastructure varied from leader to leader and from day to day. Meanwhile, the right was stirring and the menace of a "reactionary coup" was taking shape. But this threat did not rouse the *duros* from their dreams. They believed the 1J4 had nothing to fear: a coup would "deepen the contradictions"—and while doubting its imminence[239] they would welcome it. With easy assurance, the 1J4 rushed toward disaster.

Within the military, a few officers sincerely opposed any coup.[240] Two years later these "constitutionalists" would be prominent figures, but now they were just a tiny group with limited influence. They were called the "*académicos*"—the academicians. Their leader was Lieutenant Colonel Rafael Fernández Domínguez, director of the Batalla de Las Carreras Military Academy at San Isidro. Most were former classmates and were now attached to the academy. The majority were lieutenants; a few were captains.

In July, with political tensions constantly mounting, the group began to organize. "Up to that point we knew who we were and that we were opposed to a *golpe*, but we had never held any formal meetings."[241] Contacts with officers in other units were made and promises exchanged. Fernández Domínguez knew he could count on his *académicos* and on the hundred or so cadets under their command. And he believed he could rely on Lieutenant Colonel Vinicio Fernández Pérez, the commanding officer of the elite Duarte Battalion, and on about fifteen officers in the Sánchez Battalion and in the CEFA. In addition, Lieutenant Federico Piantini Colón, commanding officer of the tank detachment at the Presidential Palace, was a staunch constitutionalist.[242]

The "constitutionalists," then, composed only a handful. They were surrounded by the great mass of officers who were unwilling to "get their feet wet" and who "didn't give a damn"; men for whom the constitution was a scrap of paper and Bosch a "pain in the neck." They faced the growing cohort of officers preparing the coup: among them most of the superior officers, men who occupied the key military posts, whose orders were obeyed.

When on 25 September the moment of truth arrived, Fernández Domínguez and the *académicos* were left standing alone. Despite his promises, Lieutenant Colonel Fernández Pérez refused Fernández Domínguez's request that he send the Duarte Battalion against the capital. Nor would he yield his command of the battalion to Fernández Domínguez. At the same time, the hopelessly outnumbered constitutionalist officers within the CEFA and in the Sánchez Battalion refused to budge. Finally, Major Grampolver Medina Mercedes, one of Colonel Wessin's men, had replaced Piantini Colón as head of the tank detachment at the Presidential Palace.

But Fernández Domínguez was unwilling to give up. In haste he summoned his *académicos*. His plan: to attack the Palace, sieze the *golpistas*, free Bosch, take over the government's Radio Santo Domingo TV, appeal to the nation, isolate the rebels, and woo the opportunists among the armed forces into the legalist camp.[243] It was a grand design, but to implement it Fernández Domínguez had only one lieutenant colonel, between twenty and thirty junior officers, and approximately one hundred cadets. Bosch himself, having received a message from Fernández Domínguez, rejected the plan as too risky; the imbalance of forces was so great that an untimely intervention would only end in disaster. Fernández Domínguez abandoned his scheme. The *golpistas* appeared to have won, but for Bosch and the constitutionalist officers the game was far from over; they were already anticipating the next hand.

On 17 July 1963, General Elby Víctor Viñas Román, minister of the armed forces, had announced the dismissal of Marcial Silva, a Jesuit chaplain, and Major Rolando Rodríguez Haché of the air force. The night before, in a "resounding speech"[244] broadcast over radio and television, Bosch had denounced these two men as conspirators and demanded that they be discharged from the armed forces. Bosch appeared to have won a dramatic victory. But Silva and Rodríguez Haché were relatively insignificant figures in the brewing military plot. They were scapegoats for the real leaders—men such as General Atila Luna Pérez, air force chief of staff, General Belisario Peguero Guerrero, chief of police, and Colonel Elías Wessin y Wessin, head of the CEFA. Thus, the removal of Silva and Rodríguez Haché was less a show of strength than an avowal of impotence.

On 4 August a general assault was launched against Dominican democracy. "The recorded voice of Padre Marcial Silva"—confined to bed by an automobile accident—"pledged allegiance to the flag."[245] Thus began a series of nine "Manifestations of Christian Reaffirmation," which lasted from 4 August to 15 September. In the name of "Christ the King" and before crowds large and small, torrents of abuse rained down on the "Marxist-Leninist" president. Irresponsible orators prophesied an imminent "bloodbath," warning the country against falling into "the clutches of Communism." Once again, the name of Christ was dragged through the mud and religion prostituted by sordid interests shrouded in anonymity. The bishops kept silent, while "militant" priests acted as their spokesmen. The Reverend Tomás Abreu, chancellor of the diocese of La Vega, declared during mass that the Church "looks with favor on Catholics expressing their faith in public and combating atheistic and anti-Christian Communism."[246]

Although the Manifestations of Christian Reaffirmation met with some success, it became clear that alone they could not create the climate of chaos, the spirit of "mystic exaltation," that would give the armed forces a pretext to intervene and reestablish order and security by ousting Bosch. As the days passed, the aspiring *golpistas* grew increasingly impatient:

> The president of the republic, Professor Bosch . . . that corrupt politician . . . that faithless, Godless, unpatriotic politician . . . with the evil policies of his government is leading our people to the abyss, condemning them to starvation and poverty.
>
> We cannot understand why our people have not yet taken to the streets, demanding the three daily meals promised by the man with white hair. . . .
>
> What is happening to the armed forces, which exist to defend the Constitution? As everyone knows the Constitution has been violated thousands of times by the criminal government that now governs us.
>
> The Armed Forces have a duty to the country, and an obligation to fulfill toward the people. In the past the Armed Forces of our country did not have the support of the people, but today they do. . . . The people have faith in them, and the people are asking: What is wrong with the Armed Forces, which allow our nation's Constitution to be violated?[247]

The "democratic forces" of the country had tried in vain to overthrow Bosch. The attack by the discredited political parties failed, as did the anti-Bosch campaign in the U.S. and Dominican presses[248] and the Manifestations of Christian Reaffirmation. But two weapons remained—a general strike to be led by businessmen and the military *golpe*. On 20 September, the "Christian strike against international communism" began. In the words of Ambassador Martin: "All that summer, as the *cívicos'* opposition to Bosch continued, and as the Christian Manifestations had run their course, we had known that a general strike might be the *cívicos'* ultimate weapon. They would try to shut down both Santo Domingo and Santiago. Labor unions might join. If they could keep the cities shut down for two or three days, tension would get screwed tight, and rioting might start. Troops must quell riots."[249] At the same time the troops could rid the Presidential Palace of an inept incumbent openly rejected by the majority of his countrymen. It would be less a coup d'état than an indispensable surgical excision, demanded by an exasperated people. The goal was the same as that of the Manifestations of Christian Reaffirmation. But this, too, failed.

By 21 September, "the lock-out was falling apart in the provinces."[250] It was continuing in Santo Domingo, but only where the bourgeoisie had its stores, on El Conde Street and, to a lesser degree, on Mella Avenue.[251] The means used to assure its success were significant. Among the witnesses was Martin: "We heard the *cívicos* were paying small shopkeepers a hundred dollars each to stay closed"; "the police favored the strike."[252] *Hispanic American Report* later wrote that "shops [were] forced . . . to remain closed or else face damage from hired thugs."[253] In the working-class neighborhoods, however, the lock-out collapsed as a large number of shops were opened. Finally, by 23 September, the "businessmen's strike" was over. Its failure had been inevitable, for it was confronted with the hostility of the great masses,[254] and the unanimous repudiation of the labor unions, except, of course, for CONATRAL. The latter's hard line reflected the will of Somerford rather than that of the union's rank and file, the majority of which was sympathetic to the Bosch government.[255]

The time for "subtleties" had passed. There was only one weapon left: the military *golpe*. If the masses would not budge, then the tanks would roll in their place. Since February, Viñas Román, the armed forces minister, and Renato Hungría Morel, the army chief of staff, had been the two generals most reluctant to break the law; now they were swept along with the rest. The signatures of Viñas Román and Hungría Morel headed the list of twenty-five affixed to the "Manifesto Addressed to the Dominican People by the Chiefs of the Armed Forces and the National Police, who have deposed the Ex-President of the Republic, Professor Juan Bosch."[256] The armed forces and the police, in an impressive show of unity, closed ranks—much to the sorrow of the Dominican people.

Juan Bosch had dared to believe that in the Dominican Republic real social reforms could be realized within the context of a democratic system. Bosch was not a bad president, an incompetent administrator, or a muddle-headed politician. But his illusions clashed with the realities of his country. Thus, the defeat of his dream was inevitable.

Bosch's fall left two vastly unequal antagonists facing each other: the victorious *golpistas* and those who dreamed of guerrilla warfare. Neither group had any faith in political democracy. For the *golpistas*, political democracy threatened their social and economic privileges; while for the future *guerrilleros* it provided excessive protection for those same privileges. Bosch had hoped to stand as a buffer between these two warring forces. Now that buffer—feeble but persistent—was gone, and violence flared up again in the Dominican Republic. The *catorcistas* were preparing for martyrdom. A period of violence, repression, and injustice began once again. That period has not ended.

Chapter 4

The Triumvirate
(25 September 1963-24 April 1965)

The Dominican Republic returned to "normalcy." A military junta replaced the constitutional government of Juan Bosch. Bosch was deported on 28 September. He established himself in neighboring San Juan, Puerto Rico, where he could maintain contacts with his partisans in the Dominican Republic. Other exiled PRD leaders included Angel Miolán, Segundo Armando González Tamayo, vice-president of the Republic, and Juan Casasnovas Garrido, president of the Senate. Within four days (25-28 September), some thirty political figures—nearly all of them PRDistas—were deported.[1] A state of siege and a curfew were imposed throughout the Republic. Congress was dissolved and the constitution abrogated. Repression had begun.

But military juntas suffered from a bad press in the hemisphere; it was wiser to be "democratic." The *golpistas'* best course was to seek some "honorable" civilians to set up a triumvirate "designated by the democratic parties . . . with the approval of the Armed Forces and the National Police."[2] The "honorable" men were found: Emilio de los Santos, Manuel Enrique Tavares Espaillat, and Ramón Tapia Espinal.[3] De los Santos, the eldest and the most "honorable," was named president of the Triumvirate, which was installed on 26 September.

The "democratic" parties had been beaten in the elections, but now they shared in the spoils: four ministerial posts for the UCN, three for VRD, two for both the ASD and the PNRD, and one each for the PDC and the PPDC. Donald Reid Cabral, the former *Consejero* and *cívico* turned "independent," became minister of foreign affairs. General Viñas Román, Bosch's armed forces minister, retained his post.

Their task accomplished, the military returned to their barracks. A few decrees rewarded officers who had particularly distinguished themselves during the conspiracy. The Triumvirate created a post of general in the air force for Atila Luna Pérez, until then only an acting general. By the same process, Julio Alberto Rib Santamaría, navy chief of staff, became an admiral. Colonel Wessin, the powerful head of the CEFA, was promoted to the rank of general.[4]

Other, more important rewards were in the offing for the military *golpistas.* To topple Bosch, the *cívicos* had had to call in the armed forces; with Bosch fell the principle of the primacy of civil power. Weak and without popular support, the Triumvirate was hardly in a position to interfere in military affairs. The military barracks once again became centers of corruption to a degree that even many *cívicos* would soon find intolerable.

Several factors explain the relative passivity of the population during the coup: the thorough disorganization of the PRD, Bosch's loss of popular support, the feeling of impotence in the face of the armed forces, the wave of arrests,[5] police brutality—and the fear these engendered. To be sure, street disorders occurred, especially in the capital, primarily the acts of students, among whom far-left sympathizers predominated. They braved large contingents of police, the so-called *cascos blancos* (white helmets), while hundreds of onlookers cheered them, fleeing the minute the police closed in. The demonstrators were armed with stones; the "forces of order" carried nightsticks, rifles, and tear gas. Those who got caught were pummeled on the spot, often with rifle butts.[6] It was no contest; the sides were too unequal. At no time in those first days was the power of the new regime seriously threatened by the disorders that gripped a number of cities.

The regime needed the recognition and economic assistance of the United States. There was cause for optimism. Since the launching of the Alliance for Progress, Latin America had been shaken by several coups d'état. Some had been welcomed by Washington (Guatemala, March 1963, and Ecuador, July 1963); others were frowned upon (Argentina, March 1962, and Peru, July 1962). In Peru, where the United States had reacted as it did now in the Dominican Republic, the *golpistas* had countered with an old tactic: the promise of elections and a battle cry against Communism. After a while, diplomatic relations were restored and economic and military assistance resumed.

The same scenario unfolded in the Dominican Republic. On 26 November 1963, the Triumvirate passed a law providing for "an extremely complex sequence of five elections" leading, after two years, to the re-establishment of a legal government. The measure was so dubious that even Washington had "misgivings."[7] But the Triumvirate had other weapons in its arsenal. Like the Council of State in 1962, the new regime demonstrated its determination to fight against the "red threat." It banned the Communist parties and adopted a series of measures to combat these enemies of liberty.[8] Yet long experience had shown that the most effective weapon was to cry wolf: "Save us or we'll go Communist."[9] In the words of General Viñas Román: "If the United States refused assistance, the regime would go it alone. If this meant terror and civil war and Castro/Communist guerrilla warfare, the regime would do its best. With the United States' help, it might win; without it, it might lose."[10]

Unwittingly, the 1J4 played into the Triumvirate's hands. On 28 November it opened six guerrilla *focos* in the countryside.[11] The *duros* of the party had boasted too much, using language they could not back up. The Infrastructure existed in the capital, and, unlike 1962, now had branches in other Dominican cities, but it was a mere skeleton. Now the "reactionary coup" had occurred and the *flojos*' prophecy proved true. The *golpistas* had driven the party underground, a blow for which the *catorcistas* were ill-prepared. Hunted by the police and lacking any places of refuge, the 1J4 leaders were at a loss as to where and when to meet. In the final weeks of the Bosch regime, the Military Committee—the party's real Central Committee—allegedly had begun preparing the 1J4 for guerrilla action. In fact it had accomplished nothing. Now, in the wake of the coup, Manolo Tavárez realized that the 1J4 was in no position to launch an armed rebellion, that such a step would spell disaster not only for the *guerrilleros* but for the entire party. Manolo hesitated.

Confronted with the ambivalence of their supreme leader, two groups competed to win his support. On one side were those who urged Manolo to resist the "mountain madness": Emilio Cordero Michel, Juan B. Mejía, and Daniel Ozuna; on the other side were the *ultraduros*—among them the four *supersabios* and Polo Rodríguez. But the outcome was decided in advance: circumstances weighed too heavily in favor of self-destruction.

As early as 29 September, at the first meeting of the Military Committee after the coup, "the comrades Fidelio [Despradel], Genao [Espaillat], Juan Miguel [Román], Cruz Peralta and Polo [Rodríguez], who were in charge of the [guerrilla] zone, indicated that everything would be ready in a few days . . . and that the insurrection should be called for shortly."[12] A few days later they pretended that the preparations were completed and that peasant bases and supplies had been secured. A radio station would be available for the insurgents' use, and important sectors of the military had pledged their support. It was time to act.

But Manolo knew better. As chief of the Infrastructure, he was only too aware of the exaggerations—and the lies—of the *ultraduros*. He refused to give the order for the insurrection to begin. But the *ultraduros* pressed other, more weighty arguments. What would the Cubans think? "We cannot back out of guerrilla action. We have promised the Cubans. We have assured them all along that we were ready. We cannot pull out now. What would they think? We'd be taken for cowards."[13] And what would the Dominican people think? How could they forget that Manolo had threatened: "Listen, gentlemen of the right: if you prevent the peaceful struggle of the people, the 1J4 knows where Quisqueya's mountains are, and we will go there." [14] The party had promised too much, both to the Cubans and to the Dominicans. Now that the moment of truth was at hand, how could the *catorcistas* fail to find their way to "Quisqueya's mountains"—they who had dreamed of guerrilla struggle since 1958? Besides, what other options were there? Why wait? The *golpistas* had unleashed a wave of repression. The PRD and the PRSC would suffer little persecution. They were "reasonable" parties, open to any compromise and protected by "liberal" elements in the United States. The 1J4 was the real enemy of the imperialists—"liberals" and "conservatives" alike. No international pressure would protect the *catorcistas*. For them, the persecution would only intensify. If they waited they would be eliminated one by one.

The atmosphere was exciting, even intoxicating. Five years of dreaming about guerrilla action—so many promises and commitments. Back away now? Or believe in the impossible and chase an illusion whatever the price? Manolo hesitated. It was hard to say no. Then on 6 November a general strike mounted by the 1J4 broke out in the capital. Meant to be the prelude to the insurrection, the strike failed. And so the *ultraduros* resorted to their last weapon: black-mail. Fidelio Despradel presented Manolo with the ultimatum of his former friends. Either he would agree to take command of the insurrection, on a date to be set by the Military Committee, or they would act alone, denouncing Manolo to the people as a "traitor" and a "coward."[15]

On 26 November the 1J4 opened six guerrilla *focos*. The chief of the Supreme Revolutionary Command was Manolo Tavárez. Fearing dishonor, Manolo had yielded. He left for guerrilla action, "convinced that he was going to his death."[16]

The *ultraduros* had triumphed, but did these men who had lied about their readiness really believe in their chances for success? Polo Rodríguez—whose role was to prove decisive—did.[17] He was sincere in his illusions to the point of rejecting any meaningful collaboration with the other parties of the far left. His was the old dream of the *duros*: that after victory the 1J4 would have a monopoly of power.

From the beginning the PSP had been hostile to the idea of armed struggle. First during the Consejo, then under Bosch, the party had opposed the *guerra de guerrillas*. And now, under the Triumvirate, they maintained that opposition. They believed that "the choice of a method of struggle and of the means of development of the revolutionary movement is determined by the balance of forces between the classes, by the specific conditions of the revolutionary movement within each country. The mere existence of a despotic regime does not make armed insurrection 'the only way.' " Indeed, the party was convinced that "at this moment the premature launching of an armed insurrection can become an obstacle to the struggle against the *golpe*, since it disjoints and divides the forces opposed to the dictatorship."[18] "A revolutionary situation cannot be created artificially. Without it, ten guerrilla *focos* will prove no better than a single one in spurring, in stirring revolutions. . . . Today only small groups of workers and students—the avant-garde—favor revolution. . . . But the avant-garde cannot attribute its feelings and wishes to the masses. If the avant-garde goes into battle alone, only defeat will ensue."[19]

Any discussion between *ultraduros* and PSPistas would thus be fruitless, though ties of friendship charged the atmosphere with emotion.[20] For the MPD the situation was different. A "guerrilla" party that rivaled the 1J4 for the favor of the Cubans, it seemed ready to offer the *catorcistas* the support of its meager forces.[21] In return it demanded at least some voice in directing the guerrilla action. Polo refused. So, anticipating the *catorcistas*, the MPD began the revolt. Three of its Central Committee members—López Molina among them—four militants, and a donkey opened up the party's guerrilla *focos* near Cevicos. The adventure was stillborn, however, for that very day—24 October—the eight guerrillas (the seven MPDistas plus donkey) were arrested without a fight. The MPD's "guerrilla action" collapsed in ridicule, confirming in the eyes of many Dominicans López Molina's image as a buffoon and a traitor.[22]

Thus the *catorcistas* would go into combat alone. They nevertheless believed that they could count on the support of certain sectors of the armed forces. Since 1962, the 1J4 had maintained links with "progressive" military, mostly noncommissioned officers, but some young, low-ranking officers as well, who were least contaminated by Trujilloism and who seemed most susceptible to the party's slogans. They were only a handful. In the wake of the coup, some genuinely constitutionalist officers were ready to fight, but Polo failed to establish contacts with them, for he thought them politically "unreliable." Convinced that a guerrilla action would succeed, he would not willingly agree to the participation of "outsiders."[23] Thus by November 1963 only one officer—Captain "Gregorio"—had committed himself fully to the rebel cause. "Gregorio" commanded the Luperón Company of the elite Mella Battalion, and many *ultraduros* wanted to believe that he would eventually carry the whole battalion with him.

In addition to the *focos* in the mountains, an "urban front" was to begin operations. The *catorcista* guerrillas would precipitate, in the main cities and above all in the capital, a state of chaos and terror through a series of terrorist actions—bomb attacks on police stations, acts of sabotage, executions of "well-known criminals." The direction of the operation was entrusted to two members of the Central Committee—Roberto Duvergé and Juan B. Mejía.

For the *ultraduros*, the triumph of the guerrilla action was certain, but when would victory come? After a long struggle, like Fidel in the Sierra Maestra? A number of *ultraduros*—the most "moderate"—believed so. But this was a "pessimistic," "negative" view. Polo and some of his friends, writes Emilio Cordero Michel, a former *catorcista*, "set out on this guerrilla action as one departs on an outing—going off to the mountains to return a few days later, as conquering heroes."[24] Blind to the realities of their country, they had failed to digest the lesson of the Cuban insurrection they worshiped. To them the Dominican Republic was a dead forest of dry, rotted wood. A few sparks—the *focos guerrilleros* of the 1J4—would set it all ablaze. The flames of freedom would sweep the country as in city after city the people took to the streets in a general uprising. As in Cuba during Batista's last days, the military, craven and corrupt, would not dare to resist; they would declare themselves "constitutionalists" and beg the guerrillas for mercy. The Triumvirate would fall. As in Cuba, it would then be too late for the liberal bourgeoisie and imperialist lackeys, that is, for Bosch and his kind. Only the "guerrillas from the mountains" would be able to fill the power vacuum. The "new society" would be built—with a rifle in one hand and a hammer in the other.

The Triumvirate could have crushed the plot in advance. Two members of the 1J4's Central Committee, Leandro Guzmán and Daniel Ozuna, were arrested on 6 November and proceeded to talk.[25] Through them, the Triumvirate learned about the party's plans for an uprising and where most of the *focos* would open. But the confessions of Guzmán and Ozuna were almost super-fluous, for the 1J4 compounded its scanty preparation with almost blind impru-dence. "Everyone in Santo Domingo was aware that the 1J4 was preparing to revolt."[26] From door to door throughout "safe" neighborhoods, *catorcistas* took up collections "to buy boots for Johnny who is going off to the mountains but has no boots."[27] And when, beginning on 22 November, the guerrillas left their homes to meet their comrades at the designated places, "everyone rushed out into the streets to see the boy who was leaving to fight for his country."[28]

Where were the police? Why did they fail to intervene when it was so easy? There was no need. With a few sparks and an abundance of smoke, the 1J4 gave the Triumvirate everything it needed: a chance to regroup the civilian and military right, which was already locking horns over the spoils; but above all, a chance to scare the "liberals" in the United States and thereby speed up the in-evitable restoration of diplomatic relations and the resumption of economic aid.

So the *catorcistas* went off to rediscover "Quisqueya's rugged mountains"; many of them carried books but no food. According to *El 1J4*, there were six "guerrilla fronts" headed by a Supreme Revolutionary Command—317 men. In fact, there were only between 80 and 100 guerrillas.[29] They had wanted to believe "that victory is easy, that it is just around the corner."[30] But they soon recognized the bitter cost of their adventure. Years later, former *catorcistas* would recall the long list of errors:

The peasant bases? "There was a failure to create a social base in the guerrilla zones: that is, to have the support of the peasantry . . . who could serve as liaisons, couriers, informants, and the like. This is absolutely essential to developing a guerrilla action with any likelihood of success."[31]

Military training, physical fitness? "The feeling of comradeship was crucial in choosing recruits for the guerrilla front: comrades persecuted in the city, comrades sick and physically weak."[32] Guerrillas with any military experience were very rare.

The urban front? "They didn't do a thing."[33] "There was no organiza-tion."[34] Nothing was ready; even the avant-garde proved timid. The plan was to paralyze the cities and create chaos, but in fact the men under Roberto Duvergé and Juan B. Mejía were reduced to printing communiqués that announced the imagined successes of the half dozen guerrilla fronts opened by the 1J4 whose position was rapidly deteriorating.[35]

Arms? The 1J4 had thought the German Camilo Todemann, an employee of the government arsenal at San Cristóbal, to be a trusted ally. He sold the *catorcistas* most of the arms needed for the insurrection. Many of those arms later proved faulty.[36]

The military? Cowards, perhaps. But why should they fear the revolt of the 1J4? Captain "Gregorio," who had promised to support the *catorcistas*, took part, at the head of his company, in crushing the guerrilla front Capitán Juan de Dios Ventura Simó, commanded by Polo Rodríguez. On 10 December 1963, the soldiers of "Gregorio" killed Polo before the eyes of his fiancée, the young and ardent Josefina Lora Iglesias, the only woman to take part in the armed struggle of the 1J4.

Among the six fronts, one stood out: the front Comandante Enrique Jiménez Moya, headed by Manolo Tavárez, the supreme leader of the 1J4. Emilio Cordero Michel, one of the nine survivors of this front, recalls that out of the twenty-eight men who accompanied Manolo, "only one knew the terrain— [Domingo Sánchez Bisonó] 'El Guajiro.' " He adds that "lack of physical training" was compounded by

> the dearth of provisions. Our rations were scarcely enough to last for three days. It is true that some provisions had been previously buried, and storehouses had been set up with party money; even a pack of mules had been bought. But the storehouses had been purchased in the names of the better-known *catorcistas* in that zone, and so, when the army located the guerrilla *foco*, it was able to cut the group off from its stores by simply arresting those *catorcistas* and their families. . . . This lack of food was largely responsible for the guerrillas' rapid physical exhaustion and debility. In fact our nourishment consisted solely of *guayabas* and oranges, which, now and then, we happened to find.[37]

Manolo and his men were cut off from everything: from the "urban front," from the other *focos*, even from the *campesinos* in the region. They were tracked by the police and the army and strafed by the air force.[38] Their only contact with the outside world was listening to commercial radio broadcasts. Only one member of the front was killed, but several were sick or debilitated. In a matter of days, only about a dozen able-bodied men remained. Another survivor, Fidelio Despradel, adds that "news of the collapse of the other fronts, which came to us almost in a single blow, after 15 December, demoralize[d] us."[39] Then, allegedly in search of food, Despradel left the group with the only man who knew the region—El Guajiro—and two of the few guerrillas with military training.[40]

The remaining guerrillas thus found themselves lost in the mountains; that is, in the words of Emilio Cordero Michel, "without a guide, for there were just three of us who could read the maps and get our bearings using the compass, but the maps were highly inaccurate: where a mountain was drawn, no mountain appeared; where a river was drawn, no river appeared, and so on." In effect, the Jiménez Moya front had ceased to exist. From that point on, some wanted to surrender and accept "a pledge from the Triumvirate that came over the radio." Others "wanted to sneak back into the city and carry on the struggle in whatever way was thought best, recognizing that this phase of the guerrilla action had failed." On 21 December, "the surrender of the group was approved by a majority vote. . . . The ablest-bodied men were singled out so that we might go ahead to arrange the surrender."[41] Of these four men, one was wounded and the other three killed by a mixed patrol of the army and the CEFA a few hours later.[42] That same evening, Manolo and the men who had stayed behind with him surrendered near Alto de la Diferencia, a small village in the Manaclas region.

Manolo was doomed. At a meeting in the Presidential Palace of the Triumvirs, leaders of the "democratic" parties, and military chiefs, it had been decided that the 1J4 leader must die.[43] The decision was upheld, despite the opposition of Emilio de los Santos, president of the Triumvirate. The will of those in power was carried out near Alto de la Diferencia. The fourteen *catorcistas* still with Manolo were murdered as well, for no witness could survive. The date was 21 December 1963.

"The military debacle closed a chapter in the history of the 1J4."[44] In the six *focos*, some thirty *catorcistas* had perished; the rest had surrendered, joining in jail those who had been arrested immediately after the coup or in the weeks that followed. The party had been outlawed. The Central Committee had ceased to exist: two of its members were dead, five were in Cuba, six in jail.[45] Only two—Roberto Duvergé and Juan B. Mejía—were still free and in the country. But their prestige was seriously impaired since the urban front, which had been their responsibility, had done nothing. The party's Infrastructure was gone, and the provincial committees were in disarray. The party lacked a head. Despite his identification with the *duros*, Manolo had always been recognized, even by the *flojos*, as "the one serious, honest leader capable of unifying the masses."[46] His personality, his idealism, won respect from all, even if some bitterly opposed his methods and his decisions. Now that he was dead, a struggle for the succession gripped the party. The collapse of the guerrilla struggle exacerbated rivalries and turned antipathy to hate.

Yet the 1J4 itself survived. Its prestige was even enhanced among opponents of the Triumvirate. But a prodigious effort at organization was needed to restore the party's strength. Two qualities, heretofore lacking, were essential to such an effort: cohesion and patience. The failure of the guerrilla struggle, moreover, was to poison relations between the 1J4 and the PSP. It was rumored—and many *catorcistas* chose to believe—that the PSP had betrayed the 1J4. For the Dominican far left, the accusation would provide yet another source of division, one more reason to hate.

On 14 December 1963, a week before the death of Manolo Tavárez, Washington renewed diplomatic ties with the Dominican Republic. John F. Kennedy had been assassinated on 22 November and Lyndon B. Johnson was now in the White House. For many U.S. liberals, Johnson's recognition of the Triumvirate meant that the new president had abruptly broken with the Dominican policy of his predecessor.[47] But this was hardly the case. According to Martin,

> recognition was delayed a little by President Kennedy's death. . . . The Dominican regime had only to sit tight, maintain control, and wait. We on the other hand were being pushed hard to settle. Many things pushed us. We feared [that] a collapse of the Triumvirate might bring a reversion to a military dictatorship. We feared a leftist Castro/Communist guerrilla rising. We feared that our firm stand might encourage non-Communist young people to rise and fight and die, only to have us recognize later anyway. We feared

that if we continued to hold firm, then were forced to capitulate, we would have suffered a major diplomatic defeat. Moreover, other nations were pressing us—they wanted to recognize. We held them as long as we could, but Great Britain recognized after about a month, an extraordinarily long period for her. . . . France, West Germany, and Italy quickly recognized. . . .[48]

Little by little we retreated. Little by little we fell back from position to position. One by one we gave up our objectives, until we were left with almost nothing.[49]

By 21 November the American government had adopted its fifth in the series of changing positions vis-à-vis the *golpistas*. Compared with the first, this one "almost amounted to a rout," writes Martin.[50] The following day, John F. Kennedy was assassinated in Dallas.

Two weeks ensued, a sad December. . . . I [Martin] thought we must recognize, but could get no one to move. The entire Dominican predicament had been overtaken by events. So were we all. . . . We had accomplished all we could by withholding recognition. If civil authority weakened, we would be blamed. Nobody would benefit, except the military, and later, the Castro/Communists. We should recognize before the guerrillas gained. . . .[51] The Dominican press kept saying the guerrillas had 'opened a fourth front,' or 'a fifth front,' or 'a sixth front.' 'Front' probably meant three or four ragged men in hiding. But it sounded ominous in cables and public communiqués. *Who could be sure it wasn't—Castro had started, some say, with eleven men to take Cuba.*[52]

These two events—recognition by the United States on 14 December and the execution of Manolo Tavárez on 21 December—were twin triumphs for the Triumvirate. Yet for one of the Triumvirs, Emilio de los Santos, the victory was too painful. From the beginning de los Santos had opposed the murder of the *catorcista* leader. Naively he believed that his threat to resign would deter the would-be murderers.[53] He forgot that he was himself an expendable puppet. On 21 December, around eleven at night, the telephone rang in his home. It was the familiar voice of a "military chief": "We want you to know what has happened . . . the guerrillas have been killed in a skirmish with the Armed Forces":

—De los Santos: Is Manolo dead?
—Military chief: Him too.
—De los Santos: How many losses for the army?
—Military Chief: None.
—De los Santos: This is murder. I refuse to set foot in the [Presidential] Palace again.[54]

De los Santos resigned the next day, 22 December 1963. It was an honorable gesture, but he failed to make public the motives for his departure. He preferred to compromise where no compromise was possible, and his name, once worthy of respect, was tainted forever.

Donald Reid Cabral was nominated on 22 December by Ramón Tapia Espinal and Manuel Tavares Espaillat to fill de los Santos' post. The new president of the Triumvirate was a prominent *cívico*, a former member of the Council of State and, after the *golpe*, minister of foreign affairs. His appointment sparked a crisis within the coalition government. Four miniparties—the ASD, the PNRD, the PPDC, and the PDC—protested indignantly. No one had consulted them, an omission all the more dangerous since Reid Cabral, unlike de los Santos, was not a mere puppet. Reid Cabral was a powerful figure in Dominican politics, a member of the "Cabral-Vicini-Bermudez-Tavares family complex, one of the largest, richest and most powerful of all."[55] The men who imposed his candidacy belonged to the UCN, or, more precisely, to one of the party's most influential cliques—that of Rafael Bonnelly.

An open struggle for the spoils erupted among the *golpistas*. In vain the chiefs of the four protesting parties—Jimenes Grullón (ASD), Ramírez Alcántara (PNRD), Ramón Castillo (PPDC), Read Vittini (PDC)—demanded that Reid Cabral withdraw. He stayed on, supported by the armed forces, and the four miniparties were forced out of the government.[56] They began a period of forced abstinence that lasted much longer than they could foresee.[57]

Although the *catorcistas* had been massacred and de los Santos had resigned, a number of Dominican "moderates"[58] were optimistic. In the United States, Reid Cabral enjoyed the friendship and esteem of influential men, a particularly desirable asset in negotiations with Washington over the renewal of economic aid. Feeding on illusions, the "moderates" found in their new president admirable, indeed astonishing, qualities: "Everyone must agree that the choice of the Triumvir Dr. Donald Reid Cabral . . . is a happy one." He was considered "intelligent, understanding, flexible and liberal." Having "no need for this post financially . . . he must have a desire to serve." "He took no part in the coup, and had he been in the country, the tragedy of Manaclas would never have happened, or at least a serious effort would have been made to prevent it."[59] Even the memory of a dead brother—wrongly considered to be an anti-Trujilloist martyr[60]—enhanced the prestige of the new president, who became a hero of the "resistance." The "moderates" expected great things of Reid Cabral, the *de primera* president imposed upon the Republic by his family connections and by the interests of the Bonnelly clique. He would lead the country to free elections and stand up against the arrogant military. Reid Cabral would prevent the re-entrenchment of corruption in the Dominican Republic.

These were fond hopes, but once again a wave of corruption engulfed the country. Howard Wiarda describes the crisis:

> The overthrow of Bosch brought the traditional and family-style peculation back with a vengeance. As if trying to make up for the seven months lost during his administration, government servants engaged in a rash of corrupt practices that had not been employed since the Trujillo regime. Bribes to administration officials, for example, occurred on a scale almost matching that of the former era. Government offices became so overstaffed that many were receiving salaries without rendering any services. More importantly, the spirit of fraud which characterized every aspect of government under

the slain Generalissimo again was rampant in the public service—the enrichment of favored individuals through the expenditure of funds for public projects, self-aggrandizement through one's knowledge of pending government programs, the receipt of goods, favors or money through the performance of an official duty.[61]

It was the "Return of the Syndicate."[62] But even more flagrant was the corruption in the armed forces. The military had "served their country well" by overthrowing Juan Bosch and had proved their disinterest the next day by yielding power to the civilians. Such "probity" deserved a reward: the plunder of the nation's economy to the benefit of these modern heirs to Cincinnatus.

The military canteens—a "business legitimized by a tottering civilian government"—sprang from "the Consejo's excessive obsequiousness toward the military."[63] The canteens had always been a gold mine for corrupt officers, but the meddlesome Bosch had interfered, and business had suffered. After his overthrow, however, the top brass were free to resume their true calling—as thieves: "Through their mushrooming canteens the military imported food, liquor and all kinds of household goods duty-free and went into the wholesale business. U.S. cigarettes, for example, which sell 80 cents for a pack in the cities' stores were purchased by the Armed Forces at prices as low as 20 cents and resold to retailers at enormous profits."[64]

Ahora, the most influential Dominican weekly, described a tale of woe:

The situation worsened when the canteens . . . increased their line of imports to include even luxury items. . . . From then on commercial sales throughout the country plunged alarmingly, while the traffic in contraband soared. . . . But the crowning event was the establishment [26 June 1964] of the "National Police Canteen Company, Inc.," with an authorized capital of half a million pesos and a working capital of RD$50,000. Its principal partners, who on forming a stock company became, according to the Commercial Code, businessmen—or rather "merchants"—were the Messrs. Belisario Peguero Guerrero, president; Apolinar Alfredo Montás Guerrero, vice-president and secretary; Gaspar Salvador Morató Pimentel, treasurer and business manager; Rubén Darío Gonzáles Núñez, Hernán Despradel Brache and José de Jesús Morillo López, members of the board; and Dr. Antonio de los Santos Almarante, commissary. For those who are unfamiliar with these men, it should be pointed out that they all wear the uniform of the National Police, where they hold high ranks.[65]

Set up "in order to traffic in all kinds of merchandise, everything from dazzling jewels to exquisite imported wines, duty-free of course," the new company aroused "consternation and indignation . . . in every social, political and economic circle." The *cívicos*, who controlled the nation's commerce, were outraged as their own sales slumped. " 'Business is business' . . . , and guided by that slogan but without wishing to give a political cast to the question, the nation's businessmen and entrepreneurs met to demand that the Government do something to forestall worse evils in the offing. . . . After many long-drawn-out meetings inside the Santo Domingo Chamber of Commerce," the nine most powerful businessmen's associations demanded from the Triumvirate "the immediate suppression of the Canteens of the Armed Forces and of the Police, as well as of the commercial organizations that support and supply them."[66]

The demand was satisfied on 4 July, but victory proved illusive. The military's "business" vocation was too strong and their desire for gain too tenacious. Moreover, Reid Cabral was too dependent on the support of the military to satisfy the demands of the business community.[67] Although deprived of their "inexhaustible military canteens,"[68] the armed forces still had plenty of planes and ships. Beginning in July, smuggling—an enduring evil—experienced a "simply alarming . . . boom."[69] Naturally, the Triumvirate did nothing. In vain the Dominican press complained that only "small-time" smugglers were arrested, while the "big-time operators" enjoyed "a surprising immunity."[70] In vain the press pointed out that "the Government need not look far to find the source of the contraband":[71] "the principal and most pernicious points of illegal entry for imported foreign goods are the leading military bases—air and naval."[72]

It is no wonder, then, that the country suffered a grave economic decline. Generous authors have tried to explain the economic debacle of the Triumvirate by the drop in the world market price of sugar. But in 1964 the total value of Dominican exports in sugar was only $2.6 million less than in 1963 ($88.7 million in 1963 as against $86.1 in 1964).[73] Some even see, toward the end of the Triumvirate, a situation of "moderate upswing and slow, gradual improvement."[74] Dominican experts did not share this opinion. On 11 April 1965, the conservative *Listín Diario* commented: "A reading of the Central Bank's latest balance sheet, for this last March 31, has left a depressing, pessimistic impression, for it reveals . . . a dangerous deterioration in our monetary situation. The gross reserves on that date totalled only $33,674,082, or the lowest figure for this year. These reserves, which at the end of January amounted to $43,001,566 have consequently suffered a drop of nearly $10 million within the space of sixty days."[75]

At the same time, the nation's public debt increased dramatically. In 1964, the Dominican Republic contracted foreign debts, mostly from the United States, totaling $131,931,233 as against $15,951,040 in 1963. This assumption of debt continued at a sustained pace in the first months of 1965.[76]

Was this a "slow, gradual improvement"? On 25 September 1963, the day of Bosch's overthrow, *Listín Diario* had noted that, although the situation was still far from optimal, the government had been successful in its attempts to bolster the economy. On 11 April 1965, two weeks before the fall of Reid Cabral, the same newspaper lamented: "As long as the government fails to establish a general economic policy . . . it is almost impossible to envision a better future for our unhappy country."[77]

Extreme corruption and mismanagement were responsible for the country's economic collapse after the incipient recovery brought about by the Bosch government. One can only smile upon reading that "Reid closed the military stores" and "launched an economic policy of austerity."[78] Austerity for whom? For the laborers, for the peasants, for large sectors of the middle class, even for the soldiers and the police? Police and enlisted men were privileged in comparison with their miserable countrymen, but they, too, were wretched—mercenaries for sixty dollars a month, ill-fed and poorly lodged.[79] Bosch acknowledged that "had the *golpistas* provided work and economic prosperity, they would have won the entire country's support, even if they went on deporting and imprisoning."[80] But the people knew only suffering. The peasants remained silent beasts of burden. In the cities, however, a more politicized population grew restive. Since emerging from the deep slumber of the Trujillo Era, the urban masses had been fed on too many illusions. Now their disappointment was bitter, the ill will of the regime too cruel. Particularly after March 1964, a long string of strikes and demonstrations swept the country's urban centers. The government declared all of them illegal, and the police brutally crushed them. "Blood, pain, tears and sorrow"[81] invaded many Dominican homes.

Yet the dictatorship was not all-encompassing. A return to the *Trujillato* would not be easy: to crush a people requires prodigious power, and the *golpistas*, rent by divisions and rivalries, squandered their strength. Some freedoms remained, though diminished. The far left parties were banned, but the PRD and the Social Christians were still legal. Also legal and destined to grow was the newly founded Reformist Party of Joaquín Balaguer. The small but vociferous parties of the anti-Reid *golpistas* added to the confusion. The government, of course, kept a watchful eye out for any "abuses of freedom," especially from such irresponsible parties as the PRD and the Reformists. "People are saying . . . how things are getting tough," noted the "moderate" Pedro Fernández-Peix. "Almost no one in the Dominican Republic has managed to stage a march, . . . a meeting, . . . a demonstration; . . . there is always something to prevent it; . . . when it isn't General Peguero [Chief of Police Peguero Guerrero] . . . it's the secretary of the interior, . . . and when at last some one does succeed in obtaining a permit (miracles can happen), he 'is assigned' that Sahara that was once the old airport. . . . Good God."[82]

In the name of "harmony," the Triumvirate kept Bosch and Balaguer in exile and tried "to impose an unjustified truce, one which force[d] the parties to remain in a state of almost total inertia, while the government, with all the resources of power, carrie[d] on political propaganda obviously aimed at holding onto that power."[83] Still, the PRD recovered its strength among the broad urban mass that had been disappointed by the Bosch presidency, and that, on 25 September 1963, had "let their legally elected regime be snatched away from them without a fight."[84] Bosch, though still in exile, again became a symbol in his homeland, his lost popularity unwittingly restored by Reid Cabral and the government's supporters. In the face of the corrupt and brutal Triumvirate, the man in the street recalled the interlude of freedom under Bosch. Time had erased the disappointment—leaving only a happy memory.

José Francisco Peña Gómez and Rafael Molina Ureña; Antonio Martínez Francisco and José Brea Peña; Pablo Rafael Casimiro Castro and Virgilio Mainardi Reyna: these PRD leaders had diverging goals, but for the present they were united in a single cause—reorganization of the party. They traveled up and down the country, restructuring the committees, spreading the party's message. With them went the cadres, braving the harassment of the police. The bleak passivity of 1963 gave way to an enthusiasm reminiscent of 1962.

The party recruitment campaign, begun at the end of 1964, was a "brilliant success."[85] The PRD made gains even within the sectors that, in 1962-63, had been indifferent or hostile: the lower and the "middle" middle class, which were weary of the excessive corruption and ineptitude of the Triumvirate. Early in February 1965, a committee was created to gather signatures for a declaration of "Dominican Professionals and Intellectuals." On 27 February, the declaration appeared in *El Caribe* with over two thousand signatures. It began with an unequivocal condemnation of the coup that had toppled Bosch and continued with a thorough and devastating condemnation of the Triumvirate.[86] As Theodore Draper aptly notes, "That so many should have been willing to lend their names to such a public declaration was virtually unheard of in a country where one does not identify oneself with a deposed political exile lightly. For days, even more outspoken demands for Bosch's return to power with literally thousands of names attached to them were published, many of them with contributions by signatories of five or ten centavos."[87]

The PRD, to be sure, had not extinguished internal dissension, but the differences were no longer paralyzing. Once again, the *golpistas* had unwittingly helped, for among the PRDistas deported in September and October 1963 were Miolán and his closest partisans. In exile their struggle against Bosch went on. The Organization of PRD Exile Branches (Organización de Seccionales Perredeistas en el Exilio or OSPE) was established under their control, but they were vastly outnumbered. Their names meant little to the Dominican masses, and exile barred them from any effective political maneuvering. On 25 October 1964, the party's Fourth National Convention sealed their defeat. Over the bitter opposition of the OSPE, the 207 delegates present "unanimously acclaimed"[88] Juan Bosch president of the party.

In its public statements the PRD demanded a "return to constitutional government without elections": that is, reinstallation of Bosch as president of the Republic and restoration of the constitution of 29 April 1963. Any other solution would be a refusal to recognize the popular will, as expressed in the elections of 20 December 1962, and would mean acceptance of the coup of 25 September 1963.

This hard, "Boschist" line seemed a mere slogan to observers, a rallying cry intended to galvanize the masses; in time, it would give way to a more realistic attitude. The PRD, as everyone knew, had no partisans among the military brass, and without them nothing could be done in the Dominican Republic.

Quietly, behind the scenes, the PRD chiefs kept a watchful eye on each other. Casimiro Castro, Mainardi Reyna, and their friends were aware that, on instructions from Bosch, men like Peña Gómez and Molina Ureña—and even Martínez Francisco and Brea Peña—were conspiring. They had only vague, imprecise information, but they were opposed to any plot. Despite the unanimous vote of the convention and the defeat of the *Miolanistas*, Bosch's grip on the party machinery was far from secure.

Casimiro Castro, Mainardi Reyna, and their supporters were *electoreros*— out of conviction or, even more, out of self-interest. They believed that the PRD ought to yield to reality. With both the United States and the Dominican armed forces supporting him, Reid Cabral would never be overthrown by force. Therefore, the party should try to gain as much as it could by peaceful means, that is, by relatively honest elections. If, to achieve this, Bosch had to forego taking part in the elections, then such a sacrifice was necessary—and, for many *electoreros*, not too painful. At least the party would win some seats in Congress. Most of the *electoreros* had been congressmen in 1963—and they were nostalgic. The PRDista masses, however, and even the municipal and provincial organizations, were remote from the silent struggle waged by *electoreros* and *antielectoreros*. They were *Boschistas*—period.

The PRD remained the country's most powerful party, but there was another worthy of the term "mass": Balaguer's Reformist Party. Balaguer's own political history is an odd one. Puppet president under Trujillo, he had briefly tasted power in November 1961; a few weeks later he took refuge in the Nunciate. For the Dominican masses, his name was an object of hatred and scorn. Since March 1962 he had been in exile in New York. But in the Dominican Republic political movements had formed, choosing him as their leader. The first of these movements, in November 1962, was the minuscule PRDA, but other small groups followed. Finally, on 21 July 1963, the fusion of the PRDA with the Acción Social and the Agrario Obrero parties gave birth to the Reformist Party.[89] Balaguer was elected president of the Provisional National Directorate, and later, on 21 October 1963, at the first National Assembly of the Reformist Party, he was elected president of the party.

Balaguer's support came from powerful sectors of Dominican society, for the most part former *gente de segunda* who had risen under Trujillo. These *nouveaux riches* felt uneasy under the rule of the *cívicos* who represented the traditional *gente de primera*. But Balaguer—the "puppet" president, the sad-faced "little Doctor," the intellectual with a reputation for honesty—seemed to be popular even with many of the "children of Machepa." The reasons are difficult to explain. Perhaps it was because of the demagogic measures he took after Trujillo's death. Or maybe it stemmed from the respect that Trujillo's image still inspired in the countryside, a respect now transferred to his former servant. It might even have been a certain, intangible magnetism in a man seemingly devoid of charisma. Whatever the reason, by the spring of 1965 the Reformist Party had real strength, which was more apparent in the provinces than in the capital— a *Boschista* fief—more apparent among the lower middle class than among the "children of Machepa." Most important, the Reformists had supporters in the armed forces, and they were busy plotting. They saw no other option. Reid

Cabral refused to let Balaguer return from exile and seemed determined to hold onto power.

The clash between *duros* and *flojos* in the PRSC intensified under the Triumvirate. Reacting to the overthrow of Bosch, the Fourth National Convention had given control of the party to the *duros* on 21 February 1964. Their leaders, Antonio Rosario and Caonabo Javier Castillo, were elected president and secretary general of the PRSC. The party's National Executive Committee (Comité Ejecutivo Nacional or CEN) consisted solely of their partisans. At the Fifth National Convention a few months later (31 October 1964), the PRSC seemed to be "more unified than ever."[90] The *duros*, still in the majority, agreed to increase the membership in the CEN from six to nine to include three *flojos*: Guido d'Alessandro, Leonel Rodríguez Rib, and Josefina Padilla. But this unity was only a facade; the two factions continued to be diametrically opposed. They clashed over the nature and breadth of the social reforms the party should demand—a problem already evident in 1963. But their major conflict occurred over what attitude the PRSC should adopt vis-à-vis the Triumvirate. The *duros*, convinced that free elections under Reid Cabral would be impossible, favored the "return to constitutional government without elections" and gravitated toward the PRD; the *flojos*, however, distrusted Bosch, exalted the virtue of prudence, and preached a "limited opposition."

Relying on their majority in the CEN, the *duros* decided to ally with the PRD. But the *flojos* acted first. Although in the minority, they were enterprising and physically strong. On the night of 16 January 1965, they launched "Operation Crowbar": a group of *flojo* leaders, headed by Guido d'Alessandro and Jesús Caminero Morcelo, forced the door and took over the party headquarters. They immediately held a "convention of legitimate delegates" and elected one another to office: d'Alessandro became president, Caminero secretary general. Immediately they announced to the press that "in the present circumstances, it is undesirable, for both the nation and the PRSC, to conclude with other political groups any pact that might compromise the party's freedom of action"[91]—a nicely phrased way to refuse an alliance with the PRD. Thereupon, the newly "elected" leaders barricaded the door to the headquarters with "an iron grating, . . . heavy chains and a padlock."[92]

The situation bordered on absurdity. On the night of 20 February, the *duros* laid siege to the party headquarters. A battle ensued, both sides armed with "clubs, rocks and iron bars." When the *duros* attacked, the *flojos* counterattacked, and the two went on "dislodging each other." Then the police arrived and "dislodged them all."[93] Even though they might get into a scuffle, the *flojos* were, on the whole, well-behaved youngsters who created no great problems for Reid Cabral, so the police returned the headquarters to them on 22 February.

The PRSC was now openly split: two presidents, Guido d'Alessandro and Antonio Rosario; two secretaries general, Jesús Caminero and Caonabo Javier;

and so on. Each faction published in the Dominican press the resolutions of its supporters and excommunications of its rivals. Amid this avalanche of communiqués, it was impossible to determine who was in the majority. Perhaps the *flojos* predominated in the provinces, but the *duros* controlled the capital and the Bloque Revolucionario Universitario Cristiano (BRUC). They also had the support of CASC, though the latter had only very loose ties with the PRSC. CASC took an independent route; it bitterly opposed the Triumvirate and leaned in the direction of Juan Bosch.

Whether or not they were a majority, the *duros* achieved their goal. On 30 January 1965, in San Juan, Puerto Rico, the Pact of Rio Piedras was signed by Antonio Rosario for the PRSC and Juan Bosch for the PRD. The two parties pledged to "act as one, in a common front, in order to secure the re-establishment of the constitutional order in the Dominican Republic."[94] It was an alliance between dwarf and giant, or rather, half a dwarf, since the *flojo* leaders of the PRSC declared the Rio Piedras Pact null and void, maintaining that Antonio Rosario and Caonabo Javier "lack[ed] the capacity to represent, let alone commit," the party.[95] The agreement was vague, conceived in general terms, and the Dominican press debated its meaning. In reality the pact was nothing more than a little food for thought that Bosch served the public while, behind the scenes, he busied himself with more important matters.

In September 1963 six *golpista* parties participated in the government. By the end of December only two remained, and by April 1964, when the UCN and the VRD resigned their cabinet posts, there were none. The coalition could not survive the struggles among clans and interests. The spoils were too meager to satisfy everyone, especially since the lion's share was reserved for military leaders whose traffic in contraband paralyzed trade and threatened industry. Suddenly a number of *cívicos* discovered corruption to be a vice. To many of his old friends, "Donny" Cabral was no less than a traitor. Others, showered with favor, saw things differently. The poet Héctor Incháustegui Cabral, for instance, was named on 4 May 1964 president of the Corporation for Industrial Development of the Dominican Republic. For this coveted post, his only qualifications were his family ties to the Triumvir.

The miniparties practically vanished. No one could have said for certain whether the ASD still existed. Its leader, Juan Isidro Jimenes Grullón, was off on a long trip to Europe. But Mario Read Vittini (PDC), Horacio Ornes (VRD), and Miguel Angel Ramírez Alcántara (PNRD) still plagued the country.[96] They made a lot of noise, talking constantly about "democracy." To hear them, one would have thought they were the victims—not the authors—of the coup of 25 September 1963. Through their rhetoric, style, and the popularity of their parties an image gradually takes shape of a creature of rachitic body, shrill cry, and razor-sharp teeth.

On 21 November 1963, another miniparty was founded, the Liberal Evolutionist Party (Partido Liberal Evolucionista or PLE). It was led by Luis Amiama

Tió, with Imbert Barrera's blessing and the support of UCN dissidents. The average age of its members, according to rumor, was sixty years.[97] Perhaps the gossips exaggerated, or perhaps they confused the number of party members with their age.

The UCN—the National Civic Union—also had its problems. "It is neither a Union, nor Civic, and much less than National," aptly commented a Dominican journalist. Its "dismantlement . . . is a reality which no one here doubts."[98] The party lacked hard-core militants, but was rich in "leaders" who hated each other. Its numerous cliques gathered into two main factions, one headed by Severo Cabral y Ortíz, the other by Alcibiades Espinosa Acosta.[99] Rafael Bonnelly—shrewd and wary, a "founding father"—watched in silence, counting his partisans.

Severo Cabral quickly became a bitter enemy of "Donny" Reid Cabral, who nonetheless continued to enjoy the discreet support of Alcibiades Espinosa. On 10 February 1965, Espinosa and his friends suddenly "discovered" that they were witnessing "the start of a new dictatorship."[100] They lashed out in turn against "the arbitrary acts, the brutalities . . . of the Triumvirate."[101] Then a new event added to the confusion: Rafael Bonnelly entered the arena. Having openly broken with his old friend and protégé, Reid Cabral, Bonnelly showed himself ready to respond favorably to the "document signed by over 3,000 representatives of the Cibao region asking that, 'in view of the current political situation confronting the nation, he head a non-partisan movement, which as a moral and political force will take in under its banner all those who seek the good of the nation.' "[102] The old fox's cronies had done their work well. Was there yet another party in the offing?

Rejected by the people, attacked by the middle class, repudiated by his peers, Reid Cabral seemed alone. But, in fact, he had two powerful champions: the United States and General Elías Wessin y Wessin.

For Washington, the Dominican Republic had ceased to be a "showcase of democracy." The question was no longer one of demonstrating "freedom's alternative to the police state reforms in Cuba." The "Kennedyites" had expected Bosch to become the Dominican Betancourt; instead he proved, in their eyes, to be a dangerous demagogue. Their favor changed to distrust. Now Kennedy was dead and, on 14 December 1963, Thomas Mann became Lyndon Johnson's assistant secretary of state for inter-American affairs.[103] Mann saw Castro not as a product of the Batista dictatorship, but as the result of American mistakes. The United States, blinded by moral considerations, had cut off aid to Batista and brought about his fall. The blunder ought not to be repeated. The "Latinos" were not ready for democracy. Although the era of the Trujillo-style dictators was over, the threat of Communist subversion loomed. In the coming years the best guarantee of American security lay in "nontotalitarian dictators," and the Latin American armed forces would play a decisive role in assuring anti-Communist stability. Despite serious taints—rampant corruption and the political ambitions of certain officers—the military was indispensable. It could be hoped, of course, that a civic spirit would develop among the military, but not at the expense of the stability of the Latin American armed forces.[104]

Mann's views might seem brutal, but they did not really constitute a break with the Kennedy line, the latter's apologists notwithstanding. There were differences, but they were largely of nuance and rhetorical artifice. Regarding the Dominican Republic, Mann agreed with Ambassador Martin's appraisal of Bosch as a man who "would make an alliance with the devil himself, if he thought it could get him into office."[105] For Mann, "Bosch's failure to provide anything approaching adequate leadership when he was president, his actions during his Presidency facilitating the return of hard-core communists to the Dominican Republic . . . furnished no basis for concluding that he understood the nature of the communist design; that he would be disposed to control the communists had he understood; or that he would have been able to control them had he so desired."[106] At best, Bosch "belonged in a classroom."[107] United States interests dictated that in the future this dangerous figure be kept out of Dominican politics. "The only U.S. official personnel who talked to Bosch were F.B.I. agents who wanted him to inform them about Communists in the Dominican Republic. Otherwise the Mann-Johnson policy refused to recognize his existence."[108]

To Washington, Donald Reid Cabral, that "aggressive young businessman,"[109] represented the model of the "nontotalitarian dictator." He enjoyed the favor of the U.S. government, "even though it knew from its own [Dominican] public-opinion polls that the . . . [Triumvirate] had no popular support."[110] For almost a year and a half, from January 1964 to April 1965, the Triumvirate received massive economic assistance, "more money—about $100,-000,000 in direct and guaranteed loans—than had ever been made available to any Dominican regime before."[111]

In Santo Domingo, an "extremely one-sided Embassy"[112] carried out orders from Washington blindly, but with gusto. The new ambassador, William Tapley Bennett, was "a courtly southern gentleman, a career foreign service officer of the old school,"[113] who in his new post "seemed to know no one . . . to the left of the Rotary Club."[114] Nor was he a man to hide his sympathies. From the moment of his arrival in Santo Domingo on 22 March 1964, he struck up an extremely cordial relationship with Donald Reid Cabral—"Donny," who was so "civilized," so "realistic," so pro-American. Bennett's feelings were generally shared by his associates who regarded the PRD with a mixture of contempt and antipathy. Toward Bosch, whom he had never met, Bennett felt a violent hostility.[115]

Bennett's contacts with the *Boschistas* were extremely sparse and cold. He only dealt with the party's most "respectable" members. Peña Gómez, for example, black and "shirtless," was never received by the ambassador, nor by the ambassador's deputy, William Connett, who was also "ill at ease in the company of men improperly attired."[116] In the whirlwind of plots being devised in Santo Domingo, Bennett found it hard to take the PRD seriously. Neither lists of signatures nor fine speeches would ever topple the Triumvirate. The few U.S. diplomats responsible for maintaining contacts with the PRD leaders all sang the same tune: "You're too weak to start a revolution." The Americans saw the *Boschistas* as cowards who had stood idly by when their government was overthrown on 25 September 1963. Two months later, when the 1J4 guerrillas took to the mountains, there was not a PRDista among them. "Be realistic," advised the American diplomats. Reid Cabral sat in the Presidential Palace, Bosch was in exile. Reid Cabral alone enjoyed U.S. support—they could never repeat it enough. He alone could guarantee a period of stability. "Accept the inevitable," PRD leaders were told. "Support the candidacy of Reid Cabral for president of the Republic. In exchange, the PRD will receive economic assistance." By listening to "reason," the party, and its leaders, would prosper.

But not just the PRD opposed Reid Cabral; he faced the hostility of all Dominican political forces. The American embassy was tireless in its effort to "help him guard against his enemies."[117] In the eyes of the Dominican people, the U.S. diplomats were increasingly linked to the ambitions of one man: the Triumvir Donald Reid Cabral. Even overtly pro-American parties such as the Reformists, the PLE, and the VRD "openly questioned Bennett's partisan activity to keep Reid in power."[118]

After the United States, General Wessin, chief of the CEFA, was the power behind the throne. But the Dominican armed forces were far from cohesive. Many factions of varying importance existed.[119] The Dominican Republic had a National Police, an army, a navy, an air force—and the CEFA. If the several corps had a single trait in common, it was ineptitude among all but a few of the officers and lack of training among the rank and file. One did not enlist to answer a calling, but to get rich, or at least to trade grinding poverty for the relative security of sixty dollars a month.

The National Police, at the insistence of the American military mission, had in 1962 been increased from three thousand to ten thousand members. On paper it was a considerable force, but, as events would show, appearances were deceptive. Only the three hundred or four hundred *cascos blancos*—the shock force responsible for crushing demonstrations—had received military training.

Santo Domingo had the largest concentration of police—about three thousand men. Half of them were stationed at two principal bases: in the north, at the Palace of the National Police, the institution's headquarters, and in the southeast, in the Ciudad Nueva district, at the Fortaleza Ozama, on the Ozama River. The Fortaleza, headquarters of the *cascos blancos*, was an important arms depot. About four thousand arms were stored there, including 50-and 30-mm. machine guns.

The navy, for many Dominicans, was the clean branch of the armed forces, the one that had never been used against the people. It was untainted by the blood of the massacres of June 1959 and December 1963. No sailor had ever been seen in the streets beating citizens.[120] Moreover, the navy appeared to have played a passive role in the overthrow of Bosch. On the other hand, it was recalled that on 18 January 1962, at the time of the Rodríguez Echavarría coup, naval units had taken up positions along the coast between Santo Domingo and Punta Caucedo, threatening to open fire on San Isidro if the Council of State was not reinstated.

The navy, however, was the weakest branch of the armed forces. The "training of all naval units . . . [was] generally considered to be grossly inadequate."[121] The entire fleet consisted of two frigates, five corvettes, five patrol vessels, three landing craft, four Coast Guard vessels, three motor launches, two oilers, three auxiliaries, five tugs, and a presidential yacht.[122] There were thirty-five hundred men, but only one valuable unit: the frogmen, 100 to 150 at the most. The chief naval bases were Las Calderas, near Baní, in the province of Peravia; Haina, in the province of San Cristóbal, thirteen miles west of Santo Domingo; and Sans Souci, on the eastern bank of the Ozama, opposite the capital, housing the headquarters of the frogmen and the naval cadet school. In addition, small naval detachments were stationed in the various ports. The staff headquarters was located at La Feria, the administrative district on the western outskirts of Santo Domingo. It included only administrative personnel, more bureaucrats than military. The navy, nominally engaged in the suppression of contraband traffic, was in fact actively involved in the transport of these goods.

With twelve thousand men, the army was numerically the strongest of the nation's armed forces. But, like the other branches, it suffered from a grave lack of able officers and trained troops. There were, nonetheless, three elite units each eight hundred men strong: the Juan Pablo Duarte, the Francisco del Rosario Sánchez, and the Ramón Mella battalions. On these MAAG had concentrated its efforts, hoping to make them model units. None were further than eighteen miles from the capital. The Francisco del Rosario Sánchez Battalion was stationed at the Twenty-seventh of February camp, on the Duarte Highway linking Santo Domingo with Santiago, about four miles from the capital. The Juan Pablo Duarte Battalion was located at the Sixteenth of August camp, also on the Duarte Highway, about seventeen miles from the capital. There were four hundred additional soldiers bringing its total strength to twelve hundred men. Finally, the Ramón Mella Battalion was garrisoned at San Cristóbal, about eighteen miles west of the capital. All three battalions were equipped with model 30 machine guns (both heavy and lightweight), model 50 machine guns, and bazookas. But they had no cannon, no tanks, and no "120" mortars. The only army unit that did have cannon and "120" mortars was the 6½ Artillery. Counting 250 men, the unit was stationed near the Duarte Highway, only about one hundred yards from the Twenty-seventh of February camp.[123]

Four army units were situated inside the capital. These were not elite units in any sense, and deserve mention only because of their crucial location. (1) The

Artillería y Transportación Battalion was better known as the batallón de Transportación, after the barracks where it was lodged. It had about 350 men, primarily mechanics and chauffeurs. (2) The Compañía de Intendencia, counting between 175 and 200 men, was used for administrative tasks. At best they were inefficient bureaucrats. Their barracks were only two hundred yards from those of Transportación. (3) The Compañía Intendencia del Material Bélico, with 175 men, oversaw the war material stored in the so-called Polvorín (Powder Magazine),[124] which housed explosives, grenades, and bazookas. (4) Finally, there was the Presidential Guard: between 450 and 500 men, some lodged behind the Presidential Palace (35ta Compañía de la Guardia Presidencial), the others in barracks about three or four hundred yards away. The rest of the army—about eight thousand men—was scattered throughout the country. Every city had its Fortaleza (army barracks), which housed at most two to three hundred "ill-trained, ill-equipped, idle"[125] soldiers.

The Dominican Air Force, established in 1948, numbered between 3,300 and 3,500 men. "Unit training [was] virtually nonexistent."[126] There were three air bases, of varying importance, and a firing range on Catalina Island. The Nineteenth of November Air Base, at San Isidro, about nine miles northeast of the capital, was the seat of air force headquarters and by far the country's most powerful air base. It was also, because of rampant corruption, a "playboy's paradise."[127] The base possessed thirty P51 fighter planes, twelve Vampires, twenty-five AT6s, two B26 light bombers, a few C46 transport planes, and a couple of T33s. There were two thousand men at the base, but only one well-trained unit: the Fuerzas Especiales, a product of the fusion of the antiguerrilla corps and the parachutists. The unit had three to four hundred men and was commanded by one of the very few able officers at the base, Major Salvador ("Chinino") Lluberes Montás. The country's second air base, Colonel Piloto Juan Antonio Minaya Fernández, at Santiago, had only four P51 fighters and a single battalion, supported by an armored platoon from the CEFA (four tanks, two assault tanks, one half track).[128] Finally, the Capitán Piloto Rafael A. Davila Quezada Air Base, at Barahona, had at most four P51s, about 350 men, and a few assault tanks on detachment from the CEFA.

The Armed Forces Training Center (CEFA) was established on 5 June 1959, Ramfis Trujillo's birthday. Also located at San Isidro, the CEFA's sole raison d'être was to serve as the reigning family's elite guard. Thus the CEFA existed independently of any of the armed forces, and from its inception it was singled out for favor, in terms of both materiel and manpower. After Trujillo's death and Balaguer's exile, the Council of State allowed the CEFA to maintain its autonomy and its privileges. Even Bosch shied from interfering. Reid Cabral, of course, was interested in increasing the CEFA's power.[129]

The CEFA included around two thousand men grouped in three units: an artillery section, General Gregorio Luperón; an armored battalion, Twenty-seventh of February; and an infantry battalion, Enriquillo. Along with the neighboring Nineteenth of November Air Base, the CEFA was the country's largest military installation. This was a first element of the CEFA's power. A second was its geographical position within striking distance of the capital. But the base's main strength lay in the quality of its heavy armament. The CEFA held a monopoly on armored vehicles. Its armored battalion, Twenty-seventh of February, included between thirty and thirty-five tanks, eight to twelve assault tanks, and eight to twelve half tracks. In addition, it had the armored vehicles stationed at the Santiago and Barahona air bases and two or three assault tanks at the army's Fortaleza at Dajabón. These were only "on loan," manned by CEFA personnel and under CEFA orders. Besides the armored vehicles, the CEFA's artillery section, General Gregorio Luperón, boasted the only recoilless cannon (the Swedish Bofors) in the Dominican armed forces. Even without the Bofors cannon, the General Gregorio Luperón unit had better materiel than any army unit, for it always got the newest equipment. In light arms, however, the CEFA was no better off than the rest of the armed forces.

The CEFA did have its Achilles' heel: it lacked able officers, a surprising flaw in a supposedly elite corps. But the paradox is explained when one understands that all that was necessary to be part of the CEFA was unconditional submission to a *caudillo*, General Elías Wessin y Wessin, a capricious master and mediocre officer.

The Nineteenth of November Air Base and the CEFA, both located at San Isidro, stood one hundred yards apart. In the eyes of the people—and for many who should have known better—those hundred yards did not exist. Two bases, a single name: San Isidro, the all-powerful *conjunto* (ensemble).[130] Four thousand men under arms—three and a half times more than at any other camp—and less than ten miles from the capital; all the tanks and most of the Dominican air force: such was San Isidro. Everyone in the Dominican Republic knew that whoever controlled San Isidro controlled the country.

Since late 1961, Wessin had been head of the CEFA. The general was popular with his men, who were better housed and, above all, better fed—than their comrades elsewhere in the country. He nursed his popularity. Often he would give his men money: twenty, fifty, sometimes even a hundred dollars.[131] And many felt the pride (*civis romanus sum*) of belonging to the country's most powerful military unit. In short, the men of the CEFA seemed devoted to their general. The officers, for their part, were "yes-men"—out of necessity, out of interest, at times even out of conviction. Wessin dominated the CEFA, but this was not enough. He now turned his ambitions toward the neighboring air base.

On 24 January 1964, Colonel Ismael Emilio Román Carbuccia replaced General Atila Luna Pérez as air force chief of staff and commander of the Nineteenth of November.[132] Román Carbuccia was every bit as corrupt as his predecessor, but he was far more "flexible." Devoid of personality and of partisans, he became not Wessin's ally, but his servant.[133] The CEFA and the Nineteenth of November seemed increasingly united, strengthening in the eyes of the people the image of the *conjunto*.

Under Román Carbuccia, corruption reached new heights, provoking a reaction among a number of young officers at the base. Some of them may have reacted against this excessive corruption that had made the air force the most discredited military institution in the country; squabbling over division of the spoils and contempt for an incompetent chief may have motivated others. The weight of each of these elements is difficult to assess. It is certain, however, that an anti-Román Carbuccia current developed. The situation did not escape the attention of the U.S. military mission. The Americans would, of course, welcome any lessening of corruption within the Dominican armed forces, but only as long as cohesion and "morale" were not impaired. MAAG decided that Román Carbuccia should be replaced. Wessin had his candidate, Colonel Alfredo Segundo Imbert McGregor, whom he recommended to Reid Cabral. Of course, the Triumvir acquiesced. But MAAG, having discreetly polled the young officers at the air base, chose Colonel Juan de los Santos Céspedes, a man as pro-American as Imbert McGregor but far more respected by those he was to command.

On 18 January 1965, de los Santos was named air force chief of staff with the temporary rank of general. Without being "anti-Wessin," he was a man with his own mind—he could be an ally, not a servant. Still, Wessin retained a strong influence at the Nineteenth of November, due to the existence of a group of officers loyal to him, among whom was "Chinino" Lluberes, commander of the Fuerzas Especiales. In addition, the armored vehicles "on loan" to the air bases at Santiago and Barahona extended Wessin's influence beyond San Isidro. Barahona was already considered by some to be "Wessinist." For de los Santos, the CEFA chief was a difficult—and a dangerous—neighbor. Relations between the two generals were bound to be strained.

Dominicans identified the name of Trujillo's birthplace (San Cristóbal) with a clique of high-ranking army officers who banded together under the Triumvirate, convinced that their own interests would best be served by the return to power of Dr. Joaquín Balaguer. To accomplish this goal, they took to plotting. The principal figures of the group were Generals Salvador Montás Guerrero and Félix Hermida, Jr., Colonels Neit Nivar Seijas, Rafael Nivar Ledesma, Braulio Alvarez Sánchez, Pérez Aponte, and Rafael Leger Báez. Montás Guerrero was the army chief of staff and Alvarez Sánchez was his deputy. Pérez Aponte commanded the elite Mella Battalion, and Hermida was the army undersecretary of state.

Other *Balaguerista* officers also held key military posts: Lieutenant Colonel Giovanni Gutiérrez Ramírez, for example, commander of the Sixteenth of August camp, and Major Pedro Augusto Alvarez Holguín, commander of the Juan Pablo Duarte Battalion.[134] These men were bitter foes of the San Cristóbal Group. Unfortunately for Balaguer, his influence among his adherents was too feeble to unite them. Comprising only some of the *Balagueristas*, the San Cristóbal Group was thus relatively weak. It purported to control the army, yet, except for the Mella Battalion, it had little or no influence on the other elite army units: the Juan Pablo Duarte and Francisco del Rosario Sánchez battalions and the 6½ Artillery. The numerous Fortalezas scattered about the country were of negligible importance.

Since 8 March 1962, General Belisario Peguero had been chief of police. At the time of his appointment, he was Imbert Barrera's man, but he soon outgrew that role. While maintaining cordial relations with his old boss, Belisario Peguero wisely decided to steer his own course. He soon became a strongman, as Severo Cabral, the minister of interior and police, discovered in December 1963. The minister dared to oppose Belisario, who he felt was too corrupt. A few days later, Severo Cabral was forced to resign.[135] Belisario became rich, but ambition was to undo him. The police force was already "extravagantly numerous,"[136] yet he wanted three thousand more men, and he wanted tanks. Only the CEFA had tanks. Wessin took the request as a challenge, a threat.

These, then, were the principal known factions among the armed forces. A recognized part of the Dominican scene, they were discussed in the press, sometimes directly, sometimes implicitly. Among them, Wessin's was the strongest. Had his enemies closed ranks and had the "neutrals"[137] backed them— Wessin could have been kept in check. But they were unable to unite. For his part, Reid Cabral needed Wessin's support. Since their interests coincided, together they prepared to strike.

On 2 October 1964, the Triumvirate replaced Colonel Braulio Alvarez Sánchez of the San Cristóbal Group as army deputy chief of staff and shipped him off to Washington as Dominican military adviser to the OAS. It was only the beginning, for in January 1965 the military crisis, long expected, exploded. On 13 January, the police was stripped of the autonomy it had held since 1962 and was brought under the minister of the armed forces.[138] Five days later, Colonel Hernán Despradel Brache replaced Belisario Peguero as chief of police,[139] and Belisario was promoted to undersecretary of state and supervisor general of the police—an honorary position devoid of real power. Not satisfied, on 17 February, the Triumvirate forced him to retire. All that remained to him was the money he had stolen and a few honors: the right to wear his uniform and the right to a personal bodyguard of four.

Meanwhile the San Cristóbal Group again came under heavy fire. On 27 January, Colonel Neit Nivar Seijas, the brains of the faction, was retired "effective immediately."[140] On the same day, the post of army undersecretary of state was abolished, leaving Félix Hermida, Jr., to await a new assignment, which no doubt would never come.[141] Three weeks later (17 February), army chief of staff Montás Guerrero, already berated by his friends for having failed to intervene in behalf of Nivar Seijas, became minister of the interior, a bitter promotion since the police now served under the minister of the armed forces. The new army chief of staff, General[142] Marcos Aníbal Rivera Cuesta, had been considered a *Balaguerista*, but he now fled the sinking ship. Even Viñas Román, "the nimblest tightrope walker" in the armed forces, fell. He had foolishly opposed Wessin, daring to replace three CEFA colonels, men in Wessin's confidence, with three friends of his. Wessin refused to obey and even to receive the intruders: "A junior officer told them not to insist and bade them withdraw. He told them emphatically that if they wanted an explanation, they would get it from the Triumvir, President Reid Cabral."[143]

The explanation came like a thunderbolt. General Viñas Román had violated an unwritten law by supposing that a minister of the armed forces could give orders to the master of the CEFA. This was a serious offense. Viñas Román was no longer "worthy" of the post he had held since 19 January 1962. On 27 January 1965, Reid Cabral "temporarily"[144] became minister of the armed forces and of the National Police. Viñas Román left for Washington as the Dominican representative to the effete Inter-American Defense Board.[145]

Any possibility of a balance of power within the Dominican armed forces now seemed out of the question. Even with de los Santos replacing Román Carbuccia, Wessin remained the strong man of the Triumvirate. In fact, his power had increased. With Belisario Peguero in retirement and the San Cristóbal Group reeling from the blows it had been dealt, it appeared that no one could check Wessin's power. Nor had the San Cristóbal Group seen an end to its woes. On 12 April, Nivar Seijas was obliged to leave the country "of his own free will" for "studies" in the United States, with no date set for his return. And it was rumored that Montás Guerrero, minister of the interior, would soon be forced to retire.

"The thorniest matter—and perhaps one of highly explosive potential—[was] the forthcoming designation of a minister of the Armed Forces."[146] Many persons, civilians and military alike, were convinced that Reid Cabral, the interim minister, was paving the way for his protector: General Wessin.[147]

Against this background people spoke of elections in the Dominican Republic. Such talk had gone on for a long time. For the "moderates," the Triumvirate's raison d'être was "rooted in the offer of new elections."[148] But very soon the "moderates" were forced to recognize that in this regard the government was moving all too slowly. Finally, on 7 September 1964, after months of what they decried as a "disconcerting attitude toward the imperative return to a constitutional order,"[149] Reid Cabral set 1 September 1965 as the date for municipal, congressional, and presidential elections, with the electoral campaign opening no sooner than 1 June.

In 1966, apologists for the U.S. invasion of the Dominican Republic would write: "There was a growing suspicion, though unsubstantiated, that Reid had no intention of allowing the Dominican people to go to the polls in September 1965 to elect a constitutional president."[150] Yet one had to be blind—or hypocritical—to believe that free elections would take place in the Dominican Republic. General Wessin had been a leader of the anti-Boschist *golpe*. Since then he had clung tenaciously to his position: Bosch had been overthrown because he was a Communist. Wessin was the strong man of the Triumvirate. How could that staunch champion of "democracy" permit the Communist Juan Bosch to take part in elections and thus have another chance to deceive the honest—but naive—Dominican people? Even if Wessin had agreed, trusting his countrymen to unmask the impostor, how could he stand idly by if Bosch triumphed? Wisely, an anonymous Dominican complained: "Why should the people go to the polls, so that 25 September [1963] can happen all over again?"[151]

Reid Cabral was more subtle than his general. He had to think about public relations. The elections would be held, he said, and they would be free. But freedom did not mean license. Thus for Reid Cabral it was conceivable that there would be no elections—if the opposition proved "irresponsible." Or the elections could take place, but without the two candidates most apt to disturb the tranquillity of the "Dominican family": Bosch and Balaguer, the exiled leaders of the only two mass parties in the Republic. The Triumvir was blunt: "The participation of ex-presidents Balaguer and Bosch in the coming elections will depend on the state of public order in the country . . . ; should the present campaign of political agitation continue, it will be impossible to permit the entry of the above-mentioned political leaders."[152] But for him "every peaceful and legal movement of public opinion in support of the candidacies of Messrs. Balaguer and Bosch" was "subversive."[153]

There was a man, however, whose only concern was the welfare of the Dominican family: Donald Reid Cabral. Here was the ideal candidate. It was still too early for the Triumvir to make the happy announcement of his candidacy: not until 1 June 1965 would he communicate his decision. Yet already he had given the people reason to hope by declaring that if he chose to run, he would remain as president of the Triumvirate during the electoral campaign—one more guarantee of a "free and democratic" climate. No one was fooled. The elections, if there were any, would only serve to legalize four more years of "Donaldism." Wessin's tanks would be the lucky candidate's most persuasive electioneers. As for the United States, it had already made up its mind: with or without elections it would support Donald Reid Cabral.

But forces were at work behind the scenes, the far left, for one. Weak or strong, it was always a threat, for it was by definition well organized, powerful, and ready to strike. Its very existence provided the Triumvirate with old, but still effective, weapons for its propaganda. The Dominican Republic, warned Reid Cabral, was "the chosen center for the struggle between democracy and communism in Latin America."[154] Washington was as sensitive as ever to the "Communist threat," and its paranoia continued to play an important role in shaping U.S. policy toward the Dominican Republic. For this reason alone the far left is important. The Enriquillo movement was also preparing to overthrow the Triumvirate. The press was unaware of its existence. Reid Cabral himself, and even the Americans, began to suspect it only in early April 1965. By then it was too late.

Not even prison walls could prevent the *catorcistas* from quarreling. From a cell at La Victoria, Fidelio Despradel aspired to replace Manolo Tavárez as the leader of the 1J4. Despradel's partisans maintained that he was "wholly identified with the fallen leader."[155] To bolster this myth, they even talked of a will wherein Manolo had allegedly designated Despradel as his successor. No such will ever existed.[156] The maneuver failed, for the opposition was vehement. On 8-9 May 1964, when the Triumvirate deported some twenty high-ranking *catorcistas*, among them Despradel and the other Central Committee members who had been in jail, the 1J4 still had no supreme leader. All it had was "warring brothers," who carried on their quarrels in Europe, waiting for a chance to return clandestinely to the Dominican Republic.

Meanwhile, in Cuba, the four Central Committee members "exiled" in September 1963 went on with their training, which promised to be unusually long. These exiles were *flojos*, and the Cubans, who supported the *duros*, had no desire to see them go, since they might manage to get back to the Dominican Republic before the *duros*. The party's representative in Havana, himself a *duro*, exerted his influence with the Cubans to delay the departure of these four.[157]

Only two Central Committee members—Roberto Duvergé and Juan B. Mejía—had remained in the Dominican Republic. Duvergé was a *duro*; in the past Mejía had vacillated between the two factions; the prestige of both had been tarnished by the passivity of the urban front in November-December 1963. Thanks mainly to the efforts of Benjamín Ramos (president of the 1J4's Comité del Distrito and a *duro*) a Provisional Central Executive Committee (Comité Ejecutivo Central Provisional or CECP) was formed, in January-February 1964, around these two men. Its very name pointed to the temporary nature of the organization. It was composed of middle-level leaders, who would serve only until circumstances permitted the return of the old CEC members.[158]

From the beginning, the CECP adopted a hard line, calling on the party to prepare itself for armed insurrection. The debacle of the guerrilla action had not dimmed the "mountain madness": on the contrary, "the dead had to be avenged."[159] Such dogmatism was rhetoric, completely divorced from reality. The 1J4 had never been weaker. "There was within the party deep discouragement, a dreadful lack of morale."[160] It was a time of "atomization."[161] The provincial committees were "in fact nonexistent, except as isolated individuals acting on their own."[162] "As an organization," the 1J4 "boiled down to the Capital."[163]

Finally, the former CEC members returned from exile. First came Norge Botello, in September 1964, then Fidelio Despradel and Jimmy Durán (23 and 25 October). Next were Juan Miguel Román, Luis Genao Espaillat, and Fafa Taveras, and, on 7 January 1965, Daniel Ozuna.[164] They all entered the CECP automatically, bringing with them "their old positions and their personal rancors."[165] "Divisions within the party became more acute."[166] Everyone agreed that the Triumvirate had to be overthrown. But Reid Cabral would have to wait. The *catorcistas* faced other, far more pressing tasks. The internecine struggle promised to be bloody.

Fidelio Despradel, flanked by Juan Miguel Román and Luis Genao Espaillat, closed ranks with Roberto Duvergé. The four *supersabios* were united again. They possessed the truth, and together they strove to "purify" the party, to free it of its "petty-bourgeois" aspect. They had located the evil. Fidelio Despradel proclaimed: "Within the CECP two antagonistic political currents can be clearly distinguished": the first, the adherents of Marxism-Leninism; the second, those who wave the flag of "rightist opportunism." The Marxist-Leninists, of course, were Despradel, Duvergé, Juan Miguel Román, and Genao Espaillat. On the other hand, the *flojo* leaders—Durán, Botello, Taveras, and Ozuna—were "pseudo-revolutionaries, opportunists masquerading as revolutionaries." They had introduced into the CECP "the REAL SURRENDER and false struggle against imperialism and reaction, the REAL ABANDONMENT and false support of the means of struggle." Their program was "LIQUIDATIONIST."[167]

The *supersabios* demanded that the 1J4 be turned "shortly"[168] into a Marxist-Leninist party. Its task would be to make the "socialist revolution."[169] For Jimmy Durán and his friends, however, "skipping stages" was impossible. Whatever the ideological stance of its leaders, the 1J4 was anchored in the reality of the country. By its social composition, by its history, the party was "petty-bourgeois, anti-imperialist and anti-feudal."[170] Its leaders could not "set forth objectives that the masses . . . [did] not understand and . . . [were] not prepared to attain because of their lack of politicization and the absence of class consciousness."[171] The 1J4's role was "not to make the socialist revolution that many dream of, . . . but to mold the revolution of national liberation."[172]

For the sake of simplicity, one could say that the 1J4 was split into two main factions: the *duros*, partisans of Fidelio Despradel, and the *flojos*. But, in fact, reality was far more complex—and somewhat sordid. The divisions within the party during this period made for "a real stew."[173] Rather than only "two antagonistic political currents," there was a myriad of small factions, with personal considerations dominating infinitely more than ideological convictions. The "warring brothers" were no longer mere political rivals; they despised one another. "So-and-so is a thief!" "What's-his-name is a coward!" "That one betrayed the guerrilla movement!" "Why didn't he die at Manaclas?" These accusations were bandied back and forth by the leaders of the 1J4.

Later, the *flojos* would be accused of having returned to the country "thirsting for vengeance," of having sought "to take advantage of the guerrilla defeat to bolster their position."[174] The *duros*, who alone were responsible for that disaster, answered their critics "by exalting the mystique of the guerrilla movement."[175] With a barrage of rhetoric, they prevented any serious analysis of the events of November-December 1963. Such analysis would only have exposed their overwhelming responsibility and inability to lead the party. To these mistakes—and the refusal to recognize them—were added the criminal ambitions of men such as Duvergé, Genao Espaillat, and particularly Despradel.[176] No other 1J4 leader in the party's history showed the ambition, cynicism, and bad faith of Despradel, who was determined at any cost to take Manolo's place, but who lacked the dead leader's integrity, courage, and, above all, devotion to an ideal.

Letters of *catorcista* leaders bare the reality in that spring of 1965. "The party's problems have grown more and more acute";[177] "The specter of division . . . has become a reality, and today is threatening the very existence of the

1J4";[178] "The situation in the CECP is getting worse every day."[179] On 25 March, Fidelio Despradel ended a long-winded speech with the charge that "there is sufficient evidence to expel Fafa [Taveras] and Leandro [Guzmán] from the party and to remove Jaime [Jimmy] Durán and [Daniel] Ozuna from the leadership."[180]

The *catorcista* leaders in the CECP and in the provincial bodies were too absorbed in their quarrels to think about the party. They produced interminable documents heaping abuse on one another, or gave way—the *duros* in particular—to "ideological" lucubrations. Yet, in the words of a leading *catorcista*, they proved unable "to offer a solution to the country's economico-political crisis. The rallying cry 'return to Constitutionality' is heard a thousand times over, but no concrete steps are being taken to bring it about, and the masses feel frustrated and abandoned. Lamentably, we [find ourselves] on the margin of the situation, without plans, without tactics."[181]

The 1J4 was adrift. "The influence of the Party in the nation's problems is minimal and the party's organization is not good; moreover internal problems hinder the work of organization and prevent it from being carried out efficiently."[182] The party was "splintered in the interior,"[183] weak in the capital. "Our militants, disoriented and confused, tend alarmingly to join other parties."[184]

And yet the 1J4 had a new "military arm"—one, it must be admitted, only tenuously attached to the body—the Military Bureau.[185]

On 12 December 1963, "Baby" Mejía Lluberes secretly returned from Cuba. A *duro* and deeply committed to the idea of armed struggle, he had hoped to join the guerrilla *focos*. But already defeat was certain. Only two of the six guerrilla fronts still held out, and no one doubted that they would be crushed. The *catorcista* leaders in Santo Domingo explained to "Baby" that a decision had been made not to open any new fronts. They asked him to stay in the city and take charge of rebuilding the party's military apparatus, since the Infrastructure, which had initiated the guerrilla action, would perish with it.

They had to begin anew. The best men were either dead or in jail. Others were fearful. The plan for the new Infrastructure envisioned two stages: first, creation of a military organization in Santo Domingo, where the party had some strength; second, after it was firmly rooted in the capital, extension of the organization to the rest of the country. By April 1965, when a military revolt broke out against Reid Cabral, only the first stage had begun. The party's Military Bureau was confined to Santo Domingo, which had been divided into zones, with three or four commando units in each. Each of these units had three or four men. Although the Military Bureau numbered only about fifty men, "there were not enough [arms] to go around": sixty grenades, two Thompson machine guns, a few rifles, and some handguns.

The group was weak, but anxious to act. They had no time for the disputes that divided the CECP; they cared not at all about the "nature" of the party. They had only scorn for Jimmy Durán and his friends, whom they branded enemies of armed insurrection. They thought even the Despradel *duros* a bit "soft."

Despradel—always an opportunist—was careful not to criticize their ideas openly, but he contended that before undertaking armed insurrection, the *catorcistas* had to "rebuild the party." The Military Bureau could not wait; immediate, though modest, action was more desirable than a large-scale insurrection in some misty future.

The Military Bureau grew aloof from the 1J4. Its relations with the *supersabios* remained fairly cordial, and the appearance of party unity was maintained. But in fact the Bureau had become independent. It set off its own armed struggle, attacking isolated patrols, hitting police stations and the shops of "reactionary merchants" with grenades. A prisoner of its own eagerness, the Bureau made terrorism the core of its action. Today, "Baby" Mejía admits the dubious value of such tactics.

On 5 December 1963, four MPDistas, including Cayetano Rodríguez, returned to the Dominican Republic in a motorboat. Cayetano and two of his companions were members of the party's Central Committee. Surprised in Cuba by the coup against Bosch, they wanted to join the 1J4 guerrilla movement.[186] But they were arrested immediately, near Monte Cristi, and instead joined López Molina and his comrades in jail. Once again, it was not an impressive show, and eventually the MPD's official history would dismiss the episode as a "foolish action."[187] Thomas Mann, however, saw this event in more dramatic proportions: "In 1963 the Castro regime launched another action against the Dominican Republic by sending in a paramilitary team with weapons on the north coast of the island."[188]

In January 1964, the MPD was "in disarray."[189] Of the members of its Central Committee still in the country, only three were free.[190] The party was weakened by repression—and yet it was more "hard line" than ever. Its position was clear, if unrealistic. It demanded a return to "constitutional government without elections," though "constitutional government" was given a singular interpretation. As the party organ *Libertad* explained, it was necessary "to establish a DEMOCRATIC REVOLUTIONARY DICTATORSHIP OF THE WORKERS, PEASANTS AND WORKING PEOPLE. THIS IS THE ONLY POSSIBLE MEANING OF THE SLOGAN 'RETURN TO CONSTITUTIONAL GOVERNMENT WITHOUT ELECTIONS.' "[191] Bosch, the deposed constitutional president, "had failed to do what the Constitution of 1963 demanded."[192] His links with Yankee imperialism were well known, as were his reactionary views. So they tossed him upon the garbage heap of history. The constitution of 1963 could only be re-established "BY ARMS, BY ARMED INSURRECTION."[193] In this the MPD took a far harder line than the 1J4. In fact, its views coincided with those of the 1J4's Military Bureau: the far left should not wait for some distant D-day, but instead should immediately launch terrorist actions. That the MPD had no military strength was beside the point, since it could take credit for the few actions achieved by the *catorcistas'* Military Bureau. Perhaps the ire of the Bureau would be aroused, but no sacrifice was too great for the cause of the revolution!

So the MPD scraped along throughout 1964 and the early months of 1965. Its *líder máximo*, López Molina, was in exile, as were his chief lieutenants, Cayetano Rodríguez, Irlander Selig, Leopoldo Grullón, and the other CC members arrested between October and December 1963 and deported by the Triumvirate on 8 and 9 May 1964, along with a score of *catorcista* leaders. Cayetano Rodríguez attempted to return clandestinely to the Republic on 7 March 1965, with a group of six *catorcistas*. He was recognized at Punta Caucedo Airport (Santo Domingo) and immediately arrested with three of the *catorcistas*. López Molina, taking no unnecessary risks, remained in Paris, at the Hotel Danube. In the Dominican Republic, vacancies in the Central Committee were filled by elevating young middle-level cadres.[194]

In April 1965, the MPD was (1) a united party, with Mao Tse-tung as Allah and Máximo López Molina as his prophet; (2) a weak party, with less than three hundred members, most of them in the capital;[195] (3) a party with an "extremely reduced, almost insignificant"[196] military force: three or four rifles, a few pistols, two or three hand grenades.

Under the Triumvirate, the PSP experienced a period of internal upheaval, but its struggles were free of the violence that marked those of the 1J4. The conflicts were political, not personal, and the adversaries respected one another. The *viejos*—the founding fathers, veterans of the Era—had continued to lead the party since their return to the Dominican Republic. They alone sat on the party's top councils—the National Secretariat and the Central Committee. The most influential of these men were Juan Ducoudray Mansfield, the director of organization who doubled as secretary general, and his brother Félix Servio, director of the party weekly *El Popular*. Other important *viejos* were Pedro Mir, Nino Ramírez, Tulio Arvelo, José Espaillat Rodríguez, Justino José del Orbe, and Lisandro Macarulla.

Since the return of the party to the Dominican Republic, the *viejos*' most trusted lieutenants had been the *jóvenes*, young men such as Asdrúbal Domínguez, José Israel Cuello, Alfredo Conde, Luis Gómez, the brothers Tony and Narciso Isa Conde.[197] Most of them were university students and former *catorcistas*. To them, above all, the PSP owed its few adherents and its continuing contacts with party sympathizers. The *jóvenes* were now all middle-echelon leaders. In 1962, and even in 1963, they gladly accepted the leadership of men with the experience and theoretical knowledge they admittedly lacked. Furthermore they admired the *viejos*' "history of struggle" and shared their ideas and conceptions. There had been some friction, of course, but never anything serious. Two problems—the elections of 1962 and relations with Cuba—had caused *viejos* and *jóvenes* to clash. Like the *viejos*, the *jóvenes* believed that to oppose the elections by force would have been madness. But they did not believe that Bosch was as bad as Fiallo. They wanted the party to encourage its partisans to vote for the lesser evil, Juan Bosch, while the *viejos*, like the 1J4 *duros*, imposed a boycott of the elections. On the Cuba question, the *jóvenes*, like their mentors, were staunchly pro-Soviet. Although their sympathy for Castro had nothing of the unbounded admiration of the *catorcistas*, they would have liked the PSP to adopt a less distant stance toward the Cuban leader.

When in November 1963 the 1J4 chose guerrilla action, the *jóvenes* once again agreed with the CC's analysis, but they were quick to oppose the terms in which that analysis was expressed. For the *jóvenes*, the party's communiqués were "too cold"[198] and overstressed the 1J4's mistakes, while saluting only in passing the martyrdom of the guerrillas. For the first time, they resisted the *viejos*—an opposition made all the more impassioned by the painful memory of the old and dear friendship that linked *jóvenes* such as Asdrúbal Domínguez, the Isa Conde brothers, and José Israel Cuello to many of the *catorcistas* buried in those hills.

The final draft of the "Declaration of the Central Committee" of 30 January 1964 was the product of a bitter struggle in which the *jóvenes* went as far as blackmail, threatening not to distribute the document. They won a few concessions: some sentences were deleted, some altered. Yet even in its final form, the document was, to their minds, "unsatisfactory."[199] For the first time, opposition between *viejos* and *jóvenes* had turned bitter. The spell was broken and would never be recast.

The PSP had no military force. It was small in numbers, and its relations with the two other far-leftist parties were poor. To the *viejos* Bosch was a pawn of the imperialists; they could see no possibility for common action with the PRD. Moreover, the military was Trujilloist, motivated only by personal ambition, each faction as corrupt as the next. Finally, the masses were not politicized enough to be receptive to the party's message.

Under these conditions, it was hard to devise a strategy to combat the Triumvirate, but easy to fall from an "accurate analysis of the power relationships" into an attitude of passivity, especially as the party was forced underground. In its public statements, the PSP demanded a "return to constitutional government" through "impartial and honest elections."[200] Yet such talk was mere rhetoric. Weak and isolated, the PSP had no coherent policy. Obsessed by the problem of survival, it did not even have time for plotting.

A wind of revolt stirred within the party, and it became stronger throughout 1964. The *jóvenes* had grown up. Although they still admired the past deeds of their chiefs and respected their integrity, many were repelled by the "election" slogan of the *viejos*.[201] Rejecting the "opportunistic conceptions of the right,"[202] they took a hard line: return to constitutional government without elections. Their mentors now seemed worn out, tied to the past, unable to adapt to the times and to breathe into the party the energy and combativeness it sorely lacked. Until then, the PSP had been run by the *viejos* alone; now this monopoly was being challenged.

During the spring of 1964, and increasingly in the following months, a series of documents was drawn up by the base committees in the capital and by the student members of the PSP. These documents, sharply critical of the party line, called for a re-examination of PSP policy and tactics. Stressing the "need to make the work of leadership more collective and more agile," the documents demanded that the "norms of democratic centralism" be scrupulously respected.[203] At the same time, certain members within the CC moved away from the Ducoudray group, yet without espousing the ideas of the *jóvenes*. This was especially true of Pedro Mir, a gifted poet and the literary light of the party, and of Justino José del Orbe, prestigious labor leader of the 1940s. And then, under pressure from below, a Special Assembly (Pleno Ampliado) of the PSP was called, in October 1964, to discuss "the reasons for the lag in the growth of the party, especially among the working class." The most representative members of the lower and middle party echelons were invited to participate, along with the members of the CC.[204]

The Pleno Ampliado failed to resolve the party's problems. The *viejos* retained a majority, but new members were elected to the CC. Most were "neutrals," but two—Narciso Isa Conde and José Israel Cuello—belonged to the opposition. At last the *jóvenes* had representatives in the CC. They soon had a voice even in the party's supreme body, the Secretariat, where Pedro Mir became their spokesman. In the months that followed, the struggle inside the party deepened, and a shift in the balance of power took place within the CC. One after another, the "neutrals" sided with the emerging *jóvenes*. The *viejos* saw the relative majority they still held after October 1964 dwindle to a minority. Then, in February 1965, Narciso Isa Conde (a *jóven*) was elected to the Secretariat. Henceforth the votes were split within the supreme body: the Ducoudray brothers on the one side, Isa Conde and Pedro Mir on the other. The paralysis of the Secretariat enhanced the authority of the CC where the *jóvenes* held a majority. In February the latter won another victory when Narciso Isa Conde replaced Félix Servio Ducoudray as head of *El Popular*.

Other problems were left unresolved by the Pleno Ampliado: in particular, the problem of the return to constitutionality. Deadlocked, the delegates had postponed a decision. In February 1965, however, the *jóvenes*' time had come. Now that they held a majority, they were in a position to impose their views. A "Manifiesto" of 16 March 1965 expressed the new party line. Repudiating its "earlier proposal" for "an impartial and responsible Government to preside over an electoral process," the party demanded a return to constitutionality "without elections." The PSP had caught up, after long delay, with the position taken by the MPD and the 1J4 from the start. But it went much further. The "Manifiesto" demonstrated once again that the PSP was the only party among the Dominican far left to understand the constraints that reality placed on action. The PSP had the courage to recognize that in order to mobilize the urban masses it was necessary to give them a symbol they could identify with, not slogans imbued with a Marxism-Leninism foreign to their experience. In a nation dominated by the image of the *caudillo*, such a symbol could not be represented by a list of principles, by a constitution few had read. The symbol had to be a man: Juan Bosch.

The "Manifiesto" asserted: "A growing popular clamor is raised throughout the land in favor of Professor Juan Bosch's return to the legitimate exercise of the Government." That was easy enough to see; what distinguished the PSP was its ability to foresee the necessary consequences of this reality: "a clear slogan is needed . . . to serve as a means of orientation for all the people. A slogan of a general, indecisive nature like that of the return to the Constitution of 1963 is not enough. . . . Only the democratic way lies open: re-establishment of the popular will. . . . To reach that goal, we must adopt the slogan of the RETURN OF PRESIDENT JUAN BOSCH TO THE HEAD OF THE CONSTITUTIONAL GOVERNMENT OF THE REPUBLIC."[205]

The PSP understood what both the MPD and the 1J4 refused to see: that the only possible and still acceptable alternative to the Triumvirate was Bosch's return to power. The weakness of the far left ruled out any more "democratic" solution. For the PSP *jóvenes*, Bosch was a bourgeois leader, but not a "pawn" of the Americans; the PRD was a bourgeois party, but not an instrument of "Yankee imperialism." In their eyes, the danger that Bosch might become the Dominican Betancourt was real: this would be the final outcome of a process of degradation resulting from a presidency imposed on the nation by reactionary forces rather than one seized by the people. Thus, the *jóvenes* concluded: "The Bosch Government can be re-established in two ways: either by the struggle and mobilization of the people or by American imperialism."[206] The threat of seeing the Dominican people become masters of their fate "may drive the American imperialists to favor Bosch's return to power, in hopes of preventing this return as a result of direct action of the masses. This would inevitably impose a real democracy in the country and create better conditions for pushing the struggle toward higher goals. On the other hand, Bosch's return under the auspices of American imperialism would require not his pledge to the Dominican people, but his servility to their chief enemy." For this reason Bosch's return to the presidency had to be the result of "mass action led by the working class. The surge of spirit in a unified action of the great popular masses capable of re-establishing the government overthrown by the *golpistas* represents in itself a guarantee of democracy for the country and an indispensable step forward toward achieving the historic objectives of the Dominican people."[207]

With the "Manifiesto," the *jóvenes* of the PSP set a course and pointed a way; but even for them the path ahead was uncertain. The party was simply too weak. It had no more than two hundred members, no military power,[208] and no links with the PRD. The *jóvenes* shared the *viejos*' opinion of the Dominican military and thus were blind to "the changes taking place . . . within the Armed Forces."[209] They had heard rumors that the PRD was conspiring with the military—and they abhorred such collaboration.[210] Yet the masses followed Bosch and ignored the PSP. The task of "educating" the masses would be a long and painful one for the party activists. Still, the PSPistas believed that they had plenty of time. "We were unable to appreciate the imminence of the armed insurrection which, as a product of the situation in the country, was already in the making."[211]

Even united, the parties of the far left would have been weak; as it happened, they were divided. Relations between the MPD and the 1J4 were not bad, but both were at odds with the PSP. In 1962, the MPD had found an ideological base in support of its "ancestral" hostility toward the PSP. Along with other delegates from the Federation of Dominican Students, Cayetano Rodríguez had gone to Leningrad in July to take part in an international youth congress. At the meetings and in the hallways Cayetano first came in contact with "the clash between the Chinese and the Soviet positions." On his return to Santo Domingo, he presented a "detailed report" to the party leaders, concluding that "the Chinese position was the more correct one and ought to be supported."[212] His arguments found a receptive audience: the report was unanimously approved by the Central Committee. The MPD went Chinese, while at the same time maintaining close ties with the Cubans. A visit to China by Cayetano Rodríguez and other MPDistas in 1964[213] and a trip to Peking by José Ramírez in the spring of 1965 gave a little more substance to an ideological choice whose base was extremely fragile.

The MPD's flirtation with the Chinese was paralleled with equal intensity by the PSP's "wooing of the PCUS [Partido Comunista de la Unión Soviética]."[214] When in early 1962 the *viejos* of the PSP returned to the Dominican Republic, they enjoyed the goodwill of the 1J4. But the honeymoon ended abruptly. Polo Rodríguez, Pipe Faxas, and other former members of the MR1J4 had come back from Cuba in March. They ardently admired Castro's 26th of July Movement and violently opposed the Cuban PSP. Instinctively, they felt the same dislike for the Dominican PSP. To them, the PSP leaders were not *sabios,* old anti-Trujilloists, or "standard-bearers of Marxism," but an offshoot of the Cuban Communists, those craven opportunists who, after having supported Batista, had switched allegiance to Castro in the eleventh hour to steal the fruits of his victory.

For many *catorcistas,* the attitude of Juan Ducoudray and his friends would soon justify Polo's diatribes. The PSP *viejos* were "quite sparing" in their praise of Castro; they claimed solidarity with the Cuban revolution, but their solidarity seemed, even to some of their supporters, "very limited."[215]

The Cuban missile crisis exacerbated the differences. The PSP claimed that "in the Caribbean crisis . . . the Soviet Union has acted in conformity with the interests of the peoples throughout the world . . . and without in the slightest diminishing its solidarity with and its fraternal support of the Cuban revolution." The world had witnessed a "triumph of the [Soviet Union's] firm policy of peace."[216] The 1J4, however, cried "treason." Moscow had cravenly yielded and had abandoned Fidel. The Soviets were "scoundrels," the PSPistas, their lackeys.

In recent months the PSP had been the object of other accusations; for one, it was attacked for "stealing cadres." Since their return from exile, the party leaders had strived to set up PSP cells within other political groups, especially at the level of middle-echelon leaders and cadres. The 1J4 would have tolerated the practice had the PSP limited its infiltration to the bourgeois parties. But that was not the case: the 1J4 was a favorite PSP target. Although the PSP had little success, the ire of the *catorcistas* was intense. A second dispute centered on the problem of armed struggle. Under both the Council of State and the Bosch government, the PSP and the 1J4 took opposite stands on this question. Already intransigent toward their own *flojos*, the 1J4 *duros* quickly concluded that the so-called prudence of the PSP was nothing more than the systematic hostility of *pacifistas* toward armed struggle. Of course, in their eyes, such a conclusion only strengthened the identification of the Dominican PSP with the Cuban PSP. The *catorcista* guerrilla action of November-December 1963 aggravated tensions still more. The PSP had refused to participate and stood condemned by that refusal alone. Moreover, on 30 January 1964, at the very moment the *catorcistas* were mourning their dead and their party's defeat, the PSP issued its "Declaration of the Central Committee." The professorial tone of the document incensed the *catorcistas*.

The 1J4 *duros*, in particular, made the PSP the target of their bitterness. Drawing no distinctions between *jóvenes* and *viejos*, they "harbored a vehement hatred for anything that was PSP."[217] The rancor of an all-too-recent past was soon compounded by further differences. One was the question of the return to constitutional government, on which issue the two parties were in constant opposition. With their ill-devised slogan of "impartial and responsible elections," the *viejos* aroused against the PSP the categorical opposition of the *catorcistas—duros* and *flojos* alike. With the "Manifiesto" of 16 March 1965, the *jóvenes* in turn aroused the wrath of the 1J4. Hostile to any solution involving Bosch, the *catorcistas* accused the PSP of "transferring the whole struggle onto the person of a single man [Bosch] and of disregarding the Constitution of 1963."[218] Opposition over the Cuban question was equally fierce. Already cool before the missile crisis, relations between the PSP and Cuba had virtually collapsed by the second half of 1963. In a document of October 1965, the new party leadership said in retrospect:

> As a consequence of following the policies of the Soviet Communist Party, . . . our Party believed that, under the circumstances, it ought to limit its international relations to the above-mentioned Party and to the Soviet people.
> For more than two years [beginning with the second half of 1963] . . . no member of our party visited officially and on a party mission the Socialist Republic of Cuba, and our newspaper, taking a sectarian view, failed to adequately report the victories achieved in building socialism in that country. This sectarian outlook was the result of differences which existed between our party leadership and the leaders of the Cuban revolution, differences relating to international policy, to the ways of building socialism, to the development of the Latin-American revolution, and to the use of the

methods of struggle. We failed to understand that the strengthening of relations could contribute decisively to rectifying these supposed errors; none of us realized that we ourselves might have erred in evaluating the revolutionary process in Cuba and in the world. We sank so deeply into sectarianism that we refused to pay the necessary attention to the repeated invitations extended our leaders to visit the Socialist Republic of Cuba.[219]

The *catorcistas*' hostility toward the PSP was mild compared to that of the MPD. Party documents of the period offer vivid proof of the bitterness of the MPDistas: "The so-called 'Sino-Soviet ideological battle' . . . is nothing more than the struggle between Marxism-Leninism and modern revisionism." The self-proclaimed champion of Marxism-Leninism, the MPD waged ruthless war on the "modern Dominican revisionists" who "have entrenched themselves in the Popular Socialist Party [PSP] . . . from where they fling at the people . . . their line of treason and capitulation." The PSP "is the most destructive tool of the imperialists and oligarchists, a snake in the heart of the Dominican revolutionary movement."[220]

The MPD zealously took up the accusations hurled at the PSP by the *catorcistas*. "Cadre stealers," "opportunists," "pacifists," "Donaldists," "Boschists": anything went when it came to the PSP. *Libertad,* the MPD organ, devoted a great deal of space to diatribes against the "Dominican revisionists." The PSP was the villain of the piece. To hear the MPD, one would have thought that Juan and Félix Servio Ducoudray were in the Presidential Palace and that the Isa Conde brothers commanded the shock troops of the police. The MPD claimed that "time and again the revisionists of the Popular Socialist Party have betrayed worker strikes, paralyzed mass mobilizations, combated armed actions, supported imperialist and bourgeois schemes."[221]

Violently opposed to any common action or even to a truce with the PSP, the MPD leaders turned to the 1J4. The positions of the two parties were often similar. First, although they adopted the Chinese line, the MPDistas maintained close relations with the Cubans. The *catorcistas*, ultra-Castroists from the start, took a stance of kindly indifference toward the Chinese, and by 1964 the attitude of many *duros* was warmly sympathetic. Conversely, the leaders of the 1J4, without going as far as the MPD, felt an often vehement hostility toward the USSR, its roots tracing back to the Cuban missile crisis. Second, like the *catorcistas*, the MPDistas saw themselves as ardent supporters of armed struggle. Their attitude toward the guerrilla debacle of November-December 1963 was sympathetic: "When the insurrection fell apart, . . . the position we took was in absolute defense of the method used by the *catorcista* comrades, and although we understood that mistakes had been made in the application of that method, we refused to let those mistakes . . . be used to force the masses off their revolutionary path."[222] Third, both the MPD and the 1J4 rejected any "electoral" alternative to the Triumvirate, and both were especially hostile to a "Boschist" solution.[223]

But profound differences existed between the MPD and the 1J4, which at times stemmed from the very attitudes that united the two parties. The *cator-*

cistas and the MPDistas, vying to be Fidel's favorite, discredited each other before the Cubans. Winning favor was an obsession. Therein lay one of the causes behind both parties' striving to prove themselves the "vanguard of the revolution," one of the causes, therefore, of the "mountain madness." Further, each party felt itself superior to the other: the 1J4 because it was a giant next to the tiny MPD; the MPD because it countered the "petty-bourgeois confusion" of its rival with the wisdom of "Marxism-Leninism." Finally, the MPD's "history of struggle," and particularly the past of López Molina, aroused the distrust of many *catorcistas*. In 1960, the MPD leaders had arrived in the Dominican Republic at Trujillo's invitation—while the MR1J4 filled the jails of the regime. In 1961 came the party's "flirtation" with Ramfis, at the time the primary enemy of the *catorcistas*. Then there was the "epic" of Cevicos in October 1963.[224]

In the spring of 1965, relations between the various parties—and factions—of the far left were as follows: (1) a total break between the PSP and the MPD; (2) a total break between the PSP and the 1J4 *duros*; (3) a total break between the PSP *viejos* and the 1J4 *flojos*; (4) relatively cordial personal relations—marked by serious political differences—between PSP *jóvenes* and 1J4 *flojos*; (5) rather poor relations between the MPD and the 1J4 *flojos*; (6) "troubled" relations between the MPD and the 1J4 *duros*. These relations were good or bad according to the moment and the persons involved, but were never close enough for the 1J4 *duros* to look with favor on the MPD's proposal of a "united front." The 1J4 *duros* refused any alliance until the MPD accepted 1J4 leadership; for the MPD, equal rights had to prevail.

The Enriquillo movement brought together both civilians and military, though the two groups never merged.[225] The civilians belonged to the PRD, yet most PRD leaders opposed any plot. Adherents in the military were mostly officers, and a few noncommissioned officers joined them. Their motives varied. Some had traveled a long road before becoming "constitutionalists"; others were so in name only.

Only Bosch, in exile in Puerto Rico, knew all the secrets of the conspiracy. From the outset he had understood that force alone could undo what violence had established. And the military alone could provide that force. In 1964 he wrote:

> The only real power in Santo Domingo is the military, and if equilibrium is maintained within the ranks, the dictatorship will be long-lived. . . . Between a leader's word—or his order—and the blast of a Mauser, it is the Mauser that holds much more power. Both Dominican soldiers and policemen kill, the people have learned that by experience. . . . The leader of this moment in our nation's life cannot be the political leader, but rather the colonel able to order his men into battle. This is why, from the first day of my exile, I explained to my friends that the route to re-establishing constitutional government would be of necessity by way of the army—those few soldiers capable of fighting for a legitimate regime.[226]

It is difficult to pinpoint the exact moment when the conspiracy began. Lieutenant Colonel Fernández Domínguez was already "conspiring" on 25 September, a few minutes after the *golpe*. According to Bosch, the plotting commenced immediately after his arrival in Puerto Rico.[227] But, in those early days, no more than vague schemes and declarations of intent emerged; the means were woefully lacking. The PRD—the "civil arm" of the movement—already in disarray before the coup, was sorely weakened by the repression. The "military arm" consisted solely of Fernández Domínguez and his twenty or so *académicos*. Soon they seemed crushed as well. The Triumvirate dealt severely with this "seditious" band whose constitutionalist sentiments were only too well known and who had done nothing but conspire since the *golpe*.[228] On 14 and 15 October 1963, eighteen *académicos* were dismissed from the armed forces, and a few days later Fernández Domínguez was sent as military attaché to Spain, an elegant and hopefully effective way to dispose of a "troublemaker."[229]

Even in "exile," Fernández Domínguez continued to plot. He used every possible means to keep in touch with his men, exhorting them to action. Distance prevented him from leading the movement, but not from inspiring it. In Santo Domingo the Grupo de la Bomba—or Gas Station Group—was formed, made up of the *académicos* recently dismissed by the Triumvirate.[230] It was to prove the crucible of the constitutionalist military conspiracy, at every stage the movement's purest, most resolute element.

On 22 March 1964, a second constitutionalist group was formed during a meeting of seven noncommissioned army officers.[231] These men appealed to Captain Mario Peña Taveras, chief of administrative services at army staff headquarters, to lead them, and he accepted. The group was to be particularly active, and it occupied a vital strategic position: army staff headquarters, to which all the conspirators were attached, was on the Duarte Highway less than a mile from the Twenty-seventh of February and the 6½ Artillery camps and only a few miles from the Sixteenth of August camp.

A leader emerged who would unite the many constitutionalist nuclei that had sprouted since the spring of 1964. This was Lieutenant Colonel Miguel Angel Hernando Ramírez, chief of planning and training on the army staff and a respected officer. The Gas Station Group had won him over to the position of a "return to constitutional government without elections"; in the future he would be an unshakable constitutionalist champion.

In May 1964, a direct link was established between Hernando Ramírez and the PRD leader José Rafael Molina Ureña. In 1963, Molina Ureña had been president of the Chamber of Deputies, and, by 1964, he and José Francisco Peña Gómez were Bosch's chief representatives in the Dominican Republic.

As the months passed, Hernando Ramírez and his friends strove to broaden their support within the armed forces. They made a number of valuable "conquests": Major Manuel Augustín Núñez Nogueras, for example, deputy director of the Batalla de Las Carreras Military Academy at San Isidro. Nogueras was no Boschist; in 1963 he had not even been a true constitutionalist. But he was an honest officer and one of the few to have a sincere interest in military affairs. Before long, the corruption that had paralyzed the armed forces since Bosch's fall roused in Nogueras feelings of shame and disgust. He felt shame as he walked in the capital, in uniform, seeing the looks of scorn and hate from a people to whom any man in uniform was a thief. He felt disgust as a man of integrity trapped in the den of corruption that was the *conjunto* at San Isidro. As an able officer, he felt nothing but contempt for the incompetents around him. By its excesses, the Triumvirate accelerated Nogueras' political education. Soon his course was set. He joined the constitutionalists, and during the summer, entered fully into the conspiracy.

Nogueras' case was not unique, nor was it common. During the latter half of 1964, the constitutionalist movement made slow progress. The conspirators had adopted the model of the Trinitaria, that is, a cellular organization. Each member had to win three new converts to the cause. The procedure was nearly always the same: member X would approach an officer or noncommissioned officer who was his friend. The conversation, general at first, eventually turned, as if by chance, to the political situation in the country. Then, if his interlocutor seemed ripe, X would make an overture: "By the way, I and a group of friends . . . . " But he would never reveal the names of his co-conspirators, so as not to endanger the entire movement in case he was denounced.

The system proved highly effective because denunciations among friends were rare and the few informers were never able to give the government more than two or three names. The number of officers who welcomed the conspirators' advances was relatively high. As the economic crisis deepened, the Triumvirate became increasingly unpopular; to say "yes" to the conspirators cost nothing and might even prove useful. There were dozens ready for anything—anything but recruiting, organizing, or military tasks. "Active" members joined at a snail's pace, and superior officers, only rarely.

The PRD, meanwhile, redoubled its efforts. From exile, Bosch managed to impose a little harmony on his discordant orchestra. He concluded a de facto truce with the *electoreros* of his party; the truce hinged on a pledge that the PRD would not conspire. The slogan "return to constitutional government without elections" would be drained of meaning, but that hardly mattered. Bosch was unwilling to stir up quarrels that would only weaken the party. Devoting themselves to the reorganization of the PRD, the *electoreros* performed a useful function. Most of them no doubt hoped to carve out personal fiefs that would make them "independent." Still, for Bosch, that was no cause for concern. When the time came, they would be faced with a fait accompli.

A few PRD leaders—the *antielectoreros*—took part in the conspiracy. None of them had more than a partial picture of the movement. They fell into two groups: "moderates" and "revolutionaries." The "moderates" were latecomers, mostly former *electoreros* driven into the conspiracy by Reid Cabral's intransigence. Among them was Antonio Martínez Francisco, elected secretary general of the PRD in October 1964, who, as late as July, demanded disciplinary action against party leaders accused of conspiring.[232] The "moderates" had become convinced of the need to resort to force, but their position remained equivocal. Who would replace the Triumvirate? They wavered between a hard line—Bosch's return to the presidency until the expiration of his term (February 1967)— and a more flexible stand—installation of a military junta that would proceed to hold new elections. But for the "revolutionaries" there was only one answer: Bosch's return to the presidency without elections.

The "moderates" and the "revolutionaries" were also divided on social issues. The former—Martínez Francisco, Máximo Lovatón Pittaluga, José A. Brea Peña and others—represented the right wing of the *antielectoreros*. Once in the conspiracy, they remained what they had been: "notables" open to certain reforms if undertaken slowly and prudently. In 1963, Bosch had been too "radical" for them. If he was to return to power, he would have to slow down the pace of social reform. The "revolutionaries," however, wanted precisely the opposite. True, they were a minority within the party leadership, but they had the support of the party's young cadres. They wanted the PRD to become an instrument of real change in Dominican society. Bosch's return to the presidency—that is, the return to political democracy—was in their eyes the beginning, not the end, of a process that had to be rapid.

For the "moderates," the parties to the left of the PRD were enemies. But the "revolutionaries," while condemning the sectarianism of the *catorcista* leaders, regarded the 1J4 as an "anti-imperialist, antifeudal, anti-petty-bourgeois" force.[233] The gulf between them and the 1J4 was not deep enough to stifle their hope for an entente in the common struggle for a more just society. For the "revolutionaries," Bosch was the man who could and would realize their aspirations—he was *the* party leader. In his absence, they looked for guidance not as much to José Rafael Molina Ureña as to the young José Francisco Peña Gómez, secretary of press and propaganda within the party's Executive Committee.[234]

For Bosch, the "moderates" were unreliable, but necessary, allies. Their existence already weakened the *electoreros*, robbing them of control of the party machinery. They served another function as well. By backing Martínez Francisco for the post of secretary general at the PRD's Fourth National Convention, Bosch offered the *electoreros* a deceptive token. For *electoreros* such as Casimiro Castro and Mainardi Reyna had faith in "moderates" like Martínez Francisco and Lovatón Pittaluga: they were all part of a single family, the "notables."

The *electoreros* knew that the new secretary general had links with certain sectors of the military, but they had difficulty picturing him involved in a real conspiracy. For his part, Martínez Francisco allayed their fears as to the activities of men like Peña Gómez and Molina Ureña, "hotheads" who seemed far less of a threat now that the new secretary general was there to keep an eye on them. Bosch's support of Martínez Francisco, moreover, no doubt indicated that the former president had become more reasonable.[235]

Actually, the "moderates" had only a vague idea of what the "revolutionaries" were up to. The latter—and Bosch himself—preferred to keep their conversations with the *duro* group of Hernando Ramírez from the ears of men they distrusted. The links of the "moderates" with the military were restricted to the San Cristóbal Group and to other *Balaguerista* officers. But the "revolutionaries"—especially Peña Gómez—were engaged at the time in the very same conversations.[236]

The officers of the San Cristóbal Group wanted to overthrow the Triumvirate, but only to replace it with a military junta, which, they promised, would organize "free and honest" elections. There was reason to be skeptical, knowing Montás Guerrero, Nivar Seijas, and the rest of the clique. The first talks between Peña Gómez and Nivar Seijas (the latter was considered to be the brains of the group) took place in the summer of 1964. Agreement was swift on the negative aspect of the program: the overthrow of Reid Cabral. But agreement on what would follow Reid Cabral proved impossible.

By the autumn of 1964, other actors had entered the picture: the "moderates," led by Martínez Francisco. I believe that Martínez Francisco was lying when he later claimed to have presented the San Cristobalistas with a proposal for common action based on the formula "military junta followed by elections." Rather, his attitude was "let's act together, and then we'll see."[237] In any case, the talks dragged on. Twice toward the end of 1964, and once again in January 1965, the San Cristóbal Group considered itself ready to strike. They so informed their PRD contacts, believing that, faced with the fait accompli, the party would have no choice but to follow. But Peña Gómez, the leader of the "revolutionaries," hoped for just the reverse. Let the San Cristobalistas topple the regime, if they could. Once the mechanism had been set in motion, the PRD, strengthened by the support of the urban masses and the constitutionalist officers, would attempt to take over the Balaguerist revolt.

The San Cristóbal Group failed to realize their scheme. They lacked the means and the initiative. Then, in January-February 1965, came the military purges. The measures taken by Reid Cabral weakened the group; at the same time the constitutionalist movement within the armed forces gained strength. Finally, in early April, the forced departure of Nivar Seijas marked the end of contacts between the PRD and the now powerless San Cristóbal Group.

The hopes of the "revolutionaries" had always been lodged in Hernando Ramírez and his constitutionalist officers. After the first contacts were established in May 1964, relations with Hernando Ramírez grew increasingly cordial, leading to a formal unification in November. It was then that the Enriquillo movement was born. The lagging progress of the conspiracy tried the patience of certain of its leaders, but it could not dim their zeal. This was especially true of Fernández Domínguez. From abroad he urged his friends to act. Transferred to Santiago, Chile, as military attaché, he obtained General Viñas Román's permission to return to the Dominican Republic before assuming his new post.[238]

After a brief stopover in Puerto Rico to meet with Bosch, he arrived in Santo Domingo at the end of December 1964. Losing no time, he set 9 January as the date of the "countercoup."[239]

The plan was prepared in haste and might have been revised before put into action. But even in rough form it revealed the weakness of the resources at the constitutionalists' disposal. Of the elite army forces, only the Juan Pablo Duarte Battalion could be counted on. Yet even here their control was far from absolute. Major Alvarez Holguín, commander of the battalion, maintained an attitude of reserve, despite weeks of effort by the conspirators. This attitude was shared by his immediate superior, Lieutenant Colonel Gutiérrez Ramírez, commander of the Sixteenth of August camp, where the Juan Pablo Duarte Battalion was stationed. In the Nineteenth of November Air Base at San Isidro, the conspirators had the support of a small group of officers.

The plan called for the "battalion" garrisoned at Neiba, in the southwest, to spearhead the movement.[240] This meant three hundred men at the most, ill-trained and poorly armed. Their commander was Lieutenant Colonel Caonabo Fernández, a constitutionalist of questionable zeal. From Neiba the battalion was to advance on Barahona, the major southern town, and seize the Captain Rafael A. Davila Quezada Air Base, where the conspirators counted on the support of a few partisans. At the same time, the troops of the Sixteenth of August were to move on the capital, where they could depend on the enthusiasm of the people and the support of the Gas Station Group. The San Cristóbal Group, it was hoped, would accept the fait accompli and join the revolt.

It is fortunate that the scheme was never carried out, since its chances of success were minimal. Denounced by a colonel whom he had tried to win over to the movement, Fernández Domínguez was ordered by General Viñas Román to leave the country at once. He left for Chile, but his brief stay had happy consequences. In a conversation with police Colonel Francisco Alberto Caamaño Deñó, he convinced the latter to join the conspiracy. Later, Caamaño cooled to the movement, but he never denounced it. In the meantime, a seed had been sown in a man fated to play a decisive role for which he seemed utterly unprepared.

In January the military crisis struck. Paradoxically, these purges both strengthened General Wessin's hand and won new converts to the constitutionalist cause. There was now wide agreement that only force could stop the general. Henceforth many officers who had been reluctant would accept the constitutionalists' advances. These included officers linked to the San Cristóbal Group, whose power had been broken, and other Balaguer sympathizers. Toward the end of March, the conspirators, who already had strong influence in the Sixteenth of August, won the support of its two leading officers, Lieutenant Colonel Gutiérrez Ramírez and Major Alvarez Holguín. From then on constitutionalist control over the camp was absolute.

Other factors contributed to the growth of the movement. Some were present at an earlier stage, but their importance grew with time. No one any longer doubted the ambitions of Reid Cabral. Had the Triumvir shown a firm will to allow free elections, the movement would have collapsed. Even if he had granted only a "conditional" freedom—allowing Balaguer but not Bosch to enter honest elections—the movement would have lost adherents and failed to win new recruits. The seemingly intractable economic crisis, the exasperation of the urban population, the isolation of a government deserted even by the right, and the increasingly evident power of the PRD, also fostered the growth of the movement. Excessive corruption further irritated a number of officers, contributing to the rise of an anti-Román Carbuccia movement within the Nineteenth of November. Yet there, too, this problem persisted, despite his replacement by de los Santos.

The conspirators even had luck on their side. Colonel Caamaño and navy Captain Manuel Ramón Montes Arache, whose role was to prove decisive, joined the movement only by chance. "Won over" to the conspiracy by Fernández Domínguez, Caamaño soon backed out. But immediately thereafter he came into conflict with his superior officer, police General Belisario Peguero. Himself threatened with imminent disgrace, Belisario Peguero was unable to chastise a subordinate whom his enemy Wessin hastened to protect. Indeed, Caamaño took refuge with the CEFA. But personal differences caused a swift deterioration in his relations with Wessin. Caamaño then turned to the conspirators, bringing with him his good friend Montes Arache, who did not have the slightest interest in that odd word "constitutionality," but who felt a keen dislike for Reid Cabral and, above all, for Wessin. Montes Arache loved a good fight and rallied to the movement with the fervor of a man in a hunting party. While he joined the conspiracy for all the wrong reasons, his presence was no less important for that. As "boss" of the elite body of frogmen, among whom he enjoyed immense prestige, Montes Arache virtually guaranteed their participation.

But what the movement had gained in number of adherents since February, it lost in cohesion. Many of the latecomers felt only slight sympathy, or even indifference, toward the "return to constitutional government without elections." Others preferred a military junta. These included such *Balaguerista* officers as Lieutenant Colonel Gutiérrez Ramírez, commander of the Sixteenth of August camp, and those officers who believed that a military junta would be more acceptable to the armed forces as a whole. Still others were wary of Bosch and his "dogmatism," his "intransigence."

The original constitutionalists, centered around Hernando Ramírez, became a minority within the movement they had founded. Yet they retained control. Their prestige was great, and they were the heart of the conspiracy; without them there was only a collection of small, isolated groups. The newcomers were eager to topple the Triumvirate, but alone they were powerless, and thus had to accept conditions imposed on them. While professing loyalty to the movement's goals, many hoped to renege on their pledge once Reid Cabral had fallen.

Toward the end of March the conspirators felt strong enough to prepare for action. They elaborated the Enriquillo plan—the blueprint of the countercoup.[241] The conspirators' principal strength lay in the army. They controlled the Sixteenth of August and the 6½ Artillery and believed that their influence at the Twenty-seventh of February was such that, once the revolt had been detonated, the camp would rally at once to the cause. If so, H-hour would find them in control of two of the three elite army battalions and the heavy armament of the 6½ Artillery. That meant 1,850 men, not counting an additional 400 in the Sixteenth of August and the 100 or so stationed near army staff headquarters. In all, they counted upon a shock force of some 2,350 men only a few miles from the capital.

The conspiracy now spread to the rest of the country. At Neiba, Caonabo Fernández's "battalion" seemed assured. In Santo Domingo, the movement had infiltrated the Presidential Guard, and the commander of the Polvorín, Lieutenant Faña, was a sworn follower of Peña Taveras. Contacts were made with officers at the Fortalezas of Barahona and La Vega; at the Fortaleza San Luis in Santiago, the influence of the conspirators was particularly strong.[242] Admiral Francisco Javier Rivera Caminero, the navy chief of staff, had been discreetly sounded out, but made it clear that he preferred to remain on the side of the "forces of order." Some of his subordinates, however, including a number of superior officers, responded favorably to the conspirators' overtures, notably, as we saw earlier, navy Captain Montes Arache, head of the frogmen. Within the police, the one-time fief of Belisario Peguero, the movement made no headway. It had more success within the air force. Although they lacked influence at the air base in Barahona, the constitutionalists had partisans at the air base in Santiago, and, especially, at the powerful Nineteenth of November in San Isidro. Even among the CEFA, Wessin's preserve, the conspiracy won adherents, but only two or three superior and a few junior officers.

In 1963, the Batalla de Las Carreras Military Academy had been the cradle of the constitutionalist movement. Once the academy had been purged of Fernández Domínguez and his *académicos*, Wessin named as director one of his loyal followers, Colonel Pedro Medrano Ubiera—"a highly able but corrupt and ambitious man who [was] called Fouché." The subsequent period of calm within the academy was short-lived, thanks to its deputy director, Major Núñez Nogueras, who became one of the leaders of the conspiracy. Nogueras, however, was soon denounced. On 14 September 1964, he and two of his officers, Captain Pedro J. Guerra Ubrí, professor of tactics, and Lieutenant Federico Piantini Colón, the academy's public relations officer—both constitutionalists—were cashiered. A second period of passivity set in. "Frightened by what had happened to Nogueras,"[243] the officers at the academy broke their links with the conspiracy. Hernando Ramírez, concentrating his efforts on the Nineteenth of November, ignored the Batalla de Las Carreras. By April 1965, the constitutionalists had virtually no links with an academy in which the memory of men like Fernández Domínguez and Nogueras was still keen for the cadets. Hernando Ramírez had miscalculated.

The Sixteenth of August, the Twenty-seventh of February, and the 6½ Artillery camps formed the "center" of the Enriquillo plan; to these can be added the hundred or so soldiers at army staff headquarters, though they were bureaucrats more than soldiers. Partisans from the other military bases composed the "periphery."[244] At H-hour (5:00 A.M. or 5:30-6:00 P.M.)[245] a group of "center" units was to move on the capital. At the same time the "periphery" was to swing into action. Among the "periphery," Lieutenant Núñez Vargas, of the Presidential Guard, was to attempt to capture the Presidential Palace.

Santo Domingo, San Isidro, and Santiago were the main targets of the plan. On paper, it all looked so simple. Fifteen or twenty minutes after the outbreak of the revolt, the first constitutionalist units would enter the capital and take over the key points. There would be no resistance. The police and the Presidential Guard were judged to be weak militarily and reluctant to fight. Transportación and Intendencia were, in military terms, nonentities. Polvorín was constitutionalist. The one obstacle would be a detachment of armored vehicles from the CEFA—generally composed of ten tanks and assault tanks—permanently stationed at the palace. But Lieutenant Núñez Vargas, the constitutionalist leader in the Presidential Guard, had a certain freedom of action. If his chances for success seemed poor, he could await the arrival of the "center" units, before which the CEFA detachment would yield without a fight. Liberation of the capital would be child's play.

At San Isidro, the constitutionalists within the CEFA had volunteered to arrest Wessin. Should they succeed, the revolt would be over in a matter of minutes. Of course, they might fail. But the leaders of the Enriquillo movement looked confidently toward their numerous allies at the neighboring Nineteenth of November. The plan envisioned only two possibilities: (1) the constitutionalist officers on the base would force de los Santos to rally to the revolt; the planes would be on the runways, ready to take off should Hernando Ramírez give the signal to attack the CEFA; (2) the Nineteenth of November would declare itself neutral; the constitutionalists would lose the help of its planes, but then so would Wessin.

There remained Santiago, "capital" of the Cibao and site of the country's second largest air base. The Fortaleza San Luis (an army installation) would rally immediately to the revolt. At the Santiago Air Base, the presence of armored vehicles of the CEFA would hardly complicate the conspirators' job. The commander of the base, Colonel Francisco Ramírez Gómez, had expressed his "sympathy" through a subordinate, Captain César Fernández y Fernández, who was in contact with the plotters. Many junior officers had also pledged their support. Encouraged by good news from the capital—and backed, if necessary, by troops from the Fortaleza San Luis—the constitutionalists would easily neutralize Wessin's men. Pilots from the air base would be ready to bomb the CEFA, as they had promised.

The Enriquillo plan was based on certain requisites. First was the element of surprise; second, the simultaneous action of the "center" and the "periphery"; third, the attitude of the people, whose intended role was at once restricted and decisive.

Only a tiny "radical" minority—a few officers and above all some non-coms—favored giving arms to civilians, selected beforehand from among the "safe" militants of the PRD. But this possibility was not even considered by the conspiracy's leaders. Only constitutionalist former officers (who had never been regarded as civilians) were to be armed. The military—not the people—was to carry out the countercoup. The conspirators wanted no popular revolt, no anarchy, no useless bloodshed. The action was to come off amid order and discipline. Yet the people had an important role to play, and here is where the PRD came in. The PRDistas were to exhort the masses, both in the capital and in the other cities, to demonstrate in the streets in favor of the movement. Their support, backed by the rebels' rifles and machine guns, would prompt many senior officers to join the insurrection.

A fourth requisite was the attitude of the United States. Bosch was convinced, and the military leaders of the conspiracy agreed, that the United States would look with hostility on the countercoup, but would not act. The era of armed intervention in Latin America was over. But would the Americans at least attempt to incite Dominican officers to resist the revolt? None of the leaders of the conspiracy seems to have pondered this question. Victory would be so swift that Washington would be faced with a fait accompli before it had a chance to react.

Fifth, and finally, was the attitude of key sectors of the Dominican armed forces. The San Cristóbal Group, too weak to pursue an independent course, would, it was thought, quickly join the revolt. With a choice between Bosch and Reid Cabral, could it possibly hesitate? And the Mella Battalion, the third and the last of the elite army units, would swell the ranks of the constitutionalist forces. Within the navy, Sans Souci was constitutionalist, thanks to Montes Arache and his frogmen. Haina would soon follow, then Las Calderas.[246] Surprised by a revolt sweeping the country's major cities, Admiral Rivera Caminero would choose to be neutral at first, and soon thereafter would side with the stronger contender—the constitutionalists. He would be pressed to join the cause by many of his officers, even by those not involved in the plot. How could the navy—the "clean branch" of the armed forces—refuse to support the return to a constitutional government? And the police? They would be neutral, both in the capital and elsewhere. The Fortalezas in the provinces and the air base at Barahona? The Fortaleza San Luis at Santiago would, of course, rally to the revolt immediately. In a few other cases, support would soon come, at Neiba no doubt, and perhaps at La Vega. Elsewhere, the commanders would hesitate, then join—out of opportunism, as always. Because of its handful of planes, the air base of Barahona could play a certain role. The conspirators had no links inside the base, but they felt sure of its neutrality. The opportunism of its officers, together with public pressure, were the best guarantees.

The CEFA could have represented a formidable obstacle, but the conspirators were convinced that Wessin, his government overthrown, would bow to the inevitable. Once the Nineteenth of November had deserted, once everyone had defected, Wessin would be forced to yield in the face of a revolt growing stronger by the hour and backed by an enthusiastic populace. He would have already lost the ten or so armored vehicles stationed at the Presidential Palace; perhaps hundreds of his men would be caught by surprise in the capital, and would thus be cut off from the CEFA (see note 245 above). Many of his officers would abandon him. Why should they expose themselves to machine-gun fire from the planes of Santiago, or perhaps from the planes—even more numerous—of the Nineteenth of November? An attack by Wessin against the capital stood absolutely no chance of success. Even a CEFA attack on the Nineteenth of November would be too dangerous.[247]

Confronted with an enemy they despised, Hernando Ramírez and his officers foresaw a rapid victory. Civil war would be averted; a few bursts of gunfire would suffice. A show of force by able and resolved men would crush the will to resist of cowards and incompetents. According to the Enriquillo plan, a few hours after the outbreak of the revolt a plane would take off from the Dominican Republic and another would land near the capital at the Punta Caucedo International Airport. In the first would be Wessin; in the second, Bosch. The constitution would be restored and Bosch reinstated as president until the end of his term (27 February 1967). Victorious, the constitutionalist troops would return to their barracks amid the acclamation of a joyous populace.

Bosch, Molina Ureña, Peña Gómez, and a few other PRD leaders knew and approved of the Enriquillo plan. Their diligent activity had resulted in the Pact of Rio Piedras, the declaration of "Dominican Professionals and Intellectuals," and the lists with thousands of signatures demanding the "return to constitutional government without elections." These documents provided ample food for thought for many uncommitted officers. In addition, these men had engaged in conversations with the PRSC *duros* and the leaders of CASC, who pledged support for the movement.

Some PRD "revolutionaries" around Peña Gómez had made overtures to the 1J4.[248] Hernando Ramírez and the great majority of his officers knew nothing of these contacts. They were extremely hostile to the 1J4, which they considered to be Castro/Communist. Many of them would have deserted any movement tainted by the presence of the *catorcistas*. For the same reasons, the PRD "moderates" were also kept in the dark. Yet the overtures made to the *catorcistas* were very limited. Peña Gómez and his friends had no intention of making the 1J4 a partner of the PRD, of revealing the secrets of the Enriquillo movement, or of offering the *catorcistas* a place in the conspiracy. They simply intended to inform the 1J4, a party for which they felt a certain sympathy, about their plans: a military coup would take place, but it would be quite different from those that plagued Latin America year after year. At H-hour, the 1J4 would be alerted; its partisans could then rush into the streets, alongside the *Boschistas*, and proclaim their support for the insurrection. Constitutional government would be renewed in an atmosphere of trust between PRDistas and *catorcistas*.

News of the conspiracy reached the 1J4 leaders from other sources as well. Oscar Santana, a member of the Military Bureau and son of a PRDist "revolutionary" leader, learned of the goals of the movement from his father. Four officers in the Gas Station Group, including Jesús de la Rosa, García Germán, and "El Gato," contacted the *catorcistas*. These officers, part of the movement's "radical" minority, were closer to the 1J4 than to the PRD. They wanted the *catorcistas* to have a role, however modest, in the insurrection, in order to accentuate the movement's social aspect.

The 1J4, however, rejected all advances. No agreement was possible with the PRD. The latter could perhaps boast a few honest leaders—Peña Gómez, for one—but they, too, were only pawns in the hands of higher masters. Both *duros* and *flojos* agreed: "Today, the PRD leadership is such that . . . one can affirm it to be openly in the hands of the imperialists and the oligarchists. We refer particularly to the party's chief governing bodies, which are dominated by the upper middle class in league with representatives of the mercantile bourgeoisie (Martínez Francisco . . . Mainardi Reyna, etc.)."[249] Bosch, who had chosen to spend his exile in Puerto Rico, a colony of the United States, was still the Dominican Betancourt.[250]

Now Peña Gómez had revealed that the PRD was plotting with the military. The *catorcistas* had learned the painful lesson in November-December 1963. They believed that there existed no honest elements within the Dominican armed forces. There were only murderers: Manolo's assassins. If the PRD was plotting, it could only be with the approval of its American masters. "The Yankees have recognized the trend toward popular struggle, and want to block it."[251] The Americans would replace Reid Cabral, a worn-out pawn, with Bosch, another puppet. The PRD and its satellites, the "social pistols" (Social Christians) of Antonio Rosario and Caonabo Javier, were "preparing to become the gringos' trump card."[252] The role of the masses in this sorry drama would be to serve as the "crowd"; when no longer needed, they would be forced back to their hovels—with rifle butts. As for the fate of the far left, and especially of the 1J4: "The CIA . . . is working on it. They want another Iraq."[253]

In the face of such dark imperialist plotting, one would expect the 1J4 leaders to be alert, anxious to squeeze all the information they could out of men like Peña Gómez and Jesús de la Rosa. They did not do so. The *catorcista* leaders simply never took the *Boschistas* seriously. The PRD could continue plotting, talking endlessly with the military brass, and rejoicing over vague words of encouragement from "gringo" agents: the United States, as everyone knew, was a multitentacled octopus, each arm ignoring the others. But Reid Cabral was still Washington's darling.

The 1J4 was too absorbed by its own inner struggles to devote time to the intrigues of the PRD; Reid Cabral's enemies had already "toppled [him] a hundred times in word."[254] The Military Bureau, however, was an exception to the wave of irrationality that shook the 1J4. Paradoxically, its leaders—the "ultras," the "hotheads" of the party—were, in this instance, the only ones to show any political sense. Perhaps the explanation lies, at least in part, in the role of Oscar Santana, a prominent member of the Bureau. Through his father, he had become convinced that the conspiracy was real and that it was not a reactionary ploy. Moreover, ties of friendship bound certain leaders of the Bureau to two "radical" officers of the Gas Station Group and a captain in active service, an old-time constitutionalist. In short, the leaders of the Bureau "entered" the conspiracy, but only to come up against the studied reserve of the very men who had approached them. The Bureau offered to cooperate with the constitutionalists in preparing the revolt, but the offer was rejected. Its request for arms was turned down. Like the CECP before it, the Bureau was offered only a secondary role. It was informed of the aims of the Enriquillo movement and was asked to support the countercoup, once it had come. But the support had to be peaceful—through mobilization of *catorcista* sympathizers. Under no circumstances did the "left wing" of the constitutionalist conspiracy envision military action for the 1J4.

The Bureau agreed to these terms, realizing that it lacked the power to bargain and aware that the conspiracy was not an imperialist intrigue but a "democratic-bourgeois"[255] movement. As such, it was a step forward in the Dominican historical process, when compared with the Reid Cabral dictatorship. Moreover, the Bureau hoped to steer the mass mobilization in a more radical direction once the countercoup had begun.

At the same time, the Bureau tried to get the CECP to reconsider its contemptuous refusal. Not only did it fail, but the CECP subjected Oscar Santana to "sharp criticism and the threat of sanctions 'for having let himself be dragged into a *golpista* plot of obvious imperialist stamp.' "[256] This difference in outlook helped to aggravate relations between the Bureau and the CECP. The former continued to pursue its contacts with the conspirators—added proof of its weak ties with the party's central committee.

One last time, on 19 April, "just before the imminent unraveling of the political situation, Oscar knocked at the door of the 14th of June leadership. His hair was unkempt and he seemed nervous, gulping as he spoke:"

—I'm asking you to go—today—to a meeting with some of the PRD leaders.
—Oscar, what's up?
—Wha . . . Wha . . . What's up? Donald Reid Cabral is about to be toppled, that's what.
—Ah! Another one of your daydreams.
—No. No. No. Not at all. You really must go and talk with them. It's very serious. I've already found a house for the meeting, and I've told them you'd be there at four. You've only got half an hour.
—Damn! . . . And what the hell did you get us mixed up in this for? O.K. let's go![257]

That afternoon members of the CECP met with the representatives of the PRD. Two days later, in the evening of 21 April, the CECP formally received the information brought by the PRD, but attached no importance to it. "Somebody muttered that 'whoever pays attention to the rumors of a *golpe* has nothing else to do . . . .' Everybody agreed. [The CECP was] preoccupied with the internal and ideological struggle . . . the national political situation was not on the agenda."[258]

In April 1965, chaos reigned in the Dominican Republic. But this was nothing new. Every day in the cafés on El Conde Street, at the home of friends in the evening, or over cocktails at official get-togethers, those who were "well-informed" discussed the latest plots against the government, as they had done for so long. As Reid Cabral remarked to the author, "the *golpe* [was] our daily bread."[259] An inevitable topic of discussion was Bosch and his "endemic plot-ting."[260] The press relayed rumors that a plot to kill Reid Cabral had been un-covered that brought together such unlikely allies as "Juan Bosch and Severo Cabral, . . . Joaquín Balaguer and Luis Amiama Tió, . . . Mario Read Vittini and everyone else."[261] The PRD's contacts with the San Cristóbal Group were discussed, even though this was a well-worn topic and Montás Guerrero and the other officers of the clique were no longer a force to contend with.

Even by early April, Reid Cabral and the American embassy knew no more about the plots than did the "well informed." Then, one morning, a lieutenant in the Presidential Guard went to the Triumvir and revealed how Lieutenant Colonel Hernando Ramírez had tried to enlist him in a conspiracy against the government. The routine began: Reid Cabral summoning Hernando Ramírez, Hernando Ramírez denying the accusation, demanding—in vain—to confront his accuser. If all the officers accused of plotting had been dismissed, Reid Cabral would have been left with only Wessin and his CEFA. Faithful to his own coun-sel of prudence, Hernando Ramírez had revealed little to his denouncer. Reid Cabral did not realize that the man before him was the military leader of a vast conspiracy, the successor of Fernández Domínguez. Hernando Ramírez left the Presidential Palace absolved of all charges.

But the rumors persisted—vague stories of seditious activities among officers of the Sixteenth of August and the 27th of February camps. Henceforth, Reid Cabral realized that a conspiracy was afoot, though it appeared to be nothing but the dream of a small group of officers who would never dare to challenge the CEFA. With neither haste nor fear, the Triumvir took some precautionary measures. In the third week of April about a dozen junior officers of the Six-teenth of August and of the Twenty-seventh of February were transferred to the Fortalezas in the provinces or dismissed from the armed forces. For the con-spirators, this was an ominous warning, and on 21 April the last meeting of the leadership of the Enriquillo movement was held at Nigua. They reached the fol-lowing decision: D-day was set for Monday, 26 April; but if the Triumvirate arrested or cashiered any more constitutionalist officers, the countercoup would commence "at once."[262]

Chapter 5

The Countercoup
(24 April 1965, from Noon to Midnight)

The arrest of four army officers suspected of plotting triggered the counter-coup on 24 April, two days earlier than planned.[1] The government had just discovered the existence of a conspiracy, but still did not understand its scope and degree of preparedness. Surely this failure to grasp the strength—and the decisiveness—of the adversary alone explains the behavior of the army chief of staff, General Rivera Cuesta, who, on the morning of the twenty-fourth, summoned the four officers to army headquarters and arrived there himself with only a handful of men.

General Rivera Cuesta was unaware that the conspirators were ready to act and that army headquarters was a stronghold of the conspiracy. Nor did he know that the officer in charge of administrative services at the headquarters, Captain Peña Taveras, was one of the staunchest and most enterprising of the constitutionalists. He was also unaware that behind Peña Taveras a group of sergeants leading approximately one hundred men had joined the movement. On the other side of the river, San Isidro, the government's stronghold, was woefully distant.

History is never built on hypotheses: if only Rivera Cuesta had brought along an imposing military escort . . . if only he had picked some other place . . . if only Peña Taveras had been less resolute . . . if only the conspirators had not, just a few days earlier, taken the decision to strike. History is based on facts: Rivera Cuesta walked into a hornets' nest when he chose to arrest four army officers of influence and appeared with only a tiny escort. Event followed event with unerring logic: Rivera Cuesta arrested the four officers and was in turn arrested by Peña Taveras.

Now, approximately half-past noon on the twenty-fourth, Rivera Cuesta and his deputy Colonel Maximiliano Américo Ruíz Batista were prisoners. By a stroke of bad luck—or good luck, depending on one's viewpoint—Ruíz Batista had accompanied his chief. With a single blow, the army staff was beheaded.

Following the lead of Peña Taveras and their sergeants, the soldiers at army headquarters entered into rebellion against the Triumvirate. A page in Dominican history was irrevocably turned. The constitutionalist countercoup had begun, even if the principal leaders of the plot were not yet aware of it.

In arresting Rivera Cuesta, Peña Taveras had not acted on his own initiative; he had merely carried out the orders drawn up by the heads of the conspiracy a few days before. He deserves credit for not backing down at the last minute under the weight of the responsibility he was to assume. His action may have saved the conspiracy, for it thwarted the arrest of officers who, owing to their personal influence and their positions within the army, had an important role to play in triggering the countercoup. One of these officers, Lieutenant Colonel Gutiérrez Ramírez, commanded the Sixteenth of August camp, which the Enriquillo plan singled out for a decisive role. His arrest—and that of his comrades—two days before H-hour would have seriously undermined the conspiracy. The balance of power would have shifted to the conspirators' disadvantage, and a psychological blow would have been dealt the many officers who, having stated their support of the conspiracy, hesitated to take the last step.

For Peña Taveras, then, arresting Rivera Cuesta was a necessary defensive reaction. Both the government and the American embassy were taken completely by surprise—paralysis beset them both. One of the fundamental postulates of the Enriquillo plan was thus, at the outset, realized in full.

Yet Peña Taveras' action was not all to the constitutionalists' advantage. Surprise seized not only the enemy, but also the leaders of the conspiracy—and this was the tragicomical side to the affair. It had been decided that, if necessary, the countercoup would be set off at any time. Yet the conspirators could hardly have remained for a week at the place they were to occupy at the outbreak of the revolt, if only because their continuous presence would have aroused suspicions.

The countercoup had begun amidst a confusion that embraced both "loyalists" and rebels, civilians and military. At the moment Rivera Cuesta was arrested, most of the conspiracy's leaders sat calmly lunching at home or in restaurants.[2] As the first rebel, Peña Taveras' task was to inform these leaders that the rebellion was on. But locating them was not easy. The telephone, far more than the machine gun, was the weapon of the first hour—really of the first half day—of the constitutionalists' revolt. One by one the officers and former officers involved in the plot rushed to the posts they were supposed to occupy at H-hour. For most this was the Sixteenth of August camp, nerve center of the conspiracy. More than an hour after Rivera Cuesta's arrest—between 1:45 and 1:50 P.M.—Peña Taveras phoned José Francisco Peña Gómez, the civilian leader of the conspiracy and Bosch's delegate in the Dominican Republic. In taking action, Peña Taveras' natural reflex had been to contact other officers first—for him the military was the backbone of the movement—and only later the civilians.

Peña Gómez received Peña Taveras' call in the studios of Radio Comercial,[3] where he was delivering a speech during his party's radio program "Tribuna Democrática," broadcast daily between 1:30 and 2:00 P.M. He was therefore in an ideal position to transmit to the people the message he had just received: a group of "honest officers" had arrested the army chief of staff and announced their rebellion against the Triumvirate, in order to re-establish the government of Juan Bosch and the constitution of 1963. He urged the population to take to the streets in support of the movement.

The people of Santo Domingo responded with enthusiasm. Within minutes the streets were swarming with crowds shouting, seething, exulting, united in their opposition to the Triumvirate and their support of the military coup. Newspaper accounts tell the story: "before long there were crowds in the streets hailing the coup d'etat"; "waves of people surged through the streets of the capital shouting 'viva la libertad' . . . thousands of the capital's slum dwellers headed in the direction of the Presidential Palace."[4]

Even Danilo Brugal Alfau, a man blinded by his hatred of Bosch and the constitutionalists, paused in his litany of invective against the Dominican revolt to concede that "the movement won, from the outset, unanimous approval. Men, women, and children of humble origin exclaimed in one voice: Down with the Government! Long live the revolution!"[5] Just a few hours after the rebellion broke out, Frank Moya Pons, a young Dominican intellectual, noted in his diary:

> The din and the emotion, along with the growing throng, mounted vertiginously. Yet the police in charge of quelling acts of this sort—the *cascos blancos*—refrained from intervening violently wherever groups of rebellious citizens had formed. Quite literally the entire population of the capital rushed out into the streets. Shortly before three o'clock in the afternoon, the government radio station, Radio Santo Domingo TV . . . was occupied by a group of announcers together with political and labor union representatives of the government that had been toppled on 25 September 1963 by a reactionary coup. They invited the people to take to the streets to celebrate "the return to liberty, to constitutionality, to democracy," and so on. The people responded.[6]

At that moment the dream seemed to have come true, but only because of the initial hesitation of the police, surprised and dumbfounded by the rapid unfolding of events. The people were unarmed; the rebel officers were still at their camps, northwest of the capital. Shortly before four o'clock, the government forces, headed by the CEFA unit attached to the Presidential Palace, appeared at Radio Santo Domingo TV. The crowd surrounding the building had only its hate to hurl against the tanks of CEFA Colonel Morillo López and the machine guns of the *cascos blancos*. Resistance was futile. Government forces recaptured the radio station and arrested the "agitators," including such prominent figures as Peña Gómez, Miguel Soto (labor union leader of the PRD), and former deputy Manuel Fernández Mármol.

The retaking of Radio Santo Domingo TV by the "forces of order" marked a momentary ebb in the antigovernment movement in the capital. Moya Pons' diary continues:

> The police, on orders from a colonel [Ramón Adames Ovalle], seized the microphones and broadcast a declaration denying the existence of a coup d'état. . . . By around 4:30, the police had already moved in and begun to break up the crowds that had formed in the streets. The action of the troops, the news of the occupation of Radio Santo Domingo TV, and the

arrest of the announcers and their companions sowed confusion among the populace. Little by little the people took refuge in their homes. The battle seemed lost. I felt like weeping seeing those people, joyous and hopeful only a few minutes ago, now trudging, downcast, back to their dwellings. I felt the weight of the immense suffering that the nation had accumulated for so many years.[7]

Judging by events in the capital, the government had carried the day after a brief period of disorder. Government forces controlled the city, and a curfew was imposed. Instead of the "honest officers" who were to liberate them, the people had seen only the police and the armored vehicles of the CEFA. Bewildered, they believed that the military revolt—if it ever existed—had been stifled immediately.

The fate of the constitutionalist uprising that afternoon of 24 April, however, was not decided in Santo Domingo in that confrontation between relatively weak military forces and an unarmed populace. A battle had been lost, but not the war. The constitutionalist forces, surprised by Peña Taveras' action, were busy regrouping in their camps immediately northwest of the capital. Intact, growing in strength by the hour, they had not as yet entered into action. Nor had the government stronghold of San Isidro, nine miles northeast of Santo Domingo, entered the fray. The fate of the revolt was to be played out between these two forces, scarcely twenty miles apart. In the middle, weakly defended, lay the capital.

General Wessin received news of Rivera Cuesta's arrest shortly before Peña Gómez's announcement: "At 1:30 in the afternoon I was called by telephone. I was called in my home by Lt. Col. Rafael Polanco. He informed me that the chief of staff had been taken prisoner by Capt. Peña Taveras and a group of officers and men. . . . I immediately went to the training center [CEFA] and called an assembly of all the personnel available at this moment. I remained in my camp and waited for developments."[8]

While General Wessin conferred with his officers, a second meeting took place a few hundred yards away in which General de los Santos and the officers at the Nineteenth of November camp debated which position to adopt toward a military uprising, the strength and goals of which they knew nothing.[9]

The instinctive reactions at the two bases underline a significant fact about the famous *conjunto* of San Isidro. The CEFA and the Nineteenth of November reacted independently of each other; instead of a "summit" conference between the two commanders, they held two separate meetings. Already it was revealed, as became increasingly apparent during the hours that followed, that the *conjunto* was not nearly as united as many supposed. This attitude of "every man for himself" could only weaken the *conjunto* and explains the paralysis that gripped San Isidro and lasted until unity was re-established—by unorthodox means (see Chapter 6).

It is also significant that Generals Wessin and de los Santos both reacted by calling together their officers to decide which position to adopt, but neither moved to put himself at the service of a government whose authority he official-ly recognized. Neither felt great concern for the government upon learning of Rivera Cuesta's arrest or during the ensuing hours. The question of the survival of the Triumvirate during those hours counted for little beside the overriding question of defending their own interests. This attitude seems perfectly natural to those willing to recognize Generals Wessin and de los Santos for what they were: officers to whom respect for civil authority was a totally foreign, even per-haps a Communist notion. For those, however, who, in the face of the facts, per-sisted throughout the civil war in seeing Wessin and de los Santos as "loyalists," their behavior is difficult to justify.

At the meeting at the Nineteenth of November two groups clashed.[10] One, the "hard-liners"—led by the "Wessinist" air force officers—called for im-mediate bombardment of the rebel camps. The other, following a more flexible line, urged that contact be made with the rebels to find out their real aims and seek a possible entente. Only if talks failed should the air base resort to force. This second group, supported by de los Santos, prevailed, but only after stormy deliberations that continued until seven that evening.

What lay behind this position? The officers of the Nineteenth of November knew only that Captain Peña Taveras had taken the army chief of staff prisoner and that a number of camps had subsequently mutinied. Obviously the rebels wanted to overthrow the Triumvirate, an aim that, in itself, did not overly pre-occupy the "flexible" officers of the Nineteenth of November. Rather, their re-proach was that the insurgents had failed to consult them, but this was no rea-son for soldiers to start fighting among themselves. A military rebellion aimed at toppling Donald Reid Cabral had broken out. But Reid Cabral was merely a nice young man who had been placed at the head of the government by the armed forces, to which he was therefore responsible. Should his tenure in office create unnecessary problems, the armed forces would take back the power they had be-stowed on him and replace him with a military junta. The unhappy Reid Cabral thus posed no problem; but it was crucial to know whom—or what—the rebels hoped to put in his place. True, Peña Gómez had just announced over the radio that the aim of the movement was to return former President Bosch to power. But who could prove that he spoke for the military rebels? Even if Peña Gómez based his announcement on real pledges, who could prove they would be honor-ed? Was this not instead a tactical maneuver by the insurgents, eager to streng-then their hand by winning, through false promises, the support of the country's most powerful political party? Didn't the rebels intend to use that party to mobilize the masses and so lend an "ideological" air to their bid for power?

These considerations lay behind the decision to establish contact with the insurgents. It seemed natural to the officers of the Nineteenth of November that the Triumvirate be replaced by a military junta. Rather than the form of government, to which no objections were foreseen, the real topic of discussion would be the allotment of seats on the junta—that is, the establishment of a new balance of power within the Dominican armed forces.

This line of reasoning by the officers of the Nineteenth of November had a certain logic consistent with their mentality and with the country's military traditions. Nevertheless, changes had occurred within the armed forces, new aspirations had sprung up, far removed from the classic and sordid struggles over the nation's spoils. The embodiment of these new aspirations was Lieutenant Colonel Rafael Fernández Domínguez. Hoping to get rid of a "troublemaker," the Triumvirate had sent him abroad as a military attaché. But already in 1963, at the Military Academy Batalla de Las Carreras, a group of young officers had formed around Fernández Domínguez, and these ties and their aspirations had survived his forced departure. The group included men such as Núñez Nogueras, Lachapelle Díaz, Quiróz Pérez, and Sención Silverio. Many of them had been victims of a crackdown and cashiered from the service. The sick body had rejected the healthy organ. Yet the organ grew in importance, despite the sanctions and the threats. They were still a minority, but an active, tightly knit, resolute, influential minority—leaders of the rebel movement.

The change within the armed forces went undetected by the "traditional" officers, who, when the revolt broke out, assumed that their mutinous "comrades" were moved by the same "ideals" that guided them. This assumption was wrong, as were the conclusions drawn from it. Confounded, indignant, stunned, the officers of the Nineteenth of November woke up to their mistake on the afternoon of 25 April 1965. Henceforth the insurgents were no longer rebellious "comrades," but "Communist" rebels, as if Communists held a monopoly on integrity and loyalty to ideals. These "traditional" officers, however, should not be judged too harshly for their failure to appreciate the situation. The U.S. embassy made exactly the same error, drew the same wrong conclusions, and suffered the same rude awakening.

Once the officers of the Nineteenth of November reached their decision, they had to inform their troublesome neighbor, General Wessin. Between seven-thirty and eight o'clock that evening, Colonel Pedro Bartolomé Benoit arrived at the CEFA in his capacity as General de los Santos' emissary. His task was to inform Wessin of the stance of the Nineteenth of November vis-à-vis the military insurrection and the problem of the government's survival.

We have two versions of this meeting—Wessin's and Benoit's.[11] Despite certain discrepancies—such as Wessin's statement that his interlocutor was not Colonel Benoit but General de los Santos himself—the two versions agree on the main points, the respective positions of the CEFA and the Nineteenth of November. According to Wessin, "While I was in my camp, the chief of staff of the air force [de los Santos] came and asked me to surrender. I answered that he could surrender himself but I would defend myself . . . . I told him that this was a Communist uprising, and that I preferred to fight until the end and not to surrender. He went to the air force. At that time the only military camp that was fighting was my camp."[12]

According to Benoit, upon his arrival at the CEFA he found Wessin in conference with his officers. Benoit announced the decision of the Nineteenth of November and explained the reasons behind it. Exceeding the limits of his mandate, he even proposed that San Isidro (that is, the *conjunto*: the CEFA and the Nineteenth of November together) pre-empt the rebels by overthrowing the Triumvirate, setting up a military junta, and inviting the "other party" to join. Such a move would allow San Isidro to take the initiative and enhance its bargaining power in the forthcoming negotiations. In Benoit's account, Wessin failed to "appreciate" the stance of the Nineteenth of November and even Benoit's "goodwill." The uprising was a "Communist" plot; therefore no agreement was possible with the rebels. They had to be crushed.[13]

In brief, the two versions agree that the delegate of the Nineteenth of November (whether Colonel Benoit or General de los Santos) informed General Wessin of the air base's decision to open talks with the rebels in order to form a military junta. Wessin, a man who sees the world in black and white, regarded the decision to deal with the rebels as a signal to surrender. He favored crushing the rebels, whom he considered—or so pretended—to be Communists.

The two versions diverge, however, in their account of the inferences that Wessin drew from the "desertion" of the Nineteenth of November. Benoit recalls Wessin closing the conversation in a fit of anger and spite: "So do what you want and go to hell. I'm going to hand in my resignation."[14] In his version, however, Wessin paints himself as far more dignified and resolute. The discrepancy may be attributed in part to the conditions of Wessin's account, which was given as testimony at a hearing of the U.S. Senate. Before a highly sympathetic audience Wessin was doubtless promoting his reputation as a "fighter", fearless and faultless, who alone had the courage on that day of truth to take on the Communist dragon. In short, he was a man who could be of use some day, and who should be helped in his cruel exile.[15] According to Wessin, his reaction was sharp: "I answered that he [de los Santos] could surrender himself but . . . I preferred to fight until the end and not to surrender." His interlocutor gone, Wessin was left alone like a storybook knight ready to do battle to defend the "imperishable values" of "democracy" against the Communist threat: "At that time the only military camp that was fighting was my camp."

In his deposition before the American senators, Wessin explained how the CEFA had been fighting Communism on that Saturday evening, 24 April 1965:[16]

General Wessin: When night began to fall Saturday, I sent an infantry company with four tanks to occupy the east bridgehead of the Duarte Bridge, to protect this avenue of access to my camp.

Senator Hruska: Which end of the bridge is the east end—on the near side of the river from the camp or the far side?

General Wessin: It is on the near side of the camp. It is the side where the camp was located—the east side.
Senator Hruska: Does that mean . . . [you] had control of the entire bridge or only one end?
General Wessin: I only controlled the east part of the bridge.
Senator Hruska: But . . . [you] did not cross the bridge?
General Wessin: It was crossed later, but not at that time.[17]

Even taking Wessin at his word, it is extremely difficult to believe that he made a significant military effort in defense of the Reid Cabral government. Wessin's own account demonstrates the limits of his action: a single infantry company (176 men) and four tanks were sent to the side of the Duarte Bridge away from the city and failed to cross it. Wessin's justification: "After sending the company to the bridge, I was left with only 200 men in my camp."[18] Like a courser restrained by a boorish hand from breaking into the generous gallop prompted by his spirited nature, Wessin was prevented by a lack of troops from rushing to the rescue of the capital and "democracy," and was reduced to taking purely defensive measures.

Wishing to be impartial, I have given Wessin's version. The same impartiality requires that his story be scrutinized. Two important questions are raised: (1) Did Wessin actually order his troops to occupy the eastern end of the Duarte Bridge on the evening of the twenty-fourth? (2) Is it true that the redoubtable CEFA then counted no more than 376 men—Wessin's sole justification for failing to act? In answer to the first question, witnesses interviewed—officers from San Isidro, constitutionalist officers and inhabitants of the capital, in particular those living in the districts on the eastern side of the Duarte Bridge (Ensanche Ozama, Las Minas)—are unanimous in asserting that the CEFA troops did not take up positions at the eastern end of the bridge until early afternoon on the following day—Sunday, 25 April. If indeed Wessin dispatched his troops to the bridge on the night of the twenty-fourth, then he brought off a camouflage so flawless that not a soul, neither friend nor foe, was aware of it: not the people living in the zone of the operation—quite a feat!—or, more remarkable, the very officers who allegedly took part in it. In fact, on the afternoon of the twenty-fourth, Wessin sent four of his officers (Colonel Morillo López, Lieutenant Colonel Grampolver Medina Mercedes, Lieutenant Holguín Morilí Veras, and an officer as yet unidentified) into the capital. Their mission was to keep a close eye on developments and to take charge of the CEFA forces attached to the Presidential Palace. This was the extent of Wessin's military action on the first day of the uprising.

But the key question is not whether Wessin dispatched a company of men to the eastern end of the Duarte Bridge. This was a purely defensive measure that any commander should have taken, whether he favored talks with the rebels or steps to crush them. That Wessin failed to take this elementary course tells us nothing about his feelings toward the rebels or toward the Triumvirate. His actions bear eloquent witness, however, to his military capabilities and to the disarray that must have prevailed at the CEFA. The same appraisal is, of course, valid for the Nineteenth of November and its chief, General de los Santos. The real question is why the tanks and troops of the CEFA failed to cross the Duarte Bridge and mount an offensive against the rebel camps, or at least occupy Santo Domingo in order to protect the government from attack.

As we have seen, Wessin explained that his passivity was due to a lack of troops: "After sending the company to the bridge, I was left with only 200 men in my camp." To be sure, the CEFA had two thousand troops, but the twenty-fourth was a Saturday, and on Saturdays the men were off duty after 11:30 A.M. They were out visiting their families, and the camp was nearly empty when news of the countercoup arrived. This brilliant explanation, however, has been refuted by Wessin himself, who declared to the U.S. Senate subcommittee that on 24 April, "at 2 o'clock in the morning, or shortly thereafter, I went to my camp and confined to quarters all troops." When asked by J. G. Sourwine, the chief counsel of the Senate subcommittee, whether he had recalled "troops who were at liberty, on passes," Wessin replied: "I was able to reach those who lived in the city [Santo Domingo]." He then qualified his statement—perhaps because he realized his blunder—adding that "there were many who lived out in the country, and these I wasn't able to reach."[19] Sourwine did not press him further and went on to another question, not recognizing— or unwilling to recognize—that Wessin's statement had overturned the facts of the case. For it was no longer a question of soldiers being off duty on a Saturday morning: as Wessin said, he had confined them to quarters the previous night. And of those soldiers already "at liberty, on passes," Wessin had been able to recall "those who lived in [Santo Domingo]," but not "the many who lived in the country." The question then arises: where in fact did the men of the CEFA live? Many were housed with their families at San Isidro. Others lived at El Bonito, a little village one-half mile from the CEFA. And at Kilometer 9 of the Sánchez Highway, which links San Isidro and Santo Domingo, was a village built by Reid Cabral for the exclusive use of the men of the CEFA. In Ensanche Ozama, in Las Minas, in Villa Duarte, heavily populated districts of Greater Santo Domingo—all on the eastern side of the Duarte Bridge—lived a large number of the San Isidro military. If Wessin had been able to reach the men living in the capital, then, a fortiori, he must have been able to reach those living between Santo Domingo and San Isidro. His soldiers lived not in isolated houses high up on some cliff, but clustered in the villages just mentioned.

Are we to believe, then, that on the afternoon of 24 April, having confined his troops to quarters early that morning, having recalled those soldiers who lived near the camp, Wessin was left with only 376 men out of a total 2,000? Even a desire to whitewash Wessin's lies could not permit us to disguise truth to such an extent, turning the humble Dominican G.I., with his monthly wage of sixty dollars, into a rich rentier who, on Friday afternoon, jumps into his car and drives off to the mountains for the weekend.[20]

Yet, if lack of troops fails as an explanation, then what was the motive behind the general's refusal to dispatch his troops to save the Triumvirate, despite repeated appeals from Reid Cabral?

No document exists, no valid argument can be made in support of the thesis, advanced by some, that Wessin himself was involved in a plot (still another!) to overthrow the government of which he was the chief beneficiary. Such a thesis appears to be founded in those groundless rumors (*chismes*) that abound in the Dominican Republic.

To be sure, Wessin was suddenly faced with a particularly difficult situation on that 24 April. It was no longer a matter of overthrowing a president of the Republic after months of plotting had eliminated all the risks. Now he faced an enemy with a certain military force, whose strength he found hard to gauge. Was the Sixteenth of August alone in its rebellion? What was the real attitude of the Twenty-seventh of February and of the 6½ Artillery? Were they neutral, prorebel, or actually in league with the rebels?

Given such doubts, Wessin hesitated to act alone. The adversary had weapons far more potent than the rocks and bricks of the students. Victory might be costly, especially in terms of tanks—and tanks, not prestige, ensured his power. Within the armed forces, Wessin had wronged too many "comrades"; the responsibility for the disgrace of Neit Nivar Seijas, Belisario Peguero, Montás Guerrero, Viñas Román and many others was laid at his door. How many "comrades" would have regretted a decline in Wessin's power while they held onto theirs; how many would have lifted a finger to help the strong man whose power they both envied and feared?[21]

The attitude of the Nineteenth of November above all else drove Wessin into a corner and paralyzed him. To mount an assault on the rebels single-handedly would have meant unmanning the CEFA, while, a hundred yards away, the Nineteenth of November retained its strength intact. The unity of the armed forces—which the constitutionalists were later accused of disrupting—was such that Wessin could not be sure that de los Santos would not reach an accord with the rebels at Wessin's expense.

With no knowledge of the strength of the enemy, but all too aware of the "loyalty" of his friends, Wessin found himself in a perilous situation. To meet such a challenge would have required a firm leader ready to take risks and to exploit to the fullest those forces at his disposal. But Wessin was not made of that stuff; rather, he was like the ostrich who buries his head in the sand at the first sign of danger. For hours he did nothing, when he should have taken swift action. Surprised, confused, afraid, Wessin neglected the fundamental precaution of sending troops to the Duarte Bridge, in order to hold not simply its east end, but both ends, this being the only way to guarantee the CEFA's access to the capital. Three days later—27 April—this neglect cost him dearly.

In theory, since he was opposed to the overthrow of the Triumvirate, Wessin did not betray Reid Cabral. Yet can he be called "loyal"? Deaf to the appeals of Reid Cabral, "his" president of the Republic and minister of the armed forces, Wessin preferred to shut himself inside his precious CEFA with his men and his tanks—like the miser clutching his money box and resolved to starve rather than give it up.

If the paralysis of the CEFA can be explained in large part by the breakup of the *conjunto* of San Isidro, what explains this breakup?

General de los Santos was on good terms with Reid Cabral, but he was not the government's strong man. Therefore it was not necessarily in his interest to take too many risks to save the regime. The chief beneficiary of the Triumvirate was Wessin, a neighbor who, not content with his power over the CEFA, tended to extend his influence over the air force. A string of superior officers had already been sacrificed on the altar of Wessin's ambition. Could de los Santos be sure he would not be next? His often strained relations with Wessin offered no guarantees on this score.

The rebel movement, however, whose only goal, de los Santos believed, was to install a military junta, might offer more advantages than risks. In a new government de los Santos could easily maintain his position. He had never been wholly identified with the Triumvirate and had even lent a hand in its fall. Most important, he commanded an intact military force. In fact, he might even strengthen his position: Wessin's fall would dispel the grave threat hanging over de los Santos' control of the air force, perhaps even opening the way for him to extend his own influence over the CEFA. This would be a complete reversal— to his advantage—of the situation existing on 24 April.

For all these reasons, de los Santos had no interest in fighting to save the Triumvirate; on the contrary, his interests led him to side with the rebels, at least as long as he believed that their only goal was to set up a military junta.

For the same reasons, Wessin had no alternative but to hope to see the insurgents crushed. Any rebel movement, whether Communist, Boschist, or simply "anti-Reid Cabral," must necessarily aim at altering the balance of power in the country. But on 24 April, Wessin was the government's strong man. Any change in the balance of power could only hurt him.

Thus while de los Santos saw a chance to strengthen, or at least maintain, his position, Wessin saw only a threat to his status—the destruction, or at least a weakening, of his privileged position. The interests of the two generals collided. The breakup of the *conjunto* was a fact.

As absurd as it may seem, Reid Cabral was unaware of what was happening at San Isidro.[22] Abiding by the principle of burning his bridges only at the last moment, de los Santos was careful to conceal from the Triumvir the real position of the Nineteenth of November. Could anyone foresee what means of escape might be necessary, or whom one might in the end betray? De los Santos answered Reid Cabral's phone calls by repeated reassurances of his loyalty to the regime and by pledges to call out the air force . . . "tomorrow." Wessin, too, declared his support of the government, explaining that his inaction was due to the lack of troops and the failure of the air force to intervene ("he could not use his tanks without air support").[23]

Thus the prospects Reid Cabral faced that evening of the twenty-fourth seemed, on the whole, reassuring.[24] He had the loyal support of San Isidro, where inaction was the result of technical problems that were being resolved. The government forces held control of the capital; the rebels, isolated, dared not leave their camps. The rest of the country was quiet. The garrisons in the interior had reaffirmed their loyalty to the regime. As in Santo Domingo, the people in the cities of the interior had experienced a brief moment of excitement at the news of the uprising; as in Santo Domingo, the wave of enthusiasm had swiftly turned to sullen resignation when government forces recaptured Radio Santo Domingo TV and denied the existence of a coup. Thus it looked as though the Triumvirate would have no difficulty quelling the revolt. At 7:53 that evening, Reid Cabral informed the American embassy that he intended to "surround the rebel Camp 27th of February with loyal troops and cut off utilities there."[25] A little later, at 8:35, in a speech at the Presidential Palace that was rebroadcast over radio and television, he declared that "with the exception of the Sixteenth of August camp . . . and the installations housing Army Staff Headquarters . . . the entire country is calm, under the absolute control of the Government." And he issued an ultimatum to the rebels, summoning them to surrender "at the very latest by five o'clock tomorrow morning." Should they refuse, "the Armed Forces will carry out their assigned missions."[26]

Poor Reid Cabral was increasingly out of touch with reality. And so was the American embassy, with which he kept in close contact. False information flowed from the one to the other; mistakes were shared in perfect harmony. A queer paradox existed on that 24 April, with the Dominican president and the "big brother's" powerful embassy apparently the only ones unaware of the real situation.

While Wessin wavered and de los Santos betrayed, while Reid Cabral and the Americans were lost in fantasies, the rebels prepared to take the offensive.

The Enriquillo plan had provided for a "center" and a "periphery." At H-hour, the troops of the "center," staunch constitutionalists from the start, would occupy the capital; the constitutionalists of the "periphery," meanwhile, would neutralize any opposition within their respective branches—especially in the air force—or even win the resistors over to the rebel cause. Isolated, Wessin would have to surrender.

But the situation early in the afternoon of the twenty-fourth appeared quite unlike the one foreseen by the Enriquillo plan. Taken by surprise, the "periphery" was unable—or afraid—to act, with the result that the armed forces in the interior continued to support the government. The capital remained in the hands of the Triumvirate, and by then a surprise attack seemed impossible. At any minute, on the other hand, San Isidro might launch an offensive against the rebels. In the event of a joint thrust by Wessin's tanks and de los Santos' planes, the rebels, woefully lacking in tanks and planes and left to their own resources in camps vulnerable to attack, could offer only a hopeless resistance.

Although linked more or less closely with the conspiracy, a great many officers of the "center" balked in the face of such a prospect. But their hesitation failed to prevent the Sixteenth of August from rallying immediately to the cause. At the camp, nerve center of the movement, "everyone had joined the conspiracy."[27] The commander, Lieutenant Colonel Gutiérrez Ramírez, had no choice, since he was one of the four officers Rivera Cuesta had tried to arrest. Those who hesitated constituted a minority and were too weak to halt the course of events. Solidly constitutionalist from the beginning, the Sixteenth of August became the headquarters of Lieutenant Colonel Hernando Ramírez, leader of the revolt.

Lieutenant Colonel Salvador Escarramán Mejía, commander of the 6½ Artillery, had not joined the conspiracy. Worried, unable to decide on a stance, he wanted first to get the facts. To do so he chose—unfortunately for him—to leave his camp. Worse, he went to army headquarters—to Peña Taveras. Seeing Escarramán waver, Peña Taveras happily added this new prize to his collection of high-ranking prisoners. Escarramán shared the fate of Rivera Cuesta, Ruíz Batista, and the others. Two men who did not waver, Majors Píndaro Peña Perelló and Núñez Nogueras, took up Escarramán's vacated post. Under their leadership, the 6½ Artillery quickly rallied to the rebel side.

At the Twenty-seventh of February, however, the movement stalled. The camp commander, Colonel Carlos María Paulino Asiático, was a "traditional" officer. Odd concepts like democracy, respect for law, and the war against corruption did not particularly interest him. He was on good terms with Reid Cabral. Of course, that did not mean that he would risk his life or even his career, and the benefits it brought him, to defend the Triumvirate. His fondest wish was to avoid compromising himself before it became clear which side would prevail. He was not afraid to take a stance, provided he could be sure of being on the winning team. This was understandable in a man whose chief concern was his own future, a preoccupation shared by a great many officers during those days of crisis, until foreign armies intervened and resolved the dilemma.

Colonel Paulino Asiático therefore did not come out against the insurrection. Such a step could have proved dangerous because the rebels might indeed triumph and because he himself fell within the rebels' zone of influence: inside his own camp, a large number of officers supported the revolt. The rebels might be weak compared to San Isidro, but San Isidro was remote. All kinds of disagreeable things could happen to him before the revolt was crushed.

Colonel Paulino Asiático's response to the emissaries from the Sixteenth of August who came first to persuade, then to compel him to rally to the cause was simple. In effect he kept telling them: "Let's not be hasty, gentlemen. Of course, I'm with you. But why rush into a venture? We're all brothers. The unity of the

Armed Forces must be our chief concern. What we should do is wait, work it out. Above all, keep calm!"[28]

Even before 24 April, the Twenty-seventh of February was, of the three "center" camps, the one where the conspirators' influence was weakest. Still, their inroads were deep enough to lead the rebels to believe that, at the critical moment, a decisive, well-planned action would win over the fence-sitters, isolating the small minority openly hostile to the revolt. But the reality would prove to be quite different. The circumstances surrounding the triggering of the countercoup increased rather than reduced the number of those undecided. Paulino Asiático, who was careful not to make the same mistake as Escarramán, was in a much more secure position than the conspirators anticipated.

A brief sketch of the rebels' activities on that first day would include three phases. In the initial phase, the insurgents, already temporarily deprived of the "periphery," lacked even the full "center" which, according to the Enriquillo plan, was to spearhead the movement. Although they were entrenched at the Sixteenth of August and at the 6½ Artillery, the rebels were up against a lukewarm Twenty-seventh of February, where, outside of a small band of staunch adherents, a majority of "undecideds" dragged their feet.

Yet already during this initial phase, the first contacts were made between the Twenty-seventh of February and the leaders of the revolt. Rebel officers shuttled between the various camps. From the Twenty-seventh of February, answering Hernando Ramírez's appeal, officers went to the Sixteenth of August to get instructions. Meanwhile, envoys from the other camps and a group of his own officers pressed Paulino Asiático to align himself with the movement. At the same time, during countless private talks, they tried to win over the hesitants of the Twenty-seventh of February. With the passing of the hours San Isidro's inaction emboldened the rebels and reassured those who feared the *conjunto*.

A second phase opened between five-thirty and six o'clock, with the arrival of two rebel leaders, Colonel Caamaño and Captain Lachapelle Díaz, at the Twenty-seventh of February. Persuasion increasingly gave way to threats. Fewer and fewer officers supported the wait-and-see attitude of Paulino Asiático. The heavy armament of the 6½ Artillery, staunchly constitutionalist and close by, added special weight to the arguments of those who felt that there had been too much talk and not enough action. Paulino Asiático was soon confronted with an ultimatum: join the rebellion or face arrest. He joined, but almost immediately jumped into a car and fled.

By nine o'clock, the Twenty-seventh of February was firmly on the rebel side. A third and final phase opened, during which the rebels, having at last reestablished the unity of the "center," could now prepare to go on the offensive. Their immediate objective: occupation of the capital, a vital necessity both militarily and politically.

Yet, as in the first two, this third phase was characterized far more by diplomacy than by military activity. Around seven o'clock, the meeting at the Nineteenth of November broke up, and in accordance with the decisions taken, de los Santos endeavored to contact the rebel leaders. Shortly thereafter, during a telephone conversation with Hernando Ramírez, an agreement was easily reached whereby the next morning a delegate from the Nineteenth of November would be dispatched to the rebel camps to seek a common solution. It was a superficial agreement, so vague as to be all things to all men. For de los Santos, it meant that the rebels would spend the night in their camps, where, the next morning, they would be easy targets for his planes: a fine guarantee of "fruitful" negotiations![29] For the rebels, the agreement was further proof of the passivity of de los Santos, who granted them a few extra hours to carry out their scheme in peace.

The rebel leaders' contacts with the "outside" were not limited to de los Santos. Anxious to minimize the risks involved in occupying the capital, they launched in this last phase an impressive offensive by telephone. The telephone campaign was aimed especially at the forces that, because of their geographical position, might pose an obstacle to a rebel advance: the police, with three thousand men in the capital, and the elite Mella Battalion, which, based at San Cristóbal, was less than twenty miles from Santo Domingo. Colonel Pérez Aponte, commander of the Mella Battalion, was, like most of his officers, a member of the San Cristóbal Group. Pérez Aponte had no stake in the survival of a regime whose next victim he might be. Thus he had no reason to refuse Hernando Ramírez a support that was merely verbal. Allegedly prorebel, the Mella Battalion remained at San Cristóbal waiting for events to unfold.

Despite repeated overtures from the rebels, General Despradel Brache, the chief of police, refused to rally to the movement. Yet he also refused to go on opposing the revolt, which, because of the inaction of San Isidro and the energy of the rebels, had acquired unsuspected force. Perhaps the attitude of a large number of his officers played a part in that decision: only a few weeks before, Reid Cabral had suddenly dismissed police strong man General Belisario Peguero. This action was still fresh in the minds of those former subordinates among whom Belisario continued to enjoy great prestige.

Thus a truly odd situation existed: the chief of police was neither against the revolt (the rebels might win) nor for the revolt (they might lose), yet he found himself in the zone of an imminent rebel attack. The situation might have seemed desperate to a less nimble man. But General Despradel Brache found a way out of the impasse into which he had been driven by his own opportunism. With unsuspected mental agility, he discovered the concept of an "apolitical" police force.

Except under the brief Bosch regime, the Dominican police had always been noted for its repressive tactics. Under the Triumvirate, the police spent most of its energy beating a little common sense into the opposition. As late as the afternoon of the twenty-fourth, the police was an instrument of repression. Now it suddenly became "apolitical." It was one thing to bully a defenseless populace, quite another to confront the army's elite battalions—especially when the rebels might triumph.

And so, on the evening of the twenty-fourth, Despradel Brache answered the rebels' advances by pointing out that the exclusive duty of the police was to maintain law and order. Its role was not to get mixed up in rivalries among military factions. He made it clear that "he wanted no part of any military dispute" and that he intended to stay "neutral."[30] The military could go ahead and kill each other in their struggle for power; Despradel Brache would take cover and wait. He would emerge when the struggle was over, eager to serve the winner— and begin again his intimidation and repression of the people.

Despradel Brache's position was absurd, unreal, shocking in its cynicism and opportunism. Nonetheless the rebel leaders accepted it because it meant, in concrete terms, that the three thousand men of the police would not oppose their entry into the capital. With the San Isidro Air Base playing Sleeping Beauty, the Mella Battalion "supporting" the movement, and the police "apolitical," the way to the capital lay open.

The rebels had no illusions about Wessin's hostility to the revolt. But they were all too familiar with his "decisive" nature, his qualities as a "warrior," to fear a reaction from him. They were convinced—and events would prove them right—that the man who throughout the day had failed to order his tanks into a city occupied by friendly forces would hardly risk it at night against the enemy. But what of the army units inside the capital? The garrisons of Intendencia and Transportación, in any case negligible militarily, had already announced their adherence to the revolt, which everyone knew was motivated by sheer opportunism. The commander of Polvorín, Lieutenant Faña, was staunchly prorebel. The Presidential Guard was deeply infiltrated by the rebels. But what about the tanks of the CEFA attached to the Presidential Palace? What kind of resistance could eight tanks and four combat tanks provide?[31] The rebel units would take position in front of them, while across the river Wessin cowered at San Isidro. Just a few hours earlier, the Boschist masses of the capital had momentarily been made "wiser" by means of rifle butts and by the threat of machine guns, but not before they had loudly demonstrated where their sympathies lay. Once the rebels entered the city, the masses—heartened, elated—would, by their size alone, constitute a force that the tiny CEFA detachment would never dare to provoke.

Midnight. 24 April 1965 now belonged to history. Soon soldiers at the Sixteenth of August boarded trucks that would take them southeast, toward the capital. At about one o'clock on 25 April, the constitutionalists finally launched their offensive. According to the Enriquillo plan, it should have begun just minutes after the start of the revolt, but, owing to circumstances, a long, laborious process had been necessary. The resultant delay could have had disastrous consequences if the "loyalists" had reacted. But ineptitude, stupidity, opportunism, and betrayal barred any reaction other than police and CEFA attacks on unarmed citizens in the capital. The rebels were the first to recover the will to act. Their prize—Santo Domingo—lay within reach.

Chapter 6

From Countercoup to Civil War (25 April 1965, from Midnight to Four in the Afternoon)

At about one-thirty in the morning of 25 April, rebel units entered the capital.[1] They met no resistance. This was hardly surprising, since the San Isidro troops were at their camps and the Mella Battalion was at San Cristóbal. Inside the capital, the police were "apolitical," while the troops of Polvorín, Transportación, and Intendencia joined the rebel cause. Those that remained—the Presidential Guard and the CEFA detachment—took care to avoid any "ill-considered" act that might arouse the rebels' wrath.

Suddenly a "cry of freedom pierced the tranquil night."[2] Major Núñez Nogueras had sent one of his men to the firehouse to ring the alarm, announcing to the sleeping populace the arrival of the troops it had awaited in vain throughout the afternoon. The insurgents quickly seized the city's strategic points. But an anachronism remained that became increasingly absurd as the hours passed: Reid Cabral was still president of the Triumvirate and was still ensconced at the Presidential Palace, the one place his authority continued to hold some force. The Palace could have been taken with relative ease, for it was defended by a Presidential Guard infiltrated with rebel partisans and by a dozen or so tanks whose crews must have longed for the peace of San Isidro. A few soldiers might have died in the attack, but that was not too high a price to pay for success. The rebels could have captured the head of state and occupied the Palace, eliminating a potential pocket of resistance, but they wanted to avoid unnecessary bloodshed. In any event, Reid Cabral's fate was sealed. The Palace was now a vast prison from which he could not escape. A few hours' delay could not alter that fact.

Once again the rebels chose the path of diplomacy. The character of the Presidential Guard's commander, Colonel Julio Amado Calderón Fernández, facilitated their job and assured their success. Over the last four years Calderón Fernández had acquired a solid reputation as an opportunist. Now, at the hour of decision, he proved himself worthy of it. Calderón Fernández quickly reached an informal agreement with the rebel leaders. The Palace was neutralized. "Pro-government" within, it sheltered the ghost of a president and a few hundred apathetic soldiers. Outside was rebel territory. The CEFA troops, meanwhile, seemed to adjust easily to this odd situation.

At San Isidro, General de los Santos was surprised by the rebels' occupation of the capital. He had thought that they would answer his inaction with their own, by waiting patiently—and stupidly—in their camps for his delegate. Only then, once an agreement had been reached on the formation of a military junta, would he and the rebels march over to the Palace to "thank" Reid Cabral and inform him that he could retire, inasmuch as the armed forces no longer needed his services. In the meantime, the capital would continue to serve as a buffer zone, the police maintaining order in the streets while Reid Cabral, still chief of state but bereft of troops, sat in the Palace.

Instead, the rebels had moved into the capital. De los Santos quickly learned of this new fait accompli via the telephone, which conveyed the increasingly desperate appeals of Reid Cabral. Once again he did not act. Militarily he had little choice. Night grounded his planes and the rebels were inside the capital. Moreover, his conviction that the insurgents would eventually accept a "reasonable" solution ruled out any hasty reaction. Yet time was working to the advantage of the rebels, whose control over the city grew stronger by the hour. Barring a military response, de los Santos should at least have reacted "diplomatically," demanding that the talks between his representative and the leaders of the revolt, scheduled for the morning, be held at once. But he made no such effort. It was dawn before he talked by phone with Hernando Ramírez, their first contact since the rebel units' entry into the capital. Instead of seeking an immediate opening of talks, de los Santos asked only for a confirmation of the agreement made during their previous conversation, which was granted.[3] At eight in the morning his envoy, Colonel Enrique Pérez y Pérez,[4] left the Nineteenth of November camp. When he arrived at the Duarte Bridge, the crowd gathered there recognized him as a San Isidro officer. They set his car on fire and he was forced to flee.

The incident failed to thwart the talks since each side, confident that its position would prevail, was eager to see them proceed. The rebels phoned de los Santos and asked that he send a new delegate. Colonel Benoit was chosen. To avoid Pérez y Pérez's fate, Benoit traveled by helicopter, reaching the capital around eleven o'clock. When he landed, he discovered that Reid Cabral had resigned just a few minutes before.

Reid Cabral had spent the night in his office at the Palace, an impotent spectator to the rebels' occupation of the capital and to his own "neutralization." Glued to the telephone, he continued to ask his military chiefs—especially Wessin and de los Santos—to be so good as to save his regime. His appeals met again and again with declarations of unshakable loyalty.[5] Yet no help came.

All the while the cries of the masses could be clearly heard in the Palace: "We want Juan Bosch!"[6] It seemed a presage of defeat. Reid Cabral had only one hope: the United States embassy, *refugium peccatorum* for his tottering dictatorship for over a year. On 15 September 1965, almost five months after the uprising, Senator William Fulbright, chairman of the Senate Foreign Relations Committee, offered this assessment of his government's policy during the first twenty-four hours of the crisis:

> When the Dominican revolution began on Saturday, April 24, the United States had three options available. First, it could have supported the Reid Cabral government; second, it could have supported the revolutionary forces; and third, it could do nothing.
>
> The administration chose the last course. When Donald Reid Cabral asked for U.S. intervention on Sunday morning, April 25, he was given no encouragement.
>
> . . . If the United States thought that Reid was giving the Dominican Republic the best government it had had or was likely to get, why did the United States not react more vigorously to support him?[7]

On 24 April 1965, the U.S. embassy in Santo Domingo faced an uprising that came as a complete surprise. Such a crisis required an embassy in full force, but the U.S. embassy was half empty. Since 23 April, the day before the revolt, Ambassador Bennett had been in his native state of Georgia, visiting his mother who was seriously ill. He learned over the radio, like an ordinary citizen, that a military revolt had exploded in "his" country. Of the thirteen members of MAAG, eleven were in Panama attending a routine conference. William C. Ide, chief of mission of the International Development Agency in the Dominican Republic, was in Washington, as was Anthony Ruiz, the embassy's public safety adviser. The naval attaché, Lieutenant Colonel Ralph Heywood, was in the Dominican Republic, but remote from the theater of events. At the moment of Rivera Cuesta's arrest, Heywood was on a duck hunt in the Cibao with General Imbert Barrera. He did not return to the capital until that evening. Thus, during the early hours of the crisis, the Dominican navy was bereft of its "spiritual adviser."[8]

The embassy was headed by William B. Connett, the chargé d'affaires, who had been in the Dominican Republic five and a half months. After the fact, many chose to regard the relative brevity of his stay as a extenuating factor in the dismal failure of the embassy's actions during the first days—and especially the first twenty-four hours—of the revolt. But nearly six months' service, though no doubt insufficient in the case of a one-man mission, should have been ample time for Connett, who had already held four diplomatic posts in Latin America, to learn about the political situation of a complex yet small country. He was second in command at an embassy rich in both means and personnel, and he should have been able to count on help and briefings from his colleagues, especially those from the C.I.A. Connett's failure during the three days he headed the embassy cannot be imputed even in part to his brief stay in the country. Rather it was a personal failure and a failure of a whole team and its methods. Contrary to Fulbright's suggestion that U.S. inaction during the first twenty-four hours of the revolt can be explained by the lack of a coherent American policy, Washington's attitude resulted from the inability of its representatives in the

Dominican Republic to analyze the situation. During those first hours, the embassy piled misjudgment upon misjudgment: first, as to the relative strength of the government and the rebel forces; then, as to the rebels' aims. The embassy lagged constantly behind the unfolding of events, all the while failing to grasp their meaning or gauge their scope.

The embassy's first miscalculation—as to the relative strength of the government and the rebel forces—stemmed inevitably from two gross misjudgments: first, an underestimation of the rebels' strength and determination; second, an overestimation of the loyalty of the "loyal" forces. Most of all, the embassy seemed to know nothing about the real attitude of the Nineteenth of November, trusting de los Santos' pledges to Reid Cabral and to the American military attachés.

By mid-afternoon, the embassy's view of the situation was roughly the following: after an initial period of confusion, the "forces of order" had taken things in hand and checked the "agitators"; only two army camps were in rebellion; the rest of the armed forces, particularly the powerful *conjunto*, remained loyal to the Triumvirate. Military advantage clearly seemed to lie with the government forces. As Martin later wrote, "Washington—and the Embassy—believed the Reid government had regained control."[9] Tad Szulc, the *New York Times* specialist in Latin American affairs, confirmed this opinion in reporting a conversation he had on the evening of 24 April with the Dominican desk of the State Department: "The State Department official, quoting reports from our embassy in Santo Domingo, told me that . . . the rebellion did not seem to amount to much. He reported that loyal forces had recaptured Radio Santo Domingo . . . and that president Reid had issued an ultimatum to the military insurgents . . . to surrender . . . or face an attack by loyalist troops."[10] Dispatches from the embassy were so reassuring, in fact, that Harry Shlaudeman, the State Department's Dominican desk officer, left his office around six-thirty and went home.[11]

The behavior of the United States on 24 April was a consequence of this optimism. The U.S. may have decided to do nothing, but it is wrong to attribute its attitude to a sudden withdrawal of support for the Reid Cabral dictatorship. Quite simply, the Americans believed that the Triumvirate could control the situation without U.S. interference. Under the circumstances, it was not in the interest of the United States to identify itself with an unpopular government that, in the wake of the revolt, would be forced to take increasingly repressive measures. In particular, the United States had no desire to provoke unnecessarily "liberal" opinion on both sides of the Rio Grande by exposing itself to bitter charges of "Yankee interference." Finally, American involvement on behalf of the Triumvirate seemed even more untimely since Reid Cabral, certain that he could easily restore order, had not asked for help.

But the rebels' occupation of the capital obliged the American embassy to recognize that the rebels were stronger—and above all more resolute—than it had thought. At the same time, San Isidro's prolonged passivity aroused growing doubts, even among the Americans, as to the fidelity of the so-called loyal generals to the regime. In *Dominican Action–1965*, a semiofficial apology for the U.S. intervention, the authors wrote: "By early morning of the 25th, it had become clear that the loyal Dominican military commanders were not going to support Reid, no matter what else they might decide to do.[12] The men at the embassy learned that the Air Force officers, de los Santos and his staff, had held a meeting and agreed not to fight against their comrades."[13] The embassy now realized that only strong American pressure on the Dominican military chiefs might convince them to defend the Triumvirate—instead of contributing to its fall.[14]

At this point, Reid Cabral, recognizing his extremely weak position, turned toward the American embassy for the aid he had deemed unnecessary the day before. He asked for various forms of help: American pressure on the "loyal" generals to defend his regime, American pressure on the rebels to accept a compromise, and even American military intervention.

In the face of Reid Cabral's appeals, Senator Fulbright's question becomes truly pertinent: "Why did the United States not react more vigorously to support him?" Contrary to Reid Cabral's hopes, the American embassy appeared to adjust easily to the "loyal" generals' refusal to fight and took no steps to pressure the rebels to soften their stance vis-à-vis the regime.

The crisis reached its climax when "at 9:30 A.M. Connett went to the Palace at Reid's request after Reid had asked a U.S. Naval Attaché, assigned to the . . . Palace on orders of the Embassy, whether the United States would be willing to intervene. The attaché passed the question along to Connett and informed him of Reid's desire for a conference." During their talk, "Reid took Connett aside and told him the situation was extremely precarious. He told the Chargé d'Affaires that the Communists were taking advantage of the situation[15] and his own government forces were unwilling to act . . . . According to Connett, Reid said nothing more about U.S. intervention except to express the hope that the embassy might use its influence to persuade the rebels to stop fighting." But for Connett, the Triumvirate's time had run out: "Connett reported to Washington by cable, as soon as the conversation ended, that he had told Reid he didn't believe the United States would be able to accomplish much at that time."[16] The State Department had already agreed with Connett, obviously for the same reasons, that a "last-ditch stand" in support of the Triumvirate should be avoided in favor of a military junta.[17] This was the attitude that led Fulbright to conclude, a little too hastily, that "the United States was . . . at the outset unwilling to support Reid."[18]

No abrupt switch in the Johnson administration's feelings toward the Triumvirate lay behind the U.S. failure to act. Rather, the explanation again lies in the embassy's inability to assess the situation. Having misjudged the possibility of a revolt, miscalculated the strength of the insurgents, and mistaken the

fidelity of the "loyalists," the American embassy made one more error: it misunderstood the rebels' real aims. Too many biases prevented the embassy from
even considering that the aim of the revolt might be to return Bosch to the presidency, that the rebel movement might be "constitutionalist." Of course,
American officers would always be ready to risk their lives to return an unlaw-
fully ousted president to the White House. But what was logical, even inevitable
in the United States was unthinkable south of the border. Latin America is the
land of corruption, where democracy is abused and held in contempt, where
eternal struggle rages between the "ins" and the "outs." Although there were
a few rare exceptions, the Dominican Republic was surely not one of them:
"Far from being a professional institution dedicated to certain principles which
impel its occasional entry into politics, the Dominican Armed Forces have never
had any significant function beyond politics, except for plunder."[19] Such a
judgment was valid for the past, but it can be dangerous to use the past as a rule
for the present or to transform the lessons of history into the laws of the future.

Unfortunately for the U.S. diplomats, their experience in the Dominican
Republic could only mislead them further.[20] The Dominican officers with
whom they had the most contact were the "ins": Wessin, Belisario Peguero,
Viñas Román, Román Carbuccia, de los Santos, Rivera Caminero. They were a
sorry brotherhood—at best opportunists, and usually thieves. The Americans had
no dealings with the "outcasts," men who because of their loyalty to the democratic cause had been dismissed from the Dominican armed forces: Núñez
Nogueras, Lachapelle Díaz, Quiróz Pérez, and the other members of the Gas
Station Group. Contacts were extremely rare and formal with those officers
who, still in active service, had come to espouse constitutionalist ideals: men
such as Hernando Ramírez, Lora Fernández, and Peña Taveras. These contacts
were made even more difficult because many of these officers, driven by a nationalism exasperated for having been mocked too often, viewed their American
mentors unsympathetically. The latter, in their nonchalant exuberance, often
forgot that, unlike Puerto Rico, the Dominican Republic was not yet a "free and
associated" state. The fact that these Americans had adjusted so well to Bosch's
fall and were now openly sympathetic to the Reid Cabral dictatorship could
only estrange Dominican officers who were preparing to topple Reid and rein-
state Bosch. Peña Taveras' outburst to the American colonel on the evening of
25 April epitomizes the attitude of this group of Dominican officers (see above,
n. 14).

Unfamiliar with the leaders of the revolt, and all too familiar with the "traditional" Dominican military man, the Americans reacted to the countercoup
in the only way they knew. Without differentiating, they automatically tossed
all the officers together. This was in the best spirit of the models given everlast-
ing sanction by many U.S. scholars and in accordance with their own experience
in the Dominican Republic. They saw the constitutionalist revolt as a rebellion
of young officers—the "outs"—against the representatives of the military establishment—the "ins." Some of the rebels (the "hotheads") might have more

complex motives; they might have tired of the rampant corruption, or a few "eccentrics" might even want to go back to a democratic government. But they could only be a tiny minority. Surely, most of the rebels were motivated by the wish to get a bigger share of the perpetual feast celebrated by those in power.

Four years later, an American scholar reflected with dismal fidelity the grievous tangle of prejudices and biases that paralyzed the thinking of the American embassy:

> The major distinction between the military leaders on either side of the 1965 civil war was that of age and rank; the established leaders were of higher rank precisely because they had prevailed in previous struggles to reach the top. Dispassionate analysis of the 1965 revolution, in fact, would reveal the participation on the constitutionalist side, at least in the first days of the crisis, of some of the Dominican Republic's most discredited ex-generals, including Belisario Peguero, Atila Luna, and Santiago Rodríguez Echavarría.[21] Some of the principal constitutionalist officers were fighting primarily to win reinstatement in the Armed Forces, from which they had been fired. All these leaders, as well as a varied collection of civilian and military personalities and groups, were brought together mainly by the fact of being 'out' or, as Dominicans would say, 'abajo.'[22]

In the view of the American embassy, then, the "hotheads" were only a feeble minority within the rebel movement, and the latter was only one of many factions in the Dominican armed forces. And it was certainly not to restore Bosch to power that the other factions desired—or would accept—the overthrow of the Triumvirate. Thus the Americans saw the "hotheads" as a negligible quantity within the whole of the nation's armed forces.

As a result, the "hotheads" posed no obstacle whatever to the establishment of a military junta, the solution favored, embassy officials believed, by an overwhelming majority of the Dominican officers. Nor did the "angry young men" of the PRD, grouped around Peña Gómez, pose any real threat: first, because unarmed civilians could do very little against the armed forces;[23] second, because within the PRD a "reasonable" faction, headed by secretary general Antonio Martínez Francisco, had a reassuring "sense of reality." Moreover, the influence that the nation's other mass party, the Reformist, might still enjoy among a certain number of officers would undoubtedly favor the creation of a military junta. This was the Reformists' only hope of getting their leader, former president Joaquín Balaguer, into the Presidential Palace in the not-too-distant future. Lacking any other solution, the remaining parties of the right, all anti-Bosch, would have no choice but to press for a military junta.

The American embassy thus merrily continued to follow the wrong track. Although it had finally awakened to the highly precarious nature of Reid Cabral's position, it still failed to grasp the real aims of the rebel movement. Convinced that the rebels would readily accept the creation of a military junta, the embassy dismissed as impossible the one alternative that the United States could not accept: Bosch's return to power by means of a military revolt carried out by "radical" factions within the armed forces and within the PRD, with the active support of the masses.

Sentiment cannot guide a nation's foreign policy. The American diplomats' one and only task was to safeguard United States interests. On that morning of 25 April, the American embassy was driven to recognize, whatever personal sympathy it felt for Reid Cabral, that henceforth his interests clashed with those of the United States. Only strong pressure from the embassy could push the "loyal" generals to defend the regime. But the price for such pressure might be steep. Despite Washington's desire to keep the highly sensitive Caribbean waters free of all storms, civil war might ensue, carrying with it a host of embarrassing accusations of U.S. interference.

Such risks would have been justified, if they prevented Bosch's return to power. But they were superfluous if the alternative was a "good," "safe" military junta, a tried and true solution that posed no threat to the country's "stability." Reid Cabral had played a certain role, but now he had to step aside. The lack of continuity that Fulbright thought he saw in American policy was only apparent. If on the twenty-fourth the American embassy failed to intervene in behalf of the Triumvirate, it was because intervention seemed unnecessary— and Reid Cabral himself saw no need to request it. On the twenty-fifth the American embassy watched the Triumvirate's agony unmoved, since it was convinced that the outcome of the crisis, thoroughly acceptable to the United States, did not justify the high price of supporting the regime.

It was not a question, therefore, of an unstable policy wrenched by sudden shifts of mood; on the contrary, American policy was utterly coherent and logical. There was only one flaw: the assumptions on which it rested were completely out of touch with reality.

Connett's refusal to come to his aid shattered Reid Cabral's last illusions. Betrayed by his generals, abandoned by the American embassy, Reid was forced to admit that he had no choice. Crowds surrounded the Palace—Dominican citizens who had been crushed and suppressed too long—and violence could have erupted at any moment. Soon, at the Twenty-seventh of February, where Hernando Ramírez had transferred his headquarters, the telephone rang. At the end of the line, the voice of General Montás Guerrero, minister of the interior, informed the rebel leader of Reid Cabral's admission of defeat: "You can come and take the Palace. Donald Reid Cabral is giving it up."[24] Shortly thereafter, around eleven o'clock, about fifty military rebels, led by Colonel Caamaño and Lieutenant Colonel Gutiérrez Ramírez, arrived to take official possession of the Presidential Palace. They arrested Reid Cabral; his inglorious departure came without bloodshed and without tragedy.[25]

The rebels' strategy had paid off once again. The Palace had been taken and the Triumvir arrested without a fight. The Presidential Guard, pressured during the night by the insurgents, had virtually passed to the rebel side even before the arrest of the Triumvir.[26] At the same time, the CEFA units attached to the Palace, hated symbols of the all-powerful San Isidro, were increasingly isolated in the midst of a hostile environment. They grew more and more docile by the hour, so that when, around 9:15 that morning, a bullet from an unidentified rifle wounded the unit commander, Lieutenant Colonel Granpolver Medina, the once jittery tanks and the machine guns kept silent.[27] Soon a gentlemen's agreement was concluded with the insurgents: the CEFA tanks would leave the Palace and return to the security of San Isidro. They departed at approximately the same time that Caamaño and Gutiérrez Ramírez arrived at the Palace. Granpolver Medina's wound was the only price of the operation.

That the rebels did not try to capture Wessin's tanks is one more proof of their "flexibility," their preoccupation with avoiding all but absolutely necessary confrontation. They were convinced that, with victory practically in hand, the tanks, even if they returned to San Isidro, could do nothing to alter the course of events. The population, however, had more sense than the rebel officers, for when the tanks approached the Duarte Bridge, the crowd there refused to let them by. Only the first two tanks were able to get through; the others were abandoned by their crews and subsequently recovered by rebel officers sent by Hernando Ramírez.

When Colonel Benoit finally arrived in the capital, he faced a situation fundamentally different from the one that existed the evening before. And the change was to the detriment of the faction he represented, the Nineteenth of November Air Base. This dramatic shift was mirrored in a significant fact: it was not in a rebel camp, but in the Presidential Palace that the rebels—masters of the house—awaited him. Benoit was aware of this change. One of his first reactions on arriving at the Palace was to regret that the Nineteenth of November had not proceeded immediately after the outbreak of the revolt to arrest Reid Cabral. Air force officers would then have occupied the Palace and received the envoys from the rebel army camps.[28]

A large number of army officers surrounded Lieutenant Colonel Hernando Ramírez in the office in which he received Benoit. No civilians were present. The meeting lasted about an hour, with Hernando Ramírez as the rebels' only spokesman.[29] It was less a conversation than a dialogue of the deaf wherein, from the outset, the interlocutors spoke different tongues. Nothing they said throughout the talk could narrow the gap between them. For Benoit, it was all so plain: the rebels had triggered a revolt against the government; now they were meeting with him to find a solution to the crisis. They were all friends, comrades-in-arms, men of the same calling, who spoke the same language, and who belonged to the same "corporation."

The air force had just given proof of its goodwill. Out of consideration for its comrades in the army, it had agreed to abandon Reid Cabral, although it had no quarrel with him. Thus, an insignificant civilian had been eliminated. But now the rebels wanted another civilian, and what a civilian: Juan Bosch. Colonel Benoit was not questioning the qualities or faults of this man; he felt it might even have been a mistake to get rid of him. He was, after all, the country's constitutional president . . . whatever importance that might have. Yet it was now too late for regrets. Bosch's overthrow might have been a mistake but it was a fact. The armed forces had driven him out, and in so doing, a large number of air force officers had been compromised. How could they now agree to restore him to the presidency? Defense of their own interests forced them to oppose his return, even at the cost of civil war. A compromise solution had to be found that would safeguard the interests of all. It was not all that difficult, nor did it require any special effort at imagination: the power vacuum just created by a sector of the armed forces had to be filled, in a spirit of harmony, by the armed forces themselves. The establishment of a military junta, its composition to be decided at the highest level, was the natural and only solution.

To insist on Bosch, therefore, meant to flout completely the interests of the air force; it signified a desire to cause a schism within the armed forces, hence a civil war. This fact was so striking that only those of bad faith could fail to see it—only those who sought not a compromise but a test of strength, not agreement but division.

Benoit's reasoning was based on the need to accept the fait accompli of 25 September 1963 as an irrevocable reality. But it was precisely that fait accompli that Hernando Ramírez and his officers refused to accept because to do so meant to deny something of far greater importance—the will of the people as expressed in the elections of 20 December 1962, the first free elections since 1924. Two dates—25 September 1963 and 20 December 1962—represented radically different concepts—the old, whereby the ballot box yields to the force of arms, and the new (exalted by Bosch), whereby the force of arms yields to the ballot box and supports it, if necessary.

Alongside these reasons of principle, common sense forbade the rebels from accepting the advances of Colonel Benoit. Benoit rejected Bosch, called for a junta, and promised elections. But what value could these elections have? If the Nineteenth of November was too compromised by Bosch's overthrow to accept him at that time, how could it accept him three months hence, were he to win those much-touted elections?

Benoit's solution—a military junta followed by elections—was a compromise in name only. The Nineteenth of November never intended to discover the real voice of the Dominican people through new elections. On the contrary, its aim was to use a military junta to prevent the return of the intractable, unyielding Bosch. Under the pretext of rejecting the rebel call for Bosch's return to the presidency without elections there lurked an awkward attempt to hide a refusal of the very possibility of free elections.

Acceding to Benoit's proposal in the name of conciliation meant renouncing the ideals for which the insurgents had raised the standard of revolt. Were the constitutionalists to accept a military junta while at the same time endeavoring to remain faithful to their ideals, they would only postpone the test of strength. This would come either at the moment of the promised elections—should the other military sectors try to prevent or control them—or, should the elections take place and be free, the constitutionalists would have to fight to prevent a new military *golpe*. For it was absurd to think that the other sectors would let Bosch be elected and govern unless forced to do so. But in a test of strength, the constitutionalists would be at a distinct disadvantage. The forces that toppled Bosch in 1963, now divided and weakened, would have had the time to regroup. Having lost the advantage of surprise, the constitutionalists would have to battle under far more difficult conditions. They were a minority inside the armed forces, and the distrust engendered by their acceptance of the junta would severely undermine their strength among a Boschist—but unarmed—population.

Compromise, therefore, was impossible. Hernando Ramírez knew what Benoit was proposing, and he could never accept. Benoit, however, failed to grasp what Hernando Ramírez was saying, because the message was too new, too divorced from his experience. All Benoit could see was that the rebels were mocking the goodwill of the air force. Willing to compromise, he met intransigence; he was conciliatory, they were divisive. But why? Benoit did not know. Yet inside him echoed the warnings he had heard so many times at San Isidro: that a united armed forces is the only defense against Communism, that whoever seeks to disrupt that unity is using—consciously or unconsciously—the Communists' favorite tactic. Remember Cuba! Benoit had nothing more to say, so he left the Presidential Palace, carrying with him the painful conviction that civil war was inevitable—because the "other side" wished it.

But civil war would not yet break out. The rebels wanted peace. Convinced that de los Santos would eventually yield, they quickly got in touch with him, asking that his delegate take part in another meeting early that afternoon. When, from the house where he had taken refuge, Benoit phoned his chief to inform him of the failure to reach a compromise, he was astounded to receive orders to return to the Palace.[30]

This second meeting began at about three o'clock, preceded by a new rebel initiative. When Benoit first arrived that morning, the Republic no longer had a president. Reid Cabral had just resigned. Now, on returning, Benoit found a new president in the Palace: José Rafael Molina Ureña—a Boschist.

Benoit's initial refusal did not shake the rebels' optimism. The capital had been taken without a fight. Reid Cabral had resigned and was now a prisoner. The leaders of the movement were in the Palace, while in the streets a jubilant population manifested its support. Assuredly, they thought, the Reformist Party, despite its projunta yearnings, would join the constitutionalist movement. Its only alternative was to rally behind Wessin, a man whose hostility toward

Bosch was matched only by his hostility toward Balaguer. Hernando Ramírez was convinced that the adherence of the Reformist Party would exert a powerful influence on those Balaguerista officers still in the armed forces and on General de los Santos himself, since it was, together with the PRD, the nation's only mass party.[31]

One by one, the garrisons of the interior rallied to the cause. It hardly mattered that their sincerity often seemed dubious. The rebels, in control of the capital, did not think that the support of the garrisons was necessary for victory. All the rebels wanted was their neutrality, and the opportunism of the local commanders, the support of officers at certain military bases—at Santiago, especially—and popular pressure assured this. And although the navy had not yet declared its position, the rebels were convinced that it would soon join their side.

Although the leaders of the revolt had no illusions about the sympathies of the American embassy, they believed that the United States would be forced to accept the new situation. This conviction had been one of the axioms of the conspiracy. It was now strengthened by the embassy's inaction during the first twenty-four hours of the revolt, and in particular by a meeting called by Connett that took place shortly after Reid Cabral's fall between himself and two PRD leaders, Antonio Martínez Francisco and Máximo Lovatón Pittaluga. The talks, held in a house in the Gasque district, lasted only fifteen or twenty minutes and were thoroughly innocuous.[32] Connett warned the two against arming the populace—a Trojan horse by which the Communist threat might penetrate—and asked for assurances regarding the security of American citizens and their property. But he avoided any allusion to the crucial problem of the Triumvirate's succession. Nor did he pass judgment on the revolt, or issue any rebuke over Reid Cabral's overthrow.

Connett's attitude is easily explained. Since he regarded the establishment of a military junta as certain, he had no reason to compromise his government by involvement in internal Dominican affairs. But the significant point here is the impression that Martínez Francisco and Lovatón Pittaluga took away from the meeting. After agreeing to keep in touch with Connett through Martínez Francisco, the two PRD leaders departed with a feeling of euphoria. As they headed toward the Presidential Palace, they carried with them the illusion that the American embassy, reconsidering its position, had decided to adopt a policy of neutrality vis-à-vis the revolt. This illusion was based on a misunderstanding, and it would be short-lived. For the time being, however, the rebels believed that the opposition was limited to San Isidro, which was bereft of American support. But would there really be any opposition? Would de los Santos really fight to prevent Bosch's return to the presidency, as his spokesman Benoit pretended?

The rebels thought not. They took Benoit's words for a bluff, a tactic of intimidation aimed at obtaining by threat what the Nineteenth of November was unprepared to win by force. To succeed, de los Santos could count only on his own forces and on Wessin's, that is, his planes and the tanks of the CEFA. But the rebels were no longer isolated and vulnerable in their camps. They were in control of Santo Domingo and in symbiosis with it. To attack them would mean loosing planes against the capital—never, in all the bloody history of the nation, had this been done. How could de los Santos dare to become the most hated and scorned man in the land, to offer himself to history as the criminal who bombed a defenseless populace?

On the other hand, to send the infantry would mean venturing into the unknown, for even backed by tanks, the troops would be obliged to cross the Duarte Bridge, then pass through the maze of narrow streets in Santo Domingo. In a city of four hundred thousand inhabitants[33] solidly behind the revolt, each house could become a stronghold, each hand hurl a Molotov cocktail, each rebel soldier lead fifty volunteers. The enterprise was too dangerous. The rebels were convinced that de los Santos would shun an adventure in which he stood to lose everything—his career, his freedom, perhaps his life. In support of this conviction, they could point to de los Santos' inaction over the past twenty-four hours, a fair gauge of what was to come.

Besides, why should de los Santos agree to link his fate with Wessin's? Under a Bosch regime, he might indeed lose his position as air force chief of staff. But he was not, as he should have known, the rebels' "number one" enemy; he was not necessarily an enemy at all. In the balance of his interests, the risks of a return by Bosch, however unwelcome, should weigh far less heavily than the risks of a civil war undertaken under such difficult conditions. Thus the rebels concluded that de los Santos would yield, that firmness on their part would convince him to give up his bluff and bow to the inevitable. That left the CEFA. Wessin doubtless harbored no illusions about his future in the event of a Boschist victory. In a purged army, in a new Santo Domingo, there would be no place for him. He, after all, was the "number one" enemy, and he knew it.

But what could Wessin do alone? He had already given proof of his weakness and lack of character by failing to intervene, under far more favorable conditions, on the twenty-fourth. Antonio Llano Montes, the general's intimate and collaborator until their break in 1969, has furnished a gallant if untrue picture of what he purported to be the state of mind of the CEFA during those hours: "At the Training Center, the officers realized that only two paths lay open: they had either to take a heroic decision [to advance on the capital], or retreat to the mountains to pursue the war from there."[34] The rebel leaders took a more sober view of Wessin's reactions. Rather than retreating to the mountains, they imagined him looking for a plane to fly to Miami.

This optimistic view of the situation was shared by the various sectors of the rebel movement.[35] Their unanimity greatly facilitated the task of those civilian or military insurgents who wanted to see a Boschist solution to the crisis. At the outbreak of the revolt, the rebel military consisted of three groups: (1) the "hard-line constitutionalists," who categorically rejected any solution other than a return to constitutional government without elections; (2) the "soft-line constitutionalists," who inclined toward this same solution, but who saw it as a possibility, not a sine qua non; (3) the officers who, though not fiercely opposed to a Boschist solution, preferred the establishment of a military junta. This last group was made up primarily of that handful of Balagueristas who had individually rallied to the cause, of whom the most prominent was Lieutenant Colonel Gutiérrez Ramírez.

Within the PRD itself one finds the same basic categorization: (1) the "hotheads," led by Peña Gómez; (2) the "moderates," grouped around men like Lovatón Pittaluga and Martínez Francisco. These were the civilian counterparts to the military's hard- and soft-line constitutionalists.[36]

But the euphoria of victory swept away the doubts of the soft-line constitutionalists and of the PRD "moderates." Differences faded in that hour of apparent triumph. De los Santos would never fight; Wessin, left stranded, would yield. Why then should the rebels not go ahead and realize the highest goal of their movement? Unity, therefore, was reached between the hard-liners and the soft-liners, between the "hotheads" and the "moderates." And though the unity, based on a particular appraisal of the situation, was fragile, for the moment it sufficed. Once more the projunta sector of the movement could only follow the tide now rising even higher with popular pressure.

The "revolutionary" wing of the PRD did not wait until victory was assured. At dawn, it began urging the population to move to the Duarte Bridge, to block with a human barrier any possible offensive by Wessin. But with the news that a "San Isidro delegate" would shortly arrive in the capital, and, later, that the "San Isidro delegate" (Benoit) was at the Palace, the work of the PRD activists took on a new direction. Strategy shifted from defense to offense. Fearful of a "loss of will" among certain of their military allies and wary of an esprit de corps that might still link many officers—be they *golpistas* or *neoconstitucionalistas*—the PRD "hotheads" turned the crowds on the Presidential Palace, so that thousands of voices might cry out their will and their impatience and prevent the deliberators inside from forgetting that the goal of the movement was to return Juan Bosch to the presidency of the Republic.

Decisive action by some of the rebels, the rallying of others, and the follow-the-leader instinct of the rest held the movement to a Boschist solution, a solution made more reasonable by the general optimism and more necessary by popular pressure.

By midmorning, a rebel-controlled Radio Santo Domingo TV had begun to broadcast appeals to the senators and deputies elected in December 1962, urging them, wherever they were, to gather at the Palace. And so they came: some, like Aníbal Campagna, senator from Santiago, brimming with enthusiasm; others reluctantly, hesitant to trade the peace of their homes for the perils of the capital, but driven by the most zealous among their countrymen to become men of courage.[37] Many never arrived—lack of time thwarted some in the most distant provinces; others succumbed to shortcomings in courage or civic spirit.

But the insurgents were tired of waiting. As champions of the constitution of 29 April 1963, they needed only to apply it. Article 132 of the constitution stated that "in the case of a temporary absence of the President and of the Vice-President of the Republic, Executive Power shall be exercised, for the length of their absence, by the President of the Senate, and, in absence of the latter, by the President of the Chamber of Deputies." Bosch, González Tamayo (vice-president of the Republic in 1963), and Casasnovas Garrido (president of the Senate in 1963) were all in exile, but Molina Ureña, president of the Chamber of Deputies under the Bosch regime, was very much on hand. At approximately two o'clock in the afternoon of 25 April, in conformity with the constitution, Rafael José Molina Ureña became provisional president of the Republic. With Bosch's imposing figure looming behind him, Molina Ureña anxiously emphasized the provisional nature of his presidency. As he took office, he declared: "I assume the Presidency of the Dominican Republic provisionally, until Professor Juan Bosch, the constitutional president, returns to his native soil."[38]

And Bosch's return seemed imminent. *New York Times* correspondent Tad Szulc, in Puerto Rico at the time, wrote:

Now on this sunny April Sunday of 1965, exactly 19 months after he had been thrown out of office, Juan Bosch was getting ready for a triumphant return to the presidency of the Dominican Republic. I found him in his modest second-floor apartment on Sixth Street in the Rio Piedras section of San Juan . . . .

The apartment was full of Dr. Bosch's friends and followers, members of his Dominican Revolutionary Party. It was a joyful bedlam, with the friends embracing the former President and congratulating him on what seemed to be his victory. His wife, Carmen, and his niece and former secretary, Milagro Ortiz, were busy packing the family's belongings. Open suitcases with clothing in them were laid out on the floor. The atmosphere was electric. There was a feeling of anticipation, a sense of urgency, a readiness to return to the homeland.

Bosch expected to be able to return to the Dominican Republic the next day, perhaps even this same night. He was awaiting a military aircraft from the Dominican Republic to carry him back. It was believed it would arrive momentarily.[39]

The die had been cast. With Molina Ureña's accession to the provisional presidency until Bosch's return, the rebel movement, shedding any remaining equivocation, finally assumed its true character. Henceforth no one could speak of "rebels." The men who had arrested Rivera Cuesta and toppled Reid Cabral now claimed formally their rightful name: constitutionalists. They were men fighting to restore the constitutional government elected by the people in December 1962 and overthrown at the hands of criminals on 25 September 1963.

For the "hard-liners" of the movement, Molina Ureña's accession to the provisional presidency marked a victory and an assurance for the future. They

had called de los Santos' bluff and brought about a fait accompli that would
be hard to undo. When toward three o'clock that afternoon Benoit returned
to the Palace to discuss filling the vacuum created by the fall of the Triumvirate, he did not know that the matter had already been settled.[40]

Thus began the second meeting at the Palace.[41] Given the number of participants and the institutions they represented, it was a far more inclusive meeting than the first. In the morning, the rebel officers' sole interlocutor had been
Colonel Benoit for the Nineteenth of November. An agreement would have
created a coalition so powerful that no other force would dare stand up to it; it
would have automatically guaranteed the adherence of the rest of the armed
forces. But there had been no agreement. And so the tête-à-tête with Benoit
was replaced by a broader encounter, which included delegates from the navy
(Lieutenant Commander Emilio A. Guzmán Matos) and the police (Major Rubén
Darío González). There was even an envoy from the CEFA, Colonel Pedro
Medrano Ubiera, though he was only an auditor.[42] The army, allegedly in support of the revolt, was represented only by rebel officers: Lieutenant Colonel
Hernando Ramírez, Captain Peña Taveras, former Captain Lachapelle Díaz (of
the Gas Station Group), Colonel Emilio (Milito) Ludovino Fernández Rojas,
and Lieutenant Colonel Vinicio Fernández Pérez. The first three of these officers
were "hard-line constitutionalists"; the other two, splendid examples of opportunism. Having taken part neither in the conspiracy nor in the first phase of the
revolt, they had joined the movement on the morning of the twenty-fifth,
when victory seemed assured.[43]

There was another difference between the two meetings: in the first, the
rebels had had virtually a single spokesman—Hernando Ramírez; in the second,
each of the officers took part in the discussion. As a consequence, the first
cracks appeared in the rebels' "monolithic" front. After a while, civilians, too,
were present: Molina Ureña, the provisional president, and two other prominent
members of the PRD, Manuel Ramón Ledesma Pérez and Leopoldo A. Espaillat
Nanita, the husband of one of Molina Ureña's nieces.

The second meeting proceeded in two phases: an initial period during which
each representative stated the position of his institution; then a period of general
discussion. It was during this second phase that the three civilians entered the
room. Only then did the "loyalist" officers learn that while they were busy de-
bating the problem of how to replace the Triumvirate, a replacement had already been found. Actually, none of the "loyalists" seemed unduly alarmed,
since according to the customs of the country, a president was one of the most
dispensable of beings, especially when he was not a general commanding his own
troops, but a mere civilian.

Contrary to the rebels' hopes, not only did Benoit maintain his previous
position, but, one after the other, the navy (taking a position for the first time
since the outbreak of the countercoup) and the police (quickly forgetting its

"apolitical" calling) took his side, declaring that the only acceptable solution was the establishment of a military junta. Medrano Ubiera stayed out of the debate. His opinion was not needed; the CEFA's stand was perfectly clear. The first phase of the meeting concluded with Hernando Ramírez reaffirming his position in the name of the army.

The meeting then broke up into a series of separate conversations, with each man striving to detect his opponent's weak spot in order to isolate the "hard-liners." At this point it became apparent that, although Hernando Ramírez had spoken formally for all the rebel officers, some of them had reservations about his "hard-line" position. Benoit therefore concentrated his efforts on the two officers who seemed especially hesitant: Colonel Milito Ludovino Fernández and Lieutenant Colonel Vinicio Fernández Pérez.

Meanwhile, the Nineteenth of November began to rouse itself out of the lethargy that had prevailed ever since Rivera Cuesta's arrest. When de los Santos phoned Benoit, the latter gave his appraisal of the situation: Milito Ludovino Fernández and Vinicio Fernández Pérez show signs of yielding; the big obstacle is Hernando Ramírez. Soon after, an increasingly nervous de los Santos phoned again, this time to issue an ultimatum: should the rebels persist in rejecting a military junta, he would attack with his planes.

The discussions continued in a climate of confusion and exasperation. Suddenly, aircraft from the Nineteenth of November appeared in the sky over the capital; suddenly the Palace was strafed by the planes. Inside, consternation, disarray; for the rebels in particular, indignation and impotent rage. After the first startling moments had passed, the rebels picked up their guns and rushed outside to the Palace gardens. Benoit followed them, hoping that they would forget his role as air force spokesman, which in the heat of the moment could have cost him his life, or at least his freedom. No one spoke further of forming a military junta, of an agreement between "comrades-in-arms." They were "comrades" no longer. The civil war had begun, and at that moment, Colonel Benoit had the painful feeling that his brothers in the air force had betrayed him. They had attacked the lion while he himself sat in the lion's den, unwillingly, on orders from de los Santos. At that moment, Benoit the "negotiator" faced the most important decision of his life as a soldier: return to San Isidro to fight beside those who had just started the war, after professing to seek peace, or stay in the capital with the constitutionalists, who would accept him readily, and with them defend the constitution of 1963 and the elections of December 1962.

Benoit's choice came swiftly. His universe was small—the Dominican Republic—but he confused the "fatherland" with the armed forces. His loyalty to the latter in their hour of crisis took the concrete form of an attachment to the place where he had always lived, where he worked and had his friends: the air base at San Isidro. If he had been a part of one of the rebel camps, he would most likely have stayed on this side of the Ozama, and, with his army "comrades," fought the air force "rebels"—not for Bosch, certainly, nor for the constitution, but because he was not a man to betray his friends. Benoit, however, was a part of San Isidro; thus, he stole out of the Palace gardens to go "home," where he could make a gift of his integrity, his trust, and his devotion to the "fatherland" to unworthy men in the defense of private interests he was only vaguely, confusedly, aware of. For it was not in keeping with his habits—or his moral strength—to ask himself too many questions. That would have destroyed his little world, the illusions of a lifetime.

As we shall see, the San Isidro leaders proved adept at tapping the gold mine they had in Benoit. They exploited this honest, unsuspecting man, using him until the end, and when he was no longer needed they dropped him. When he was retired from the service two years after the revolt, Benoit still failed to comprehend what had happened in the Dominican Republic, what had destroyed him. He collected articles and letters exalting his stance; he used the word "Communist" a lot, though rather undiscerningly. But despite the articles and the letters, his self-confidence was shaken. Anxious to persuade others—and, more so, himself—of the justness of his position, Benoit, alone in a land where to be friendless is dangerous, had become one of the revolution's victims.[44]

After more than a day of wavering, de los Santos had decided on war. Two officers, Lieutenant Colonel Juan René Beauchamps Javier and Major Salvador ("Chinino") Lluberes Montás, "helped" him make the decision: they "went to see General de los Santos . . . and they forced him to give the order to strafe the national [presidential] palace. . . . Major Lluberes surrounded the air force headquarters and Lt. Col. Bochan [sic] at gunpoint ordered General de los Santos to give the order to strafe the positions held by the rebels."[45] The same story, though weighed down by his customary and often fallacious rhetoric, was told by the Cuban refugee Llano Montes, who, as Wessin's counselor and friend, was in a good position to know what was happening at San Isidro:

> That same Sunday, two officers . . . [of San Isidro] performed an action that probably saved the nation from a Communist victory. One of them, Major Lluberes, chief of the Special Forces battalion, went to General Wessin and asked him for a X100 tank in order to carry out a mission in the vicinity of the camp. The general gave the necessary orders to Colonel Perdomo [Rosario], chief of the Armored Battalion, and that same morning [actually around four o'clock in the afternoon] Lluberes was in command of a powerful tank driven by two sergeants. Accompanied by Lieutenant Colonel Beuchamps [sic] Javier, Lluberes set off in his jeep toward air force headquarters. Placing the tank in front of the building, the two officers went upstairs to General [de los] Santos Céspedes's office. The general was in the middle of a meeting with some of the officers of his staff, and scarcely took note of the presence of Beauchamps and Lluberes, who entered with machine guns in their hands. Colonel Beauchamps walked over toward the general, while Major Lluberes, his shoulders pressed against the door, his machine gun fixed on the officers, watched their every movement. When he was a few feet from de los Santos, Beauchamps, pointing his

weapon at him, said: "General, either you give the order to bomb the Palace or we all die here." Visibly nervous, de los Santos replied: "Calm down, Beauchamps, let's examine the situation." But Beauchamps, raising his voice, answered: "There's nothing to examine, general. At stake here are the lives of us all and the fate of the country." And he added: "Wasn't it enough for you to see television to realize that they're going to shoot us all?"[46] De los Santos scanned the room, waiting for some reaction from his officers. But they were silent. Then the general picked up the phone and gave the order to strafe the Palace and the Radio Santo Domingo TV transmitters. Moving toward the window, de los Santos could see the tank trained on his headquarters.[47]

Thus two Wessinist officers—one from the CEFA, the other a Nineteenth of November hard-liner—showed de los Santos the "right" path. But if de los Santos' role appears less than heroic (he gave the order at gunpoint), Wessin does not emerge looking much better. Overcome by the events, he reacted to the countercoup with utter passivity, as if paralyzed. His own description of his activities during those hours of crisis sums it up well: "I remained in my camp, and waited for developments."[48] Faced with such a commander, two subordinates seized the initiative.

At the moment that de los Santos received the order to send the planes into action, the representatives of the various factions of the armed forces were gathered at the Presidential Palace. It seems paradoxical that Wessin, or officers tied to his interests, chose an act of war to stop the talks, particularly since Wessin, unlike de los Santos, had absolutely no contact with those engaged in the discussions.[49] He was therefore unaware that the talks were deadlocked; for all he knew, they might be moving toward an agreement. Viewed more closely, however, the paradox vanishes. The night before, during his talk with Benoit, Wessin had already rejected any kind of negotiations with the insurgents—he wanted them crushed. The reasons for this attitude could not be altered by Reid Cabral's fall. If Wessin ever had doubts as to the rebels' feelings toward him, Hernando Ramírez removed them once and for all when, that morning, he barred Colonel Medrano Ubiera, the CEFA envoy, from entering the office in which the meeting with Benoit was to take place (see n. 42 above). Benoit's reaction to this incident—he watched Medrano Ubiera's departure in silence, raising not the slightest protest—mirrored the Nineteenth of November's position in this crisis.

It was evident, in conditions such as these, that if a military junta was set up, any agreement between the rebels and the air force would damage the CEFA. And it was clear that the navy, the police, or what was left of the Balaguerist forces would never raise objections in defense of Wessin's endangered interests. De los Santos had threatened to send in the air force if the rebels rejected the creation of a military junta: his goal was to reach an agreement with the rebels. But a reconciliation between the "divided brothers" was precisely what Wessin and his clique feared most; thus, the "Wessinists" had to break off the negotiations forcibly and bring the Nineteenth of November, willingly or unwillingly, back to the fold, implicating it in an irreparable rupture. Only then could the CEFA, having broken out of its isolation, plunge into the civil war to defend its interests.

Thus, shortly before four o'clock on the afternoon of the the twenty-fifth, two gun-toting Wessinist officers forced General de los Santos, the air force chief of staff, to give the order to bomb the Palace, triggering civil war in the Dominican Republic.[50] It is possible that, faced with the rebels' refusal to accept a military junta, de los Santos might in the end have chosen to fight, as he threatened to do. Or he might have yielded, agreeing to Bosch's return as president. But these questions will always stand unresolved. "Chinino" Lluberes and Beauchamps Javier, interested paladins of a crippled Wessin, took it upon themselves to lift the burden of decision from de los Santos' shoulders.

Chapter 7

The Balance of Power
at the Outbreak of the Civil War
(the Evening of 25 April)

At the moment the first rebel units entered the capital on 25 April, the military balance of power was roughly as follows:

The rebels commanded approximately 2,350 men; they controlled the three insurgent camps, Sixteenth of August (1,200 men), Twenty-seventh of February (800), 6½ Artillery (250), and the army headquarters (about 100).

If "government forces" refers to those troops which, out of loyalty, discipline, or mere interest, stood ready to obey the orders of their commander in chief, Donald Reid Cabral, then no such forces now existed in the Dominican Republic. Even Wessin, though opposed to the revolt, acted like an independent *caudillo*, wholly detached from the central authority. Ignoring Reid Cabral's appeals, he remained in his camp, refusing to intervene despite his ability to do so.

The "neutrals" included Wessin and the entire Dominican armed forces with the exception, of course, of the few units constituting the rebel movement. Generally speaking, military "neutrality" had two distinctive traits: (1) it gave a decisive advantage to the rebels because "neutrals" would stay out of their struggle against the Triumvirate; (2) all the "neutrals" believed the civilians had no business getting mixed up in a quarrel among the military. Therefore any popular demonstration had to be crushed—an easy task since the people, after a moment of exaltation, had sunk back into passivity. Thus, for the time being, the population played no active role.

The political parties were similarly inactive. When the countercoup broke out, no party supported the Triumvirate; none was about to weep over the possible fall of Reid Cabral, even though they were divided by insurmountable differences regarding his succession.

As for the American embassy, no more need be said except to recall that, blinded by its mistakes, it played no role on the evening of the twenty-fourth.

Thus, as we saw at the end of Chapter 5, error, confusion, fear, and bad faith had tilted the balance of military power in the rebels' favor—2,350 to 0. So they occupied the capital and arrested the Triumvir.

Some sixteen hours later, at about four o'clock in the afternoon on the twenty-fifth, the air force attack marked the start of the civil war. Molina

Ureña's accession to the provisional presidency until Bosch's return made the revolt's purpose clear to all. The new balance of power was particularly complex.

Within the armed forces, the trend toward "neutrality" was widespread among the very officers who proclaimed aloud their adherence to the constitutionalist movement and to the government it had set up. To record mechanically these declarations of support would be to view the events through a distorting lens. For this reason a distinction must be drawn between "hard-line" and "opportunist" constitutionalist units. The latter were units whose commanders, though opposed to Bosch's return to power, were ready to resign themselves to it should that be the will of the mighty. Yet even such a distinction will not allow us to divide the nation's armed forces into two large camps—constitutionalists ("hard-liners" and "opportunists") and "loyalists."[1] To assume such a division would be to underestimate the cleverness of those Dominican military chiefs whose major preoccupation on the twenty-fourth, the twenty-fifth, and always, was to be in a position to demonstrate to the eventual victor, whoever he might be, that they had been on his side from the start. So it is necessary to add a third category, the "uncommitted," including both the "apolitical" and the "undiscoverable." This leaves us with the schema:

(1) Constitutionalist forces
    (a) "hard-line"
    (b) "opportunist"
(2) "Loyalist" forces
(3) "Uncommitted" forces
    (a) "apolitical"
    (b) "undiscoverable."

In addition to the military, we shall consider the civilian sector, which took on a new dimension after the liberation of the capital by the rebel forces. Two aspects will be analyzed: the political parties and the masses. Finally, we shall consider the reactions of the United States government, represented in Santo Domingo by an embassy entirely divorced from reality.

THE ARMED FORCES.

The "hard-line" constitutionalist units were concentrated in the capital, the only city solidly in their hands. Since midnight of the twenty-fourth, their number had increased only slightly. The liberation of the capital led the 450 to 500 men of the Presidential Guard to rally the rebel side. The strong personal prestige of navy Captain Montes Arache ensured the adherence of the 100 to 150 navy frogmen. And slightly more than 100 sailors joined the movement when, won over by young constitutionalist officers, they piled into trucks and drove out of the base at Las Calderas, arriving in the capital on the twenty-fifth. All told, the "hard-line" constitutionalist units now numbered between 3,000 and 3,200 men, all army men except the 200 to 250 sailors. It was a force relatively feeble in numbers, but impressive in the quality of the units that comprised it.[2]

The Dominican armed forces were discussed in Chapter 4. Of the three elite battalions in the army, two—the Francisco del Rosario Sánchez and the Juan Pablo Duarte battalions—made up the backbone of the constitutionalist forces, that is, 1,600 out of the 2,700 army men in revolt. Their firepower was enhanced by the 6½ Artillery's heavy armament and by the munitions seized when the rebels liberated the capital and captured the arms depots at the Palace and the Polvorín. Even Wessin's monopoly of armor was broken when a few armored vehicles were captured as the CEFA soldiers fled the capital. And the frogmen, despite their small number, were a trump whose value should not be underestimated. Antonio Llano Montes writes: "Besides the . . . usual military training, [the frogmen] were expert at judo, expert underwater swimmers, specialists in underwater sabotage, and almost all of them were excellent marksmen." In short, "they were undoubtedly fine fighters, with no lack of valor."[3] Coming from a man who on principle judged his enemies scurrilously, this is high praise.

But a serious weakness undermined the "hard-line" constitutionalist forces. Their units were swarming with officers whose opportunism approached—and often overlapped with—treason. In Chapter 6, the rebel officers at the outbreak of the revolt were classified in three groups: (1) "hard-line constitutionalists," (2) "soft-line constitutionalists," (3) "projunta officers." The alliance between the first two groups had favored the provisional presidency of Molina Ureña; it was based on a mere impression—on a "certain"assessment of the situation. But once San Isidro chose to fight, this optimistic view was doomed to fade. And as optimism gave way to the hard fact of civil war, so vanished the resolve of a great many "soft-line" officers. The "projunta" ranks, meanwhile, had been swollen by the adherence of a group of opportunistic officers. Many had joined on the twenty-fourth because, stationed in the rebel camps, they had thought it dangerous to resist. This was true of a large number of officers of the Twenty-seventh of February. Others had followed, particularly in the morning of the twenty-fifth, because their principles required then to join a winning team. The outbreak of hostilities, however, proved that victory had yet to pick her favorites, and this increasingly distressing uncertainty was to have disastrous consequences on ever so many "loyalties." Yet the constitutionalists held a trump whose potential importance could be gauged only by the testing of the hours. This was the presence within other units of officers linked to the movement— the "periphery"—particularly at San Isidro and Santiago.

The "loyalist" stronghold was at San Isidro, nine miles from the capital. Because of the persuasive tactics of Lieutenant Colonel Beauchamps Javier and Major Lluberes, the *conjunto* had recovered its unity. After more than twenty-four hours of paralysis, it finally began to function. "We became united again,"[4] Wessin later testified.

San Isidro had four thousand men, of which two thousand belonged to the CEFA, the others to the Nineteenth of November. The Fuerzas Especiales, between three and four hundred men, were an elite corps, in the same class with the constitutionalist battalions Juan Pablo Duarte and Francisco del Rosario Sánchez. In light arms, the *conjunto* held no advantage over the constitutionalists; heavy armament, however, was another story. The artillery, especially in the General Gregorio Luperón group, was equipped with materiel superior to that of the 6½ Artillery. The constitutionalists, like the CEFA, had mortars, but the *conjunto* held a monopoly in recoilless cannons. Even worse, de los Santos' adherence gave the "loyalists" absolute control of the skies, since the constitutionalists had no aircraft. The monopoly of the Nineteenth of November could be challenged only by the air base at Santiago and, to a lesser extent, by the one at Barahona. Hence, the importance of their stance was obvious. Despite Wessin's loss of the tanks at the Presidential Palace, he could still count twenty-five or thirty, in addition to several combat tanks and about ten half-tracks. The day before, the constitutionalists had had no armored vehicles; now they faced the enemy with the very vehicles it had lost: about ten tanks. But they lacked the trained personnel to man those tanks.

During the period of the conspiracy the constitutionalists had forged links with officers of the CEFA and the Nineteenth of November. The Enriquillo plan had placed little faith in the CEFA conspirators, since they were too few, and it had failed to exploit the possibilities at the Batalla de Las Carreras Military Academy. The leaders of the conspiracy expected the Nineteenth of November officers linked to the movement to move into action once the counter-coup had been set off. But this never happened. During three telephone conversations in the morning and early afternoon of the twenty-fifth between Major Núñez Nogueras and officers at the Nineteenth of November, the officers justified their passivity by pointing out that since de los Santos had not yet taken sides, any action from them would be untimely. By the time of the fourth conversation, it was too late: "It's all over. We've been taken prisoner!"[5] Whether due to circumstances or their own inadequacies, the conspirators at the air base failed to seize the opportunity to play a role in those first confusing hours. At the outbreak of the civil war de los Santos was unable to count on the unswerving loyalty of all his officers, but the risk of open mutiny was thwarted when, on the afternoon of the twenty-fifth, those officers most suspected of constitutionalist sympathies were arrested. There was no "Chinino" Lluberes or Beauchamps Javier among the constitutionalists at the Nineteenth of November.

The Military Academy—for Wessin, a "viper's nest"—counted 9 officers, 144 cadets, and 10 or 12 noncommissioned officers.[6] Its armament consisted of X1 mortars, light model 30 machine guns, a few heavy machine guns, and some bazookas. After Major Núñez Nogueras and two other officers were cashiered on 4 September 1964, conspiratorial activity virtually died out at the Academy. But the Academy had been profoundly marked by men like Lieutenant Colonel Fernández Domínguez and Núñez Nogueras, and would continue to be "a haven for persons whose heads were full of strange ideas."[7]

From the beginning, the Academy was sympathetic toward those across the river who had raised the flag of revolt. Unlike the officers at the Nineteenth of November, the *académicos* moved into action. An academy officer later wrote:

> Though from the first it was our idea to turn our backs on Wessin, it wasn't until Sunday, after we officers had reached agreement, that the departure was planned, for up until Sunday (the twenty-fifth) the departure had not been plotted among us as a group, because of distrust among the officers. At noon on Sunday part of us nine officers who later left decided to abandon the Academy and join the people, even though to do so it would be necessary to take with us as a prisoner any officer not in agreement with our goal. Some of the oldest cadets had knowledge of the agreement and were with us; the others would not be told of the plan until it was under way so as to prevent a betrayal to the CEFA. The ten or twelve recruits who later accompanied us were also not told about the plan until it was under way, except for a sergeant major who from the outset had taken part in the planning. The plan was not communicated to the CEFA officers, because they seemed wary of the "académicos." The CEFA officers lunched that Sunday in the Academy mess hall, carrying their guns, a sign that they distrusted us, and that was why none of them were told, so as to prevent our being discovered.

Soon after the outbreak of the civil war the *académicos* went into action: "We left the Academy in the evening of the twenty-fifth. Only three officers and a few soldiers, who were absent when we left the compound, remained behind."[8]

San Isidro faced a fresh threat. But the scope of that threat would depend on what use the new "rebels" made of their forces and on the energy of their leaders.

A peril far graver than the Academy's defection threatened San Isidro, a peril inherent in the nature of a system dominated by corruption. San Isidro was weakened from within. First, it lacked qualified officers. With a few rare exceptions ("Chinino" Lluberes, for one) the level of competence— starting with Wessin—was exceedingly low. The rank and file, too, was seriously impaired. Some of San Isidro's men may have thought it necessary to fight because they had been infected with virulent anti-Communist propaganda, out of loyalty to their chiefs, or to thwart what they saw as a threat to their privileged status. Yet it is clear that whereas many rebel soldiers could identify with the cause for which they were asked to fight, for the great majority of "loyalists" such identification was altogether impossible.

On the morning of the twenty-fifth, when a rebel victory seemed assured, the military leaders of the interior suddenly revealed their love for democracy, until then a jealously guarded secret. Declarations of adherence to the movement poured in from all the army bases around the country except the Fortaleza of San Juan de la Maguana.[9] The air bases at Santiago and Barahona followed the trend.

To avoid a long and tedious enumeration, we shall use Santiago as a model. Santiago was the nation's second-ranking city, heart of the Cibao—the Republic's richest region—a city whose military significance was enhanced because it headed one of the country's four military zones and controlled the second most important air base. In Santiago, the fresh enthusiasm of Colonel José R. Félix de la Mota, army commander of the military zone, suddenly knew no limits. Fearing that the democratic spirit that had seized him might not be visible enough to the victors, around ten in the morning he unexpectedly appeared "for a drink" at the house of Don Antonio Guzmán, a rich landowner of the region, a personal friend of Juan Bosch, and one of the foremost PRD leaders in the city. He left only after repeatedly declaring his support of the constitutionalist movement, claiming to one and all that he was "on the side of the people."[10] Soon the radio broadcast this message:

> By means of the present communiqué, the joint commands of the National Army, the Dominican Air Force, and the National Police of the Northern Zone, with their seat at Santiago, announce to the people, for its information: That, conscious of their obligations as military men and identified with the people's cause, they have decided to support the people's appeal, and hereby declare their solidarity with the military movement originating in Santo Domingo.
> Signing this communiqué are:
>
> —José R. Félix de la Mota
>   colonel in the National Army
>   commander of the National Army's 2d Brigade
>
> —Caonabo Jaquez Olivero
>   colonel in the National Police
>   commander of the Northern Department[11]
>
> —Francisco A. Ramírez Gómez
>   colonel in the Air Force
>   commander of the Santiago Air Base
>
> —Miguel A. Calderón Cepeda
>   captain in the National Army
>   adjutant to the commander of the National Army's 2d
>   Brigade.[12]

Soon, either to avoid clashes with the people or out of fear of fraternization between civilians and military, "the entire Armed Forces [were] confined to quarters."[13] Even the presence of the police on Santiago streets became discreet, and the few policemen still to be seen appeared to prefer the role of unconcerned bystanders.[14] Soon the military authorities turned to the PRD leaders to ensure order, since the local authorities installed by the Triumvirate had fled.

Such was the facade; behind it, at Santiago and elsewhere, lurked a very different reality.

The hierarchy was respected; military power, both in form and in fact, was still in the hands of senior officers who had no sympathy for this disquieting military revolt. The junior officers remained passive in their subordinate positions. Yet some of them belonged to the conspiracy and should have profited from the situation to secure the support of their units. This was an enterprise demanding a taste for fresh responsibilities, rather than a blind respect for rank.

Although enthusiastic and emboldened the people remained unarmed; weapons were the monopoly of the armed forces and the police, a monopoly easily justified by the apparent absence of any threat to the constitutionalist victory. The garrisons in the interior were "unanimous" in their support; San Isidro would not fight.

But this sudden constitutionalist veneer was so thin that the slightest touch, the slightest pressure, would have rubbed it off. Would the constitutionalists be able to transform these verbal vows, made when their victory seemed assured, into real support, now that their victory was openly contested? Or, losing even the neutrality of these dubious adherents, would they find themselves facing open hostility? Nothing was settled. The game had just started. The dynamism of civil war was about to impose its disrupting rhythm, whereby every apparent but unproved gain would be constantly called into question, every pledge of loyalty broken as fast as it had been made.

Sometime during the night of the twenty-fourth, General Despradel Brache discovered the "apolitical" calling of his National Police. Only a few hours later, however, his spokesman, Major González, was at the Palace expressing the open hostility of the police to Bosch's return to the presidency and adopting the position of the Nineteenth of November. The air force attack then cut off the negotiations, marking the start of the civil war. Logic demanded that the police, faithful to Major González's declarations, support San Isidro against the rebels. But such a stance would have been wholly out of keeping with the opportunism of Despradel Brache. During the meeting at the Palace, it was easy for González, backed by the delegates of the Nineteenth of November and the navy, to take a "hard" line, breaking sharply with the previous night's prudence. But the hail of machine-gun fire from the skies swept away all the threats; words now had to yield to action. With civil war beginning, San Isidro and the fleet were remote; the constitutionalists were inside the capital, supported by an enthusiastic populace unwilling to submit. This was too much for Despradel Brache. At the moment of decision, he suddenly remembered that the forces under his command were not to get mixed up in disputes among the military. The police were "apolitical!"

For Despradel Brache, "apolitical" meant a refusal to fight as long as the enemy could defend itself, a willingness to serve the Boschistas if they were to triumph. But it also meant that, should they find themselves at bay, the constitutionalists would be forced to hold off an enemy within their very stronghold—Santo Domingo—unless they had the foresight to crush that enemy while there was still time.

In Santo Domingo on the afternoon of the twenty-fifth, the former chief of police, General Belisario Peguero, was waiting to flee to San Isidro. In a remarkable example of continuity in command, the current chief of police, General Despradel Brache, waited to do the same. There were three thousand police in the capital, many of them scattered among a series of small, militarily indefensible stations spread throughout the various districts of the city. And there were two larger bases, the National Police Headquarters and the Fortaleza Ozama, far from inconsequential on paper . . . but then, on paper, San Isidro should have crushed the rebels at the outset.

Less sophisticated than the forces in the capital under Despradel Brache, the police and their commanders elsewhere in the country did not pretend to be apolitical. Their attitude toward the revolt evolved, as we saw in Santiago, from one of open hostility to one of "sincere" support.

At the meeting at the Palace on the afternoon of the twenty-fifth, the naval representative, Lieutenant Commander Guzmán Matos, had supported the stance of the Nineteenth of November. But the position of the navy was far from clear. Would it cling to its "hard" line, which had completely surprised the constitutionalists, or, after a few threats, would it finally join the revolt? The question was justified, given the highly "discreet" position adopted by Admiral Rivera Caminero on learning of the countercoup. Hence the classification of the navy as "undiscoverable."

On the afternoon of the twenty-fourth, Rivera Caminero was at navy headquarters in the western sector of the capital, on the outskirts of the city in the La Feria district. The tiny Dominican fleet was scattered, some ships in the Santo Domingo harbor, others at various ports throughout the country. When news of the revolt came in, Rivera Caminero reacted by unleashing a "high seas operation"; by two o'clock the first ship left Santo Domingo while those at other Dominican ports hastened to join the bulk of the fleet in a predetermined spot on the high seas, not far from the capital. Militarily, this was a sound maneuver—a regrouping of forces in anticipation of battle. But the behavior of Rivera Caminero lent a special character to the move. The admiral vanished, leaving La Feria for a quieter spot—Haina, according to Rivera Caminero himself;[15] the high seas, according to others. From his refuge, wherever it was, he sent declarations of support to Reid Cabral, until the moment when, like de los Santos, he announced that he had no intention of defending the Triumvirate.[16] Then there was silence, until his delegate arrived at the Presidential Palace. In the meantime, however, segments of the navy—the frogmen, the seamen of Las Calderas—had joined the movement.

Once again, after Guzmán Matos' departure from the Palace, the curtain fell. When it rose again, eleven hours later, it was to reveal Rivera Caminero mounting the steps to the Palace, this time to announce his support of the Molina Ureña government (see Chapter 8).

THE CIVILIAN ELEMENT.

Several problems arise in attempting to define the positions of the various political parties at the outbreak of the civil war. No party leaders, except, of course, some in the PRD and their allies in the PRSC, expected the Boschistas to set off a coup d'état on 24 April 1965 or any other date. In fact, the Boschista leaders themselves—not to mention the Social Christians—did not expect the countercoup to break out on the twenty-fourth. Surprise made a swift reaction more difficult, particularly for those parties which, unlike the PRD and the PRSC, were surprised not only by the timing, but by the very fact of a military uprising. Doubts as to the insurgents' actual aims heightened the confusion. Moreover, the period under consideration was especially brief: scarely twenty-eight hours elapsed between the outbreak of the countercoup and the start of the civil war.

For the historian the gathering of information on the positions of the various political parties during those twenty-eight hours poses problems of its own. Government control was maintained in the capital until the early hours of the twenty-fifth, and until midmorning in the other cities. In these circumstances, radio and television, except for a brief lapse on the afternoon of the twenty-fourth, could broadcast only the government's views. With the collapse of the Triumvirate, the constitutionalists took over the airwaves, and although the voice was new, it still broadcast only one version. The newspapers as well offer little to ease the historian's task. What, indeed, could they add? Most political parties had better things to do than publish manifestos, which might in the near future be transformed into incriminating evidence. Except in rare cases, ambiguity best served the interests of the political parties during those early hours of the Dominican crisis.

The gravity of these problems varies from party to party. Our interest in them also varies, according to the importance of each party, its role in the upcoming struggle, or the reactions provoked by its mere existence: for example, the red of the far left was to provoke the highly touchy American bull to a paroxysm. We shall examine, in turn: (1) the microparties of the right; (2) the Reformist Party; (3) the parties of the Rio Piedras Pact; and (4) the parties of the far left. We shall not, however, consider all the parties existing at the time in the Dominican Republic. The Alianza Social Democrática of self-proclaimed Marxist Juan Isidro Jimenes Grullón and the Partido Nacionalista Revolucionario of "Corpito" Pérez and Dato Pagan, two "old Communists," will not be included in our discussion. These "pocket-parties"—minuscule even compared to the microparties of the right—played no role. Their leaders were not even in the country.

The Church and the trade unions deserve only a brief word. The Church could not sympathize with a revolt aimed at restoring to power a man who had aroused its distrust, often even its hostility, and with whom it had clashed bitterly two years earlier. Of the major unions, FOUPSA-CESITRADO was in the

PRD camp, and the leaders of CASC, already aware of the conspiracy, stood staunchly behind the principle of a "return to constitutional government without elections." The leaders of CONATRAL, however, linked to the American embassy and to the interests of the country's conservative sector, could only oppose any effort to bring back to power a man whose fall they had hailed some nineteen months earlier.

Deeply hostile to Reid Cabral, the leaders of the microparties of the right[17] applauded a revolt to overthrow him. Even more violently anti-Bosch, however, they would fiercely oppose the return of a man they had helped to topple.

It is impossible to know exactly at what point the rightist leaders realized that the rebel movement was Boschist. Molina Ureña's accession to the provisional presidency, however, must have shocked them into recognition; the steadily growing role of the masses and the fraternizing between civilians and military intensified their fears. During the Triumvirate they had fought bitterly among themselves, against Reid, against Wessin. But now there was no alternative. Henceforth San Isidro's cause was theirs:

> And they beat their heads bloody,
> brawling over the plunder,
> calling the others greedy jerks
> and themselves the good guys.
> We see them endlessly hating
> and fighting each other. Only then
> when we no longer nourish them
> are they suddenly together as one.[18]

These leaders could hardly have hoped to help defeat the Boschistas by using their influence with the people. For most Dominicans, the parties of the right had ceased to exist—if indeed they had ever existed. Mobs had already set fire to some of their offices. When Héctor Aristy, vice-president of the Partido Liberal Evolucionalista and an ambitious young man undaunted by self-contradiction, hastened to the Twenty-seventh of February to join the revolt, he was received coldly.[19]

These old "captains" of politics, in the worst sense, had often lacked popular support. In the December 1962 elections, no one had rallied around their tattered flags; only the UCN drew any support, and it quickly ceased to be a mass party. Their strength lay elsewhere: in money, in contacts with the U.S. embassy, the military, the clergy.[20] These were assets that would not count for much if the struggle was brief, but they could be exploited if the constitutionalists failed to win a swift victory.

For the Reformist Party Reid Cabral's will to cling to power and his "flexibility" in the means to that end barred the path to the Palace. The Balagueristas had attempted to answer this arrogance by a military coup. Even though the revolt that finally broke out was not theirs, it was aimed at toppling the man who prevented Balaguer from returning to the Republic. The presence among the movement's apparent leaders of officers like Gutiérrez Ramírez and Alvarez Holguín, men known to be sympathetic to Balaguer, could only reassure the party. Through Reid Cabral, the rebels struck at Wessin, the archfoe of the Balagueristas.

On 25 April, in a statement to the Associated Press, Balaguer showed a cautious sympathy for the rebel movement, which he saw as "the people's rejection of bad Government." He attributed the revolt above all to "the Triumvirate's reluctance to hold free and honest elections."[21] Already on the evening of the twenty-fourth, Colonel Pérez Aponte, commander of the Balaguerist Ramón Mella Battalion, promised Hernando Ramírez his support. Though only a verbal pledge, this promise nonetheless contrasted favorably with the attitude held at the moment by the other military chiefs in the country.

Early on the morning of the twenty-fifth, Balaguerist and PRD activists mingled in a common effort to mobilize the people at the Duarte Bridge in order to form a human barrier against a possible thrust by Wessin's tanks. Yet when it was made known that a representative of the Nineteenth of November (Colonel Benoit) had arrived at the Presidential Palace to begin negotiations, the Duarte Bridge witnessed the first incidents between the Boschistas and the Balagueristas. The latter took a dim view of the PRD effort to assemble crowds around the Palace to press for Bosch's return to the presidency and against the installation of a military junta, just the opposite of what the Reformist Party wanted. Clashes broke out between activists on both sides, each giving orders to the people and countering the instructions of the other ("To the Palace!"— "No, stay at the bridge!"). Once the Triumvirate had fallen, the prime motive for unity collapsed. Henceforth, the two parties pursued opposite ends.

From New York, Balaguer indicated his own wishes for a solution to the crisis: "The formula best suited to bringing peace to the country would be a new popular election."[22] Balaguer's partisans in the Dominican Republic were not surprised. Such a solution had been the Reformist Party's rallying cry from the start. And during the conspiracy, it had been the stumbling block that had shattered the unity of action between Balagueristas and Boschistas. The PRD leaders had no illusions about the sentiments of the Reformist leaders concerning a Boschist solution to the crisis, for such a solution postponed indefinitely the dreams of power of Balaguer and his partisans. They were convinced, however, that once Bosch was installed, the Balagueristas, faced with the alternative of an uncertain and risky alliance with Wessin, would yield and accept Bosch as president. Certainly, the Balagueristas knew that they could depend on Bosch's fairness and that under him there would be no more exiles. Balaguer would be free to return to the Dominican Republic and devote himself to strengthening his party and planning his future electoral campaign.

But this belief was illusory. Francisco Augusto Lora, at the time Balaguer's number one spokesman in the Dominican Republic, has stressed the impasse facing the Reformists, torn between Scylla and Charybdis—between Bosch and

Wessin. According to Lora, this impasse paralyzed the party, and it did not emerge from its paralysis until four long months later, with the establishment of the Godoy government.[23] But Lora has unjustly reproached both himself and his colleagues. From the outset, the Reformist Party rejected any position that would have reduced it to a passive bystander, a role too much in conflict with its aspirations. The choice between Scylla and Charybdis was made. On the afternoon of the twenty-fifth, or on the morning of the twenty-sixth, Lora and other Balaguerist leaders arrived at San Isidro.

Their trip was a carefully guarded secret. The constitutionalist cause had to be thwarted. Civil war was now not only necessary, but desirable. It remained for others, however, to take up arms and break the rebels' drive and the masses' ardor, and so incur the people's hate. Hiding its ties to San Isidro and urging Wessin to fight—yet hoping to see him weakened—observing an official neutrality and preaching moderation, the Reformist Party preserved its freedom of action and prepared for the future.[24]

The Reformists' adherence to the constitutionalist cause would have created a common front between the nation's two mass parties and made massive U.S. intervention in Dominican internal affairs more difficult. It might have influenced the attitude of certain Dominican military chiefs. In particular, it might have spurred the officers of the elite Mella Battalion to rally firmly to the constitutionalists. Militarily, that would have been a considerable addition.

It is difficult to measure the immediate import of the Reformist Party's anticonstitutionalist stance. The Reformistas were believed to enjoy the support of broad sectors of the population—but the constitutionalists could hardly complain about their lack of popular support during those fateful days. As for the military impact, the addition of the Mella Battalion to the anticonstitutionalist cause might, on 27 April, have proved decisive—and yet, because of deep-seated rivalries among the "loyalists," it lost nearly all its significance (see Chapter 9). Thus, in the short run, the Reformistas were less important than one might have thought; yet here again, as with the "microparties" of the right, they could assume greater significance should the struggle be prolonged.

At the outbreak of the civil war, the PRD "moderates" and "hotheads" had just come together in mutual acceptance of the position of a "return to constitutional government without elections." This unity may seem artificial, since it rested on an optimistic view of the situation that events were soon to belie. But a decisive step had been taken with Molina Ureña's accession to the provisional presidency. From that moment on, it became particularly difficult for the "moderates" to back out. To do so would be to betray the movement and yet would not influence the masses in the capital, the majority of whom were won over to the "hothead" line. And so, the PRD entered the civil war. A party created to win elections, not to fight armed struggles, the PRD found itself immersed in an enterprise for which it was totally unprepared.

At the outbreak of the countercoup, the two leaders of the PRSC's *duro* wing, Antonio Rosario and Caonabo Javier, were abroad, but their absence did not seem to weaken the Social Christians' support of the constitutionalist cause. Probably under the impact of the rebels' first victories, the leaders of the party's *flojo* wing, Guido d'Alessandro and Jesús Caminero, announced their adherence.[25] The PRSC's unity suddenly seemed restored.[26] Yet the party's contribution to an armed struggle against San Isidro would be minimal. Not only did the PRSC match the PRD in lack of military training and "guerrilla" mentality, but it had far fewer partisans.

The PRSC, moreover, had lost any influence it had had on CASC, the powerful labor federation of Social Christian leanings. Run by energetic leaders jealous of their prerogatives, CASC clung to its independence and did not wait for instructions from the PRSC before acting.

If, in the short run, the Social Christian contribution to the constitutionalist cause was practically nil, in the long run it offered certain advantages. In the extended period of "trench warfare" that followed the United States military intervention, the presence of the PRSC held out a guarantee of "democracy" to a movement "tainted" by the participation of the far left.[27] And the PRSC's links with the Christian Democratic family in the world, though not to be overestimated, were of some use, especially in Chile and Venezuela.

The reactions of the far left during these first twenty-eight hours encompassed points of conjunction and important divergences.[28]

Surprise was a reaction common to all the far-leftist parties. They were aware that the PRD was plotting with the military, but they never thought that anything would come of it. Moreover, they had only a very vague knowledge of the conspiracy. The leaders of the far left were thus totally unprepared for an event they had dismissed with a frivolity skirting mindlessness. Lacking a precise strategy, they were forced to improvise a line of conduct. This was particularly difficult, since the various leaders were scattered when news of the military coup broke. At dawn on Saturday, 24 April, for instance, the *catorcista* leader Amín Abel Hasbún set out for Puerto Plata, 147 miles north of Santo Domingo, to get married. Others "were taking a siesta or were at some beach when, at 1:55 in the afternoon, José Francisco Peña Gómez announced the arrest of the army chief of staff and the uprising at the 16th of August Military Camp."[29] Peña Gómez's announcement inaugurated a phase of regrouping, during which the absent leaders sought to return to the capital.

The MPD was in particular difficulty, with the four chief members of its Central Committee unavailable. The party's *caudillo*, López Molina, deported on 8 May 1964, was still in France. Cayetano Rodríguez, also deported on 8 May and later arrested trying to re-enter the country clandestinely, had just been transferred because of ill health from La Victoria Prison to the Padre Billini Hospital in the capital, where he remained under police surveillance. José Ramírez ("El Conde"), the Central Committee member who during López Molina's absence had gained the most authority, was in China. Maximiliano Gómez ("El Moreno"), the fourth leading member of the Central Committee, was at home, in San Pedro de Macorís, but returned to the capital that same evening in time to take part in the Central Committee meeting.

The leaders of the far left were granted a breathing spell when, on the afternoon of the twenty-fourth, the tide of the rebel thrust in the capital ebbed. It was a chance to pause and plot a strategy. But, to do so, they had to meet, and thus first to get in touch, an undertaking far more difficult than one would think for parties in which goodwill too often substituted for solid organization. They also needed to find safe meeting places. Each of these leaders was in danger of being arrested by patrols prowling the streets. They cautiously determined to wait until nightfall.

A second reaction common to the parties of the far left was distrust. They had condemned the PRD conspiracy as a reactionary ploy. The conspiracy had given birth to the countercoup, and the far left censured both. Nevertheless, the judgment of the various parties—and of the many factions within them—regarding the conspiracy was not unanimous; it ranged from the blind intransigence of the MPD to the open-mindedness of the 1J4's Military Bureau, from the narrow sectarianism of the *catorcistas* to the more flexible sectarianism of the PSP *jóvenes*.

Our statement must therefore be qualified. Although an instinctive distrust characterized the initial reaction of the far-leftist leaders, it varied in intensity from group to group, the 1J4's Military Bureau representing a special case, as in the preceding period.

A party's attitude toward the conspiracy—that is, its dogmatism—determined the speed with which that party was able to face reality. The first to do so was naturally the PSP. During the night of 24-25 April, the party's Central Committee met to decide on a stance.[30] There were two possibilities:(1) the party could take refuge in inaction, distrusting any military revolt, or (2) it could act, in the hope of steering the coup d'état in a democratic direction.

A number of factors made the Central Committee members' choice less difficult. First, their condemnation of the conspiracy had never been absolute. They rejected the means by which Bosch was trying to return to power, but not the principle. Then there were other reasons, linked to the events of the preceding hours—events which unfolded even as they met. First was the attitude of the people. The population supported the revolt—nobody doubted that; even militants of the far left were swept up in the general enthusiasm. The PSP leaders, anxious not to "cut themselves off from the masses,"[31] were impressed by the intensity of enthusiasm, the fervor of popular support. The Central Committee also considered the attitude of the rebel troops. The first rebel units had just entered the capital; fraternizing between civilians and military was evident and not always limited to hugs and words: weapons, though still in small numbers, were being distributed to the people.

The Central Committee chose, therefore, to support the revolt, but its distrust of the military lingered. The PSP's task would thus be to "democratize" the coup. This goal could be reached only by working through the masses: by integrating with them, by bringing to them the dynamism and the political consciousness of the party's militants. In this way, the masses might become more than sheep trailing blindly behind the PRD and might impose a democratic stamp on the rebel movement—the one safeguard for the future. Above all, the PSP had to prevent the rebel officers from establishing a military junta. This concern was in no way unique; the same preoccupation absorbed the PRD activists.

But the PSP contributed more significantly. Suddenly the walls of the capital were plastered with posters urging "arms to the people—PSP." The party "called on all the people to take up arms in behalf of the Constitution. The slogan was appropriate, because it gave a popular tone to what might have been a cold military coup."[32] Thus there was an important difference between the PSP's position (soon adopted by the MPD and the 1J4) and that of the PRD. As a party, the latter remained loyal to the decision made during the preparation of the countercoup: that civilians should not be armed. But this in no way prevented many PRD militants from urging that arms be distributed to the people.

Long before 24 April, the 1J4 took a more intransigent stand than did the PSP. The *catorcistas* were equally adamant in rejecting both the kind of plot in which the PRD was engaged and any Boschist alternative to the Triumvirate. The PSP *jóvenes* acknowledged the risk that Bosch might become a Betancourt. The 1J4's verdict was in: Bosch *was* the Dominican Betancourt. Within the party, however, the Military Bureau kept aloof from this witch hunt. Although its estimate of the PRD and its leader more or less overlapped with that of the PSP *jóvenes*, the Military Bureau went further. It regarded not only Bosch's return but also the PRD military conspiracy as the best possible solution, given the balance of power within the Republic. Furthermore, of the Dominican far left, only the Bureau believed the Boschistas capable of triggering the revolt.

Because of its unsectarian assessment of the goals of the conspiracy and its faith in the conspiracy's realization, the Military Bureau was surprised by the timing, not by the outbreak of the revolt on 24 April. Unlike the Central Committees of the three parties of the far left, therefore, the Bureau was not compelled to improvise completely in the hours that followed. Its choice to support the revolt had already been made.

Although the revolt had broken out, the insurgents were still in their camps and the government forces still in control of the capital. The weakness of the Military Bureau forced it into a hateful passivity relieved only by the hope of imminent activity. "Forego action, but be ready to act as soon as the situation permits"[33]—the Military Bureau tried to send these instructions to the various commandos under its direction. At the same time, the Bureau attempted to reach the members of the CECP to persuade them to support the revolt. During the night of 24-25 April, the first meeting took place.[34] But the representatives of the Military Bureau faced the same intransigence they had met during the previous months. Some members of the CECP, the *flojos* in particular, now conceded that the revolt might not be an imperialist "trick." Yet they remained as passive as the *duros*, who saw the threatening shadow of the Pentagon behind every rebel officer. Indeed, both groups came to the same conclusion: the safest course was to wait. But the first rebel units were already in the capital! It was too much—the frustrated leaders of the Military Bureau walked out of the meeting.

The members of the Bureau had again failed to persuade the leaders of their party. The Bureau, however, had long felt itself autonomous inside a party where personal ambitions and factional struggles had reduced discipline to a vague memory. There was no formal rupture, no excommunications. But between the passivity of the CECP and the exalted crowds in the streets, the leaders of the Military Bureau had made their choice: "We decided to act on our own."[35]

Early the next morning the CECP met. The people's support of the rebels and the fraternizing between civilians and military were realities. It became more and more difficult to shut one's eyes to these facts, particularly since the 1J4 now found itself trapped in an intolerable position. In the number of its adherents and sympathizers, the 1J4 was the "mass party" of the Dominican far left, the only party that was more than just a cluster of cadres. But it was also the most undisciplined. The bulk of its partisans had already engaged in open, enthusiastic support for the revolt. The CECP found itself increasingly isolated. Memories of December 1962 were revived: the people were clamoring for elections, but the 1J4 Central Committee ordered a boycott of the polls; the people voted en masse, and the party covered itself with ridicule. In November 1963, plunging into guerrilla action, the 1J4 had similarly failed to understand the nation's temper. The martyrs of Manaclas had turned a tragicomedy into an epic, yet the defeat dealt the party a crushing blow. The betrayal—both real and imagined—surrounding that defeat aroused a distrust that soon exceeded the bounds of good sense. Now the party leadership had once again chosen a solitary route. But this time there was more to pay than the ridicule of a disastrous electoral abstention or the somber heroism of a hopeless cause. This time the price would be shame for those cowering in a corner while in the streets the people fought to recover their liberty. The thought of "being discredited with the masses"[36] was especially intolerable for young men who had already proved their eagerness to plunge into the struggle even against good sense. A majority in the CECP took shape, calling for action, even at the risk of falling into the "imperialist trap." Besides, due either to a serious analysis of the events of the past few hours or to a compulsion to act, the risk now seemed slight.

Yet a minority balked. Although it now conceded the possibility that the Boschist rebels were not acting at the behest of Washington, it wanted more information, more time to think. This group was made up of many *duros*, but the balance was tipped by those among Despradel's friends, especially Juan Miguel Román, who joined the *flojos* in clamoring for action.

The first steps were taken under the impetus of this newly formed majority. In their conception, if not in their details, they were like those taken by the Central Committee of the PSP a few hours earlier; the same preoccupations inspired them. The city was divided into several zones, each headed by a CECP member ("zone chief") supported by a group of cadres. The chief was responsible for "organizing" the zone. His main job was "to rouse and direct the masses"[37] in his sector so that, under the prodding of the 1J4 activists, the people would cease to be the blind executants of the PRD's will and would demand the "democratization" of the revolt.

Of the parties of the far left, the MPD suffered the most harrowing evolution.[38] When the Central Committee met late in the evening of the twenty-fourth, its verdict was decisive: the revolt was an imperialist trap and the MPD would not be taken in. The party would "stand aside."[39] The best-known leaders—those most likely to be arrested—were to remain in hiding; the others were to gather news and try to maintain contact with the party cadres and with the 1J4. Needless to say, no contact was envisaged with the PSP. But in the face of "rampaging imperialism," few dared to emerge from their prudent passivity. In fact, according to our information there was no communication among the parties of the far left, neither between the MPD and the 1J4 nor between the latter and the PSP. A few MPD members, left to themselves, "fell into the trap," and joined the crowds acclaiming the rebels.

As the hours passed and the sun came up, a little light managed to reach even the MPD leaders. Shaken by the complexity of the situation, the Central Committee relaxed its stance. In the morning, "informally and from mouth to mouth,"[40] the Central Committee ordered the party cadres to join in all the demonstrations so as to steer them in a "democratic" direction. Distrust lingered, however—until swept away in the afternoon by the machine-gun fire from the San Isidro airplanes. The bourgeois nature of the coup remained, but the MPD no longer saw it as an imperialistic trap.

Nor did the 1J4. That afternoon, the party's CECP met again to get its bearings. The decisions made at the earlier meeting had been adopted over the objections of a group of especially "prudent" leaders and had at times been implemented with a timidity born of distrust. But the air assault against the Palace furnished final, decisive proof. A new zeal fired the members of the CECP. The hours lost seemed all the more grievously wasted now that all doubts had fled.

The emergent civil war gave new dimensions to a revolt that the *catorcistas* had thought to be a "bourgeois-democratic" coup at best. The bounds of that coup had exploded. It was up to the 1J4 to exploit this unexpected opportunity and to shoulder the responsibilities that went with it.

A guerrilla party, one that had always advocated armed struggle as the only answer to the nation's ills, the 1J4 believed that this was the chance that, seventeen months earlier, they had sought in vain in the mountains of Quisqueya. The CECP was determined not to lose it.

Designating a three-man Political Committee (Jimmy Durán, Fidelio Despradel, Pin Montás), the CECP set out "with all of its energy to take over the movement."[41] But the 1J4, a "battered, debilitated body, stricken in all its parts,"[42] had few resources at its disposal, even less than in November 1963. Its military force was a myth. Arms were woefully lacking and internal divisions were tearing the party apart. To a large extent the very composition of the Political Committee reflected the factional strife: Fidelio Despradel represented the *duros*, Jimmy Durán the *flojos*. Pin Montás was chosen because, within the CECP, he usually represented the students, the most important and most prestigious group in the 1J4. The times demanded unity, but the CECP "brothers," unable to reach an agreement, were forced into a compromise whose fragility might soon become evident.

Militarily the PSP and the MPD were even weaker than the 1J4, but at least had greater cohesion. The divisions within the PSP's Central Committee were free of the venom that marked those within the CECP. The MPD leadership, for its part, was monolithic.[43] Despite the lack of arms and the near nonexistence of commandos, the parties of the far left held a trump: cadres trained in armed struggle and leaders capable of directing it, men schooled in the art of guerrilla warfare at the best "universities": in Cuba and China. This was an asset whose value only time could gauge. Many rebel officers, of course, knew their trade, but they would have to act under totally unfamiliar conditions. The new balance of power within the constitutionalist camp would depend in part on their capacity to adapt to these unfamiliar conditions and on their resolve. And it would depend on the reaction of the PRD. The party leaders, Bosch above all, enjoyed an overwhelming popularity and had the support of the rebel officers—but nothing had prepared them for the violence of a civil war.

Events would provide the answer. For the moment, the far left was preparing to seize its chance. Because of the number of its followers and the mystique of its martyrs, the 1J4 was the most able of the parties of the far left to aspire to an important role, despite the divisions that racked it. But to play that role, it needed weapons. That was the first concern of the 1J4—and of the PSP and the MPD as well.

The overwhelming majority of the people backed the Boschist movement.[44] This had been demonstrated on the afternoon of the twenty-fourth, when the streets in the capital and in other cities were suddenly filled with crowds answering with a long-repressed passion Peña Gómez's appeal. And although police intervention and the rebels' apparent passivity repulsed this explosion of enthusiasm, the people's support in Santo Domingo was confirmed and renewed when the first rebel units entered the capital. A few hours later, hearing that Santo Domingo had been liberated, the people of the cities in the interior in turn emerged from their torpor. Soon, when the local police and army garrisons declared their neutrality and then their support, the last reins on enthusiasm fell away, an enthusiasm already brought to a pitch by the news of Reid Cabral's arrest.

In Santiago the people "were jubilant in celebrating the overthrow of the Government. Thousands of vehicles moved in caravans through the streets of this city. The people in the cars called for the return to Constitutional Government 'without elections.' "[45] San Francisco de Macorís "was enthusiastic in celebrating the success of the movement that began yesterday in Santo Domingo." In San Juan de la Maguana, "as soon as the populace learned of the constitutionalist victory, they filled the streets, shouting praise to the young soldiers who had boldly imposed the rights of the people." And in other cities: "According to news that come in from all the towns in the north, the fall of the Triumvirate is being celebrated with joy everywhere."[46] The reaction was the same throughout the land.

The celebration revealed a significant political fact. Along with the PRD, the Reformist Party was considered to have great popular support. On 25 April one looked for that strength in vain. During these critical days the crowds in the streets described by the Dominican papers were hailing the name of Bosch and demanding a "return to constitutional government without elections." Nowhere did the masses demonstrate in support of Joaquín Balaguer. His lack of support cannot be explained by accusing the papers—*El Caribe* and *Listín Diario*—of bias. True, they were often biased—but never in favor of Bosch. Unless the Reformistas recruited the bulk of their adherents from among a "silent majority," Balaguer's prestige was overestimated, at least in the cities. Or else, at the decisive moment, the legendary figure of Juan Bosch, the first freely elected president in almost forty years, prevailed over Trujillo's last president, even among large numbers of Balagueristas.

This conclusion, moreover, does not contradict the testimony of those few persons—including the brother-in-law of a former Reformist Party vice-president—who have insisted that, amid the crowds shouting their joy and their demands, voices were heard hailing the name of Joaquín Balaguer. This was not only possible, but normal. Our concern, however, is to discover the feelings of the majority of the people who filled the streets. And the evidence overwhelmingly supports our contention that the people supported Bosch. Because the documents are wanting, however—a gap only teams of Dominican sociologists can fill[47]—it is impossible to extend this conclusion to the rural population. The only clue we have is that, late in the morning on the twenty-fifth, answering the appeals that came over the radio, the first contingents of peasants began to arrive in the cities to demonstrate their support for the Boschist cause.

Although the reaction in the countryside is still poorly understood, the picture in the cities is clear. In Santo Domingo, the nerve center of the revolt, rebel troops and jubilant crowds joined forces in a common cause: the return to power of former President Bosch. In the other cities, the local police and army garrisons responded to the enthusiasm of the population by keeping to their barracks in sullen resignation. In the face of this passivity from the forces of repression, the apparatus of the Triumvirate collapsed. The civil authorities set up by the regime fled, demonstrating—at last—their full comprehension of the people's feelings. The deserted buildings awaited only the arrival of the Boschistas to give them new life. Although the rebels did not interfere with the newspapers,[48] they took over the radio stations and broadcast the directives of the movement.

These directives called on the people to mobilize, to demonstrate their support, and thus, by the sole weight of their presence, to dissuade the "neoconstitutionalists" among the military from returning to their former loves. Indeed, in Santiago, the Fortaleza San Luis seemed almost fragile when a sea of several thousand people from every quarter of the city threatened to engulf it.

It was natural, though regrettable, that the heady freedom after a long period of repression would lead to excesses in crowds unchecked by the police. It is not the excesses that ought to surprise us, but rather how few and innocuous they were. The wrath of the people fell quite naturally on what they saw as the symbols of the evils they had suffered. Angry crowds attacked the headquarters of certain parties identified with the overthrow of Bosch's constitutional government. In Santiago, "the offices of the National Civic Union (UCN) and the Liberal Evolutionist Party (PLE) were sacked"; in Santo Domingo, "the headquarters of the Dominican Revolutionary Vanguard, the [National] Civic Union, and the Liberal Evolutionist Party" were put to the torch. Also burned were "the printing room and offices of the *Prensa Libre*,"[49] a newspaper that in 1963 had stopped at nothing to precipitate Bosch's overthrow.

The ire of the crowds was directed as well against the property of certain figures linked to the Triumvirate. But these attacks were rare. The Dominican press reports only two such incidents during the first twenty-eight hours of the revolt: one in Santo Domingo ("mobs sacked the Reid and Pellerano company"), the other in Santiago ("[and they sacked] the office of the radio commentator Rafael Rivas Jerez"). Rare acts of vandalism unconnected with any political motive also took place: in Santiago, for example, "two bars were sacked."[50]

Other acts of unreported violence may have occurred. Sometimes, however, the reports were categorical, as in the case of San Francisco de Macorís, the nation's third largest city, where, despite an exalted populace, "no incident of any kind stemming from the events ha[d] . . . been recorded."[51] Even recognizing the possibility of omissions in the newspaper accounts, it is clear that in this hour of triumph the Dominican people showed a moderation all the more commendable for the absence of any restraining force. Victory came amid a feeling of goodwill despite the violence and suffering of the past.

For at least a part of the demonstrators, however, goodwill did not exclude the desire for arms. This desire was especially strong in the capital. The attitude of the rebel troops inspired confidence, but memories of the recent past prevented this confidence from being absolute. Moreover, the disquieting proximity of San Isidro and the fear of an imminent attack by the CEFA tanks aroused in many an urgent desire to secure the means to defend themselves. The rallying cries of the far left thus fell on ready ears. The desire for arms existed in the other cities as well, where the sincerity of the adherence of the local garrisons fooled few. The Enriquillo plan, however, had envisioned only a secondary role for the civilian sector: the people were to be called on to demonstrate their support, but arms were to remain exclusively in the hands of the military.

In Santo Domingo these instructions were not followed in full. To understand why, two phases must be distinguished. During the first—from the outbreak of the countercoup up to the entry of the first rebel units into the capital—the orders were strictly obeyed. This is easily explained, since the rebels were isolated in their camps and physically cut off from the populace in the capital. Arms were distributed to fewer than fifty former officers[52] who, linked in varying degrees to the conspiracy, had hurried to the rebel camps on learning of Rivera Cuesta's arrest. This initial distribution of arms, limited and selective, was in complete accordance with the provisions of the Enriquillo plan. During the second phase, however—from the entry of the first rebel units into the capital until the start of the civil war—a change occurred. When the rebels entered the city around 1:30 A.M., they did not strictly follow their orders not to arm the population.[53] Popular pressure was great; crowds acclaiming the rebels and exalting their "democratic spirit" were asking for weapons.

It was not always easy to refuse their insistent demands, especially for those few officers and noncoms who, during the period of the conspiracy, had bowed only reluctantly to the categorical refusal of the great majority of their comrades to arm civilians. Other officers, moved by the acclamations of the crowd and fearful that an overly stubborn refusal might dispel their sudden aura as "democratic officers," sometimes abandoned the "orthodox" position they had always held. Still other officers were, at first, gripped by worry. Too many precious hours had been lost since Rivera Cuesta's arrest, hours during which the enemy might have regrouped. The rest of the armed forces remained hostile. Although the capital had been liberated without a fight, a victory made easy by the complicity of the night, daybreak might bring a violent riposte from San Isidro. If so, the population should be in a position to contribute to the defense.[54]

Soon, guided by the first glimmers of dawn, long lines of civilians filled the highway leading from Santo Domingo to the rebel camps. They came not only to declare their support but to ask for arms. Most of the time they met with a refusal. Despite the actions of some individual officers in contact with the crowds in the capital, the orders still held: civilians should not be armed. It was easier to follow orders at the camps, where the senior commanding officers more easily controlled their subordinates, and where military tradition held sway, dampening somewhat the electric atmosphere coming from the capital.

The refusal, however, struck a serious blow to the hopes of those eager to share in their own liberation, for it aroused distrust as to the true intentions of officers wearing a uniform long dishonored. For those who had made the trek on foot, the disappointment was all the more bitter. To mitigate these reactions and prevent distrust from engendering a current of hostility, Hernando Ramírez issued the order encouraging civilians to make Molotov cocktails. His aim was not to block an assault by Wessin's tanks, a danger the rebel command discounted, but to give those who had been refused arms the feeling that, despite the refusal, they were wanted as partners in the events.[55]

In rare cases, the rebels distributed arms at the camps. Thus, at about ten in the morning, several "radical" sergeants, profiting from the momentary absence of their superiors, hastened to arm the civilians around them with weapons they had just taken from a depot.[56]

Thus, in one way or another, some civilians received arms, despite the orders of the rebel command. Naturally, no one knows how many. But exaggeration should be avoided and a distinction drawn between what happened after the outbreak of the civil war and what took place in the hours preceding the strafing of the Presidential Palace.

The "radical" officers and noncommissioned officers constituted a small minority. Others, for reasons noted earlier, followed their example. The decisions—isolated and sporadic—were made individually. In each instance the officers distributed only those few arms that could be spared—in all probably between three and five hundred weapons. At the outbreak of the civil war, most of the citizens of Santo Domingo had no arms; the parties of the far left were distressed by the shortage of weapons. Still, although quantitatively insignificant, these first distributions were very important in another sense. Even the "radical" officers had felt that only "trustworthy" civilians should be armed. This might have been possible had lists of such civilians been prepared. But since orders were not to arm civilians, there were no lists on 24 April. Arms were therefore distributed without knowing whether the man getting a rifle was a PRDist, a Communist, a Balaguerist, or a criminal who later would use the weapon to improve his stock in trade. But, given the highly charged atmosphere permeating the capital, the distribution could be carried out in no other way.

In the other cities there was no such indiscriminate distribution of arms; indeed, none were distributed. Far more than the "orthodox" constitutionalist officers in the capital, the local commanders elsewhere were loath to arm a people they considered their enemy, a people aspiring to break with the past. The crowds in the streets were offering enthusiastic support to a revolt that the officers themselves had joined only out of opportunism. Nor could there be any question of individual initiative whereby, out of conviction, weakness, or the exaltation of the moment, officers could have armed the population. The troops were confined to their barracks, which made fraternizing physically impossible.

The populace had little or no faith in the sincerity of the rallying of the local garrisons, and demonstrators, especially the far leftists, called for arms, yet the atmosphere was not charged with the kind of exasperated hate that would have been needed to impel an unarmed people to attack barracks in search of arms. The mood was one of victory, but in a spirit of goodwill. The game had been played—and won—in Santo Domingo; the local commanders, whether they liked it or not, would have to go along. In fact, they had already fallen into line. San Isidro was remote, often too remote for its shadow to dim the people's triumph.

Moreover, the local PRD leaders appealed for moderation. Surprised by the events, still disorganized, but convinced that the revolt had succeeded, they urged the people to mobilize. Still, they opposed taking drastic measures made unnecessary by certain victory. Such measures were dangerous because the leaders lacked arms and because nothing in their experience had prepared them for such bold action.

Then, shortly before four in the afternoon, General de los Santos' aircraft attacked the Presidential Palace. San Isidro's unity had been re-established; the shadow of the *conjunto* now threatened the entire nation.

THE U.S. EMBASSY

At approximately five-thirty on the afternoon of 25 April, four PRD leaders arrived at the American embassy. Two of them—Antonio Martínez Francisco and Máximo Lovatón Pittaluga—had met earlier in the day with the American chargé d'affaires, William B. Connett. During the six hours since that first meeting a series of grave events had taken place. The two men were anxious to discover the reactions at the oddly silent embassy. They were accompanied by Antonio Guzmán, the rich and respected landowner from the Cibao, and Enriquillo del Rosario Ceballos, the Bosch government's ambassador to Washington.[57]

They came to take the pulse of the U.S. embassy, but they wanted something else as well. Shaken by the attack on the Presidential Palace and distressed by the idea that civil war might overrun the country, they wanted Connett to intervene with the San Isidro generals to dissuade them from launching their planes against the capital. Their hopes were nourished on the illusion that Connett had shown a "reasonable" attitude earlier in the day: having issued no rebuke, he had tacitly accepted the constitutionalist victory. But what they took to be a "reasonable" attitude was the product of a misapprehension: Connett's conviction that the rebels would agree to resolve the crisis through the classic procedure of establishing a military junta. Molina Ureña's accession to the provisional presidency had dispelled this misunderstanding.

Similarly, the visit to the embassy quickly dispelled the illusions of the PRD leaders. These "honorable men," the respected notables, did not even get a chance to talk with Connett, who was "too busy to receive them."[58] Instead, they had to settle for Arthur E. Breisky, the embassy's second secretary, who was "very nervous, hostile,"[59] not there to listen, but to accuse. The movement was Communist, whatever its initial goals. The Dominicans' denials and explanations were futile. Breisky declared that the American embassy was unable to intervene to prevent new air attacks, for "we have no contact whatever with San Isidro."[60] The only reasonable solution would have been to establish a military junta. But this the rebels had refused. So ended the talk, and the accused withdrew, having been judged guilty.

Although crushed by their reception, the PRD leaders failed to grasp the true import of the Americans' hostility. At no point during the meeting had

Breisky threatened them. But their last illusions would have crumbled had they been able to read the telegram that Connett sent, a half hour before their visit, to the State Department:

> The Air force has decided to fight to block return of Bosch and Wessin y Wessin has agreed to support the Air Force.[61]
>
> Situation extremely confused and no identifiable authority is exercising any effective control over the government.
>
> ALL MEMBERS OF THE COUNTRY TEAM FEEL BOSCH'S RETURN AND RESUMPTION OF CONTROL OF THE GOVERNMENT IS AGAINST U.S. INTERESTS IN VIEW OF EXTREMISTS IN THE COUP AND COMMUNIST ADVOCACY OF BOSCH RETURN.

Breisky, pressed to intervene to stop renewal of the bombings, told the PRD leaders that the embassy had "no contact whatever with San Isidro." Yet Connett had already written:

> I have reluctantly agreed to the De Los Santos—Wessin plan even though it could mean more bloodshed. But it is the only way to forestall a leftist takeover. No one is governing in the Palace. Merely talking talking, according to Rivera Caminero.[62]
>
> The country team is against a show of force by the U.S. at this time. Our attaches have stressed to the three military leaders, Rivera [Caminero], De los Santos and Wessin, our strong feelings everything possible should be done to prevent a communist takeover.[63]

The court had passed sentence. No appeal could be made. The constitutionalist movement had to be crushed even if it meant more bloodshed. This was the unanimous judgment of those Americans present. No U.S. military intervention was foreseen; the embassy was relying on Wessin's tanks, de los Santos' aircraft, and Rivera Caminero's warships. But what if Wessin, de los Santos, and Rivera Caminero proved unequal to their task? The goal was set; the means would depend on the circumstances.

Chapter 8

The Civil War (until Dawn of 27 April)

The strafing of the Presidential Palace marked the outbreak of the civil war. But this reality escaped Hernando Ramírez, the military chief of the constitutionalist movement. That morning, he had viewed Benoit's ultimatum to be a bluff. Now he regarded the air force attack as no more than de los Santos' desperate effort to lend credence to that bluff. For him not a civil war, but a war of nerves had begun. De los Santos would yield if the constitutionalists held firm. The day passed without any further air attacks and without Wessin's tanks advancing on the capital. In the enemy's apparent passivity Hernando Ramírez saw evidence of weakness and indecisiveness that nourished his hopes.[1]

Meanwhile, in the middle of the night, a man who had fled the city thirty-six hours earlier returned. At about one in the morning on the twenty-sixth, Admiral Rivera Caminero, navy chief of staff, mounted the steps of the Palace. Had he come to announce his adherence to the cause? Not at all, according to his own account.[2] His story, more a tribute to his imagination than to his honesty, recalls a "shirtless" stranger "rubbing his bare foot with his finger" while lolling in a chair in Reid Cabral's old office.[3] "Six blue-eyed, blond-bearded men dressed in olive drab, obviously not Dominicans," were grouped around Molina Ureña in the second-floor office where he received his visitor.[4] Rivera Caminero's tale, with the half-naked civilian in the presidential seat, was meant to arouse indignation and to strike fear. The foreigners around Molina Ureña did not go unnamed; on the contrary, fearing that the details ("blue-eyed, blond-bearded") might escape his interviewer (the author), Rivera Caminero was explicit. They were Russians. Their presence was proof that the international Communist conspiracy was there, its coils already wrapped around Molina Ureña and ready to encircle the entire Republic.

Given these circumstances, Rivera Caminero's talk with Molina Ureña was brief. According to Rivera Caminero, Molina Ureña exclaimed: "Bosch will be very glad when he hears that the navy is on our side." "I have not come here to yield, but to discuss," interrupted the admiral. But what did they have to discuss in the face of irrefutable proof of Communist intervention, which the rebels obligingly displayed to the admiral? The rebels wanted a test of strength, a fratricidal struggle; Molina demanded that the navy bomb San Isidro. "Impossible—at San Isidro there are also civilians," shot back navy Captain Francisco Amiama Castillo, who Rivera Caminero claims accompanied him. Yet, thirty-six hours later the fleet bombarded the capital and its more than four hundred thousand inhabitants.

219

Faced with the resolve of Rivera Caminero and Amiama Castillo, upright men unlikely to yield, international Communism was forced to throw off its mask, and promises gave way to threats. The two officers were about to be arrested. But in the Palace garden the handful of sailors who had escorted Rivera Caminero "realized" what was happening on the second floor. They entered the Palace and posted themselves at the foot of the steps—unopposed. In his account, Rivera Caminero glossed over these points, but it mattered little. Tiny details must not stand in the way of the grand finale. Rivera Caminero slowly descended the staircase, alone, for Amiama Castillo had conveniently disappeared. He walked backward toward his men, clutching a machine gun, his gaze fixed on the rebels watching him impotently from the second floor.

Such is Rivera Caminero's version, a fantasy all the more ludicrous for the myriad of details meant to impress but that only turn the hero into a clown and the episode into the unconvincing ending to a third-rate western.

The constitutionalists' version is more sober, free of heroics or histrionics, almost banal in its simplicity. According to those present—Molina Ureña, Espaillat Nanita, Hernando Ramírez, Lovatón Pittaluga, Ledesma Pérez, and Frank Moya Pons—Rivera Caminero told Molina Ureña that the navy was "with the people" and declared himself at the orders of "Mr. President."[5] Shortly thereafter, senior navy officers appeared on radio and television to announce their decision to support the revolt.[6] Following Rivera Caminero's example, others went to the Palace to declare their adherence. Two days later one of these, navy Captain Olgo Santana Carrasco, became the navy's representative within the military junta set up at San Isidro "to fight Communism."[7] It even seemed that the navy's adherence might take the form of concrete acts; early on the morning of the twenty-sixth, when de los Santos' planes renewed their bombing raids on the capital, a few navy units returned the gunfire of the Dominican air force.[8]

Rivera Caminero's visit bolstered the constitutionalists' optimism. "The Navy is ours," exulted Molina Ureña after the admiral's departure.[9] San Isidro appeared to be completely isolated. The garrisons in the interior continued to affirm their support. The police were "neutral" in the capital and "constitutionalist" elsewhere. Besides the *conjunto*, only the navy had remained. Now it, too, had joined the cause, and Rivera Caminero "seemed sincere."[10]

It is not difficult to understand how in such circumstances Hernando Ramírez, and others with him, could have believed that the enemy would eventually submit. The balance of power as they saw it, the characters of Generals de los Santos and Wessin and their attitude since the outbreak of the countercoup all seemed to weigh far more heavily than the machine gun bursts from the skies a few hours earlier, after which there came no other military action.

But Hernando Ramírez's confidence, still justifiable on the night of 25-26 April, became increasingly removed from reality as the hours passed. Clinging to an optimism explicable only as a blind will to escape the bitter truth, Hernando Ramírez continued to affirm, up until the early hours of the twenty-seventh, that San Isidro would never dare to fight, that the Dominican Republic would never experience the throes of civil war.[11] The illusion was belied by the facts, and to cling to it one had to deny those facts.

On the twenty-sixth, beginning at five-thirty in the morning, the air attacks were renewed, more violently than before. The primary targets were the Juan Pablo Duarte Bridge and the Radio Santo Domingo TV antenna. The air force also attacked the Twenty-seventh of February and the Sixteenth of August camps, the President Peynado Bridge, and the intersection of Duarte Avenue and Lieutenant Amado García Guerrero Avenue.[12] At nine-thirty, the Presidential Palace was bombed. The raids claimed their first victims; casualties mounted quickly. Yet Hernando Ramírez persisted. The attacks were of a "limited" nature;[13] de los Santos was only trying to intimidate him, to step up the war of nerves; he did not wish—or dare—to go all the way. Even if de los Santos had wanted to act, his officers would never have permitted it. The constitutionalists at the Nineteenth of November would make their weight felt, and others would join them, in order to forestall a shameful bombardment of the capital and prevent a fratricidal war between Dominicans.

Wessin's tanks stood poised at the eastern end of the Duarte Bridge, but had not tried to cross it. Hernando Ramírez was certain that Wessin would never dare to fight. The American embassy opposed the revolt; the PRDistas' stormy talk with Breisky on the afternoon of the twenty-fifth had proved that. From the start of the conspiracy Hernando Ramírez had expected the United States to disapprove of a revolt aimed at toppling a regime it protected, but he failed to grasp the violence of this disapproval. Most important, he never thought, nor even imagined, that its hostility to the revolt would drive the United States to take drastic steps.[14] After the inevitable fit of temper, Washington would accept the fait accompli; men like Bosch and Hernando Ramírez were hardly Fidel Castros or Che Guevaras. Hernando Ramírez had no doubts about his own anti-communism, and it seemed absurd to him that anyone could entertain such doubts.

Hernando Ramírez's illusions were understandable, and were shared by others around him. The months elapsed since Bosch's fall had not fully erased the vision that some held of a "certain" America: the America that in the name of the Alliance for Progress had allegedly helped defeat the Trujillos and later had allegedly supported the Bosch government. It was an America that had never existed. Thirty years after Franklin Delano Roosevelt proclaimed the principle of nonintervention, reasonable men had difficulty imagining an American military intervention against an uprising that threatened no vital U.S. interest. Yet there were other means short of military intervention whereby Washington could deny the rebels their victory. In particular, the United States could encourage the "natives" to fight among themselves—the "good" against the "bad," the San Isidro generals against the insurgents. Then Wessin and de los

Santos would not be alone, and their champion's influence would chill the ardor of many an officer in the rebels' own camp, men who at that moment still called themselves constitutionalists.

In the capital the situation of the constitutionalist forces grew worse and worse. Within the "hard-line" constitutionalist units were a host of officers knit together for a moment, at the start of the revolt, by the energy of some of their comrades, then by the certainty of victory. But the air raid on the afternoon of the twenty-fifth dealt an initial blow to the confidence of a number of these officers. Of course, other officers continued to share Hernando Ramírez's belief that the raid was only a bluff. By the following morning, however, when the air strikes resumed, only a few still held to that view. In addition, the increasingly widespread sense of the disapproval and the hostility of the American embassy distressed a great many officers. The time for boasting had passed. Faced with the challenge from San Isidro, every man now had to shoulder responsibility to the utmost, to commit his life, his future. Some did so, men who were able to stand by the cause they had espoused and who, in the teeth of peril, redoubled their efforts, hardened their will. Their number was greater than most observers have claimed, but their efforts were lost in an incredible confusion, in an atmosphere poisoned by betrayal.

Aversion to Bosch's return to the presidency; reluctance to pay for his return with a civil war; distrust of the growing role of the popular masses; desire to ensure, by a military junta, the possibility of Balaguer's prompt return to power: these were the centrifugal forces that regained the upper hand once the constitutionalist victory no longer seemed assured. For all too many officers the goal was no longer the victory of a revolt in whose success they had ceased to believe; the goal was now to disengage their allegiance from a cause to which, for the most part, they had rallied reluctantly and opportunistically.

Some deserted, seeking refuge at the embassies or with friends. Others stayed on, but they were not to be found at the front (if one can speak of a front), not to be seen at the head of their men. Bravery would have enlarged their role—one they wished to deny. It could have turned a "momentary weakness," a "painful error," into guilty obstinacy, something too difficult to justify later on before the victors of San Isidro. They stayed on, and their presence only increased the constitutionalists' woes, the tension, the confusion. Afraid of the isolation that desertion would bring, afraid that desertion alone would not be enough to spare them the wrath of the victors while ensuring the hatred of the vanquished, they wanted the entire rebel movement to submit along with them. They wanted the rebel leaders to bow to San Isidro's demands and resign themselves to the establishment of a military junta. They besieged Hernando Ramírez, a man wasted by illness (on 25 April he suffered an attack of his chronic hepatitis) and faced with a task for which he was unprepared. They urged him to surrender. They crowded into the hallways of the Presidential

Palace, spreading their recriminations, their fear, the example of their weakness, the very picture of betrayal.

Before long, rumors began to circulate of a plot against Hernando Ramírez. His removal would eliminate the chief obstacle in the path of capitulation to San Isidro. And there was talk of contacts between the enemy and certain "constitutionalist" officers who regretted their momentary adherence to the revolt. For those officers, treason would be the price of a pardon from San Isidro.

There was no proof, however, and there is none to this day. Although the attitude of a number of officers justified suspicion, confusion prevented a serious investigation. Those officers who refused to surrender felt surrounded not only by cowards but by traitors. Yet how could the traitors be identified? The senior officers were particularly suspect. Some, of course—such as Hernando Ramírez, Lora Fernández, Núñez Nogueras—were above suspicion. But others dragged their opportunist pasts behind them. They had not taken part in the plot; they had joined the cause late and from the pressure of events rather than from inner conviction.[15] Now, during these difficult hours, their behavior confirmed the suspicions aroused by their pasts.

Where should the line between opportunism and treason be drawn? A fifth column had come into play. But how could its members be known? Which orders were to be followed, which spurned? The principle of hierarchy, on which every army is based, was called into question; but at the time there was no substitute structure.

Among the soldiers in the "hard-line" constitutionalist units were many who missed the real meaning of the struggle—often poor peasants who had joined the army for a meal, which, although bad, at least was steady. At the outbreak of the rebellion they had followed their officers, as they had been accustomed to doing. Perhaps this time they obeyed with a little more enthusiasm owing to Bosch's great prestige; perhaps, instead, they followed with anxiety, since the enterprise might prove dangerous, and they had not become soldiers out of any love of adventure. At the start, the ease of the affair, the enthusiastic support of the people, the feeling—ever so new—of being hailed, respected, must have been a pleasant, stimulating surprise. But the feeling was short-lived. The first machine gun bursts from de los Santos' planes on the afternoon of the twenty-fifth sparked many fears that were confirmed at dawn the next day when the raids were resumed and expanded. They had followed their officers, but many of those officers now abandoned them to apply pressure on Hernando Ramírez, or simply to desert.

Their disarray was soon exacerbated by another important event. At approximately noon on the twenty-sixth, a station came on the air identifying itself as Dominican Armed Forces Radio—Radio San Isidro.[16] As Llano Montes later explained, "It was necessary to establish a radio station to broadcast the viewpoint of the Armed Forces [that is, the viewpoint of Wessin]. . . . The job was given to a friend of the military, Máximo Fiallo. . . . Within a few hours the equipment was set up and everything ready for transmitting."[17] Radio San

Isidro unleashed a violent campaign in which hate poured out in slander and lies, a campaign reinforced by the leaflets dropped on the capital from de los Santos' planes.[18]

The "viewpoint" of the armed forces was simple: the revolt was Communist. This was hardly a new theme. Trujillo had used it, and it had been pushed to the height of absurdity to justify the overthrow of Bosch. But it was a theme guaranteed a certain success among those in the leisure classes—the *gente*— who since time immemorial had been accustomed to judging everything through the distorting lens of fear—fear of losing their privileges. For those who might have resisted such arguments—the wretched masses, particularly, who made up the majority of Santo Domingo's population—San Isidro had another message. The revolt had failed; "liberation" of the capital was at hand. Nothing could prevent the vengeance of the victor from coming down on those who had dared to resist. And on whom would that vengeance fall more terribly than on the soldiers who had "betrayed"? Pardon would be granted all those who, recognizing in time the error of their ways, gave up this desperate struggle. A firing squad awaited those who persisted in linking their fates with the agony of the "Communist" revolt.

These threats were given particular force by the machine-gun bursts overhead, victory cries seemingly confirmed by the many "constitutionalist" officers abandoning their troops. Desertions also began among the rank and file in the constitutionalist units.[19] Some simply gave up the fight, trading their rifles for civilian clothes; they tried to get home, in the vain hope that the walls of their houses would shelter them from the wrath of the victors. By nightfall of the twenty-sixth, the first deserters appeared in the vicinity of La Vega, a city of the Cibao some seventy-five miles from Santo Domingo.[20] They carried a message of defeat. Still other soldiers, following the example of some of their superiors, did not desert, but "withdrew" from the struggle by taking refuge within Transportación and Intendencia, officially constitutionalist but by then becoming the gathering place for all those who no longer wanted to fight on the rebel side.

The constitutionalists answered San Isidro's propaganda with their own. As masters of the capital they controlled Radio Santo Domingo TV, the only Dominican television station and the radio station with the most powerful transmitter.[21] In the name of liberty and democracy, anarchy took over at Radio Santo Domingo TV. The people backed the revolt, which had been set off in their name. Now thousands flocked to the station to demonstrate their support—or simply to see the inside of a place that until then had been off limits to them.

Radio San Isidro functioned under military discipline. Soldiers were stationed at the entries and let in only a privileged few. Everybody was at his post, everybody had his task.[22] At Radio Santo Domingo TV, however, crowds jammed the hallways, wandered into the studios, grabbed hold of the microphones. No one was at his post—no one had a post: everyone wanted to "help," adding to the confusion. When the Palace phoned to issue orders and instructions, unfamiliar voices answered. Messages were given to strangers. Sometimes they were relayed, sometimes they got lost in the shuffle.

Radio Santo Domingo TV was later blamed for the violence of its transmissions, its "hysterical broadcasts . . . urging the people into the streets to sack the homes of the pilots and to defend the Palace."[23] But its appeals for restraint—"Once more, we urge the owners of liquor stores, bars and restaurants not to sell alcoholic beverages in order to prevent disorders and accidents"[24] — were forgotten. Also forgotten was the confusion, the lack of leadership and control, the chaos in which "everybody did what he pleased."[25] Anyone with enough muscle could push his way through the crowd, take over a microphone, and appear on TV. *El Caribe* reported: "Throughout the day, hundreds of persons, civilians and military, who support the [rebel] army, have appeared on Radio Santo Domingo's radio and television channels, urging the people to fight for the 'return to constitutional government.' "[26] These persons were finally free to shout out what they had been unable to utter since the fall of Bosch. They could at last throw off the frustration of years of repression. Some among them were undoubtedly demagogues, hotheads, or left-wing extremists. Was moderation or calm possible with the planes from San Isidro spewing their machine-gun fire and bombs on the capital?

Amid the chaos, however, announcers ("strangers improvising")[27] strove to combat the San Isidro propaganda and to prevent defeatism from gripping the people. They would have to persuade the population that the constitutionalists in the capital were not alone, that the rest of the armed forces supported the revolt. Radio Santo Domingo TV announced: "Urgent; last minute report. The people are informed that the military garrisons of the following provinces have joined the forces that are loyal to the Constitution and President Bosch." The announcer read a list of twenty-three of the country's twenty-six provinces. "This means that the military garrisons of the entire country are with the people, the 1963 Constitution and President Bosch." The enemy was isolated, and the full might of the constitutionalist forces was about to crush him: "Attention, attention. Much attention. We have been informed that military contingents are arriving in the capital from several parts of the country. Contingents from San Cristóbal, San Francisco de Macorís, San Pedro de Macorís, La Vega, Santiago have already arrived." As late as the twenty-seventh, before being silenced by the planes, Radio Santo Domingo TV broadcast: "An official report announces that all army and air-force units stationed at Santiago are on the way to the capital to give their support to the people." Those fearing an unopposable attack on the capital by San Isidro were reassured: "Every rooftop in Santo Domingo has been transformed into a military post. We have machine guns set up everywhere. Artillery . . . ready to check any attack from the forces of reaction."

On other occasions, in an atmosphere of chaos growing worse by the hour, Radio Santo Domingo TV relayed alarming—and often unfounded—reports: "Warning to the people. There are a number of red trucks, of the . . . [unintelligible] make, going around soldiers in the service of Wessin y Wessin. . . . Be on guard, people. Fight those red trucks, of the . . . [unintelligible] make, belonging to Elías Wessin y Wessin. They are against the people and the restored Constitution."[28]

The Enriquillo plan had envisioned a bloodless coup, with the masses playing only a secondary role. The people were to pour out into the streets of the capital and all the towns of the Republic to express their support for the revolt. But their liberation would be granted them, not fought and won. Now the vision of a bloodless coup collapsed before the reality of a civil war. Over Radio Santo Domingo TV unfamiliar voices urged the population to fight for its own liberation: "Do not be afraid. Get out on the streets, Dominican people, to defend your constitutionality. Swarm into the streets of the capital." The celebrations were off: "Everybody to the Cañita bridge.[29] Everybody armed, because the forces disloyal to this movement are infiltrating through there [a false report]. So everybody with clubs, stones, firearms, even barehanded, fight for this [unintelligible]."[30]

Relatively few arms had been distributed to or seized by the people. "The people's weapon, beginning that Sunday [25 April] was the Molotov cocktail!" Radio Santo Domingo TV offered "practical instruction in making Molotov cocktails . . . by unknown speakers bedecked with cartridges and with machine guns slung over their shoulders."[31] As the aircraft dropped their bombs, appeals were broadcast to San Isidro, to the officers and soldiers of the CEFA, calling on them to "respect the Constitution, . . . join in a fraternal embrace with the people, . . . obey the dictates of your heart; do not betray your conscience. Imprison the men who make you fight the people, your brothers, the law and freedom."[32] Wives pleaded with their husbands, daughters with their fathers, as "numerous family members of the pilots bombing the city" appeared on television "appealing to the pilots to stop the raids" and calling on them to " 'unite with the people' in the struggle against 'the forces of reaction.' "[33] Sometimes threats followed the appeals: "Attention, attention. We have just been informed that the homes of the family members of the pilots flying . . . have been surrounded and that these people will be seized and taken hostages to the bridge . . . so that if this area is bombed by the rebels [that is the "loyalists"—rebels to the constitution of 1963] their families will pay for it."[34]

Radio Santo Domingo TV experienced three days of frantic activity until the twenty-seventh, when it was silenced by de los Santos' aircraft. In capable hands, with leadership and a central authority, the station could have played a positive role of extreme importance; gripped by anarchy, its role was at best uncertain. The station managed, up to a point, to galvanize the populace and to combat Radio San Isidro's defeatist propaganda, even if to do so meant resorting to lies about "military contingents" that never arrived because they had never left. But the vehemence of the novice announcers; a rhetoric "disconcertingly reminiscent of the early days in Havana after Castro's assumption of power";[35] irresponsible threats that happily were never realized (the pilots' families as hostages at the Duarte Bridge)[36]—all exposed the movement to attack from those looking for an excuse to accuse the constitutionalists of indulging in the worst excesses and of being Castro/Communist in character or inspiration.

Until the afternoon of the twenty-fifth, the sense of victory had sent the crowds into the streets, muting any feelings of hatred or violence. By the twenty-sixth—after repeated bombings—the victory that had seemed within reach still remained to be won. The civil war had begun. Added to the hate that envelops every fratricidal struggle was the exasperation of a people who believed they had come to the end of their woes—only to find that the way was barred. The crowds were powerless in the face of the machine gun fire, powerless against the generals who sat ensconced at sinister San Isidro, the country's most powerful military base. The dead, however, cried out for vengeance; hate demanded a target. At least for the moment, San Isidro was out of reach, but other enemies of long standing were at hand: the rich, the "oligarchs," and, above all, the police.

Violence gripped the city. Excesses were committed. Pillaging broke out. "Gangs of rioters . . . [began] to prowl at the edge of the residential districts to the west and at the approaches to the highway north, where the homes are very isolated, breaking into the dwellings of wealthy Dominicans."[37] Yet there was never an "orgy of plunder and pillage," contrary to what one American commentator has claimed.[38] This was an invention of those who saw the very existence of the revolt as an intolerable challenge—and affront. "On the whole, the pillaging [was] limited."[39] There were no "turbas [mobs] . . . deployed to loot, burn, sack, intimidate, and kill."[40] "Hungry youths, armed, passed in front of grocery stores and kept walking."[41]

Against the police, however, the people unleashed their wrath with a violence that at times seemed unbounded. There were some terrible incidents. Marcel Niedergang has written: "Liquidation of the . . . police informers is beginning again, as at the end of 1961. It's a sinister manhunt, accounts settled on street corners and at homes in the northern suburbs, executions in which all the hate accumulated by the people against the police is given vent . . . . At Villa Consuelo [a district of the capital], the force of an entire police station is attacked by bands of summarily armed civilians and cut down on the spot."[42] The police chiefs reiterated their declarations of neutrality, but to no avail. In the hope of escaping the violence of the masses, the police "adhered" to the revolt. "The National Police is on the side of the people," announced a committee of police officers over Radio Santo Domingo TV on the morning of the twenty-sixth. "On the side of the people"—and against San Isidro: "If the members of . . . [the National Police] do not fire at Wessin's planes, it is because their arms are of short range and unable to shoot down aircraft."[43] But this declaration was also in vain. The vengeance of the mobs swept down on this symbol of an accursed past that had seemed dead at last, but that some now meant to resurrect.

The rage of an oppressed people, apparently forgotten on the morning of the twenty-fifth, was fired with fresh intensity by the threat from San Isidro. At times the violence was rash, but all too often it was necessary. The police were "neutral," the police "adhered"—yet few were taken in by this neutrality, this adherence. As long as victory seemed assured, the police's equivocal position had little importance; opportunism would be the best guarantor of their behavior. But the air raids changed all that. Although disorganized and in the grip of panic, the police were nonetheless a hostile force within the heart of the constitutionalist zone, a force that at any moment could stir and strike the rebels in the back, while they faced an attack from San Isidro.

The far left recognized this danger. PSP "revisionists" and MPD "dogmatists," leaders of the CECP and of the Military Bureau of the 1J4: all agreed that the police had to be eliminated as a military force. It was not merely a matter of attacking an enemy who could at any moment mount its own attack, of helping therefore to win the fight against San Isidro. Much more was at stake. The people had to be armed so that the revolt would not be simply a "cold military coup."

Some weapons had been handed out by the military even before the first wave of air raids. More arms followed,[44] and more still were abandoned by deserters or traded in by them for civilian garb. Whatever arms could be found at the armories were appropriated, sometimes with the help of the constitutionalist military, who made sure that no looting took place under the pretext of confiscating weapons. This was the case at the Oliva shop (El Conde Street) that specialized in the sale of hunting equipment. At around noon on the twenty-sixth,

> a band of youths and a few soldiers broke down the door . . . . At least two soldiers went in, but no civilians; the latter stayed at the entrance.
>
> One of the soldiers entered the store while a second stood guard behind the grating to keep civilians out and prevent any possible looting.
>
> The soldier inside gathered the arms and gave them to the soldier standing guard, who distributed them to the civilians. And so it went for the munitions.
>
> There was a group of about fifty persons waiting for weapons.[45]

At times civilians acted alone, without the help—or the opposition—of the military. Nor did the police offer any opposition. Thus, again on the morning of the twenty-sixth, a band of youths—mostly *catorcistas*—broke into Read's Hardware and seized the arms there.[46] The crowd even found weapons at the Presidential Palace when "with the first strafing of the Palace, one of the doors to the arms depot was knocked out, permitting a great many persons in the area to arm themselves."[47]

The far left was not satisfied; only a limited number of weapons had been obtained,[48] and these had been "gifts"—or, at least, taken without a fight. The people had to learn to win the instruments of their liberation, for only then would they be capable of defending their rights: against Wessin and de los Santos now, but against Bosch and his "constitutionalist" officers too, should that one day prove necessary. The old slogan of the 1J4 Military Bureau—arms torn from the hands of the enemy—was now taken up by the entire far left. But this harmony was not the result of consultations between the leaders of the various parties of the far left, inasmuch as the feverish unraveling of events made all contacts necessarily episodic and superficial.[49] Rather, it was the result of an instinctive reaction to an event—or series of events—that seemed suddenly to bring the future nearer. It would be a revolution and not just the uprising of a group of officers; it would be an action by the masses, a brotherly mingling in the streets of civilians and military, a popular cry in answer to the threat from San Isidro. Now the words of Aimé Césaire had meaning for Santo Domingo: "Suddenly a great outcry lit up the silence. We—the slaves—had burst our chains; we the downtrodden; we the cattle with our hoofs of patience."[50]

On the afternoon of the twenty-fifth, even before the air raid on the Palace, the Dominican far left carried out its first military action since the outbreak of the revolt. At Parque Independencia, in the heart of the city, members of the 1J4's Military Bureau attacked and disarmed some *cascos blancos*. They were not acting on their own, but were following the orders that the Military Bureau had just given its commandos.[51] Yet by itself, the Military Bureau, for all the martial qualities of its members, could realize actions only of limited scope: attacks on the few police patrols bold enough to venture into the streets and forays against several small neighborhood police stations.

Even united, the far left would have been unable to set off a large-scale offensive against the police. Very few had military training or arms.[52] Even without this obstacle, the far left had abundant cause to hesitate. Acting alone, without the cooperation of the people, the PSP, 1J4, and MPD would risk cutting themselves off from the masses. At the same time they would expose themselves to possible repression—now or in the future—from the "constitutionalist" military, in whom they had little confidence.

This time, however, the far left was not alone. This time its will—to tear arms from the enemy—coincided with that of an enraged people. It coincided as well with the will of groups of constitutionalist soldiers and noncommissioned officers,[53] and it was in accordance with the reality of the situation: the police was no longer the enemy of the far left alone, but of the entire constitutionalist movement.

By the evening of the twenty-fifth the people's offensive against the police had begun. Groups attacked patrols in the streets and struck at the first police stations. The strategy called for groups of soldiers, often led by "radical" noncommissioned officers, to direct the attack.[54] Their training and weapons made them the spearhead of the action. Behind them stood the civilians, some of whom now had firearms but lacked the time or the chance to learn how to handle them. Others were armed more simply with Molotov cocktails, iron bars, clubs. One by one the police stations fell. The small ones were hit first, but as the mobs armed and the violence mounted, bigger and bigger stations were seized, the police at times being slaughtered.

Panic heightened. Resistance seemed impossible, as did relief. Hundreds of policemen fled the various neighborhood police stations to take refuge in the two spots that might offer them safety: the Fortaleza Ozama and the National Police Headquarters. Many were cut down in the streets, even though some had shed their uniforms, vainly hoping to escape recognition. On the twenty-sixth groups of civilians joined by soldiers advanced toward the Fortaleza Ozama and the Police Headquarters.

The besiegers controlled the streets around the two bases, but they did not dare to launch an attack. They were no longer facing mere neighborhood police stations, but the two main police bases whose size alone inspired awe. Inside were hundreds of heavily armed policemen. In fact, the bases were in the grip of panic. The hundreds of policemen who, abandoned by their superiors, had taken refuge there were hardly welcome reinforcements; they brought with them news of disaster and massacre—police stations seized by mobs, policemen killed. Their accounts heightened the distress of the besieged, as fear turned to terror. The officers should have reorganized and taken charge of their men, but the only example they set was of their own fear. The few rare exceptions—above all, Lieutenant Colonel Rafael Guzmán Acosta at the National Police Headquarters—were not enough.[55] At that point the intervention of the rebel high command could have been decisive. It had the heavy armament that the civilians lacked—the few tanks taken from Wessin, especially. And it had soldiers with the requisite training.[56] A large number of those soldiers, abandoned by their superiors, deserted; others, often led by "radical" noncommissioned officers, began to act as small, independent units, taking part in the raids on the police stations, in particular. But where the officers had grown with their task, their units remained disciplined, as, for example, the company in the Parque Independencia area, under Major Núñez Nogueras. These units, led by competent, determined officers, could have constituted the spearhead of an action against Police Headquarters and, then, the Fortaleza Ozama. They would have brought the civilian groups what they lacked: leadership, firepower, and the capability of mounting a large-scale action. But as night fell on Santo Domingo, Hernando Ramírez's troops did not advance against Police Headquarters or the Fortaleza Ozama.[57] Hernando Ramírez still believed that San Isidro would yield, that de los Santos would recognize his impotence, that Wessin would give up the struggle. A day later Hernando Ramírez would understand his error, but by then it would be too late. With support from both the air and the sea, Wessin's tanks would have attacked the city, precipitating the constitutionalists' darkest hour.

Intervention by the constitutionalist units and occupation of Police Headquarters and the Fortaleza Ozama would, of course, never have decided the conflict. The struggle would be decided at San Isidro, the enemy's stronghold. As early as the evening of the twenty-fifth, this fact was clear to a number of officers, and a struggle for influence began around Hernando Ramírez. The "optimists," like their leader, believed that de los Santos was bluffing, that it was a matter of time before the enemy acknowledged his defeat. The "pessimists" were convinced that Wessin and de los Santos, aided and abetted by the American embassy, would fight. San Isidro wasn't bluffing; in the face of the threat, all the constitutionalists could do was bow and beg for mercy. Both the "optimists" and the "pessimists," for different reasons, came to the same conclusion: it would be a mistake to launch an offensive against San Isidro.

The constitutionalist movement's "young Turks" clashed with this coalition. These were mostly young officers—lieutenants and captains—and a few superior officers: Major Lora Fernández, Major Núñez Nogueras, navy Captain Montes Arache. Like the "pessimists," they believed that de los Santos and Wessin, with support and encouragement from the American embassy, would try to crush the revolt. Yet they refused to concede. To sit and wait for San Isidro to attack was absurd; action should be taken before the *conjunto* could reorganize,[58] before de los Santos' aircraft had a chance to demoralize the constitutionalist forces, before U.S. influence had time to bolster the morale of the "loyalists" and undermine the faith of too many "constitutionalists."[59]

The "Young Turks" favored an all-out thrust against the *conjunto*.[60] The operation would be carried out at night. The attackers would have the cover of darkness, limiting the effectiveness of the planes. But Hernando Ramírez rejected this plan. Although the operation was possible, it carried serious risks. The constitutionalists' real strength stemmed from the support they received from the population. Their stronghold was Santo Domingo, where tens of thousands of civilians kept guard, where each street—each house—was a rampart. To march on San Isidro would mean leaving that protective embrace to confront in his lair an enemy with, on paper, nearly four thousand men under arms. True, San Isidro was in disarray, a great many of its officers gripped by panic, and others, especially in the air force, in sympathy with the rebels. True, morale was low, disorganization rife, as evidenced by the painless departure of the cadets on the evening of the twenty-fifth. But how could this disarray and disorganization be assessed? Above all, how could they be measured against the risks? To hurl the best constitutionalist units against San Isidro in a decisive attack meant to stake the fate of the revolt on a single card. If the attack failed, the defeat of the rebellion was almost inevitable.

There was another means which fell between an all-out attack and passivity. This was to launch a commando raid against San Isidro. The limited number of men involved would have heightened the element of surprise while lessening the consequences of a possible defeat. As early as the evening of the twenty-fifth, this scheme was put forth by a number of officers—largely those who favored an all-out attack but were aware that such an attack stood almost no chance of winning Hernando Ramírez's approval. On the twenty-sixth, they received valuable support when navy Captain Montes Arache, the head of the frogmen and one of the most prestigious constitutionalist officers, presented Hernando Ramírez with a concrete proposal. Montes Arache would swim, at night, across the Ozama River to "loyalist" territory to stage an attack on San Isidro. Forty frogmen and Colonel Caamaño, his longtime friend, would go with him. Montes Arache asked Hernando Ramírez for authority to undertake the action and for the arms necessary to succeed: four mortars, two model 30 machine guns, a certain number of grenades, and some explosives (especially TNT).

Montes Arache did not intend to conquer San Isidro. His aim was to clip its wings: to infiltrate the Nineteenth of November, destroy at least a portion of the aircraft on the runways, and, if possible, sabotage the runways themselves by means of explosives and mortar fire. Although the outcome was in no way assured, the undertaking stood a good chance of success. The frogmen's training was excellent and particularly suited to this kind of operation. The Ozama River posed no significant obstacle; San Isidro was less than ten miles away. The attackers would advance under the cover of darkness; the enemy's disarray and weak security measures strengthened the chances for a successful *coup de main*.[61]

For a moment, Hernando Ramírez was convinced; then he fell back on his first position: wait and see. And while Hernando Ramírez waited, the country waited with him. As the outcome of the revolt hung in the balance, worried officers—at Barahona, at San Francisco de Macorís, at a number of other bases—struggled to predict the future. When at first it looked as if the revolt would triumph, the commanders of the various units in the interior had hastened to join the movement. But then San Isidro strafed the Palace, and the constitutionalists lost the initiative. Perhaps the rebels had won only the first round.

Twenty miles from the capital, at San Cristóbal, the elite Mella Battalion also waited. On the evening of the twenty-fourth, its commander, Colonel Pérez Aponte, had assured Hernando Ramírez of his support. On the twenty-fifth and again on the twenty-sixth, Pérez Aponte renewed his pledge in a series of telephone conversations with the constitutionalist leader, but he failed to act. When Hernando Ramírez asked for reinforcements, Pérez Aponte gave him advice, pointing out the need to avoid a fratricidal war and the importance of getting the military to reach an accord. As the hours slipped by, the Mella troops still had not arrived. Before long it was 27 April.[62]

At Santiago, site of the country's second most important air base,[63] Colonel Ramírez Gómez, base commander, had joined the rebellion: he was a "constitutionalist." But now he, too, waited. Instead of bombing San Isidro, his planes stayed on the ground. A number of pilots were sympathetic to the revolt, yet they hesitated, afraid to seize the planes and attack the *conjunto*. Finally, on the morning of the twenty-sixth, Lieutenant Francisco María Hidalgo, commander of the base's small armored battalion, forced a decision by blocking the runway with his tanks.[64] Hidalgo, a "Wessinist," was determined that no plane would take off to attack San Isidro. But what of the Fortaleza San Luis, the army base less than two miles away? Colonel de la Mota, commander of the base, had "enthusiastically" joined the revolt on the morning of the twenty-fifth, when the rebels appeared to have triumphed. The air attacks on the capital quickly cooled his ardor. The Fortaleza, however, counted a large number of officers sympathetic to the revolt. Some had even taken part in the conspiracy. The Enriquillo plan had envisioned their intervention. Yet on the twenty-fourth they failed to act. Now would they dare to act, forcing de la Mota to "persuade" the air base to move against San Isidro? Would they dare, if necessary, to arrest de la Mota and take command of the struggle themselves?

These officers were not alone. The population also supported the revolt. Around the Fortaleza were massed "more than 10,000 citizens of Santiago and neighboring towns."[65] Never had the walls of the Fortaleza seemed so fragile. Caught between the crowd outside and a determined band of officers inside, how could de la Mota resist? How could Ramírez Gómez himself resist? And what, then, could Hidalgo do with his handful of tanks?

But the constitutionalists at the Fortaleza lacked the courage of their convictions. While they talked and reflected, hours slipped away. The crowds in the streets were waiting. News from the capital was bad; the rebels there needed help. Impatient, the crowds called for weapons. Arms had been refused them on the morning of the twenty-fifth (why did they need them since the revolt had succeeded?) And arms were refused them in the hours that followed (they were "led to believe that distribution was unnecessary since the military command supported the constitutionalist movement").[66] Officially, de la Mota was a "constitutionalist"; officially, Ramírez Gómez was no "loyalist." Arms were never delivered.

To be sure, the PRD leaders in Santiago were not fooled by de la Mota's intrigues, nor did they harbor any illusions concerning the real position of the air base.[67] Given the total deficiency of the constitutionalist officers at the Fortaleza, it was up to the PRD to direct the struggle. The people looked to them for guidance—insofar as the people looked to leaders at all.[68] The PRD leaders had to act—but what should they do? Should they occupy the Governor's Palace? Issue proclamations in support of the revolt? Make speeches? Those would be vain gestures. San Isidro was preparing to crush the revolt. In Santo Domingo, the battle had begun, but in Santiago the commanders clung to "neutrality." Under these conditions, to act could only mean to seize arms, for once civil war has struck, arms alone have the power to make themselves understood. To act meant hurling the people against the Fortaleza, if such were the price of forcing the "constitutionalists" inside to join the ranks of the revolt. With the Fortaleza in their hands, the constitutionalists could approach the air base on a very different footing.

The action involved risks; blood would undoubtedly be shed. But if it were done quickly and decisively, the operation could prove less costly than anticipated. De la Mota was wavering; many of his officers and soldiers would refuse to fire on the crowd; and in the face of the people's resolve, proconstitutionalist officers might overcome their fears.[69] Arms could be had by confiscating them from civilians, by attacks on small police stations, and, especially, by getting them from Santo Domingo.[70]

To arm the people and attack the Fortaleza were revolutionary acts. But there were no revolutionaries among the Boschist leaders of Santiago;[71] there were only honest democrats, good bourgeois who wanted to see a peaceful return to the moderate, constitutional government of Juan Bosch. An armed populace? For them as well this was too new, too shocking a notion. They had been waiting for a military countercoup that would unfold in calm. They were not yet ready to storm the Bastille.

The PRD wasted hours in futile talks with men who were only too eager to gain time—Colonel de la Mota and Major Joaquín A. Méndez Lara, second in command of the Fortaleza. About four hundred former soldiers—"trustworthy" men, "tried and true democrats" whom "it would be fine" to arm—were gathered at the Old Cemetery. But de la Mota and Méndez Lara were unwilling to grant the PRD leaders' request for weapons. They did not refuse outright, for they, too, were "constitutionalists." But they demanded guarantees, ostensibly to be sure that Communists and hooligans would not be armed. De la Mota asked for a list of those who would receive the hundred rifles he might give. Smelling a trap, the PRD leaders demurred;[72] hours passed, while at the Old Cemetery the former soldiers waited.

The crowd, meanwhile, was growing more and more impatient. Anxious to reassure them, the local commanders issued another communiqué, the second since the outbreak of the revolt. They were on the side of the people, they repeated; they even invited Wessin to "lay down his arms."[73] What more could one ask? While continuing their futile negotiations, the Boschist leaders were concerned lest the population resort to violence. "There was even a [constitutionalist] leader who urged the people to go back to their homes, 'because the military [was] on their side.' " A few days later "the home of this very leader . . . was raided" by the police.[74]

The evening of the twenty-fifth went by, then the twenty-sixth. The Constitutionalist Military Command could easily have intervened. Hernando Ramírez was fully aware of the real sentiments of de la Mota and Ramírez Gómez.[75] All that was needed to redress the situation was a little reinforcement from the capital: some weapons, a few soldiers—about a hundred staunch constitutionalists.[76] But again Hernando Ramírez failed to seize the chance.[77] At dawn on Tuesday, 27 April, Santiago was still, officially, constitutionalist. In Santiago, the military awaited the outcome of the decisive battle about to take place in Santo Domingo before throwing off their masks. They did not have to wait long. At that moment Wessin was preparing to hurl his tanks against the capital.

The cadets who had left the Military Academy on the evening of the twenty-fifth had headed "east, toward San Pedro [de Macorís]."[78] They had met with no obstacle, and, a few hours later, they entered the city in triumph. One of the officers who led them later wrote: "Upon our arrival in San Pedro de Macorís, we sent a delegation to the commander of the local Fortaleza. The commander surrendered the Fortaleza to us and put himself at our disposal with arms and men.[79] . . . We received an extremely warm welcome from the people, and material as well as moral support. We were now in authority. The police kept to themselves, hiding in their station until we evacuated the city."[80] Except for the capital, San Pedro de Macorís was the only city in the Republic controlled by a military force that was genuinely constitutionalist. The cadets had dared to "betray" Wessin. And yet the Enriquillo plan had not counted on their support. Nowhere had the "periphery" dared to stir themselves out of their prudent passivity: it was the cadets who crossed the Rubicon.

Now, with dawn of the twenty-sixth, the cadets and their officers had a grand opportunity, if only they dared seize it. Behind them lay San Isidro, which, for the moment at least, had too many problems to pose a serious threat. Before them stretched the eastern part of the country—La Romana, Higüey, Hato Mayor, El Seibo—a vast territory with a power vacuum waiting to be filled. The great majority of the population backed the revolt; the small army and police garrisons—ill-armed and poorly trained—hesitated to choose sides. Controlled by the cadets, San Pedro de Macorís, gateway to the eastern region, might have become the springboard for a blitz in that direction. True, 150 men were scant for an undertaking of this scope, even in the exceptional conditions in which it would have to be carried out. But the captain who commanded the San Pedro army garrison made available to the cadets the Fortaleza, with its personnel and armaments. Profiting from the paralysis of the local garrison, those arms could have been distributed to civilians chosen from among members of the PRD, in collaboration with the party's local committee. Groups of armed civilians solidly officered by cadets could have been organized, and a part of that mixed force could have swept down on La Romana and repeated the operation. La Romana would have been the first step in the liberation of the eastern region; thirty-three miles of good road was all that lay between it and San Pedro de Macorís. A working-class city, a city with revolutionary traditions,[81] La Romana represented an invaluable prize for the constitutionalist cadets.

Arm civilians? The cadets were disciplined; they obeyed their officers. But their officers were not revolutionaries. It was one thing to defy Wessin, quite another to arm the people. The people would not be armed. The cadets would not advance to La Romana.

When, on the evening of the twenty-fifth, the cadets quit San Isidro, the *conjunto* faced a fresh threat. The extent of that threat, however, would depend on how the new rebels used their forces and on the energy of their leaders. Ultimately, the cadets failed to raise the banner of revolt in the east, on San Isidro's left flank; they, too, sank into inaction. The twenty-sixth and a part of the twenty-seventh passed quietly in San Pedro de Macorís, where the cadets disturbed no one and no one thought of disturbing them. The two days were spent "taking measures to defend the town in anticipation of an attack by the CEFA." On the afternoon of the twenty-seventh, planes from San Isidro strafed San Pedro de Macorís, at which point the few officers from the Academy who were leading the cadets "decided to abandon [their] positions." After spending two days setting up the town's defenses, the cadets fled San Pedro de Macorís, hoping that, by taking a circuitous route, they would reach the capital without encountering the enemy. After a long detour—"taking the road to Sabana de la Mar, crossing Samaná Bay, then reaching Sánchez"—they finally arrived in the neighborhood of Santo Domingo "by way of the Cibao." It was 29 April; in two days the cadets had traveled well over two hundred miles, and no one had tried to stop them. "The military and the police [of the various localities] paid us no attention and didn't block our way." Since they did not know the situation in Santo Domingo, they sent out scouts once they neared the city. But the scouts never returned. Then in a group, arms and all, in uniform, the cadets and their officers entered the capital "with no idea that we might be attacked."[82] Such confidence is hard to explain, inasmuch as the scouts sent out to determine the situation in the city had failed to return.

In Calle César Nicolás Penson, near the Presidential Palace, stood the barracks of the Corps of Adjutants of the president of the Republic, occupied, on 29 April, by a score of "loyalist" soldiers. Suddenly, at the end of the street, the cadets appeared. As one of the officers of the cadets later told it, "we offered no resistance, because at first we believed that they were on our side."[83] Harsher, but still candid, is the version by Morilí Holguín, the CEFA lieutenant who headed the small band of "loyalists." "They [the cadets] let themselves be captured like children." "Halt," shouted Holguín "and they halted." "Drop your arms," he yelled, "and they dropped them."[84] One hundred and forty-four cadets together with a score of noncommissioned officers and officers—including a major and two captains—were taken prisoners by a lieutenant and around twenty men, with no resistance.

And so, in a lonely street in the capital, the "epic" of the constitutionalist cadets ended ingloriously, unspectacularly. Perhaps those youths most needed a determined chief, an officer capable of drawing all the inferences from the bold action taken on the afternoon of the twenty-fifth. They had no such officer.

Chapter 9

San Isidro's Gamble Fails (from Dawn of 27 April to the Afternoon of 28 April)

27 April. Sunrise over Santo Domingo, the rebel bastion. Radio San Isidro is alive with invective. The day of decision is at hand. San Isidro readies itself for the final blow, the grand offensive that will crush the revolt.

With their machine guns and their bombs, the planes could undermine a people's will to resist and weaken enemy defenses. But they could not occupy territory or conquer a city. That required the infantry, so Wessin and de los Santos prepared to send in the troops to take the capital: Operation Mop Up.[1]

In the harbor stood the warships of the Dominican navy. Twenty-four hours earlier, the navy had been "constitutionalist." Rivera Caminero had gone to inform Molina Ureña of the navy's adherence, and "he had seemed sincere." His officers had hastened to follow suit, some at the Presidential Palace, others on Radio Santo Domingo TV. But that was twenty-four hours earlier, when the constitutionalists seemed on the verge of victory, and pressure from the American embassy had not yet had time to take effect. Now, one day later, Rivera Caminero and his men had thought it over—with the help, of course, of the U.S. naval attaché.[2]

27 April. Sunrise over Santo Domingo, a battered city. The navy is no longer "constitutionalist." It has taken sides against the "Communist" revolt.[3] Reconciled at last, the generals and the admirals hatch their plot to crush the rebels. At 3 A.M., Rivera Caminero told U.S. officials that "the Dominican Navy and Air Force were planning an all-out attack on the rebels, starting with a heavy bombardment."[4] Operation Mop Up was ready to begin. But there were American citizens in Santo Domingo, and they had to be lifted out of the hellfire about to consume the city. Already on the twenty-sixth, the U.S. embassy had decided to evacuate its nationals, and Connett had asked the two sides for a cease-fire to permit their safe evacuation. Some would be lifted by helicopter from the Embajador, the luxury hotel on the western outskirts of the capital. Others would be evacuated by ship from Haina, a port seven miles from Santo Domingo. Both the constitutionalists and the "loyalists" agreed to cooperate fully. The evacuation was to begin at six o'clock the next morning. Thus there were no air raids as the twenty-seventh dawned; a cease-fire was in force until eleven o'clock.

Would the opposing sides take advantage of the lull to negotiate? Even if they did, was there any chance for a solution other than the submission of one

party to the other, the vanquished yielding to the victors? The "loyalists" saw
victory close at hand, but the constitutionalists still did not feel the full brunt of
defeat. With no ground for agreement, the negotiations collapsed before they began; the adversaries could not even agree on a place to meet. The time had
passed when de los Santos and Wessin sent delegates to the constitutionalists
at the Presidential Palace. Now San Isidro was calling the plays. It was the generals' turn to choose the place where the rebels would be advised of the winners'
conditions. The constitutionalists were not to negotiate, but to yield; should
they balk, said "loyalist" navy Captain Milo Jiménez Reyes, "we are going to
destroy them."[5]

The Americans informed the constitutionalists of San Isidro's demands.
At about nine in the morning on the twenty-seventh, Hernando Ramírez met
with American officers for the first time since the outbreak of the countercoup.[6] They told him that if he wanted to negotiate, he and Molina Ureña
would have to go to Haina and board one of the Dominican warships in the
harbor. San Isidro's envoys would be waiting there. Hernando Ramírez refused,
as did Molina Ureña, who received the same message from Breisky, second secretary at the American embassy.[7] The two leaders insisted that the talks be held
at the Palace.

Lieutenant Colonel Thomas Fishburn, U.S. Air Force attaché, relayed the
refusal to Jiménez Reyes:

> Fishburn: President Molina talked with his staff and says that he
> wants to guarantee the safety of the people of the Chief of
> Staff of the Navy and the Chief of Staff of the Air Force.
> He wants to talk, but he wants to talk in the Palace. Do you
> understand? Over.
>
> Jiménez Reyes: Wait a minute. [Noise and Silence.] [8]
>
> Fishburn: Hello!
>
> Jiménez Reyes: No. Eh! Hello! Eh. Fishburn. Eh? If they want to talk they
> have to come here [Haina].
>
> Fishburn: That's your decision?
>
> Jiménez Reyes: Yes. That's our decision. If they are going to talk they
> are . . . they are going to talk here. If not we are going to
> destroy them.
>
> Fishburn: All right. I will call back and tell them . . . tell you what
> they say. All right?[9]

The constitutionalists, meanwhile, sought a compromise. Molina Ureña proposed that the talks be held at the Colombian embassy, but Jiménez Reyes refused, telling Fishburn: "We are not going anywhere. If they want to talk, they
are going to talk here. That's our position."[10] The constitutionalists wanted to
negotiate. Molina Ureña made a major concession. He would send two personal
representatives to Haina: his close adviser and PRD leader Leopoldo Espaillat
Nanita and Colonel Caamaño, his minister of interior.[11] It was not enough.
Perhaps not even the unconditional acceptance of their demands would have
satisfied the "loyalists." The truce was still in force. Seeing his latest proposal rejected, Molina Ureña might yield altogether. But so what? Confident of victory

and of their ability to easily crush the revolt, the "loyalists" were no longer willing to wait. They were eager to launch Operation Mop Up. "Loyalist" navy Captain Rafael Rivas told Jiménez Reyes: "We're going to have to start to move fast."[12]

Early resumption of hostilities could endanger the evacuation of U.S. citizens. Fishburn protested, telling Jiménez Reyes: "The message I received from the Air Force said that they will give us until eleven o'clock to move the Americans out. Now we have had trouble at the Embajador. They have been shooting into Americans, . . . into groups of Americans and there is a delay in moving them. Do you understand?"[13] A premature renewal of hostilities would break the truce and destroy the last hopes, however slim, of a negotiated surrender of the rebels. But Fishburn's only concern was for the safety of the Americans, and he easily came to terms with the "loyalists": "Can you guarantee that you will not fire or bomb the route between the Embajador and Haina?" he asked. Promptly Jiménez Reyes promised: "Oh yes. Of course, of course. If no . . . we are not going to bother with your movements there. The bombardment is going to be here."[14] The guarantee granted, Operation Mop Up could begin at last.

Shortly before noon, Dominican warships, lined up along the shore of the capital, opened fire in the direction of the Presidential Palace and the Duarte Bridge.[15] The air force had already gone into action, surpassing in violence its exploits of the previous day. Bombs were dropped in the area of the Palace and Radio Santo Domingo TV, on Ciudad Nueva, and on the northern sector of the city. But the fiercest strikes were aimed at the districts bordering on the western approaches to the Duarte Bridge. The terrain had to be prepared for the troops of the CEFA to minimize the resistance they might encounter in their advance.[16] The air force bombed for an hour and a half, then began a series of strafing raids. Behind the bridge, on the east bank of the Ozama, the tanks and the infantry waited patiently for the planes to finish their job.

At the Palace, seat of the constitutionalist government, bad news poured in: San Isidro was bombing, the navy had deserted to the enemy, and the Duarte Bridge was a scene of carnage, its defenders massacred even before the enemy infantry had launched an attack. Molina Ureña found himself increasingly isolated. The crowd had fled in the wake of the raids. Contacts with the outside had been cut. The Palace phones were out.[17] The speech he was scheduled to deliver at noon could not be broadcast because Radio Santo Domingo TV had been hit by a bomb and had gone off the air. Only the strident voice of Radio San Isidro could still be heard.

Everything seemed lost. For Lovatón Pittaluga, Molina Ureña's minister of foreign affairs, resistance was futile. The carnage must stop. The constitutionalist cause had collapsed under the awful weight of the bombs. San Isidro had triumphed. Only foreign mediation could soften the victor's demands and, above all, temper his vengeance.

Lovatón undertook this lonely mission on his own, turning to the Colombian ambassador, Jesús Zarate Moreno, who, in the absence of the Papal Nuncio,[18] was the dean of the diplomatic corps.[19] Although he was eager to help,

Zarate Moreno could do nothing. Only the United States embassy could help Lovatón Pittaluga. It alone had the necessary contacts with San Isidro.

Still fresh in Lovatón's mind was the hostile, nearly violent welcome he had received at the U.S. embassy on the afternoon of the twenty-fifth. That is why he had turned to Zarate Moreno. Now he had no choice but to return to the U.S. embassy. There he asked to see Connett, but the chargé d'affaires refused to receive him, alleging that he was very busy with the arrangements for the evacuation of American nationals. Because of this refusal, Lovatón met for the second time in less than forty-eight hours with the embassy's second secretary, Arthur Breisky, who was accompanied by Alfonso Arenales, a political officer.

The meeting was brief. As the minister of a moribund government, Lovatón Pittaluga could offer nothing. He asked for a truce and an end to the bombings. He thought that Molina Ureña and Hernando Ramírez would now submit to San Isidro's demands and accept the installation of a military junta. He asked for an abrupt halt to the military operation, which by then was in full swing and seemed assured of a quick success, even if the cost in human lives would be high. In return, he offered negotiations that could prove difficult, with new delays that might strengthen the morale of the "rebels" while weakening the will of the "loyalists."

It was too little and too late, and Lovatón was acting on his own, without any mandate. Breisky turned down his appeal, claiming that the United States embassy had no contacts with San Isidro. That was a patent lie, and Lovatón knew it, but he understood the message: the United States had no intention of halting Operation Mop Up. His last hopes destroyed, Lovatón left the embassy. Instead of returning to the Palace, he took refuge at the Mexican embassy. Molina Ureña's government now had no foreign affairs minister.[20]

Yet all was not lost. Wessin's tanks and the "loyalist" infantry had finally launched their attack, crossing the Duarte Bridge,[21] but the defenders held out, refusing to acknowledge defeat. The planes and warships had performed their bloody work: "Hundreds of bodies were strewn about the ground . . . [witness to the] great destruction wrought by the air force and by the shelling of the Navy."[22] If the tanks were to reach the Avenida Duarte, the battle would be lost. If from there they penetrated further south into the Avenida Mella, the revolt would be crushed. Between the western entrance to the bridge, now controlled by San Isidro, and the Avenida Duarte stood five streets: Manzana de Oro, Josefa Brea, Dr. Betances, Juana Saltitopa, and José Martí. There were hundreds of bodies in those streets, but even more survivors, resistors armed with machine guns, rifles, and Molotov cocktails. Behind every window, at every street corner, on every roof stood soldiers, young officers, civilians, even women and children. It was a disorderly, disorganized mass, and the great majority had no military training. The "loyalists" advanced, occupying Manzana de Oro and Josefa Brea streets. The advance was arduous, and each foot took a costly toll in lives. "The defenders fought like cornered bulls."[23]

So the battle went on. But for the leaders of the movement—both civilian and military—it hardly mattered. They had abandoned all hope of victory. Although Molina Ureña remained in the Palace, other civilian leaders followed the example of Lovatón Pittaluga and sought asylum in foreign embassies. By the afternoon of the twenty-seventh, virtually the entire PRD leadership had deserted.[24] To find them, one had simply to make the rounds of the embassies. Peña Gómez, the most popular PRD leader after Bosch, was safe at the Mexican embassy while the PRDist masses were dying near the Duarte Bridge. With Peña Gómez were Antonio Martínez Francisco, secretary-general of the PRD, and two other high-ranking party leaders, José A. Brea Peña and Pablo R. Casimiro Castro.

Although he was increasingly isolated, Molina Ureña refused to give up. True, the defenders at the bridge were holding out, but where were Caamaño, Hernando Ramírez, and Montes Arache? They had lost their nerve. Professional soldiers, the top constitutionalist officers judged the situation from their habitual viewpoint, the only one they had ever known. On the side of the revolt stood the people, a chaotic mass of civilians brandishing arms that, more often than not, they did not know how to handle. They had no military training and knowledge of combat techniques. The elite forces of the revolt—the Sánchez and Duarte battalions—had ceased to exist. Some of the soldiers had deserted; others lay lifeless in the battle-scarred streets. Still others went on fighting, but the number of deserters grew by the hour and those soldiers who still resisted found themselves inextricably entangled in the disorderly mass of civilians, lost in confusion and despair. Discipline was gone; no effort to organize seemed possible. On the enemy side stood the "professionals" led by their officers, with heavy armament—tanks, planes, cannons—that the rebels lacked.

Very little was expected from the forces in the interior. Santiago Rodríguez Echavarría had failed in his effort to "revolutionize" the Santiago Air Base, which clearly was hostile to the revolt (see Chapter 8, n. 77). Nowhere had the "periphery" dared to act, and now it was too late. From San Cristóbal, the elite Mella Battalion, a fresh force unscathed by the ravages of the civil war, was on the move toward the capital. At approximately two o'clock in the afternoon, news arrived at the Palace that the first units of the battalion had entered the western outskirts of the city, in the La Feria district. But the Mella Battalion—"constitutionalist" on the twenty-fourth, on the twenty-fifth, and still on the twenty-sixth—had not come to succor the beleaguered defenders. The Mella was now in the "loyalist" camp.

Between La Feria and the Palace, no force stood to block the advance of this new foe. The men fighting to halt the relentless drive of San Isidro were massed near the Duarte Bridge. The Mella troops had only to advance a few miles to take the defenders from behind and crush all resistance, if, in fact, they met any resistance.

Whereas Molina Ureña—a "tranquil man," a civilian and "hardly a great captain"[25]—refused to surrender, Hernando Ramírez, Caamaño, and Montes Arache had given up. Taking the route that Lovatón had followed a few hours before, the rebel military command beat a path to the U.S. embassy. Later in the day, Benjamin Ruyle, the embassy's first secretary, reported to Washington:

At about 3:00 P.M. on April 27 Col. F. Caamaño Deñó and Col. [sic] M. A. Hernando Ramírez, accompanied by 6 other persons in uniform, appeared at the Embassy. They were shown into Ben Ruyle's office. The principal spokesman was Col. Hernando Ramírez, but Col. Caamaño also spoke,[26] and there was no disagreement among the group that they had come to the Embassy to ask it to bring about a cease-fire. The members of the group stated repeatedly that "this massacre must stop; this shedding of blood must end" (referring to the air attacks on the National Palace and on the western Duarte Bridge approaches). Some of those present commented that they were exhausted, complitely [sic] worn out, and could not carry on. Ruyle asked Hernando Ramírez wether [sic] the cease-fire should be understood to be based on the group's willingness to see the formation of a junta, looking toward the holding of elections. Hernando's reply was affirmative; there was no demurral from anyone present.[27]

This was surrender. No one among that group could nurse illusions about the sincerity of San Isidro's pledge of elections. A military junta would be set up, and the constitutionalists would be powerless to oppose the arrogance of the victors. And yet the "constitutionalist" officers had taken up arms to erase the shame of 25 September 1963, to reestablish constitutionality, smashed by the violence of a coup. Now they crowded into the American embassy, having come "on their own initiative, behind the back and in disregard of"[28] Molina Ureña, their president, who still refused to surrender.

Whatever the extenuating circumstances, their action was nothing but a coup d'etat against Molina Ureña. It was the same as renouncing their status as "constitutionalist" officers. They had "abandoned . . . the struggle, while [in the Palace] Dr. Molina Ureña, together with a tiny number of die-hards, . . . put up with the bombing."[29] Yet in a last-minute surge of dignity, one of them commented that "they were in agreement concerning the matter, but that they could not proceed without the approval of the 'President.' "[30] None of the officers present objected to this flash of "constitutionalism." Ruyle drew the obvious conclusion, suggesting that "the group's first order of business should be to communicate with Molina; if the group could not act without Molina's approval, this approval should be sought urgently before other steps were taken." Escorted by a small band of constitutionalist officers, Ruyle himself went to the Palace in search of Molina Ureña. In his report, he described the scene he found: "The Palace was filled with rubble, broken glass and other debris, and seemed eerily devoid of life. Molina was finally located, surrounded by 8 or 10 persons, both civilians and military, huddled in a tiny corridor deep inside the Palace on a ground floor. No other living souls were in evidence in the Palace or in the area extending for several blocks around it." Molina Ureña refused to abdicate: "In his usual soft-spoken manner, but with intense emotion, he avowed his intention to remain in the Palace and die, if necessary, rather than betray the Dominican people and their aspirations for liberty and democracy."[31] But the evidence of defeat was overwhelming. He was alone, abandoned by the principal military leaders of the movement. At the American embassy, on the verge of taking the final step, those leaders had hesitated, acknowledging that "they could

not proceed without the approval of the 'President.' " Yet they were convinced that resistance was hopeless, that a continuation of the struggle meant only
useless slaughter. How long, under these conditions, would they continue to
seek the consent of their president, whose stubborn refusal they saw as blind
intransigence?

Upon Ruyle's departure, Molina Ureña was subjected to a variety of pressures. These pressures went in only one direction, for those eager to carry on the
struggle were not at the Palace to plead their cause, but in the streets, near the
Duarte Bridge, braving Wessin's tanks. So, "before the awkward situation of
lacking the support of his military leaders, already acting without his consent,"[32] Molina Ureña gave in.

At around four in the afternoon, Ruyle was at the U.S. embassy giving his
report to Ambassador W. Tapley Bennett, who had just returned to the country.[33] Suddenly,

> someone interrupted to announce Molina Ureña standing outside the front
> door of the Embassy . . . . Ruyle went to the front door to find Molina
> Ureña standing quietly at attention, surrounded by the officers who had
> been in the Embassy earlier, together with most of those Ruyle had seen
> with Molina in the National Palace, a total of about 16 persons.
>
> Asked whether he wished to enter, Molina silently nodded his head.
> When the door was opened, he advanced one step, unbuttoned his jacket,
> removed his small pistol and handed it to an aide, walked slowly through
> the door. All of those with Molina accompanied him into the Ambassador's
> office.[34]

After a four-day absence, Bennett had returned in time to witness the surrender
of the revolt. Before him stood the defeated leaders. The decisive meeting—
the "unhappy interview with W. Tapley Bennett, the interview of sorry
fame"[35]—could now begin.

Ruyle felt both compassion and esteem for the vanquished chief: esteem
for Molina's undaunted courage at the Palace; compassion for Molina, "standing quietly at attention" outside the embassy door, his every gesture an admission of defeat, yet fraught with dignity. But Bennett felt neither compassion
nor esteem for Molina. On the contrary, he felt a violent hostility and scorn.
This scorn is apparent in the report he sent to Washington: "Molina Ureña, nervous and dejected, was trying hard to carry himself as a constitutional president
and failing miserably."[36]

With Bosch's return to the presidency blocked and a military junta in the
offing, Ruyle believed that the U.S. embassy could have and should have accepted the role of intermediary, a role that could have spared the lives of hundreds. Risking his own life under the bombs, he had gone to see Molina Ureña at
the Palace. But Bennett rejected that role: "I declined courteously proposals
made by Molina that I attend negotiations with the dean of the dip corps and representatives of the church. I said I had no authority to participate and the U.S.
view was that accord should be reached by dominicans talking to dominicans."
Bennett's suggestion—"Dominicans talking to Dominicans"—was, of course, an

impossibility. His refusal to mediate dashed the last hopes of the constitutionalist leaders, leaving them little choice: asylum in an embassy or death in the streets. Bennett's description of the closing moments of the meeting, brilliant in style and bitterly ironic, paints some of his visitors "lingering as though trying to avoid going out again into [the] cruel world."[37]

All versions of the meeting agree on the fundamental issue—Bennett's refusal to mediate, a fact acknowledged by Bennett himself. There is disagreement, however, as to the way in which the ambassador treated his guests. They say he was "gruff;" he describes his conduct as "courteous."[38] "Courteous"— perhaps. Yet Bennett's own account shows him, like a schoolmaster righteously indignant with some naughty pupils, upbraiding the vanquished. All the frustration of a man who failed to foresee and to understand was given vent in his telegram to the State Department:

> I made clear our emphatic view senseless shedding of blood must end, at same time reminding them that it was their actions on Saturday which initiated this fratricide and called forth counter-reaction . . . . I underlined and reiterated there was no question communists had taken advantage of their legitimate movement,[39] having been tolerated and encouraged by PRD. I noted that in spite of fact PRD democratic party they had in effect given communists free rein, especially through military distribution of arms to civilians in large numbers, their tolerance of widespread looting and physical mistreatment of innocent persons. I said there was much talk of democracy on their part, but this did not impress me as road to get there. I came down strongly on disgraceful incident at Hotel Embajador where American lives were wantonly placed in peril this morning; was this an example of democracy in action?[40]

Thus, instead of mediation, the constitutionalists were given a lesson in "democracy"; when it ended, they were sent back into the cruel world. For some— including Caamaño and Montes Arache—this meant the road to the Duarte Bridge in search of an honorable death; for the majority it meant seeking asylum at the various embassies.

At this point the Molina Ureña government ceased to exist, its president abdicating and choosing asylum at the Colombian embassy.

Poor Molina. He had been called to the presidency on 25 April "until Professor Bosch, the constitutional president, returns to his native soil." Bosch's return had seemed imminent: "the next day, perhaps even this night." In his apartment in San Juan, Bosch's suitcases had been readied for the flight home. But the reaction of San Isidro made his return impossible.[41] And, instead of a brief, smooth transition, Molina Ureña had had to face the violence of civil war.

He was an interim president but lacked the authority of his office. To the extent that there was a central constitutionalist power during those first days of the revolt (25-27 April), such power rested in the hands of the military, especially Hernando Ramírez, the undisputed leader of the "hard-line" constitutionalist officers. It was the military who, on the twenty-fifth, conducted the negotiations with San Isidro, both in the morning and in the afternoon.[42] It was Hernando Ramírez who decided how the constitutionalists should react to San Isidro's challenge. He made the crucial decisions not to attack the *conjunto*, not to attack the Fortaleza Ozama and National Police Headquarters, and to show "flexibility" toward the "constitutionalists" in Santiago. And it was Hernando Ramírez who, at dawn on the twenty-seventh, offered Rivera Caminero the post of armed forces minister in the constitutionalist provisional government (see above, n. 3). Molina Ureña was never consulted: "Should I [Hernando] make the decision, Molina will have to accept it."[43] Early in the afternoon of the twenty-seventh, the constitutionalist military leadership went to the American embassy "behind the back and in disregard of" the provisional president.

In the face of such behavior by officers claiming to be the standard-bearers of a constitution, it is easy to fall into a facile irony. Too aware of their role—"We're the ones who made the countercoup; without us nothing would have been possible"[44]—and subject to the baleful influence of their milieu—Dominican society itself—many of those officers had only a vague notion of the principle of military submission to civil authority.

But there were other reasons for their attitude that mitigate a judgment that otherwise would be too harsh. First, the countercoup had been undertaken to re-establish "constitutional" government. Such a government was identified with the image of Juan Bosch: idol of the Dominican masses, charismatic leader, *caudillo*. But Bosch was absent. In his place, against a background marked by *caudillismo*, Article 132 of the 1963 constitution dictated a substitute, Molina Ureña, who had undeniable qualities, but was a good party functionary rather than a decisive leader. His position, moreover, was weakened by the provisional nature of his power. Yet above all it was San Isidro's challenge, hurled on the afternoon of the twenty-fifth, that explains and in part justifies Molina Ureña's self-effacement. Whether it meant civil war or was just a bluff, the reaction of San Isidro created a dramatic situation that could be resolved only by the threat or use of force. Thus, Molina Ureña, the civilian, naturally yielded power to the military, to Hernando Ramírez, the leader of the only organized force in the revolt. As president of the Republic, Molina Ureña's role was largely restricted to acts devoid of real substance: a few decrees, a few speeches, a few ministerial appointments.[45]

Given the circumstances, it is easy to paint Molina Ureña as a sorry little civilian completely overwhelmed by events, paralyzed by a crushing burden. Indeed, he was no "great captain," no man to dominate events. Yet, in the darkest hour of the revolt, when Caamaño and Montes Arache—tomorrow's heroes—lost heart, Molina Ureña refused to give up. Rather than an object of scorn or amusement, Molina Ureña became a figure of pathetic nobility: "huddled in a tiny corridor deep inside the Palace," but "wearing a coat and tie in spite of the heat."[46] Alone, abandoned, sure of defeat, Molina chose to die rather than sur-render. And when at last he yielded, he did so with honor; defeated but digni-fied—this is how he appeared to Ruyle at the door of the American embassy.

After Bennett's exhausting diatribe, it would have been dramatic had Molina followed Caamaño and Montes Arache to the Duarte Bridge, seeking the death which an hour earlier he had faced without fear. Dead or alive, he would have earned a place in the pantheon of Dominican heroes. But history has no room for myth, and its heroes reveal their flaws. Whereas Bennett's diatribe revived the resolve of Caamaño, Montes Arache, and a few others, it dealt a final blow to Molina Ureña, who, since that morning, had been subjected to extreme pressure: from the enemy, announcing defeat; from his comrades, urging surrender.

Yet it was not Molina Ureña's decision to forego the Duarte Bridge and seek asylum in the Colombian embassy that was later censured by his old as-sociates. Peña Gómez had done the same, and his prestige had grown during the course of the revolt. But Molina Ureña's asylum went on too long. Deaf to the appeals of his comrades and insensitive to the responsibilities of his position, Molina Ureña let days—then weeks—go by.[47]

A countercoup transformed into a revolt, a revolt radicalized by American intervention: a new world dawned and asserted itself. If Molina had been part of the battle at the Duarte Bridge and had shared with the people those hours of triumph and grief, he might have understood. But he was not there. The walls of the Colombian embassy stifled and distorted the cries of that newborn world. As a man of order, a man of law, Molina Ureña was not touched by the brother-hood born of common suffering that claimed to embrace even the far leftists, for they, too, died confronting the same enemy, the American aggressor and its Dominican lackeys (see Chapter 10).

That new world should have been his, but he hesitated, letting the gulf widen day by day. Yielding at last to pressure from his party (his prolonged absence was excellent fuel for enemy propaganda), Molina joined the constitu-tionalist bastion at Ciudad Nueva.[48] But it was too late; he was a stranger among men he no longer understood and who resented his vacillations, too often taking them for proof of treason. The suspicions and the accusations embittered Molina, widening the gulf still further.[49]

After the end of the civil war, Molina Ureña broke completely with the constitutionalist movement. Thus one of the most eminent of the constitutiona-list leaders renounced his past and put his talents at the service of the Balaguer regime,[50] a regime that makes a bitter mockery of "conciliation" and, in the name of the "law," hunts down those calling for a more just future.

Along with Molina Ureña, Hernando Ramírez also quit the constitutionalist stage on 27 April, seeking refuge in the Ecuadorean embassy. An able officer who enjoyed the respect of his comrades, Hernando Ramírez had replaced the absent Fernández Domínguez in the spring of 1964. Having only limited sym-pathy for Bosch, he had become a Boschista in the name of "constitutionality." As the military chief of the conspiracy, he had planned a coup that, despite an entirely unorthodox aim—re-establishment of a legal government instead of the eternal military junta—was to be effected by orthodox means, with the armed forces playing the leading role, the populace in a walk-on part, and the far left offstage. But San Isidro's reaction on the twenty-fifth had unleashed civil war. As events unfolded, their intensity and their violence surprised and shook this conscientious, honest officer, who could never have foreseen anything but the order and calm of a bloodless military coup.

Hernando Ramírez revealed the limits of his personality. He was not the man to direct a civil war, not the man to lead in a common struggle the armed populace that already, and with mounting fury, surged into the desolate streets of Santo Domingo. Helpless to dominate events, he chose to deny their existence. He persisted in believing that San Isidro would finally yield (see Chapter 8).

As the twenty-fifth dawned, Reid Cabral was in fact a prisoner at the Palace, but it took him several hours to realize his impotence and to draw the necessary conclusions. Wise enough to forbear, the constitutionalists' patience was rewarded. Without a fight, without any effort, they arrested the Triumvir. Hernando Ramírez thought that San Isidro would in time give up as well. The breach within the Dominican armed forces would be quickly healed; Dominican soldiers would not have fired on other Dominican soldiers. On the twenty-seventh, Hernando Ramírez finally understood, but for him it was too late. Twice that afternoon he made the sad pilgrimage to the American embassy.

Later, Hernando Ramírez did not follow Caamaño and Montes Arache to the Duarte Bridge. His illness, no doubt, prevented his going; he sought refuge in an embassy, missing the chance to add a new, more human, dimension to his experience, the chance to discover, as Caamaño and Montes Arache did, the Dominican people whom he probably never knew except across barracks fences. And it leaves a bitter taste, a question without an answer: would Hernando Ramírez have gone to the Duarte Bridge had he not been ill? Would he have been able, above all, to take part in the metamorphosis of that "band of bold and determined men" who, at the bridge, "rediscovered, unwittingly, the gestures and commands of the loyalist officers fighting alongside the people of Barcelona in July 1936"?[51]

On 12 June, his illness cured, Hernando Ramírez joined his former officers at Ciudad Nueva. On 16 June, during a violent American attack against the constitutionalist zone, he was hit by grenade fragments. The wound no doubt seemed a godsend, since it offered him an "honorable" excuse to flee a place where he already felt himself a stranger.

Political reasons explain in part the alienation of Hernando Ramírez.[52] Not having shared in the metamorphosis of his fellow constitutionalist officers, he considered the radicalization of the revolt unjustified and dangerous.[53] But personal motives were even more important. True, Hernando Ramírez had escaped Molina Urena's painful experience. No one doubted his loyalty; no one accused him of treason. Upon his arrival at Ciudad Nueva, he was named "counselor to President Caamaño"—a bitter irony for a man unable to forget that he had been the leader of the constitutionalist forces. "Counselor" to his former subordinate, Hernando Ramírez would have liked to become Caamaño's mentor, his éminence grise—the only way, perhaps, to sweeten the bitterness of wounded pride. He was full of advice on political and military matters. But he had just arrived and was plunged into an atmosphere that was utterly foreign to him. He himself has emphasized that, as a "counselor," he was treated with respect, consideration, and courtesy. During his absence, however, others had shared with Caamaño the most dramatic moments of the revolt: the battle at the Duarte Bridge, the shock of the American invasion, the first gropings of the consititutionalist government, the agony of the northern districts of the capital, and the painful apprenticeship of negotiating with the invaders' representatives. A small core of men had formed and grown close. Too preoccupied with the achievements of his own past, Hernando Ramírez was unable to become part of the present. Wounded, he left Ciudad Nueva, even though a hospital was functioning there. Once treated, he went into a self-imposed exile (29 July) in Puerto Rico.[54]

At the very moment that Molina Ureña, Hernando Ramírez, and so many others escaped into embassies, newspapers around the world were preparing to announce the defeat of the constitutionalist movement. "The military-civilian revolt aimed at restoring former president Juan Bosch to power . . . collapsed tonight at the end of a day of savage fighting," wrote the *New York Times*; San Isidro's forces "swept into the city with tanks and men," reported the *Washington Post*.[55] Betrayal and physical force had joined hands to crush the revolt. Betrayal—by Rivera Caminero, the Mella Battalion, de la Mota and Ramírez Gómez in Santiago, and others who followed their example; betrayal abetted and blessed by the American embassy, whose attachés had stressed to Rivera Caminero, de los Santos, and Wessin that everything possible should be done to prevent a "Communist takeover." Yet to complete their victory, the "loyalists" would have to occupy the capital, finishing the "liberating" work of the planes and warships.

Beginning in the early afternoon, the "loyalist" infantry launched its attack.[56] Having crossed the Duarte Bridge, the troops pushed ahead toward the Avenida Duarte, meeting fierce resistance. Meanwhile, farther west, inside the city, stood Montás Guerrero's Mella Battalion. Had it advanced the few miles to the combat zone it would have caught the rebels in a crossfire and made further resistance impossible. But Montás was a Balaguerista, and Wessin was Balaguer's enemy. Montás belonged to the San Cristóbal Group, a recent victim of a crackdown by Wessin and Reid Cabral. Montás himself had been directly affected: on 17 February, he had been forced to give up his position as army chief of staff for the far less important post of minister of the interior. For the moment, Montás and Wessin, Balagueristas and Wessinistas, were united in their opposition to Bosch's return to power. But the impending defeat of the constitutionalists undermined that unity. In the days ahead, as in the past, Wessin's ambitions would represent the chief obstacle to those of the Balaguerist officers. Montás Guerrero's presence in the capital proclaimed his right to share in the spoils of victory. But the price of victory would be Wessin's alone. Thus the Mella Battalion failed to advance, failed to close in on the bridge from the rear and strike the forces that, by their sacrifice, drained Wessin's strength. Despite the planes and the ships, despite the support of the American embassy and the betrayal of all too many "constitutionalists," Wessin was alone. His men would have to confront the enemy by themselves. The hour of truth had come; Wessin's defeat was at hand.

Shortly before five o'clock, the "loyalist" forces reached Calle José Martí, the last of the five streets lying between the Duarte Bridge and the Avenida Duarte. One last push—two hundred yards more—and they would reach Avenida Duarte. But the "loyalist" forces never made it. Harried by rebel counterattacks, they gave ground. Again they went on the offensive, but again they had to retreat. As night fell, darkness favored the defenders. Wessin's troops abandoned the terrain they had won so painfully that afternoon. Once more, they crossed the Duarte Bridge, but this time in the direction of San Isidro. Shortly after six o'clock, they withdrew to the eastern bank of the Ozama. The "loyalist" offensive ended in defeat; Operation Mop Up had backfired.

Later many people would speak of the "miracle at the bridge." Indeed it was a miracle to all—be they constitutionalists, "loyalists," or other observers—who had concluded that the constitutionalist cause was lost even before San Isidro launched its offensive. On the twenty-sixth and in the morning of the twenty-seventh, the air force, eventually joined by the navy, had tried to destroy the people's will to resist. They had hoped to turn Operation Mop Up into a walkover—to occupy ground already won and perhaps to crush the last nests of "Communist" resistance. The "miracle" took shape when, despite the bombs and machine-gun fire, hundreds of soldiers and thousands of civilians massed at the Duarte Bridge to block the entry of the CEFA forces. De los Santos and Rivera Caminero had failed. There would be no walkover; the CEFA would have to fight at the bridge.

And so the contest was on. On one side stood men—civilians and military—who had chosen to defy death. Their motives—be they noble or mean[57]—were varied but powerful: powerful enough to drive them to endure the murderous bombings and confront San Isidro's tanks and infantry. On the other side stood troops that had never fought in the streets of a city nor faced an enemy able to defend itself. Nor had hours of bombing familiarized them with the specter of death. For them too, it was a baptism of fire.

Why were they there, advancing under rebel fire? To defend Wessin's interests or the few benefits they derived from their relatively privileged status? Or were those "soldiers of the Christian, democratic West" risking their lives to crush this fresh "Communist aggression" and safeguard the "eternal values" restored by the coup of September 1963 and the dictatorship of the Triumvirate? In any case, they advanced, obeying orders. How many would have been there if they had had the choice?

Wessin's tanks were hampered by the narrow streets between the Duarte Bridge and the Avenida Duarte. The lack of coordination between tanks and infantry and other such errors made by the CEFA officers aggravated the situation.[58] Yet it would be quite unfair to place responsibility for those blunders on Wessin. The general was careful to stay away from the site of the battle because "his death would have been an irreparable loss to the cause being fought." He remained at San Isidro in his office, out of range of any stray bullets.[59]

The rebels' morale was bolstered with every passing hour. The resistance ceased to be an illusion: it was real. At the same time, San Isidro's morale declined. The walkover was transformed into a nightmare, as victory was stubbornly denied. Marcelino Zapico writes: "Very quickly it became clear that the San Isidro military lacked the force to enter the city. They had the aircraft and the ships, but they didn't have the army necessary to prevail over the constitutionalist troops and the armed militiamen."[60] Just how many men would Wessin have needed to break the constitutionalist resistance? "Ten thousand," according to Llano Montes.[61] Perhaps. But Wessin did not have ten thousand men.[62] The battle was unequal and retreat inevitable.

Yet, at least on the surface, the constitutionalists had won only a defensive victory, and although it salvaged a gravely compromised situation, it failed to settle the conflict. Driven from the capital, San Isidro's troops still occupied the eastern approaches to the Duarte Bridge. The air force and the navy were still "loyalist." Even in Santo Domingo, the rebel bastion, the constitutionalists were not the sole masters. In the western districts, the National Police Headquarters and the two barracks of Intendencia and Transportación were potential threats to constitutionalist control. The important Fortaleza Ozama in Ciudad Nueva and a few police stations throughout the capital were still in the hands of the police.

Is it really possible to speak of "constitutionalist control" of the capital? The Molina Ureña government had come apart, most of the civilian and part of the military leaders had taken refuge in the embassies, officers had lost control over their troops. Given these conditions, was the constitutionalist movement, despite its victory at the bridge, anything but a riot? Were the rebel forces anything but mobs, somewhat well armed, but neither disciplined nor cohesive; mobs condemned to wander aimlessly about the streets of the capital, "terrorizing whole neighborhoods and indiscriminately firing weapons"?[63] Many "observers," the U.S. embassy among them, concluded that, unable to exploit their success and alienating by their excesses the moderate elements who had supported the revolt, the rebels would succumb to a new "loyalist" offensive. San Isidro would doubtless take advantage of the lull afforded by the enemy's disarray, and Montás himself, finally perceiving the seriousness of the threat, would agree to coordinate his action with Wessin. The embassy's optimism was shared in Washington, where, on that evening of 27 April, a feeling of confidence still prevailed as to the outcome of the struggle. Events in Vietnam, much more than the Dominican crisis, occupied the attention of the U.S. government.[64]

At this point a crucial role was played by a group of rebel officers, led by Colonel Caamaño, who now emerged as the leader of the revolt. Coming from the U.S. embassy, Caamaño, Montes Arache, and a few other officers had arrived at the Duarte Bridge shortly after five in the afternoon, in time to take part in the final phase of the battle and link their names with the glory of the victory. Their part in that battle was far from decisive, yet the importance of their presence should not be underestimated, for it gave the defenders the feeling that they were not alone, that their leaders had not all defected. And in exploiting the victory and reorganizing the revolt, they did play a decisive role. The hundreds of soldiers and young officers who took part in the battle needed leadership. Now Caamaño and Montes Arache, senior officers worthy of confidence, had arrived. Their presence proved their attachment to the common cause and the sincerity of their support. Moreover, rifts among constitutionalist officers had disappeared. No longer was the "atmosphere poisoned by betrayal" (see Chapter 8). The ordeal of the last few days, and of the last few hours especially, had effected a natural purge, banishing the opportunists and the weak to the embassies and the homes of friends. Those who remained—braving the tanks, after standing up under the planes—were all "hard-liners." Now they gathered around Colonel Caamaño, the officer of highest rank among the constitutionalists, Molina Ureña's minister of the interior and Hernando Ramírez's choice as his successor.

Only navy Captain Montes Arache, by virtue of his rank and prestige, could have challenged Caamaño's primacy and thus threatened the restored unity of the constitutionalist armed forces. But a capricious lust for power was not one of Montes Arache's many faults. He put his talent and influence at the service of the man he recognized as Hernando Ramírez's successor: "Francis" Caamaño, his long-time friend. And with Montes Arache's support went that of the frogmen, an elite and, in the presence of their chief, disciplined force.

Of course, the constitutionalist military was only a minority among the mass of armed civilians. Three days earlier, an open, direct collaboration between the people in the capital and a Caamaño, a former high-ranking officer in the *cascos blancos*, would most likely have been unthinkable. It was the PRD that, by its presence and its identification with the revolt, assured the people of the sincerity of those officers who suddenly proclaimed themselves "constitutionalists." Now there was no longer a PRD to speak of, even if PRD masses swarmed in the streets. Bosch was still the leader and symbol of the revolt, but he was in Puerto Rico, and Molina Ureña and Peña Gómez were hiding in embassies.

No other party could have filled the power vacuum. Weak, divided, lacking charismatic leaders, the far left had trouble enough reorganizing its own forces. So the military was called on to fill the void. What no bloodless coup could ever have achieved was accomplished by San Isidro's savagery. Under the hail of machine-gun fire, during the raids on the police stations and the fighting at the

Duarte Bridge, a strong link had been forged based not on words but on shared suffering. It mattered little that, for the moment, the PRD had ceased to exist as an organized party; the constitutionalist military and the people had no more need of intermediaries. The PRD cadres and the Boschist masses now turned toward men like Caamaño and Montes Arache. The constitutionalist movement had found new leaders and would not break down into a riot.

Backed by his officers, Caamaño immediately set to work reorganizing the rebel forces. Surely it is an exaggeration to maintain that "Caamaño and Montes Arache were [already] in full control of the city";[65] surely order and discipline were still only relative. But the process had begun. And to carry it through, the constitutionalists could count on several highly competent military leaders, a populace that recognized those leaders as their own, and a passive foe.[66]

As the hours passed, confusion and anarchy gradually gave way to a degree of order. The constitutionalists of Santo Domingo got very little sleep that night as efforts to reorganize went on without interruption or respite. By the next morning, 28 April, it was clear that the rebels had reorganized themselves during the night and had gained new spirit and determination to win.

This new determination seized military and masses alike. For the constitutionalist military, there was no turning back. The civil war was a fact. Any chance for compromise had passed; victory alone would heal the breach within the armed forces. For the masses, a miracle had been accomplished. "Always they had been at the mercy of men with guns. Now, for the first time in their history, the people had guns, and they had forced the tanks to retreat. They were beating the armed forces that symbolized their centuries of misery. . . . They realized for the first time that they possessed a strength they never had before imagined could be theirs."[67] The constitutionalist movement had overcome the crisis caused by the lack of resolve of certain chiefs and the betrayal of others. A new spirit animated its ranks. The defensive phase had ended. Already in the morning of the twenty-eight, Caamaño led a successful attack by a combined force of military and armed civilians against the important police station located in the neighborhood of the Palace of Justice. It was the first time that a constitutionalist officer led such an attack—evidence of the new and more aggressive attitude on the part of the constitutionalist command. And this was only the first step: the next would be the rapid occupation of the few enemy ("neutral") strongholds still left in the capital; then a massive attack against the *conjunto* would take place.[68]

At San Isidro, meanwhile, "a severe test of nerves [was] in process."[69] Betrayal and physical force had joined to crush the revolt. But the revolt had triumphed. The "rabble" had endured the bombings, broken the thrust of the infantry, and thrown the attackers back across the Duarte Bridge. The tanks of the CEFA, the symbol of Wessin's power, had been forced to beat a retreat before civilians. Camped on the eastern bank of the Ozama were the survivors of the rout. Having failed to overcome rebel resistance, would they be able to halt a rebel offensive? "[CEFA] Colonel Morillo López was sent to survey the situation at the Duarte Bridge, where he found only a few loyalist troops; they were tired and frightened, and their morale was alarmingly low. Upon Morillo's return to San Isidro, the generals made an attempt to recruit more troops from neighboring garrisons; they could get a reinforcement of only twenty-five men."[70]

In Santo Domingo, Caamaño and Montes Arache were reorganizing the rebel forces; at San Isidro, panic gripped the numerous generals.[71] "It is not an impressive show," complained Ambassador Bennett; "Wessin is not making a very aggressive showing."[72] As best it could, the American embassy gave aid and comfort to "its" generals. Early on 28 April, when General de los Santos urgently asked the American embassy to provide fifty walkie-talkie radio sets, Bennett immediately seconded the request.

If it had taken many hours for the embassy in Santo Domingo to begin to realize the extent of Wessin's defeat, it took Washington even longer. Once again, there was no difference between Washington and the embassy as to the aims of U.S. policy. But now, for the first time since the twenty-fifth, a difference arose as to the means. The State Department, taken by surprise by the gloomy forecast of the embassy, initially refused to deliver the walkie-talkies, stressing its opposition to actions that would increase the visibility of the U.S. role, "unless the outcome should actually be in doubt."[73] For the embassy, the outcome was indeed in doubt—hence the request for the walkie-talkies. For Washington, the embassy was overreacting—hence the refusal. The refusal was given by a "hard-liner," Undersecretary Thomas Mann—soon to be a favorite target of the "liberals" in Washington.

Bennett was right—although he still failed to realize the full extent of the "loyalist" collapse. He, who had been so optimistic, now fought against Washington's optimism. He first tried to convince Assistant Secretary for Inter-American Affairs Jack Hood Vaughn by telephone. Then, after Vaughn invited him to make his argument by cable, he did so, at 1:43 P.M. in dramatic terms that left Washington little choice: "The issue here now is a fight between Castro-type elements and those who oppose. I do not wish to be over-dramatic but we should be clear as to the situation. If we deny communication equipment and the anti-rebel forces lose for lack of heart we may well be asking in the near future for landings of marines to protect U.S. citizens and possibly for other purposes. Which would Washington prefer?"[74] The question was rhetorical. Soon after the cable was received, McGeorge Bundy, special assistant to the president for national security affairs, authorized the delivery of the walkie-talkies.[75]

Among the many weaknesses besetting the "loyalist" generals was an absence of coordination, a result of their rivalries. American diplomats, striving to palliate the problem, "urged the formation of a junta" in the hopes that "the fragmented military forces would reunite and restore order."[76] In the early afternoon of 28 April the "loyalists" at San Isidro finally installed a military junta. Its president: Colonel Benoit, "a virtually unknown air force officer."[77]

Flanking Benoit were two other unknowns: Colonel Enrique A. Casado Saladin, for the army, and Captain Olgo M. Santana Carrasco, for the navy.[78]

The group was hardly a "combat junta." One of Benoit's first acts was to telephone the United States embassy "to ask for 1,200 U.S. marines to help restore order." Bennett refused to acknowledge this hard evidence of the moral bankruptcy of his protégés, cabling the State Department: "I do not believe the situation justifies it . . . . Logically the junta forces should be able to control the situation." But "the situation [was] not very logical,"[79] he added; short of military intervention, the American embassy was prepared to go to great lengths to weaken the constitutionalist cause and thus ensure the generals' victory. On the afternoon of the twenty-eighth, the Americans kidnapped Antonio Martínez Francisco, secretary-general of the PRD, from the Mexican embassy, where he had sought asylum the day before. In the words of José Moreno, Martínez Francisco "received a phone call from Arthur Breisky, Second Secretary at the U.S. Embassy, who asked him to come to the embassy to discuss important problems with W. T. Bennett. Martínez agreed, and a car arrived to take him from the Mexican embassy. Inside the car he found a loyalist colonel and a CIA agent who took him at gunpoint to San Isidro."[80] Convinced that he was going to be shot, Martínez Francisco was shaking so hard while in Benoit's office that he was unable to drink the cup of coffee that Benoit offered him.[81] He emerged a while later, and—"of his own free will and without the least coercion[!] "—went before the microphones of Radio San Isidro to read a statement "in which he declared that the revolution had been sidetracked from its goals, and, in consequence, he was inviting the militants of his party to lay down their arms."[82] The militants of the PRD, however, ignored this "free" and "uncoerced" advice.

But the abduction of a constitutionalist leader and logistic support (especially those fifty walkie-talkies) were merely half measures. In no way could they allay the generals' terror. A specter haunted San Isidro: the people flooding out of Santo Domingo, overwhelming all resistance and inundating everything in their path, a human deluge that would sweep over the *conjunto*, a scant nine miles from Santo Domingo. Against such a flood, the warriors who had not hesitated to bomb a defenseless populace saw only one barrier: the United States armed forces.[83] Shortly after five that afternoon, Bennett at last accepted the truth:

> CRITIC, CRITIC, CRITIC.
> Regret report situation deteriorating rapidly. San Isidro pilits [sic] tired and discouraged. [Police Chief] Despradel says cannot control situation. MAAG chief went to San Isidro, found [former Police Chief] Belisario Peguero there in an hysterical mood, urging "retreat,"[84] number of officers weeping. Benoit requests U.S. troops formally. The country team is unanimous that the time has come to land the marines. American lives are in danger. Proposes marine beachhead at Embajador Hotel. *If Washington wishes*, they can be landed for the purpose of protecting evacuation of American citizens. I recommend immediate landing.[85]

It was 5:16 P.M. The U.S. naval task force stationed off the coast of Santo Domingo was engaged in the evacuation of American citizens. But soon its role changed. At 6:53 P.M., the commander of the Marine Expeditionary Unit aboard the task force was ordered to send five hundred armed marines ashore.[86] Thinly disguised as a "humanitarian intervention,"[87] the United States invasion of the Dominican Republic had begun. San Isidro's nightmare was nearly over. Soon U.S. troops would act as a shield between the "loyalist" generals and the "rebel hordes." The shield would then give way to the sword.

Chapter 10

The Triumph of Might
(The "Solution" of the Crisis.
Its Immediate Aftermath:
The Provisional Government
of García Godoy)

With the landing of the marines the "Dominican phase" of the revolt came to an end.[1] Triumphant on the afternoon of 28 April, the constitutionalists could no longer hope for victory. But how crushing would their defeat be?

On the evening of the twenty-eighth, President Johnson announced the U.S. intervention in the Dominican Republic to the American public and to the world. There was no mention of a "Communist threat":

> The United States Government has been informed by military authorities in the Dominican Republic that American lives are in danger. These authorities are no longer able to guarantee their safety, and they have reported that the assistance of military personnel is now needed for that purpose.
>
> I have ordered the Secretary of Defense to put the necessary American troops ashore in order to give protection to hundreds of Americans who are still in the Dominican Republic and to escort them safely back to this country. This same assistance will be available to the nationals of other countries, some of whom have already asked for our help.[2]

At this stage, both the American government and its representatives in Santo Domingo still hoped to avoid a flagrant military intervention with serious repercussions not only in the United States but especially in Latin America. The Americans believed that the mere presence of the marines might be enough to discourage the rebels and encourage the "loyalists,"[3] who, of course, would also receive secret logistical support from the United States.[4] Thus, the 536 marines that landed on the evening of 28 April took no part in the fighting. They restricted themselves to positions around the American embassy and in the area around the Hotel Embajador, far from the combat zones and in the middle of the evacuation operation. A low-key intervention, one easily disguised as a humanitarian action: this was Johnson's policy on 28 April.

For a few hours, the policy seemed almost to succeed. The news that the marines had landed in the area around the Hotel Embajador caused a "general wavering"[5] among the constitutionalists, seriously compromising the efforts at reorganization begun after the victory at the Duarte Bridge. Nearly everyone was

256

convinced that the American troops would spread throughout the city and "crush the revolt."[6] "It's all over," thought *catorcista* leader Jimmy Durán.[7] Who could stand up against United States omnipotence? Many constitutionalists—both civilians and military—deserted the movement. Others stayed on, but according to "Baby" Mejía, "they all seemed paralyzed, as if waiting for something to happen."[8]

At that moment, the marines could have occupied the whole city "with very little effort."[9] But they did not advance. Washington was waiting for San Isidro to take the offensive. "Operation Clean Up is afoot and very soon the city will be free of the Communist mob," blared Radio San Isidro, which played the "Stars and Stripes Forever" between attempts at intimidation. "[I] believe that with determination your plans will succeed," Bennett declared in a "personal message of encouragement"[10] to Colonel Benoit.

Once more Bennett failed to understand the situation. The United States intervention, even in its currently limited form, had no doubt saved San Isidro, since it both halted the already well-advanced disintegration of the "loyalist" forces and paralyzed their foes. But it could not restore San Isidro's offensive capabilities. Wessin and the other generals were waiting for the Americans to "clean up" Santo Domingo for them. The struggle against Communism was, after all, a common effort; the generals' contribution would be to remain in the country and hurl their planes against the rabble. According to former Ambassador Martin, the State Department "asked why San Isidro had lost its will to fight."[11] The answer was evident: it never had one.

Once again, the constitutionalists seized the initiative. Their paralysis had lasted less than twenty-four hours. Beginning on the afternoon of the twenty-ninth, many constitutionalists returned, reassured by the Americans' seeming passivity or prompted by a feeling of shame at having run away on the twenty-eighth.[12] On the evening of the twenty-ninth, the Constitutionalist Military Command, which had begun to form around Colonel Caamaño in the wake of the victory at the Duarte Bridge, issued its first tract. Responding to Radio San Isidro, the tract called for "unity between armed civilians and soldiers" in order to "defeat decisively the criminal Wessin and his gang . . . . Cities are not won from the air; they are won on the ground, and so Santo Domingo will never be taken nor our people vanquished in their democratic struggle. Our arms and our breasts will block their drive. We will accept no solution but the complete reestablishment of constitutional government with Professor Juan Bosch as President of the Republic."[13]

Words quickly turned to deeds. On 30 April, Caamaño and his officers organized an attack against the Fortaleza Ozama, seat of the *cascos blancos*, using mixed civilian and military commando units. It was the first offensive action taken by the constitutionalist movement since the landing of the marines. The *cascos blancos* put up almost no resistance, and the Fortaleza, with its depot of four thousand arms, fell to the rebels. In the eyes of the Constitution-alist Military Command, this was only the first step. Next they would take Transportación, Intendencia, and the National Police Headquarters. Then it would be San Isidro's turn.

But it was too late. Even before the fall of the Fortaleza Ozama, Washing-ton finally understood. The generals' inaction on the twenty-ninth dispelled any lingering illusions. That afternoon Washington agreed to Bennett's request to land the remaining marines aboard the task force (1,166 men); they were not, however, to intervene in the combat zone. A few hours later, the Johnson ad-ministration realized that additional—and more momentous—steps were nec-essary to defeat the revolt. At 2:30 A.M. on Friday, 30 April, 2,500 men of the Eighty-second Airborne Division landed at San Isidro. It was the beginning of a massive military build-up that within ten days would reach a peak of 23,000 American troops on Dominican soil, almost half as many as were then serving in Vietnam. Also on 30 April, Johnson gave the public its first glimpse of the real nature of his "humanitarian intervention." "There are signs," he announced, "that people trained outside the Dominican Republic are seeking to gain control. Thus the legitimate aspirations of the Dominican people and most of their lead-ers for progress, democracy and social justice are threatened and so are the prin-ciples of the inter-American system."[14]

Two days later, on 2 May, Johnson took up the theme again, much more forcefully: "Communist leaders, many of them trained in Cuba, seeing a chance to increase disorder, to gain a foothold, joined the revolution. They took increas-ing control. And what began as a popular democratic revolution, committed to democracy and social justice, very shortly moved and was taken over and really seized and placed into the hands of a band of Communist conspirators."[15]

Johnson could no longer have hidden the political character of the Ameri-can intervention. Because of San Isidro's ineptitude and the constitutionalists' resilience, the United States was landing thousands of troops instead of the hun-dreds they had hoped would suffice. These troops began to play an active role in the conflict—the only way to save the "loyalists." On 30 April, the para-troopers of the Eighty-second Airborne Division pushed out of San Isidro to-ward the capital. Attacking the constitutionalists, they captured the Duarte Bridge and proceeded to secure an area of several blocks on its western approach, that is, in rebel Santo Domingo. Their superior firepower gave them a decisive edge, but unexpected resistance slowed their advance.

That same day, the marines fanned out from the area around the Hotel Embajador and occupied nine square miles in the western sector of the city, where they set up the so-called "International Security Zone" (ISZ) under U.S. control. Then, in a surprise attack on the night of 2-3 May, the paratroopers advanced along a narrow front from the bridgehead on the western approaches of the Duarte Bridge through the capital in order to line up with the marines of the ISZ. They set up a "corridor" bisecting Santo Domingo from the northeast to the southwest.[16] The constitutionalist forces were thus cut in two, confined to the Ciudad Nueva district in the southeast and the *barrios altos* in the north-east. To go from one zone to the other they had to pass through several check-points established along the "corridor." They were searched, and at times arrested. No one with arms was allowed through.

In spite of American psychological and military pressure the revolt did not collapse. After the victory at the Duarte Bridge, this was a second miracle. Al-though forced on the defensive, the constitutionalists carried on with their effort at internal reorganization; Colonel Caamaño's election to the presidency of the Republic on the night of 3-4 May was a first manifestation of that effort. The constitutionalist government tried to govern the limited sector still in its hands. It gave itself a structure: a cabinet, a military staff, and a Congress. It re-organized the armed forces and was even active on the international scene. There was still confusion and disorganization in Ciudad Nueva, but not the chaos that would allow the United States to use anarchy and blind violence as an excuse for launching a "humanitarian" police action and occupying the entire consti-tutionalist zone.

Yet Washington did not remain passive. Since the military junta was too discredited,[17] another government had to be found to challenge that of Caamaño. John B. Martin, Kennedy's ambassador and now Johnson's special envoy, took on the job. He acted swifty. His chief sources of information were the American embassy and his old friend Tony Imbert Barrera.[18] In a few hours, Martin "understood" everything. On 2 May, he held a press conference to announce his conclusions: "What began as a PRD revolt had in the last few days fallen under the domination of Castro/Communists and other violent ex-tremists."[19] "I felt the situation demanded a third force," he later wrote.[20] The president of this "third-force" government, Imbert Barrera, was at hand, as was a second member, Colonel Benoit. On 28 April, the generals had chosen Benoit to head the military junta; now they ordered him to scuttle his junta and join the new Government of National Reconstruction (Gobierno de Reconstruc-ción Nacional or GRN).[21] But the search for civilian members—"citizens of rec-ognized character"[22] who would impart a semblance of respectability to the enterprise—proved more difficult. Martin solicited a number of *honorables*. Some, constitutionalists[23] or "neutrals," refused; others, though hostile to the revolt, were smart enough not to compromise themselves in a government cer-tain to be hated and that would last just long enough for the Americans to come up with a less awkward solution.

At last, after several days, three civilians accepted: Alejandro Zeller Cocco, an engineer who, until then, was an unknown, and Carlos Grisolía Poloney, elected senator for the UCN in December 1962 and very active under the Trium-virate first as a minister of labor and then as governor of Puerto Plata.[24] The third was a relatively well-known bookseller, Julio Postigo. A friend of Juan Bosch, he was an excellent recruit for the GRN. Like Zeller Cocco, he had no political standing, but he enjoyed a reputation for honesty that his two col-leagues lacked. "Postigo had joined Imbert's government, a rival to Caamaño's

Bosch-inspired government," exulted Martin. "If ever a man joined a government not for himself but for his country, it was Julio Postigo."[25]

Postigo's case is indeed special. He agreed to join a government formed "on the influence and advice of President Johnson"[26] for motives other than political ambition or the wish to enrich himself. Postigo believed—or was led to believe—that that government was the only alternative to an American military offensive against the constitutionalist redoubts. And yet he could not be persuaded that the rebel movement was dominated by the Communists.[27]

On 7 May 1965 the Government of National Reconstruction was born. It had been constituted, it proudly announced to the Dominican people, with the blessing of the San Isidro military, Johnson's special envoy Martin, and Ambassador Bennett.[28] The birth certificate of this "third-force government" plainly betrayed the parentage:

> On this seventh day of May 1965, the undersigned, Members of the Government Military Junta, . . . have resolved the following:
> (1) to confer full powers on General Antonio Imbert Barrera—so that he might preside over and constitute a new Government in the way he deems fittest;
> (2) to declare the dissolution of the Junta so as to render feasible the above-conferred mandate.[29]

On 9 May, with the agreement of the American embassy, the new government cashiered Generals Belisario Peguero, Salvador Montás Guerrero, Atila Luna Pérez, and Félix Hermida, Jr., Admiral Julio A. Rib Santamaría, and Colonel Marcos Aníbal Rivera Cuesta; Generals Manuel M. García Urbáez and Renato Hungría Morel were retired.[30] Two days later they were all deported to Puerto Rico. But this act of "good will" (the officers in question were famous for their corruption) fooled no one: seven of these men had already been stripped of their commands, and the eighth, Montás Guerrero, a personal enemy of Imbert Barrera and of Wessin, had been deeply compromised by his inaction on 27 April (see Chapter 9). Yet Rivera Caminero, whose fleet had bombarded the capital, became minister of the armed forces; Jiménez Reyes was named navy chief of staff, and Colonel Jacinto Martínez Arana—a "hard-liner"—became army chief of staff.[31] De los Santos remained as air force chief of staff, and Wessin retained command of the CEFA. "They have killed the flies but left the beetles," Caamaño correctly observed.[32]

In the meantime, at the seat of the OAS in Washington, the Latin American delegates hid their countries' feelings of impotence under a flood of rhetoric. The United States had neglected to inform them of a military intervention in open contravention of articles 15 and 17 of the OAS charter.[33] Faced with a fait accompli that stirred a wave of resentment in Latin America, would the delegates dare to answer Washington's arrogance with a condemnation (contrary to the tradition of the organization)? A first meeting of the OAS Council on 29 April, and a second the following day brought the answer: although the Council resolved to convene the Tenth Meeting of Consultation of Ministers of Foreign Affairs in order to study the "situation created by the armed struggle in the Dominican Republic,"[34] the resolution failed to mention the armed intervention of the United States in the internal affairs of a member state.

Of course, there was the inevitable "difficult" minority in the OAS: Mexico, Chile, and Uruguay as a rule; others on occasion. Washington's job, therefore, would be to assemble the necessary majority of "consenters" and at the same time to confine the exasperation of the dissidents within limits compatible with the "dignity" of the organization. As usual, the OAS complied, an occasional tantrum being followed at once by a return to its accustomed docility thanks to Washington's vigorous reprimands.

The OAS refrained from condemning the unilateral actions of the United States. Better still, on 6 May, by the creation of an Inter-American Peace Force (IAPF), it provided a legal base for the illegal presence of American troops on Dominican soil. Proposing the establishment of the IAPF on 3 May, the United States "seemed extremely confident that it would be adopted quickly." But the proposal met with "stiff and unexpected opposition."[35] Three days of feverish activity followed, during which the United States bombarded the OAS "with hortatory, then commendatory statements." In the words of the *New York Times*, "it was apparent that there was growing impatience in the Administration. . . . It was also clear that the U.S. was not awaiting OAS sanction before continuing its military steps in the Dominican Republic."[36] On 5 May, in a "freewheeling talk," Vice-President Hubert Humphrey expressed his indignation at the recalcitrance of the Latin Americans and called on "the OAS to discard its 'dressing gown' of aloofness," berating it for its ignorance of the "realities of life." Proclaimed Humphrey, "the OAS ought to learn how to provide for law and order . . . lest we have to garrison place after place to uphold law and order and to protect the lives of citizens."[37]

Thus, the OAS submitted to the "realities of life." Fourteen votes were needed to carry the resolution, but on 6 May only twelve Latin American nations joined the United States in voting to create an Inter-American Peace Force. In order to make the count, the vote of José Antonio Bonilla Atiles was added to the thirteen others. Bonilla Atiles, minister of foreign affairs under the Council of State, was the Dominican delegate to the OAS under Reid Cabral. But the fall of the Triumvirate had left the Dominican Republic with two rival governments, neither of which was recognized by the other nations of the hemisphere. Neither, therefore, should have been allowed to vote.[38] But never mind that. Washington needed that vote, so a man—Bonilla Atiles—was turned into a country. The trick—legal legerdemain that heightened the ridicule engulfing the OAS—succeeded. And yet the dissident minority refused to draw the necessary conclusions and continued in an organization that flouted its own charter and the most elementary rules of international law.[39]

And the farce continued. On 12 May, Honduras became the first Latin American nation to contribute troops to the IAPF. "A majority of Latin American states are now expected to follow suit, with probably more than 10 nations making at least token contributions," optimistically commented the *New York Times*.[40] The *Times* was wrong. Faced with an outraged public opinion, several governments took care to avoid such an unpopular action.[41] Only six Latin American nations sent contingents to the IAPF:[42] Brazil, 1,152 men; Honduras, 250; Paraguay, 178; Nicaragua, 159; Costa Rica, 21; and El Salvador, 3. Haiti's *tontons macoutes* were absent from the IAPF. This was unfortunate—they would have been in good company. Soldiers from five dictatorships marched side by side in Santo Dominigo in defense of Dominican "democracy." And with them marched twenty-one Costa Rican policemen, a "ludicrous contribution to this international farce."[43]

Hugo Panasco Alvim, a Brazilian general, was given command of the IAPF. Modestly, the United States contented itself with the second-in-command, General Bruce Palmer, commander in chief of the American occupation forces. Not a diplomat, Palmer told the press that "if the OAS and the U.S. government get into a policy conflict, I would have to follow the guidance of my government."[44]

A Special Committee of the OAS composed of delegates from five "safe" countries—Argentina, Brazil, Colombia, Guatemala, and Panama—had been in Santo Domingo since 3 May. At the Tenth Meeting of Consultation of Ministers of Foreign Affairs of the OAS, the committee received a mandate to "offer . . . its good offices to the Dominican armed factions" and "carry out an investigation into all the aspects of the present situation in the Dominican Republic that have led to the convening of the [OAS] meeting."[45] Jerome Slater has aptly summed up the role of the Special Committee:

> . . . There is nearly unanimous agreement among United States, Dominican, and Pan American Union officials that . . . the committee was lackadaisical, easily aroused to petulance, and generally incompetent.
>
> Not only that, but the committee seemed to go out of its way to antagonize the constitutionalists, and soon had so compromised its mediating status as to dissipate whatever chance it might have had to arrange a compromise. . . . Within a few days . . . the committee had publicly accused the constitutionalists of tolerating Communist infiltration of their movement and had issued a report asserting that had the United States not intervened the Dominican revolution "could rapidly have been converted into a Communist insurrection." . . . The committee ignored or even sanctioned massive violations of the military status quo it had been charged with maintaining. On May 2 the committee "authorized" the United States to create the so-called neutral zone of refuge in Santo Domingo by extending American lines directly across the middle of the city, thus creating an unbroken line of U. S. military power all the way to the San Isidro Air Base. (In a revealing indication of what *it* thought of the Special Committee, the State Department told the U. S. Embassy to proceed with the move even if the committee refused its permission. . . .)

Similarly, the committee failed to prevent or even to condemn the Imbert junta's blatant violations of the ceasefire,[46] including the major attack in mid-May on constitutionalist forces in the northern sector of the city. . . . Indeed, there were reports that the chairman of the Special Committee, Ricardo Colombo of Argentina, personally favored military action against the constitutionalists, despite his explicit mandate to maintain the ceasefire.[47]

The committee in fact was acting as a stopgap, while, behind the scenes, the United States pondered what policy to follow. The constitutionalists had survived the psychological trauma of 28 April and the damage since inflicted on them by the American troops. Depicted only a few days earlier as a horde of bloodthirsty savages, they quickly earned the respect of important voices in the American press, including the *New York Times*, the *Washington Post*, and the *Wall Street Journal*. American liberals were becoming increasingly critical of Johnson's Dominican policy. Not only did the "humanitarian" intervention appear to have been a pretext, but Communist influence within the constitutionalist movement seemed to have been grossly exaggerated. This assessment was shared even by certain government officials and many senators. Although Johnson's Dominican policy continued to enjoy the support of a large majority of the American public, the sweet unanimity of the first days was shattered by the revolt of the liberals.[48] In Latin America, moreover, the propaganda tours of Averell Harriman and Teodoro Moscoso failed to placate an anger aggravated by a feeling of impotence. And, in the United Nations Security Council, the United States was in an increasingly uncomfortable position because the world body, breaking with a long history of inaction, seemed ready to intervene for the first time in an area that the OAS regarded as its preserve.[49]

Faced with "rebels" unwilling to surrender, but anxious to avoid a "Budapest," the United States decided to open negotiations with the constitutionalists. But neither Ambassador Bennett nor special envoy Martin, both discredited in the eyes of the constitutionalists, could effectively negotiate with them. The talks were too important to be left to the five puppets of the OAS Special Committee or to José A. Mora, the OAS secretary-general, who also happened to be "visiting" Santo Domingo. On 13 May, four Americans holding high-ranking posts in the Johnson administration arrived in Puerto Rico: two "hard-liners"—Thomas Mann, undersecretary of state, and Jack Hood Vaughn, assistant secretary of state for inter-American affairs; and two "liberals"—McGeorge Bundy, special assistant on national security affairs, and Cyrus R. Vance, deputy secretary of defense. The "Guzmán talks" were under way. With one hand, the United States government offered the rebels a chance to negotiate; with the other, it struck hard to encourage its interlocutors to be reasonable. Parallel with the "Guzmán talks" ran Operation *Limpieza* ("Clean Up").

The strategically situated *barrios altos* were the capital's slums. To the south, the "corridor" separated them from Ciudad Nueva; to the west was the

ISZ occupied by the Americans; to the north, the Isabela; to the east, the Ozama, these two rivers marking the boundary with San Isidro's territory. The constitutionalists, firmly entrenched at Ciudad Nueva, where the government machinery and the leadership of the political parties were located, had only slight control of the *barrios altos* and but a rudimentary military organization there. According to Tad Szulc, who was in Santo Domingo at the time: "In contrast to the situation in their downtown stronghold, . . . the rebels in the north did not have an organized defense plan. Most of the rebel forces in the north were irregulars and they lacked the intricate system of defenses and roadblocks that existed in the downtown area."[50] Unlike a successful attack against Ciudad Nueva, the occupation of the *barrios altos* would not end the civil war. But the international repercussions of the latter would be far less serious—only slums were involved—and, above all, it would be easier to deny U.S. complicity. To attack Ciudad Nueva, Imbert Barrera's troops had to cross the American "corridor," while to invade the *barrios altos* they had the advantage of a common frontier.

On 14 May, in flagrant violation of the truce concluded nine days earlier, the GRN launched Operation *Limpieza*. The operation—an offensive against the *barrios altos*—included more than two thousand GRN troops that had been reorganized and reequipped by the Americans with tanks, cannon, and walkie-talkies. The assault went on for eight days (14-21 May) despite worldwide indignation and a unanimous vote in the UN Security Council calling for a ceasefire in which the United States had had to join. It ended only after the last foot of the *barrios altos* had been taken and the last resistors massacred.[51]

From Ciudad Nueva, the constitutionalists looked on helplessly at the carnage. Loyal to their "humanitarian" mission, the American soldiers prevented the rebels from crossing the "corridor" with arms—a "corridor" whose checkpoints were "manned by U.S. troops and by troops of the . . . military junta" and across which "truckloads of armed junta policemen and soldiers"[52] moved freely and uninterruptedly.

But United States responsibility went even deeper; on 20 May, the *Washington Post* reported that "U.S. Marines and paratroopers gave both direct and indirect help to the forces of General Antonio Imbert Barrera today as Imbert's junta troops captured the rebel-held Radio Santo Domingo and conducted a house-by-house clean-up of rebels in the northern sections of the city."[53] "Incidents" of this kind had been going on day after day since the fourteenth. They were necessary, for the resistance of the *infelices* was heroic. Morilí Holguín, a CEFA lieutenant who participated in the attack, later remarked: "They never surrendered: they fought with a courage and a determination that we lacked. It was only natural: they were fighting for something; we, only for our pay."[54]

The idea of a "Guzmán solution"[55] apparently took shape during the second week in May, in the course of conversations held in San Juan between

Bosch and members of the "Puerto Rico Group"—Luis Muñoz Marín, Teodoro Moscoso, and Jaime Benítez—who acted as intermediaries between Bosch and Washington.

Antonio Guzmán, a rich Cibao landowner linked to the *gente de primera* and brother-in-law of former Minister of the Armed Forces General Viñas Román, was a special case within the PRD. A "moderate," he had nothing in common with the Peña Gómez-style "hotheads." The peasants who worked his lands were somewhat better paid and better treated than those working for other *latifundistas*. But Antonio Guzmán was not a man who would push for real changes in Dominican society. According to former Ambassador Martin: "He was no revolutionary, simply a devoted friend of Bosch, with whom he had grown up." And he had a special quality: "he was friendly to the United States."[56]

Significantly, after the American military intervention, Antonio Guzmán did not remain with the constitutionalists entrenched in Ciudad Nueva, but returned to Santiago, where no one bothered him. Significantly, too, he was one of the men whom Martin wanted to see in the GRN, under Imbert Barrera.

Late on the morning of 14 May, Guzmán, who was to preside over a "Government of National Reconciliation" (or "Government of National Concord"), quit the peace of his beautiful Santiago home and twelve hours later stepped off an American plane in San Juan, Puerto Rico, where he had his first talk with Bosch. The following day, at Muñoz Marín's country house, Antonio Guzmán met with "Mr. Jackson,"[57] McGeorge Bundy, Jaime Benítez, and Cyrus Vance. The meeting lasted from eight in the morning to ten at night, but the only agreement that emerged was to pursue negotiations in Santo Domingo. From the start, disagreement had arisen over two points that proved crucial throughout the negotiations. First was the "Communist aspect of the Dominican problem" and the measures to be taken against it: "The Americans asked that this aspect be handled as follows: deportation of those persons that they would designate as Communists or establishment of a detention camp [at Samaná] to house them."[58] Second was the question of who would be named to the key posts within the armed forces. Guzmán had not had the time to draw up a list of officers to be appointed to the key positions of chiefs of staff and minister of the armed forces. Because of his sporadic contacts with the constitutionalist movement, moreover, he had only a superficial knowledge of the officers around Caamaño. Yet the few names he put forth were curtly rejected by the Americans.[59]

These two problems—especially the first—were at the heart of the talks on 15 May. Other points raised by Guzmán were skimmed over. In particular, when Guzmán pointed out that certain "San Isidro officers" ought to leave the country, the Americans answered simply that "in that case San Isidro [would] surely demand a counterpart"[60]—that is, the departure of constitutionalist officers.

On 16 May, Guzmán returned to the Dominican Republic. This time he took up residence in Santo Domingo, choosing to stay not in Ciudad Nueva, but at the home of one of his sisters in the ISZ. Negotiations were renewed between Guzmán, assisted by the moderate Salvador Jorge Blanco, and Bundy, accompanied by Dominican desk officer Harry Shlaudeman. The constitutionalist government had given prior approval, in principle. Guzmán kept Caamaño informed of the talks, but often without providing important details.[61]

The negotiations made swift progress. By the evening of 23 May, agreement had been reached on the following points: (1) Guzmán would be called on to terminate the mandate accorded Juan Bosch "on the basis of the constitution of 1963. Immediately [Guzmán will] issue a call for a national plebiscite ... to take place within sixty days. This plebiscite will allow the people to reaffirm— or to reject—its support of this constitution. Full observation by the OAS [will] be solicited." (2) "Mr. Guzmán will form a Government of National Reconciliation. This government will rest on a broad base. The cabinet members will represent a vast body of political, economic and social viewpoints."[62]

The composition of the cabinet had raised a number of difficulties. On 15 May, the Americans demanded that Guzmán preside over a coalition government that would include members of the GRN, "moderate" constitutionalists, and Reformists. Guzmán replied that "if Balaguer agrees to support the Government, one of his men will receive a seat in the Cabinet."[63] No GRN member, however, would sit in the cabinet. Generally speaking, Guzmán claimed the right to choose his own ministers—a right he was quickly forced to renounce. In the end, the list of cabinet members was drawn up jointly by Guzmán, Bundy, and Shlaudeman. Aside from the minister of the armed forces, it included three Reformists, five "independents," and two "moderate" PRDistas. In addition, a member of the GRN, the innocuous Postigo, was to be named minister without portfolio. In a memorandum to Bundy, Guzmán wrote: "During our conversation on Monday night, 17 May, you had agreed to our request that no member of the 'opposition' be allowed to sit on the cabinet. Nevertheless, to prove our conciliatory spirit, both myself and the Constitutional Government reverse our position and accept the inclusion in the cabinet of an opposition member, preferably Postigo."[64]

Even on the two crucial questions—the Communists and the armed forces— an agreement had been reached. Bundy had dropped his initial demand that the "Communists" be deported or placed in a detention camp. But Guzmán had to pay a high price for this concession. In a secret memorandum he pledged that:

(1) The Government of National Concord will place under strict surveillance those persons identified as Communists or pro-Communists, and, should it be determined that any law whatsoever has been broken, they will be immediately arrested. All other measures necessary to meet the threat of Communist subversion will be adopted after appropriate consultation with the United States government. . . .

(2) The United States Government will hold at the disposal of the Government of National Concord a staff adequately trained and possessing a perfect command of the Spanish tongue so as to aid in the identification of Communists and pro-Communists and in the control of their activities . . . .

(3) The measures necessary to contain the Communist threat will be the object of continuous consultations between our two governments. The United States government reserves the right to re-examine the provisions of the agreement contained in this memorandum in the event that the measures taken under same should prove insufficient.[65]

On the question of the armed forces, Guzmán's original position had been that "We will name the minister of the armed forces. The army chief of staff must be a constitutionalist officer; San Isidro, on the other hand, can pick the air force and navy chiefs of staff, but it cannot be one of the military who bombed the people. Wessin, de los Santos, Rivera Caminero, and Martínez Arana will have to leave the country. They will receive diplomatic missions abroad."[66]

Guzmán later tempered his stand. He remained adamant about reserving the post of army chief of staff for a constitutionalist, but he agreed that a "neutral"[67] be named minister of the armed forces. Before 22 May, Guzmán and Bundy had already agreed on Major Lora Fernández—a constitutionalist—as army chief of staff, and on Colonel José N. González Pomares—a "neutral"—for air force chief of staff. Guzmán's stance on the armed forces minister was that "I pose no objection to the naming of Colonel de León, the present attaché of the Dominican embassy in Washington, whom you [Bundy] had originally suggested."[68] All that remained was to choose the navy chief of staff. Captain Amiama Castillo was offered the post, but refused, professing unwillingness to serve under a "Communist" constitution—that of 1963! Guzmán then proposed that the Americans pick from a list of three names that included navy Captain Miguel A. Cintrón Romero, a "neutral" with "loyalist" sympathies.[69]

In the Dominican Republic and among United States liberals the outlook was optimistic. The Guzmán solution would be "a dramatic reversal in the American position towards the Dominican conflict," observed the *New York Times* with satisfaction.[70] But, for various and complex reasons, the Guzmán negotiations failed. For one, Imbert Barrera opposed from the outset a solution that would undermine his ambitions. Yet his opposition never seemed to worry Bundy.[71] Imbert Barrera was a puppet whose generals obeyed him solely because he enjoyed American support. On instructions from Washington, they would have abandoned him, forcing his resignation—which is precisely what happened, at the end of August, with the Godoy solution.

The real obstacle to the Guzmán solution came from Washington. We still have only an imperfect picture of what went on in the highest spheres of the Johnson administration, but it is clear that a fissure had appeared from the first days of the negotiations. On one side were the "liberals," who believed that the Communist peril had been exaggerated and that Guzmán's concessions were sufficient to guarantee U.S. interests; on the other were the "hard-liners," who saw the Communist peril as a fact and thought the Guzmán solution "did not offer enough guarantees."[72]

Certain Dominican forces played a role as well, though they managed to stay in the background. It appears certain that Jimmy Pastoriza, a dynamic spokesman of business interests with important friends in the State Department, went to Washington to lobby against the Guzmán solution. It also appears that the Reformist Party, after first accepting the "liberal compromise" in the belief that it was the irrevocable decision of the United States, reversed itself when it realized that the compromise had staunch enemies in Washington and that an arrangement more in the interests of the party could be secured. But in neither case is there conclusive proof.

One thing, however, is certain. On the night of 23 May, Guzmán on the one side and Bundy and Shlaudeman on the other came to complete agreement on the crucial questions of the Communists and the top armed forces posts. Yet on the morning of the twenty-fourth, "the American representatives oddly resubmitted proposals concerning these two questions," even though they were "points already agreed on by both parties."[73] In fact, McGeorge Bundy had been overtaken by events. His position was disowned by Washington, when, at the last minute, he received "a set of new instructions which in effect meant a death warrant for the Guzmán negotiations."[74]

Visiting Guzmán on the morning of the twenty-fourth, Bundy did not try to reopen negotiations on a new basis. The Johnson administration wanted new men to conduct any future talks with the constitutionalists. The "hard-liners" in Washington had persuaded Johnson that Guzmán was too close to Bosch, too closely linked to the rebels. Someone else would be chosen to lead the provisional government that, sooner or later, would be installed in Santo Domingo. On the morning of 26 May, McGeorge Bundy flew back to Washington. Over the previous twelve days the constitutionalists had suffered two grave reverses: a military defeat (the occupation of the *barrios altos*) and a diplomatic setback (the failure of the Guzmán solution).

The opposing forces in Santo Domingo in early June were:[75]

1.   The Constitutionalist Camp

There are three aspects to the constitutionalist microcosm: the territorial, the political, and the military.

The constitutionalist territory was confined to Ciudad Nueva. This relatively small area, inhabited by lower-middle and middle-class families, was the heart of Santo Domingo. It included the banking district, the telephone exchange, the most important department stores, and the harbor.

Politically, the constitutionalists claimed a president of the Republic, Colonel Francisco Alberto Caamaño Deñó; the constitution of April 1963; a cabinet, dominated by the PRD; a Congress, made up of the debris of the one elected in December 1962 and, like the cabinet, dominated by the PRD; and five political parties: the PRD, the PRSC, the 1J4, the MPD, and the PSP.

The military organization of the constitutionalists included a commander in chief, Colonel Caamaño, in his capacity as president of the Republic; a minister of the armed forces, navy Captain Montes Arache; a general staff, headed by Major Lora Fernández; the commando units, armed bands of civilians and military, the infrastructure of the constitutionalist armed forces; and "military supervisors" providing a formal link between the general staff and the commando units, one supervisor for each of the four zones comprising the constitutionalist territory.

The commando units represented the most interesting and most problematical aspect of the constitutionalist movement. Because of their very nature and because they have been only partially studied, it is hard to pinpoint their strength, structure, and influence within the movement. On paper they numbered more than six thousand men.[76] But this figure is deceptive, since a large number of these units had no military value and existed solely as centers for regrouping and mutual aid.

The commando units of a certain military standing—somewhere between two and three thousand men—can be divided into five categories: units composed entirely of military men; those made up of civilians and military and controlled by the military; those controlled by the Central Committee of a political party; units of the *caudilloist* type; and the "tiger" commando units, where discipline was most lax and where dangerous inclinations toward theft and pillage existed. Two commando units—those of Peña Taveras and the frogmen of Montes Arache—were made up solely of military: more than 150 well-armed men, nearly all with machine guns—an elite corps devoted to their chiefs, a formidable Praetorian Guard within the little world of Ciudad Nueva. To these two units must be added those under military direction—between six and seven hundred men.

Militarily, the parties of the far left played a modest role. The PSP was influential in the San Lazaro, a commando unit that was well disciplined and adequately armed, but contained only between 50 and 60 men; moreover, few PSPistas had military training. The MPD controlled the commando Argentina (on paper 140 men, in reality no more than 100). But the MPD adopted a position at once absurd, yet coherent with the odd past of the party. The MPD refused to risk its few cadres in a struggle "dominated by the bourgeoisie." Therefore the Argentina hardly participated in military actions and remained inactive when the Americans launched a powerful offensive against Ciudad Nueva on 15-16 June. This position was not due to cowardice, but simply to that impervious political stupidity so typical of the party's past. The stance of the MPD led to very hostile reactions in Ciudad Nueva. Thus, after the American attack on 15-16 June, many constitutionalists, particularly those from the commando units that had fought, demanded that the MPDistas be disarmed and expelled to the American-occupied ISZ.

There was, of course, the 1J4, the "giant" of the far left. The party of Manolo Tavárez had reached 24 April wracked by bitter divisions. Instead of uniting the 1J4, the civil war only increased its internal conflicts. Because of his cowardice, Fidelio Despradel lost all chance of rallying the *catorcistas* around him. The death on 19 May of Juan Miguel Román, the only *supersabio* to show any courage, left a void that could not be filled. Nor was any *flojo* in a position to take over the party's leadership. Jimmy Durán, the most able of the *flojos*, had never enjoyed great prestige; he was soon discredited by the failure of an absurd guerrilla operation that he led in the southwest.[77] Another *flojo*, Fafa Taveras, distinguished himself by his courage, but he was politically naive and lacked charisma. Despradel's ambitions finally dealt the party's hope for unity a mortal blow when by a "coup d'état" in early June he tried to replace the CECP by a National Secretariat of seven members with himself as president and his partisans holding the majority of the seats. Most of the *catorcista* leaders refused to recognize the new leadership.

A semblance of unity was restored a few days later by a meeting of the cadres at the Apollo Theater, where the CECP and Despradel's secretariat were replaced by a five-member Provisional Political Committee (CPP). But in reality the 1J4 had ceased to exist as a political party. Even the distinction between *duros* and *flojos* had lost all meaning. There were only "barons," over whom the new CPP had no control. Some of these barons, like Norge Botello, Fafa Taveras, and "Baby" Mejía showed great military ability and became leaders of important commando units. But they were independent *caudillos* rather than *catorcista* leaders and had better relations with Caamaño and the constitutionalist government than with the other members of the former CECP or the ineffectual CPP.

So the 1J4 failed. Divided, leaderless, it was only the shadow of a party.[78] What stinging irony! Where were all those Communist "supermen" that haunted the American leaders?

Little need be said of the PRSC. It served only as an organ of propaganda in the face of international public opinion. Otherwise, it contributed nothing, either politically or militarily. As for the PRD, after the rout of 27-28 April most of its leaders played only a minor role. The one exception was Peña Gómez, who, through his self-sacrifice and political acumen, redeemed his serious lapse of 27 April. And most importantly there was Bosch in Puerto Rico, far from Ciudad Nueva. The distance only partly dimmed a still brilliant prestige. The masses in Ciudad Nueva and the rank and file in the commando units were for the most part "Boschistas." But the PRD lacked military chiefs. That vacuum had been filled by Colonel Caamaño who, only a few weeks earlier, was a policeman feared by the people of Santo Domingo. Once again, the far left had failed.

These, then, are the decisive elements in any analysis of the constitutionalist movement: the charisma of Bosch, the political leader; the appeal of Caamaño, the military leader; the failure of the far left.

The relationship between Caamaño and the commando units was crucial. The latter may have seemed unstable, but they held together for four months. They were largely autonomous. No hierarchy existed and orders were rare. The "zone supervisors" acted far less as "commanders" than as justices of the peace, whose job was to resolve disputes among the various commando units, most often with the help of other commando leaders. But there were limits to that autonomy. The commando leaders recognized the political authority of the Caamaño government. They were kept informed, in broad outline, of the negotiations with the Americans through the meetings of the G-5, an extraofficial body created by Caamaño wherein Caamaño or his delegates met two or three times a week with the leaders of the most powerful commando units. But no votes were ever taken during the meetings.

If Caamaño had nurtured any personal ambitions or if a break had occurred between him and the PRD, an extremely difficult situation would have arisen at Ciudad Nueva. But no break took place, even though relations between the colonel and the party of Juan Bosch were cool at times. Without the PRD's support, the constitutionalist movement would have ceased to exist, becoming the revolt of a handful of officers and "far leftists." Everyone, even the *catorcistas* and the MPDistas, recognized that the PRD was indispensable at Ciudad Nueva. Lacking political ambition, Caamaño accepted that reality all the more easily.

The PRD, in fact, dominated the political life of Ciudad Nueva. It held sway over the negotiations with the United States, and on those few occasions when the constitutionalist movement took a decisive vote, the PRD, controlling the cabinet, the Senate, and the Chamber of Deputies, had an absolute majority. Caamaño always yielded.

2. The Government of National Reconstruction (GRN)

Except for the constitutionalist redoubt at Ciudad Nueva and the ISZ, the GRN controlled all Dominican territory. On 28 April, the landing of the marines swept away any lingering doubts commanders outside the capital might have had. At once, and with one voice, they pledged their allegiance to the Benoit junta, then to the GRN. The "disorders" ceased. The police and the army "valiantly" cleared the streets of the unarmed crowds. The civil authorities installed by the Triumvirate reappeared, confirmed in their functions by the new leaders. The "agitators" were rounded up.

If only certain foreign newsmen could have been expelled from the country! *Le Monde*, the *New York Times*, the *Washington Post*—these were Communist-dominated papers whose correspondents were in the pay of Moscow. But "loyalist" hearts ached to see even *El Mundo* of San Juan, Puerto Rico, which had applauded the "anti-Communist" character of the American intervention, join the campaign of calumny against the legal Dominican government, a government created by Washington. *El Mundo* could write: "Travelers report that the city of Santiago and all the towns between Santiago and the capital are heavily guarded by units of the Army and the Police . . . . These same sources report . . . that discontent is cropping up all over regarding the possibility of a prolongation of General Imbert Barrera's Government." And *El Mundo* could indulge in invidious comparisons between a rally organized on 26 May by the GRN and one by the "rebels" the day before, at which "a torrential downpour . . . neither reduced attendance nor dampened the people's enthusiasm, as the crowd stood listening to the speeches for over an hour." The report went on:

Unlike the rally that took place yesterday in the International Security Zone outside the offices of the president of the Government of National Reconstruction . . . today's was an act of the people. The GRN rally was a meeting of ladies—mostly the wives of public officials and the military; today's was the doing of workers, students, and common folk.

A comparison between the two events seems to indicate clearly the gulf dividing the two movements claiming power in the Dominican Republic.[79]

The GRN also failed to win the support of the Reformist Party. Balaguer, who returned to the country on 28 June—against the wishes of Imbert Barrera but with the approval of the Americans—declared that "the drama triggered by the revolutionary outbreak on 24 April can have no other denouement than the establishment of a provisional government charged with the specific mission of leading the nation to honest elections."[80] The statement was an affront to Imbert Barrera and his clique, who had repeatedly insisted that the GRN was precisely that provisional government. Even the church held back, taking a position close to that of the Reformistas—just like the "d'Alessandro faction" of the PRSC and CONATRAL. Too many Dominican leaders were already looking to the future, and nearly everyone in the country understood that, in the eyes of the Americans, Imbert Barrera was only a temporary answer. Only a few leaders of "democratic" parties came out in support of the GRN: Ramírez Alcántara (PNRD), Severo Cabral (PAR), and Horacio Ornes (VRD).

Imbert Barrera was only a puppet. He had absolutely no authority over the GRN's military chiefs and enjoyed no prestige among the armed forces. At the outset, the strong man was Wessin. But his star quickly faded. The *caudillo* went down with his precious CEFA, victims of the constitutionalist revolt. An unforgivable disappointment to the Americans and far too compromised in the eyes of the urban masses, for whom he was the symbol of evil, Wessin was a perfect scapegoat. This left Rivera Caminero, corrupt but intelligent—a man who, as minister of the armed forces, seemed to have luck on his side. Around him formed a clique: Martínez Arana, once Wessin's protégé and the new army chief of staff; Jiménez Reyes, the navy chief of staff; de los Santos, the air force chief of staff, never one of Wessin's admirers.

But in fact the GRN had no real "strong man." There were only the Americans, who controlled everything. They reorganized and equipped the "loyalist" forces. Thousands of U.S. soldiers occupied the country; others were aboard ships just off the coast. American planes and American tanks were masters at the Nineteenth of November, where they left little space for the "natives." A hundred yards away stood the CEFA, ridiculous against such competition. And American money, the banner of many "loyalists," paid the salaries of the GRN, the salaries, therefore, of the military.

On 3 June, a second ad hoc committee of the Tenth Meeting of Consultation arrived in Santo Domingo.[81] American Ambassador Ellsworth Bunker presided, flanked by two confederates: Ambassadors Ilmar Penna Marinho of Brazil and Ramón de Clairmont Dueñas of El Salvador. Negotiations between the Americans and the constitutionalists were reopened, but under conditions far different from those set down in the Guzmán solution. From the outset, Bunker proposed a formula "wholly contrary to the return to the constitutional order of 1963."[82] Trench warfare—both military and diplomatic—replaced the rapid tempo of the Guzmán negotiations. Thus began a war of attrition that lasted for nearly three months and forced the constitutionalists to abandon their essential objectives one after another.[83]

On 10 June, during its first meeting with the ad hoc committee, the constitutionalist Negotiating Committee reiterated its demands: installation of a government presided over either by Guzmán or another "moderate" from Ciudad Nueva. This government would remain in place until 27 February 1967, the date when the mandate voted Juan Bosch on 20 December 1962 expired. Its legal instrument would be the constitution of 1963, which, however, would be submitted to a referendum. The Congress elected in December 1962 would be reconvened.[84] But on 23 June, "in the face of the military superiority of the invaders," the constitutionalist government made a vital concession. It accepted the principle of a provisional government with a "neutral" as president, a government whose charter would be an Institutional Act drawn up in advance in the course of the negotiations. Elections would take place between six and nine months after the installation of the provisional government.

Still the constitutionalists clung to three demands:

(1) The Inter-American Peace Force will withdraw from the country . . . no later than a month after the establishment of the Provisional Government. . . .

(2) The Armed Forces will be subject to the exclusive authority of the Provisional Government, the constitutionalist military retaining their respective ranks,[85] including those who at the outbreak of the Constitutionalist Movement were, by Decrees of the Constitutionalist Government, reinducted into the Armed Forces from which they had been cashiered after 25 September 1963. . . .

(3) The Provisional Government will be subject to an Institutional Act inspired by all the economic and ethico-social gains, human rights and public liberties of the Constitution of 1963. . . . The Constitutional Government considers that in order for this Act, once it is approved, to hold the force of law, . . . it must be voted by the National Congress.[86]

After 30 June, the negotiations focused on the search for the man to preside over the provisional government. The constitutionalists put forward lists of candidates, all "neutrals." But Ambassador Bunker had only one name to offer: Héctor García Godoy.

Few constitutionalists knew the candidate personally, though most knew about his past and his family ties. A *de primera* Dominican, ambassador under Trujillo, and minister of foreign affairs in the last weeks of the Bosch regime, Godoy belonged to that breed of men always "on top." In 1964 he had been one of the vice-presidents of the Reformist Party, but he had quit that post to become vice-president of the Tabacalera, the country's most important cigarette manufacturer (at the time his nephew, Ramón Cáceres Troncoso, was a Triumvir).

"Señor Godoy is a man of experience," affirmed Bunker, "with no ties to either of the warring factions." And "he fully meets the requirement that the new Chief of State be known in the country and *above all* in diplomatic circles."[87] The constitutionalists' opposition was futile; the candidates they proposed—all "neutrals"—were rejected by the ad hoc committee. Finally, on 7 July, Bunker declared "categorically"[88] that "having received the lists of all the available candidates, we have reached the following conclusion: . . . Señor Héctor García Godoy [is] the answer to the problem."[89] The constitutionalists had no more doubts; Godoy's candidacy was not a "suggestion; . . . it was an imposition."[90] They were faced with an ultimatum. If they refused, what price would they pay?

The movement's leaders met the following day. Only seven of those present had the right to vote: the representatives of the three "democratic" parties (Peña Gómez for the PRD, Andrés Lockward for the PRSC, Juan B. Mejía for the 1J4); the representatives of the cabinet, the Senate, and the Chamber of Deputies (three bodies dominated by the PRD); and the representative of the constitutionalist military staff, Major Lora Fernández. Colonel Caamaño and three other members of the Negotiating Committee took part in the debate, but did not vote.[91]

Should they reject the Godoy solution the rebel leaders foresaw two consequences: an American assault in force against Ciudad Nueva, or a break, formal or real, in the negotiations.

The danger of an American assault on Ciudad Nueva seemed very real to the constitutionalists. A truce had been signed after the American-supported GRN occupation of the *barrios altos*. But new incidents took place every day, though these exchanges of fire between the commandos and the Americans were generally not very serious. On 15 June, however, two days before the Bunker committee made public its proposals for a "solution to the Dominican crisis,"[92] one incident assumed dramatic proportions. This time the exchange of fire did not subside after an hour or so—the American troops had launched an offensive. Only a part of the American forces were engaged, but their superior firepower was overwhelming. The offensive lasted for close to thirty-six hours. Yet there was no rout; the commandos put up fierce resistance. Hour by hour, however, they were forced to give ground—nearly a quarter of their territory.

The constitutionalists feared a new attack. How long would they be able to hold out if the Americans attacked in full strength? "A day or two," admitted Juan B. Mejía, the 1J4 representative at the 8 July meeting.[93] The constitutionalists had world opinion and the United Nations on their side; a bloody American drive against Ciudad Nueva would raise an outcry. The United States could even find itself in hot water again in the Security Council, as it had over the *barrios altos*. But that battle had continued in spite of the Security Council resolutions. "By the time the United Nations gets around to taking action," argued Peña Gómez, "we will be lying in our graves" and "our people . . . will have lost a whole generation of revolutionaries."[94]

Rather than provoking an attack on Ciudad Nueva, rejection of Godoy could mean "an end to the negotiations and the possible withdrawal of the ad hoc Committee of the OAS."[95] Or the Americans might choose to formally continue the negotiations while turning them into a fruitless game: infrequent meetings at which the constitutionalists would submit new lists of candidates only to see them rejected, one at a time. Finally a "compromise" would be reached, whereby the Americans would show their "goodwill" by dropping Godoy's candidacy. "Another representative of the country's ruling class [would] be chosen and the will of the mighty Northerners [would] always prevail."[96]

Indeed even time favored the Americans. They could wait, while the constitutionalists needed a rapid solution. In Ciudad Nueva, several thousand persons were crowded into a few square miles. A *cordon sanitaire* cut off this entrenched camp from GRN territory: that is, from the rest of the country. In May, the constitutionalists had hoped to "break the siege" by stirring up guerrilla operations in the interior, "exporting" men and arms from Ciudad Nueva. The attempts proved disastrous—the last of them, at San Francisco de Macorís in late May, was a particularly grievous debacle. After that, even the 1J4 "hotheads" abandoned all hopes of a "second front."

The constitutionalists had hoped that international pressure would force the Americans to search with them for a rapid negotiated solution. Now, at the crucial meeting of 8 July, the PRD representative of the cabinet expressed a bitter truth: "The world's once ardent attention to our cause has cooled as the days have passed and has been directed at other areas in which problems of worldwide interest are also being debated. The very sector of the international press that was virtually monopolized by our affair has fallen away as well, and we are ceasing to be front-page news, occupying the inside pages of the newspapers."[97] At the same time in Ciudad Nueva, demoralization set in: "The Senate of the Republic has sufficient evidence to affirm here that the morale in which the revolution [was] born is not the morale that now reigns among the commandos and among the people."[98] "The people are weary and long for a solution. Every day some new incident indicates this weariness. I must say here . . . that the despairing populace seeks relief from its misery and hardship."[99]

The problem of provisions had worsened, unemployment was rife, and the feeling of helplessness was becoming more and more crushing. The forced inactivity of the commandos made it increasingly harder to impose discipline.

These conditions led the constitutionalist government to accept the candidacy of Héctor García Godoy[100] on 8 July. But the negotiations dragged on for another two months, for there remained other points on which the "rebels" had to yield. The most important of these—the question of the top military posts—was finally resolved when both the constitutionalists and the Americans agreed that "the Provisional President will handle military questions directly and will be the one to make the decisions on matters of such consequence, inasmuch as said Government will hold the exclusive right to distribute military commands."[101]

Godoy, in fact, had launched an intensive "electoral campaign" in Ciudad Nueva that led him on a round of visits to party leaders, government officials, military officers, and even several commando units. He played his role skillfully, making many promises and winning the trust of a large number of constitutionalists, who now thought of him as a "man of goodwill" and sympathetic to their cause. Specifically, Godoy promised to name constitutionalist or "neutral" officers to the top military posts. The feeling that there was no alternative enhanced his credibility. To insist that Godoy commit his pledges to paper, which he refused to do, would have been "to maintain a rigid stance out of touch with reality and to play into the enemy's hands."[102]

The constitutionalists were also forced to yield on the question of the Inter-American Peace Force. Initially they had demanded that the IAPF leave the country a month after the installation of the provisional government, but the ad hoc committee had refused. They next asked that, once the provisional government was installed, Godoy be given the authority to decide when the foreign troops should withdraw, but this, too, was rejected. The position of the ad hoc committee was that the withdrawal of the IAPF would be determined by the Tenth Meeting of Consultation of Ministers of Foreign Affairs.[103] Days passed. The ad hoc committee adamantly maintained its position. Once again the constitutionalists gave in. The most they could obtain was a reservation in the final draft of the agreement to the effect that "the 'Constitutionalist Government' . . . considers that it is the exclusive and sovereign right of the Provisional Government to determine the date of the withdrawal . . . [of the IAPF] from Dominican territory."[104] On 29 August, the consitutionalist Negotiating Committee and the OAS ad hoc committee gave their final approval to the texts of the Institutional Act and the Act of Dominican Reconciliation, documents on which depended the installation of Godoy's provisional government.

But what of Imbert Berrera? From the outset he had opposed "any compromise with the Communists"—that is, any solution that impinged on his power. His opposition, however, carried little weight. Both the Americans and Godoy dealt directly with the military chiefs of the GRN, who were all the more understanding since they knew their interests were not threatened, as later events proved.

On the evening of 30 August, Imbert Barrera appeared on television to declare his refusal to sign the Institutional Act and the Act of Dominican Reconciliation and to announce his resignation. "We have been the victims of a coup d'état," Colonel Benoit, another member of the GRN, would later complain.[105] Imbert Barrera had been informed of the demise of the GRN by Rivera Caminero, minister of the armed forces, and by the joint chiefs of staff—Martínez Arana (army), de los Santos (air force), and Jiménez Reyes (navy)—all of whom put their signatures to the Institutional Act and the Act of Dominican Reconciliation the following day. General Despradel Brache, chief of police, also signed the acts.

On 3 September 1965, the provisional government of Héctor García Godoy was installed. One phase of the Dominican crisis had ended. Another began.

Godoy's cabinet included not only "loyalists" and "neutrals," but also persons sympathetic to the constitutionalists. In addition, the new president immediately revoked the autonomy of the CEFA and forced Wessin out of the country. Thus, some observers have hastily concluded that Godoy intended to be impartial toward both sides. They forget, of course, that in the Dominican Republic power stems not from a cabinet position but from control of the armed forces. And they fail to realize that the troops of the CEFA remained under the control of "loyalist" officers and that Wessin's departure was an empty gesture that in no way affected the strength of the "loyalists."[106]

The men whom Godoy appointed to the key positions of minister of the armed forces, joint chiefs of staff, and chief of police were Rivera Caminero, Martínez Arana, de los Santos, Jiménez Reyes, and Despradel Brache, respectively. These officers had occupied the same positions in the GRN. Other "loyalist" officers served under them. Their appointments were the price that Godoy had agreed to pay to become the provisional president of the Dominican Republic. Whether he was an eager or a reluctant accomplice, his government could never have been neutral: the "loyalists" controlled the armed forces and the police, and thus the country—with the approval of the United States.

One event will perhaps best give the feeling of those months of the provisional government: the incident at the Matúm Hotel, on 19 December 1965. The facts can be outlined briefly: at dawn on the nineteenth a caravan of cars left Santo Domingo. About one hundred constitutionalists drove to Santiago to attend a mass in memory of Lieutenant Colonel Fernández Domínguez, who was killed in action four days after his return to the country on 14 May. Among them were some of the major leaders of the revolt: Caamaño, Montes Arache, Lachapelle Díaz, Lora Fernández, Héctor Aristy, and many others. After mass in Santiago they all went to the Matúm Hotel. There, at 9:30 A.M., several hundred troops of the Dominican air force and army, supported by tanks and cannons, attacked them. The unequal battle lasted for eight hours, but the attackers were unable to storm the hotel, despite their superior armament. At last, at 5:30 P.M., the IAPF enforced a cease-fire.

The incident shows not only the criminal intentions and the military ineptitude of the "loyalists," but also raises a grave question about the role of the IAPF. From Santo Domingo, the helicopters of the IAPF could have reached Santiago in less than an hour. The cease-fire could have been enforced in the morning. The "loyalists" were not in the habit of opposing the orders of their

American protectors, and no one has ever claimed that they disobeyed that day in Santiago. Yet the IAPF intervened only at 5:30 P.M. after eight hours of fighting. One wonders whether the IAPF waited several hours because it was in collusion with the "loyalists" and wanted to give them the time to storm the hotel and kill Caamaño and the other constitutionalist leaders. If this is true, then the IAPF intervened only after it became obvious that the attack had failed and that a longer delay could not be justified.

If the IAPF was indeed an accomplice, at what level was the initial decision taken? Did Generals Panasco Alvim and Palmer—both bitterly hostile to the constitutionalists—act on their own initiative? Or was the matter first referred to the U.S. embassy and Washington?

There is no hard evidence to prove the complicity of the IAPF—and yet nobody has ever explained its otherwise astonishing inaction.

The aftermath of the Matúm incident is also highly significant. Godoy could not remain completely passive before a flagrant aggression that had created an uproar in the country and brought the masses of the capital to the brink of revolt. There is little doubt that he disapproved of an attack that in his opinion brought unnecessary violence against the vanquished and openly flouted his own authority.[107]

The country waited while the provisional president appointed a three-man commission of inquiry. Finally, on 3 January 1966, Godoy broadcast his conclusions to the Dominican people. "This is not a time to establish guilt," he announced[108]—a bitter disappointment for those who realized where the responsibilities lay and had hoped that the president would be able and willing to enforce the law. To decrease the tension in the country, Godoy explained, thirty-four officers, including the key military leaders on each side, would have to leave the Dominican Republic as military attachés or on a study mission to Israel. Among them would be the constitutionalists Caamaño (as military attaché to England), Montes Arache, Lachapelle Díaz, and Peña Taveras, and the "loyalists" Rivera Caminero, de los Santos, and Martínez Arana.

By 22 January, the constitutionalists who were on Godoy's list had left the country; Godoy had assured them that if they set an example, the "loyalists" would have to follow suit.

But the "loyalists" refused to leave. Thus they placed themselves in open insubordination against the provisional government—and yet in the country there were thousands of soldiers of the IAPF whose task was to help to enforce the authority of the Dominican president. It would have been simple for the IAPF to compel the rebel "loyalist" officers to obey. But these officers were no vulgar constitutionalists; they were not the "extremists" who had forced the United States to intervene in April 1965 and who had then defied Washington's authority for four long months. These officers were the "loyalists," the "good guys" whose allegiance went not to a Dominican constitution or to an "anti-American" Dominican president (Bosch), but to the United States. Therefore, a compromise was necessary. From early January to the end of February, a tragi-comedy unfolded in Santo Domingo—or rather, it was a tragedy for Dominican democracy and for the constitutionalists, but a comedy for the "loyalists."

In this bizarre scenario, Godoy threatened at times to resign or to appeal to the OAS, but in the end did neither. The United States and the IAPF constantly proclaimed their support for the provisional president, but showed an extreme reluctance to compel the "loyalists" to obey, while in Santo Domingo a general strike was held in an effort to force Godoy to be firm. Finally, amid flows of rhetoric, a "moderate" solution was reached that was acceptable to both sides, that is, to the "loyalists" and Godoy. The solution was as follows: Rivera Caminero went to Washington as military attaché, but he was the only "loyalist" to leave. De los Santos and Martínez Arana resigned as chiefs of staff to become deputy ministers of the armed forces. These were far less important positions, but in exchange they were allowed to remain in the country. Above all, these three officers were replaced in their key positions by three other "loyalists," comrades-in-arms who had fought with them against the constitutionalists and who shared their hatreds and their "political views." Thus, Colonel Enrique Pérez y Pérez became minister of the armed forces with the rank of general; Colonels Elio Osiris Perdomo Rosario and Juan Nepomuceno Folch Pérez became, respectively, army and air force chiefs of staff, also with the rank of general. This, then, was the "moderate" outcome of the Matúm incident. Eleven prominent constitutionalist officers left the country in the naive belief that Godoy would then adhere to his pledges. On the side of the aggressors, the only casualty was Rivera Caminero. Benoit, Imbert Barrera, Wessin, and now Rivera Caminero were the victims of the Americans' cosmetic operations, sacrificed on the altar of a false impartiality that changed the names of the champions of the indispensable pro-American stability, while leaving the power of that faction intact. But no one among the constitutionalists could make up for the loss of Francisco Caamaño.

The Matúm incident and its aftermath were only the most striking moments of the bitter drama that began for the constitutionalist military on 3 September 1965. They evacuated Ciudad Nueva to be herded into an abandoned army camp on the outskirts of the capital, where the exits were controlled by the IAPF. There they remained throughout the presidency of Godoy. At times the IAPF prevented them from leaving the camp, in order to "avoid incidents," while the "loyalists" controlled the country.

Time after time, Godoy promised the constitutionalist officers that he would act, that he would reincorporate them and their men into the armed forces, and that they, too, would receive command of military units. Godoy was an excellent, smooth diplomat; moreover, the constitutionalists felt that they had little choice. They had left their stronghold of Ciudad Nueva and were now isolated outside of the capital. Should they prove "insubordinate," the IAPF would certainly be all too happy to reduce them to obedience.[109]

The weeks went by, and the promises were never honored—Godoy kept asking for a little more patience, a little trust . . . there were still so many obstacles to overcome: the opposition of the Americans, that of the "loyalists." Meanwhile, Caamaño and his officers left the country, as did the constitutionalist cadets, who in late March were sent to Chile to "continue their military studies."[110]

Deprived of their leaders, demoralized, some of their numbers assassinated in the streets of the capital—and yet still hoping against hope—the constitutionalist military placed their faith in promises that would never be respected. Under Godoy no constitutionalist officer ever received a military position of any importance. Contrary to what he repeatedly had promised, Godoy reintegrated only two of the many constitutionalist officers that the Triumvirate had cashiered: former Captain Lachapelle Díaz on 20 January and former Major Núñez Nogueras on 2 March 1966. Others kept hoping, encouraged by the cases of Lachapelle and Núñez Nogueras. Then the day came, after the election of Balaguer, when Godoy told them that "he regretted it, but outside pressures made it impossible for him to reintegrate them into the armed forces."[111]

But the suffering of the constitutionalist military under Godoy was only part of the suffering of the Dominican people. Acts of violence against the population marked the period of the provisional government. A few of the victims belonged to right-wing groups. But the great majority of those killed by "unknown" assassins—or openly by the police and the armed forces—were *Boschistas* or supporters of the far left, as were those who suffered arrest, beatings, and persecution. Such was the lot of the vanquished.[112]

This was the climate surrounding the electoral campaign. Two major candidates shared the field: Bosch and Balaguer. Too "unsophisticated" to follow the rhetoric of the United States and the Godoy government, the Dominican people understood a simple reality: in September 1963 the armed forces had overturned Bosch's electoral victory. Then, in April 1965, the United States had invaded the country to prevent his return to the presidency. The constitutionalist bid for power had been crushed, and the Matúm incident, its aftermath, and the daily acts of violence were a constant reminder of that defeat. The Yankees and their "loyalist" protégés controlled the country, and if Bosch won the elections, they would drown his victory in blood.

To a people who had endured so much violence, Joaquín Balaguer brought a promise of peace. Only a select few knew that his Reformist Party had already joined San Isidro against the constitutionalists before 28 April and had later opposed the Guzmán solution. Those who knew kept silent. But everybody could remember that the "little doctor with the sad face" had criticized both the *golpe* of September 1963 and the Triumvirate; he had greeted the counter-coup and then had remained ostensibly neutral throughout the civil war, refusing to support the GRN. The all-powerful Americans were now his friends, and the armed forces reserved their hatred for Bosch. But Balaguer did not attack Bosch—in fact he hardly attacked anyone. His was a message of peace and social reform. Bosch, however, could not promise peace.

Balaguer's supporters were free to fan out through the countryside, where the *Boschistas* were hounded by the police. Balaguer barnstormed the country, making eloquent speeches, while Bosch, back from exile on 25 September 1965, stayed in Santo Domingo. His life was in constant danger, and throughout the campaign he left his house on only three occasions. It is likely that Bosch was a reluctant candidate, torn between a desire to win and the realization that his victory would be followed by a new and more bloody *golpe*.[113] His speeches lacked their habitual vitality, and he failed to expose the "social-reformer" Balaguer—but then Bosch had never understood the real character of Trujillo's last president,[114] and probably saw in him, at that time, the only man who could offer peace and a modicum of social reforms to the Dominican people.

On 1 June 1966, the elections produced the inevitable result: Joaquín Balaguer was elected president of the Republic with 57 percent of the vote, to Bosch's 39 percent.[115] Stressing that the elections were free, many American observers have triumphantly concluded that this outcome represented a repudiation of Juan Bosch. Some have even contended that the electoral results vindicate President Johnson's policies and prove that the United States helped the Dominican people make a free choice. The elections on 1 June 1966 were technically free. Fraud at the polls in favor of Balaguer, if at all extant, was limited, and certainly not sufficient to give him the presidency. But we have already seen that in a larger and deeper sense the elections were not free at all. Taking this into account, a strikingly different conclusion emerges. It is truly impressive that in spite of such odds, 39 percent of the Dominican people still dared to vote for Juan Bosch.

To the surprise of those who remembered him as Trujillo's puppet, Balaguer soon proved that his sad, uncharismatic face concealed the personality of one of the most skilled Dominican leaders of this century, a man of great energy and unusual intelligence. By gaining control of the armed forces, he guaranteed the "favorable" climate necessary for his reelection in 1970 and 1974. But the social reforms have remained an empty promise. The years have passed, world opinion hardly remembers that in 1965 a constitutionalist revolt took place in the Dominican Republic, and only now and then a few lines in the American and European press recall the existence of that unhappy country. Yet today murders, arrests, and persecutions go on in the Dominican Republic because this is the only way for a minority in power to maintain "order" and "peace" in face of a populace denied even the most elementary social justice.[116]

Chapter 11

The Pax Americana

In a deeper sense, the Dominican crisis began with the arrival of Christopher Columbus at the fair island of Hispaniola. But this study deals with one particular crisis, that of 1965. Thus our starting point is the death of Trujillo. The Jefe was killed, and this no one should regret. Yet his demise was not brought about by the *manolistas* of the Movimiento Revolucionario 14 de Junio; the MR1J4 had been crushed in January 1960. Trujillo was eliminated by those who, after serving the master, turned against him, not to change Dominican society, but to protect their own interests.

They killed Trujillo, but power eluded them and the interlude of Balaguer-Ramfis and Balaguer-Rodríguez Echavarría followed. The inauguration of the second Council of State signaled the defeat of "neo-Trujilloism." But the new rulers represented another scourge of Dominican history: the *gente de primera*.

True, elections took place in December 1962, and they were largely free. But does it matter? Real power remained in the hands of the armed forces, and the armed forces were still corrupt and hostile to social reforms and political democracy.

From 1962 to 24 April 1965, many actors crisscrossed the scene of Dominican politics. But a myriad of names can be reduced to a small group of key protagonists: the U.S. government, the Dominican armed forces, the *gente de primera*, Juan Bosch. The Dominican people, in whose name all spoke, were an object rather than a protagonist, and the Dominican far left—Washington's nightmare—was strong only in the minds of its enemies.

What role did the 1J4, "giant" of the far left, actually play on the Dominican scene between 1962 and 1965? The party made one mistake after another—these have been pointed out throughout this book. Among its leaders, some were unworthy—and this, too, has been mentioned. Is the story of the 1J4, then, a comedy?

The 1J4 was doomed from the outset—not because of its mistakes, but because of its very nature, because of its message. The 1J4 represented the Dominican contingent of the rebel battalions that mounted the Castroite offensive throughout the Western Hemisphere in the 1960s. Its ideology and its message were not necessarily wrong—each of us will draw a different conclusion, according to his or her political views. But the Dominican "reality" would not tolerate such a party. Nor would the American "big brother." The 1J4 was indeed correct when it claimed in 1962 that the December elections were a farce, not because they were rigged, but because political democracy was not possible in the Dominican Republic. In a matter of months those who overthrew the very moderate Juan Bosch proved this point. To escape its fate, to escape a succession of defeats, the 1J4 would have had to change not only its tactics, but its nature and its ideology as well. It would have had to become a reformist party—moderate and pro-American. Thus, the party had no alternative. Its story was a tragedy, not a comedy. If at moments one error or another appears absurd, lending a farcical aura to the play, recall that the protagonists were battling forces that no "sane" man would have dared to defy. Even if one leader or another proved unworthy, petty, jealous, or corrupt, the majority of the *catorcistas* braved death and imprisonment with courage and idealism. They tower over this period of Dominican history and may well serve as an example for those who will someday recover the glorious flag of national liberation and social reform of the 1J4 warriors.

And the Dominican masses throughout these years? The peasants' only role was to cast their ballots in the December 1962 elections. They chose Juan Bosch, then disappeared from the scene. Centuries of history had taught them to endure and obey. Trujillo made the lesson still more vivid. It was a remarkable feat, daring to defy their *patrones* on election day in 1962. To expect more in so short a time is to forget Dominican reality. Bosch was overthrown too soon for this reality to change in the countryside. Then came the return to "normalcy" of the Triumvirate.

The urban masses, especially those in the capital, were more active than the peasants, but their role was still subordinate. They had neither the strength nor the requisite degree of political consciousness to assert themselves as a major actor throughout the period. In 1963, their support for Bosch would not have prevented the *golpe*. During the Triumvirate, their "Boschism" helped to create a political climate that influenced many constitutionalist officers. But the Enriquillo plan assigned them only a minor part, reserving the key one for the military. Only after the civil war began did the masses of Santo Domingo assume a decisive role. It was then that they found the appropriate means to act: weapons and the will to use them at the risk of their lives. For the few hours after the battle at the Duarte Bridge, Dominican "reality" changed drastically. Then the U.S. intervened and the dream was shattered.

After the long humiliation of the Era of Trujillo, the *gente de primera* recovered the government in 1962, with the Council of State. But on 20 December of that year the Dominican masses elected the upstart Juan Bosch as president of the Republic, and the "elite" saw its ambitions crushed. The nightmare ended, however, with the *golpe* of 25 September 1963. The Triumvirate offered the *gente de primera* a new chance, but they failed to seize it. They thought the threat of Juan Bosch was gone for good: the PRD would never be able to topple the Triumvirate. The armed forces had crushed the 1J4 and its *guerrilleros* in December 1963 and had killed Manolo Tavárez, the party's only charismatic leader. If the *gente de primera* saw a danger, it came only from the *nouveaux riches* of the *Trujillato*—those *de segunda* who had acquired wealth and power during the Era and whose interests were now represented by Joaquín Balaguer and his Reformist Party. But Balaguer was in exile, and his supporters in the armed forces were not strong—indeed, they grew weaker with the passing months.

This apparent security proved a curse for the *gente de primera*. They perceived no threat from below, hence no need for any change. And so they refused to grant those minimal social reforms and that modicum of honesty in government that might have helped to defuse the exasperation of the urban masses and reduce the appeal of Juan Bosch. Above all, they fought each other over the spoils and spurned their potential allies, the *nouveaux riches* of the Era.

The *gente de primera* can invoke only one factor in their defense: the heavy burden they chose to shoulder when they sought the help of the armed forces to overthrow Juan Bosch. They bought an ally at a staggering price, for the generals were even more corrupt than the *de primera*.[1] The suffering of the Dominican people during the Triumvirate was in part the inevitable result of this alliance.

During the Triumvirate, also the generals failed to grasp the danger from below. The Dominican officers had known fear in 1962, in the wake of the collapse of the Trujillo empire. In the months following the death of the Jefe, the armed forces had been on the losing side. They had blindly supported Ramfis until November 1961, but Ramfis left in defeat, deserting them. The majority of the military then switched their support to Balaguer and Rodríguez Echavarría, but they, too, had been defeated. Who, then, would protect the armed forces? A cold fear haunted the military chiefs: fear of retribution, fear of being alone against the *gente de primera*, the Dominican people, the political parties, the United States. If the Americans really wanted a democratic Dominican Republic, what would happen to the military chiefs, to their careers that had blossomed under Trujillo, to their privileges and their stolen riches? Above all, would they have to atone for thirty years of crime?

But the Americans wanted anti-Communist stability more than democracy in the Dominican Republic as well as in the rest of the hemisphere. The Castroite offensive had to be crushed—indeed, this was the first priority, and there was no time for "unnecessary" purges, for retribution and punishment. Such as they were, the Dominican armed forces had a decisive and "positive" role to play. The United States was not their enemy, but their protector and friend. This was a key element of the Latin American policy of John Kennedy and then of Lyndon Johnson—a clear example of continuity between the two administrations.[2]

Thus the Dominican armed forces recovered from their great fear. The last lingering doubts disappeared during the Bosch administration. The *gente de primera*, the bishops, "democratic" political parties, and rightist newspapers all beseeched the military to save the Fatherland—what a dramatic change in such a short period! And the military chiefs acted; they saved the Fatherland and entered the period of the Triumvirate reinvigorated and self-assured. They were free now, much freer than they had ever been under Trujillo, for the Jefe had combined graft and privileges with strict controls and sudden punishments.

Now they could steal and oppress. They were needed, for without them Donald
Reid Cabral would not last one day. They were indispensable, for only they
could guarantee anti-Communist stability in the Dominican Republic—a "vital"
contribution to the defense of the "free world" against the red threat, a contribution justly appreciated by their good American friends.

Wessin, de los Santos, Rivera Caminero, Belisario Peguero: who could have
stopped their robbery, had they only remained united! But they fought among
themselves over the spoils. They believed that the diverse factions in the armed
forces were united by a common, sacred bond: passion for graft and undying
hostility toward Bosch. While they squabbled, the Enriquillo movement organized in secret. Its aim was to return Bosch to the presidency.

Juan Bosch was arrogant and vain. He sought not friends, but followers.
He was not the leader of a modern political party, but a *caudillo*. He was an excellent novelist, but not a political theorist, nor, indeed, a towering figure of
Latin American politics. But this *caudillo* wanted social change, this arrogant
man believed in political democracy and, above all, he was scrupulously honest
with public money. He loved his country and his countrymen—as children, perhaps, rather than brothers, but even this represented a drastic change in Dominican political life.

Bosch was not overthrown because he was arrogant and vain. Nor was he
overthrown because of mistakes he made during his short administration. He was
doomed from the start because his message and his promises were directed to the
masses, the powerless *infelices*. His qualities, not his mistakes, led to his
downfall. His search for social reforms and honest government arrayed against
him the *gente de primera*, already exasperated by their electoral defeat at the
hands of a *de segunda*. His nationalism and particularly his deep belief in political democracy cost him the support of the Kennedy administration. The
Americans were unable to accept real, rather than formal Dominican independence. Above all, they wanted Bosch to persecute the "Castro-Communists."
He refused. This was a capital sin.

Not even the Kennedy administration could have saved Bosch in 1963,
had it so desired. American economic aid and pressure on the Dominican military might have enabled the Bosch government to survive a few months longer,
but the final outcome would have been the same. To give democracy a chance in
Santo Domingo, the United States should have used all its influence in 1962 to
purge the Dominican armed forces. This Washington would not do. By 1963 it
was too late. The threat of severing diplomatic relations and cutting off all economic and military aid could not have prevented the *golpe*. The Kennedy administration had used this same threat in 1962 to dissuade the Argentinian and
the Peruvian armed forces from overthrowing their constitutional governments,
governments that enjoyed warm U.S. support. But when the Argentinian military overthrew President Arturo Frondizi on 29 March 1962, Washington failed
to act. When the Peruvian military seized power on 18 July of the same year,
American resolve lasted only a few weeks. On 17 August the United States

recognized the Peruvian military junta and resumed economic aid. Shortly thereafter, military assistance began anew.

The same policy considerations that were behind the Alliance for Progress first led Washington to oppose the military *golpes* in Argentina and Peru, then set severe limits to U.S. reactions once the *golpes* had taken place. As already stated, the U.S. aim was to maintain an anti-Communist stability throughout the hemisphere. The Kennedy administration believed that over the long term this stability would best be guaranteed by pro-American and bitterly anti-Communist governments that would also be willing to attack "the long run sources of the Communist appeal—poverty, hunger and ignorance"[3]—by introducing some social reforms. President Frondizi in Argentina and Raúl Haya de la Torre in Peru belonged to this "democratic left" as defined in Washington; hence the Americans opposed the *golpes*.[4] But once the military had acted, the Kennedy administration concluded that it could not afford to "punish" the *golpistas* too severely without further endangering the very aims of its Latin American policy. The interrruption of economic aid might destabilize the economies of Argentina and Peru. An economic crisis would increase social tensions and thus play into the hands of the "Castro-Communists." The interruption of military aid would weaken the armed forces of those two countries. The Peruvian and Argentinian military might not be democratic, but at least they were staunchly anti-Communist.

In the Dominican Republic, as elsewhere in the hemisphere, the lessons of Argentina and Peru were not lost. The Dominican military knew that their weakness was a source of strength in dealing with the United States: the Americans would have to forgive them, for they were the only bulwark against Communism.

Thus, even if Washington had supported Bosch, by 1963 there were clear limits to its power to influence the weak, ineffective Dominican armed forces.

But the Kennedy administration was deeply disillusioned with Bosch. Kennedy, the liberals claim, backed the "democratic left" throughout Latin American. They point to his support for Betancourt, Figueres, and Paz Estenssoro. They fail to explain, however, that in order to belong to the circle of the "good boys" a Latin American leader had to prove his qualifications according to the narrow and arbitrary criteria set by the Kennedy administration. Nor was it only the Communist danger that explained American imperial behavior. If a Communist Caribbean represented the ultimate threat to the American empire, U.S. ambitions and extreme sensitivity in the region long antedated Marx, the Soviet Union, and Castro. The United States had inherited these ambitions from "mother" England. After the Louisiana Purchase, Thomas Jefferson had hankered for the annexation of Cuba to the extent that in 1809 he thought of making a deal with Napoleon whereby the French emperor would help the United States acquire Cuba in exchange for a free hand in South America and Mexico.[6] And if the might of the British fleet frustrated the annexationist dreams of Jefferson, James Monroe, and John Quincy Adams, the American drive toward the Caribbean intensified throughout the nineteenth century and finally exploded in all its violence after 1898, reaching its climax under Woodrow Wilson. The "Good Neighbor Policy" avoided fresh military interventions—they were not necessary, since in the only case where the United States saw its imperial interests threatened (the Grau San Martín government in Cuba, 1933-34), the overthrow of the culprit was swiftly obtained by more subtle, but still effective, means.[5] No new challenge arose in the region throughout the Roosevelt and Truman administrations. The overthrow of Arbenz in Guatemala (1954), the Bay of Pigs (1961), and then the missile crisis (1962) proved once more that the Caribbean was still the heart of the American empire and that Washington intended it to remain so. Against this historical background, and with the usual American sensitivity exasperated by Castro's challenge, Bosch came to the presidency in 1963.

Beyond any shadow of doubt, Juan Bosch was a man of the "democratic left"; therefore, according to the rhetoric of the Alliance of Progress, he should have enjoyed U.S. support. But he was too independent; he bluntly refused U.S. control and "advice." This alone would have cost him membership in the "Democratic left made in USA." At the same time, the ill will, resentment, and suspicion it generated were exacerbated by his position on the "Communist" issue. By Washington's standards, Bosch was "soft on Communism."

Under the superficial cloak of rhetoric of the Alliance for Progress, Kennedy's Latin American policy took no risks. Social change and political democracy would be encouraged only as long as they did not conflict with U.S. interests in the Western Hemisphere; otherwise they would be opposed. The paranoia created by Castro's challenge ran high in the circles of the Kennedy administration. Too often there was no place for real members of the democratic left, but only for the "safe" ones. Juan Bosch was not one of the latter. Neither was Arévalo of Guatemala nor Miguel Arraes of Brazil, among other members of the democratic left elsewhere in the continent.[7]

If this was Kennedy's policy, it is difficult to agree with Kennedy's liberal admirers, who condemn the Johnson administration for its Dominican policy during the Triumvirate. Opposition to "Boschism" was indeed a proof of continuity rather than a break with Kennedy's policies. Once we recognize this reality, it becomes clear that at the time there was little the United States could do beyond supporting Donald Reid Cabral.

At most one might be tempted to berate the Johnson administration for its hostility to Balaguer. The latter was as "reliable" as Donny, but enjoyed much more popular support. Yet even this criticism is not well founded. Large sectors of the Dominican armed forces—Wessin's faction, above all—were bitterly hostile to Balaguer while seemingly willing to back or at least tolerate Reid Cabral. And the support of the military, rather than that of the population, was the requisite for the survival of a Dominican president. Thus Reid Cabral was a better candidate than Balaguer and deserved U.S. support.[8] Indeed, this choice seemed increasingly wise. By the spring of 1965 the "troublemakers" of the San Cristóbal Group in the armed forces and Belisario Peguero in the police had lost all or most of their power. Lists of signatures would never topple Reid Cabral and return Bosch to the presidency. The "elections" promised for September 1965 would be a farce even if they took place. The far left was weak, and the anti-Reid Cabral "rebels" among the *gente de primera* could do nothing but complain and invoke that sacred term—"political democracy." If only the U.S. embassy and the CIA station in Santo Domingo had discovered the existence of the Enriquillo movement in time, Reid Cabral could have remained in power in spite of the corruption and economic problems of his Government—and Lyndon B. Johnson would have been spared much grief.[9]

But the Enriquillo movement was not discovered, and the constitutionalist revolt began on 24 April. Indeed, in the space of five days, two different revolts took place. First came the countercoup. Had it been successful on 25 April, Bosch would have returned to power in orderly fashion. The crowds in the streets still had only a few weapons, and the protagonists of victory would have been the constitutionalist military. Hernando Ramírez and his officers wanted to re-establish the constitutional government and eradicate corruption from the armed forces. Such was the extent of their "radicalism." With few exceptions, their urge for social reform was modest; they were violently anti-Communist and felt little community with the Dominican masses. In this respect, they were close to the "notables" of the PRD and had little in common with that party's "hotheads," led by Peña Gómez.

It is obvious that the constitutionalist military would have been influential in a Bosch administration. It is equally clear that their influence would have played a "moderating" role. Other officers—the *Balagueristas* and the crowd of opportunists who were joining the revolt or had already joined the conspiracy—would have called for even more "moderation." The constitutionalist victory would have reduced their influence, but they still would have represented a considerable force.

Finally, there was Juan Bosch. His desire for social reform was deep and sincere, but he was less "radical" than a Peña Gómez, more sensitive to fiscal and economic constraints and to the need for political compromises. In this regard, he occupied an intermediate position between the two major factions of his party, "notables" and "hotheads."

Thus, insofar as history allows us to speculate, one can conclude that the success of the countercoup would have resulted in a moderate answer to the Dominican dilemma. A new Bosch administration would have sought social reforms while rejecting "radical" or "hasty" solutions. It would have been anti-Communist, but respectful of political democracy. It would have felt no sympathy for the "totalitarian" solutions of Cuba and the Soviet bloc, but would have opposed U.S. imperialism in the Western Hemisphere and asserted the national sovereignty of the Dominican Republic. In short, it would have been a government of the "democratic left"—but not of that "democratic left" that enjoyed Washington's favor.

Early in the afternoon of 25 April, the constitutionalist victory seemed both imminent and peaceful. Then the planes of San Isidro began to attack the Presidential Palace. There would be no bloodless and orderly return to constitutional government. The countercoup gave way to the harsh reality of a civil war.

Two days of drama ensued. The constitutionalist forces lost ground. On 27 April, the battle at the Duarte Bridge should have dealt the death blow to the revolt. Instead, it marked the rebels' triumph.

A day later, U.S. troops landed in Santo Domingo, precluding a constitutionalist victory. Without the American intervention, Juan Bosch would have returned to complete his term as president of the Dominican Republic, and the great aim of the constitutionalist movement, already within reach on 25 April, would finally have been achieved. Bosch's return, however, would not have been the result of the countercoup. The countercoup had failed, and by 28 April a new revolt had defeated San Isidro.

The urban masses of Santo Domingo had found their weapons and had rallied to battle San Isidro. While the constitutionalist military collapsed as an organized force, while so many officers deserted or betrayed, the people won the battle at the bridge. This abrupt change in the role of the population marked a striking difference between the countercoup and the revolt as it appeared on the twenty-eighth.

Thus the events of those days decreased the relative importance of the constitutionalist military in the rebel camp. But they also promised momentous consequences for the armed forces as a whole. Gone were the opportunists who had joined the constitutionalist military movement, gone were the *Balaguerista* officers. A rebel victory in the civil war would have forced a much more radical purge inside the armed forces than the one foreseen by the leaders of the Enriquillo movement. De los Santos, Rivera Caminero, and their cronies had chosen to side with Wessin. For them and many like them, there would now be no place in the new Dominican armed forces—not even the reduced one that many of them could have maintained had the countercoup succeeded on 25 April.

Finally, those days of struggle had left an indelible mark on many hard-line constitutionalist officers, particularly on those who participated in the battle at the Duarte Bridge. They had fought not for, but with the people. They had experienced the valor and self-sacrifice of the *infelices* and the betrayal and cowardice of so many of their fellow officers. Their relation to the population, hence their attitude toward social change, could never be the same.

One does not need to be a prophet to predict that a Bosch government returning to power after 28 April would have been more "radical" than if it had come to power as a result of the countercoup. There would have been more urgency for, and less resistance to, social reforms. But one needs a powerful imagination—and much naiveté or bad faith—to conclude that on 28 April the revolt had fallen under any degree of "Castro-Communist" influence. Many U.S. politicians and scholars—liberals and conservatives alike—have proclaimed such a "truth." They have offered no proof other than their all-pervasive fear

and at times their dogmatic belief that in a situation of chaos and civil war—
when the *infelices* find their weapons and fight—the "Communists" will play an
ever-increasing role.[10] It is, however, no slight to the valor of the Dominican
"Castro-Communists" to state that in Santo Domingo on 24 April the far left
was painfully weak and that it remained so throughout those days of struggle.
Contrary to the belief of many Americans, the Dominican far left had neither
supermen nor charismatic leaders. The country's only charismatic leaders at the
time were Juan Bosch, and, to a certain degree, Joaquín Balaguer. And if some
members of the far left had military training, so did the constitutionalist officers. Though many PSPistas, MPDistas, and, above all, *catorcistas* armed themselves between 25 and 28 April, they remained a small minority in a sea of
armed civilians. Finally, when on 27 April the Molina Ureña government collapsed and most PRD leaders sought asylum in embassies, the leaders of the 1J4
stood at the Duarte Bridge. But the great majority of the civilians who fought
at the bridge were *Boschistas*, among them many young cadres of the PRD.
Once the battle was over, they did not turn to the 1J4 for leadership. While
waiting for the long yearned-after return of their *caudillo*, Juan Bosch, they
turned toward the constitutionalist officers, and in particular toward Colonel
Caamaño.

On 28 April, the U.S. military intervention began, robbing the constitutionalists of victory. Few critics or defenders of the intervention have lent any
credence to the claims of the Johnson administration that the marines landed
to protect foreign and Dominican lives. It was not the first time that an
American president had resorted to this pretext to mask an aggression against
a weaker neighbor. Wilson, for one, had done so to justify his intervention in
Haiti in 1915 and in the Dominican Republic in the following year. The lie was
as flagrant in 1965 as it had been on previous occasions. The real question is:
why did Washington decide that the revolt had to be defeated even at the cost of
military intervention? Was this decision an aberration, or was it justified given
the framework of U.S. policy?

Many American liberals, once convinced that on 28 April there was no
danger of a Communist takeover, began to criticize the intervention as a blunder
and a return to the "big stick" that represented a betrayal of Kennedy's policy
toward the Western Hemisphere and in particular toward the Dominican Republic. These same liberals, however, have failed to deny the right of the United
States to intervene had the revolt been Communist-dominated.

To assess the liberal critique, we need to look back at the period of 24-28
April. On two occasions in those five days the Johnson administration made
critical decisions in regard to the Dominican Republic. On the afternoon of 25
April, it resolved that the revolt had to be crushed. Three days later, Johnson
landed the marines. On the surface, the latter was the more momentous of the
two decisions; in fact, the opposite is true. The landing of the marines was the

inevitable outcome of the conclusion reached on 25 April. This conclusion, in turn, was not a sudden whim, but the logical result of decades of U.S. policy toward the Dominican Republic and the Western Hemisphere. Lyndon Johnson did not create this policy, but inherited it from his predecessors.

On the afternoon of the twenty-fifth, the U.S. embassy in Santo Domingo realized at last that the rebels' aim was not the installation of a military junta, but Bosch's return to the presidency. The embassy therefore concluded that the revolt had to be crushed. In the words of Chargé d'Affaires Connett, one of the reasons was "Communist advocacy of Bosch return"[11]—a statement that may seem pathetically absurd since we have seen at length how the parties of the far left reacted to the news of the countercoup. Instead of rejoicing, they feared another CIA "trick."

But what the far left thought is irrelevant here. Relevant is what the embassy knew, or believed it knew. Ignorance allied with paranoia and fear can be very dangerous. The embassy knew that the PSP, at least since the "Manifiesto" of 16 March 1965, had been openly advocating Bosch's return to the presidency. The public statements of the 1J4 were more ambiguous, for the party stressed the importance of the 1963 constitution and played down the role of Juan Bosch, while at the same time asking to be included in the Pact of Rio Piedras. We have seen what was behind this official rhetoric and that the 1J4 really stood against Bosch. But fear and prejudice led the embassy to a conclusion diametrically opposed to reality: behind its ambiguous statements, the 1J4 concealed its outright support for Bosch.

In this light it becomes easier to understand how Connett could conclude that the "Communists" were advocating Bosch's return to the presidency. Moreover, in the course of the twenty-fifth the PSP, then the 1J4, and finally even the MPD decided to support the revolt and hence, by implication, Bosch's return. The embassy completely missed the real significance of the position of the far left, both before and during the countercoup, but this hardly matters. The same lack of sophistication and the same biases had characterized Washington's judgment about the "Communist threat" in Latin America for many years. In the specific case of the Dominican Republic, they had from the beginning crippled the ability of the Kennedy administration to think and evaluate.

Is a man guilty by association? Did "Communist advocacy of Bosch return" prove in any way that Bosch himself had ties with the "Communists"? Had the Communists in Venezuela and Costa Rica advocated the election of Betancourt and Figueres, would this have reflected on the shining image of those champions of the "democratic left made in USA"? But here there is a key difference. Bosch was already guilty, he was already banned from the circle of the "good boys." He was "soft on Communism." In the inspired words of Kennedy's ambassador, John B. Martin, Bosch was "a reckless political plunger, willing to risk everything, including the democratic system itself, to gain a personal political objective"; he was a man who in 1962 already had "reached an understanding with certain Communists."[12] Why, then, in 1965 should the U.S. government and its Dominican embassy fail to suspect Bosch of having reached another secret agreement with the Communists? Of course, there was no proof. But had there been any proof for Martin's conclusions in 1963?

And so we have, on 25 April 1965, a man who is "soft on Communism," and whose return the Communists are advocating. This same man, while president, has also shown a dangerous "anti-American" nationalism.

This, then, is the rationale for the U.S. decision of 25 April 1965, a rationale all the more compelling if we realize that the decision was momentous only in hindsight. At the time it appeared to be of modest importance, nearly banal.

Neither San Isidro nor the embassy was contemplating a U.S. military intervention. The "loyalists" would do the job; alone they would crush the revolt. All the United States had to do was to whisper a few inspiring words to some Dominican military chiefs (Rivera Caminero, for example). Not even American logistical support would be necessary. Washington would hide its hand and remain "neutral"—indeed, Franklin D. Roosevelt and his celebrated Sumner Welles had intervened much more actively in Cuba in 1933-34, while inaugurating the "nonintervention" policy of the United States.

For more than two days, Washington's policy seemed successful. The constitutionalists lost ground and San Isidro grew stronger while the United States remained "neutral." Since everything went so smoothly, the administration paid relatively little attention to the crisis throughout 26 and 27 April.[13] Thus, in spite of the incident at the Hotel Embajador and the heavy fighting in the capital on the twenty-seventh, the United States calmly proceeded to evacuate its nationals: there was no need to play up the humanitarian angle since the "good guys" were winning.[14] Nor was there a place for OAS involvement in a crisis destined for such a happy ending.

On the morning of 28 April the nightmare suddenly began. San Isidro had lost the battle at the bridge and was in the grip of panic. If three days earlier the United States had concluded that the constitutionalist revolt was against American interests, what now emerged was an intolerable threat. In Santo Domingo the United States saw chaos, armed mobs, the collapse of the armed forces (bulwark against Communism), even the collapse of the Molina Ureña government and the PRD: ideal conditions for a "red" takeover. The specter of a second Cuba was suddenly not a distant possibility, but an immediate reality. Given the American paranoia, to expect a more sophisticated conclusion, whether under Kennedy or Johnson, is absurd.

Yet the Johnson administration was not "trigger-happy." Even the embassy understood the political cost of military intervention. When Colonel Benoit asked for the landing of 1,200 marines early in the afternoon of the twenty-eighth, Bennett cabled his opposition to the State Department.[15] Only after he realized that the collapse of San Isidro was imminent (for once the embassy was correct in its assessment of the situation) did the ambassador endorse Benoit's plea. If anything, Bennett had waited too long before accepting the debacle of his protégés as reality. Even after the landing of the marines, however, Bennett went on hoping that the rebels would be defeated without actually committing U.S. troops to the fight.[16]

If the Embassy hesitated, Washington was even more cautious, as proved by its refusal, throughout the morning of the twenty-eighth, to deliver the fifty walkie-talkies to the "loyalists." Washington relented only in the early afternoon, after renewed pressure from the embassy.[17]

But after Bennett's dramatic telegram of 5:16 P.M., what else could Johnson have done except intervene? What would Kennedy have done?

Johnson and his advisers, "liberal" or "conservative," could judge only according to the evidence they had. This evidence was provided by the embassy and the CIA reports, all unanimous in stressing that a rebel victory would lead to a Communist takeover, and that such a victory was imminent.

Johnson had no room for maneuvering. There was obviously no time. "Never a second Cuba" was the imperative rule of U.S. policy in the Western Hemisphere, a rule accepted by one and all, a basic tenet of the Kennedy legacy, one that nobody challenged. In 1965 that rule seemed more compelling than ever. How could the United States tolerate a second Cuba in the Caribbean when it was intervening against a Communist takeover in faraway Vietnam? How weak the administration would appear, to friend and foe alike! Now was not the time for a philosophical discussion on whether a second Cuba would indeed represent such a threat to the United States as to warrant military intervention. American public opinion and the U.S. Congress would be pitiless to a president who had failed in the decisive moment—especially in the Caribbean, heartland of the American empire.[18]

Should Johnson have waited until he had more evidence? He had no reason to distrust the reports of his embassy. Above all, a delay would have meant the collapse of San Isidro and the consolidation of the rebels' victory. A "constitutionalist" government would then have been created—with or without Bosch—and in all probability it would prove cunning enough to hide its Communist tendencies, while underneath the degree of Communist influence would constantly increase. An American military intervention after the conclusion of the civil war would have been much more flagrant, and therefore much more costly in political and probably also in military terms. Given the constraints of U.S. policy, Johnson chose the lesser evil: an immediate, but limited, military intervention that could give San Isidro the possibility of recovering, while disheartening the rebels and enabling the United States to pretend that its intervention was for humanitarian purposes. None of those with Johnson when he ordered the landing of the marines dissented. Yet these were "liberals" of the Kennedy vintage: Dean Rusk, Robert McNamara, McGeorge Bundy, George Ball, and Bill Moyers.[19] A few days later, Johnson sent another "Kennedy man" to Santo Domingo as his special representative: John B. Martin, a self-proclaimed friend of the Dominican people and "expert" on Dominican affairs. Martin concluded that on 28 April the Communist threat was real—thus vindicating the hard-liner Bennett.

Eager to prove that the decision to intervene was an aberration rather than the consequence of a larger U.S. policy that antedated Johnson, some liberal critics have followed yet another line of attack. After stressing the obvious blunders of the embassy they have gone one step further, contending that the embassy was the image of the administration it served. Under Johnson, the U.S. embassy in Santo Domingo was hopelessly biased, and its prejudices led to the intervention. Under Kennedy, they argue, there would naturally have been a much more "liberal" embassy. Many of the blunders would have been avoided and no intervention would have taken place.

The major errors of the embassy that led to the intervention can be separated into two groups: (1) "objective" mistakes: the failure to discover the existence of the Enriquillo movement, the underestimation of the strength of the revolt on 24 April, and the failure to realize its constitutionalist aim until the afternoon of 25 April; and (2) "subjective" mistakes: the conclusion that Bosch was "soft on Communism," the failure to understand the real attitude of the far left toward Bosch, and the belief in the imminence of a "Communist takeover" on 28 April.

It should by now be obvious that the "subjective" mistakes were not the result of the failures of specific individuals, or even of a specific group of men (the so-called Johnson-Mann hardliners). They were rather the logical consequence of a set of perceptions common to both the Kennedy and Johnson administrations and largely shared by liberals and conservatives alike.

A more perceptive embassy might have avoided the "objective" mistakes. To do so, however, it needed not to be more or less "liberal," but only more skilled. The Johnson administration may be criticized for having sent men of limited abilities to the Dominican Republic, but this has nothing to do with their being "liberals" or "conservatives," nor is there any reason to suppose that Kennedy would have sent more able men. In fact, if Ambassador Martin is an example, the contrary would have been true.

Finally, had the embassy been more perceptive, the intervention might have been avoided, but not as a result of a more liberal policy. A more competent embassy, and in particular a more efficient CIA station, might have uncovered the existence of the Enriquillo movement in time for Reid Cabral to thwart the conspiracy. And had the embassy learned that Peña Gómez had made overtures to the IJ4, its hostility toward the *Boschistas* would have grown stronger still. More able American personnel might at least have discovered the rebels' real aims at a time when the revolt could easily have been crushed.

If the decision to intervene can easily by explained and justified within the framework of U.S. foreign policy, what then about the failure of the Johnson administration to consult the OAS before landing the marines and its management of the crisis once the military intervention had begun? On these points, too, many and diverse criticisms have been made against the administration.

It is certainly a bitter irony that Senator Robert Kennedy chose to attack the Johnson administration for its failure to consult the OAS before sending troops to the Dominican Republic.[20] The senator's brother had totally ignored the existence of the OAS when he launched the Bay of Pigs operation, an aggression that represented a flagrant violation of the organization's charter.[21] A few months later, during the crisis of the "Wicked Uncles," President Kennedy had gently pushed the OAS to the sidelines, and, finally, during the missile crisis, he did not wait for OAS approval before deciding how the United States would act. On all those occasions, Robert Kennedy, the most influential member of his brother's administration, failed to express the slightest disapproval at such neglect of the OAS. Indeed, he would have been a fool had he objected. Whenever it considers its vital interests at stake, no great power subordinates its decisions to the vote of an international organization unless considerations of Realpolitik, but not of legality, compel it to do so. In this regard, President Kennedy was following the example of his predecessor, Dwight D. Eisenhower, who had acted with sovereign contempt for both the OAS and the United Nations during his aggression against Guatemala in 1954.[22]

If in April 1965 vital American interests were not threatened, the United States should not have intervened. If, however, vital American interests were at stake, then to seek OAS approval before intervening would have been, to say the least, irresponsible. First, there was the time factor—a rapid decision was needed, but the OAS is not noted for its speed, and most Latin American delegates in its councils excel in verbosity. Above all, the OAS might have refused to approve a military intervention in the Dominican Republic, whether a unilateral one by the United States or a collective one by the organization. Seven states out of twenty would have sufficed for a negative vote. Then what would Washington have done? Would it have sent troops in spite of the OAS disapproval? Even the OAS would have found it difficult to swallow such a humiliation. Or would Washington have bowed to the decision, while still believing vital U.S. interests were in danger? Judging from the record, this is not what President Kennedy would have done. Thus the Johnson administration made the "correct" decision: it landed the marines without requesting OAS approval, but paid lip service to the organization.[23]

Of the many criticisms that have been directed at the Johnson administration for its management of the crisis in the period following the landing, one is so obviously correct that even many apologists of the administration's Dominican policy have conceded the point. The authors of the semiofficial *Dominican Action—1965, Intervention or Cooperation?* have stated the case as suavely as possible: "the reasons for the U.S. landing were ineptly explained to the public."[24]

In his efforts to convince the American people that his Dominican policy was just, Lyndon Johnson lived up to the image of a Texan that had haunted him throughout the "aristocratic" Kennedy administration: he acted like a bull in a china shop. Here, rather than in the substance of policy, lies the striking difference between Johnson and Kennedy, who had so skillfully extricated himself from the ruins of the Bay of Pigs operation and, in the minds of the American people, transformed his blunder into something akin to a personal triumph.[25]

Johnson had committed no blunder, at least not within the framework of U.S. values and foreign policy. Throughout the crisis he enjoyed the support of a large majority of the American public and Congress. But this was not enough for him. He had to convince not once, but ten times; he had to convince even the minority that disapproved. In order to do this, he presented a generous mixture of a little truth with a flood of outright lies, gross exaggerations, bombastic statements, and irrelevant generalizations. The result was pathetic and counterproductive.

To discredit the constitutionalist movement and to prove that the U.S. "humanitarian intervention" had been indispensable, Johnson did not merely point to the inevitable excesses that had taken place in the first days of the revolt: he invented atrocities the rebels had never committed. To demonstrate the reality of the "red threat" in Santo Domingo, he did not merely say that there had been a danger of a Communist takeover; he stated categorically that on 28 April the revolt had been "seized and placed into the hands of a band of Communist conspirators,"[26] thus charging himself unnecessarily with the burden of proof, when "not even the most zealous Red-hunters could document that statement."[27]

Most Americans supported his decision to land the marines, but Johnson was stung by criticism from the few who disapproved, and as a result he overreacted. He who had been sincerely reluctant to intervene created the impression of a jingoistic, irresponsible president.

While Johnson stumbled from one faux pas to the next—dutifully imitated by some members of his cabinet and lesser figures of his administration—in Santo Domingo an inept embassy and an equally inept CIA station added their contribution to the public relations blunders of their government. With a determination worthy of a better cause, they fed the American press an unending list of "flagrant" examples of rebel "atrocities" and "concrete" proof of the Communist takeover. The "proof" and "examples" were such obvious falsifications that with little effort an honest and competent journalist could easily have exposed them. Some American journalists did so, with devastating effect. Having arrived in Santo Domingo ready to believe in the integrity of their embassy and the correctness of their government's policy, they became bitter critics.[28]

An imperialist power always needs a few fabrications to mask its aggressive policies. Thus the United States had an interest in pretending that it had intervened on 28 April for humanitarian reasons. Indeed, one can even understand why between 14 and 21 May the administration stubbornly pretended that it was neutral in the civil war, while in Santo Domingo the U.S. military helped the "loyalist" offensive against the *barrios altos*. But the drama of the Johnson administration is that it became caught in a web of lies and contradictions that were, for the most part, not only flagrant but unnecessary. These blunders, however, hardly affected a majority of the American people and their elected representatives, who supported Johnson's Dominican policy to the very end.

A minority in Congress, in the press, and throughout the land, however, reacted negatively. Most of these critics would have approved the landing of the marines had there been a Communist danger, but once they understood that no such danger existed, they condemned the intervention. They were shattered by the realization that their president was lying to them. The credibility gap had been opened. It would never close. Behind the Dominican crisis loomed Vietnam, and the bitter taste left by the former was soon transferred to the latter. Senator Fulbright, the powerful chairman of the Senate Foreign Relations Committee, "realized that if Johnson was lying to him about the Dominican Republic, he might be doing the same about Vietnam."[29] At the time, not many were as perceptive as Fulbright—but the number would soon increase.

Although he blundered in his public relations offensive, Johnson aptly led the Dominican crisis to a pro-American conclusion. By mid-May, the administration had begun its efforts for a "negotiated" solution. Given the surprising resilience of the constitutionalists, the alternative would have been a "Budapest"—obviously feasible from a military standpoint, but extremely costly in political terms.

The administration has been condemned by many liberal critics for its decision to abandon the Guzmán formula. Indeed, it is on this issue that the first differences between liberals and hard-liners appeared inside the U.S. government.

To assess the validity of the liberal critique, and thus to pass judgment on the administration's policies, two questions must be answered. Were the Guzmán and the Godoy solutions similar or different? If different, which one best served the interests of the United States?

Antonio Guzmán was an admirer and close friend of Juan Bosch; he was a constitutionalist, however moderate. Héctor Godoy was a political opportunist, with strong ties to powerful anticonstitutionalist groups;[30] he felt no hatred for Juan Bosch and the rebel movement, but he was a pliant man, one who would accept the "realities of life" whatever their price. The Guzmán solution would have divided control of the armed forces between constitutionalists and "loyalists"; the Godoy solution gave complete control of the military to the latter. Thus the two formulas were strikingly different: the first represented a real compromise; the second, a compromise in name only.

Which formula, then, would best serve the interests of the United States? The Guzmán solution offered little hope for stability. Civil wars seldom end with a reconciliation between "enemy brothers," and for the Dominican Republic, such a reconciliation would have been impossible. Stability required that one of the two sides be crushed—it would have been absurd for the United States to desire the defeat of their "loyalists."

The United States had invaded the Dominican Republic; the aggression had radicalized the constitutionalist forces and the Dominican urban masses while transforming the mild antipathy that many felt toward the Americans into deep hostility. And if Bosch and his supporters were "unrealiable" or "soft on Communism" before 28 April, the intervention had certainly not helped to lead them toward the "right path." To believe otherwise required a great deal of naiveté.

The United States had already paid the political cost of the intervention. For Washington to retreat from the Dominican Republic without full guarantees for the future would have been absurd. Only the Godoy formula offered such guarantees.

Some have argued that the Dominican Republic "was a comparatively easy place for the United States to intervene and from which to withdraw" and that "it seems likely that military intervention in the Caribbean bears fewer costs and risks for the United States than it would in any other area."[31] There is no reason to dispute this obvious truth; nevertheless, the Johnson administration should receive credit for avoiding the twin pitfalls—a "Budapest" and a Guzmán solution. In mid-May, the administration had acted in haste, in fear of the political cost of a prolonged intervention. By the end of the month, it had recovered from the shock. Throughout the summer, the constitutionalists were urging a rapid solution, while Ambassador Bunker appeared in no hurry. The United States had realized that it could afford to wait, that time would play in its favor. Only a massive U.S. attack on Ciudad Nueva could rekindle the interest and the indignation of international public opinion; the United Nations was ineffectual and the OAS docile. Events have proved that the Johnson administration made the right decision; the intervention was a success. It was successful in the short term because three months of a skillful blend of carrot-and-stick policy led to the installation of the Godoy government and its inevitable consequence: the election of Joaquín Balaguer as president of the Republic in June 1966. The intervention was a success in the long term because this same Balaguer has remained in power ever since—and it is now 1977.[32]

Looking back at the period of the Godoy government, certain liberal critics of the Johnson administration have reached a very peculiar conclusion: "Héctor García-Godoy was an independent, progressive democrat, and his mandate was to provide a liberal transitional government that would make it possible to hold genuinely free elections, thus giving the moderate forces within the constitutionalists a real chance to attain their primary objective, the return of Bosch to the Presidency."[33] If this were true, it would render Johnson's Dominican policy completely incoherent; and the rejection of the Guzmán solution would become a flagrant blunder.

But this statement, of course, is far from true. We have seen the real meaning of the Godoy formula and how this "liberal, transitional government" made

Bosch's victory at the polls in June 1966 highly unlikely. And if by a quirk of fate Bosch had won, how long would he have lasted? To topple him would have required no new U.S. military intervention. Between April 1965 and June 1966, the United States had prepared the ground well enough. In June 1966, the Dominican armed forces were in the hands of officers who had fought against the "rebels" during the civil war and who now felt not hostility, but hatred, for Bosch and his constitutionalists. How long would they have tolerated a Bosch government—a day, a week, a month? This is the only relevant question. Without a doubt, they would have overthrown Bosch. Certainly they would have had the power to do so. Had the United States wanted to leave a free choice to the Dominican people in June 1966, had it wanted to make of the elections something more than a painful farce, it should have avoided the particular cast of the Godoy solution. In particular, it should have prevented "loyalist" control of the armed forces and the sad fate of the constitutionalist military during the provisional government. Here again, no one could doubt that Washington had the power to do so. Instead, the United States chose to transform the elections into a farce. Such action was logical, given U.S. imperial interests and its policy throughout the crisis.

However successful in the short term, the U.S. intervention in the Dominican Republic would have failed if the Balaguer government had proved either unfriendly to American interests or unable to sustain itself. But this has not been the case. It is true that the civil war and the intervention brought about a radicalization of Dominican politics. Anyone walking in Santo Domingo in the late sixties could see the oppressive presence of army and police patrols, an obvious symbol of a very tense situation; any political observer could feel ferment among the masses and see the clear signs of the activity of a radicalized opposition. But the repression has been stronger than the opposition, the blows of the regime have been devastating, and Balaguer has shown his ability to survive. In February 1973, Caamaño was killed by Dominican troops a few days after landing with nine men in the southwest of the Republic. He had been in Cuba since 1967 and had become a sincere believer of the *foco* theory. His faith in it persisted even after the Cubans had recognized its failure. Returning to his country to make a dream come true, Caamaño paid with his life, as Manolo Tavárez had done nearly ten years earlier.[34]

Bosch is now in the Dominican Republic and is still the major leader of the opposition, but years of frustration and defeat have decreased his charisma. In November 1973, he and a nucleus of devoted followers abandoned the PRD to create a more militant and revolutionary party, the Partido de la Liberación Dominicana (PLD). Peña Gómez, for many years a friend, follower, and protégé, has broken with Bosch and remains at the head of the PRD. Abandoning the revolutionary positions of the late sixties, he is now moving back to a "moderate" stance, probably the result of years of frustrated hopes—another victory for Joaquín Balaguer and his American protectors. And while it is too early to assess the potential of the PLD, so far the new party has been weak, despite the efforts of its members.[35]

The far left has received continuous blows; its list of brave martyrs has grown endlessly. Otto Morales, Amín Abel, Maximiliano Gómez, and so many others: beautiful names, glorious examples for Dominican youth . . . but they are dead, and too many of their followers have been jailed or exiled, or have deserted the cause, pressed by the need to support their families or the fear of a repression that becomes ever more precise and effective.

Rather than democracy, the Dominican Republic has what is euphemistically called a "strong government." In a climate of uninterrupted violence, this "strong government" has granted elections every four years, so that naive or biased observers could claim that the regime is democratic.

While U.S. aid, high sugar prices, and the exploitation of new mineral resources have brought about some years of economic growth, it is impossible to speak of any social or economic progress for the Dominican masses. Hunger, unemployment and underemployment, lack of education and social services are still the lot of the *infelices*, both in the cities and the countryside. Awaiting "troublemakers" who dare to complain are the police and the armed forces, the anti-Communist champions of "Dios, Patria, and Libertad"—"their" God, "their" Fatherland, and "their" freedom.[36]

The sufferings of the Dominican people hardly matter, however, if we want to assess whether or not the intervention was successful. What is important is that Joaquín Balaguer, the former servant of Trujillo, the skilled friend of the Americans, is still in power after eleven years of murder and oppression—eleven years in which Dominican events have created no worries for Washington, and the situation has been kept under control. Perhaps in a not too distant future the Dominican people will free themselves of this regime of violence and will move toward a more just society. But for eleven years the Balaguer formula has proved successful.[37] This is no small accomplishment for the United States, no little vindication for Lyndon Johnson and the policy he executed but did not create.

The intervention "stabilized" the Dominican Republic, but what about its impact on U.S. foreign relations, in particular those with Latin America? The OAS was once more prostituted and public opinion in the hemisphere reacted with outrage—that is, in those countries where opinions could still be expressed.

But what did it matter? The OAS had been prostituted long before, by Eisenhower and by Kennedy; the Latin American governments were already used to American violence, and their shallow cries of indignation were not new. True, the Second Special Inter-American Conference to be held in Rio was postponed from June to November 1965 because of the U.S. intervention in the Dominican Republic. Also true is that the idea of a permanent inter-American peace force—so dear to the United States—received its deathblow as a result of the Dominican intervention. But the concept had been doomed from its inception, and the crisis only accelerated its official demise. Besides, the death of Che

Guevara two years after the Dominican revolt, in October 1967, marked the end of the guerrilla offensive of the 1960s. A few U.S. military advisers and some CIA agents had sufficed to help the Bolivian army, probably the worst in South America, defeat Che's last challenge. Now there was no need for a permanent inter-American peace force designed to defeat the Castroist offensive throughout the hemisphere.

It is highly arbitrary to attribute to Dominican events any influence in the new trends that appeared in U.S.-Latin American relations in the late 1960s. The real causes of these trends were rather the U.S. loss of prestige in Vietnam, increasing economic conflict between the United States and its Latin "brothers," and the emergence of new, less subservient regimes in Peru and Panama in October 1968, whose coming to power had nothing to do with the Dominican crisis.

If anything, the intervention had some positive repercussions for U.S. imperialism in the Western Hemisphere. It showed to friend and foe alike that while it had failed to destroy Castro, the American tiger had lost none of its teeth. Castro felt that threat in April and early May 1965: would the United States, in the wake of its Dominican intervention, leap to a greater banquet and move against Cuba? Paradoxically, the crisis damaged the prestige of the Cuban leader in some circles. In the Western Hemisphere, voices were heard from the far left senselessly criticizing Castro for his "passivity" while the Americans invaded a neighboring country—as if there were something he could have done. At the same time, the Soviet Union, by its passivity throughout the crisis, anticipated the American reaction to the Soviet intervention in Czechoslovakia three years later: the Caribbean area was still a closely guarded sphere of influence of the United States, just as Eastern Europe was of the Soviet Union.

To conclude this sad story one last observation is in order. The 1960s witnessed the offensive of Castroism throughout Latin America. The *focos guerrilleros* spread in many countries of the Western Hemisphere; sometimes with lightning speed, at other times more slowly, all were crushed. But the Dominican revolt, a democratic movement owing nothing to Castro and in no way following the Cuban model, came close to success. It afforded a unique opportunity for the Dominican people to break the chains of oppression. It could have shown a new, non-Cuban road toward social change in Latin America. Instead, the Pax Americana prevailed.

Post Scriptum

In May 1978, in a presidential election that saw him pitted against the PRD candidate, Antonio Guzmán, Balaguer at last allowed a free ballot. The result was predictable: he lost. A military coup to prevent the proclamation of the results was stillborn. It is now likely that Guzmán will ascend the presidency of the Dominican Republic thirteen years after the failure of the "Guzmán solution."

The era of Balaguer has come to an end. The old president for once committed a grievous error: to allow free elections without having previously secured the results by other, less democratic means. Had he become the victim of his own rhetoric? Did he truly believe that he was the choice of the Dominican people?

It is too early, however, to divine the future. Times have changed, and the PRD, since the break with Bosch, has become increasingly "moderate." Guzmán himself, never a "radical," is now freed from the "pernicious" influence of Bosch—this had been his major fault, in the Americans' eyes.

Above all, there are the armed forces, the children of the intervention. Their power remains intact, posing a mortal threat to the Guzmán administration. Will they move swiftly to overthrow the new president, or will they remain "loyal"—and if so, what will be their price? Will Guzmán be their captive, as was the case in Guatemala for another reformist who won free election in an unfree country, Julio César Méndez Montenegro?

The United States bears a part of the responsibility for Balaguer's misfortune. The Carter administration applied pressure on the Dominican president to hold free elections and, above all, against the incipient military coup once it appeared that Guzmán had won. Few will criticize Washington for such interference. But those who see too readily a dramatic change in American policy ought to remember that Guzmán and the "new" PRD have neither the means nor the will to "misbehave." They do not threaten the pro-American stability imposed on the Dominican Republic by Johnson's policies and twelve years of Balaguer; to the contrary, a less corrupt and more reform-minded government would give more legitimacy to this stability, and would defuse the danger, however distant, of a popular explosion.

Appendix I

The United States and the Assassination of Trujillo

In early 1960, a small group of Dominicans, gathered around retired General Juan Tomás Díaz, began plotting the overthrow of the regime.[1] Fourteen men formed the core of the conspiracy. One of them, Lieutenant Amado García Guerrero, was no doubt motivated by idealistic considerations, as was probably true for another, Livio Cedeño Herrera.[2] But the other twelve—some members of the *gente de primera*, others representatives of the *nouveaux riches* of the Era—were men who had willingly served Trujillo, reaping the benefits and enduring the humiliations the Jefe heaped upon his servants. Now they turned against him. They were motivated by fear for their own security and privileges, which were threatened by the agony of the regime (see Chapter 1), and by desire for a revenge that at last seemed possible.[3] They were also spurred on by ambition for the power and riches they could seize as the heroes who vanquished the dictatorship. They had no desire for social reform, nor any interest in political democracy. If successful, "they had no intention of holding elections."[4]

Their plan to overthrow the regime was simple: Trujillo had to be assassinated. But they could seize power after his death only with the complicity of a key army officer.

In early 1961 they found such a man: Minister of the armed forces General Juan René ("Pupo") Román Fernández. Román Fernández, married to a niece of Trujillo, had received both money and preferment from the dictator, but he, too, felt that the time for betrayal had come. He promised the conspirators that immediately after the death of Trujillo he would arrest and if necessary execute the other members of the reigning family, place Juan Tomás Díaz in command of the powerful military base of San Isidro, and neutralize any *trujillista* reaction inside the armed forces. He would act only after he had received decisive proof of the death of the Jefe: the conspirators would have to show him the corpse.

In the evening of 30 May 1961, outside Ciudad Trujillo, the conspirators ambushed and killed Trujillo. But they drove in vain to the general's house with the dictator's corpse hidden in the trunk: Román Fernández was not at home.

By chance, General Arturo Espaillat, a staunch *Trujillista*, had witnessed from afar the Jefe's assassination. Unable to save Trujillo, his concern now was to save the regime. As he recounts in his book, "I swung the car around and sped back to the capital to give the alarm. . . . I headed for the home of General Román [Fernández]. As chief of the Armed Forces he should be the first to know. I had not the slightest reason to doubt his loyalty." Thus Román Fernández learned of Trujillo's death not from the conspirators, but from an energetic man determined to save the regime, who had come to him for assistance. Román Fernández was an opportunist, but he was also a coward. Meekly he left with Espaillat to help crush the plot, perhaps in the absurd hope that his own complicity would not be discovered. Espaillat, himself a knave, but a brave one, has aptly commented: "He should have shot me. When he walked out of the house [with me], he doomed his coup and himself. I was the only one who knew Trujillo had been assassinated. He knew I would take immediate action."[5]

Unable to find Román Fernández, the conspirators knew they were lost. In panic they scattered in search of refuge.

What role did the United States play in the conspiracy? From 1961 until 1975, this question remained shrouded in mystery. Many indices pointed to American complicity with the group around Juan Tomás Díaz, but there was a dearth of concrete proof. Some useful information was contained in the "Proceso instruido con motivo de la muerte del Generalisimo Trujillo" (in particular in the deposition of Huascar A. Tejeda Pimentel), but it was never made public, nor is its evidence conclusive. Outside of the American government only three men had direct knowledge of the role played by the United States: the leader of the conspiracy, Juan Tomás Díaz, and two men who served as intermediaries with the Americans: the Dominican "Plutarco Acevedo" and Wallace Berry ("Wimpy"), an American citizen who was a close friend of one of the plotters.

Juan Tomás Díaz's lips were sealed forever on 4 June 1961, as he tried to escape arrest. After the death of Trujillo, Wimpy was detained briefly, then allowed to flee the country because of his government's protection. He later returned to the Dominican Republic, but refused to indulge in "revelations" or interviews. As for "Plutarco Acevedo," the police failed to discover his identity. His real name was Angel Severo Cabral y Ortíz,[6] and he died four years later, without having revealed his secrets.

In November 1975, a committee of the U.S. Senate, chaired by Senator Frank Church, published a report on *Alleged Assassination Plots* [of the United States] *Involving Foreign Leaders*. The committee investigated U.S. responsibility in the assassination or attempted assassination of Patrice Lumumba, Fidel Castro, Rafael Trujillo, Ngo Dinh Diem, and General René Schneider. While many questions still need to be answered, the report is an authoritative source on the role played by the United States.[7]

In early 1960 the American government decided that U.S. interest demanded the end of Trujillo's rule. According to the Church report, "increasing American awareness of Trujillo's brutality and fear that it would lead to a Castro-type revolution caused United States' officials to consider various plans to hasten his abdication or downfall."[8] Of course, Trujillo's brutality was nothing new, and the "increasing awareness" of it on the part of U.S. leaders stemmed from political rather than moral considerations.

In both 1960 and 1961, official and unofficial American emissaries tried to persuade Trujillo to relinquish power in the Dominican Republic. Among these envoys were U.S. ambassador to the Dominican Republic James Farland, Senator George Smathers, William D. Pawley (a former diplomat, prominent businessman, and Trujillo's friend who had played an analogous role for the U.S. government in December 1958 with another friend, Fulgencio Batista in Cuba), and finally, in April 1961, former Undersecretary of State Robert D. Murphy, who was sent for this purpose by President Kennedy. They all failed to achieve their goal, as did the OAS sanctions, the special import fee decreed by the Eisenhower administration against Dominican sugar, and the many other public manifestations of Washington's disapproval.

But at the same time the United States was trying to "hasten" Trujillo's "downfall" by other, more concrete means. In the spring of 1960, Ambassador Farland made initial contact with the "moderate," "pro-United States"[9] group of Juan Tomás Díaz. From the outset, the Americans were aware that the conspirators planned to assassinate Trujillo, and they approved. On 1 July 1960, Assistant Secretary of State for Inter-American Affairs Roy Rubottom and Acting CIA Director General C.P. Cabell approved the delivery of twelve "sterile" (that is, untraceable) rifles with telescopic sights to the conspirators by means of air drops.

But the conspirators requested that the delivery be postponed. They were not ready to act, and the air drops therefore represented an unnecessary risk.

Throughout the remaining months of 1960 and the winter of 1961, various U.S. officials maintained close contact with Juan Tomás Díaz. After diplomatic relations were broken off in August 1960, Ambassador Farland departed, and his role fell to the U.S. consul, Harry Dearborn. Little progress was made, however, since the conspirators still lacked a key man in the armed forces.

Only when General Román Fernández had joined the plot did the conspirators feel ready to move. In response to their request, CIA headquarters approved on 10 April the dispatch of four machine guns to be used in the assassination of Trujillo.[10] The weapons arrived in Santo Domingo on 19 April, but were never delivered to the conspirators because at that very moment Washington's policy underwent a drastic change as a result of the debacle at the Bay of Pigs. Indeed, by 17 April, CIA headquarters realized that the invasion had failed and concluded that "precipitous action should be avoided in the Dominican Republic until Washington was able to give further consideration to the consequences of a Trujillo overthrow and the power vacuum which would be created."[11] In early 1960, the United States had begun to plot the overthrow of the dictator because it feared that in the long term his regime might lead to a social explosion and thus increase the danger of a "Castroist" solution in the Dominican Republic. But the fiasco at the Bay of Pigs, and the resulting increase in Castro's prestige heightened the fears of the Americans and led them to a different conclusion. The short-term danger was now paramount. In the words of a CIA headquarters cable: "filling a vacuum created by assassination [is] now bigger question than ever [in] view [of] unsettled conditions in Caribbean area."[12] A few days later, because of these same considerations, the National

Security Council and President Kennedy concluded that the United States should not initiate the overthrow of Trujillo until it could be sure that a pro-American government would be able to assert itself in Santo Domingo.

Thus, by May 1961, the Dominican policy of the United States had reached an impasse. Washington still believed that in the long run a continuation of the Trujillo regime represented a danger to U.S. interests, but it now refused to plot the dictator's overthrow because of the immediate danger a power vacuum would pose. On 5 May, as a defensive measure, the National Security Council "agreed that the task force on Cuba would prepare promptly both emergency and long-range plans for anti-Communist intervention in . . . the Dominican Republic"[13]—tantalizing words that lead one to believe that a U.S. military intervention was contemplated if necessary to prevent a "second Cuba." While searching for a new Dominican policy, Washington instructed its representatives in the country not to deliver the machine guns to the conspirators and to tell them they should not proceed with their plans to assassinate Trujillo.[14] The administration probably believed that the conspirators would not dare to act without American permission in spite of Consul Dearborn's reports predicting an imminent assassination attempt. This may be why the administration was surprised by the news of Trujillo's death.

The Church report, which is the major source on the U.S. role in the death of Trujillo, is at once categorical and ambiguous. It is categorical in acknowledging that the United States was involved in plots to assassinate Trujillo, Fidel Castro (from 1960 to 1965), and Lumumba (1960-61). It is ambiguous, however, regarding the other major question it deals with: At what level in the U.S. government was American participation authorized? In this respect, the report submits:

> We are unable to draw firm conclusions concerning who authorized the assassination plots. Even after our long investigation it is unclear whether the conflicting and inconclusive state of the evidence is due to the system of the plausible denial or whether there were, in fact, serious shortcomings in the system of authorization which made it possible for assassination efforts to have been undertaken by agencies of the United States Government without express authority from authorities above those agencies.
>
> Based on the record of our investigation, the Committee finds that the system of Executive command and control was so inherently ambiguous that it is difficult to be certain at what level assassination activity was known and authorized. This creates the disturbing prospect that assassination activity might have been undertaken by officials of the United States Government without its having been incontrovertibly clear that there was explicit authorization from the President of the United States. At the same time, this ambiguity and imprecision leaves open the possibility that there was a successful "plausible denial" and that a Presidential authorization was issued but is now obscured.[15]

In the case of the Dominican Republic, a curious picture results if we assess U.S. responsibilities according to what the Church report has been able to prove.

In the Eisenhower administration, only senior CIA officials and Assistant Secretary Rubottom knew of the assassination plot and U.S. complicity in it. President Kennedy and the members of his cabinet were kept in the dark until early May 1961—that is, once the issue had become academic since the CIA had already stopped its support for the assassination of Trujillo in the wake of the Bay of Pigs disaster. Until then Kennedy had believed (as had Eisenhower before him) that his government sought the overthrow of Trujillo and was ready to provide weapons and other materials to dissident groups in the Dominican Republic with whom contacts had already been established, but that it in no way contemplated assassination. Once he learned the truth, Kennedy not only approved the CIA decision to discontinue the assassination effort, but he went so far as to send a lofty cable to consul Dearborn two or three weeks later, stating that the United States "as a matter of policy cannot condone assassination."[16] But he reacted, otherwise, with perplexing forbearance. According to the Church report, there is no record that any U.S. official involved in the assassination plot was ever reprimanded or censured.[17] Should one conclude that John Kennedy was an extremely weak president who stood in awe of the CIA even after the Bay of Pigs? Or rather did Kennedy, like Eisenhower before him, know and approve of the plot from the outset, a reality that the Church committee has been unable to prove only because of a wall of lies? Although there is no definite proof, the conclusion of Church committee member Senator Howard Baker, Jr., seems particularly sound:

> It is my separate view that on balance the likelihood that Presidents knew of the assassination plots is greater than the likelihood that they did not. The impression stems from the record, of course, but as well from observing and hearing the witnesses testify and by applying the usual courtroom tests for determining the worth and value of the witnesses' testimony: the demeanor of the witnesses while testifying; the completeness or the incompleteness of their statements; whether the testimony has the ring of truth; prior consistent or inconsistent statements; inconsistencies in the course of their testimony before the Committee; the probability or improbability of their testimony; their means of knowledge; their interest in the subject. All of these things are best judged by observing the testimony of the witnesses.[18]

Appendix II

The Dominican Far Left from its Beginnings until January-February 1962

1. THE POPULAR SOCIALIST PARTY
(PARTIDO SOCIALISTA POPULAR OR PSP).[1]

In the six-month period from November 1939 to May 1940, nearly five thousand Spanish refugees arrived in the Dominican Republic, driven from their homeland by Franco's victory. Among them were some Communists. Jesús de Galíndez, a Spanish refugee, later wrote: "The Communists were few in the midst of the mass of refugees, but from the very first they reacted with their characteristic discipline and dynamism. Already in the ships, they established their first cells."[2]

The Communist "virus," however, had infected the Dominican Republic even before the arrival of the Spaniards. Trips abroad had brought many Dominican youths into contact with the Marxist doctrine. Having been converted, they returned to the Dominican Republic and tried to spread the hitherto unknown ideology.[3] Such was the case of Fredy Valdez, a pioneer of Marxism-Leninism in the Dominican Republic. A youth in the early 1930s, Valdez took part in a conspiracy against Trujillo and was forced to escape to Cuba, where he became a Communist. In 1938 he was able to return to the Dominican Republic, thanks to an amnesty granted by the regime. He came back with one aim, the result of long discussions with his Cuban Communist friends: to dedicate his energies and his life to the creation of a Communist party in his own country. Once in the Dominican Republic, he moved to Barahona, where some members of his family lived. In Barahona, the major town of the southwest and one of the most important working-class centers of the country, he organized a series of legal activities designed to "link him with the people."[4] Foremost among these activities was the establishment of the Casa del Obrero, a school for illiterate workers. He thus succeeded in winning over "the most enlightened workers of the zone and in creating the first Marxist cells."[5]

Other cells and study groups, composed primarily of middle-class elements, were set up in various parts of the country by men such as Heriberto Núñez in El Seibo and Julio Raúl Durán in Santiago. At this initial stage in the development of Dominican Communism the "Spanish refugees, bearers of Marxism"[6] made their contribution. Their experience and their talent for organization gave a powerful boost to groups that were still in their infancy, accelerating what was surely an inevitable process.

In the years from 1940 to 1943 intense clandestine activity took place. Spanish and Dominican Communists joined hands in a common effort of organization and proselytism. Some paid with their lives, but others were ready to take their places. Leaders of inestimable value began to stand out from the working class. The names of Mauricio Báez, Luis Guillén, Justino José del Orbe, and Jaime Nils will always tower over the Dominican labor movement. At the same time, some middle- and upper-class youths who had been studying at universities abroad returned to the country and joined the movement, taking their places at the forefront of the struggle. Among them was Pericles Franco Ornes, who had been converted to Communism while in Chile. Today Franco Ornes has moved away from the ideals of his youth, but for approximately ten years—until the mid-fifties—he was one of the best and most influential leaders of Dominican Communism.

By 1943, separate Communist groups existed in the country, mainly in Barahona, San Pedro de Macorís, La Romana, El Seibo, Santo Domingo, Santiago, and La Vega. The next step was logical: unification of these groups into a single movement. Two preliminary meetings were held in September and December 1943. Then, on 27 February 1944, the constituent congress of the first Communist party in the history of the country was held in Santo Domingo. The new party at first took the name Partido Democrático Revolucionario Dominicano, but soon thereafter it became the Partido Socialista Popular (PSP), after Cuba's Communist party. The Cuban PSP provided the link between the Dominican and the international Communist movements and gave encouragement and advice.

The Dominican PSP was a tiny, clandestine party with fewer than two hundred members, but it was resolute and geared for action. It had sprung up amid a society crushed by an implacable dictatorship. Persecution was relentless. Fredy Valdez was arrested in 1944, and soon other leaders—Francisco A. ("Chito") Henríquez Vásquez, Félix Servio and Juan Ducoudray Mansfield, Pericles Franco Ornes, Manuel Lorenzo Carrasco, and Ramón Grullón Martínez—were forced to seek refuge in foreign embassies, which they left only to go into exile in 1945. In spite of the terror and the arrests, the party survived. Its goal—to fuse all the forces of the "democratic opposition"—was ambitious. A first step was taken in the last months of 1944, with the establishment of the Dominican Revolutionary Youth, the youth movement of the party, "intended to group together all the young people yearning to fight against tyranny and for the establishment of a democratic regime."[7] Then, in early 1945, a National Liberation Front was formed and soon included a few dozen non-Communist professionals. In the distance was the supreme goal: a general strike of an insurrectionary nature that would topple the regime, a vision born in the wake of the Allied triumph over Hitler and the illusions that that victory roused. A new wind seemed to be stirring in the world. In the Caribbean arc, dictatorships were crumbling. In Cuba in 1944, Batista accepted defeat at the polls. Also in that year, Jorge Ubico was toppled in Guatemala, and Isaías Medina Angarita met the same fate in Venezuela in October 1945. The men who replaced the vanquished dictators, Ramón Grau San Martín, Juan José Arévalo, and Rómulo Betancourt, represented a violent break with the past and a hope for the future.

In the Dominican Republic, Trujillo, finely attuned to the needs of the moment, began a "parody of liberal indulgence,"[8] but it looked as though it might not be enough. Within the university, long the epitome of abject conformity, agitation began.[9] In the streets of the capital, a new, disturbing phenomenon was seen: young people were distributing and posting subversive propaganda in public places throughout the city. Even the workers movement, completely passive since 1930, seemed to be aroused to new demands. And in Washington the State Department showed an unusual coldness toward the regime.[10]

Then, in January 1946, a strike broke out in the sugar fields of La Romana and San Pedro de Macorís; it was the only successful strike during the entire Trujillo Era. It was well organized, and Trujillo did not dare to crush it by force. The Communists played a decisive role. Mauricio Báez, the "brains" of the strike, was a Communist leader and, according to the regime, "the most dangerous, active and intelligent of them all."[11] Four years later he paid for his courage with his life; Trujillo's thugs assassinated him in Havana, where he had taken refuge.

Trujillo was preparing to strike, but to destroy his enemies, he had to identify them. And of his enemies, the most active and brave were Communists. In mid-1945, he sent Ramón Marrero Aristy to Havana, who was there joined by Virgilio Díaz Grullón. Both were government officials with relatively untarnished reputations. Their task was to contact Dominican Communist leaders in Havana and persuade them that Trujillo wanted to "democratize" the country; thus they could return to the Dominican Republic and organize a public, legal communist party.[12]

The talks began in Havana, probably in late 1945, at first through the intermediary of the Cuban communists, particularly Blas Roca and Fabio Grobart. In the spring of 1946, a final agreement was reached between Trujillo's two emissaries and the Dominican communist leaders, Ramón Grullón, Chito Henríquez, and Félix Servio Ducoudray, who represented the Central Committee of their party. The PSP exiles would return to the Dominican Republic. In exchange, they asked that a workers' congress be held in the country. The congress would be organized by a committee of three Communists and three Trujilloists. The Communist-dominated Confederación de Trabajadores de Cuba (CTC) and the leftist Confederación de Trabajadores de América Latina (CTAL) would be invited to participate.

Thus the Communists accepted the dictator's challenge, pretending to trust the guarantees he offered them. But why? According to Galíndez, "Trujillo's game was obvious, and the Communists must have realized that in the long run it could not go on forever. What did they hope to gain? Perhaps [they believed that] the Dominican people, under the dictatorship for sixteen years, would see the Communists as the only ones with enough courage to go into the streets and defend their program."[13] "We had realized," explains PSP leader Justino José del Orbe, "that Trujillo should be fought in the Dominican Republic, and not from exile."[14] It was a "unique opportunity," adds Félix Servio Ducoudray, "and the party had to try it, even if it meant enduring repression later."[15]

And so, for the PSP, the "semi-legal days of 1946-47"[16] began. On 14 September 1946, in Ciudad Trujillo, the PSP held its first public meeting—the first allowed any opposition party since the beginning of the Era. A week later, a second public meeting was held at San Pedro de Macorís, and a third on 11 October at Santiago. Each time, the PSP had asked and been granted permission from the authorities. A fourth meeting was to be held in the Parque Colón in the center of the capital on 26 October, the day the first issue of *El Popular*, the party organ, was scheduled to appear.

On the morning of 26 October, *El Popular* was on the newsstands of Ciudad Trujillo; a few hours later, Communist orators began to address a few hundred people in Parque Colón. Suddenly, "General Joaquín Cocco, Jr., at the head of his Veteran Corps, interrrupted the meeting, . . . breaking it up with clubs, after which his mob went on with its rampage wrecking and pillaging the party's headquarters at the corner between Parque Enriquillo and the Avenida Duarte."[17] Since truth—especially Trujilloist truth—is many-faced, General Cocco's men were merely "peaceful citizens" out for a stroll in Parque Colón "without worries of any kind." The Communists, who were "in a state of extreme tension and excitement" and "many of them . . . quite drunk," had "unjustifiably" attacked the strollers with "clubs and knives." Then, "in the confusion, many of the red demonstrators fought amongst each other," as did "a certain Mara, a prostitute that the communists had recruited that night" and who wounded "a worker called Robinson . . . without realising that he was one of her companions." In the end, the Communists, "frenzied by the sight of blood, . . . tore down the platform, . . . piled up the wreckage and set fire to the timber."[18]

The agony of the PSP had begun. Although the party was still legal, it was increasingly subject to the violence of "popular indignation." Proclaiming itself Marxist-Leninist, but careful at the same time to stress its respect for legality, the PSP strove desperately to win time[19]—time to spread its message and sow the seeds of the future.

But time was running out. In Washington, the "Braden policy" gave way to the demands of the Cold War. Henceforth, anti-Communism and not "love of democracy" would be the touchstone in judging the leaders of Latin America.

The Trujillo regime was recovering. In January 1946, the strikes at La Romana and San Pedro de Macorís had given the dictator his most difficult moment: "Trujillo himself had felt the chill of the general strike."[20] But that was the last of the strikes. If, in September of that year, the National Workers' Congress seemed to stir a new breath of hope,[21] it was only a brief illusion. With the congress over and the foreign delegates gone, the wave of repression struck the cities. And it paid off. In the midst of a populace quickly made "wise," the PSP activists became more and more isolated, febble shadows lost in the vast desert of the Trujilloist terror.

Gone were the considerations of internal order and international prestige that had prompted the "parody of liberal indulgence" and the legalization of the Communist party. The farce had lost its raison d'être. In addition, it seemed clear that it would be impossible to identify any other clandestine Communists in the Dominican Republic.[22] Trujillo's "triumphant" re-election on 16 May 1947 heralded the end of the party. "A unanimous outcry arose from the Dominican people demanding the dissolution of the PSP. . . and the prohibition of all communist activity." Trujillo "listened to the outcry of his people [and] . . . on June 8th . . . he sent a patriotic message to the National Congress together with a Bill which prohibited the existence in our country of communist and other groups of similar tendencies as legal parties."[23] This marked the end of the semi-legality of the PSP. Trujillo unleashed a reign of terror and virtually destroyed the party. All its members who were unable to escape to foreign embassies were arrested.[24]

In February 1949, by some strange quirk of tyranny, the PSPistas were freed, but they were subjected to strict police surveillance. All political activity was closed to them. They were seen as "lepers" by the "good citizens" and shunned by those who, while sympathetic to their cause or impressed by their courage, were reluctant to compromise themselves by a dangerous intimacy. Soon the repression began anew. In August 1949, Fredy Valdez was arrested, followed by Pericles Franco Ornes. Tensions mounted, yielding to anguish when "we [PSPistas] received news that they were planning to go ahead with a big round-up. But we had no place to hide."[25]

A "liquidationist tendency" appeared in the party. (The term was coined scornfully some seventeen years later under far less dramatic conditions by youths blinded by their hate of "revisionism.")[26] The "liquidationists" expressed the predominant view of the party that the conditions to develop the revolutionary struggle in the country did not exist; they proposed a massive exodus of the party members abroad.

The PSP's dream had been shattered. Fredy Valdez, "pioneer of Marxism-Leninism"; the first cells, the study groups, the arrival of the Spanish refugees, "bearers of Marxism"; the establishment of the first Dominican Communist party, the Revolutionary Dominican Youth, the National Liberation Front; the strike of January 1946 and the "semi-legal days of 1946-47"; and, further ahead, the dream that justified the risk, the pains: the general strike of an insurrectionary nature to be organized and headed by the Partido Socialista Popular, the great mass party destined to liberate the country. Where did all the dreams go? Time had betrayed the hopes of the PSPistas. Some died, victims of tyranny, like Fredy Valdez, murdered by the police on 27 January 1950, in the San Francisco de Macorís prison. Others, even more numerous, abjured the party, terrorized by the repression. In the spring of 1950, several dozen men left the Venezuelan and Mexican embassies, where they had sought refuge a few weeks earlier to go into exile; they represented the entire Central Committee of the party and the majority of its members.

The PSP was now a small group of refugees struggling to survive in the sterile life of exile while in the Dominican Republic the fruits of their labors shriveled: the few cells that the PSP had left behind when most of its members went into exile were swiftly destroyed.[27] In exile, the Dominican Communists faced not only the hostility of the dictators of the hemisphere but also that of the "democratic" regimes. In Cuba, Carlos Prío Socarrás placed four of them in a detention center—a prelude to deportation. Only in Arbenz's Guatemala did the PSP refugees find a haven and the chance to engage in some political activity, publishing *Orientación* and *Vanguardia*, the organs of the party in exile. But the respite was brief. Arbenz's overthrow in 1954 forced a new migration. Some fled to Costa Rica; Félix Servio Ducoudray went to Argentina; still others came ashore in the United States, especially New York.

But the "heart" of the party established itself in Mexico, around Pericles Franco Ornes, Julio Raúl Durán, and Juan Ducoudray, and the publication of *Orientación* began again.[28] Cut off from the masses and from its homeland, the PSP stagnated, its links with the Dominican Republic going from "highly precarious" to "nonexistent."[29] At least the party was spared the internal dissension that so often plagues the inactivity of exile. Gradually and smoothly, Pericles Franco Ornes yielded power to Juan Ducoudray. In 1956, some members were expelled from the party (and immediately founded the Movimiento Popular Dominicano), but that was an isolated case, "the only serious case of insubordination during this whole period."[30]

The years dragged by. Suddenly, in January 1959, Castro's triumph seemed at last to open up new horizons. In the spring, an anti-Trujilloist expedition was organized in Cuba under the unifying banner of the Movement of Dominican Liberation (MLD).[31] The Central Committee of the PSP agreed to participate in the movement; it was the only one of the parties in exile to join the MLD. Of the 185 men who reached the Dominican Republic on 14 and 20 June 1959, nineteen were members of the PSP. Half of the Central Committee—six out of thirteen members—were among those nineteen. The price of the adventure was paid in blood. All the PSPistas were killed. Along with the martyrs of the period 1944-50 and the victims of Trujillo that followed, these men belong to the "Honor Cadre of the PSP."[32]

Rich in glory, but deeply wounded, the PSP returned to its former stagnation. It had no contacts with the underground movement that developed in the Dominican Republic during the second half of 1959. Moreover, it remained virtually absent from the Dominican scene during the first eight or nine months that followed the death of Trujillo, since the Dominican government, in cooperation with Washington, had barred all exiles known or suspected of having Communist sympathies from entering the country. Those who tried to come back, like Tulio Hostilio Arvelo Delgado of the PSP, were deported. Only three PSPistas, whose affiliation with the party was unknown, did manage to return during that period. One of them, a member of the Central Committee, "stayed for a week, then left the country never to come back." The other two remained and infiltrated the AP1J4.[33]

2. THE FOURTEENTH OF JUNE
MOVEMENT (CATORCE DE JUNIO OR 1J4)[1]

A. The Revolutionary Movement 14th of June
(Movimiento Revolucionario 14 de Junio or MR1J4)

Having adroitly rounded a cape, the Trujilloist ship of state seemed headed for triumph when the decade of the 1950s began. The democratic winds that had stirred the Caribbean and Central American area in the previous years had given way to the victory chant of the dictators. The Dominican exiles had met defeat upon defeat in their efforts to overthrow the regime from abroad. Inside the country, the opposition had been crushed and the PSP practically destroyed. Economic growth and the warm friendship of the United States increased Trujillo's power and prestige. The Dominican people could do nothing but submit.

Years passed. In December 1956, a group of rebels in neighboring Cuba succeeded in getting a foothold in the mountains of Oriente province. To everyone's amazement, Batista's men were unable to dislodge them. Within months, the adventure had become an epic. Soon, by way of Radio Rebelde, the voice of Castroism could be heard in the northwestern regions of the Dominican Republic. A new language penetrated the Dominican Republic, that vast Trujilloist concentration camp. Stirring ill-defined hopes, this new language was a powerful stimulus in "awakening certain sectors of the Dominican youth."[2]

In 1957, in the town of Monte Cristi, Manolo Tavárez and his wife Minerva "began to envision the possibility of creating a resistance movement."[3] They were not alone. Small groups organized throughout the Dominican Republic. This was an initial phase, a first timid and uncertain step. Trujillo's secret police had proved efficient, and the practice of denunciation—even among members of the same family—was too widespread for potential opposition suddenly to break the chains of fear. There were clandestine cells in a number of cities, but at this stage they were only isolated groups, vegetating in their own private worlds, unaware, most of the time, of each other's existence.

Suddenly, on 31 December 1958, Batista's regime collapsed, and the dictator fled to the safety of Ciudad Trujillo. Castro's rebels came down from the mountains to enter Havana in triumph. Cuba was free, and in the Dominican Republic potential rebels took heart. The Cubans had proved that a Batista could be overthrown. Dream had become reality. Could the Dominicans not re-enact the Cuban epic and enter a liberated Santo Domingo after having crushed Trujillo?

Then, on 14 June 1959, anti-Trujillo exiles landed at Constanza; six days later others disembarked at Maimón and Estero Hondo, to liberate their country. Within a few agonizing days, all but a handful had been massacred. But their very defeat was a victory. Their courage, their desperate boldness, and their sacrifice set an example. According to Jimmy Durán Hernando, one of the future leaders of the 1J4, the actions at Constanza, Maimón, and Estero Hondo created a "guilt complex, as if we were responsible for the murder of those people."[4] They "broke the dike of fear and doubt that existed among us and, as a result, opened up the possibility for . . . the swift development"[5] of the underground movement. "We had finally realized that it was not from without, but from within that Trujillo had to be overthrown."[6]

A new phase of increased activity led to the unification of the underground movement. In the course of this process, the Monte Cristi group, led by Manolo Tavárez and his wife Minerva, stood out for its dynamism.[7] Manolo assumed the role of coordinator, and by mid-October close contacts had been established among the major clandestine groups existing in the northern and central regions of the country (Monte Cristi, Santiago, Moca, Salcedo, San Francisco de Macorís).[8] Toward the end of October, Manolo sent emissaries to the capital and to the east and south of the Republic to contact centers thought to be in existence or to create ones where they were lacking. After a few weeks of intense activity, thirteen underground leaders, representing groups from the various regions of the country, met near the town of Mao on 10-11 January 1960. There they united the several resistance organizations in a single movement, chose leaders, and adopted a program.[9]

Thus was born the Revolutionary Movement 14th of June (Movimiento Revolucionario 14 de Junio or MR1J4). The name referred to the date of the landing at Constanza. Manolo Tavárez was named president; Leandro Guzmán Rodríguez, his brother-in-law and loyal supporter, treasurer; and "Pipe" Faxas Canto, also very close to Tavárez, secretary-general. The rest of the group formed the Central Committee.

The *manolistas* dominated the meeting at Mao. Their desire for reforms was sincere, if somewhat confused. The great doctrines of world politics—Communism, capitalism, socialism, in their many guises—were empty words for men who had seen the Era of Trujillo. But they wanted changes in the Dominican Republic. They knew that it would not be enough to overthrow Trujillo; the very roots of the Dominican tragedy—poverty, injustice, illiteracy—had to be attacked. How, they did not know. But Radio Rebelde filled them with dreams and desires. Castro's revolution held them under a spell. For them, it meant struggle against dictatorship, defense of national dignity, and striving for social change.

The invaders of June 1959 had been crushed, but the tracts they had brought with them remained. Those tracts contained their program, the *Programa minimo del Movimiento de Liberación Dominicana*. It demanded "a broad-scaled Agrarian Reform to give the peasants possession of the land, the right to organize for the working class and the peasants, and the right to strike as an instrument in the proletarian struggle." It would initiate "an effective campaign against illiteracy, a sweeping reform of the educational system, and a comprehensive system of social security affording protection to the young, the old and the unemployed."[10] Manolo, Minerva, and their friends read this message.[11] They vowed to honor the sacrifice of the dead "by adopting the program of the heroes of Constanza."[12] At Mao, they forced its adoption on the "traditionalists," for whom the movement could have no other aim beyond the elimination of Trujillo—that is, a return to 1930.

The "traditionalists" were in the majority,[13] but Manolo's charisma, his prestige, and his friendship with most of the delegates led to the adoption of his program. And although some of the "traditionalists" gave in only "grudgingly,"[14] one consideration made the concessions easier: the need to eliminate Trujillo. The rest was nothing but words, fine speeches of idealists that would fade in time, at the moment of truth.

This, then, was the origin of the 1J4. It was a hybrid movement that carried from the start the seeds of its own undoing. The social background of its members was homogeneous; they were, for the most part, well-to-do youth. More precisely, the rank and file belonged to the middle class and the leadership primarily to the upper middle class.[15] But in the movement were deep divisions between the champions of social change and the champions of immobility. For the time being, the hatred of the tyrant masked the rifts between the *progresistas* and the *tradicionalistas*. But what would happen when Trujillo was gone? What would become of the bonds of friendship, of kinship, that for the moment softened relations between the *catorcista* leaders? How far would the *progresistas* go in their wish for reforms? Would they remain united, or would they split into factions, quarreling over the pace of social change?

At Mao, no such thoughts burdened the delegates. The Trujillo question was foremost, so there was unity and even optimism. The regime was increasingly plagued by problems within and without: a deteriorating economy, a growing chill from the United States, militant hostility from the new governments in Caracas and Havana. The *catorcistas* had been receiving promises of help from abroad. Two months before Mao, a member of the MLD, Irlander Selig del Monte, had come from Puerto Rico "to promote contacts with the home front."[16] In mid-October 1959, he met with Pipe Faxas, a leader of the underground in the capital. As Faxas later recounted: "He [Selig] told me that the movement in exile had become unified; therefore we would be receiving all its help. He assured me that he had a chance to get money, arms, etc. from the Venezuelan consul in Puerto Rico [Luis Alcalá] who had spoken to him of aid; Venezuela was ready to offer all it could."[17]

Also in the fall of 1959, a member of the "home front," Jorge Lama Mitre, had gone to New York to speak with Alfonso Canto, one of the leaders of the MLD. Lama Mitre returned home ecstatic: Canto had promised arms and money and announced that the MLD was preparing to organize a new invasion. After relaying the good news, Lama Mitre hurried back to New York on 14 December

1959, "hoping to make the final arrangements."[18] At the same time, in the Dominican Republic, the conspirators were busy selecting places on the coast where arms could be brought into the country.[19]

The meeting at Mao (10-11 January 1960) thus proceeded with "the highest degree of optimism."[20] Lama Mitre was still in New York, but the delegates were confident of his success. In their minds, they already caressed the arms they had not yet received; they already saw the columns of the MLD landing in the Dominican Republic. But it was not to be a replay of June 1959. The invaders would not find a terrorized country, slaves with uncomprehending stares, distrustful, even hostile. This time the 1J4 would be there, determined, powerful, its cells spread throughout the country, ready to strike. At H-hour, a wave of sabotage would strike the regime, followed by a general uprising of the *catorcistas*. The only task remaining for the MLD would be to put an end to the agony of the regime. Trujillo would be overthrown from within, not from without.[21]

Who distorted the facts: Canto, Lama Mitre, or the men of the "home front"? Who was to blame for these cruel illusions? All were, in part, each driven by the same dream. But the reality was different. In December 1959 and January 1960, the MLD, in New York as in Puerto Rico, was only a glorious banner held aloft by a few brave but impotent men. The MLD had been created during the adventurous euphoria surrounding the triumph of the 26 of July Movement with the aim of eliminating Trujillo; the debacles at Constanza, Maimón, and Estero Hondo had destroyed the movement. Perhaps, in time . . . but for the *catorcistas*, time was running out.

The rapid growth of the underground movement over recent months was a source of danger.[22] What, in fact, did the young bourgeois of the 1J4 know about underground work? They were brave, but inexperienced dilettantes. They had no one to advise them, no model for clandestine organization if not the romantic, archaic example of the Trinitaria, the secret society founded by Duarte in 1838. Their security precautions were a mockery, utterly insufficient for what was to come.

In fact, the movement was doomed. On 18 December 1959, an informer, Andrés Norman Montero, joined the movement. Before the end of December, he visited Johnny Abbes, the chief of military intelligence, with a list of victims. But the Trujilloist officials were in no hurry. They preferred to learn more about the movement, in order better to destroy it. Montero did his job—indeed it was all too easy. On 10 January 1960, while the underground leaders were meeting at Mao, the crackdown began. The Trujilloists arrested Federico José Cabrera and took him to *La 40*—not a prison but a torture center. The next day he was joined by Marcos Pérez Collado, who had "won" Montero for the movement. On 13 January, Manolo Tavárez was arrested at Monte Cristi, while other MR1J4 members were seized at various points throughout the country. Those *catorcistas* still free recognized that they had been betrayed. But what could they do? They had no arms, no hiding places, and the embassies were all being watched. They could do nothing but wait—and the wait was brief. The arrests came "in great, shuddering waves, . . . not by the hundreds, but by the thousands."[23] Not only the MR1J4istas themselves but also their families and often their friends were arrested. The principle governing the repression was to arrest them all and let God sort them out. Within a few weeks, perhaps even before the end of January, the movement was completely broken.

B. The Political Group 14th of June
(Agrupación Política 14 de Junio or AP1J4)

On 8 July 1961, thirty-nine days after the death of Trujillo, seven former members of the MR1J4 formed a Provisional Executive Committee "to study the conditions under which the Movement would take part in the political struggle."[24] Ramfis and Balaguer were beginning the first steps of their "democratization," while the vast majority of the members of what was once the MR1J4 continued to rot in Trujillo's prisons. Others were dead, by execution and torture. A privileged few had been allowed, after some months in jail, to go into exile. Now, under pressure from the OAS, the regime began releasing its prisoners. In July, the former *catorcista* leaders were freed, including, on the twenty-sixth, Manolo Tavárez, Leandro Guzmán, and Pipe Faxas.

In a general assembly on 30 July, the former prisoners[25] founded the Agrupación Política 14 de Junio (AP1J4), the direct heir to the MR1J4, the underground movement crushed by Trujillo. Manolo Tavárez was named president, Leandro Guzmán, secretary-general. The mystique of martyrdom surrounded the new party; its past already belonged to legend. Conquered by a history of glory, the urban youth brought the party massive and enthusiastic support. The young found in Manolo Tavárez a leader with charisma: his past, his eloquence, his youth, and then the tragic fate of his beautiful, unforgettable wife, Minerva Mirabal, a victim of the struggle for freedom.[26]

Thus in the summer of 1961, the future seemed bright for the 1J4. The struggle, of course, was far from over. Trujillo's successors still clung to power. But that power was waning; the people were stirring. The day of liberation could be glimpsed in the distance, the day when at last a new society would be built. But what kind of society? The AP1J4 itself did not know the answer. It retained the hybrid character of its forefather, the MR1J4. Of the eleven members on its Central Executive Committee (CEC), five were also—and above all—leaders of the reactionary UCN.[27] Manolo Tavárez and his *progresista* friends had failed to grasp the true nature of the UCN (see Chapter 2); they saw in it a faithful ally and accepted the idea that one person could belong to both the 1J4 (a political party) and the UCN (allegedly a "civic-patriotic" organization!).

The 1J4 contained not only *cívicos*, but Communists. In 1960, two young anti-Trujilloists, Fidelio Despradel Roque and José Israel Cuello Hernández, met members of the PSP while in exile. A new world appeared to them. They were seduced and became Communists.[28] After Trujillo's death, the two returned to the Dominican Republic in August 1961. Keeping their PSP membership a secret, they joined the 1J4. Their talents, their honorable past, and their friendship with many *catorcista* leaders gained them influence within an organization rich in heroes but tragically poor in men with political experience.

Following a strategy that the PSP would use later (see Chapter 4), Despradel and Cuello attempted to "capture cadres" within the 1J4—a slow process, made all the more painful by the need for secrecy. Finally, in autumn, the first PSP cell in the 1J4 was established.[29] It consisted of five or six members; one of them, José Israel Cuello, soon became the codirector of the *El 1J4*, the party organ. Two others, Fidelio Despradel and Máximo Bernard, were brilliant cadres, valued by their *catorcista* comrades. The 1J4 had one other Communist cell, but it was independent of the PSP. Its three members were R. Alfredo Manzano Bonilla, a CEC member and chief of the party's radio propaganda; Ramón A. ("Chino") Ferreras, editor in chief of *El 1J4*; and Alberto Malagón, who, with Cuello, became codirector of the paper.

Thus, in the autumn of 1961, Communist infiltration of the 1J4 appeared in two forms: the PSP cell and the Manzano group. Yet their influence should not be exaggerated. The Communists were only a few, and the positions they occupied within the 1J4, while important, were not crucial. Except for Alfredo Manzano, none of the "infiltrators" belonged to the hard-core leadership of the party, and Manzano himself grew increasingly isolated within the CEC.

In the middle, between the *cívico catorcistas* and the Communist *catorcistas*, stood the mass of youthful *manolistas*. But those youths, the militants as well as the leaders, were politically naive. Thirty years of dictatorship had taken their toll: "Many [of us] were fresh out of jail, . . . never having read a book." But they were pressured into action; there was no time for reflection. The Trujillo clan remained in power. The time had come to plunge into the struggle against the Trujillos and against their henchman, Balaguer. For the youth *catorcistas*, it was "a period of deep confusion. We were up in the air. All kinds of people offered to lead us."[30] They were caught up in an ideological conflict in which contradictory influences collided.

The *manolistas* of the summer and autumn of 1961 were "Castroites." But theirs was a diffuse brand of Castroism, a sentimental Castroism that, for the time being, rejected "the risks of Communism that threaten[ed] the established democratic order in America," while "reaffirming its Social Christian posture."[31] Indeed, in September 1961, a group of *manolistas* went off to study and learn at the Institute of Political Education in San José, Costa Rica, under Don Pepe Figueres, Washington's friend and Castro's enemy.[32]

Within this ideological conflict, there was one constant element: "an impetuous, even fierce nationalism.[33] But the *manolistas* could not blame the distant Soviet Union for the trampled dignity of the tiny nations of the Caribbean. It was not the Soviets who occupied the Dominican Republic between 1916 and 1924 or who, later on, offered tokens of friendship to Rafael Leonidas Trujillo.

Between July and mid-November 1961, the *manolistas* were careful to avoid mentioning too loud the outrages of U.S. imperialism. But they could never forget. "Better civil war than [American] intervention."[34]

As long as the Trujillos clung to power, the 1J4's weaknesses remained hidden. But then, on 17 November, Ramfis left the Dominican Republic. Two days later, the "Wicked Uncles" had been defeated. Once again, but for the last time, the 1J4 and the UCN appeared united when, on 27 November, the general strike against Balaguer broke out.

Then, unexpectedly, the romance was over. On 2 December, the UCN entered into negotiations with the government. A week later, it pulled out of the general strike. This "treason" on the part of a "faithful ally" provoked the 1J4 to an intransigence that it was unable to sustain. The party's supporters were urged to carry on the "struggle in the streets," but their number dwindled.

The *manolista* leaders of the 1J4 "were fired by patriotic passion, were honest, and were good fighters, but they had not had time to study their people."[35] They failed to grasp—and never did grasp—an important truth: "the needs and the problems of . . . [the] great Dominican masses were different from those of the middle-class youth." Their feelings, therefore, were also different. "Middle-class youths have a highly developed political conscious-ness, revolutionary consciousness. Middle-class youths do not always fight for economic reasons in the same way they fight for patriotic reasons, nationalistic reasons, and revolutionary reasons." But "the great masses," those "men and women with no place to sleep and nothing to eat, begging for a peso, wandering in our streets, . . . do not feel the same patriotism as the revolutionary youths of the middle class. They are affected far more by their material problems than by their spiritual needs."[36]

The Dominican people had fought for more than five months, giving example after example of their courage and their will. But the economic crisis went on. Unemployment grew worse by the day, hunger grew more and more harsh, and the children's tears became increasingly desperate. But in 1961 the political consciousness of the masses, the basis from which action might have been taken, had not reached more than a primitive and insecure stage. How could it have been otherwise after thirty years of Trujillo?

To a weary, hungry populace, Manolo Tavárez's party proved unable to offer any constructive suggestions. Against the hard fact of the Council of State, all they could set was a nebulous Government of National Unity (GUN). "The slogan had a nice ring,"[37] but it masked a void.[38] On the one hand, the 1J4 de-manded that the struggle go on; on the other hand, the party failed to justify its demand in a language comprehensible to the masses. The middle-class revolu-tionary youths proved to be prisoners of their own contradictions, of their lack of clarity. The masses deserted them.

At this point the 1J4 made its dramatic break with the PRD. All through-out the summer of 1961, the *catorcistas* viewed Juan Bosch and his friends with reserve; they were too "soft" in their opposition to Trujillo.[39] But it was only in December 1961 that the PRD dropped its anti-Trujilloist mask and committed open treason, first by refusing to support the general strike against Balaguer and then by accepting the Council of State. For Manolo and his friends, distrust turned to hatred and scorn. "Bosch was the scum of exile"[40] and the PRD was "Trujillo's party [P.D.] with an R in the middle."[41]

Only the mood of the times, the bitterness, frustration and inexperience of the *catorcistas* can explain their unreasonable stand, the absurdity of which today strikes the very people who took it. Then, however, the sentence was without appeal; the UCN and the PRD were confounded in a single verdict. The consequences of this attitude would be obvious a few months later, in December 1962, at the time of the elections (see Chapter 3).

The break with the UCN helped diminish the ambiguous nature of the origins of the 1J4. On 4 January 1962, José A. Fernández Caminero and the four other *cívico* members of the CEC quit the 1J4. But their tardy departure was that of a fifth column pulling out after a brilliant sabotage operation. Fernández Caminero's reward came swiftly. On 8 January, he was named a minister; seven weeks later, he became a member of the Council of State.

Too many disappointments and failures accelerated the radicalization of the 1J4. All traces of that "Social Christian posture" to which *El 1J4* had once alluded were swept away. *Catorcistas* would no longer study at the Institute of Political Education in San José, Costa Rica. Only Cuba remained as a guide and an example for Manolo and his friends.

In February 1962, the 1J4 cracked down on its left wing. The CEC expelled Alfredo Manzano and forced his friends, Alberto Malagón and Chino Ferreras, to resign. At the same time, the party destroyed the PSP cell. Given a choice between expulsion and a total break with the PSP, Fidelio Despradel and Máximo Bernard chose the latter, while José Israel Cuello decided to leave the 1J4. But these measures were aimed much more at the "fractionalism" of the guilty members than at their ideology. Marxist solutions had begun to sway men who had failed and who were looking for answers to the needs of the future and an explanation for the defeats of the past.

3. THE DOMINICAN PEOPLE'S MOVEMENT (MOVIMIENTO POPULAR DOMINICANO OR MPD)[1]

The Movimiento Popular Dominicano was founded in Havana on 27 February 1956 "by a group of militants from the Partido Socialista Popular, a break provoked by the revisionist tendencies of the ruling camarilla . . . [tendencies] which attained their peak with the meeting in Moscow of the Twentieth Congress of the Communist Party and its consequent 'policy of de-Stalinization.' These revisionist tendencies in turn brought the militants and the ruling camarilla into total opposition over the method of combatting the Trujilloist tyranny."[2]

This is the official version of the origin of the MPD, written in 1965 by the party's Political Committee. It evokes a smile. This break with Soviet "revisionism" had already taken place in February 1956, well before the results of the Twentieth Congress were known, let alone analyzed. Here are the MPD-istas turned champions of orthodoxy, precursors of the Chinese and the Albanians. They were very strange precursors, indeed, since the founders of the new party included such notable anti-Communists as Julio César Martínez and Tiberio Castellanos. Obviously, the official version must be revised.

In January 1956, half a dozen members were expelled from the PSP. These included the two men who were to dominate the history of the MPD: Máximo López Molina, whose distinguishing feature was his ambition to be *the* leader, but who in the PSP was not even a member of the Central Committee; and Andrés Ramos Peguero, the "hardest of the hard-liners," a man who was brave and honest, but who could think only of armed struggle—all the rest was for him "cheap politicking."[3] The PSP had many courageous men, but no place for irresponsibles.

For some time, in their Cuban exile, Máximo—the thinker—and Andrés—the man of action—had tried to create their own organization outside the PSP. When the latter's Central Committee ordered them to dissolve their small group, they refused and were expelled.[4] Now they were on their own, with only a few followers. But, like all self-respecting men in the cruel world of exile, they needed a party. They were in touch with other "orphans" in Cuba: the anti-Communists Julio César Martínez, Tiberio Castellanos, and their friends. The two tiny groups fused, giving birth to the MPD, one of the most absurd creations of the Dominican exile.

The contradiction is too flagrant to be ignored, and the official party history strove to justify it by altering the facts and, above all, by choosing to explain nothing: "Although our founding fathers upheld the Marxist-Leninist doctrine in all its purity, the precarious conditions of exile in a land ruled by Batista's tyranny, which forced the Marxist Dominican exiles to disband, perverted the goals of the founders, to the point of having to take in political exiles from the Trujillo regime who had neither a Marxist background nor a Marxist consciousness, some of whom went immediately from betrayal to paid anti-Communist militancy."[5]

The "founding fathers" of the MPD needed a banner to mask the vast ideological vacuum and to provide this highly unlikely amalgam with a raison d'être. They decided that that banner would be "the method of struggle against the Trujilloist tyranny." The MPDistas preached that the people had to overthrow Trujillo. Exile was fruitless; the exiles had to get back to the Dominican Republic at all costs to join the "masses," educate them politically, and prepare them for armed struggle. To maintain, as the PSP "cowards" did, that the absence of necessary objective conditions rendered such a program impossible meant choosing a shameful passivity, which is to say, in the last analysis, isolating themselves from the masses.

This was an attractive program, sincerely held by some. But reality played no role in it. What of Trujillo's absolute control over the country, the passivity of the population—in a word, the absence of the necessary objective conditions? The MPD was bold in its affirmations, but in its deeds it proved just as cautious as the "cowards" of the PSP. LIke the PSP, it chose to remain in exile, postponing the liberation of the Dominican people.

The boldest of the MPDistas attempted in their Cuban exile the struggle that seemed chimerical in their own country. They joined Fidel Castro and the 26 of July Movement in the insurrection against Batista. Andrés Ramos Peguero, in particular, attained the rank of captain in the Rebel Army in the Sierra Maestra, and others attained lesser ranks. One of the party's founders, Pablo Antonio Martínez, died in defense of Cuban freedom on 13 March 1958.[6]

After Castro's triumph, the MPD refused to take part in the expedition being mounted by the Movimiento de Liberación Dominicana (MLD) against Trujillo, claiming that it "was cut off from the Dominican masses and consequently was doomed to destruction."[7]

Indeed, such lucidity on the part of the MPD is startling. It goes against the usual behavior of the party, past and future. Future historians of the MPD, should there be any, will face the task of explaining so flagrant a contradiction. Here it is enough to take note of it.

In 1960, the party finally succeeded in getting back to the Dominican Republic, but in a way that brought into question the integrity of its leaders. Having just annihilated the MR1J4, but faced with a difficult international situation, Trujillo designed a new version of his 1946 "parody of liberal indulgence." One of the pawns in his new strategy would be the MPD. He invited the MPD leaders to return to the Dominican Republic and offered them guarantees. The MPD accepted, as the PSP had done in 1946.[8] This decision, still criticized today with violent partisanship, was an act of courage. Above all, it was in line with the fundamental doctrine of the party: "Struggle From Within or Trujillo Forever."[9] Trujillo could be toppled only from within.

On 4 June 1960, MPD president Máximo López Molina and secretary-general Andrés Ramos Peguero arrived from Cuba "with a bristling manifesto and little else." A week later, they opened the party's headquarters in "a small, rotting building"[10] in a working-class district of Ciudad Trujillo.

By the time López Molina and Ramos Peguero came to the Dominican Republic, the party had at last rid itself of some of the ambiguities of its origins. The official history of the party proudly states that with the triumph of the Cuban revolution (which had a decisive influence on the MPD), the resignations of Julio César Martínez and Tiberio Castellanos, and the MPD's plans for the struggle against Trujillo, "the liberal-bourgeois element of the party was reduced to a very secondary status."[11] López Molina and Ramos Peguero became the uncontested leaders of the twenty or thirty men who made up the MPD. They claimed to be well-versed Marxist-Leninists.[12] What these two "founding fathers" might have assimilated of Marxist-Leninist doctrine is a sorry tale. From its "Marxist beginnings" until today, the MPD has been distinguished by its "in-fantilism," its narrow sectarianism, and its all-too-frequent penchant for irres-ponsible solutions.

In any case, in June 1960, López Molina and Ramos Peguero preferred to be more flexible. Marx and Lenin were brushed aside. Though the two leaders took "leftist" positions, they shunned adopting specifically "Communist" stances. In fact, their statement of principles was that of the Movimiento de Liberación Dominicana, "based on the defense of sovereignty and the realization of agrarian reform." Their flexibility enabled López Molina and Ramos Peguero to receive the support of "numerous elements among the middle and lower middle classes that opposed Trujillo and co-operated economically because they failed to see the true classist orientation of the MPD."[13]

This first period of legality for the MPD proved to be briefer still than that of the PSP in 1946-47. On 29 August, just eight weeks after the party had been legalized, the police watched in Ciudad Trujillo while a mob beat up perhaps one hundred members and sympathizers of the MPD and wrecked the party head-quarters. "Agents of the SIM [Servicio de Inteligencia Militar] then appeared and herded the disillusioned oppositionists off to jail."[14] With the destruction of the headquarters, the movement entered its first underground phase. A violent wave of persecutions and murders of MPD members began. López Molina and Ramos Peguero ended up in jail. Many other leaders and militants were as-sassinated.

Looking back at the period of legality of June-August 1960, the party's official history points out that the MPD failed to develop a clandestine appar-atus, and, therefore, once the crackdown had begun, "the majority of the party members were cut off from one another, since the headquarters had been the sole link between the MPDistas."[15] One might ask how a clandestine apparatus might have helped the MPD, since the party's secretary of finances, Mario Jerez Cruz, a member of the small Central Committee set up in Ciudad Trujillo, was a government agent.[16]

And yet the efforts of López Molina and Ramos Peguero had not been com-pletely in vain. Received at first with extreme distrust ("many people came to believe that our movement was a 'trap' at the service of Trujillo"),[17] the two leaders saw their prestige grow "as their opposition developed and as the Govern-ment began to strike." By its presence, "the MPD filled a void." Above all, it began to forge links with a sector of Dominican society "that would never aban-don it";[18] the marginal population of the capital, the lumpenproletariat, which was impressed perhaps by their looks as much as by their words: they were "without a clean shirt, a pair of socks or a shoelace among them."[19]

A few months later, on 6 May 1961, Joaquín Balaguer, the puppet president of the Republic, once again legalized the MPD—another fluctuation in the government's "parody of liberal indulgence." Three weeks before Trujillo's death, López Molina and his friends returned to the Dominican political scene as the only legal opposition group. But again, the parenthesis would be brief. Within a few weeks—before the summer was over and well before the end of the Era—the MPD had been reduced to a wretched little group at bay. The UCN and the 1J4 had become the giants of the opposition, with the PRD following at a distance.

Any other outcome would have been surprising. The support of the young middle-class revolutionaries might have turned the MPD into the leading party of the Dominican far left. But the 1J4 had already swept them away. The martyrdom of the June 1959 invaders, the tragedy of the MR1J4, had left too deep a mark on youth who were eager to commit themselves to a noble cause and redeem their fathers' crimes with their own blood. With their eyes fixed on the prisons holding Manolo Tavárez and his friends, these young middle-class revolutionaries stood firm. Even before the AP1J4 was formed, they were *catorcistas*.

There were, of course, some rare exceptions: students who had joined the MPD at the time of the party's first legal period from June to August 1960. With their help, the MPD began its effort to win over the university. During the last week of June, MPD students led by Leopoldo Grullón and Miguel Genao strove to create a Federation of University Students so as to "organize and give impetus to the national student struggle"[20]—in the hope, of course, that it would be led by the MPD.

Yet, at a time when it was still the only organized force of the opposition, and when the university students lacked leaders, organization, and experience, the MPD failed to seize its chance. On 13 July the FED was created, but only two of the nineteen members of its first Provisional Committee belonged to the MPD. Moreover these two, Leopoldo Grullón and Miguel Genao, were elected more for their personal prestige than for their party affiliation.

Soon repression struck the MPD. Although all the opposition groups suffered from the violence of the regime, the MPD, the pariah among the opposition, was hit hardest. Political reasons explain its outcast status: its "ultraleftist" leaders, its violent anti-Yankeeism, its confused Marxist faith at a time when Castro-Communism loomed as a continuing nightmare in Washington! But there were social reasons as well. In spite of the handful of students in its ranks, the MPD was still the party of the unemployed and the down-and-out, the sectors of the population on which its message had some impact. Where in the slums would the MPD find those ladies of high society and impeccable manners to send before OAS committees to plead the cause of its jailed members? The "ladies" available to the party were for the most part the type that the "gentlemen" of the OAS would allow in only through the service entrance.

On 7 July, an "indignant mob" sacked MPD headquarters to avenge the fire at Radio Caribe (see Chapter 2), in which several thousand demonstrators took part and for which the MPD was, of course, held responsible. Party members were arrested with mounting frequency, throwing the MPD into disarray and bringing all activity to a virtual halt, while at the same time the "democratic" opposition was taking its first steps. Tracked by the police, López Molina went into hiding.

A desire to escape the repression and to save the party probably explains one of the most unsavory episodes in the history of the MPD—the party's "romance" with Ramfis Trujillo, at a time when he was the foremost enemy of the people. Four years later, during their first precongress, the MPD delegates did their best to present this squalid episode in a favorable light. "Ramfis [had] made clear his desire to avenge himself on the [U.S.] imperialism that had killed his father . . . [by] giving the leftist forces some arms. Because our leaders overestimated the contradictions between the remains of tyranny and imperialism, and because we overestimated our own strength, we accepted the offer of arms. The repression ordered by Ramfis himself and by Balaguer came down on us before the offer ever materialized."[21]

The MPDistas are, however, too indulgent of their past sins. The "leftist forces" vaguely mentioned in the official version consisted in fact of the MPD alone. Furthermore, López Molina, not Ramfis, initiated the conversations in mid-September. He hoped to win privileges for the MPD, a highly anti-American party, "by exploiting [Ramfis'] hate for the Yankees who had assassinated his father."[22]

Was López Molina's real goal to get arms? He received none, but he did manage to obtain what probably interested him most: "a lessening of the repression against the party."[23] Ramfis had already spent much time trying to convince the United States of the need for a "strong" government—his own—which alone was capable of challenging the red threat. He had reason to spare, at least for the time being, the MPDistas, who had unexpectedly become so "reasonable." He would thus increase the "Castro-Communist" threat in the eyes of an oversensitive Washington.

This, then, was the "romance." Previously the favorite target of the regime, the MPD at last felt a certain respite. It was free to reorganize; it had new headquarters, a small printing press, and a leader, López Molina, at last free from the need to hide since he enjoyed Ramfis' personal protection.[24]

The romance ended abruptly, however. Ramfis' tolerance of the MPD aroused Washington's ire and endangered the image he had been at pains to create—that of a militant anti-Communist. Thus on 22 October the police showed up in force at MPD headquarters. The district attorney announced that the party had been declared illegal and that the headquarters were closed.[25] Repression struck again, and the party was unable to withstand the blows. The MPD experienced an even more serious crisis than the one it had suffered earlier that summer. When the Trujillo empire finally fell (19 November), the party was a negligible force.

López Molina, who had been sought by the police since 22 October, was arrested on 14 November and deported eight days later. Ever since many Dominicans have contended that Ramfis had "hidden him in one of his country estates."[26] This is not impossible. But can one conclude that López Molina was the "pocket Communist" of the Trujillos? Can one cry betrayal? As far as I have been able to determine, the question here is instead one of a serious manifestation of ultraopportunism of the rightist variety mixed with a strong dose of political stupidity, a phenomenon far from unique in the history of the party.

Appendix III

Art Buchwald and the "Humanitarian Intervention"

"REVOLUTION AND A HUMANITARIAN REASON NAMED SIDNEY"

When the story of the Dominican Republic's revolution unfolds, you may hear about a great unsung hero whose name is Sidney.

Nobody knows Sideny's last name, but the whole course of the revolution would have been changed if it hadn't been for him.

Sidney was an American tourist visiting Santo Domingo when the fighting broke out. As you may remember, President Johnson sent in Marines to protect Americans who could possibly be hurt. Unfortunately, the evacuation went off so fast that in 24 hours there wasn't an American left in the capital except Sidney.

When Sideny showed up at the pier to be taken on board ship, he was stopped by a Marine colonel who said, "I'm sorry, you can't leave, sir."

"Why not?" Sidney wanted to know.

"Because we've been sent here to protect Americans and you're the only American left. If you leave, we'll have to pull out."

"Nuts to that," said Sidney. "I want to get out of here. They got a bunch of crazy people in this town."

"My orders are to keep you here, sir. We made a mistake in evacuating the Americans too fast, and now, we need you more than you need us."

"That's not my problem" Sidney said. "I want to go on that ship out there."

Two Marine sergeants raised their guns. "It's not possible, Sidney," the colonel replied. "If the OAS arrived and found no American here for us to protect, we would be in a very sticky position. But you'll be perfectly safe. President Johnson is sending in 10,000 more troops to protect you."

"To protect me?"

"Yes sir. We're going to build a nine-mile perimeter around you so nobody can get near you. I assure you nothing can go wrong."

Sidney took his bags and went back to the hotel.

The next morning he was visited by the general in charge of the paratroopers. "Are you okay, Sidney?"

"Yeah, I'm okay. But I want to go home."

"Just be patient and everything will be all right."

While the general was talking, a platoon set up a machine gun on the balcony. Two tanks were parked in front of the hotel and an antiaircraft gun was placed on the roof.

"What's all that for?" Sidney wanted to know.

"Just to see that no one hurts you. You're very precious to us."

"Yeah, well, if I'm so precious, why don't you get me the hell out of here?"

"We will, as soon as we feel it's reasonably safe. For the moment you're the only humanitarian reason for our being here."

"I don't know what's going on, but all I know is I'm being held as a hostage."

"Sidney, have you ever heard of the Monroe Doctrine?"

"Yeah, I guess so."

"Well, you're part of it. Your name will go down in history books with Teddy Roosevelt and Admiral Dewey. When school teachers ask their pupils who saved the Dominican Republic from going Communist, the children are going to have to answer, 'Sidney.' "

Just then the phone rang. The general picked it up.

"It's the President, Sidney. He wants to speak to you."

"Yes, sir, Mr. President. No, I'm just fine. I'll stay here as long as you want me to. That's nice of you to say. You're a good American too."

(Art Buchwald, CAPITOL PUNISHMENT
Washington Post, 6 May 1965)

Notes

CHAPTER 1

1. The size of the pre-Colombian population of the Americas is still the object of heated debate. For Hispaniola, the two foremost authorities on the subject, Frank Moya Pons and Roberto Cassá, give different estimates: six hundred thousand and two to three hundred thousand, respectively. These figures can be considered the upper and the lower limits of the population of the island at the time.

There is no debate, however, as to what happened after the arrival of the Spaniards: by 1514 no more than twenty-six thousand natives remained, even though some forty thousand Indians had been "imported" from the Bahamas between 1508 and 1513. By the 1530s, the native population was virtually extinct through deliberate massacres, starvation, physical and moral exhaustion, and the inevitable collapse of the birth rate. Epidemics played a role, too, but were not as decisive as many have claimed. See Roberto Cassá, *Los Tainos de la Española* (Santo Domingo: Editora de la Universidad Autónoma de Santo Domingo, 1974), ch. 6, and Frank Moya Pons, *La Española en el Siglo XVI, 1493-1520* (Santiago, D. R.: Universidad Católica Madre y Maestra, 1971), ch. 2. For a different view, see Angel Rosenblat, *La población indigena y el mestizaje en América* (Buenos Aires: Institución Cultura Española, 1954), p. 102, and Troy S. Floyd, *The Columbus Dynasty in the Caribbean, 1492-1526* (Albuquerque: University of New Mexico Press, 1973), pp. 13, 74-75, 161, 171, 191-92.

2. Médéric Louis Elie Moreau de Saint-Méry, *Description topographique, physique, civile, politique et historique de la partie française de l'île Saint-Domingue . . . ,* 2 vols. (Philadelphia, 1797), 1:5. Other sources give slightly different figures.

3. "The inhabitants were so poor that in 1669 when a ship came at last with 400 slaves to be sold in Santo Domingo, the colonists could buy only 140, although the ship remained in the harbor for more than five months trying to sell its cargo" (Frank Moya Pons, *Historia colonial de Santo Domingo* [Santiago, D.R.: Universidad Católica Madre y Maestra, 1974], p. 205. Moya Pons is the foremost authority on Dominican colonial history).

4. Ibid., p. 208.

5. Franklin J. Franco Pichardo, *Los Negros, Los Mulatos y La Nacion Dominicana* (Santo Domingo: Editora Nacional, 1970), p. 72. Other authors give different figures. Indeed, the contrast was dramatic not only in the number, but also in the treatment of the slave and free colored populations. This was due not to differences in nationality of the slaveholders, but to the diverse economic infrastructures of the two colonies. Plantation agriculture made much harsher demands on the slaves than a cattle society where, by the very nature of their work, slaves could be of real use only if given some freedom of movement and trust. Other variables (security, for example) helped determine the treatment of slaves and free coloreds. While it would take too much space to develop these points here, the result is relevant to us. If we refer to the three basic meanings of "treatment" introduced by Eugene Genovese—"day-to-day living conditions," "conditions of life," and "access to freedom and citizenship" (*In Red and Black: Marxian Explorations in Southern and Afro-American History* [New York: Vintage Books, 1968], ch. 7)—we may conclude that the treatment of slaves and free persons of color was relatively mild in Santo Domingo from all three points of view. This, in turn, would be a key reason for the relative lack of racism in the Dominican Republic after that country's independence (see also below, n. 21).

For a good introduction to the problem of comparative slavery in the Western Hemisphere, see Genovese, *In Red and Black*; Gwendolyn Midlo Hall, *Social Control in Slave Plantation Societies, A Comparison of Saint-Domingue and Cuba* (Baltimore: Johns Hopkins Press, 1971); Magnus Mörner, *Race Mixture in the History of Latin America* (Boston: Little, Brown, 1967), esp. ch. 8; and C. Vann Woodward, *American Counterpoint: Slavery and Racism in the North-South Dialogue* (Boston: Little, Brown, 1964), esp. ch. 3.

For an overview of slavery and race relations in colonial Santo Domingo, see Moya Pons, *Historia Colonial*. Additional sources may be found in the Bibliographical Essay.

6. C. L. R. James, *The Black Jacobins* (2d ed. rev.; New York: Vintage Books, 1963), p. 74. Written in 1938, James's book still remains by far the best work on the Haitian Revolution. More recent authors include José L. Franco (*Historia de la Revolución de Haiti* [Havana: Academia de Ciencias de Cuba, 1966]) and Thomas O. Ott (*The Haitian Revolution, 1789-1804* [Knoxville: The University of Tennessee Press, 1973]). But they add very little and leave out a great deal.

7. Emilio Cordero Michel, *La Revolución Haitiana y Santo Domingo* (Santo Domingo: Editora Nacional, 1970), pp. 40-41.

8. The mulattoes, an intermediate group, vacillated between the two major contenders, constantly hoping to be accepted by the whites, but the latter rejected and betrayed them.

9. Juan Bosch, *Composición social dominicana: Historia e interpretación* (2d ed. rev.; Santo Domingo: Editora Arte y Cine, 1970), p. 137.

10. The term "Dominicans" is used loosely here. There were the slaves, the *peones*, the little folk: a mass of wretched souls whose function was to serve their lords. The lords— the *hateros* and a few ranking officials, all whites—preferred to think of themselves as Spaniards (whenever they could think beyond their economic interests and social privileges).

11. The best analysis of this controversial period is in Moya Pons, *Historia Colonial*, ch. 18.

12. Juan Bosch, *Trujillo: Causas de una tiranía sin ejemplo* (2d ed.; Caracas: n.p., 1961), pp. 84-85.

13. Moya Pons, *Historia Colonial*, p. 421.

14. "Manifiesto de la parte del Este de la Isla, antes Española o de Santo Domingo, sobre las causas de su separación de la República Haitiana," 16 Jan. 1844, reproduced in Emilio Rodríguez Demorizi, ed., *Documentos para la Historia de la República Dominicana*, 3 vols. (Ciudad Trujillo: Academia Dominicana de la Historia, 1944), 1:8-17.

15. Howard J. Wiarda, *The Dominican Republic: Nation in Transition* (New York: Praeger, 1969), p. 27.

16. Sumner Welles, *Naboth's Vineyard: The Dominican Republic, 1844-1924*, 2 vols. (Washington, D.C.: Savile Books, 1966), 2:900-901. Welles, a child of his time and his milieu, has been justly accused of "a racial prejudice directed principally at Haitians" by even so conventional a writer as Selden Rodman (*Quisqueya: A History of the Dominican Republic* [Seattle: University of Washington Press, 1964], p. vi).

17. Reading what American scholars have written about the Dominican Republic, one is struck by their superficiality. Too often one finds an author content to repeat uncritically the conclusions of another. His style may be dazzling, but he will have made no attempt to verify the facts. Thus many myths have persisted, and the two volumes by Sumner Welles continue to be venerated as "exhaustive and eloquent" (Rodman, *Quisqueya*, p. vi). But Welles's book is neither eloquent nor exhaustive. Although he had access to an abundant documentation and devoted more than one thousand pages to a period of less than eighty years, Welles neglects almost completely the economic and social components of the period he considers. He has produced not a history of the Dominican Republic, but a massive manual of diplomatic history on rare occasions brilliant, all too often mediocre, very biased, and never free of racism. By glorifying the book well beyond its very limited value, too many authors have copied from it with a serene conscience, repeating uncritically its often false and arbitrary judgments.

For some typical examples of distortion in regard to the Haitian occupation see Wiarda, *Dominican Republic*, pp. 27-28 (in general a very good book); Rodman, *Quisqueya*, pp. 47-50; John Bartlow Martin, *Overtaken by Events: The Dominican Crisis from the Fall of Trujillo to the Civil War* (Garden City, N.Y.: Doubleday, 1966), p. 20; Robert D. Crassweller, *Trujillo: The Life and Times of a Caribbean Dictator* (New York: Macmillan, 1966), p. 19; T. D. Roberts et al., *Area Handbook for the Dominican Republic* (Washington, D.C.:

U.S. Government Printing Office, 1966), pp. 35-36; T. E. Weil et al., *Area Handbook for the Dominican Republic* (Washington, D.C.: U.S. Government Printing Office, 1973), pp. 37-38.

18. Letter of Simón Bolívar to Alexandre Pétion, Sept. 1816, cited by Paul Verna, *Pétion y Bolívar* (Caracas: n.p., 1969). Among the many authors who write on the independence of Spanish America, Verna is a welcome exception, the only one who tells of the generous and decisive aid given by Pétion to Bolívar in the latter's darkest hours (1815-16), at a time when the United States and Britain remained, at best, completely indifferent.

19. The major proponents of this trend are Juan Bosch, Hugo Tolentino Dipp, Emilio Cordero Michel, Juan Isidro Jimenes Grullón, Pedro Andrés Pérez Cabral, Franklin J. Franco Pichardo, and Frank Moya Pons, the most "moderate" of the group. To date (1977) Moya Pons is the only one to have published a book on the Haitian occupation (*La Dominación Haitiana, 1822-1844* [Santiago, D.R.: Universidad Católica Madre y Maestra, 1972]). The others have expressed their views through articles, conferences, and university lectures.

20. "Llamado a los fidelísimos Naturales y Habitantes de la Española," 10 June 1820, cited in Franco Pichardo, *Los Negros*, pp. 124-29. Italics added.

21. For a brief but excellent presentation of race relations in nineteenth-century Santo Domingo and their colonial antecedents, see Harry Hoetink, *El Pueblo Dominicano, 1850-1900, Apuntes para su Sociología Histórica* (Santiago, D.R.: Universidad Católica Madre y Maestra, 1971), esp. pp. 296-312; by the same author see in English, "The Dominican Republic in the Nineteenth Century: Some Notes on Stratification, Immigration and Race" in Magnus Mörner, ed., *Race and Class in Latin America* (New York: Columbia University Press, 1970), esp. pp. 96-121.

The democratizing influence of the Haitian occupation combined with the Dominican Republic's colonial background (see above, n. 5) enabled the country to begin its independent life in 1844 as a society relatively free of racism, certainly more so than neighboring Cuba, the British Caribbean, or Brazil (which had all developed as plantation societies). The creation of an economically powerful white social elite in the last decades of the nineteenth century and then the U.S. occupation (1916-24) increased prejudice based on color, but could not erase the impact of the historical elements already mentioned. Indeed, although race is still an important determinant of social status, throughout this century the Dominican Republic has remained relatively free of racial tension.

In addition, as we have already seen, the events of the period from the Haitian Revolution to the end of the Haitian occupation led to a decrease in the number of whites and, to the great sorrow of racists, "darkened" the Dominican population. In fact, because of the number and political importance of blacks and mulattoes, the United States refused to recognize the Dominican Republic throughout the latter's first period of independence (1844-61)—a special treatment that the Dominicans shared only with "black" Haiti.

While estimates concerning the racial composition of the population vary greatly, today the majority are considered to be mulatto (about 67 percent); of the rest, the black minority outnumbers the white.

22. "As always happens in such cases, there were members of the petty bourgeoisie who joined the *hateros*. [Tomás] Bobadilla was one of these" (Juan Bosch, "Sicología de las clases en la República Dominicana; para la ampliación y aplicación de la tesis: Dictadura con Respaldo Popular," *Ahora*, no. 310 [20 Oct. 1969], p. 19). These collaborators— Bobadilla, Manuel María Gautier, Félix María del Monte, Manuel María Valencia, and others—belonged to a small group of bureaucrats who had served under the Haitian administration.

23. The following generals succeeded to the presidency during the period 1844-61: Pedro Santana: 1844-48; Manuel Jimenes: 1848-49; Buenaventura Báez: 1849-53; Pedro Santana: 1853-56; Manuel de Regla Mota: 1856; Buenaventura Báez: 1856-58; José Desiderio Valverde: 1857-58; Pedro Santana: 1858-61.

24. Juan Bosch, *Composición social dominicana: Historia e interpretación* (1st ed.; Santo Domingo: Publicaciones Ahora, 1970), p. 200.

25. Hugo Tolentino Dipp, *La Traición de Pedro Santana* (Santo Domingo: Impresos Brenty, 1968), p. 29.

26. Rodman, *Quisqueya*, p. 64.

27. Tolentino Dipp, *Traición*, pp. 28-29.

28. From the same country, a precedent springs to mind. By 1809, the "Dominicans" had driven out the French only to place themselves again under Spanish rule. But an important distinction must be made: in 1809 the "Dominicans" renounced the chance to be independent; in 1861 they surrendered an independence already savored for many years.

29. These were the events: On 14 September 1863 a provisional government was set up in Santiago with General José A. Salcedo as president. Following a *pronunciamiento* he was replaced by General Gaspar Polanco on 10 October 1864. Polanco broke his pledge of amnesty to Salcedo, who was shot on 5 November. On 28 January 1865 yet another *pronunciamiento* bore fruit. Polanco was replaced by Benigno Filomeno de Rojas. But Rojas, too, was ousted, and General Pedro Pimentel "convinced" a national convention to elect him provisional president of the republic (25 March 1865).

30. Bernardo Pichardo, *Resumen de Historia Patria* (Santo Domingo: Editora del Caribe, 1969), pp. 191-92.

31. Juan Isidro Jimenes Grullón, *La República Dominicana: Una ficción* (Mérida, Venezuela: Talleres Gráficos Universitarios, 1965), p. 66.

32. Charles C. Tansill, *The United States and Santo Domingo, 1798-1873: A Chapter in Caribbean Diplomacy* (Baltimore: Johns Hopkins University Press, 1938), p. 363.

33. Hartmont would receive a commission of £100,000. The Dominican government would get only £ 320,000 and would have to pay £ 58,900 annually for twenty-four years. To guarantee the loan, "the entire resources of the Republic, both real and hypothetical, were pledged" (Welles, *Naboth's Vineyard*, 1:359).

34. Dana Munro, *Intervention and Dollar Diplomacy in the Caribbean, 1900-1921* (Princeton: Princeton University Press, 1964), p. 81. As for the "gullible investors": "It was later reported that a considerable number of French holders of Dominican bonds were Catholic peasants in France who were under the impression that they were buying securities of the Dominican religious order" (ibid.).

35. See U.S., Department of State, *Papers Relating to the Foreign Relations of the United States, 1904* (Washington, D.C.: U.S. Government Printing Office, 1905), 45:270-71 and 274-79. (Since 1932, these documents have been published under the title *Foreign Relations of the United States: Diplomatic Papers*, and hereafter will be cited as *Foreign Relations*, with year.)

36. The choice of a "financial agent" from among the officers of the Santo Domingo Improvement Company "seemed a logical arrangement to the State Department, but it had an unfortunate effect on the Dominicans, who still hated everything connected with the company" (Munro, *Intervention and Dollar Diplomacy*, p. 96).

37. Welles, *Naboth's Vineyard*, 2:616.

38. Munro, *Intervention and Dollar Diplomacy*, p. 98. The Italian Embassy "asserted that the Improvement Company award infringed upon the prior rights of Italian creditors and that the United States should either permit Italy to 'collect the quota due her directly from the customhouses of the Republic assigned for this purpose' or assume the obligation to pay the Italian claims if the United States had already occupied these customhouses" (ibid.).

39. Olney to the American ambassador in London, Thomas F. Bayard, Instruction No. 804, 20 July 1895, in U.S., *Foreign Relations, 1895*, 35:558.

40. *Proceedings of the Academy of Political Science* (New York) 7, no. 2 (July 1917): 383, cited by Scott Nearing and Joseph Freeman, *Dollar Diplomacy: A Study in American Imperialism* (New York: Monthly Review Press, 1969), p. 122.

"The inevitable effect of our building the Canal must be to require us to police the surrounding premises. In the nature of things, trade and control, and the obligation to keep order which go with them, must come our way" (Secretary of State Elihu Root to H. M. Flagler, 3 Jan. 1905, cited in Philip C. Jessup, *Elihu Root*, 2 vols. [New York: Dodd, Mead, 1938], 1:471).

41. In December 1902, Germany and Britain, soon joined by Italy, began a blockade of Venezuelan ports to force the dictator of that country, General Cipriano Castro, to satisfy the long outstanding claims of their citizens. Before acting, they were careful to inform the American government of their intentions. In response, Secretary of State John Hay notified the British ambassador that "the United States viewed with regret any resort to force on the part of European powers against the Republics of Central and South America, but they

could not object to any action taken by them with the view of obtaining redress for injuries inflicted on their subjects, provided such action did not contemplate any territorial acquisition" (U.S., Congress, Senate, *Venezuelan Arbitration . . . Appendix to Case of Great Britain*, Sen. Doc. 119, 58 Cong., 3 sess., pp. 782-83, cited by Munro, *Intervention and Dollar Diplomacy*, p. 69). Roosevelt himself had declared as much in his message to Congress (December 1901), and he "evidently had Venezuela in mind" (ibid, p. 67).

But Roosevelt, as he later admitted to the German ambassador, had underestimated the reaction of American public opinion to a European show of force against Venezuela. Cries of indignation arose in the United States against such a "flagrant violation" of the Monroe Doctrine. The three European powers quickly accepted arbitration of their claims against Venezuela and lifted the blockade on 19 February 1903. Even so, largely because of the reaction of the American public, Roosevelt decided that "a second attempt by foreign powers to collect debts by force would simply not be tolerated" (President Roosevelt to Theodore Roosevelt, Jr., 10 Feb. 1904, cited by Munro, *Intervention and Dollar Diplomacy*, p. 76). For an excellent analysis of the crisis, see Howard K. Beale, *Theodore Roosevelt and the Rise of America to World Power* (New York: Collier Books, 1967), pp. 135-37 and 369-70.

42. Welles, *Naboth's Vineyard*, 2:621.

43. "Message from the President of the United States, Transmitting a Protocol of an Agreement between the United States and the Dominican Republic, Providing for the Collection and Disbursement by the United States of the Customs Revenues of the Dominican Republic, Signed on February 7, 1905," 15 Feb. 1905, in U.S., *Foreign Relations, 1905*, 46:334-35.

44. Hay to Dawson, telegram, 30 Dec. 1904, ibid., p. 298.

45. Melvin M. Knight, *The Americans in Santo Domingo* (New York: Vanguard Press, 1928), p. 27.

46. For the full text of the protocol, see U.S., *Foreign Relations, 1905*, 46:342-43.

47. Knight, *Americans in Santo Domingo*, p. 28. The two American negotiators were Minister Dawson and Commander Dillingham of the U. S. Navy; the latter was sent to Santo Domingo as a special commissioner to help Dawson.

48. Dawson to the State Department, Jan. 1905, in U.S., *Foreign Relations, 1905*, 46: 309.

49. Two clear examples of this "understanding" are the Tariff Law of 1910 and the Agricultural Concessions Law of 1911. Written by American experts, the Tariff Law was designed to foster the importation of U.S. manufactured products, even when this went against the interests of the Dominican economy and the Dominican consumer. A year later, the Agricultural Concessions Law was enacted. This Magna Carta of the foreign sugar industry granted the sugar producers—Americans in the majority—generous privileges. See in particular Knight, *Americans in Santo Domingo*, pp. 45-48.

50. Munro, *Intervention and Dollar Diplomacy*, p. 259.

51. Knight, *Americans in Santo Domingo*, p. 29.

52. In the case of President Victoria, the American government decided that "the recommendations should be backed up by sending a warship with a landing force" (Munro, *Intervention and Dollar Diplomacy*, p. 262). But Victoria proved "reasonable," and the marines went home after spending almost two months on board their transports.

53. A detailed analysis of Wilson's policy toward Latin America is outside the scope of this chapter. Works such as those of Arthur S. Link (*La política de Estados Unidos en América Latina, 1913-1916* [México, D.F.: Fondo de Cultura Económica, 1960]) and Dana G. Munro (*Intervention and Dollar Diplomacy*), while useful, present an idealized view of Wilson's Latin American policy. A short but good overview is in Gordon Connell-Smith, *The United States and Latin America* (New York: Wiley, [1974]), pp. 132-45. Some perceptive studies on specific aspects of Wilson's Latin American policy are Robert Freeman Smith, *The United States and Revolutionary Nationalism in Mexico, 1916-1932* (Chicago: The University of Chicago Press, 1972), chs. 1-7; Peter Calvert, *The Mexican Revolution, 1910-1914: The Diplomacy of Anglo-American Conflict* (Cambridge: Cambridge University Press, 1968); Hans Schmidt, *The United States Occupation of Haiti, 1915-1934* (New Brunswick, N. J.: Rutgers University Press, 1971). However, there is still no good overall analysis of Wilson's Latin American policy.

54. Munro, *Intervention and Dollar Diplomacy*, p. 274.

55. As a prize-fight promoter, Sullivan had been accused of appropriating box-office receipts. Then, as a law student at Yale, he was sued for nonpayment by the tailor who made his graduation suit. When at Yale, he won a valuable watch as a prize for oratory, but lost it, he explained, in a "scuffle in Waterbury." Later, as a New York lawyer, he distinguished himself for his ties with underworld and gambling figures. But he was prominent in Irish ward politics in New York, and his political work in the 1912 electoral campaign made him a "deserving Democrat." A post as diplomat appealed to him "because the salary would enable him to pay his debts." He was particularly drawn to the Dominican Republic because of his friendship with Samuel Jarvis, who had recently founded the Banco Nacional of Santo Domingo. Jarvis, himself a "deserving Democrat," used his influence to help Sullivan to obtain the post. See Knight, *Americans in Santo Dominigo*, pp. 53-54; Munro, *Intervention and Dollar Diplomacy*, p. 275; and Arthur S. Link, *Wilson: The New Freedom* (Princeton: Princeton University Press, 1956), pp. 107-10.

56. Munro, *Intervention and Dollar Diplomacy*, p. 301. In Munro's judgment, "it is extraordinary that the American government should have attempted for several months to deal with so potentially dangerous a situation [as the one that existed in the Dominican Republic] through a representative who was completely discredited" (ibid.). While in Santo Domingo, Sullivan used the Banco Nacional of his friend Jarvis as a downtown office and its personnel for interpreters. He persistently overdrew his account and was rebuked by the State Department. For an official report on Sullivan's conduct while in Santo Domingo, see *Santo Domingo Investigation: Copy of the Report, Findings and Opinion of James D. Phelan, Commissioner Named by the Secretary of State, with the Approval of the President, to Investigate Charges against the United States Minister to the Dominican Republic*, 8 May 1915. Short of stating openly that Sullivan had taken bribes, the report was devastating.

57. William W. Russell, United States minister to Santo Domingo beginning in September 1915, had held the same post under Taft. His views of the country had long been all too clear: "Only complete control by our Government would permanently insure order and justice, but any degree of control would be beneficial" (Letter, 19 Sept. 1912, in U.S., *Foreign Relations, 1912*, p. 366).

58. Note delivered by Russell to the Dominican foreign minister, 19 Nov. 1915, in U.S., *Foreign Relations, 1915*, p. 336. Italics added. The note became known throughout Latin America as "Russell's No. 14."

59. The drama of the "Haitian precedent" seemed about to be replayed. Wilson had sought to "grant his protection" to the Haitians, too, and with the same results. But in 1915, during a civil war, particularly bloody and repugnant acts of violence occurred in Port-au-Prince. There was, however, no threat to American lives, and the violence of Port-au-Prince could hardly have shocked the American government: in many parts of the United States, Negroes and other "lesser breeds" were often lynched and on occasion burned alive in front of festive crowds. But Wilson seized the "humanitarian" pretext to justify an intervention that would have occurred in any case. On 28 July the marines landed in Port-au-Prince; they soon occupied the whole country. Suddenly the Haitian leaders, until then so "obstinate," became "reasonable." In September the Haitian legislature "elected" as president of the Republic Philippe Dartiguenave, a puppet chosen by the marines. Dartiguenave hastened to sign a treaty satisfying Washington's demands for military and economic control: the very demands that "Russell's No. 14" was to inflict on the Dominicans. By far the best analysis of the U.S. intervention in Haiti is in Schmidt, *United States Occupation of Haiti*, esp. chs. 3 and 4.

In Santo Domingo, in April 1916, the atrocities that characterized the Haitian scene ten months earlier were clearly missing. But General Desiderio Arias, the most powerful of the rebel *caudillos* who were on the point of toppling President Jimenes, was guilty of the most atrocious of all crimes. Arias, long the *bête noire* of the State Department, was considered by the United States to be "pro-German."

60. A detailed analysis of the causes of the U.S. intervention is outside the scope of this chapter. Briefly, however, they can be summarized as follows: (a) security considerations that were pushed to the limit of the absurd created an urge to preempt the nonexistent German "threat" in the Caribbean and the "threat" presented by the allegedly "pro-Ger-

man" *caudillo* Arias (see above, n. 59); (b) for Washington, this flagrant violation of international law was mitigated by its contempt for the Dominicans and their rights as an independent state; (c) the Wilson administration's harsh intolerance led it to perceive as insults and hostile acts the refusal of the Dominican leaders to submit to American dictates; (d) the realization that the rag-tag Dominican armed forces would be unable to offer any effective resistance minimized the cost of an intervention and helped to eliminate any restraint in Washington. While economic considerations were not the primary motivation for the intervention, United States economic dominance was, in Wilson's eyes, a tool to foster political control—hence the two elements are tightly intertwined.

There is as yet no study that provides a satisfactory analysis of the background of the 1916 U.S. intervention in the Dominican Republic. The works most often cited, in particular Munro's *Intervention and Dollar Diplomacy* and Welles's *Naboth's Vineyard*, sacrifice analytical depth in order to present the policy of the United States as favorably as possible. Since the causes of Wilson's interventions in Haiti and the Dominican Republic are largely the same, any interested reader should consult Schmidt, *United States Occupation of Haiti*.

61. Knight, *Americans in Santo Domingo*, p. 97. For a brief discussion of the literature on the U.S. occupation, see the Bibliographical Essay.

62. Edwin Lieuwen, *U.S. Policy in Latin America* (New York: Praeger, 1965), p. 43. In the same vein, Abraham Lowenthal has written: "For eight years American military and civilian personnel ruled the Dominican Republic directly, taking over every branch of public administration. American troops attempted to impose order, American officers trained and commanded a Dominican Constabulary, American revenue agents collected taxes, American engineers built roads and bridges, American bureaucrats set up a civil service system and reformed the post office, and American educators revamped the Dominican Republic's schools" (*The Dominican Intervention* [Cambridge, Mass.: Harvard University Press, 1972], p. 9).

63. The military government's public work program also included "other scraps of roads, some bridges, improvements to trails, harbor works and public buildings." This was a "good beginning," but no leap forward. Moreover, $2,918,536—nearly half of the $6,688,-536 spent on these works—was borrowed money, which merely added to the burdens of any future Dominican government (Knight, *Americans in Santo Domingo*, pp. 102, 107).

For the forced labor (*corvée*) that the Americans imposed in Haiti, and the accompanying violence they meted on the Haitian peasants, see Schmidt, *United States Occupation of Haiti*, pp. 100-107, and Suzy Castor, *La Ocupación Norteamericana de Haiti y sus consecuencias (1915-1934)* (México, D.F.: Siglo XXI, 1971), pp. 91-93.

64. Munro, *Intervention and Dollar Diplomacy*, pp. 317-18.

65. Knight, *Americans in Santo Domingo*, p. 89.

66. Ibid., p. 34.

67. The Americans controlled property worth $33,697,632; the Dominicans $1,344,541. The remainder of the sugar estates, worth roughly $5 million, belonged mostly to Italians or to Dominico-American or Italo-American companies. It should be added that these are the evaluations that were given for tax purposes and thus are low (ibid., pp. 138-39). For a discussion on the sugar industry and the Military Government, see also Bruce J. Calder, *Some Aspects of the United States Occupation of the Dominican Republic* (Ann Arbor, Mich.: Xerox University Microfilms, 1974), esp. ch. 7.

68. Knight, *Americans in Santo Domingo*, p. 122, and Frank Moya Pons, *Manual de Historia Dominicana* (Santiago, D.R.: Universidad Católica Madre y Maestra, 1977), p. 492.

69. Knight, *Americans in Santo Domingo*, pp. 90-91.

70. Munro, *Intervention and Dollar Diplomacy*, p. 321.

71. Letter of Msgr. Adolfo A. Nouel, archbishop of Santo Domingo, to Russell, 20 Dec. 1920, cited by Emilio Rodríguez Demorizi, *United States Military Intervention* (Ciudad Trujillo: n.p., 1958), p. 12.

72. Judge Schoenrich, memorandum, 11 Dec. 1919, cited by Munro, *Intervention and Dollar Diplomacy*, p. 321.

73. Knight, *Americans in Santo Domingo*, p. 109.

74. Rodríguez Demorizi, *United States Military Intervention*, p. 11.

75. Martin, *Overtaken by Events*, p. 29 (reprinted by permission of Doubleday and

Company, Inc.). Martin, who served as U.S. ambassador to the Dominican Republic in 1962-63, remarked in his memoirs: "In those eastern provinces, years later, anti-Americanism remained" (ibid.). These provinces saw the most pronounced growth of American sugar plantations, whose rapid expansion displaced a large number of the local peasants. From the dispossessed the rebels drew many men and much of their support.

76. Msgr. Nouel to Russell, 20 Dec. 1920, cited by Rodríguez Demorizi, *United States Military Intervention*, pp. 12-13. American atrocities in the Dominican Republic were not aberrations. In those same years American troops were perpetrating even worse crimes in Haiti, after having spread death and desolation in the Philippines a few years earlier.

In rare instances, when a scandal exploded, congressional inquiries were held, only to result in whitewashes. This was the case for the much-touted Senate inquiry on Haiti and Santo Domingo held in late 1921 and 1922 by a special select committee chaired by Senator Medill McCormick of Illinois (U.S., Congress, Senate, *Inquiry into Occupation and Administration of Haiti and Santo Domingo, Hearings before a Select Committee on Haiti and Santo Domingo*, 2 vols., 67 Cong., 1 and 2 sess. [Washington, D.C.: U.S. Government Printing Office, 1922]).

On other occasions, and for the same reasons, a few scapegoats were tried. Thus in the Dominican Republic, Captain Charles Merkle, U.S.M.C., was arrested in October 1918 — and allowed to commit suicide with a revolver purposely left in his cell by two fellow officers rather than face charges. After his death, the Military Government brushed off Merkle's numerous atrocities as isolated incidents attributable to his German ancestry: Captain Merkle, wrote Military Governor Thomas Snowden, "was a German who used the well-known German methods on the native population until the authorities found him out" (quoted by Calder, *Some Aspects of the United States Occupation*, pp. 168-69).

77. Bruce Calder aptly comments on the deeply ingrained antiblack prejudice of most marine officers and men: "North American racism found a fertile field in the Dominican Republic, 'a country whose people', Military Governor Harry Knapp noted, 'are almost all touched with tarbrush . . . .' " Calder continues: "The Marine prejudice caused them to look down upon Dominicans generally, but the problem was even worse among the peasants of the East, poor and darkerskinned than many other citizens of the Republic. Furthermore the Marines' racist culture had accustomed them to patterns of white superiority and black subservience in both the northern and southern United States. Their experience at home led them to expect similar behaviour abroad, a fact which led to abuses on the part of the Marines and bitterness on the part of the Dominicans. Myriad comments in military documents betray the Marines' view on race. The commander of all Marine operations in the East from 1917 to 1919, Colonel George C. Thorpe, referred to the guerrillas as 'the black savage enemy.' . . . In a more philosophical mood, he noted 'the instinctive antagonism between the white and the colored races', adding that 'no white nationality has less sympathy with colored races than the American; i.e. the American goes further than any other people in its race prejudice' " (*Some Aspects of the United States Occupation*, pp. 153-54).

78. By the end of the Wilson administration, it became obvious even to Washington that the military occupation of the Dominican Republic was no longer necessary to maintain U.S. political and economic domination over that country. Instead, it only served as a needless irritant in U.S. relations with other Latin American nations and exposed the hypocrisy of the anti-imperialist claims of the United States before Europe and Japan. In October 1922, with the consent of the State Department, a provisional government was set up in the Dominican Republic. The following year, the Dominican people elected a Congress and in March 1924 a president of the Republic. The last American troops pulled out in September. In exchange, the evacuation treaty of July 1924 forced the Dominicans to recognize as valid hundreds of orders, regulations, and contracts of the U.S. military government. Additionally, the United States was guaranteed control over the customs receivership until the extinction of the foreign debt. Three differing points of view on this subject are given by Joseph R. Juárez, "United States Withdrawal from Santo Domingo," *Hispanic American Historical Review* 17, No. 2 (May 1962): 152-90; Dana Munro, *The United States and the Caribbean Republics, 1921-1933* (Princeton: Princeton University Press, 1974), esp. ch. 3; and Julio Ortega Frier, *Memorandum relativo a la intervención de Sumner Welles en la República Dominicana* (Santo Domingo: Ediciones del Taller, 1973).

79. Report of Major Thomas E. Watson, 30 Sept. 1920, cited by Crassweller, *Trujillo*, p. 45.

80. Jesús de Galíndez, *La Era de Trujillo: Un estudio casuistico de dictadura hispano-americana* (Buenos Aires: Editorial Américana, 1962), pp. 162, 166.

81. A few facts, as significant as they are amusing: the Dominican Republic was the first Latin American country to declare war on the Axis. It lagged a day behind the United States in the case of Japan, but redeemed itself by declaring war on Germany and Italy the very day these two countries declared war on the United States.

Naturally, Trujillo had shown well before December 1941 how willing he was to follow Washington's lead. On 4 December 1939, the Dominican Republic had offered the United States the full use of its territory in order to "ensure the continental defense." U.S. warships and military planes could use "as often as they desire" the country's "harbors, bays and territorial waters," and American forces could remain in the Dominican Republic as long as the United States thought "necessary or expedient." Edward Guerrant rightly concludes: "This was an amazing offer. It was virtually a blank check for the forces of the United States to make use of the territory of the Dominican Republic as they saw fit. . . . The United States obtained the right to use bases in a number of other nations, but never on such favorable terms as those granted by the Dominican Republic"(*Roosevelt's Good Neighbor Policy* [Albuquerque: The University of New Mexico Press, 1950], p. 155).

82. Phillips to Roberto Despradel, Dominican ambassador to the United States, *Washington Post*, 17 Aug. 1934.

83. DeLesseps Morrison, mayor of New Orleans and later (1961-63) President John F. Kennedy's ambassador to the OAS, during a visit to the Dominican Republic, 2 July 1946, cited by Emilio Rodríguez Demorizi, *Cronología de Trujillo*, 2 vols. [9-10] [Ciudad Trujillo: Impresora Dominicana, 1955], 10:124. The *Cronología* is part of *La Era de Trujillo: 25 años de historia dominicana*, a set of twenty volumes published to celebrate the twenty-fifth anniversary of the Era.

84. See Myron Taylor, United States delegate to the Evian Conference, to Secretary Hull, telegram, cited by Eliahu Ben Elissar, *Le Facteur juif dans la politique étrangère du IIIe Reich* (Paris: Editions Julliard, 1969), p. 435.

85. According to Arturo Espaillat, once Trujillo's chief of intelligence, the dictator had "price lists for the purchase of some U.S. Congressmen. An ordinary, run-of-the-mill Representative would cost about $5,000 or less. A few House Committee Chairmen could be had for about three times that much, depending on the committee. Senators came higher, of course. A chairman of a key committee could run from $50,000 to $75,000" (*Trujillo: The Last Caesar* [Chicago: Henry Regnery, 1963], p. 81). Espaillat is not always reliable—in this case, his price lists might not be exact, and some of the lurid details that he gives might be exaggerated. But there is no doubt that Trujillo bought some members of the U.S. Congress, State Department officials, and journalists, among others. In the 1940s the case of Congressman Hamilton Fish, ranking Republican member of the House Committee on Foreign Affairs, became famous. His abrupt change of heart toward Trujillo, followed by the "mysterious" deposit of $25,000 into his account in a New York bank, was exposed by *Time*, 17 Aug. 1942. There were many like Hamilton Fish in the 1950s, but fear of libel charges and political pressures have shrouded in a welcome anonymity the names of the powerful men who sold themselves to Trujillo.

Espaillat, *Trujillo*, esp. ch. 8, is the most explicit on the subject. Brief but good accounts are provided by Crassweller, *Trujillo*, pp. 323-25, and Howard J. Wiarda, *Dictatorship and Development. The Methods of Control in Trujillo's Dominican Republic* (Gainesville: University of Florida Press, 1968), pp. 140-41.

In addition to bribery, Trujillo used blackmail. During their visits to the Dominican Republic, many prominent Americans were generously provided with women and then secretly photographed in compromising situations—Trujillo's "blackmail photographic library was extensive" (Martin, *Overtaken by Events*, p. 35).

86. In a short article, Frank Moya Pons offers the best presentation of the history and fortunes of the Dominican church before the Era of Trujillo ("Notas para una historia de la Iglesia en Santo Domingo," *Eme Eme Estudios Dominicanos* [Santiago, D.R.], 1, no. 6 [May-June 1973], pp. 3-18).

Throughout the colonial period, the church shared in the fortunes of the colony. It was rich in the early years of the sixteenth century, and it became desperately poor in the later decades, above all after the "depopulation" ordered by Philip II. Its situation improved notably in the eighteenth century, but then came the Haitian Revolution, with its consequences in Spanish Santo Domingo. The Church had just begun a modest recovery under "Stupid Spain" (1809-21), when the curtain rose on the most trying period of its history: the Haitian occupation (1822-44).

The clergy was intransigent in its hostility to the Haitians. Archbishop Pedro Valera y Jimenes "refused to accept his pay from the [Haitian] Treasury as a Haitian citizen, and declared in a letter to President Boyer that he was a subject of His Majesty the King of Spain" (Pichardo, *Resumen de historia patria*, p. 82); many priests conspired against the new rulers.

Thus provoked, the Haitians reacted with vigor, confiscating Church property and deporting a large number of priests. By the time the country gained its independence in 1844, the Church was practically crushed. Thereafter, the Church's efforts to recover its lost property met the opposition of the groups that had acquired them from the Haitian state. The resulting tensions between church and state culminated in a break of relations in 1853. In the end the Dominican Church failed to recover its lost properties, and, unlike its counterparts in most other Latin American countries, by 1930 was relatively poor; there were few clergymen, and all too often they were ill-equipped for their spiritual mission.

87. Wiarda, *Dictatorship and Development*, pp. 141-42.

What Trujillo got out of the bargain can be summed up in a sentence: with a loyalty worthy of a better cause, the clergy never missed a chance to demonstrate ardent support for the regime. The tone was set by Msgr. Ricardo Pittini, archbishop of Santo Domingo, a man of "pliant heart and conscience" (Crassweller, *Trujillo*, p. 382) and lavish in his praise of the dictator.

But the Church's blessing came from far beyond the Republic itself. In Rome two popes—Pius XI and Pius XII—showed their approval: there were decorations, which the Jefe relished, special blessings, and, in 1954, the highly un-Catholic annulment of Trujillo's first marriage. And in Boston, Cardinal Francis Joseph Spellman, a powerful prince of the Church and influential in American politics, applauded Trujillo's "religious and anti-Communist policies" (ibid., p. 325), blind to the rest.

In return for such devotion, Trujillo gave to the Catholic Church a privileged status relative to other faiths. Above all, he granted generous economic benefits both to the Church as an institution and to individual priests as well. The Church became rich, and the number of priests increased, with dozens arriving in the country from abroad, especially from Spain.

For additional information on the relations between the Church and Trujillo, see especially Crassweller, *Trujillo;* William L. Wipfler, *The Churches in the Dominican Republic in the Light of History* (Cuernavaca: Centro Intercultural de Documentación, 1966), pp. 59-101; Wiarda, *Dictatorship and Development*, esp. ch. 7; see also, by the same author, "The Changing Political Orientation of the Catholic Church in the Dominican Republic," *Journal of Church and State* 7, no. 2 (Spring 1965), pp. 238-58, and *Dictatorship, Development and Disintegration*, 3 vols. (Ann Arbor, Mich.: Xerox University Microfilms, 1975), vol. 1, ch. 6.

88. Only the official party—the Partido Dominicano, founded in 1931—remained.

89. During 1938-42, there were twenty-nine "resignations" from sixteen Senate seats. Only three senators finished their terms. During the same period, the House saw ninety-eight "resignations" from fifty seats. Five constituencies changed congressmen four times each and several others three times each. The day after it was organized, on 17 Aug. 1938, the House accepted the "resignations" of seven representatives. And so it went, with only one exception, in the first legislature of the Era, when the Senate preserved a degree of stability. For details, see especially Galíndez, *La Era de Trujillo*, pp. 111-14.

90. "I was told of a prominent minister who was humiliated by Trujillo at a cabinet meeting, but who reacted by declaring: 'El Jefe es justo hasta cuando castiga' " (ibid., p. 195).

91. The Trujillo regime affected not only the economic but also the social structure of the country. At the end of the Era (1961) as in 1930, the Dominican Republic was a two-class society, where a small upper class dominated an immense mass of very poor (the *infelices*) with only a small middle sector (*gente de segunda*) in between. Many changes, however, had intervened during the Era. In 1930 the country's upper class was represented by

the *gente de primera*, a small group of families—hardly more than one hundred—interrelated by blood and marriage. Trujillo broke the political power and weakened the economic position of the *gente de primera*. Above all, many families *de segunda* joined the upper class. Their elevation was due to the arbitrary whim of the dictator to whose favor they owed their sudden riches and official status and who forced them upon a resentful *gente de primera*. Thus in 1961, and in contrast to 1930, the Dominican upper class consisted of two antagonistic sectors: the *gente de primera* and the *nouveaux riches* of the Era. With Trujillo dead, their clash was inevitable, for the *gente de primera* sought to regain their previous exclusive status. They constantly condemned the *nouveaux riches* as *Trujillistas*, forgetting, of course, that they, too, had collaborated in the crimes of the Era and were thus equally responsible. From 1962 to 1965, the *gente de primera* dominated the government during the Council of State (January 1962 to February 1963) and, after the interlude of Bosch, during the Triumvirate (September 1963 to April 1965). The *nouveaux riches* were able to regain a share of political power only in 1966. By that time, however, the shock of the civil war of April to August 1965 had taught a precious lesson to the *gente de primera*, who, albeit reluctantly, would now be ready to collaborate with their enemy brothers in the Dominican upper class in defense of the status quo.

The *gente de segunda* increased numerically during the Era as a result of the economic growth, however skewed, of that period and the vast expansion of state functions. Of course, they had no political power. Above all, they lacked during the Era, as they would lack in the years after Trujillo, any feeling of cohesion, of common identity.

The size of the Dominican middle class varies according to different authors. For Juan Bosch, it comprised by the early 1960s nearly two hundred thousand adults, or about 15 percent of the population. But many of those he includes in the "lower middle class" could easily be added to the mass of *infelices*.

There will be no specific discussion of the Dominican proletariat. The subject would be of importance in a work devoted to the social structure of the Dominican Republic, but not for our purpose. The Dominican proletariat increased in size during the Era because of the "industrialization" that took place, but was still extremely small. It had no class-consciousness and played no independent role throughout the 1960s—nor, indeed, does it now. Neither the leadership nor the rank and file of the two Dominican communist parties of the 1961-65 period (MPD and PSP) belonged to the proletariat.

For sources on the social structure of the Dominican Republic, see the Bibliographical Essay.

92. Dominican Republic, Secretaría de Finanzas, *Informe de la República Dominicana ante la reunión del Consejo Inter-Americano Económico y Social al nivel de expertos* (Santo Domingo, 1962), p. 2. The *Informe* is also the source for the percentages cited above.

93. Wiarda, *Dominican Republic*, p. 40, and Bosch, *Trujillo*, p. 175. For further information on Trujillo's economic empire see Wiarda, *Dictatorship and Development*, ch. 5; Bosch, *Trujillo*, chs. 13, 14; Germán E. Ornes, *Trujillo: Little Caesar of the Caribbean* (New York: Thomas Nelson, 1958), ch. 15; and Crassweller, *Trujillo*, ch. 16.

94. Jesús de Galíndez was a Spanish exile who, after a few years in the Dominican Republic (1940-46), moved to New York. There he became a prominent and well-informed critic of the Trujillo regime, having good ties with Latin American exiles and the U. S. "liberal" academic community. In February 1956, he presented a doctoral dissertation at Columbia University entitled "The Trujillo Era," a well-documented and shattering critique of the dictatorship. On 12 March 1956, Galíndez mysteriously disappeared. All evidence indicates that on Trujillo's orders he had been kidnapped from the streets of New York, transported to a nearby airport, and flown, drugged, to the Dominican Republic, where he was killed. Galíndez's relative prominence and the *démarches* of his friends gave the case some notoriety, but police investigations were inconclusive, and soon the affair lost its place in the news. Nor had it in any way affected the warm relations between the Eisenhower administration and the Dominican regime.

Early in December, however, the car of Gerald L. Murphy, a young American pilot with the Dominican airline, was found abandoned in Ciudad Trujillo. Murphy, too, had disappeared and was presumed dead. It soon became evident that the Galíndez and the Murphy cases were related. Murphy had piloted the plane that brought Galíndez back to the Dominican Republic. He knew too much, he talked too much, and thus he had to die. All clues pointed to the Dominican Republic.

Trujillo had violated the first rule of the game: assassinations were allowed, but not of American citizens. Gerald Murphy's American parents were "tireless in their demands for justice," and his American fiancée "knew a great deal and was willing to talk" (Crassweller, *Trujillo*, p. 314). Two congressmen from Murphy's home state, Senator Wayne Morse and Representative Charles O. Porter, were among the rare critics in Congress of the Trujillo dictatorship. With the help of such influential newspapers as the *Washington Post* and the *New York Times*, they transformed the affair into a *cause celèbre*, while the American public grew increasingly indignant over the murder of an "American boy" in one of those "banana Republics." The Eisenhower administration felt no desire to strain its warm relations with Trujillo, but the pressure of a large sector of the press and public opinion forced it out of its lethargy. At last the State Department broke its "strange silence" and began to press the Dominican government, "demanding a truthful account of what had happened to Gerald L. Murphy" (*Washington Post*, 24 March 1957. In that same issue, the *Washington Post* commented that "it would have been better if the Department had also shown concern for Galíndez").

Under the sudden American pressure, the Trujillo regime desperately tried to prove its innocence, but proceeded in such a clumsy way that it only succeeded in making its guilt more evident, thus further exasperating the American public and press, and forcing the State Department to adopt a harsher tone. At the same time in the United States, a series of trials and investigations sparked by the Galíndez-Murphy case spectacularly revealed the pervasive activities in the country of agents and public relations men at the service of Trujillo.

As a result of the Galíndez-Murphy case, Trujillo's prestige suffered a heavy blow in the United States, and the Eisenhower administration had to cool its relations with the Dominican Republic. If no further development had occurred, however, the case, which was never officially solved, eventually would have lost its impact, and in time relations between Washington and Ciudad Trujillo would have returned to their habitual warmth. But unforeseen political developments soon took place elsewhere in Latin America, and in turn negatively affected Washington's attitude toward the Dominican regime. Thus, rather than a parenthesis, the Galíndez-Murphy case marked the beginning of the end of an era.

For further information on the subject, see Elena de la Souchère, *Crime à Saint-Domingue: L' Affaire Trujillo-Galíndez* (Paris: Editions Albin Michel, 1972); Wiarda, *Dictatorship and Development*, pp. 151-53; Crassweller, *Trujillo*, pp. 311-23; Ornes, *Trujillo*, pp. 309-38.

95. Crassweller, *Trujillo*, p. 344.

96. Trujillo's propaganda claimed that the conduct of the "communist agent" Betancourt had been "so scandalous . . . that the Dominican Republic published a 'White Book' denouncing to the governments and peoples of South America the misbehavior and attacks of Rómulo Betancourt" (Dominican Republic, Ministry for Home Affairs, *White Book of Communism in Dominican Republic* [Madrid: Gráficas Rey, 1958]). The best account is in Charles D. Ameringer, *The Democratic Left in Exile, The Antidictatorial Struggle in the Caribbean, 1945-1959* (Coral Gables, Fla.: University of Miami Press, 1974), ch. 2.

97. Crassweller, *Trujillo*, p. 421. For a more detailed discussion of U.S. policy toward Trujillo from 1959 to 1961, see below, Appendix I and Chapter 2.

98. Crassweller, *Trujillo*, p. 421.

99. For the June 1959 invasion and the history of the underground movement (Movimiento Revolucionario 14 de Junio or MR1J4), see Appendix II.

100. [Catholic Church, Conferencia del Episcopado de la República Dominicana] "Carta pastoral colectiva del Episcopado de la República Dominicana en ocasión de la fiesta de Nuestra Señora de la Altagracia," 25 Jan. 1960, in *Documentos de la Conferencia del Episcopado de la República Dominicana, 1955-1969* (Santo Domingo: Imprenta Amigo del Hogar, 1969), pp. 39-44.

101. No one has yet given a definitive explanation of why Trujillo ordered the massacre that resulted in the slaughter of fifteen to twenty thousand Haitians in October 1937. The most plausible explanation is the one given to me by a former official of the regime. Shunning a direct answer, the man recounted a "little incident" that took place in the Dominican Republic toward the turn of the century. There was a governor in a western province

who, to cut down the Haitian population in the region—and, above all, to prevent a new in-flux—ordered three Haitian men accused of theft to be castrated in the public square. Salt was then applied to their wounds, and they were driven across the border. The maiming had the desired effect: the Haitian population in the province dropped off over the next few years.

The tale may not be true, but it is significant. During the 1930s, Trujillo was increasingly troubled by the peaceful—but to him intolerable—presence of tens of thousands of Haitians in the Republic. The Haitians were an "inferior" people bringing "barbarous" customs into the country and "Africanizing" the population, which the government insisted was of Spanish stock. The infiltration was particularly apparent in the border areas, "more Hai-tianized year by year" (Crassweller, *Trujillo*, p. 150). Did Trujillo try to "Dominicanize the border" by massacre and the terror that followed? This was the conclusion suggested by my interlocutor, a reliable and usually knowledgeable source.

102.   Organization of American States, OAS Official Records, OEA/Ser. F/II. 7, *Report of the Inter-American Peace Committee to the Seventh Meeting of Consultation of Minis-ters of Foreign Affairs* (Washington, D.C.: Pan American Union, 1960), Appendix D, p. 5. See also Chapter 2, below.

103.   Crassweller, *Trujillo*, p. 413.

104.   Organization of American States, Council, Subcommittee to the Special Com-mittee, *Informe de la Subcomisión sometido a la Comisión Especial para dar cumplimiento al mandato recibido por el Consejo de acuerdo con la Resolución I de la Sexta Reunión de Consulta de Ministros de Relaciones Exteriores* (Washington, D.C.: Pan American Union 1961), pp. 6-7. Italics added.

105.   Exportation to the Dominican Republic of petroleum and petroleum products, trucks, and spare parts was suspended (see ibid., p. 8).

106.   Wiarda, *Dictatorship and Development*, p. 161.

107.   For this economic crisis of the regime, see [Dominican Republic] Oficina Nac-ional de Planificación, *Bases para el desarrollo nacional: Análisis de los problemas y pers-pectivas de la economía dominicana* (Santo Domingo, 1965); Manuel José Cabral, *Trayec-toria de la economía dominicana, 1950-1966* (Santiago, D.R.: Universidad Católica Madre y Maestra, 1967), and Wiarda, *Dictatorship and Development*, pp. 160-64.

108.   See Appendix I.

CHAPTER 2

1.   See Appendix 1.

2.   For a portrait of the two survivors—Antonio Imbert Barrera and Luis Amiama Tió—see n. 216 below.

3.   See decree 6729 and law 5545 of 2 June 1961, in *Gaceta Oficial* 8579, 7 June 1961, pp. 5, 7.

4.   *Hispanic American Report* 14, no. 5 (July 1961), p. 412.

5.   *New York Times*, 2 June 1961, p. 8.

6.   "On the evening of June 4, General Juan Tomás Díaz . . . and Antonio de la Maza Vásquez were machine-gunned to death in the Plaza Independencia, . . . in the heart of Ciudad Trujillo." Less than forty-eight hours earlier, "secret police machine-gunned one of the suspected killers [Lieutenant Amado García Guerrero] at a private home in downtown Ciudad Trujillo" (*Hispanic American Report* 14, no. 6 [Aug. 1961], p. 503).

7.   Ibid.

8.   Juan Bosch, *Crisis de la democracia de América en la República Dominicana*, 3d ed. (México, D.F.: Centro de Estudios y Documentación Sociales, 1965), p. 20.

9.   Quoted by *Hispanic American Report* 14, no. 6 (Aug. 1961), p. 503.

10.   Juan Bosch, *Trujillo: Causas de una tiranía sin ejemplo*, 2d ed. (Caracas: n. p., 1961), p. 178.

11. Harry Kantor, *Patterns of Politics and Political Systems in Latin America* (Chicago: Rand McNally, 1969), pp. 168-69.

12. Congress had instructed the president to reallocate the large Cuban quota (over 60 percent of U.S. sugar imports) by increasing existing domestic and foreign suppliers' shares of the U.S. market according to a specified formula, which automatically resulted in a near quadrupling of the Dominican quota. In vain Eisenhower asked for legislation that would deprive the Trujillo regime of "a large sugar bonus embarassing to the United States in the conduct of our foreign relations throughout the hemisphere." Unable to overcome the opposition of the powerful friends the Jefe still had in Congress–chiefly the Democratic Senators James Eastland (Mississippi) and Allen Ellender (Louisiana)–Eisenhower proved his determination by imposing a fee of two cents per pound on Dominican sugar. This fee, which was later increased to 2.5 cents per pound, canceled the so-called premium, that is, the difference existing at that time between the U.S. price and the world price, thus depriving the Dominican Republic of a $22 million windfall. For a more detailed account, see Pope G. Atkins and Larman C. Wilson, *The United States and the Trujillo Regime* (New Brunswick, N.J.: Rutgers University Press, 1972), pp. 115-21.

13. Bosch, *Trujillo*, p. 148.

14. Although the Caribbean Legion represents a fascinating chapter in the history of the region, no satisfactory work on the subject has yet been published. In English the best source is Charles D. Ameringer, *The Democratic Left in Exile* (Coral Gables, Fla.: University of Miami Press, 1974), pp. 59-110; also useful is John Patrick Bell, *Crisis in Costa Rica* (Austin and London: The University of Texas Press, 1971), esp. ch. 5. In Spanish, Oscar R. Aguilar Bulgarelli, *Costa Rica y sus hechos políticos de 1948* (San José: Editorial Costa Rica, 1969), contains much valuable information. Finally, among the many accounts written by participants, the most interesting is the most partisan: Rosendo Arguello, Jr., *Quienes y como nos traicionaron* (México, D.F.: published by the author, 1954).

15. See Organization of American States, Documentos Oficiales/Ser. F/III. 5, *Quinta reunión de consulta de ministros de relaciones exteriores* (Washington, D.C.: Pan American Union, 1961), pp. 108-16 and 207-18.

16. Christian Herter, speech, 12 Aug. 1959, to the Fifth Meeting of Consultation of Ministers of Foreign Affairs of the OAS, San José, Costa Rica, in *Department of State Bulletin* 41 (July-Dec. 1959): 301.

17. Christian Herter, speech, 13 Aug. 1959, to the Fifth Meeting of Consultation of OAS Foreign Ministers, in ibid., p. 303.

18. Jerome Slater, *The OAS and United States Foreign Policy* (Columbus: Ohio State University Press, 1967), pp. 185-86.

19. See *Inter-American Efforts to Relieve International Tensions in the Western Hemisphere, 1959-1960* (Washington D.C.: Department of State Publications, 1962).

20. Organization of American States, Official Records, Ser. F/II. 7, *Report of the Inter-American Peace Committee to the Seventh Meeting of Consultation of Ministers of Foreign Affairs* (Washington D.C.: Pan American Union, 1960), Appendix D, p. 5.

21. Slater, *OAS and United States*, p. 190.

22. Arthur M. Schlesinger, Jr., *A Thousand Days: John F. Kennedy in the White House* (Boston: Houghton Mifflin, 1965), p. 185.

23. Dean Rusk, speech, 25 Jan. 1962, to the Eighth Meeting of Consultation of Ministers of Foreign Affairs of the OAS, Punta del Este, in *Department of State Bulletin* 46 (Jan.-June 1962): 275.

24. John F. Kennedy, "The Lesson of Cuba," address before the American Society of Newspaper Editors, Washington, D.C., 20 April 1961, White House press release in *Department of State Bulletin* 44 (Jan.-June 1961): 659.

25. *New York Times*, 4 June 1961, sec. 4, p. 4.

26. Organization of American States, Council, Subcommittee to the Special Committee, *Informe de la Subcomisión sometido a la Comisión Especial para dal cumplimiento al mandato recibido por el Consejo de acuerdo con la Resolución I de la Sexta Reunión de Consulta de Ministros de Relaciones Exteriores* (Washington, D.C.: Pan American Union, 1961), Appendix III, p. 46.

27. Venezuela took a particularly hard line: its Foreign Minister Marcos Falcón Briceño "threatened that his country might withdraw from the OAS if the economic sanctions imposed on the Dominican Republic were lifted. He said that Venezuela would continue to

oppose the lifting of sanctions until free and supervised elections were held and the family and associates of the former dictator ousted from power" (*Hispanic American Report* 14, no. 6 [Aug. 1961], p. 565). Caracas' intransigence clashed, in the months to come, with Washington's more flexible stance, and at times even limited Washington's freedom to maneuver.

28. Organization of American States, *Informe*, p. 1. It was, to be exact, a "Subcommittee to the Special Committee" set up "to carry the mandate received by the Council pursuant to Resolution I of the Sixth Meeting of Consultation of Ministers of Foreign Affairs" (ibid., pp. 1-2).

29. Press conference, 22 June 1961, in *Department of State Bulletin* 45 (July-Dec. 1961): 56.

30. Organization of American States, *Informe*, p. 29.

31. John B. Martin, *Overtaken by Events: The Dominican Crisis from the Fall of Trujillo to the Civil War* (Garden City, N.Y.: Doubleday, 1966), pp. 81, 31.

32. Schlesinger, *Thousand Days*, p. 769.

33. Ibid.

34. *Hispanic American Report* 14, no. 8 (Oct. 1961), p. 698. The hard line taken by Venezuela, which "vigorously opposed" (ibid.) any compromise with the Trujillos, was especially influential, since the Venezuelan government enjoyed the respect of both the new administration in Washington and a number of Latin American governments.

35. Moscoso was then the U.S. coordinator of the Alliance for Progress. From 1950 to 1960 he had been in charge of the Economic Development Administration of Puerto Rico, and then, for a few months, U.S. ambassador to Venezuela. Morales-Carrión, a former undersecretary for the Commonwealth of Puerto Rico (1953-61), became, in 1961, deputy assistant secretary of state for inter-American affairs. Muñoz Marín was in himself an institution. Founder and president of the Popular Democratic party of Puerto Rico, he had been governor of the island since 1948, a post he assumed after seven years (1941-48) as president of the Senate.

36. Interview with Arturo Morales-Carrión.

37. Schlesinger, *Thousand Days*, p. 769.

38. DeLesseps S. Morrison, *Latin American Mission: An Adventure in Hemisphere Diplomacy*, ed. and intro. by Gerold Frank (New York: Simon & Schuster, 1965), p. 114.

39. The absence of diplomatic relations and the viselike grip of the dictatorship on Dominican society left Washington particularly ill-informed about the actual state of the country. Indeed, a Senate committee has written in this regard: "On June 1, 1961, Robert Kennedy dictated four pages of personal notes reflecting his contemporaneous thoughts on the situation in the Dominican Republic. A review of these notes evidences considerable concern regarding the lack of information available in Washington as to events in the Dominican Republic. The notes end with the following statement: 'The great problem now is that we don't know what to do because we don't [sic] what the situation is and this shouldn't be true, particularly when we have known that this situation was pending for some period of time' " (U. S. Congress, Senate, Select Committee to Study Governmental Operations with Respect to Intelligence Activities, *Alleged Assassination Plots Involving Foreign Leaders: An Interim Report*, 94 Cong., 1 sess. [Washington, D.C.: U. S. Government Printing Office, 1975], pp. 214-15. To gather information, in September, Kennedy sent John B. Martin, "one of the best American reporters" (Schlesinger, *Thousand Days*, p. 769), to the Dominican Republic. For a discussion of this presidential fact-finding mission, which lasted a little less than a month, see Martin, *Overtaken by Events*, pp. 64-82.

40. Schlesinger, *Thousand Days*, p. 769, speaking of Morales-Carrión.

41. Interview with John C. Hill, then U.S. consul in Ciudad Trujillo.

42. *New York Times*, 7 Aug. 1961, p. 3.

43. Organization of American States, *Informe*, p. 1.

44. Ramfis Trujillo, press conference, in *Hispanic American Report* 14, no. 6 (Aug. 1961), p. 504.

45. José Arismendi ("Petán") Trujillo, a brother of the late dictator, commanded at his Bonao fief a paramilitary force—"los Cocuyos de la Cordillera" ("the Fire Beetles of the Cordillera")—of some thousand men.

46. *Hispanic American Report* 14, no. 6 (Aug. 1961), p. 505. *El Caribe's* "pro-Communist line" was part of a "tactic of intimidation" that, beginning in January 1960, but

without great conviction, Trujillo tried out "as a cynical leverage against the United States" (Robert D. Crassweller, *Trujillo: The Life and Times of a Caribbean Dictator* [New York: Macmillan, 1966], p. 425). It was a complete failure.

47. Editorial, *New York Times*, 8 June 1961, p. 34.

48. Decree 6737 of 6 June 1961, in *Gaceta Oficial* 8579, 7 June 1961, p. 14.

49. Decree 6828 of 26 June 1961, in *Gaceta Oficial 8584*, 30 June 1961, pp. 17-18.

50. Ambassador Augusto Arango, head of the OAS subcommittee sent to the Dominican Republic, to Juan Bosch, president of the Dominican Revolutionary party, cable, 13 June 1961, in Organization of American States, *Informe*, Appendix IV, p. 47.

51. Editorial, *New York Times*, 8 June 1961, p. 34.

52. *Hispanic American Report* 14, no. 6 (Aug. 1961), p. 506.

53. Editorial, *New York Times*, 8 June 1961, p. 34.

54. *Hispanic American Report* 14, no. 7 (Sept. 1961), p. 607.

55. *New York Times*, 17 June 1961, p. 2. Ramón Castillo was secretary of the party's Puerto Rico branch; Nicolás Silfa was secretary of the New York branch. Angel Miolán was the party's secretary general. "Although the PRD sent three delegates, political responsibility for the party's actions [in the Dominican Republic] was vested primarily in Angel Miolán" (Bosch, *Crisis de la democracia*, p. 21).

56. Bosch, *Crisis de la democracia*, p. 11. Juan Bosch was one of the founders of the party, together with Angel Miolán, Enrique Cotubanama Henríquez, and the brothers Virgilio and Rafael Mainardi Reyna.

57. The PRD did not have three thousand—nor even three—members in a Dominican underground that had been virtually extinct since January 1960. Unlike the Movimiento de Liberación Dominicana, the PRD had no contacts with the underground even in 1959 when the latter existed as the Movimiento Revolucionario 14 de Junio (MR1J4). For the MR1J4, see Appendix II.

58. Martin, *Overtaken by Events*, p. 179.

59. Ibid., p. 71.

60. Schlesinger, *Thousand Days*, p. 769.

61. Ibid., p. 773.

62. Morrison, *Latin American Mission*, p. 126. By the time of Trujillo's death, Bosch had won considerable fame as a novelist, essayist, and short-story writer. His principal works include: *La Mañosa*, a novel; *Hostos el Sembrador*, an essay on the life and work of Hostos; *Camino Real* and *Muchacha de la Guaira*, short stories.

63. *Hispanic American Report* 14, no. 7 (Sept. 1961), p. 608.

64. The letter, dated 11 July, was published in *El Caribe*, 17 July, pp. 8-9. The group's Provisional Executive Committee was headed by Viriato Fiallo, president; José Antonio Fernández Caminero, vice-president; Luis Manuel Baquero, secretary general. Among its members were: Antinoe Fiallo, brother of Viriato, and two women, Asela Morel and Minetta Roques.

65. The abbreviation 1J4, and not AP1J4, which is more exact, is current in the Dominican Republic and will be used hereafter.

66. "With the period of clandestinity swept away by the deed of 30 May [Trujillo's assassination], the former *Movimiento Revolucionario 14 de Junio*, faithful to its political nature . . . rises openly to political life as the *Agrupación Política 14 de Junio* in the General Assembly convened last July in this capital, so as to begin the people's struggle, accepting the guarantees provided by the government" (Manuel Aurelio [Manolo] Tavárez Justo, speech given in the Parque Colón, Ciudad Trujillo, 16 Sept. 1961, in *El 1J4*, no. 5, 17 Sept. 1961, p. 7). For the MR1J4, as well as for a more detailed account of the first months of the new party, see Appendix II.

67. Florangel Cardenas, "La Universidad de Santo Domingo. Un trayecto difícil: De la Tiranía a la libertad" (II), *Renovación*, no. 141 (14-20 Oct. 1969), p. 8. An examination of the newspapers of the period amply supports the accuracy of this statement.

68. There were two brief exceptions—in 1945-46 and 1959—but both times, especially 1945-46, only a fraction of the students were involved. See also Appendix II.

69. Armando A. Hoepelman, student in the School of Arts and Sciences, speech given at the "Doctor Defilló" Building of the Ciudad Universitaria, Ciudad Trujillo, 13 July 1961, cited by Cardenas, "La Universidad de Santo Domingo" (II), p. 9.

70. Martin, *Overtaken by Events*, p. 81.

71. Kennedy, at a "top meeting," 28 Aug. 1961, cited by Schlesinger, *Thousand Days*, p. 771. "United States officials believe that the regime of President Joaquín Balaguer is facing an increasing danger from powerful military groups that oppose his policy of restoring political freedoms and preparing for general elections next May" (*New York Times,* 13 Sept. 1961, p. 29).

72. *New York Times*, 3 Oct. 1961.

73. Martin, *Overtaken by Events*, p. 64.

74. Schlesinger, *Thousand Days*, p. 770, referring to the meeting on 28 Aug.

75. Kennedy at the 28 August meeting, cited by Schlesinger, *Thousand Days*, p. 770.

76. Balaguer, "PROCLAMATION," 31 May 1961, in *Gaceta Oficial* 8577, 2 June 1961 (Special Edition), p. 7.

77. Balaguer, *"FUNERAL ORATION* delivered by Dr. Joaquín Balaguer, President of the Dominican Republic, at the burial service for Generalissimo Dr. Rafael L. Trujillo Molina, Benefactor of the Fatherland and Father of the New Fatherland, in the parish church of the Fair City of San Cristóbal, on the second of June in the year 1961," in ibid., p. 11.

78. Speech given before the United Nations General Assembly, 2 Oct. 1961, in *El Caribe*, 3 Oct. 1961, p. 9.

79. Press conference, 26 Oct. 1961, in *El Caribe*, 27 Oct. 1961, p. 13.

80. Press release 605, 5 Sept. 1961, in *Department of State Bulletin* 45 (July-Dec. 1961): 523.

81. See *Latin American Mission*, p. 137.

82. *New York Times*, 14 Sept. 1961, p. 10.

83. Morrison, *Latin American Mission*, pp. 137, 140. Martin's "presidential fact-finding mission" (see n. 39 above) led him to the same conclusion. See *Overtaken by Events*, p. 81.

84. "Wherever it [the OAS mission] stopped, it found the opposition wanted the sanctions maintained" (*New York Times*, 17 Sept. 1961, p. 37).

85. *New York Times*, 14 Sept. 1961, p. 10.

86. *El Caribe*, 22 Sept. 1961, p. 1, and 23 Sept. 1961, p. 1. Because the Dominican Republic has a presidential system, a majority in the cabinet is nonetheless a "minority" before the president.

87. *Hispanic American Report* 14, no. 9 (Nov. 1961), p. 795. Aware of the increasing weakness of the regime, the Dominican church was changing its previous position of support in hopes of building bridges to the "democratic" opposition.

88. Press conference, 11 Oct. 1961, in *El Caribe*, 12 Oct. 1961, p. 1.

89. See the Executive Committee's open letter (30 Sept. 1961) to Balaguer, excerpts of which were printed in *El Caribe*, 1 Oct. 1961. The complete text of the letter, published as a tract, is in the library of the Universidad Autónoma de Santo Domingo. The exile of the eleven officers was the sixth of eleven conditions laid down in the letter. For the PRD's and the 1J4's position, see n. 99 below.

90. Press conference, 11 Oct. 1961, in *El Caribe*, 12 Oct. 1961, p. 1. In its open letter of 30 Sept. the UCN demanded that the government "abolish the post of Head of the Joint Chiefs of Staff, whose current titulary [Ramfis Trujillo] will be absent from Dominican soil during the period of transition; that is, he will leave prior to the establishment of the Provisional Government, and will not return until the establishment of the Constitutional Government."

91. Editorial, *El 1J4*, no. 10 (21 Oct. 1961), p. 2.

92. *El Caribe*, 13 Oct. 1961, p. 1.

93. Martin, *Overtaken by Events*, p. 80. For an analysis of the Dominican far left of the period, see Appendix II.

94. Interview with Thomas Mann. No doubt the myth of the "twelve men" shows a very poor understanding of the insurrection against Batista, but this is beside the point. What matters here is the kind of thinking Mann reveals, for his attitude was widely shared.

95. As an apostle of democracy, Morrison was far from the best choice, at least from the Dominican point of view. As mayor of New Orleans, Morrison had received the Trujillos with "profound courtesies" (Crassweller, *Trujillo*, p. 275), a welcome further magnified by the Dominican press. Within the Dominican Republic, which he visited on various occasions, Morrison made it a point to sing Trujillo's praises (for an example, see Chapter 1, p. 22). In

April 1956 the Dominicans learned that a "park and an avenue" in New Orleans had been named for Trujillo. At the same time, Trujillo's brother Héctor was made an "honorary citizen" of the city (Máximo Lovatón Pittaluga, "Efemerides–1956," in my personal archives).

96. Morrison, *Latin American Mission*, pp. 116-17, 124-25.

97. The role of Emilio Rodríguez Demorizi during that period went well beyond the limits of a minister of education and arts. At that moment, his relations with Ramfis were especially close. In conversations with the author, the former government official emphasized again and again the Americans' obsession: "It was against the far left that the United States applied the strongest pressure, even to the point of furnishing–forcing on us–lists of 'Communists' they wanted deported." The Dominican government, of course, took full advantage of the situation; deportation and denial of entry permits struck "Communists" and "leftists" indiscriminately, "leftists" often including those to the right of center. However, Ramfis refused for a short while to deport "selected" Communists, since they were needed at home as part of his "Communist scare" tactics, which would call for a strong government–the Trujillo government–as a deterrent. (See also Appendix II).

98. Martin, *Overtaken by Events*, p. 80.

99. On 9 October, the 1J4 broke off the talks: "In view of the present historic events through which our country is passing, the establishment of a Coalition Government is impossible" (1J4: "14 JUNIO NO VA A COALICION," open letter to Balaguer, in *EL 1J4*, no. 9 [14 Oct. 1961], p. 3). At the same time the UCN held to its eleven demands as formulated in the open letter of 30 September (see n. 89 above). Only after these conditions had been met–which for the regime would have meant surrender–could substantive negotiations begin. The latter would not consider the coalition government proposed by Balaguer, but rather the establishment of a Council of State. Balaguer could be its president, but he would have to share power with six other men, to be chosen by mutual agreement (!) with the opposition. Even the PRD, the least intransigent opposition group, declared through its secretary general Angel Miolán that it "would not take part unilaterally in any negotiation proposed by the government, since to do so would wreck the unity of the Opposition, betraying the Dominican people" (Angel Miolán, press statement in *El Caribe*, 11 Oct. 1961, p. 1). *El Caribe* commented: "This unexpected decision of the Dominican Revolutionary party–whose moderate stance toward the regime had aroused suspicion among the other opposition groups–has dashed the government's most strenuous efforts to date . . . to find a path to resolving the national crisis . . . . Although the Revolutionary party is considered to be the smallest opposition group in numbers, its position regarding a Coalition Government has been closely watched by the other opposition groups because of the influence and political stature of its exiled leader, Juan Bosch" (*El Caribe*, 11 Oct. 1961, p. 1).

100. Statement (14 Nov. 1961) before the "Special Committee of the Council of the OAS considering the situation in the Dominican Republic," in *Department of State Bulletin* 45 (July-Dec. 1961): 931.

101. In early November, Ramfis Trujillo was head of the joint chiefs of staff. Major General Virgilio García Trujillo was army chief of staff. Major General Fernando A. Sánchez, Jr., a militant *trujillista*, was air force chief of staff. Ramfis's brother-in-law, Colonel Luis J. León Estévez, was head of the powerful Centro de Entrenamiento de las Fuerzas Armadas (Armed Forces Training Center). And there were others: Augustín R. Pluyer Trujillo and José García Trujillo, brigadier generals, and Major General Pedro Vetilio Trujillo Molina. Moreover, no voice beyond that of the Trujilloists was heard among the Dominican armed forces; no urge to rebel–not even the faintest wish–was felt, except perhaps deep inside, out of sight.

102. Joint communique, 27 Oct. 1961, signed by the UCN, the 1J4, and the PRD, extracts published in *El Caribe*, 27 Oct. 1961, p. 1. Like the UCN's open letter, the full text of the communiqué, published as a tract, is in the library of the Universidad Autónoma de Santo Domingo.

103. Luis M. Baquero, secretary general of the UCN, statement, 9 Nov. 1961, in the Washington *Evening Star*, 10 Nov. 1961, p. A-10. With the aim of blocking even a partial lifting of the sanctions, Viriato Fiallo, president of the UCN, and Manolo Tavárez, president of the 1J4, went to Washington (7 November). They were accompanied by the two secretaries general: Luis M. Baquero (UCN) and Leandro Guzmán Rodríguez (1J4).

104. Joint communiqué, 27 Oct. 1961, signed by the UCN, the 1J4, and the PRD.

105. Editorial, *El Caribe*, 15 Nov. 1961, p. 5. *El Caribe* followed the government line all the way.
106. Statement by the Partido Dominicano (Trujillo's official party), broadcast over the radio and reprinted in *El Caribe*, 15 Nov. 1961, p. 4.
107. Editorial, *El Caribe*, 15 Nov. 1961, p. 5.
108. Ibid.
109. Joint communiqué, 27 Oct. 1961, signed by the UCN, the 1J4, and the PRD.
110. The primary source for Ramfis' story is a series of talks with Emilio Rodríguez Demorizi and a lengthy interview with John C. Hill, at that time U.S. consul general in Ciudad Trujillo.
111. Ramfis Trujillo (July 1961) as quoted by Rodríguez Demorizi. The remarks were made in connection with Rodríguez Demorizi's delivery of a request by Miolán for permission to stage a public rally.
112. Although I was unable to obtain any of the letters written at that time by María Martínez de Trujillo to her son Ramfis, passages were quoted from memory by two men familiar with them: Hill and Rodríguez Demorizi. Their versions match point for point. According to Hill and Rodríguez Demorizi, Ramfis was the target of equally violent reproaches from nearly all members of the Trujillo clan.
113. *Hispanic American Report* 14, no. 11 (Jan. 1962), p. 992.
114. Interview with a former top official of the regime and close friend of Ramfis.
115. *Hispanic American Report* 14, no. 11 (Jan. 1962), p. 992.
116. *El Caribe*, 19 Nov. 1962, p. 7.
117. The victims were Luis Manuel Cáceres Michel, Pedro Livio Cedeño Herrera, Modesto Eugenio Díaz Quezada, Luis Salvador Estrella Sadhala, Roberto Rafael Pastoriza Espaillat, and Huascar Antonio Tejeda Pimentel.
118. *New York Times*, 20 Aug. 1961, p. 29. During the June 1959 invasion, "it was Ramfis, together with Trujillo and Johnny Abbes, who made the decision (contrary to Trujillo's practice in comparable situations) to execute systematically every prisoner who was taken alive . . . . They were massacred, . . . [and] Ramfis in person lent his hand to these savage executions" (Crassweller, *Trujillo*, pp. 365-66).
119. José Arismendi Trujillo Molina, in an interview granted to and published in *Ahora*, no. 96 (20 Feb. 1965). This was confirmed to me by Rodríguez Demorizi: "Ramfis called them. He had decided to get out, and he wanted to give the Yanks a slap in the face."
120. *El Caribe*, 16 Nov. 1961, p. 1.
121. Interview with Hill. "Once again, the highest American authorities were caught unawares" (Editorial, *New York Times*, 21 Nov. 1961, p. 38). As for the Dominican opposition, the presidents and secretaries general of the UCN and the 1J4, the two leading opposition groups, were in Washington (see n. 103 above). They were able to return only after the departure of the "Wicked Uncles."
122. Indeed, at the same time the crisis of the "Wicked Uncles" was developing, anti-Castroist forces were mounting an offensive in the OAS Council (see p. 49 below).
123. *New York Times*, 20 Nov. 1961, p. 3. "Tell Hill that we owe the failure of the *golpe* to him" (interview with Rodríguez Demorizi).
124. "On the recommendation of the United States, the Special Committee of the Organization of American States has already postponed further consideration of a proposal [made by the U.S. itself] on withdrawing the suspension of trade with the Dominican Republic in certain products" (Dean Rusk, "United States Considers Measures on Dominican Republic," press release 799, 18 Nov. [1961], in *Department of State Bulletin* 45 (July-Dec. 1961): 931.
125. *Washington Star*, 19 Nov. 1961, p. A-1.
126. "United States Considers Measures," p. 931.
127. *Washington Star*, 19 Nov. 1961, p. A-1.
128. *New York Times*, 20 Nov. 1961, p. 1.
129. Excerpt from a tract, printed in the *New York Times*, 20 Nov. 1961, p. 4.
130. Statement from the Santiago air base issued on the afternoon of 19 November, in *New York Times*, 20 Nov. 1961, p. 1.
131. Interviews with Hill and Rodríguez Demorizi.
132. Lovatón Pittaluga, "Efemerides—1961."

133. Editorial, *New York Times*, 20 Nov. 1961, p. 30.
134. Ibid., p. 3.
135. Balaguer, speech given on 23 Nov. 1961, in *El Caribe*, 24 Nov. 1961, p. 2.
136. *International Organization* 16 (1962): 256.
137. "Although neither the Soviet Union nor Cuba are mentioned in Colombia's resolution, everyone in the OAS knew its purpose was to bring Cuba's role out into the open and then decide what to do about it" (Morrison, *Latin American Mission*, p. 149).
138. William S. White, "Diplomatic Victory for U.S. End of the Trujillo Regime Is Termed Lesson for U.S. in Dealing with Evil," *Evening Star*, 22 Nov. 1961, p. A-11.
139. Editorial, *New York Times*, 21 Nov. 1961, p. 38.
140. Editorial, *New York Times*, 20 Nov. 1961, p. 30.
141. Balaguer, speech given on 19 Nov. 1961, in *El Caribe*, 20 Nov. 1961, p. 1.
142. Balaguer, speech given on 23 Nov. 1961, in *El Caribe*, 24 Nov. 1961, p. 1.
143. Ibid.
144. Balaguer, speech given on 19 Nov. 1961, in *El Caribe*, 20 Nov. 1961, p. 1.
145. Only the leading political forces will be considered here. The two Dominican Communist parties, too weak to play a major role, will be omitted. The first of these parties, the Popular Socialist party (Partido Socialista Popular or PSP), had regained only a shaky foothold in Dominican politics; the second, the Dominican Popular Movement (Movimiento Popular Dominicano or MPD), already on the scene at the time of Trujillo's death, was virtually forced out of action by the violent repression that struck in mid-October. Because of the interest raised by the "Communist question," however, the history of these two parties and their role in the political life of the nation until January 1962 will be treated separately (see Appendix II). A third group, the Partido Nacionalista Revolucionario (PNR), was just a handful of intellectuals. From its beginnings, the "party's" following consisted of two men—"Corpito" Pérez Cabral, the president, and Dato Pagán Perdomo, the secretary general—along with a few members of their families. An analysis of the PNR would boil down to a biography of Pérez Cabral and Pagán Perdomo. This would be a fruitless, if fascinating, exercise, since the PNR's political role was nil.
146. *Unión Cívica* (the party organ), no. 4 (26 Aug. 1961), p. 1.
147. *New York Times*, 15 Dec. 1961, p. 19.
148. Martin, *Overtaken by Events*, p. 71.
149. Only a brief sketch of the party is given here. For a more detailed analysis, see Appendix II.
150. Martin, *Overtaken by Events*, p. 72.
151. Robert Berrellez, "Dominicans Appear Headed to Dictatorship," *Washington Star*, 13 Dec. 1961, p. A-5.
152. Martin, *Overtaken by Events*, pp. 72, 81.
153. Bosch, *Crisis de la democracia*, p. 25.
154. Ibid., esp. chs. 2-5, and personal interviews with Bosch are the chief sources. Many conversations with a great number of prominent Dominicans strengthen my conviction that what Bosch wrote in his book on these issues—and enlarged upon in our talks— does not stem from some later reconstruction born of the political pressures of the moment, but corresponds closely to his thinking in 1961.
155. Quotes in the above paragraphs are from Bosch, *Crisis de la democracia*, pp. 17, 24, 25, 44, 47.
156. Thomas P. Whitney, "In the Wake of Trujillo," *New Republic*, 11 Dec. 1961, p. 8.
157. See *Crisis de la democracia*, pp. 40-59, and Bosch's *El Proximo paso: Dictadura con respaldo popular* (Santo Domingo: Impresora Arte y Cine, 1970), pp. 84ff.
158. Balaguer, speech given on 23 Nov. 1961, in *El Caribe*, 24 Nov. 1961, p. 2.
159. Among these, "the Dominican Bar Association led a call for a general strike against the government" (*El 1J4*, no. 16 [29 Nov. 1961], p. 3).
160. "Comunicado de los Jefes de Estado Mayor de las Fuerzas Armadas de Aire, Mar y Tierra," 22 Nov. 1961, in *El Caribe*, 23 Nov. 1961, p. 1. The rural population continued to play no role in the political life of the nation. For the PRD's position, see p. 60 below.
161. See decrees 7305 and 7309 of 22 Nov. 1961, and decree 7321 of 24 Nov. 1961 in *Gaceta Oficial* 8621, 23 Nov. 1961, pp. 26, 28-29, and *Gaceta Oficial* 8629, 22 Dec. 1961, pp. 11-12. As the vice-presidency had been abolished, the minister of the armed forces, "in

the event of a definitive vacancy in the office of President of the Republic . . . shall occupy
the Presidency of the Republic . . . for the remainder of the term" (Constitution of 2
Dec. 1960, Art. 58).

162. *New York Times*, 29 Nov. 1961, p. 1.
163. Whitney, "In the Wake of Trujillo," p. 8.
164. Editorial, *New York Times*, 12 Dec. 1961, p. 42.
165. *New York Times*, 29 Nov. 1961, p. 26.
166. *Hispanic American Report* 14, no. 12 (Feb. 1962), p. 1096.
167. Whitney, "In the Wake of Trujillo", p. 8.
168. Out of the flood of decrees and laws, of particular importance were: (1) Law
5674 of 23 Nov. 1961, "which changes the name of the Capital City of the Dominican
Republic to Santo Domingo" (*Gaceta Oficial* 8621, 23 Nov. 1961, pp. 5-6; (2) Law 5785
of 4 Jan. 1962, "which confiscates and declares state property all the assets, bank accounts,
stocks and bonds that were the property of Rafael L. Trujillo Molina, his sons, his wife,
his mother and his other relations" (*Gaceta Oficial* 8632 bis, 4 Jan. 1962, pp. 14-16). For
more information see especially these issues of the *Gaceta Oficial*: 8621 (23 Nov. 1961);
8622 (30 Nov. 1961); 8624 (1 Dec. 1961); 8627 (16 Dec. 1961); 8629 (22 Dec. 1961);
8632 bis (4 Jan. 1962); 8633 (5 Jan. 1962); 8633 bis (7 Jan. 1962); 8634 (8 Jan. 1962);
8637 bis (12 Jan. 1962).
169. Whitney, "In the Wake of Trujillo," p. 8.
170. *New York Times*, 5 Dec. 1961, pp. 1, 10.
171. *Evening Star*, 5 Dec. 1961, p. 10.
172. Interviews with Hill and Morales-Carrión.
173. "Dominican Republic: Revolution Aborted," *Time*, 8 Dec. 1961, p. 36.
174. "U.S. Expresses Concern over Events in Dominican Republic," State Department statement of 1 Dec. 1961, in *Department of State Bulletin* 45 (July-Dec. 1961): 1003.
175. *Evening Star*, 1 Dec. 1961, p. A-1. "One man shouted to United States correspondents: 'Why did you bring those boats? To defend assassins? Yankees go home!' Some
echoed this and shouted, 'Get the Yankees' " (ibid.). This and similar episodes were reported by American newsmen.
176. "The opposition leaders . . . blamed the United States, which has deployed a naval
task group off the Dominican coast, for supporting President Balaguer and the military
against a solution 'supported by a majority of the Dominican people.' 'This is a historic
error that will affect not only the future of this country, but all America. The people are
being pushed toward extremist solutions,' said Dr. Fiallo, the 66-year-old physician who is
president of the National Civic Union" (*New York Times*, 1 Dec. 1961, p. 16). Finally,
"on December 15 the State Department announced for the first time the withdrawal of the
Second Fleet 'some ten days' previously" (*Hispanic American Report* 14, no. 12 [Feb.
1962], p. 1097).
177. Editorial, *New York Times*, 12 Dec. 1961, p. 42.
178. On 21 November "the sanctions subcommittee [of the OAS] had returned to the
Dominican Republic for its third and last investigating mission." It spent only five days in
the country, "and therefore played no part in the December negotiations" (Slater, *OAS and
United States*, p. 200). The committee subsequently showed "admirable" discretion. Having
gone "to investigate whether President Balaguer's government remains a threat to the peace
and security of the hemisphere" (*Evening Star*, 20 Nov. 1961, p. A-6), the committee "delayed publishing" its report until the crisis appeared to be over and Kennedy had come out
"supporting the lifting of sanctions." In early December, "when the resistance of the armed
forces was at its peak, Dr. Fiallo sent a telegram to the Sanctions Committee requesting
'its urgent presence.' " But his request was met with a rebuff. "The Latin American States
were not prepared to go quite that far in stretching the non-intervention doctrine, and the
United States feared that the presence of the OAS would limit its freedom of maneuver in
the delicate negotiations" (Slater, *OAS and United States*, pp. 200-201). "One has the right
to ask: What has happened to the Organization of American States?" (Editorial, *New York
Times*, 12 Dec. 1961, p. 42). The answer? In the name of nonintervention it looked the
other way while the United States, an OAS member, went eagerly to work. And when the
U.S. had what it wanted, the OAS took a look, and nodded approval. This farce was to be
repeated again and again.
179. "Dominican Republic: Riots and Reactions," *Newsweek*, 11 Dec. 1961, p. 51.

180. Rodríguez Echavarría had been elevated to the rank of general on 18 June (decree 6794, in *Gaceta Oficial* 8582, 24 June 1961, p. 18).

181. One of them, General Andrés Rodríguez Méndez, Subsecretary of the Armed Forces, "was held to be sympathetic to the National Civic Union's proposals," and was banished to Washington on 28 November as Dominican delegate to the ineffectual Inter-American Defense Board (*New York Times*, 29 Nov. 1961, p. 26; see also decree 7348 of 28 Nov. 1961, in *Gaceta Oficial* 8625 bis, 13 Dec. 1961, p. 75). A week later his career lay in ruins. In one day he was dismissed from his post with the Inter-American Defense Board (decree 7369 of 4 Dec. 1961, in *Gaceta Oficial* 8360, 29 Dec. 1961, pp. 12-13) and cashiered from the armed forces (decrees 7367 and 7369 of 4 Dec. 1961, in *Gaceta Oficial* 8627, 16 Dec. 1961, pp. 12-14). In the wake of Rodríguez Mendez's fall "five officers resigned and accused Major [sic] General Pedro Rafael Rodríguez Echavarría . . . of attempts to lead the country to a 'military dictatorship' " (*New York Times*, 4 Dec. 1961, p. 1). One of the dissidents was Lieutenant Colonel José N. González Pomares, deputy air force chief of staff, who "headed a list of thirteen signatories to a letter issued last night that said that General Rodríguez Echavarría had 'betrayed the patriotic ideals and the thirst for liberty of our people joined together as we are in the sole inspiration of the 19th of November' " (ibid., p. 16).

182. Interview with Rodríguez Demorizi, at the time minister of education and "Balaguer's personal representative in the talks" (*New York Times*, 8 Dec. 1961, p. 24). According to Rodríguez Demorizi, Hill's role was particularly important. For the absence of the PRD and the 1J4 from the talks, see below, pp. 58-60.

183. *Washington Star*, 9 Dec. 1961, p. A-3.

184. Balaguer, press conference, 10 Dec. 1961, in *New York Times*, 11 Dec. 1961, p. 1.

185. *New York Times*, 11 Dec. 1961, p. 1.

186. Ibid., p. 2.

187. *Hispanic American Report* 14, no. 12 (Feb. 1962), p. 1095.

188. State Department statement, in *New York Times*, 12 Dec. 1961, p. 24.

189. *New York Times*, 12 Dec. 1961, p. 24.

190. Balaguer, speech given on 17 Dec. 1961, in *El Caribe*, 18 Dec. 1961, p. 1.

191. *New York Times*, 18 Dec. 1961, p. 1.

192. UCN communiqué, 19 Dec. 1961, in *Unión Cívica*, 23 Dec. 1961, p. 7.

193. Editorial, *Unión Cívica*, 23 Dec. 1961, p. 7.

194. "U.S. Welcomes Dominican Solution of Political Difficulties," White House press release (Palm Beach, Fla.), 20 Dec. 1961, *Department of State Bulletin* 46 (July-Dec. 1961): 128.

195. 1J4, "El 1J4 SIEMPRE AL LADO DEL PUEBLO. COMUNICADO AL PUEBLO DOMINICANO," 6 Dec. 1961, in *El 1J4*, no. 18 (7 Dec. 1961), p. 1.

196. 1J4 communiqué [28 or 29 Nov. 1961], in *El 1J4*, no. 16 (29 Nov. 1961), p. 1 (the capital letters are in the original text).

197. 1J4, "El 1J4 SIEMPRE AL LADO DEL PUEBLO," p. 1.

198. 1J4, "14 de Junio asume posición frente a crisis nacional. Comunicado al pueblo dominicano," 30 Dec. 1961, in *El 1J4*, no. 26 (3 Jan. 1962), p. 13.

199. 1J4, open letter to Balaguer ("14 de Junio no va a Coalición"), 9 Oct. 1961.

200. 1J4, "14 de Junio asume posición," pp. 2, 13.

201. Interview with Jaime (Jimmy) Durán Hernando, at the time a "middle-level" cadre in the 1J4.

202. *El 1J4*, no. 28 (10 Jan. 1962), p. 1.

203. 1J4, "14 de Junio asume posición," p. 13.

204. Interview with Jimmy Durán.

205. Bosch, *Crisis de la democracia*, p. 47.

206. The communiqué in which the PRD announced its position was printed in *El Caribe*, 2 Dec. 1961, p. 1.

207. Bosch, *Crisis de la democracia*, p. 53.

208. *El Caribe*, 25 Dec. 1961, p. 1.

209. Bosch, *Crisis de la democracia*, p. 77. Nicolás Silfa, a PRD leader, was expelled from the party in January 1962 for having accepted a cabinet post in Balaguer's government.

210. Interviews with Hill and Morales-Carrión (the word is Hill's).
211. Bosch, *Crisis de la democracia*, pp. 77-78.
212. Read Barreras resigned on 1 March. He was replaced by José A. Fernández Caminero, the minister of health and social security and, like Read Barreras, a leading *cívico*.
213. *New York Times*, 18 Dec. 1961, p. 13.
214. *El Caribe*, 25 Dec. 1961, p. 1. To get an idea of the UCN's predominance within the new government, these facts should be emphasized: (1) not only did the UCN hold four votes out of seven on the Council, but it was almost certain that, with Balaguer gone, a *cívico* would be chosen as the Council's seventh member; (2) Bonnelly, a *cívico*, was already in line as Balaguer's successor to the Council presidency; (3) the cabinet was almost entirely *cívico*.
215. Interview with Morales-Carrión. Amiama Tió and Imbert Barrera "came out of hiding" almost immediately after the promulgation of "total amnesty for all persons who took part in the assassination on the night of 30 May . . . and in the plot leading up to same" (Law 5683/art. 3 of 28 Nov. 1961, in *Gaceta Oficial* 8622, 30 Nov. 1961, p. 23).
216. Although he never reached the highest rungs on the Trujilloist ladder, Imbert Barrera held a series of important and lucrative posts: inspector general of the railways, supervisor general of the National Lottery, and assistant administrator of the department in charge of personal documents. In 1949, at the time of the anti-Trujillo invasion at Luperón, Imbert Barrera was governor of the province of Puerto Plata. Luperón was within his jurisdiction, and in the inevitable crackdown that followed, he distinguished himself by his "severity." In this he had the help of his brother, Major Segundo M. Imbert Barrera, the province's military commander and, in the words of a former official of the regime (who has requested anonimity) "a real animal". On 23 March 1956, Segundo Imbert Barrera was sentenced to thirty years at hard labor—one of the regime's rare acts of justice. A close friend of José Arismendi Trujillo, Antonio Imbert Barrera was, in May 1961, director of Mezcla Lista (Ready Mix), a firm whose principal shareholder was Francisco A. Martínez Alba, Trujillo's brother-in-law.

Luis Amiama Tió, who in the early 1950s held the important post of president of the administrative council of Ciudad Trujillo, devoted himself chiefly to business. His career thrived, largely because of his friendship with Danilo Trujillo, who was probably also responsible for Amiama Tió's receiving on 26 Nov. 1960 the "Estero Hondo Medal" (Estero Hondo was one of the sites where the June 1959 invaders were massacred). However, during the last years of the regime, Amiama Tió suffered a series of bad financial setbacks. He had been rescued once before from bankruptcy by Danilo when, in the spring of 1961, he found himself in a jam again, having defaulted on a loan from Danilo by failing to meet the due date (30 April 1961). All his assets were mortgaged and he was on the verge of ruin. But Trujillo's death plucked him just in time from the maw of disaster. Later, in one of its last acts, the Council of State annulled the debt, though it was flagrant, and even awarded the debtor an indemnity (Resolution 6194 of 19 Feb. 1963, in *Gaceta Oficial* 8743 bis, 8 March 1963, pp. 11-18). A "national hero" could hardly be in the debt of a Trujillo.
217. "[My] participation in the events of 30 May had been for the benefit of the ultimate salvation of the people of this nation," pompously declared Antonio Imbert Barrera, the "hero" fresh out of hiding ("Larga Odisea de Imbert y Amiama Tió," *El 1J4*, no. 18 [7 Dec. 1961], p. 12).

Strictly speaking, Imbert Barrera was the only tyrannicide to survive. Amiama Tió, like six other of the fourteen hard-core conspirators, did not take part in the attack.
218. On 25 July 1956 he became senator from the province of Sánchez Ramírez. His predecessor was also a priest, Monsignor Felipe Sanabia. Both were worthy delegates of an overly compliant Church. Suddenly unwilling to serve in a Trujilloist Congress, Pérez Sánchez resigned on 6 Dec. 1961 (*El Caribe*, 7 Dec. 1961, p. 9).
219. Nicolás Pichardo "had the good luck to be out of office when Trujillo was killed" (interview with Lovatón Pittaluga). Pichardo, a protegé and close friend of Anselmo Paulino—a "sinister man" (Crassweller, *Trujillo*, p. 227) who for a few years was the regime's number two figure—had begun a brilliant career as a *Trujillista*, notably as minister of interior and police and minister of public health. But Paulino's fall (August 1954) brought Pichardo down as well. He had to give up his political ambitions and be content to practice medicine. He was too cautious, however, to show his resentment, and as long as Trujillo was alive he never joined any conspiracy.

Eduardo Read Barreras, a lawyer who had held a number of ambassadorships during the Era, was still "high up" in the administration—president of the Supreme Court—when Trujillo was killed.

220. Bosch, *Crisis de la democracia*, p. 71. Here in outline is the career of Rafael Francisco Bonnelly: 1942: senator from the province of Santiago and secretary of the Senate; 10 July 1944: minister of interior and police; 22 January 1946: minister of labor and economy; 27 April 1948: attorney general of the Republic; 4 August 1948: secretary of state without portfolio; 26 March 1949: rector of the University of Ciudad Trujillo; 28 February 1953: minister of the presidency; 31 March 1954: minister of education and fine arts; 4 August 1954: ambassador to Spain; 30 June 1956: minister of interior; 27 September 1956: minister of justice and labor; 11 September 1957: ambassador to Venezuela (during Pérez Jiménez's dictatorship).

See the relevant issues of the *Gaceta Oficial*, and also Emilio Rodríguez Demorizi, *Cronología de Trujillo*, 2 vols. (Ciudad Trujillo: Impresora Dominicana, 1955), 10:37, 70, 121, 125, 138-39, 235, 264). Bonnelly also served his master as a lawyer. In 1948 he was state's attorney at the important trial of anti-Trujillo "criminals"—the so-called Cayo Confites case. The "criminals" were sentenced in absentia (23 September) to thirty years hard labor and damages amounting to $13,256,000. Trujillo did not fail to requite this loyal servant. On various occasions the Jefe showed his appreciation: in painful moments, when he went to Santiago to attend the burial of Bonnelly's mother, and in happier times, as when with his wife he made the trip to Santiago to act as "sponsor" at the wedding of Luisa Amalia Bonnelly Battle, Bonnelly's daughter (Rodríguez Demorizi, *Cronología de Trujillo*, 10:267).

In his memoirs, John Martin, Kennedy's imperceptive—and confused—ambassador to the Dominican Republic (1962-63), defended his friend Bonnelly as "a decent, sensible, patriotic, upright, intelligent man" whom he "liked from the outset" and who "certainly . . . was not so tainted by Trujillismo that he was unacceptable as the President of the Consejo." Martin argued that "Bonnelly was not in principle a Trujillista. He had the contempt for Trujillo's blunders, crudities, and cruelties that so many Santiago oligarchs feel" (*Overtaken by Events*, p. 89). The defense is peculiar and pitifully inadequate. The facts speak for themselves; Bonnelly's past cannot be erased with a stroke of the pen. The "contempt" Martin evokes in Bonnelly's behalf only deepens our own contempt for Bonnelly, a man who served for over fifteen years in the highest echelons of the Trujillo regime while harboring nothing but scorn for his boss.

221. Bosch, *Crisis de la democracia*, p. 19.

222. Because of his anti-Trujilloist background, Viriato Fiallo was picked to be the party's standard-bearer and its candidate for the presidential elections.

223. Eventually Bonnelly became an eternal candidate for the presidency. Overtaken by the events of the spring of 1965 (see ch. 4), this game stallion was raring to "sacrifice" himself in the presidential sweepstakes the following year, in which he brought up the rear. Undaunted, he tried again in 1970, but this time he never made it to the starting post. He was a man in search of a party; the PRD snubbed him, and the other parties already had their candidates. So Bonnelly went home to sit it out, waiting for the day when he could offer himself for some new "sacrifice."

224. Editorial, *Unión Cívica*, 28 Dec. 1961, p. 10.

225. Emilio Rodríguez Demorizi, "Journal," in my personal archives.

226. Ibid. This brief account of the events in the Parque Independencia is based chiefly on Rodríguez Demorizi's "Journal" and on *Ahora*, no. 2 (31 Jan. 1962), pp. 54-55. For another, certainly biased, version, see Pedro Rafael Rodríguez Echavarría, "Hice salir a los Trujillo," *Ahora*, no. 45 (second biweekly issue of November 1963), pp. 11-12, and also his interview granted to and published in *Ahora*, no. 242 (1 July 1968), p. 8.

227. Rodríguez Demorizi, "Journal." The official toll was four dead.

228. Martin, *Overtaken by Events*, p. 154.

229. The junta included: Huberto Bogaert, president; Antonio Imbert Barrera; Luis Amiama Tió; Armando Oscar Pacheco; Enrique R. Valdez Vidaurre, commander and navy chief of staff; Neit R. Nivar Seijas, lieutenant colonel in the army; Wilfredo Medina Natalio, major in the air force. There are clear indications that Balaguer was Rodríguez Echavarría's accomplice during these dramatic events. He undertook to find a president for the new junta. Profiting from his long-standing friendship with Huberto Bogaert, who at the time was "ill and ill-informed of the events" (interview with Rodríguez Demorizi), Balaguer sum-

moned him to the Presidential Palace. Only "at the insistance of Dr. Balaguer" (Emilio Rodríguez Demorizi, "Sintesis cronologica, 1916-1966," in Bernardo Pichardo, *Resumen de historia patria* [Santo Domingo: Postigo, 5th ed., 1969], p. 431) did Bogaert agree to become president of the junta. At the same time, Balaguer tried—and failed—to persuade a leading *cívico*, Donald Read Cabral, to take part in the junta, pointing out that "it was his duty to sacrifice himself" (Rodríguez Demorizi, "Journal").

230. Imbert Barrera and Amiama Tió later claimed that they had agreed to take part in the junta only after they were threatened, if they refused, with being thrown to the vengeance-starved Trujilloists (see their statements in *Ahora*, no. 2 [31 Jan. 1962], pp. 54-55).

231. See *Ahora*, no. 2, (31 Jan. 1962), p. 55. Rodríguez Demorizi's "Journal" gives the best account of the events of these three days (16-18 January).

232. Interview with Hill.

233. *New York Times*, 18 Jan. 1962, p. 1.

234. "As a general rule" the U.S. "does not officially offer the right of asylum" in its embassies (Martin, *Overtaken by Events*, p. 541). Imbert Barrera and Amiama Tió were "guests" of the American government ("They were lodgers," says Rodríguez Demorizi's "Journal").

235. Rodríguez Echavarría continued to cashier dissident officers even after the inauguration of the Council. It was either a "Communist plot" (8 January) or—Rodríguez Echavarría was eminently fair-minded—a "Trujilloist plot" (13 January). Meanwhile, anti-Balaguerist forces were becoming "increasingly irritated by Rodríguez Echavarría's discovery of plots invisible to any other eye" (*Hispanic American Report* 15, no. 1 [March 1962], p. 36).

236. Rodríguez Echavarría was deported, while Balaguer left of his own free will and with a safe conduct from the government. When the news came out, the 1J4 took to the streets in a series of violent demonstrations against the Council. To the *catorcistas*, the Council was guilty of releasing criminals who by all rights should have been brought to justice. The demonstrators turned their wrath against the U.S. embassy as well, which issued visas to the two exiles. San Juan, Puerto Rico, was their first stop, whence, a few weeks later, they flew on to New York.

CHAPTER 3

1. [Dominican Republic] Oficina Nacional de Estadistica, *República Dominicana en cifras* (Santo Domingo, 1968), p. 4, table 5. The percentages are figured for 7 August 1960.

2. Inter-American Development Bank, *Progreso Socio-económico en América Latina. Quinto Informe Anual–1965* (Washington, D.C., 1966), p. 597. In 1960, approximately 16,385 square miles (2,638,600 hectares) were "devoted to farm and cattle production" (Inter-American Development Bank, *Progreso Socio-económico en América Latina. Cuarto Informe Anual–1964* [Washington, D.C., 1965], p. 513). Compared with 1950, this represented an increase of slightly more than 2,173 square miles (ibid.).

3. Gifford E. Rogers, *Régimen de la tenencia de la tierra en la República Dominicana* (Santo Domingo: International Development Services, December 1962), p. 6.

4. [Dominican Republic] Oficina Nacional de Planificación, *Plataforma para el desarrollo económico y social de la República Dominicana*, 2 vols. (Santo Domingo, November 1967), 1:10. "Trujillo had forced many of the campesino squatters off the good lands and taken them over for himself . . . . As a sop to the dispossessed peasants, he instituted a much-publicized agrarian reform program which meant that they were resettled in the less fertile hillsides. Deforestation and the subsequent erosion made these lands almost worthless with the result that the subsistence existence of the campesinos declined still further throughout the 1950's" (Howard J. Wiarda, "The Aftermath of the Trujillo Dictatorship: The Emergence of a Pluralist Political System in the Dominican Republic" [Ph.D. dissertation, University of Florida, 1965], p. 309).

5. Universidad Nacional Pedro Henríquez Ureña, Instituto de Desarrollo Económico y Social, *Promoción popular dominicana* (Santo Domingo: Ediciones Culturales, 1968), p. 22. The study covers the period 1966-67. But agrarian reform after Trujillo's death was so modest that changes compared to 1960 were infinitesimal. In 1960, 44 percent of the farms were "operated by others than the owners" (Rogers, *Agrarian Reform*, p. 103).

6. Peter Dorner et al., *Agrarian Reform in the Dominican Republic: The Views of Four Consultants* (Madison, Wis.: University of Wisconsin, Land Tenure Center, 1967), p. 42. "The country has much good land, . . . good seasonal water supplies, a favorable climate" (Cyrus W. Maddox, *Some Factors Involved in Meeting the Agricultural Requirements of the Dominican People* [Santo Domingo: International Development Services, March 1964], p. 1.

7. Wiarda, "Aftermath of the Trujillo Dictatorship," pp. 306-7. Wiarda's dissertation is the best study on the Dominican Republic for the period 1962-63. On some issues I consider it weak—for instance, his treatment of the far left; and I sharply disagree with some of his conclusions. But on many aspects of Dominican political and socioeconomic reality during this period it is outstanding.

8. Ibid., p. 307.

9. "In the urban areas the population supplied with drinking water is less than 40 per cent and only 5 per cent [of the water] can be regarded as first class. In the rural area . . . 99.5 per cent are without running water"([Dominican Republic] Oficina Nacional de Planificación, *Perspectivas de la economía dominicana para el periodo 1967-1968*, 3 vols. [Santo Domingo, 1967], 2:78).

10. Wiarda, "Aftermath of the Trujillo Dictatorship," pp. 307-8. Wiarda is here referring to the "vast Southwest," but similar conditions prevailed in other parts of the country.

11. Universidad Nacional Pedro Henríquez Ureña, *Promoción popular dominicana*, p. 21. "The average Dominican is underfed." "The daily intake of between 2,500 and 3,000 calories represents an adequate Dominican allowance." Results of a study by the Dominican government, however, "show an estimated caloric intake per capita of 2,113.52 for the year of 1959. In comparison, the Foreign Agricultural Service of the United States Department of Agriculture estimates the Dominican caloric intake to be 1,950 per capita for the year 1958" (Maddox, *Agricultural Requirements of the Dominican People*, pp. 76, 11, 9).

12. [Dominican Republic], *Plataforma para el desarrollo*, p. 141.

13. [Dominican Republic], *República Dominicana en cifras*, p. 4, table 5. From 1950 to 1960, the rural population dropped from 76.2 percent to 69.7 percent of the total population. Nevertheless, because of the growth in population (a rate of increase of about 3.6 percent per year), the rural population rose, in absolute numbers, by about 500,000—from 1,627,464 to 2,124,980. In 1960, the country's five most populous cities (after Santo Domingo) were: Santiago: 85,640 (1950: 56,558); San Francisco de Macorís: 27,050 (1950: 16,083); La Romana: 22,310 (1950: 14,074); San Pedro de Macorís: 21,820 (1950: 19,875); San Juan de la Maguana: 21,630 (1950: 9,920).

14. John B. Martin, *Overtaken by Events: The Dominican Crisis from the Fall of Trujillo to the Civil War* (Garden City, N.Y.: Doubleday, 1966), p. 139. Martin served as Kennedy's ambassador to the Dominican Republic in 1962-63. His voluminous memoirs are extremely valuable, although not for the reason intended by the author. With gross intellectual arrogance Martin gives his perceptions—or rather his misperceptions—of the Dominican Republic, its key political leaders, and the events that occurred during his stay as ambassador and in the weeks immediately thereafter. Above all, he provides with incredible naiveté a wealth of information not available elsewhere on the Dominican policy of the United States and on the Dominican "right," both civilian and military.

15. [Dominican Republic], *Plataforma para el desarrollo*, p. 14.

16. [Dominican Republic], Oficina Nacional de Planificación, *Bases para el desarrollo nacional: Análisis de los problemas y perspectivas de la economía dominicana* (Santo Domingo, 1965), pp. 7-8. Significant as well was "the impossibility of free movement within the interior of the country and especially to the capital" ([Dominican Republic], Oficina Nacional de Planificación, Misión Tripartita y Misión del Instituto Latinoamericano de Planificación Económica y Social de las Naciones Unidas, "Informe interno sobre la estrategia de desarrollo y el plan bienal 67-68" [Santo Domingo, 1966], unpaginated).

17. [Dominican Republic], *Bases para el desarrollo*, pp. 7-8.

18. [Dominican Republic], "Informe interno sobre la estrategia de desarrollo."

19. [Dominican Republic], *Plataforma para el desarrollo*, pp. 16, 17.
20. Inter-American Development Bank, *Progreso Socio-económico en América Latina. Cuarto Informe Anual–1964*, pp. 509ff. The GNP has been figured at current prices. In 1960 Dominican exports totaled $174,428,655; in 1961 they fell to $143,147,623. At the same time, a sudden drop in domestic consumption (see also Chapter 1, pp. 28-29) decreased imports from $87,002,913 to $69,489,393, thus maintaining a surplus in the balance of trade ($87,405,742 in 1960; $73,658,230 in 1961) (Dominican Republic, Oficina Nacional de Estadistica, *Comercio exterior de la República Dominicana–1965* [Santo Domingo, 1967], 13:1).
21. Martin, *Overtaken by Events*, p. 88.
22. Abraham F. Lowenthal, "Foreign Aid as a Political Instrument: The Case of the Dominican Republic," *Public Policy* 14 (1965): 149.
23. Wiarda, "Aftermath of the Trujillo Dictatorship," p. 200.
24. George Walker, "Report on Activities of BCIU [Business Council for International Understanding] in the Dominican Republic–1962," in my personal archives.
25. Wiarda, "Aftermath of the Trujillo Dictatorship," pp. 151, 152.
26. Ibid., pp. 191-92.
27. Martin, *Overtaken by Events*, pp. 204, 203.
28. See ibid., pp. 451, 470.
29. Dorner et al., *Agrarian Reform in the Dominican Republic*, p. 41. For the text of the law (Law 5879), see *Gaceta Oficial* 8671, 14 June 1962, pp. 3-23.
30. Martin, *Overtaken by Events*, p. 114. "Though the Council's plans had called for the resettlement of no less than 2,500 campesino families on new lands before its mandate expired, the government came nowhere near this goal. By the end of its term [February 1963] . . . a total of only 822 new landowners had been settled" (Wiarda, "Aftermath of the Trujillo Dictatorship," p. 333).
31. *New York Times*, 27 Jan. 1962, pp. 2, 1.
32. *Hispanic American Report* (May 1962), p. 230.
33. *Hispanic American Report* (Nov. 1962), p. 810.
34. Martin, *Overtaken by Events*, p. 242.
35. Ibid.
36. Ibid., p. 8. The most recent law banning all Communist activity had been promulgated by Balaguer on 14 July 1961 (Law 5576, in *Gaceta Oficial* 8587, 20 July 1961, pp. 26-29). The law remained in force under the Council.
37. *Gaceta Oficial* 8640, 26 Feb. 1962, pp. 9-11.
38. Martin, *Overtaken by Events*, p. 100.
39. Ibid., p. 100. The parties, even the UCN, protested the deportations. Although the UCN was the government party, it could not forget that general elections would be held in a few months, and looked after its public image. Nevertheless, the Council did a very good job, as Martin implied (despite the contradiction) when, commenting on the parties' attitude on this issue, he explained that they were seeking "the votes of the deportees' relatives"– a waste of time for a few dozen votes. Martin eventually acknowledged the Council's zeal, particularly that of Councilmen Imbert Barrera and Amiama Tió. Discussing the period following the missile crisis, he notes that "they [Imbert Barrera and Amiama Tió] were busy . . . deporting Castro/Communists" and that "the deportations took an uglier turn– not only Castro/Communists themselves but also their lawyers. Then Spaniards. Then others" (ibid., pp. 99, 247). In all, the Council deported several hundred persons, including a few dozen Trujilloists; the rest allegedly "Castro/Communists" or at least "leftists." In addition, some exiles were still barred from returning to the country.
40. Ibid., p. 100.
41. Here only a general outline will be given. We will return to many of the problems introduced here later in this chapter, and especially in Chapter 4. For the far left before February 1962, see Appendix II.
42. On 26 January 1962 the first "active" member of the "old guard," Tulio Hostilio Arvelo Delgado, entered the country. He had tried twice before (on 24 Dec. 1961 and on 8 Jan. 1962), only to be immediately deported (interview with Arvelo Delgado). Little by little, under the Council, the members of the party's Central Committee trickled back to Santo Domingo, most of them clandestinely. But two members of the Central Committee–

Pedro Mir and Félix Servio Ducoudray—were unable to return until Bosch's accession to the presidency (27 Feb. 1963).

43. FOUPSA (later FOUPSA-CESITRADO) was the first labor federation created (17 Sept. 1961) after Trujillo's death. Throughout the period 1962-65, FOUPSA-CESITRADO was one of the three "giants" of the Dominican labor movement, along with the National Federation of Free Workers (Confederación Nacional de Trabajadores Libres or CONATRAL) and the Autonomous Federation of Christian Unions (Confederación Autónoma de Sindicatos Cristianos or CASC). For a detailed account of Dominican labor during these years, see Howard J. Wiarda, "The Development of the Labor Movement in the Dominican Republic," *Inter-American Economic Affairs* 20, no. 1 (Summer 1966), pp. 41-63.

44. Interview with Tulio Arvelo.

45. *El Popular* saw the "forced resignation" of Sánchez Cordoba as a "capitulation by FOUPSA's leaders" to "official subsidies and the promise of imperialist dollars" (*El Popular*, no. 6 [18 May 1962], p. 7). In 1962 the Dominican far left lost control of the labor movement. FOUPSA, the most "leftist" of the big labor federations, lost much of its influence to both CONATRAL ("created, supported, and financed by the U.S." [Wiarda, "Development of the Labor Movement," p. 57]) and CASC, which was at the time closely linked with the Partido Revolucionario Social Cristiano. The far left lost control of what was left of FOUPSA, when, in September 1962, FOUPSA merged with the Federation of Dominican Workers (Central Sindical de Trabajadores Dominicanos or CESITRADO). The new organization—FOUPSA-CESITRADO—became the "worker arm" of the PRD. The 1J4 maintained a fairly strong influence within a number of unions, but these were, on the whole, of minor importance.

46. Interviews with José Israel Cuello, Asdrúbal Domínguez, and Félix Servio Ducoudray.

47. Interview with Asdrúbal Domínguez.

48. Movimiento Popular Dominicano (Comisión Política), *Documentos del primer pre-Congreso del partido de la clase obrera* (Santo Domingo: n.p., 30 Sept. 1965), p. 23.

49. Andrés Ramos Peguero, quoted in interview by Cayetano Rodríguez.

50. Interview with Cayetano Rodríguez. During this period, López Molina and Ramos Peguero were the "real heads of the party. The other members of the Central Committee were only an Advisory Committee" (interview with Cayetano Rodríguez).

51. Movimiento Revolucionario 20-10, "Que nuestra sangre caiga sobre el Consejo de Estado," tract [early May 1962], in my personal archives.

52. *El Popular*, no. 88 (21 June 1966), p. 18.

53. MPD, *Documentos*, p. 23.

54. After his arrest, Ramos Peguero ceased to play a role in the MPD, and López Molina became the party's only *caudillo*. Released in 1965, during the civil war, Ramos Peguero became the leader of a small ultraleftist group and was killed by the police in 1973.

55. Interview with Cayetano Rodríguez. As we shall see in Chapter 4, during the Triumvirate the military strength of the MPD was nonexistent.

56. Martin, *Overtaken by Events*, p. 308.

57. Though it is impossible to determine how much each party benefited from this shift in allegiance, it is certain that the PRD penetrated in force into the rural areas and the 1J4's growth was restricted to the cities. The reasons are: (1) the influence with the rural population of a clergy violently hostile to the 1J4's "Castro/Communism"; (2) the police made it virtually impossible for the 1J4 activists to propagandize among the peasants; (3) the 1J4's message was too radical for a peasantry just emerging from the long night of Trujilloism; (4) the 1J4's language—the language of urban middle-class youths—made communication difficult.

58. 1J4 (Grupo Anti-Transformista), "La Revolución dominicana, el partido proletario y el 14 de Junio: Tesis revolucionaria en defensa de la clase obrera y contra el transformismo" (Santo Domingo, 6 July 1966), p. 13.

59. Interview with Jimmy Durán, CEC member.

60. Interview with Norge Botello, CEC member.

61. 1J4 (Grupo Anti-Transformista), "La Revolución dominicana," p. 14.

62. Interviews with Emma Tavárez and Marco Rodríguez, both partisans of the *duro* faction.

63. In particular, Félix María Germán and his friends were virtually barred from the party, as confirmed by their resignations in November 1962. The *flojos* on the CEC held their seats, but a number of their partisans were denied leadership of several provincial committees. Although the *flojos* recovered some of their influence after the *duros'* failure of November to December 1962, they lost it again during the following year.

64. Interview with Rafael ("Baby") Mejía Lluberes, president of the 1J4 youth and member of the Infrastructure.

65. Interview with Jimmy Durán.

66. 1J4 (Grupo Anti-Transformista), "La Revolución dominicana," p. 14.

67. The vivid memory of the "Boschist betrayal" of November 1961 to January 1962 (see Appendix II) continued to weigh heavily in the attitude of many 1J4 leaders—the *duros,* especially—until the outbreak of the constitutionalist "countercoup" in April 1965.

68. See the 1J4's communiqué of 16 December 1962, in *El Caribe,* 18 Dec. 1962, p. 23. The PSP and the MPD took the same stance. These two parties, both outlawed, could not participate in the elections; they could have invited their supporters to vote for Bosch, but they rejected this course.

69. Interview with Jimmy Durán.

70. Martin, *Overtaken by Events,* p. 114.

71. Ibid., p. 81.

72. In 1962, out of a total budget of $125,990,087.86, more than a quarter—$33,-414,580.60—was allotted to the Ministry of the Armed Forces. An additional $11,923,064 went to the Ministry of Interior and Religion—in other words, most of it, to the National Police. In 1963, out of a budget with total expenditures of $167,287,868.06, "only" $32,849,869.55 went to the Ministry of the Armed Forces, but the sum allotted to the Ministry of Interior and Religion rose to $29,280,101.60, an increase of nearly 200 percent. For more details on the 1962 and 1963 budgets, see Law 5734 of 30 Dec. 1961 (in *Gaceta Oficial* 8632, 31 Dec. 1961, pp. 3-56) and Law 6149 of 31 Dec. 1962 (in *Gaceta Oficial* 8725, 31 Dec. 1962, pp. 3-70).

73. The armed forces totaled around 19,000 men: 3,500 in the navy, between 3,300 and 3,500 in the air force, and 12,000 in the army. To these must be added the 2,000 soldiers of the Armed Forces Training Center (Centro de Enseñanza de las Fuerzas Armadas or CEFA) and about 10,000 police. For further details, see Chapter 4.

74. The military chiefs did not belong to the *gente de primera,* but to that class of *nouveaux riches* that had taken shape under Trujillo, to the prejudice of the old families. Yet the Council's attitude cannot be explained simply by a thirst for revenge; the military chiefs posed a threat to the monopoly of power and national wealth coveted by the *cívicos.* The time would come when there would be a need for an alliance between these jackals and wolves. But for the moment the *cívicos* saw no threat to their ambitions on the side of the "populace." It was desirable, therefore, to subordinate the Trujilloist military to civil power, since that power lay in the hands of the *gente de primera.*

75. Martin, *Overtaken by Events,* pp. 118, 115.

76. Ibid., pp. 117, 118.

77. Ibid., pp. 94, 118.

78. Ibid., p. 117.

79. Wiarda, "Aftermath of the Trujillo Dictatorship," p. 100. Colonel Wessin y Wessin was the commander of CEFA, the country's most powerful military base. From 1963 to 1965, he played a crucial role in the political life of the Republic.

80. Martin, *Overtaken by Events,* pp. 141, 145, 141. See also Larman C. Wilson, "United States Military Assistance to the Dominican Republic, 1916-1967," paper delivered before the Seminar on the Dominican Republic, Center for International Affairs, Harvard University, 20 April 1967, p. 65. For an excellent survey of Kennedy's policy toward the Latin American armed forces see Willard F. Barber and C. Neale Ronning, *Internal Security and Military Power* (Columbus: Ohio State University Press, 1966).

81. Wiarda, "Aftermath of the Trujillo Dictatorship", p. 99. From February to September 1963, however—the period of the Bosch administration—the police showed an uncharacteristic lack of brutality toward the civilian population.

82. Martin, *Overtaken by Events,* p. 194.

83. Ibid., pp. 205, 230, 204, 223, 217, 223, 204-5, 213, 217, 205. The two "national

heroes" were not part of the armed forces, yet on 1 November the Council appointed them generals, effective 27 February 1963, the day the Bosch government would be inaugurated. For this episode, see Martin, *Overtaken by Events*, especially pp. 252-56.

84. Ibid., p. 681.

85. Wiarda, "Aftermath of the Trujillo Dictatorship," pp. 243, 244.

86. *El Caribe*, 2 Dec. 1961, p. 12. The communiqué is dated 29 November. See also interviews with Josefina Padilla Deschamps, a former leader of the PRSC, and Alberto Guzmán Rodríguez, a former cadre of the same party.

87. Howard J. Wiarda, ed., *Dominican Republic: Election Factbook, June 1, 1966* (Washington, D.C.: Institute for the Comparative Study of Political Systems, 1966), p. 25.

88. Interview with Josefina Padilla.

89. FRAGUA was made up of "Marxists" from the PSP and the MPD and, especially, of "Castroists" from the 1J4. In the university elections of 25 May 1962, the group won fourteen of the twenty-seven seats on the Executive Committee of the FED. But the BRUC (at the time called Bloque Democrático Revolucionario Universitario or BDRU) was a close runner-up, with twelve seats. A third group, the University Radical Revolutionary Front (Frente Universitario Radical Revolucionario or FURR), which was PRDist, won only one seat.

For a fine analysis of the student movements inside the University of Santo Domingo from 1961 to 1966, see Florangel Cardenas, "La Universidad de Santo Domingo. Un trayecto difícil: De la Tiranía a la libertad," *Renovación*, no. 140 (7-13 Oct. 1969) to no. 151 (3-9 Feb. 1970).

90. The best-known case is that of the Jesuit Marcial Silva. A chaplain at the San Isidro Air Base, Silva played an important role, during 1962, in the beginnings of the Dominican social-christian movement. Then, in 1963, he distinguished himself by his relentless plotting against the Bosch government.

91. *Hispanic American Report* 15 (July 1962): 417. Actually, there were four *cívicos* on the Council: Rafael Bonnelly, Nicolás Pichardo, José Fernández Caminero, and Donald Reid Cabral.

92. Martin, *Overtaken by Events*, p. 119.

93. Ibid., p. 267.

94. Editorial, *Unión Cívica*, 11 Dec. 1962, p. 6. "Noble and long-suffering Dominican people" became "a favorite Fiallo phrase from the summer of 1961" (Martin, *Overtaken by Events*, p. 267).

95. Martin, *Overtaken by Events*, p. 268.

96. Ibid., p. 267.

97. Ibid., p. 89.

98. Juan Bosch, *Crisis de la democracia de América en la República Dominicana*, 3d ed. (Mexico City, D.F.: Centro de Estudios y Documentación Sociales, 1965), p. 72. To the *gente de primera*, Balaguer was an upstart. He was "of humble origin, son of a Puerto Rican immigrant, and in his youth had worked in a grocery store" (ibid.).

99. After Trujillo's death, the *gente de primera*, represented by the UCN, sought to recover their monopoly of power. Late in realizing the threat from the PRD, during most of 1962 they concentrated their attacks on the *nouveaux riches* of the Era. Until 1963 and the formation of Balaguer's Reformist Party, no major political group represented the *nouveaux riches*.

100. Wiarda, "Aftermath of the Trujillo Dictatorship," pp. 252-53.

101. Martin, *Overtaken by Events*, p. 135.

102. *Hispanic American Report* 15 (Jan. 1963): 1012.

103. Whereas the leadership of the UCN was drawn from the *gente de primera*, that of the PRD consisted of *gente de segunda*. Among the PRD leaders Máximo Lovatón Pittaluga, scion of a *de primera* family, was "very much an exception" (interview with Ivelisse Prats-Ramírez de Pérez).

104. Wiarda, "Aftermath of the Trujillo Dictatorship," p. 315.

105. Martin, *Overtaken by Events*, p. 179.

106. Norman Gall, "Ferment in the Caribbean," *New Leader*, 10 June 1963, p. 8. In an "orthodox" electoral campaign in the Dominican Republic the candidate left the capital

only rarely to swing through the country's major cities. He arrived in state ("cavalcades of big cars") and was given a lavish reception by the local notables. He greeted his admirers in the city's best hotel, delivered a "historic" speech in the main square, and, after a party at the local club *de primera* and a good night's sleep, departed.

107. Martin, *Overtaken by Events*, p. 267.

108. Gall, "Ferment in the Caribbean," p. 8.

109. For the PRD as an "organization of exiles"—in contrast to the UCN and the 1J4—see Chapter 2, pp. 38-39.

110. Bosch, never a brilliant student, dropped out of school in the third year of the *bachillerato*. So he didn't even have a bachelor's degree.

111. Bosch, speech, in *El Caribe*, 14 Nov. 1962, p. 11.

112. Cited by Bosch, *Crisis de la democracia*, p. 86. Bosch notes: "To explain to the young of the Party how they ought to express themselves to the masses, I held up the example of a gentleman . . . *de primera* loaded with [university] degrees who in his radio speeches often used the expression 'eso entraña una traición a la ética revolucionaria' ['that entails a betrayal of revolutionary ethics']. I drew their attention to the fact that the word 'entraña' to the people meant 'animal intestines,' which they called 'mondongo'; that the word 'ética' meant nothing to the masses, and that had somebody from that sector of society considered it, it was with the meaning 'consumptive,' which it had in certain areas. So, the phrase 'eso entraña una traición a la ética revolucionaria' was taken by the people to mean this gibberish: 'that animal intestines betrayal of the revolutionary consumptive.' To the people, of course, this was Greek" (ibid.).

113. Ibid., p. 87.

114. Ibid., pp. 87-89. "I never preached harmony with the *tutumpotes*; what I preached was that we forget about the poor *caliés* and devote ourselves to solving the problems of the people. But I always pointed out to the people who their real enemies were: not Petán [Trujillo] or Ramfis—already out of the country—but that clique which had always exploited the Dominican masses, whether under Santana, Heureaux, or Trujillo" ("Declaraciones exclusivas de Juan Bosch sobre los problemas nacionales," Bosch's interview with Eduardo Sánchez Cabral in *Ahora*, no. 91, 16 January 1965, p. 16). For the origins of the term "tutumpote" see Bruno Rosario Candelier, "Connotaciones Socio-semánticas de 'Tutumpote' e 'Hijo de Machepa' " (*Eme Eme Estudios Dominicanos* [Santiago, D.R.] 4, no. 23 [March-April 1976], pp. 3-14).

115. Bosch, *Crisis de la democracia*, pp. 88, 89, 81. "The phrase 'hijo de Machepa' ['child of Machepa'] is relatively old in Santo Domingo. It dates back at least to the time of the Haitian domination [1822-44]. It appears that it was used to designate the children of a very poor Santo Domingan woman named Josefa Pérez, alias Machepa, and by extension the children of the poor and the poor themselves were then called 'children of Machepa' " (Frank R. Moya Pons, letter to the author, Santo Domingo, 11 May 1972). See also Rosario Candelier, "Connotaciones Socio-semánticas."

116. Martin, *Overtaken by Events*, p. 284.

117. The article appeared in *La Nación*, 12 December 1962, p. 5.

118. *Hispanic American Report* 15 (Feb. 1963): 1112.

119. *El Caribe*, 14 Dec. 1962, p. 1.

120. "Declaración del Episcopado Dominicano," 15 Dec. 1962. The text appeared in *El Caribe*, 16 Dec. 1962, p. 1.

121. Bosch, *Crisis de la democracia*, p. 117.

122. *Unión Cívica*, 11 Dec. 1962, p. 7.

123. *Unión Cívica*, 13 Dec. 1962, p. 1.

124. Ibid.

125. Quoted by Martin, *Overtaken by Events*, p. 268.

126. Martin, *Overtaken by Events*, p. 268.

127. Ibid.

128. "Juan versus Láutico: El Debate del año," *Ahora*, no. 24, 1st biweekly issue of Jan. 1963, p. 13.

129. Bill Fritts, "Juan Bosch y sus amigos," *Sarasota Herald Tribune*, reprinted in *Ahora*, no. 45 (2d biweekly issue of Nov. 1963), p. 18-C.

130. Wiarda, "Aftermath of the Trujillo Dictatorship," p. 112.

131. See articles 3 and 22 of the "Bosch" constitution of 29 April 1963.

132. Cited by Martin, *Overtaken by Events*, p. 327.

133. See Articles 22, 23, and 24 of the constitution of 29 April 1963. For an overall picture of the economic content of the constitution, see Articles 13 to 34.

134. Article 66/1. Even foreigners benefited from the spirit of the new constitution: "The deportation or expulsion of any foreigner from Dominican territory will be effected only in virtue of a judgment pronounced by a competent tribunal upon fulfillment of the legal formalities and procedures" (Article 66/2).

135. Still worse, the constitution legitimized "opposition directed towards protection of those human rights sanctioned above [Articles 58-80], not excluding the other rights established by this Constitution and others of the same nature or that may result from the sovereignty of the people and of the democratic regime" (Article 81).

136. See Articles 43, 48/2, and 49.

137. See Articles 42 and 46.

138. [Catholic Church, Conferencia del Episcopado de la República Dominicana] "Declaración del Episcopado de la República Dominicana sobre la Constitución de la República," 25 April 1963, in *Documentos de la Conferencia del Episcopado de la República Dominicana, 1955-1969* (Santo Domingo: Imprenta Amigo del Hogar, 1969), p. 94. The new constitution threatened the "stability of the family" all the more in that it sanctioned "the absolute equality of rights for husband and wife, including in economic matters" (Article 46).

139. "The Concordat is a bilateral treaty and there was never any mention of disregarding it" (Juan Bosch, "Why I Was Overthrown," *New Leader*, 14 Oct. 1963, p. 4).

140. [Catholic Church], "Declaración del Episcopado," p. 94. The bishops also condemned the constitution for its alleged ignorance of "the historical, particular, Catholic reality of the Dominican people" (ibid.). Yet one of the primary aspects of that reality was the widespread cohabitation.

141. Wiarda, "Aftermath of the Trujillo Dictatorship," p. 108.

142. Bosch, quoted by Wiarda, "Aftermath of the Trujillo Dictatorship," p. 226.

143. Decree 9/art. 2 of 4 March 1963 (in *Gaceta Oficial* 8743, 7 March 1963, pp. 18-33), cut the salaries of more than 300 high officials in the government and the diplomatic corps. The savings realized amounted to $107,185 a month ($6,250 for the Dominican embassy in Washington). Article 1 of the same decree (ibid., pp. 10-18) wiped out 150 "soft jobs" (again in the government and the diplomatic corps), a savings to the Dominican Treasury of $75,740 a month. Decree 102 (articles 1 and 2) of 3 April 1963 (*Gaceta Oficial* 8750, 3 April 1963, pp. 11-31) further cut jobs and salaries.

144. *Hispanic American Report* 16, no. 3 (May 1963), p. 258. On 26 February, the day before he acceded to the presidency, Bosch signed a notarial document in which he declared that, for his term of office, "he and his family would live solely on the pay he earned as a public official" (*El Caribe*, 27 February 1963, p. 1).

145. Wiarda, "Aftermath of the Trujillo Dictatorship," p. 192.

146. Martin, *Overtaken by Events*, p. 716.

147. Bosch, quoted by Theodore Draper, "Bosch and Communism," *New Leader*, 14 Oct. 1963, p. 10.

148. Article 73 of the constitution of 29 April 1963.

149. Bosch, speech, 16 July 1963, in *El Caribe*, 17 July 1963, p. 1.

150. Martin, *Overtaken by Events*, p. 531. Article 20 of the constitution of 29 April 1963 denied public officials the right to strike.

151. "¿Resucitará FENEPIA?", *Ahora*, no. 69 (10 Aug. 1964), p. 47.

152. Martin, *Overtaken by Events*, p. 457. It was not by means of police clubs, a method dear to the government before his and to those that followed, that Bosch "destroyed FENEPIA." For a brief analysis of Bosch's fight against FENEPIA, see "¿Resucitará FENEPIA?" *Ahora*, no. 69 (10 Aug. 1964), pp. 47-48, and Miguel San José, "Cuando Bosch le cantó el Requiem a la huelga la sabía fracasada de antemano," *Ahora*, no. 33 (2d biweekly issue of May 1963), pp. 21-22. See also Wiarda, "Aftermath of the Trujillo Dictatorship," pp. 212-13.

153. Bosch himself admitted: "We had not as yet been able to launch any significant program that would give work to the unemployed" ("Why I Was Overthrown," p. 3).

154.   Alvaro Montalvo, "¿Cual sería el resultado de una ruptura entre Bosch y el PRD?,"
Ahora, no. 41 (2d biweekly issue of Sept. 1963), p. 4.
155.   Wiarda, "Aftermath of the Trujillo Dictatorship," pp. 192, 226-27.
156.   Ibid., p. 316. For an analysis of the errors of the Bosch government in the area of
land reform, see Rogers, *Agrarian Reform*, pp. 140-44.
157.   The law, which set "ceiling prices for sugar and molasses sold abroad," stipulat-
ed:
"art. 1:   The Ministry of Industry and Commerce, through the Commission for the Protection of Sugar and the Promotion of Sugar Cane, shall set the average price
f.o.b. in Dominican ports for all the sugar and all the molasses produced in the
country for sale abroad during the current year.
"art. 2:   The ceiling prices for sugar, free of duty, shall be set at RD$5.82,5 per 100
pounds, and for molasses at RD$0.12,85 per gallon.
"art. 3:   A duty shall be levied accruing to the State, consisting of a sum equal to the difference between the ceiling prices set in the above article for sugar and molasses
and the average annual price for these same products sold abroad . . . .
"art. 4:   The revenues collected from the duty levied by this law shall be distributed as
follows:
—75 per cent . . . for social works, according to these priorities: construction of
communities in the sugar-cane areas (sugar mill grounds), construction of aqua-
ducts and rural hospitals in those and other areas;
—15 per cent . . . for construction of local roads throughout the country;
—10 per cent . . . at the disposal of the Executive Power for the dissemination of
popular culture" (Law 23 of 7 May 1963, in *Gaceta Oficial* 8761, 15 May 1963,
pp. 10-12).
158.   Wiarda, "Aftermath of the Trujillo Dictatorship", p. 322.
159.   Ibid., pp. 223-25. See also Bosch, *Crisis de la democracia*, chap. 16.
160.   Editorial, *Listín Diario*, 25 Sept. 1963, p. 6.
161.   Martin, *Overtaken by Events*, p. 227.
162.   Ibid., p. 329.
163.   The PN accepted the labor portfolio in the person of Silvestre Alba de Moya—
a generous reward for a party that in the elections had polled less than 1 percent of the
votes. The other parties solicited by Bosch were the UCN, the ASD, the VRD, and the
PNRD.
164.   There were of course, especially in Santiago, *de primeras* who refused to join the
crusade. But they were few. And even among them, the overwhelming majority preferred
an attitude of "neutrality" to an active role in defense of constitutionality.
165.   Víctor Alba, "Historia de una iniquidad: Los Generales y los personajillos contra
el pueblo dominicano," *Panoramas*, no. 6, supplement (Mexico City, Nov.-Dec. 1963), p. 7.
Paradoxically, at the outset of Bosch's presidency the UCN tried to pin another charge on
him: "that his government was being run by the U.S. 'imperialists.' . . . The target . . . was
the intensely nationalistic Dominican people" but "the . . . charge . . . provided the UCN
with little advantage. . . .The President himself was an intense nationalist and often made
it abundantly clear that he brooked no interference from the outside" (Wiarda, "Aftermath of the Trujillo Dictatorship," p. 62).
166.   "The bond holding the [Civic] Union together came unbound, setting its
members at odds" ("Es cosa tan seria . . . que se llama política," *Ahora*, no. 38 [1st biweekly issue of Aug. 1963]. The UCN, the only "democratic" party to show some strength
at the polls, underwent a serious internal crisis. Seven of its twenty deputies had already declared themselves independent: Arevalo Cedeño Valdez (La Altagracia); Miguel A. Brito
Mata (Santiago); Gilberto Martínez M. (Duarte); Rodolfo R. Pichardo P. (Monte Cristi);
Juan S. Santoni Vivoni (La Romana); Carlos R. Guzmán Comprés (Espaillat); Arturo G.
Muñiz Marte (Puerto Plata). The struggle among factions tore apart what was left of the
party. The will to oust Bosch and to erase forever the consequences of 20 December 1962
was the single thread tying the divided party together.
167.   One example is Bosch's opposition to the decision of General Atila Luna Pérez,
air force chief of staff, to buy "twelve Hawker Hunter Mark VI jet fighters and other equipment from the British at a cost of about five million dollars" (Martin, *Overtaken by Events*,
p. 532). "Only to an irresponsible person could it occur that a bankrupt country, its people

dying of hunger, could afford to spend . . . millions of dollars on war planes" (Bosch, *Crisis de la democracia*, p. 190). General Luna Pérez, however, stood to lose hundreds of thousands of dollars in commissions—more than enough reason to set off a coup. For this episode, see especially Martin, *Overtaken by Events*, pp. 532-33, and Bosch, *Crisis de la democracia*, p. 190.

168. The phrase comes from Peter Nehemkis, *Latin America: Myth and Reality*, 2d ed. rev. (New York: Mentor, 1966), p. 118.

169. Monsignor Hugo E. Polanco Brito, bishop of Santiago, speech delivered in Santiago, 11 Aug. 1963, in *Listín Diario*, 14 Aug. 1963, p. 7.

170. Monsignor Polanco Brito, speech delivered in Santiago, 21 July 1963, in *El Caribe*, 25 July 1963, p. 1. "This was an obvious reference to Bosch who, with his white hair, was often referred to as 'the lamb' " (Wiarda, "The Changing Political Orientation of the Catholic Church in the Dominican Republic," *A Journal of Church and State* 7, no. 2 [1965], pp. 238-254).

171. [Catholic Church] "Declaración del Episcopado Dominicano dirigida a la autoridad pública, dirigentes políticos, laborales y patronales con reflexiones sobre la situación socio-política del país," 31 July 1963, in *Documentos de la Conferencia del Episcopado de la República Dominicana*, p. 97.

172. Monsignor Polanco Brito, speech, delivered 11 Aug. 1963.

173. The Papal Nuncio, Monsignor Emanuele Clarizio, took a more moderate stand. He was a critic of the Bosch regime, but apparently he opposed the bishops' irresponsible attitude (to no avail).

174. Interview with Dr. Ivelisse Prats-Ramírez de Pérez, PRD leader and dean of the School of Humanities at the University of Santo Domingo.

175. It is worth reflecting on one of the bitterest accusations hurled at Bosch by a rabid Miolanista: "The Party's activists and PRDistas in general ought not to forget how the doors of the Presidential Palace as well as those of most of the Ministries and State Enterprises were closed to them. The Party had asked its committees throughout the land to send lists of the activists and comrades most in need of jobs. Those lists were sent by the Party to the President's office where they were pigeonholed" (Roberto Frias, *Origen de las diferencias entre Juan Bosch y Angel Miolán* [Santo Domingo: n.p., 1966], p. 16). Two conceptions collided here: the idea that the state ought to serve the winning party, and the idea that the state ought to serve the people. Hence the charge that "Bosch turned his back on the Party." (ibid.).

176. Although Bosch's *caudillismo* was tempered by a number of extenuating circumstances, it was nonetheless real.

177. Declaration by the provincial bodies of the PRSC at the meeting of the party's National Directorate, 4 August 1963, in *Listín Diario*, 5 Aug. 1963, p. 12.

178. Interview with Alberto Guzmán Rodríguez.

179. The *duro* (or, as it was then called, "*revolucionario*") faction "abstained from taking part in the elections and withdrew its candidates" (*Listín Diario*, 2 Sept. 1963, p. 1). Thus, the party's National Executive Committee (Comité Ejecutivo Nacional) was made up wholly of *flojos*: Carlino González Batista, the party's president; Alfonso Moreno Martínez, first vice-president; Guido d'Alessandro, second vice-president; Leonel Rodríguez Rib, secretary general; and five other *flojos*, including Josefina Padilla, the Social Christians' 1962 candidate for president of the Republic. Of the two chief leaders of the *duros*, Caonabo Javier Castillo was expelled from the National Directorate, and Antonio Rosario was summoned before the party's disciplinary tribunal, which was dominated by the *flojos*. But the coup d'état took place, rekindling the struggle between the two factions.

180. *Hispanic American Report* 15, no. 12 (Feb. 1963), p. 1112.

181. Wiarda, ed., *Dominican Republic*, p. 40.

182. Jerome Slater, *Intervention and Negotiation: The United States and the Dominican Revolution* (New York: Harper & Row, 1970), p. 11.

183. *Washington Post*, 10 Jan. 1963.

184. Lowenthal, "Foreign Aid," p. 151; Slater, *Intervention and Negotiation*, p. 11.

185. Bosch, *Crisis de la democracia*, pp. 156-57. Bosch admitted: "Dealing with me wasn't easy—I'm aware of that—because I was highly sensitive to everything affecting Dominican sovereignty" (ibid., p. 155).

186. Bonnelly, quoted by Martin, *Overtaken by Events*, p. 93.

187.   Martin, *Overtaken by Events*, p. 280. For an excellent analysis of Martin's personality, see Slater, *Intervention and Negotiation*, pp. 59-63.
188.   Martin, *Overtaken by Events*, pp. 308-309. When president of Guatemala (1945-51), Arévalo had offered help to Juan Bosch and other Dominican exiles in their struggle against Trujillo. Thus it would have been indeed an "aberration" had Bosch failed to invite Arévalo. Washington's reaction is indicative of the intolerance of the Kennedy administration.
189.   Wiarda, "Aftermath of the Trujillo Dictatorship," p. 403.
190.   For Bosch's ambivalent view of the Alliance for Progress, see the discussion in his *Crisis de la democracia*, pp. 140-59.
191.   "The official United States position was that we welcomed European aid in Latin America. . . . But at the same time the Overseas deal meant that the generators and everything else needed for the dams would be bought in Europe—sales which should have been ours" (Martin, *Overtaken by Events*, p. 370). For the text of the contract, see "Resolución no. 2 del Congreso Nacional, que aprueba el contrato suscrito entre el Gobierno Dominicano y la Overseas Industrial Construction Ltd para la construcción de diversas obras," 15 March 1963, in *Gaceta Oficial* 8744, 17 March 1963, pp. 5-18.
192.   For this affair, see especially "Resolución no. 5 del Congreso Nacional, que revoca la aprobación dada al contrato celebrado entre el Estado Dominicano y Thomas A. Pappas and Associates, para la construcción y operación de una refinería petrolera," 28 March 1963, in *Gaceta Oficial* 8750, 3 April 1963, pp. 3-6.
193.   See Martin, *Overtaken by Events*, pp. 353, 355.
194.   They were all the more "provoked" inasmuch as the constitution decreed that "only Dominican citizens have the right to acquire landed property." Possible exceptions were provided for—"according to law" and "whenever by so doing it suited the national interest"—but only for buying land "in urban areas" (Article 25).
195.   *Overtaken by Events*, p. 415. Of the OAS, Bosch said: "At the moment, the OAS is unresponsive to the needs of the hemisphere. It had some success in the past, but today it is not a suitable instrument for resolving the continent's conflicts. The OAS lacks popular support in Latin America, and lacking popular support it lacks the political vigor necessary to an organization of its kind" ("La OEA no tiene respaldo popular—afirma Bosch," interview granted Santiago Estrella Veloz, in *Ahora*, no. 36 [1st biweekly issue of July 1963], p. 14).
196.   Martin, *Overtaken by Events*, pp. 357-58, 465, 201.
197.   Ibid., pp. 389, 481, 505, 504.
198.   Interview with Arturo Morales-Carrión.
199.   Interview with a high official in the State Department.
200.   Slater, *Intervention and Negotiation*, p. 13.
201.   Williams to Martin, cited by Martin, *Overtaken by Events*, p. 389.
202.   Martin, *Overtaken by Events*, p. 451. In fact, the Bosch government received very limited aid from the United States. Cole Blasier states: "All or almost all AID loans and grants for fiscal year 1963 were committed before Bosch became president and the account had a negative balance for fiscal year 1964. AID records made available to me show only a $3.5 million loan for housing under the Social Progress Fund signed on February 28, 1963, and the authorization of a $4.8 million loan in fiscal year 1964 to complete a prior Food for Peace Agreement." (*The Hovering Giant: U.S. Responses to Revolutionary Change in Latin America* [Pittsburgh: University of Pittsburgh Press, 1976], p. 303, n. 26).
203.   In his memoirs, Martin relates a conversation he had with Bosch on the afternoon of 24 September:

"I said, 'We have talked several times about bringing a carrier in and taking you aboard for lunch, Mr. President' [this was a method used often in 1962 to underscore U.S. support for the Consejo].
Bosch said, 'Could we do that now?'
'We might, though I don't know how much time we have—it's late.'
Bosch thought a minute. Then he said, 'Could you get them please?'
I said, 'If you want a carrier, I'll ask for an alert on it.'
'Yes, I would be very grateful.'
'But I'll have to ask you this now—do you want Marines to land?'
He said, 'No.' " (*Overtaken by Events*, p. 565.)

Bosch asserts that he rejected Martin's offer (interview). With or without Bosch's approval, however, Martin undoubtedly asked the State Department to send in a carrier.

204. Martin, *Overtaken by Events*, p. 565. Martin had told Bosch to "call a special session of Congress. Tell them, first, to enact something like our Smith Act. Second, tell Congress to stop travel to Cuba . . . . Third, tell them to enact a law permitting deportations" (ibid., p. 562).

205. Ibid., p. 570.

206. Ibid., pp. 329, 344, 330. Martin adds that "the alternatives were probably as bad or worse" (ibid., p. 330), but never in the course of his memoirs does he lash out against Bonnelly, Fiallo, or even Imbert Barrera with the vehemence he reserves for Bosch.

207. Ibid., pp. 504, 505. Cass is quoted by Martin on p. 504.

208. Wiarda, "Aftermath of the Trujillo Dictatorship," p. 408.

209. Ibid., p. 298.

210. Ibid.

211. Editorial, "¡Buenos días, señor Presidente!" *El 1J4*, no. 85 (1 March 1963), p. 2.

212. Editorial, *El Popular*, no. 20 (10 Dec. 1962), p. 2.

213. PSP (CC), "¡No votar!" 8 Dec. 1962, ibid., p. 6.

214. "¡Buenos días, señor Presidente!"

215. *El Popular*, no. 25 (30 March 1963), p. 2.

216. Interview with Asdrúbal Domínguez.

217. *El Popular*, no. 25 (30 March 1963), p. 11. For the Latin American far left, Betancourt was a symbol of evil. He hid the true nature of his regime under the guise of social reform. But in fact he was a servant of U.S. imperialism and an implacable foe of those who desired social justice and independence. He was doubly dangerous: his semblance of reform and populist jargon "put to sleep" the masses, giving them a false hope for the future.

218. "Many PSP sympathizers are delighted about that party's coming out of hiding, but . . . they are not concealing their fear at a possible trap being laid . . . when the list of the names of its members is sent to the Electoral Tribunal on requesting the PSP's admittance" (Fernández-Peix, "Se comenta," *Ahora*, no. 35 [2d biweekly issue of June 1963], p. 30).

219. Interview with José Israel Cuello.

220. MPD, *Documentos*, pp. 25-26.

221. Ibid., pp. 26, 27.

222. The MPDistas have claimed: "Our efforts at organization in the countryside were hampered by the military repression maintained by the reaction during the Bosch regime" (ibid., p. 26). In fact, like its far-leftist "brothers," the MPD completely neglected the countryside and concentrated its activity in the cities, especially the capital.

223. 1J4 (Grupo Anti-Transformista), "La Revolución dominicana," p. 13.

224. Ibid.

225. Interviews with Emma Tavárez and Marco Rodríguez.

226. Interview with Emilio Cordero Michel, CEC member.

227. Interview with Norge Botello, CEC member.

228. Interview with Jimmy Durán, CEC member.

229. Emilio Cordero Michel, letter, in my personal archives.

230. The *flojos* had no long-term strategy. They regarded armed insurrection as impossible, yet they also rejected the idea of elections. They were caught in a vicious circle from which they had not yet found a way out and which could only weaken their position vis-à-vis the *duros*.

231. Interview with Fafa Taveras, CEC member.

232. Emilio Cordero Michel, letter, in my personal achives.

233. Interview with Emma Tavárez and Marco Rodríguez.

234. Interviews with *catorcista* leaders. The Cuban position doubtless corresponds to what at the time was Castroist strategy for Latin America. But the *duro* leaders of the 1J4 bear their share of responsibility. Eager to increase their audience among the Cubans and to destroy the "competition" of the MPD (see Chapter 4), the *duros* fed Havana false information as to the party's strength. This was the same tactic that certain PSP leaders used with the Soviets (interview with José Israel Cuello), but its effectiveness depends more than anything else on the "victims' " wish to be duped.

235. Fidelio Despradel, Juan Miguel Román, Roberto Duvergé, and Luis Genao Espaillat. Their adversaries called them "smart boys."
236. Interview with Emma Tavárez and Marco Rodríguez.
237. Interview with Emilio Cordero Michel.
238. Interview with Norge Botello.
239. Manolo Tavárez, the party chief, was preparing for a trip to Algeria (interview with Emma Tavárez).
240. The information in this section derives primarily from interviews with Lieutenant Lorenzo Sención Silverio, Lieutenant Ernesto González y González., Lieutenant (Ret.) Manuel Ramón García Germán, and Major Manuel A. Núñez Nogueras.
241. Interview with Lieutenant Lorenzo Sención Silverio.
242. To this list should be added a handful of officers at the San Isidro Air Base and a few others scattered among various garrisons in the interior.
243. Interview with Lieutenant (Ret.) Manuel Ramón García Germán. See also *Ahora*, no. 133 (23 May 1966), p. 14.
244. Miguel A. Hernández, "¿Cumplirá Bosch? Meditaciones con motivo de la trama golpista," *Ahora*, no. 38 (1st biweekly issue of Aug. 1963), p. 15.
245. *Listín Diario*, 5 Aug. 1963, p. 1.
246. *Listín Diario*, 11 Aug. 1963, p. 1.
247. Editorial, Emisora Radio Antillana, Santo Domingo, 12 Aug. 1963, in *Listín Diario*, 15 Aug. 1963, p. 4.
248. "The stories were printed first in the United States, then reprinted in the Dominican Republic, where Bosch's enemies—who had inspired them in the first place—displayed them to the military as proof that 'even the impartial United States press' considered Bosch dangerously 'soft on Communism' " (Martin, *Overtaken by Events*, p. 455). For a stinging critique of a certain brand of American "journalism," see Bosch, *Crisis de la democracia*, pp. 150-53.
249. Martin, *Overtaken by Events*, p. 547.
250. *Listín Diario*, 22 Sept. 1963, p. 1.
251. "Several employees in shops on Calle El Conde and Avenida Mella said that they were not supporting the lock-out, but that their bosses had closed the stores without telling them, so that they had to go home" (*Listín Diario*, 21 Sept. 1963, p. 4).
252. Martin, *Overtaken by Events*, pp. 553, 548.
253. *Hispanic American Report* 16 (Nov. 1963): 871.
254. See *Listín Diario*, 23 Sept. 1963, p. 1.
255. See Wiarda, "Aftermath of the Trujillo Dictatorship," p. 296.
256. See *Gaceta Oficial* 8791, 30 Sept. 1963, pp. 5-12. The Manifesto was signed by the minister of the armed forces, the three chiefs of staff, the chief of police, and twenty other generals and colonels—including the two "national heroes," Generals Imbert Barrera and Amiama Tió.

CHAPTER 4

1. *New York Times*, 29 Sept. 1963, p. 38.
2. "Acta de Juramentación del Triunvirato," 26 September 1963, in *Gaceta Oficial* 8791, 30 Sept. 1963, p. 13.
3. Emilio de los Santos was considered a "good old man" (interview with Ivelisse Prats-Ramírez de Pérez). He came from an upper-middle-class family, well-to-do but not wealthy. Strictly speaking, he was not *de primera*, but he could be useful to them, and they readily adopted him. He was one of those rare Dominicans who, under Trujillo, had refused to add his voice to the chorus of sycophants. Despite pressure, he never joined the official party. In 1962, he was named president of the Central Electoral Committee, where he again won respect. Public opinion gave a share of the credit for the country's first free elections since 1924 to "don Emilio."

Altogether different was Manuel Enrique Tavares Espaillat. He was neither "good" nor "old." Young, rich, ambitious, he belonged to one of the most powerful *de primera* families. He was a member of the UCN and had served under the Council of State, first as minister of finance and then as president of the Industrial Development Corporation of the Dominican Republic. For Tavares Espaillat, as for many other *de primera*, Bosch's victory was an insult and a threat. Together with his fellow *cívicos*, he had battled the "demagogue." Now he was coming back to claim "his" place.

Ramón Tapia Espinal, scion of a relatively humble family, had grown up under the wing of Rafael Bonnelly, his professor, during the Era, at the University of Santo Domingo. On graduating from law school, the young Tapia had gone to work in Bonnelly's law office. During the *belle époque* of the Council, Bonnelly had him named minister: first, of industry and commerce, then of the presidency. In September 1963, as Tapia became a Triumvir, it was Bonnelly–by proxy–who took a seat in the government.

4. Decree 22/arts. 1-4 of 4 October 1963, in *Gaceta Oficial* 8792, 5 Oct. 1963, p. 20. But Luna Pérez failed to get his Hawker Hunters (see Chapter 3, note 167): Great Britain stopped the sale (John B. Martin, *Overtaken by Events: The Dominican Crisis from the Fall of Trujillo to the Civil War* [Garden City, N.Y.: Doubleday, 1966], p. 613).

5. "General Belisario Peguero Guerrero, chief of the National Police and a strong opponent of Communism and Castroism, said in an interview that 700 persons had been arrested since Wednesday [25 September] morning in Santo Domingo alone. Other estimates place the number of arrests well in excess of 1,000" (*New York Times*, 27 Sept. 1963, p. 1).

6. This description is based chiefly on the *Listín Diario* of 26, 27, and 28 Sept.1963.

7. *Washington Post*, 15 Dec. 1963. See Law 68, in *Gaceta Oficial* 8812, 30 Nov. 1963, pp. 4-5.

8. Law 6 and 8 October 1963 "prohibits the organization existence, and activities of the Communist parties and lays down further provisions" (*Gaceta Oficial* 8793, 9 Oct. 1963, pp. 17-19). Law 62 of 23 November 1963 bears on the "application of penalties for violation of the provisions which prohibit entry into the country of persons appearing on lists given to transport companies" (*Gaceta Oficial* 8811, 27 Nov. 1963, pp. 3-4). Law 144/ art. 1 of 19 February 1964 states that "any person traveling to a country behind the 'Iron Curtain,' to Communist China, or to Cuba without authorization from the Executive Power will be barred from reentering the country for a period of two years after his leaving the last of those countries" (*Gaceta Oficial* 8834, 20 Feb. 1964, p. 7).

Law 6 was aimed at the PSP and the MPD, but not at the 1J4, which was declared illegal only on 2 December 1963 (Law 77, in *Gaceta Oficial* 8813, 5 Dec. 1963, pp. 20-21). In fact, persecution of the *catorcistas* had begun on the very day of the coup, and their headquarters were sacked and closed by the police.

9. Martin, *Overtaken by Events*, p. 596.

10. General Viñas Román, armed forces minister under the Triumvirate, to Spencer King, counselor to the American embassy in Santo Domingo, cited in ibid., p. 606.

11. In this section on the guerrilla struggle of the 1J4 I have had recourse, beyond abundant written documentation, to a series of interviews. Following are the names of the leading actors interviewed and their positions as of late 1963: Fidelio Despradel, member of the 1J4's CEC and a participant in the guerrilla action of November-December 1963; Emilio Cordero Michel, member of the 1J4's CEC and a participant in the guerrilla action; Marco Rodríguez, member of the 1J4's CEC (in Cuba at the time); Jimmy Durán, member of the 1J4's CEC (in Cuba at the time); Norge Botello, member of the 1J4's CEC (in Cuba at the time); Fafa Taveras, member of the 1J4's CEC (in Cuba at the time); "Baby" Mejía Lluberes, middle-level cadre in the 1J4; María Elena Muñóz Marte, middle-level cadre in the 1J4; Carmen Josefina ("Picky") Lora Iglesias, guerrilla member of the 1J4; "Marcelo," guerrilla member of the 1J4; Emma Tavárez, middle-level cadre in the 1J4 and sister of Manolo Tavárez; Evelio Hernández Brito, middle-level cadre in the 1J4 and worker leader at the government armory at San Cristóbal; Felix Servio Ducoudray, member of the PSP's National Secretariat and CC, Narciso Isa Conde, middle-level leader in the PSP; Asdrúbal Domínguez, middle-level leader in the PSP; José Israel Cuello, middle-level leader in the PSP; Luis René Sánchez Cordova, member of the MPD's CC; Monchín Pinedo, member of the MPD's CC; Antonio (Tonito) Abreu Flores, middle-level cadre in the PRD; Ivelisse Prats-Ramírez de Pérez, middle-level cadre in the PRD; Juan Isidro Jimenes Grullón, president of the ASD; Pedro Manuel Casals Victoria, leader of the ASD and minister of finance under the Triumvirate; and Emilio de los Santos, president of the Triumvirate.

12. Leandro Guzmán, at the time secretary general of the 1J4, letter, 12 April 1965, Mexico City, D.F., in my personal archives.

13. These remarks, according to a 1971 interview with José Israel Cuello, were made to him by Fidelio Despradel. Whether the sentence has been reported with absolute accuracy after a gap of eight years is beside the point. What is certain is that fear of the Cubans' contempt was a chief motive in driving the *ultraduros*—Fidelio included—to guerrilla action.

14. Manolo Tavárez, speech, 14 June 1962, in *El Caribe,* 16 June 1962, p. 5.

The Dominican Republic is often referred to by the pre-Columbian Indian name of the island, Quisqueya ("Mother of all nations").

15. Interview with Emma Tavárez and Marco Rodríguez.

16. Interview with Emma Tavárez.

17. Polo Rodríguez often figures prominently in the pages ahead. This is because he was, during that period, the most active 1J4 leader. It was Polo, notably, who wielded real control over the Military Committee and the Infrastructure. It was Polo to whom the *ultraduros* looked as their leader. And it was Polo who led the talks with the 1J4's potential allies.

18. PSP (CC), "¡La Lucha del pueblo puede derrotar la dictadura!," Santo Domingo, 23 Nov. 1963, p. 9, in my personal archives.

19. PSP (CC), "Declaración del Comité Central del PSP," Santo Domingo, 30 Jan. 1964, pp. 3-4, in my personal archives.

20. I am thinking in particular of the last talks that took place at the Universidad Autónoma de Santo Domingo between university leaders of the PSP and certain university leaders of the 1J4 preparing to take part in the guerrilla action. Old, firm bonds of friendship united them. The PSPistas were convinced that defeat—and probably death—awaited their friends. Some of the *catorcistas* knew this, too. Yet they went, like Manolo, "fearing dishonor" (interviews with José Israel Cuello and Asdrúbal Domínguez).

21. The MPD had practically no "armed wing" left (see Chapter 3). But everything is relative. The 1J4 was so weak militarily that even the MPD's contribution could have been of use.

22. Some have asserted that López Molina went to Cevicos only after having informed General Belisario Peguero, chief of police, and having arranged with him the conditions of his arrest. Thus the whole affair was merely a shameful charade designed to hoodwink the public.

But for this author there is more truth in the view of those who see the "epic" of Cevicos not as an act of treason, but as another manifestation of the party's ultraleftist puerility and of its *vanguardismo en la insurrección*. According to this version, López Molina, faced with the impossibility of an accord with the 1J4, had wanted to steal a march on the *catorcistas* and win for the MPD a place in history as the party that started guerrilla action in the Dominican Republic—which, he hoped, would not fail to impress the Cubans.

In 1965, the official party chronicle perfunctorily explained that "in October 1963, our organization saw itself forced, because of the repression in the capital, to transfer men and arms to the mountains of Cevicos without having all the conditions necessary to take such a step. This attempt at an insurrection was a total disaster and was used by the [PSP] revisionists to discredit the method of armed struggle" (Movimiento Popular Dominicano [Comisión Política], *Documentos del primer pre-Congreso del partido de la clase obrera* [Santo Domingo: n.p., 30 September 1965], pp. 28-29).

23. For the same reason, Polo chose not to help certain young cadres of the PRD—Rafael Gamundi Cordero, for instance—who were trying to organize a PRDist column to take part in the 1J4 guerrilla action.

24. Emilio Cordero Michel, "Ningún movimiento armado aislado de las masas puede triunfar," interview with Bolívar A. Reynoso, in *¿Qué?* 1, no. 6 (1971), p. 14.

25. For Ozuna, we have only the oral testimony of Emma Tavárez and Marco Rodríguez, who claim to have read the record of his interrogation. For Leandro Guzmán, however, we have two documents: (1) "Interrogatorio practicado al nombrado José Ramón Leandro Guzmán Rodríguez en relación a asuntos que le interesan a la Policía Nacional," Santo Domingo, D.N., 8 November 1963, and (2) "Interrogatorio adicional al ingeniero Leandro Guzmán Rodríguez en relación a asuntos que le interesan a la Policía Nacional," Santo Domingo, D.N., 11 November 1963. Both documents have recently been published in

a special issue of *Ahora* on occasion of the tenth anniversary of the guerrilla action (*Ahora*, no. 524 [26 Nov. 1973], pp. 50-53).

26. Interview with Ivelisse Prats-Ramírez de Pérez.
27. Interview with Emma Tavárez.
28. Interview with Josefina Lora Iglesias.
29. *El 1J4*, 5 Dec. 1963, p. 1. In each front, alongside the commander, there was a "political adviser."
30. Cordero Michel, "Ningún movimiento armado," p. 14.
31. Ibid.
32. Ibid.
33. Interview with María Elena Muñóz Marte.
34. Interview with Marco Rodríguez.
35. By around 15 December, five of the six fronts had ceased to exist. For the sixth and last front, see pp. 113-14 below.
36. Todemann, "fully aware that he was selling them [the *catoicistas*] unusable arms, urged them to take to the hills" (statement by Juan José Matos Rivera, a 1J4 leader who took part in the guerrilla action, in *El Caribe*, 26 Jan. 1965, p. 10). No one doubts that Todemann betrayed the 1J4. Many assert that he was a government agent, though we have no proof.
   The 1J4's other contacts at the San Cristóbal arsenal were much less important. Their job above all was to get munitions for the party. Almost all of them were arrested after the coup (interview with Evelio Hernández).
37. Cordero Michel, "Ningún movimiento armado," p. 14. Cordero Michel was the front's "political adviser."
38. One pilot, Lieutenant Hugo Víctor Manuel Román, chose to flee in his plane to Puerto Rico rather than take part in the air operations against the guerrillas.
39. Interview with Fidelio Despradel, in ¿*Qué*? 1, no. 4 (1971), p. 15. Despradel was the front's commander, but the presence of Manolo Tavárez, the guerrilla action's supreme commander, reduced him automatically to second in command.
40. Another version supported by some former guerrillas contends that Fidelio, fearing for his life, deserted the guerrilla action. Whatever the truth, Fidelio was captured and lived; of his three companions, only *El Guajiro* was killed.
41. Cordero Michel, "Ningún movimiento armado," p. 15. Five guerrillas refused to surrender and left the group. It proved a lucky decision: they are among the few survivors of the front.
42. The episode is described by Cordero Michel—the sole survivor—in his interview in ¿*Qué*? ("Ningún movimiento armado," p. 15). Richer in details is the letter he sent a few weeks after his arrest to the editor of the *Listín Diario*, who chose not to publish it. A copy of the letter is in my personal archives.
43. Interviews with Emilio de los Santos, Juan Isidro Jimenes Grullón, and Pedro Manuel Casals Victoria. Emilio de los Santos took part in the meeting.
44. Interview with Marco Rodríguez.
45. Manolo Tavárez and Polo Rodríguez had been killed in the guerrilla action. In Cuba were the four "exiles" of 13 September 1963 (Norge Botello, Jimmy Durán, Fafa Taveras, Hugo Toyos) and Marco Rodríguez, who a few days before the insurrection had been sent to Havana to inform the Cubans of the 1J4's plans. The six leaders jailed in Santo Domingo were Leandro Guzmán and Daniel Ozuna, arrested on 6 November, and Emilio Cordero Michel, Fidelio Despradel, Luis Genao Espaillat, and Juan Miguel Román, captured during the guerrilla action.
46. Cordero Michel, "Ningún movimiento armado," p. 15.
47. See in particular Theodore Draper, *The Dominican Revolt: A Case Study in American Policy* (New York: Commentary, 1968), p. 8.
48. Of the motives for recognition that Martin names, the first two are by far the most important.
49. Martin, *Overtaken by Events,* pp. 722, 613, 611. "At first, the mild U.S. pressures focused on ways to return to constitutional rule, although not, let it be noted, to Bosch" (Jerome Slater, *Intervention and Negotiation: The United States and the Dominican Revolution* [New York: Harper & Row, 1970], p. 16). " 'I take it we don't want Bosch back,' " Kennedy told Martin on 3 October 1963. " 'No, Mr. President.' 'Why not?' 'Be-

cause he isn't a President' " (Martin, *Overtaken by Events*, p. 601). In fact, the American government's "First Position" required "in exchange for recognition: Free political activity for non-Communist parties; restoration of some semblance of constitutionality by the appointment of Casasnovas [Casasnovas Garrido, president of the Senate] to head the Triumvirate; reconstitution of the Cabinet to include PRDistas; removal of Wessin and Luna [Pérez] ; honesty and efficiency in running the former Trujillo properties; social and economic reforms in accordance with the *Alianza*. We hoped for a presidential election in one year and on a new Constitution later" (ibid., p. 600). "On October 24, a month after the golpe, we cabled the Second Position to the Embassy for action. This scenario abandoned entirely the idea of constitutionality and nearly abandoned the idea of getting rid of the military golpistas" (ibid., p. 611). "And so on—we kept falling back to a Third Position, then a revised Third Position, then a Fourth Position, then a revised Fourth Position—it was all so complex we had to keep a flow sheet" (ibid., p. 612).

50. Martin, *Overtaken by Events*, p. 620.

51. Ibid., pp. 629-30. "I called Dungan and told him we must delay recognition no longer. Dungan agreed and said he would call George Ball. Early next morning—it was December 10, a Tuesday—Ed Martin [assistant secretary of state for inter-American affairs] called a meeting. He said that at George Ball's request he had drafted a paper recommending recognition of both Honduras [a coup had taken place there on 3 October] and the Dominican Republic by next Monday at the latest" (ibid.).

52. Ibid., pp. 629-30, 631, italics added. For reasons we have already mentioned, the *golpistas* wanted the American "liberals" to worry. And so, for example, "the Nuncio saw Bonnelly privately and sent word strongly recommending we recognize now. Bonnelly was frightened. He said the military seemed unable to cope with the guerrillas. An Air Force pilot had defected. The Triumvirate was fast losing power and talking, as usual, of quitting. U.S. recognition was essential, he said" (ibid., p. 631).

53. Interview with Emilio de los Santos. De los Santos' assertion has been corroborated in interviews with Juan Isidro Jimenes Grullón and Pedro Manuel Casals Victoria.

54. Interview with de los Santos, who chose, however, not to disclose the officer's name. For de los Santos, the tragedy was all the more grievous since among those killed at Las Manaclas was the engineering student Jesús Antonio (Tony) Barreiro Río, to whom he was godfather.

55. Martin, *Overtaken by Events*, p. 11.

56. See decree 363 of 26 December 1963, in *Gaceta Oficial* 8822, 31 Dec. 1963, pp. 19-20.

57. The case of Juan Isidro Jimenes Grullón is unique. Hatred for Bosch together with political ambition had led him to conspire with the worst elements of Dominican society. Many of his friends in the party were dishonest. Of them, it is fitting to speak ironically of "abstinence." Juan Isidro, however, was not a thief.

58. By "moderates" I mean those who condemned the coup but who believed that it was necesssary to accept the fait accompli, any other path being too dangerous. They could only hope that the government would show "goodwill." This was the party of "constructive opposition," represented by a series of *de segunda* professional associations and, in the press, by the *Listín Diario* and, especially, *Ahora*.

59. Quotations are from the following, respectively: Fernández-Peix, "Se comenta," *Ahora*, no. 49 (20 Jan. 1964), p. 13; Ciriaco Landolfi, "Soluciones a la crisis nacional: La Fórmula de Santiago," *Ahora*, no. 60 (10 May 1964), p. 18; Fernández-Peix, "Se comenta," *Ahora*, no. 49 (20 Jan. 1964), p. 13; Eduardo Sánchez Cabral, "Donald Reid Cabral," *Ahora*, no. 75 (26 Sept. 1964), p. 8. At the time of the massacre, Reid Cabral was on a state visit to Israel.

60. Three of the hard-core members of the conspiracy against Trujillo—Luis S. Estrella Sadhala, Juan Tomás Díaz, and Antonio de la Maza—had found refuge with Robert Reid Cabral a few hours after Trujillo's assassination. But the facts bely the legend: "As soon as he learned of the death of the Generalissimo, [Robert Reid Cabral] demanded that we leave" (Marcelino B. Vélez Santana, deposition, 6 June 1961, in "Proceso instruido con motivo de la muerte del Generalisimo Trujillo," Servicio Judicial [Ciudad Trujillo, 8 August 1961], p. 2. Dr. Vélez Santana had been forced to accompany the three conspirators to Reid Cabral's). At that point, Antonio de la Maza "pulled out his pistol and threatened him" (Luis Salvador Estrella Sadhalá, deposition, 5 June 1961, in "Proceso instruido,"

p. 3). Further, "Juan Tomás Díaz and Antonio de la Maza held the child [one of Reid Cabral's sons] hostage and threatened him with this" (ibid.). The hiding place was subsequently uncovered by the SIM, and Robert Reid Cabral was arrested and interrogated; he was then released—a rare occurrence in those days. He commited suicide soon thereafter. His fate, however tragic, still does not make him an anti-Trujilloist hero.

61. Howard J. Wiarda, "The Aftermath of the Trujillo Dictatorship: The Emergence of a Pluralist Political System in the Dominican Republic" (Ph. D. dissertation, University of Florida, 1965), pp. 193-94.

62. The phrase is borrowed from John P. Roche, "Return of the Syndicate," *New Leader*, 14 Oct. 1963, pp. 5-8.

63. Alvaro Montalvo, "Las Cantinas Militares: ¿Siguen siendo el principio del fin?" *Ahora*, no. 60 (10 May 1964), p. 7. The military canteens date from the American military occupation (1916-24). They were abolished by Trujillo and re-established by the Council of State.

64. Wiarda, "Aftermath of the Trujillo Dictatorship," p. 177.

65. "¿Quién ganó con el cierre de las Cantinas?" *Ahora*, no. 66 (10 July 1964), p. 12. General Belisario Peguero was the chief of police, and Colonel Hernán Despradel Brache was the officer picked by Reid Cabral a few months later to take Belisario Peguero's place (see below).

66. Ibid., pp. 11-13.

67. From now on, the name Donald Reid Cabral and the term Triumvirate will be used synonymously as the Triumvirate became increasingly identified with its president. Tapia Espinal was forced to resign (8 April 1964) because of a "disagreement with a sector of the Armed Forces" ("¿Qué hubo del 'Tercer Triunviro'?" *Ahora*, no. 71 (29 Aug. 1964). Tavares Espaillat soon followed (27 June), "declaring that 'it is well known . . . that I don't feel myself cut out for the arduous work of politics' " (ibid.). The real reason behind the resignation was a "disagreement" with Reid Cabral. The vacancy left by Tapia Espinal's departure was immediately filled by Dr. Ramón Cáceres Troncoso, a *de primera* and former member of the UCN, who under the Council of State had been first an ambassador and then minister of finance. Forced into "abstinence" by Bosch's victory, he was renamed ambassador—first to the OAS, then to Rome—under the Triumvirate. No successor replaced Tavares Espaillat. By July 1964, therefore, the Triumvirate, while keeping its name, was transformed into a de facto Duumvirate, and a most peculiar one at that. For only Reid Cabral, "the No. 1 Triumvir," enjoyed "freedom of speech" (Fernández-Peix, "Se comenta," *Ahora*, no. 72 [5 Sept. 1964], p. 21). Cáceres Troncoso was the silent, ever-consenting partner. He had no "disagreements" with anyone; indeed, one hardly knew he existed.

68. "El apocalipse económico: La Verdad desnuda sobre los contrabandos. ¿Son invulnerables los contrabandistas dominicanos?" *Ahora*, no. 90 (9 Jan. 1965), p. 5.

69. Editorial, *Listín Diario*, 22 Dec. 1964, p. 6.

70. "El apocalipse económico," p. 6.

71. *Listín Diario*, 28 Dec. 1964, p. 1.

72. "El apocalipse económico", p. 5.

73. Dominican Republic, Oficina Nacional de Estadistica, *Comercio exterior de la República Dominicana: 1964* (Santo Domingo, 1966), 12:2.

74. Howard J. Wiarda, "The Development of the Labor Movement in the Dominican Republic," *Inter-American Economic Affairs* 20, no. 1 (Summer 1966), p. 62.

75. Editorial, "La Situación monetaria," *Listín Diario*, 11 April 1965, p. 6.

76. For the debt figures, see [Dominican Republic] Banco Central de la República Dominicana, *Deuda externa de la República Dominicana* (Santo Domingo, November 1966), table 5. By the "Loan Agreement" 517-K-66 of 9 February, the U.S. government agreed to lend the Dominican government, through AID, as much as $10 million (see Law 610 of 11 February 1965, in *Gaceta Oficial* 8926, 20 Feb. 1965, pp. 7-13). A week later, a new agreement was concluded regarding a million dollars in credit (see Law 625 of 20 February 1965, in *Gaceta Oficial* 8929, 28 Feb. 1965, pp. 26-45). On 22 February and 26 March, the Triumvirate ratified Loans 517-L-004 and 517-K-003, concluded with Washington on 30 November 1964 and 18 August 1964, respectively, that totaled $5.5 million (see *Resolución* 626 of 22 February 1965, in *Gaceta Oficial* 8930, 6 March 1965, pp. 3-22, and *Resolución* 678 of 26 March 1965, in *Gaceta Oficial* 8939, 8 April 1965, pp. 8-21).

77. "La Situación monetaria," p. 6.
78. Martin, *Overtaken by Events*, p. 638.
79. "Despite the budgetary allocations for the armed forces, and the items corresponding to the feeding of its members, the soldiers are poorly fed. Who is to blame for this? The string of Mess officers, whose appointment is revolving and who for the most part take on that post with the idea that it's a *jicotea* to reap profits by way of purchase commissions . . . . One has only to hear the complaints from the non-coms and the enlistees about the ill-prepared and at times unsanitary chow to be appalled.

"Another problem in many military installations is the state of deterioration of the buildings, particularly as regards sanitation. Plumbing out of order and leaks all over the place. Yet . . . no funds ever appear to recondition those quarters, or no one bothers about it . . . .

"The armed forces have a large annual budget, and these anomalies cannot be explained if not as negligence by those in charge concerning such vital aspects of military life as the proper feeding of its members and the good estate of its quarters" ("La Semana dominicana," *Ahora*, no. 99 [13 March 1965], p. 20).
80. Juan Bosch to Dr. Ramón Pina Acevedo y Martínez, letter, 27 May 1964, San Juan, Puerto Rico, in my personal archives.
81. "Otra huelga de chóferes," *Ahora*, no. 61 (20 May 1964), p. 7.
82. Fernández-Peix, "Se comenta," *Ahora*, no. 67 (20 July 1964), p. 17.
83. "Profesionales e intelectuales dominicanos," 27 February 1965, in *El Caribe*, 27 Feb. 1965, p. 1.
84. Bosch to Pina Acevedo y Martínez, 27 May 1964.
85. "La Semana dominicana," *Ahora*, no 93 (30 Jan. 1965), p. 10.
86. "As a result of the unhappy events of September 1963, the country suffered the loss of its democratic institutions, and, after the abuse of every human right, corruption, and administrative chaos, economic crisis promptly arrived." The declaration condemned, among other things, "An ill-conceived economic policy aggravated by governmental irresponsibility and corruption," which "has wrecked the most dynamic and important sectors of the nation's economy; . . . the frightening increase that has occurred in the public debt in less than a year; . . . the alarming management of the National Budget; . . . the so-called Agrarian Reform, [which] has been nothing but an instrument of political demagogy; . . . the destruction of the sugar industry, . . . brought about because of political reasons, mismanagement, and the lack of planning as to production volume, costs, and marketing of its products; . . . the government's passivity . . . in the face of the unfair competition created by contraband" ("Dominican Professionals and Intellectuals," p. 1).
87. Draper, *Dominican Revolt*, pp. 25-26.
88. *Listín Diario*, 26 Oct. 1964, p. 1. The OSPE refused to recognize the legality of the convention and continued to publish communiqués attacking the party's "Boschist" line, but its influence was virtually nil. On 28 November 1965, the adventure ended with Angel Miolán's expulsion from the party.
89. See Reformist Party communiqué in *El Caribe*, 23 July 1963, p. 9.
90. Statement by Antonio Rosario in *Listín Diario*, 1 Nov. 1964, p. 1.
91. Statement by *flojo* leaders to *El Caribe*, 18 Jan. 1965, p. 16.
92. *Listín Diario*, 21 Feb. 1965, p. 4.
93. Ibid., p. 1.
94. Article 1 of the pact. The complete text was printed in *Listín Diario*, 1 Feb. 1965, p. 4.
95. *El Caribe*, 2 Feb. 1965, p. 1.
96. Ramón Castillo had in early 1964 incorporated his PPDC into the Reformist Party. His decision was to prove judicious. On 30 May 1966, Balaguer was elected president of the Republic and Castillo was handed the portfolio of interior and police (decree 1 of 1 July 1966, in *Gaceta Oficial* 8995, 6 July 1966, p. 3).
97. Fernández-Peix, "Se comenta," *Ahora*, no. 83 (21 Nov. 1964), p. 19.
98. Fernández-Peix, "Se comenta," *Ahora*, no 90 (9 Jan. 1965), p. 8; ibid., no. 86 (12 Dec. 1964), p. 8.
99. On 26 December 1964, Severo Cabral was expelled from the UCN, after having himself named president of the party by his followers (29 November). On 11 April 1965, he

founded a new political group, the Revolutionary Action Party (Partido de Acción Revolucionaria or PAR).

100. UCN (*Comité Central Ejecutivo*) "Declaración de Bonao," in *El Caribe*, 13 Feb. 1965, p. 1. Much more than "the culmination of a long process" (UCN, statement by the Directorate, in *Listín Diario*, 15 Feb. 1965, p. 1), the rupture resulted from "a quarrel between Dr. Alcibiades Espinosa . . . and the Triumvir Reid Cabral" ("La Semana dominicana," *Ahora*, no. 96 [20 Feb. 1965], p. 10).

101. UCN (*Comité Central Ejecutivo*), statement, 26 March 1965, in *Listín Diario*, 7 April 1965, p. 1.

102. "La Semana dominicana," *Ahora*, no. 104 (17 April 1965), p. 39. On 17 January, Bonnelly had opposed Reid Cabral's possible candidacy for president of the Republic, declaring that "elections in which any of the current government leaders take part will fail to satisfy public opinion" (*El Caribe*, 18 Jan. 1965, p. 1). A few weeks later he doubled the dose, warning that "the present Dominican state is fast headed toward collapse and is proving radically unfitted for the full exercise of its fundamental duties" (*Listín Diario*, 11 April 1965, p. 4).

103. After having been deputy assistant secretary of state for inter-American affairs (1950-51), Mann had served as the deputy chief of mission at the American embassy in Athens and as counselor of embassy in Guatemala City. In 1955 he was named ambassador to El Salvador, a post he left in 1957 to become assistant secretary of state for economic affairs (1957-60), and then assistant secretary of state for inter-American affairs (1960-61). In 1961 Kennedy appointed him ambassador to Mexico.

104. Interview with Mann. For Mann, "totalitarian dictators" are those who exercise absolute and arbitrary power over the lives of their people and who regard the nation's patrimony as their personal property. "Nontotalitarian dictators" are more "responsive" to public opinion and to the needs and wants of their people. They do not attempt to rule by force and terror alone, but recognize that their regime could not be maintained for long without the support of a large sector of the population.

105. Mann, cited by Max Frankel, "Secret U.S. Report Details Policy Shift in Dominican Crisis," *New York Times,* 14 Nov. 1965, p. 32.

106. Mann, unpublished manuscript, courtesy of the author.

107. Interview with Mann.

108. Draper, *Dominican Revolt*, p. 16.

109. Martin, *Overtaken by Events*, p. 6.

110. Frankel, "Policy Shift in Dominican Crisis," p. 32.

111. Draper, *Dominican Revolt*, pp. 15-16.

112. Interview with a high official of the State Department.

113. Slater, *Intervention and Negotiation*, p. 17.

114. Marcel Niedergang, *La Révolution de Saint-Domingue* ([Paris] : Plon, 1966), p. 39.

115. Benjamin J.Ruyle, the embassy's first secretary, was the only one to show, even while supporting the Triumvirate, any human warmth and understanding in his relations with the PRD leaders. Information concerning relations between the U.S. embassy and the PRD during this period derives primarily from interviews with the PRD leaders José Rafael Molina Ureña, José Francisco Peña Gómez, Antonio Martínez Francisco, Máximo Lovatón Pittaluga, Manuel Ramón Ledesma Pérez, and Enriquillo del Rosario Ceballos.

116. Niedergang, *La Révolution de Saint-Domingue*, p. 39.

117. Frankel, "Policy Shift in Dominican Crisis," p. 32.

118. Draper, *Dominican Revolt*, p. 22.

119. Data regarding the materiel and the manpower within the various branches of the Dominican armed forces (with the exception of number and type of navy units) derive from interviews with Dominican officers, whose names will be withheld for obvious reasons. The figures refer at all times to the period of the Triumvirate and, wherever possible, to April 1965; sometimes, as in the case of the armored vehicles of the CEFA, they are approximate.

120. President Balaguer has made good that oversight. Today sailors share in keeping the peace within "mixed patrols" that prowl the streets of the capital whenever tensions are especially high. Now the navy, too, is guilty of clubbing citizens.

121.   T. D. Roberts et al., *Area Handbook for the Dominican Republic* (Washington, D.C.: American University, 1966), p. 401.

122.   Larman C. Wilson, "United States Military Assistance to the Dominican Republic, 1916-1967," paper delivered before the Seminar on the Dominican Republic, Harvard University, Center for International Affairs, 20 April 1967, p. 61.

123.   The unit's—and the camp's—official name was "Agrupamiento de Artillería" (Artillery Group). But "6½ Artillery" is the name used by the officers in the Dominican army themselves, and this is the name I prefer to use to designate both the unit and the camp. The entire zone around "Kilometer 7" of the Duarte Highway was known as the "Twenty-seventh of February Military Zone," which included the Twenty-seventh of February camp, the 6½ Artillery, and army staff headquarters.

124.   The name of the depot was generally used to designate the unit.

125.   Martin, *Overtaken by Events*, p. 118.

126.   Roberts et al., *Area Handbook*, p. 402.

127.   Martin, *Overtaken by Events*, p. 533.

128.   The number of armored vehicles given here applies to those on the base on 24 April 1965. Apparently the number remained fairly constant throughout the period of the Triumvirate.

129.   Only after the civil war did the CEFA lose its autonomy. On 4 September 1965, the provisional government ordered that "beginning on the date of this decree the military organization or body known as the Armed Forces Training Center will be incorporated into the forces of the military corps of the Nation" (decree 26, in *Gaceta Oficial* 8946, 24 Sept. 1965, p. 35).

130.   Inside the *conjunto*, opposite the CEFA, also stood the Batalla de Las Carreras Military Academy, with slightly over one hundred cadets. It was dependent on the CEFA for administrative matters (supplies, salaries, and service personnel), and on the armed forces ministry for matters of technical operation (curricula, operational rules, etc.).

131.   In an interview with the author, Morilí Holguín, a CEFA lieutenant during the Triumvirate and a Wessinist of long standing, underlined with evident relish this "generosity" of his general. He failed to realize, however, that by the same token he had accused Wessin of corruption. Where did Wessin get those "hundreds of dollars per month" which he distributed to his soldiers? His monthly salary did not exceed $700, and since he came from a modest background, he should not have had a personal fortune.

132.   Decree 428/art. 2, in *Gaceta Oficial* 8827, 25 Jan. 1964, p. 16.

133.   Throughout this section, the information often derives from interviews with Dominican officers; again, names are withheld.

134.   The degree of "Balaguerism" of these officers varied. Gutiérrez Ramírez, for instance, was considered to be "one hundred per cent" Balaguerist. Alvarez Holguín was Balaguerist mostly through Gutiérrez Ramírez's influence.

135.   See decree 320 of 12 December 1963, in *Gaceta Oficial* 8818, 21 Dec. 1963, p. 24.

136.   "La Semana dominicana," *Ahora*, no. 92 (23 Jan. 1965), p. 7.

137.   That is, General de los Santos and the navy.

138.   Law 574 in *Gaceta Oficial* 8919, 20 Jan. 1965, pp. 15-16.

139.   Colonel Despradel Brache was also given the "temporary rank of General" (Decree 2004 of 18 January 1965 in *Gaceta Oficial* 8921, 31 Jan. 1965, p. 31). We have met this officer before—as a director of the National Police Canteen Company.

140.   Law 595, in *Gaceta Oficial* 8921, 31 Jan. 1965, pp. 24-25.

141.   Law 592/art. 2 of 27 January 1965 (in *Gaceta Oficial* 8921, 31 Jan. 1965, pp. 23-24) abolished the four undersecretariats of state for the army, navy, air force, and police. The former undersecretaries were to "return to their respective corps for assignment of duties" (ibid.). Three months later, at the fall of the Triumvirate, General Hermida was still "without duties."

142.   As was customary in the Dominican Republic, with his promotion to army chief of staff Colonel Rivera Cuesta was also awarded the temporary rank of general (see Decree 2134 of 17 February 1965, in *Gaceta Oficial* 8932, 13 March 1965, p. 12).

143.   "La Semana dominicana," *Ahora*, no. 93 (30 Jan. 1965), p. 7.

144.   Law 591/art. 1, in *Gaceta Oficial* 8921, 31 Jan. 1965, pp. 24-25.

145. Viñas Román held this post until 15 September 1966, when he was retired.
146. "La Semana dominicana," *Ahora* no. 97, (27 Feb. 1965), p. 8.
147. Several authors explain the military crisis of January-February 1965 as Reid Cabral's valiant effort to cleanse the armed forces. They miss the whole point: the military purge was due only to a struggle for power inside the country, involving equally corrupt factions. For this erroneous view, see for instance Abraham Lowenthal, *The Dominican Intervention* (Cambridge, Mass.: Harvard University Press, 1972), pp. 43-44.
148. Alvaro Montalvo, "¿Qué hay de elecciones?" *Ahora*, no. 56 (30 March 1964), p. 8.
149. Guillermo Perallón, "¿Qué opina usted de las elecciones?" *Ahora*, no. 74 (19 Sept. 1964), p. 7.
150. Georgetown University, Center for Strategic Studies, *Dominican Action—1965: Intervention or Cooperation?* Special Report Series #2 (Washington, D.C.: Center for Strategic Studies, 1966), p. 3.
151. Perallón, "¿Qué opina usted de las elecciones?" p. 7.
152. Press conference, 26 February 1965, in *Listín Diario*, 27 Feb. 1965, p. 1. Reid Cabral maintained this position in the weeks that followed. Thus, on 22 April 1965, at his last press conference, his answer to a question about Bosch's and Balaguer's possible participation in the elections was that "the government has on several occasions expressed itself on that subject, and at the moment sees no reason to alter that position" (*Listín Diario*, 23 April 1965, p. 4).
153. H. Ruiz Berges, "Un comentario político," *Listín Diario*, 7 March 1965, p. 6.
154. Reid Cabral, press conference, 26 February 1965, *Listín Diario*, 27 Feb. 1965, p. 4.
155. Eduardo Sánchez Cabral, "Entrevista con Fidelio Despradel," *Ahora*, no. 75 (26 Sept. 1964), p. 7.
156. Interviews with Emma Tavárez, Marco Rodríguez, and Emilio Cordero Michel.
157. Interviews with Norge Botello, Fafa Taveras, and Jimmy Durán.
158. Besides Duvergé, J. B. Mejía, and Ramos, the CECP consisted of Emma Tavárez, Pedro Bonilla, Pin Montás, Homero Hernández Vargas, Amín Abel Hasbún, Amiama Vargas, Ivelisse Acevedo Gautier, and two or three unidentified individuals.
159. Interview with Emma Tavárez.
160. Interview with Emma Tavárez and Marco Rodríguez.
161. Interview with "Baby" Mejía Lluberes.
162. Interview with Emma Tavárez.
163. 1J4 (Grupo Anti-Transformista), "La revolución dominicana, el partido proletario y el 14 de Junio. Tesis revolucionaria en defensa de la clase obrera y contra el Transformismo," (Santo Domingo, 6 July 1966), p. 10, among my personal papers.
164. The arrival in Cuba of a new, and less sectarian, 1J4 delegate played an important part in ending the "training" of Norge Botello, Jimmy Durán, Hugo Toyos, and Fafa Taveras (interviews with Norge Botello, Jimmy Durán, and Fafa Taveras). Three members of the old CEC—Emilio Cordero Michel, Hugo Toyos, and Leandro Guzmán—returned to the Dominican Republic only after the civil war (April-September 1965) had ended. A fourth member—Marco Rodríguez—had managed to return during the summer of 1964. Perhaps because he was traumatized by the death of his brother Polo, he never took part in the meetings of the CECP, of which he was a rightful member, and ceased to play a role in the life of the 1J4.
165. Interview with Emma Tavárez. The middle-level leaders admitted to the CECP yielded their seats to the newcomers—a less than smooth transition. On 24 April 1965, the CECP consisted of Jimmy Durán, Norge Botello, Fafa Taveras, Daniel Ozuna, Fidelio Despradel, Roberto Duvergé, Juan Miguel Román, Luis Genao Espaillat, and Juan B. Mejía. In addition, two of the party's organizations—the Worker Bureau and the 1J4 University Youth (Juventud Catorcista Universitaria or JECAU) were represented, with the right to vote, on the CECP. The delegates were, most often, Pedro Bonilla for the bureau, and Pin Montás for the University Youth.
166. Interview with Norge Botello.
167. Fidelio Despradel, "Esquema de la intervención de Fidelio Despradel" (Santo Domingo, 25 March 1965), in my personal archives.

Of Juan B. Mejía, who I earlier termed a *vacilante*—sympathetic to the *flojos* but afraid to clash with the *duros*—Despradel said: "Ample theoretical ability. Rational outlook on life." Yet "at times he mistakenly adopts positions scornful of the masses" (that is, whenever he supported the *flojos!*), and is "unstable emotionally and therefore unstable politically, though not in the sense of his theoretical positions (these could not be more correct), but rather in the sense of his practical attitude towards the party's problems" ("Esquema"). Despradel ended with an "appeal to Juan B. Mejía . . . to take a strong stand against the opportunism of the right and to unite with all the Party's revolutionary sectors" (ibid.).

168. Interview with Jimmy Durán.
169. Leandro Guzmán to Antonio Vásquez, letter, 2 April 1965, Mexico City, D.F., in my personal archives.
170. Interview with Jimmy Durán.
171. Emilio Cordero Michel, letter, 6 April 1965, Mexico City, D.F., in my personal archives (although in exile, Cordero Michel kept in constant touch with the party's developments).
172. Interview with Jimmy Durán.
173. Interview with Josefina Lora Iglesias.
174. Accusations still repeated to the author, in 1970, by Fidelio Despradel.
175. Interview with Marco Rodríguez.
176. Juan Miguel Román seems to me to represent a case apart among the *supersabios*. He erred in putting his faith in Despradel, but his motives were pure.
177. Daniel Ozuna to Emilio Cordero Michel, letter, 9 April 1965, Santo Domingo, in my personal archives.
178. Emilio Cordero Michel to Daniel Ozuna, letter, 17 April 1965, Mexico City, D.F., in my personal archives.
179. Emilio Cordero Michel to Daniel Ozuna, letter, 19 April 1965, Mexico City, D.F., in my personal archives.
180. Despradel, "Esquema".
181. Daniel Ozuna to Emilio Cordero Michel, letter, 10 Feb. 1965, Santo Domingo, in my personal archives.
182. Daniel Ozuna to Emilio Cordero Michel, letter, 9 April 1965, Santo Domingo, in my personal archives.
183. Interview with Fafa Taveras.
184. Daniel Ozuna to Emilio Cordero Michel, letter, 31 March 1965, Santo Domingo, in my personal archives.
185. Interviews with "Baby" Mejía have furnished most of the information on the Military Bureau. This evidence has been verified through interviews with Marco Rodríguez, Jimmy Durán, Fafa Taveras, Emma Tavárez, and Cayetano Rodríguez. In the following section, the quotes come from "Baby" Mejía.
186. Interview with Cayetano Rodríguez. With him Irlander Selig del Monte (CC), Leopoldo Grullón Ruiz (CC) and Francisco Ramos Peguero were arrested. Other CC members, including Baldemiro Castro and Luis René Sánchez Cordova, were still in Cuba. For a brief account of the episode, see *Ahora*, no. 524 (26 Nov. 1973), p. 8.
187. MPD, *Documentos*, p. 30.
188. Interview with Max Frankel, in *New York Times*, 9 May 1965, sec. 4, p. 3.
189. Interview with Monchín Pinedo.
190. The most important of these was José Ramírez ("El Conde").
191. *Libertad*, Nov. 1964, cited in MPD, *Documentos*, p. 33.
192. *Libertad*, 9 April 1965, p. 14.
193. *Libertad*, Nov. 1964, cited in MPD, *Documentos*, p. 33.
194. Among these was Maximiliano Gómez ("El Moreno"), who very quickly assumed an important role in the life of the party. "El Moreno" became the party's chief following the civil war of 1965 and was assassinated in Brussels on 23 May 1971. His killers have yet to be identified.
195. The MPD divided its following into four categories: (1) "professional militants" (full-time party workers); (2) "militants"; (3) "organized sympathizers"; (4) "sympathizers." Only those in the first three categories were considered party members.
196. Interview with Cayetano Rodríguez.

197.　Besides a number of party documents, my principal sources for the PSP's internal struggles are interviews with the *viejo* leaders Félix Servio Ducoudray, Justino José del Orbe and Tulio Arvelo, and the *jóvenes* José Israel Cuello, Narciso Isa Conde and Asdrúbal Domínguez.

198.　Interview with José Israel Cuello.

199.　Interview with Asdrúbal Domínguez.

200.　PSP (CC), "Unámonos para rescatar las libertades" (Santo Domingo, 25 Sept. 1964), in my personal archives. "In setting forth under the Triumvirate the unhappy and mistaken proposition of an 'impartial and responsible government that would preside over elections,' the party strayed from the Marxist conception of the state and encouraged the electoral solution, which was not backed by the great masses, committing a serious tactical blunder" (Partido Comunista Dominicano [PCD], "Documento autocrítico del Comité Central del Partido Comunista Dominicano (PCD)" [Santo Domingo, 15 Oct. 1965], p. 6, in my personal archives).

201.　From now on the words *viejo* and *jóven* will carry a political meaning, distinguishing the two currents dividing the party.

202.　PCD, "Documento autocrítico del Comité Central," p. 6.

203.　PSP (CC), internal document (untitled) Santo Domingo [mid-March 1965], in my personal archives.

204.　PCD, "Documento autocrítico del Comité Central," pp. 2, 4.

205.　PSP (CC), "Manifiesto" (Santo Domingo, 16 March 1965), p. 1, in my personal archives. Even though they were a majority, the *jóvenes* still did not enjoy absolute control of the party. The Ducoudray faction retained enough influence to carry on a vigorous rearguard action. Thus they succeeded in delaying for nearly a month the publication of the "Manifiesto" which should have come out in February.

206.　PSP (Comisión de Educación y Propaganda del Comité Central), "A los Militantes," (Santo Domingo, 16 March 1965), in my personal archives.

207.　PSP (CC), "Manifiesto," pp. 3-4.

208.　"In the struggle against ultra-leftism, which regards armed insurrection as the only solution in all circumstances without taking into account the conditions necessary for its development, our Party rightly upheld the position of utilizing all methods of struggle and the proper one in each case. Despite that, in its acts, our Party neglected preparations for armed insurrection and the military training of its members" (PCD [CC], "El Partido y la insurrección de abril: Documento autocrítico del Comité Central," in *El Popular*, no. 78 [16 Aug. 1965], pp. 8-9), and it "reduced the importance of the armed method, [and] restricted its course and practical activity to nonviolent forms of struggle" (PCD, "Documento autocrítico del Comité Central," p. 7). In April 1965, the PSP could count on a Military Committee that existed in name only, on a handful of cadres with military training, and on a rifle and two or three revolvers.

209.　PCD, "Documento autocrítico del Comité Central," p. 7.

210.　It should be stressed, to prevent any misunderstanding, that the PSP had only extremely vague–and indirect–knowledge of the PRD's conspiratorial activities.

211.　PCD (CC), "El Partido y la insurrección," p. 8.

212.　Interviews with Cayetano Rodríguez, Luis René Sánchez Cordova, and Monchín Pinedo. The quotes come from Cayetano Rodríguez.

213.　"In May 1964, a number of Central Committee members who had been in jail for several months were deported. The deportation was put to advantage in order to strengthen and develop our Party's international relations. On 12 July 1964, the MPD delegation was welcomed in Peking by the Deputy Prime Minister of the People's Republic of China, Liu Nin Yi. The following day our delegation was received by the President of the Chinese Communist Party, comrade Mao Tse-tung, with whom views were exchanged on imperialism and contemporary revisionism" (MPD, *Documentos del primer pre-Congreso*, pp. 30-31). See also *Ahora*, no. 122 (7 March 1966), pp. 12-13.

214.　PCD, "Documento autocrítico del Comité Central," p. 8.

215.　Interview with Asdrúbal Domínguez. Asdrúbal explains this attitude by the doubts the *viejos* had about "Castro's ideological steadfastness."

216.　Editorial, *El Popular*, no. 19 (24 Nov. 1962), p. 2.

217.　Interview with José Israel Cuello. This hostility was to have repercussions within the university, where the *catorcistas* attempted to have the PSPistas expelled from positions of leadership inside FRAGUA. The scheme failed because of the great personal prestige of the PSP university leaders, particularly Asdrúbal Domínguez and Narciso Isa Conde. In time, an uneasy coexistence was restored within FRAGUA.

218. "Una aclaración oportuna," *El 1J4*, 31 March 1965, p. 1.

219. PCD, "Documento autocrítico del Comité Central," pp. 8-9.

220. MPD, *Documentos del primer pre-Congreso*, p. 44.

221. Ibid., p. 60.

222. Ibid., p. 29.

223. The three points analyzed above take into account, for the 1J4, only the views of the *duros*. The positions of *duros* and *flojos* were, however, very close on the first and third points.

224. Two other, lesser points of friction were the MPD's alleged "cadre snatching" at the 1J4's expense, and the communiqués through which the MPD tried to take credit for the terrorist activities of the 1J4's Military Bureau.

225. The chief sources of information for this section are interviews with the PRD leaders Juan Bosch, José Francisco Peña Gómez, José Rafael Molina Ureña, Antonio Martínez Francisco, Máximo Lovatón Pittaluga, Manuel Ramón Ledesma Pérez; with the PRD cadres Tonito Abreu Flores and Bonaparte Gautreaux Piñeyro; with Henry Molina Peña, secretary general of CASC; with Donald Reid Cabral, president of the Triumvirate (for p. 158 only); with the constitutionalist military, Lieutenant Colonel Miguel Angel Hernando Ramírez, Major Manuel Augustín Núñez, Nogueras, Lieutenant (Ret.) Manuel Ramón García Germán, Lieutenants Lorenzo Sención Silverio and Ernesto González y González, Sergeant Polonio Pierret. For the sources on the relations between the PRD and the 1J4, see note 248 below.

226. Juan Bosch to Ramón Pina Acevedo y Martínez, letter, 27 May 1964, San Juan, Puerto Rico, in my personal archives.

227. Interview with Bosch. For Fernández Domínguez see Chapter 3.

228. Fernández Domínguez intended to set off a "countercoup" on 10 October, but he lacked the means. He had only the pledge of the commander of the Fortaleza at Barahona, who, at the last minute, changed his mind.

229. For Fernández Domínguez see decree 125 of 21 October 1963, in *Gaceta Oficial* 8800, 29 Oct. 1963, p. 26. For a list of the eighteen *académicos* cashiered, see *Listín Diario*, 18 Oct. 1963, p. 5. Following are the names of some of the officers who later played an especially important role: Captain Héctor Lachapelle Díaz, commander of the cadet corps; Captain Rafael Armando Quiróz Pérez; Lieutenant Lorenzo Sención Silverio, adjutant to the director of the Military Academy; Lieutenant José René Jiménez Germán, instructing officer and officer in charge of physical education and sports; Lieutenant Ernesto González y González, instructor in charge of the official register and public relations. For simplicity, later references to these and other officers later cashiered by the Triumvirate will not take the designation "former," since during the April revolt they were reintegrated into the armed forces by the constitutionalist government.

230. One of the cashiered officers, Captain Lachapelle Díaz, became the manager of a gas station (*bomba de gasolina*) owned by his brother-in-law. The station became the habitual meeting place of the other *académicos* discharged from the armed forces.

231. A quartermaster sergeant, four sergeants (including Polonio Pierret), and two corporals.

232. He wanted notably to have Molina Ureña brought before a disciplinary board (interviews with José Rafael Molina Ureña, Máximo Lovatón Pittaluga, Manuel Ramón Ledesma Pérez, and Tonito Abreu Flores).

233. Interview with José Francisco Peña Gómez.

234. Molina Ureña belonged by right to the "revolutionary" group because of his full adhesion to the "return to constitutionality without elections." He was, however, much closer to the "moderates" by virtue of his social views and his feelings toward the 1J4.

235. It goes without saying that the "moderates" also served as a screen—for roughly the same reasons—vis-à-vis the Triumvirate and the U.S. embassy.

236. The "revolutionaries'" contacts with the Hernando Ramírez group took place in an atmosphere of absolute discretion. The Triumvirate, the U.S. embassy—and even the "well-informed" among the public—only suspected the PRD of conspiring, unsuccessfully,

with the San Cristóbal Group. The screen played a role here, too. By focusing the "enemy's" attention on what was to them a secondary front, Bosch and the "revolutionaries" were better able to hide the real plot in which they were engaged.

237.   After Balaguer's election to the presidency of the Republic, Martínez Francisco accepted the portfolio of minister of finance, breaking with the PRD and becoming a virulent detractor of Bosch. In a 1970 interview with the author, Martínez Francisco was anxious to present his conspiratorial activities in the most "subdued" light possible—understandable for a man who served in the Balaguer regime. To prove his allegations, moreover, he offered to discuss them, in the author's presence, with his former political allies Máximo Lovatón Pittaluga and Manuel Ramón Ledesma Pérez, but quickly changed his mind when Lovatón Pittaluga and Ledesma Pérez agreed to the confrontation.

238.   A Dominican officer serving abroad as a military attaché can return to his country only with the permission of his superiors.

239.   The term "countercoup" will be used throughout to underscore the nature of the constitutionalist movement, which aimed at erasing the effects of the coup of 25 September 1963 and at re-establishing the status quo ante.

240.   Besides the Ramón Mella, Juan Pablo Duarte, and Francisco del Rosario Sánchez battalions, the other army battalions counted eight hundred men only on paper. Each battalion was stationed in a province's chief town, but its forces were spread among a network of little garrisons scattered throughout the province.

241.   The plan was drawn up by three officers of the Gas Station Group—Captains Lachapelle Díaz and Quiróz Pérez, and Lieutenant Sención Silverio—and revised by Lieutenant Colonel Hernando Ramírez.

242.   The movement had adherents at other Fortalezas as well, but they were minuscule groups of no importance.

243.   The above quotations are from a letter of a constitutionalist officer to the author.

244.   The terms "center" and "periphery" are my own.

245.   Hernando Ramíre z had decided to wait until the eve of D-day to choose one of the two times. An important consideration was the fact that Monday through Friday the soldiers of the CEFA went off duty at 4:30 P.M. (11:30 A.M. on Saturday). Many of these soldiers usually went to the capital, which was less than ten miles away. The countercoup triggered, they would be trapped in the city—the "center" units' first objective. At the Sixteenth of August, the Twenty-seventh of February, and the 6½ Artillery camps, off-duty hours began at 5:00 P.M. At the Sixteenth of August Lieutenant Colonel Gutiérrez Ramírez could easily delay leave for thirty or sixty minutes, so that H-hour would find all the soldiers at the camp. This would have been more difficult at the Twenty-seventh of February and the 6½ Artillery, since the commanders of those camps were not part of the conspiracy. But in any case, the soldiers who had left those camps could easily have been "recovered" once the troops of the Sixteenth of August had occupied the city.

246.   Haina was thirteen miles from the capital, and the Enriquillo plan expected the frogmen to assume immediate control over the base. At Las Calderas the constitutionalists had a large number of partisans.

247.   The conspirators' line of reasoning was that should the CEFA attack, the air base's infantry would keep the assailants at bay, giving the planes time to take off and bomb the CEFA. Soon the "center" units would arrive at San Isidro. Wessin would be crushed. This logic already led the leaders of the conspiracy to exclude the possibility of an attack by the CEFA on the Nineteenth of November camp.

248.   In addition to the interviews noted above (see note 225), the principal source of information on the relations between the 1J4 and the Enriquillo movement is interviews with these 1J4 leaders: Norge Botello, Jimmy Durán, Fafa Taveras, Fidelio Despradel, "Baby" Mejía, Marco Rodríguez, and Emma Tavárez.

249.   1J4 (CECP), "La Unidad del pueblo. Estrategia de la reacción. El pacto. El frente. Nuestra situación. Conclusiones," confidential document intended for the party's local committees, Santo Domingo [late March or early April 1965], p. 1, in my personal archives.

250.   In the eyes of the *catorcistas*, both *duros* and *flojos*, Bosch's overthrow in 1963 was merely one episode in the struggle in Washington between the Pentagon and the State Department—divided in their means but pursuing the same end.

251. Rafael Francisco (Fafa) Taveras Rosario and Amín Abel Hasbún, "Se aproxima otro 24 de abril," *Claridad*, no. 28 (22 April 1969), p. 1. Fafa Taveras was at the time a member of the CECP. Amín Abel was president of the Federation of Dominican Students and the leader of the 1J4 University Youth.

252. Daniel Ozuna to Emilio Cordero Michel, letter, 17 Feb. 1965, Santo Domingo, in my personal archives. The PRSC "is divided into two wings: one (the 'Yuyo' [Guido d' Alessandro] faction) that at this very moment is serving the reactionary forces at home and abroad; the other [the *duros* of Antonio Rosario and Caonabo Javier] will do so at a later date" (1J4 [CECP], "La Unidad del pueblo," p. 2). "Social pistols" was the far left's pet nickname for the members of the PRSC.

253. Taveras Rosario and Abel Hasbún, "Se aproxima otro 24 de abril," p. 1.

254. Ibid., p. 2.

255. Interview with "Baby" Mejía.

256. Taveras Rosario and Abel Hasbún, "Se aproxima otro 24 de abril," p. 2 Because of his family ties, Oscar Santana was chosen by the Military Bureau to be its representative with the conspirators.

257. Ibid., p. 2.

258. Ibid. Some U.S. scholars, not too familiar with the Dominican far left, have been taken in by the fact that in its official communiqués the 1J4 asked to be included in the Pact of Rio Piedras. They have hastily concluded that the *catorcistas* favored "the immediate reinstallation" of Bosch to the presidency. They fail, however, to realize that this was a facade, similar to the one put up by the 1J4 in 1963 during the Bosch government. In both cases the 1J4 wanted to appear "moderate" in the eyes of the masses, who were clearly Boschist. In 1965 the *catorcistas* also strove to embarrass the PRD by forcing it to refuse publicly a cooperation that the 1J4 never wanted. Hence a paradox: the 1J4 asked for some form of cooperation with the PRD, but the latter refused. In secret, however, a wing of the PRD made limited overtures to the 1J4—only to be rebuffed. No wonder a superficial analysis may have confused many observers. For an example of such confusion see Lowenthal, *Dominican Intervention*, p. 56.

259. Interview with Donald Reid Cabral.

260. Frankel, "Policy Shift in Dominican Crisis," p. 32.

261. "La Semana dominicana," *Ahora*, no. 96 (20 Feb. 1965), p. 7.

262. Interview with Hernando Ramírez.

CHAPTER 5

1. These were: Lieutenant Colonel Giovanni Gutiérrez Ramírez, Major Eladio Ramírez Sánchez, Major Juan María Lora Fernández, and Captain José Aníbal Noboa Garnes.

2. Mario's, especially, was packed with conspirators. At one table sat former officers, members of the Gas Station Group, the constitutionalist elite: men like Lachapelle Díaz, Jiménez Germán, Bobadilla Ubico, Quiróz Pérez, Gerardo Brito, and Sención Silverio. At another table sat navy Captain Montes Arache and the Italian Ilio Capozzi, instructor of the frogmen. But Mario's was not the headquarters of the conspiracy. There was nothing mysterious about this gathering of constitutionalists; they were brought together, quite simply, by a shared taste for good food (interview with Lieutenant Sención Silverio).

3. A private radio station, owned by José Antonio Brea Peña, a wealthy businessman and the PRD's secretary of finances.

4. Quotes are from *Listín Diario*, 25 April 1965, p. 1 and *El Caribe*, 25 April 1965, p. 12, respectively.

5. Danilo Brugal Alfau, *Tragedia en Santo Domingo: Documentos para la historia* (Santo Domingo: Editora del Caribe, 1966), p. 13. Brugal Alfau served during the conflict as director of public relations of the anticonstitutionalist Gobierno de Reconstrucción Nacional of General Antonio Imbert Barrera. (For comments on his book, see the Bibliographic Essay.)

6. Frank R. Moya Pons, "Notes of 24 April 1965," in my personal archives.

7. Ibid.

8. U.S., Congress, Senate, Committee on the Judiciary, Subcommittee to Investigate the Administration of the Internal Security Act and Other Internal Security Laws, *Communist Threat to the United States through the Caribbean: Hearings: Testimony of Brigadier General Elías Wessin y Wessin*, 89 Cong., 1 sess., 1 October 1965 (Washington, D.C.: U.S. Government Printing Office, 1965), p. 15.

9. Interview with Colonel Pedro Bartolomé Benoit, officer at the Nineteenth of November.

10. These pages (163-64) are based primarily on seven conversations with Colonel Benoit in the spring of 1969. Two other officers of the air base, who later confirmed Benoit's version, asked not to be named.

11. Interviews with Wessin and Benoit. See also U.S., Congress, *Testimony of Brigadier General Elías Wessin y Wessin*.

12. U.S., Congress, *Testimony of Brigadier General Elías Wessin y Wessin*, p. 156.

13. This was, except for a nuance or two, the argument made at the meeting that afternoon by the Wessinist officers of the air force.

14. Interview with Benoit.

15. At the time of his testimony (October 1965), Wessin was enjoying a gilded exile in Miami, after being deported by the provisional government of Héctor García Godoy (see also Chapter 10, n. 106).

16. Not to be overlooked is the fact that Wessin was testifying before representatives of a foreign power, however "friendly." Imagine an American general, or former general, giving testimony before the Dominican Senate!

17. U.S., Congress, *Testimony of Brigadier General Elías Wessin y Wessin*, p. 157. Roman L. Hruska (Rep.-Neb.) was one of the two senators (the other was Thomas J. Dodd, Dem.-Conn.) taking Wessin's testimony.

18. Ibid.

19. Ibid., p. 156.

20. Neither Senator Dodd nor Senator Hruska, so alert when it came to spotting a "Castro/Communist" plot—especially one of Sino-Soviet origin!—noticed this gaping contradiction in Wessin's story.

21. On 27 April, during the "loyalist" offensive against the capital, General Montás Guerrero gave stunning proof of this "solidarity" (see Chapter 9).

22. The paragraph that follows is based primarily on an interview with Reid Cabral.

23. Georgetown University, Center for Strategic Studies, *Dominican Action–1965: Intervention or Cooperation?* Special Report Series # 2 (Washington, D.C.: Center for Strategic Studies, 1966), p. 15.

24. Interview with Reid Cabral.

25. Georgetown University, Center for Strategic Studies, *Dominican Action–1965*, p. 13.

26. *Listín Diario*, 25 April 1965, p. 14. Reid Cabral's speech aimed at giving the impression that the government was dealing from a position of strength: only two camps were in rebellion, the country was calm, and an ultimatum had been issued to the rebels. The majority were convinced. Yet on others the speech had the opposite effect. They believed the revolt—if one ever existed—had been crushed. Now they learned, from the head of state himself, that not only had there in fact been a rebellion, but that the rebels were still holding out.

27. Interview with Sención Silverio.

28. This line of reasoning and the various positions adopted were reconstructed from long talks with officers who, on 24 April, found themselves in the "center" camps.

29. In addition to the sources mentioned above, talks with Colonel Benoit have furnished information used here.

30. Antonio Llano Montes, *Santo Domingo: Barricadas de odio* (México, D.F.: Editores Mexicanos Unidos, 1966), p. 109.

31. These are the figures cited by *El Caribe*, 25 April 1965, p. 5. Despite numerous interviews, I have been unable to determine the actual number of tanks and combat tanks at the Presidential Palace on the twenty-fourth. There were, in any case, no less than seven and no more than twelve.

CHAPTER 6

1. The only troops then involved were four to five hundred soldiers from the Francisco del Rosario Sánchez Battalion. The rebels, who knew their adversaries, considered such a force sufficient to occupy the center of the city—their immediate objective—and thus left the bulk of their troops in reserve at the camps. The latter were close enough so that, if needed, reinforcements could be brought into the capital without delay. This proved unnecessary, however, and not until a few hours later did the bulk of the rebel forces enter the city, leaving small units behind in the camps (interviews with Lieutenant Colonel Hernando Ramírez, and Lieutenants Sención Silverio and García Germán).

2. *Hymn to the Constitutionalist Revolution* by Aníbal de Peña.

3. Interviews with Sención Silverio and Hernando Ramírez.

4. Pérez y Pérez was chosen because before entering the air force he had long served in the army. Therefore he was thought to have a number of friends among the rebel officers, which would lighten his task as negotiator.

5. Interview with Reid Cabral.

6. *El Caribe*, 26 April 1965, p. 9.

7. U.S., Congress, Senate, "The Situation in the Dominican Republic," speech delivered on the floor of the Senate on 15 September 1965, *Congressional Record*, 89 Cong., 1 sess., III, pt. 18 (Washington, D.C.: U.S. Government Printing Office, 1965), p. 23856.

8. Even worse, when Heywood returned to the capital, rather than being sent immediately after Admiral Rivera Caminero, navy chief of staff, he was "assigned to the [Presidential] Palace on orders of the Embassy" (Georgetown University, Center for Strategic Studies, *Dominican Action—1965. Intervention or Cooperation?* Special Report Series #2 [Washington, D.C.: Center for Strategic Studies, 1966], p. 16). No doubt this decision was due largely to excessive optimism about Rivera Caminero's "loyalty." The situation in Washington was no more coherent. President Johnson was at Camp David for the weekend. Jack Hood Vaughn, the assistant secretary of state for inter-American affairs, was in Cuernavaca, Mexico, attending a conference of Western Hemisphere intellectuals. Robert B. Sayre, Jr., the deputy assistant secretary of state for inter-American affairs, and William Bowdler, White House staff specialist for Latin America, had only recently assumed their posts. At the CIA the new director, Vice Admiral (Ret.) William F. Raborn, Jr., had just been appointed and would not take over his post until 28 April.

9. John B. Martin, *Overtaken by Events: The Dominican Crisis from the Fall of Trujillo to the Civil War* (Garden City, N.Y.: Doubleday, 1966), p. 646. Martin's testimony is especially significant inasmuch as on 29 April he was called on by President Johnson to serve as his personal representative in the Dominican Republic. Preparing for his mission the next day in Washington, Martin was briefed by the leading actors on the American side and read the cables and papers of those first days (see ibid., p. 640).

10. *Dominican Diary* (New York: Dell, 1966), p. 16. Abraham Lowenthal adds: "Thus assured by the embassy, the Dominican desk officer at the State Department in Washington briefed Benjamin Read, the department's Executive Secretary, at 6:30 P.M.; Read decided that it was not necessary to alert Secretary Rusk about the crisis" (*The Dominican Intervention* [Cambridge, Mass.: Harvard University Press, 1972], p. 66).

11. The Dominican press, reporting the news received from Washington, noted the optimism prevailing at the State Department (see especially *Listín Diario*, 25 April 1965, p. 1, which cites Shlaudeman as a source).

12. The obvious contradiction of this statement can only be explained as a bias far beyond the bounds of "academic impartiality." By what stretch of the imagination can officers be called "loyal" who, at the same time, are said to have decided to drop the government they have set up?

13. Georgetown University, Center for Strategic Studies, *Dominican Action—1965*, p. 15.

14. The meeting took place on the afternoon of 24 April. The betrayal by the "loyal Dominican military commanders" should, therefore, have been patently clear to the American embassy by the evening of the twenty-fourth, and not "by early morning of the twenty-fifth." If the American embassy erred on this point, then the question arises as to how such

a blunder could have occurred. Although I do not pretend to solve this riddle, I can set forth various tentative explanations.

First, the absence of part of the embassy staff played a definite role, especially regarding contacts with the local military chiefs. Of the sixteen American officers assigned to "assist" their Dominican colleagues, only five (the three attachés and two members of MAAG) were in the country on the twenty-fourth. Since Colonel Heywood did not return to the capital until evening, only four U.S. officers were present during the first few hours. Obviously, such a restricted staff limited the embassy's chances to "work in the field." Even these few men were ineptly employed. Heywood, for one, was assigned to the Presidential Palace (see n. 8 above), but he would have rendered far greater service chasing after Rivera Caminero, to show him that the path to heaven lay in loyalty to the Triumvirate. Apparently no American military personnel were at San Isidro during those decisive hours. Thus embassy personnel could not obtain firsthand reports, relying instead on whatever the various Dominican military chiefs were disposed to tell them. Until the early hours of the twenty-fifth, this was the same old tune—pledges to support the government. The embassy's chief source of information, it seems, was the Palace, where Reid Cabral's optimism belied reality.

Finally, the embassy was late in contacting the rebels. It was nearly midnight before an American colonel arrived at the Sixteenth of August camp. His mission, however, met with little success. To the American's question, "what's going on here?", Captain Peña Taveras replied: "what's going on here is a problem for Dominicans and will be solved by us Dominicans" (interview with García Germán). The American colonel, unaccustomed to such treatment from his Dominican protégés, did not press the issue, and withdrew. Until Reid Cabral's fall, this was the embassy's only contact with leaders— civilian or military—of the rebellion. Admittedly, Peña Taveras' sharp words to the American colonel were hardly of a nature to fill the embassy with hope about its chances of influencing the rebels.

15. The surest way to get American aid, as experience had shown, was to invoke the "Communist threat".

16. Georgetown University, Center for Strategic Studies, *Dominican Action-1965*, pp. 16, 17. Ever since, Reid Cabral has constantly denied that he asked for United States military intervention. But Senator Fulbright's assertion that "Donald Reid Cabral asked for U.S. intervention on Sunday morning, April 25th" ("Situation in the Dominican Republic," p. 23856) supports the version given here.

17. Lowenthal, *Dominican Intervention*, p. 70.

18. "Situation in the Dominican Republic," p. 23857.

19. Abraham F. Lowenthal, "The Dominican Republic: The Politics of Chaos," in *Reform and Revolution: Readings in Latin America*, ed. Arpad von Lazar and Robert R. Kaufman (Boston: Allyn & Bacon, 1969), p. 40.

20. The word "diplomat" is used here in a broad sense, to include the members of MAAG and the military attachés. In a country like the Dominican Republic, these people engage in activities far exceeding simple military functions, at times relegating these to a secondary role.

21. On the contrary, "dispassionate analysis" of the Dominican revolution would show that the Generals Belisario Peguero and Atila Luna Pérez were never invited by the rebels to join the movement, either before 24 April or after. Better still, when early on the morning of the twenty-fifth, convinced of a rebel victory, the two men came to declare their adherence, they were shown the door by the rebel leaders. And they were not alone; other officers, notably General Hungría Morel, offered their adherence, but were refused. Only a strongly biased analysis could blame the rebels for this episode. Nor did these "discredited ex-generals" support the revolt "at least in the first days of the crisis"; already on the evening of the twenty-fifth, that little band of opportunists was gathered at San Isidro, where the values they embodied were being defended. If at all, the rebel leaders could be blamed for having rejected, out of an overly scrupulous concern for preserving the purity of the movement, the adherence of men—especially Belisario Peguero—who, because of their influence, might have been of use of them.

Santiago Rodríguez Echavarría, for his part, participated in the conspiracy and stayed with the movement until he was arrested by the "loyalists" at Santiago on 27 April. Again, wouldn't "dispassionate analysis" show that, far from being one of the "most discredited ex-generals," he enjoyed a well-deserved prestige?

22. Lowenthal, "Dominican Republic," p. 42.

23. Up until the morning of 25 April, arms had been distributed to the population only erratically (see Chapter 7).

24. Interview with Hernando Ramírez.

25. Ramón Cáceres Troncoso, the second Triumvir (see Chapter 4, n. 67), was at the Palace with Reid Cabral from the first hours of the uprising. But in the middle of such important events, I have found it hard to remember the negligible presence of this "invisible" member of the Triumvirate.

After their arrest, the two Triumvirs were confined in an office on the Palace's third floor. Three hours later, "when the planes attacked the Palace, the rebels took Reid and Cáceres Troncoso below to a safer floor." But their captivity was brief, for that evening "colonel [sic] Giovanni Manuel Gutiérrez told Reid and Cáceres he could no longer guarantee their lives if they remained in the Palace. Reid was given the choice of going to the Police Headquarters or to the home of a friend, José Antonio Caro. . . . Reid chose Caro, and the two former leaders were put into an ambulance which passed safely out of a side gate of the Palace . . . . From this time on Reid remained in hiding with friends until he left in June" (Georgetown University, Center for Strategic Studies, *Dominican Action—1965*, pp. 21, 22).

26. In fact it is hard to determine who actually "arrested" Reid Cabral. Sención Silverio, notably, maintains that it was Lieutenant Nuñez Vargas of the Presidential Guard who, judging the situation propitious, took Reid Cabral prisoner, carrying out the task assigned to him by the Enriquillo plan. Reid Cabral, however, has confirmed my version of the event. This somewhat byzantine dispute is significant because it reveals the confused state at the Palace. It is probable that, although Reid Cabral was formally arrested by Caamaño and Gutiérrez Ramírez, he had been, since Connett's departure, a de facto prisoner, his freedom of movement restricted, by tacit agreement, to his office and, perhaps, the corridor. Hence Sención Silverio's version: Reid Cabral was already a prisoner before the arrival of the officers sent by Hernando Ramírez.

27. Interview with Morilí Holguín. In April 1965, Holguín served in the CEFA as a lieutenant and was one of the four officers sent by Wessin to the Palace on the twenty-fourth (see Chapter 5).

28. Interview with Benoit.

29. The sources for this meeting are interviews with Benoit and Hernando Ramírez. Although these two officers were on opposing sides, their stories match.

30. Interview with Benoit.

31. Interview with Hernando Ramírez.

32. The sources for this meeting are interviews with Máximo Lovatón Pittaluga and Antonio Martínez Francisco. Their versions, deriving from separate interviews, coincide. Their agreement carries additional weight because Lovatón Pittaluga and Martínez Francisco have taken different political paths since the start of the Balaguer regime—that is, well before these interviews. The former remained in the PRD, while the latter became minister in the Balaguer government.

33. According to the *Listín Diario*, which cites as its source the Office of Statistics and Census, the population of Santo Domingo in 1964 was 420,440 (*Listín Diario*, 24 April 1965, p. 1-A). The figure, however, may actually have been higher.

34. Antonio Llano Montes, *Santo Domingo: Barricadas de odio* (México, D.F.: Editores Mexicanos Unidos, 1966), p. 118.

35. It was also adopted by the overwhelming majority of more or less opportunistic "neutrals," which explains the flood of converts to the revolt on the morning and early afternoon of the twenty-fifth.

36. The PRD *electoreros* (see Chapter 4) should also be considered, but they had no hold on the population of the capital and were overwhelmed by events because the counter-coup, which they rejected, had burst.

37. At times comical incidents took place: suddenly the local congressman cannot locate his car—or has run out of gas; he is the victim of some strange indisposition; he (and he alone) discovers that he is needed at home. But a car is found, the gas arrives, and suddenly there he is, almost without knowing how, in a car speeding toward the capital.

38. *Listín Diario*, 26 April 1965, p. 1.

39. Szulc, *Dominican Diary*, pp. 26-27.

40. Interview with Benoit.

41. My sources are conversations with five of the participants: Hernando Ramírez, Benoit, Molina Ureña, Manuel Ramón Ledesma Pérez, and Leopoldo A. Espaillat Nanita. Given the importance of the meeting, I also discussed the event with persons who, though they were not present, were well informed of what went on. The list embraces men as far apart as Admiral Rivera Caminero and Máximo Lovatón Pittaluga. I have often had recourse to this practice, but I have been careful never to lose sight of the difference between direct and indirect testimony. In this case I also had a joint meeting with Colonel Benoit ("loyalist") and Lovatón Pittaluga (constitutionalist). It was the first time since the outbreak of the civil war that Benoit and Lovatón Pittaluga met, and their meeting proved to be highly interesting as regards the talks in the Presidential Palace and a number of other issues. I would like to thank them heartily.

42. Sent by Wessin, Medrano Ubiera had arrived at Hernando Ramírez's office in the Palace while the latter was greeting Benoit. Hernando Ramírez welcomed the Nineteenth of November's delegate, but he barred the CEFA's representative from the office where the meeting was scheduled. The constitutionalist leader claimed that since the CEFA was not an independent branch of the armed forces, it had no right to send a delegate. This justification, formally correct, had little connection with the reality. Hernando Ramírez refused to admit Wessin to his tête-à-tête with de los Santos because he realized—as he has conceded to the author—that an agreement with the number one enemy of the constitutionalist movement was neither possible nor desirable. His answer (as reported by Benoit) to Medrano Ubiera's identifying himself as an envoy from Wessin—"We don't recognize Wessin"—is revealing. As for Wessin's assertion that his camp "was fighting" the rebels as early as the evening of the twenty-fourth, no other position being possible since the insurgents were Communists, (see Chapter 5), we can see now that this proud attitude did not rule out less bellicose measures.

Significantly, Benoit himself was completely unaware of the arrival of a CEFA delegate (interview with Benoit). If relations between the two elements of the San Isidro *conjunto* had been normal, it would have been natural to send the two delegates together. Their separate arrivals tell much about the less than friendly relations between the Nineteenth of November and the CEFA. Even more significant was Benoit's behavior during the incident unfolding before him—no words, no protest as his CEFA "neighbor" departed.

43. The full extent of these two officers' opportunism, especially that of Milito Fernández—"king of the opportunists"—would appear in all its splendor in the days ahead. Also present, according to some witnesses (notably Colonel Benoit), were two other constitutionalist officers: navy Captain Montes Arache and Lieutenant Colonel Servando Alfredo Bounpensiere Morel (the former a "hard-liner," though by nature more than by political conviction; the latter a "soft-liner," at best). These two officers, however, seem to have played no great role during the talks.

44. This portrait derives from long talks with Benoit.

45. U.S., Congress, Senate, Committee on the Judiciary, Subcommittee to Investigate the Administration of the Internal Security Act and Other Internal Security Laws, *Communist Threat to the United States through the Caribbean: Hearings: Testimony of Brigadier General Elías Wessin y Wessin*, 89 Cong., 1 sess., 1 October 1965 (Washington, D.C.: U.S. Government Printing Office, 1965), pp. 157, 161.

Beauchamps Javier was deputy director of the CEFA; Lluberes Montás was the commander of the Special Forces of the Nineteenth of November (see Chapter 7) and one of the "Wessinist" officers at the air base.

46. Radio Santo Domingo TV was already in constitutionalist hands, but if Beauchamps actually spoke these words, it is hard to know what he meant, since the broadcasts assumed a violent tone only after the air force attack (see Chapter 8).

47. Llano Montes, *Santo Domingo*, p. 119. For the most part, Llano Montes' version seems to me worthy of trust in this instance because it is "neutral" in the sense that, for once, it aims to heighten neither his friend Wessin's "glory," nor the rebels' "ignominy."

48. U.S., Congress, Senate, *Testimony of Brigadier General Elías Wessin y Wessin*, p. 156.

49. This statement is based on interviews (see note 41 above). De los Santos was the only one to phone; Medrano Ubiera, the CEFA delegate, never contacted his chief during the meeting.

50. After attacking the Palace, the planes also strafed the rebel camps before flying back to the Nineteenth of November.

CHAPTER 7

1. For convenience, the term "loyalist" will continue to be used to describe the anti-constitutionalist forces. The term is a misnomer, but is used in the literature on the subject, with quotation marks by the most honest authors, without quotation marks by the rest.

2. In theory one should add the 700 to 725 men of Polvorín, Intendencia, and Transportación (see Chapter 4) who were stationed in the city and declared for the revolt. But their military weight was negligible and, except for the Polvorín, their loyalty to the cause was highly suspect.

3. Antonio Llano Montes, *Santo Domingo: Barricadas de odio* (México, D.F.: Editores Mexicanos Unidos, 1966), pp. 124, 125.

4. U.S., Congress, Senate, Committee on the Judiciary, Subcommittee to Investigate the Administration of the Internal Security Act and Other Internal Security Laws, *Communist Threat to the United States through the Caribbean: Hearings: Testimony of Brigadier General Elías Wessin y Wessin*, 89 Cong., 1 sess., 1 October 1965 (Washington, D.C.: U.S. Government Printing Office, 1965), p. 157.

5. Interview with Núñez Nogueras.

6. These data derive from a report written after the civil war by an academy officer for a senior constitutionalist officer. The report is among my personal papers. For reasons of security, the names of the two officers cannot be printed.

7. Ibid.

8. Ibid. For the story of the cadets, see Chapter 8.

9. Its commandant was Colonel Juan Esteban Peréz Guillén, later army chief of staff under the Balaguer regime.

10. Interviews with Silvestre Antonio Guzmán and with his wife, Renée Klang de Guzmán.

11. The Santiago police, then, did not go along with General Despradel's idea that the institution was "apolitical."

12. *Listín Diario*, 26 April 1965, p. 1.

13. Ibid., p. 9.

14. The problem of control of the radio stations best enables us to follow the behavior of the police. Again, Santiago will serve as an example. Still "progovernment" on the evening of the twenty-fourth, the Santiago police lost its enthusiasm during the night, under the impact of the news pouring in from Santo Domingo. Early on the morning of the twenty-fifth, when bands of civilians seized the local radio stations, the police kept aloof. Yet during the night, police officers had removed the crystals from the stations, making them unusable (interview with Pedro Manuel Casals Victoria). But this was only a half-measure, depriving the "pro-government" forces as well as the rebels of the chance to use the radios. Above all, this cautious behavior is remarkable in policemen accustomed to using violence against unarmed civilians—and in Santiago, on 25 April 1965, the civilians were unarmed. This new moderation—this failure to beat the "rabble" into line—is evidence of the hesitation forced on the police by the events taking place in the capital. Later in the morning, when two clandestine radio stations—"La Voz del Pueblo" ("The Voice of the People") and "Ondas del Valle" ("Valley Radio")—began to broadcast, the police again did nothing. Constitutionalist sympathizers soon found new crystals to replace those removed from the transmitters. The radio stations in the city began to respond to the appeals of the two clandestine stations by forming a chain. Before long, all the Santiago radio stations were

broadcasting—in unison—the constitutionalists' slogans and directives. And the police remained passive, with one exception. On the morning of the twenty-fifth, "the police closed down a local radio station for a half an hour" (*El Caribe*, 26 April 1965, p. 10). The incident, however, was isolated and brief; it was most probably the work of some underling acting on his own, insensitive to the needs of the times—one more proof of the confusion besetting the police. The about-face became complete as officers took to the airwaves to announce, in the name of Colonel Jaquez Olivero, that the police were joining the revolt.

15. Interview with Rivera Caminero.

16. Interview with Reid Cabral.

17. There were: the Revolutionary Action Party (Partido de Acción Revolucionaria or PAR); the Christian Democratic Party (Partido Demócrata Cristiano or PDC); the Liberal Evolutionist Party (Partido Liberal Evolucionista or PLE); the Democratic Nationalist Revolutionary Party (Partido Nacionalista Revolucionario Democrático or PNRD); the National Civic Union (Unión Cívica Nacional or UCN); and the Dominican Revolutionary Vanguard (Vanguardia Revolucionaria Dominicana or VRD).

18. Bertold Brecht, "Die Ballade von Wasserrad," in *Die Rundköpfe und die Spitzenköpfe* (Frankfurt am Main: Suhrkamp Verlag, [20 vols., Complete Works] 1967), 3:1008. Translated for the author by Dr. Brewster Chamberlin.

19. Contrary to what he later pretended, Héctor Aristy had nothing to do with the conspiracy, as I have learned in conversations with Peña Gómez, Molina Ureña, Hernando Ramírez, Sención Silverio, and several other figures who played key roles in organizing the countercoup. Aristy suddenly became a "constitutionalist" on the morning of the twenty-fifth. At first, he was received coldly by the rebels as one more opportunist climbing aboard the bandwagon. But when many early leaders deserted, his courage and decisiveness allowed him to assume a central role. As a valued adviser to his old friend and new leader of the revolt, Colonel Caamaño, Aristy became one of the key figures of the constitutionalist movement. But he was never the *deus ex machina* whose instructions were merely repeated by an allegedly incompetent Caamaño. Yet this was the impression Aristy tried to give to the visitors who poured into the constitutionalist zone, as well as to the author three years after the revolt, during a lengthy conversation in Paris. Aristy's unbounded ambition, taste for intrigue, and opportunism tarnished his actions. Perhaps every revolution needs such a figure, but no revolution could be proud of him.

20. Their contacts among the Church hierarchy were particularly close with the bishops and the Jesuits (there were at the time 175 Jesuits in the country, 60 percent of them of Cuban origin).

21. *El Caribe*, 26 April 1965, p. 1.

22. Ibid.

23. Interview with Francisco Augusto Lora, at the time first vice-president of the Reformist Party.

24. It is impossible to prove conclusively that the Reformist leaders were at San Isidro during these crucial days. The Reformists still safeguard the myth of their "neutrality" and present themselves as those who preached conciliation at a time when rivalries among factions were tearing the country apart. Because of that myth, in 1970 a Reformist leader could dare to attack Wessin—once again an enemy after a brief interlude—by recalling that he "showed no pity to women and children when he mercilessly bombed an unarmed city" (statement by José Oscar Bonnelly, secretary of organization of the Reformist municipal directorate of Santiago, 8 May 1970, in *El Nacional*, 9 May 1970, p. 24). Yet "the widows, the orphans and the mutilated victims of that man's barbarity" (ibid.) have more than Wessin to curse. The Reformist Party and others along with it were accomplices.

At the time of my interview with him, in February 1970, Lora had a special interest in defending the myth of "neutrality." As a candidate for president of the Republic in the elections to be held three months later (16 May 1970), he was already preparing to woo PRDist votes.

That the Reformist Party is still in power, imposing a climate of repression, deters those who, in other circumstances, would give valuable testimony. They justifiably fear reprisals. Those who spoke of the presence and activities of the Reformist leaders at San Isidro did so with extreme reluctance and on condition that their names be withheld. I can only respect their wishes. In one case, my source was a senior officer of the *conjunto*, an eyewitness; in another, an eminent figure in the business world.

In addition, Abraham Lowenthal mentions that Lora "sped to San Isidro to confer with Generals Wessin and De Los Santos and other military figures" (*The Dominion Intervention* [Cambridge, Mass.: Harvard University Press, 1972], p. 76), but he too does not give his sources.

25. *El Caribe*, 26 April 1965, p. 16.

26. But not for long. As soon as the U.S. military intervention had demonstrated that the constitutionalists would be denied the right to victory, Guido d'Alessandro and his friends hastened to return to a more "reasonable" position. They condemned "the unilateral intervention of the United States as an act in violation of our Sovereignty," but took care to rail against "the underhanded, powerful and well-organized efforts of the far-leftists to control and capitalize on a revolutionary movement of deep democratic roots" (PRSC, "Manifiesto al Pueblo Dominicano" [Santo Domingo, n.d.], p. 1). By proclaiming their conviction that the threat of Communist dictatorship was as real as that of San Isidro, they took up a theme dear to American propaganda and undermined the official stance of the constitutionalist government, with which they had already ceased all collaboration.

That was the price they had to pay to demonstrate to the American invader their "independence of mind," their "impartiality," and so claim a role as responsible interlocutors.

27. Despite the defection of its *flojos*, the PRSC was considered throughout the crisis—both at home and abroad—to be one of the five parties supporting the constitutionalist government of Colonel Caamaño. This assessment is easily explained. Whether it had been a majority or a minority during the Triumvirate, the Guido d'Alessandro faction lost the backing of most Social Christian militants throughout the civil war. The group's "reasonable" posture was regarded as a betrayal; its statements found only a tiny audience. It was in the constitutionalist zone that *Pueblo*, the PRSC organ—and *Revolución Obrera*, CASC's organ—were published. Both newspapers staunchly supported the Caamaño regime. After emerging from the throes of the civil war, the PRSC became the party of the *duros* Antonio Rosario and Caonabo Javier. Guido D'Alessandro's place would be in Montevideo, as ambassador of the Balaguer regime.

As the years have gone by, the resolve of the PRSC *duros* has increasingly weakened. Balaguer's regime has proved corrupt and undemocratic, but able to remain in power. Firm opposition meant estrangement from the soft jobs and perquisites the government could offer. The longer the opposition lasted, the more painful this abstinence became for many Social Christian leaders. Thus, with the passing of time, the PRSC has become increasingly "moderate" and "realistic" (and as a result the university youth of the BRUC has broken with the party to create an independent organization, the Comités Revolucionarios Camilo Torres, CORECATO, whose opposition to the regime remains uncompromising). Finally, after the 1974 presidential "elections"—in which Balaguer had himself re-elected for four more years—the leaders of the PRSC found a new, genial formula of "constructive" opposition: the party would remain in the opposition, but its members would accept high positions in the government.

28. For this section I have had recourse, along with abundant documentation, to a series of interviews. The principal figures interviewed are: from the 1J4: Norge Botello, Fidelio Despradel, Jimmy Durán, and Fafa Taveras, all members of the CECP, "Baby" Mejía, leader of the Military Bureau, and María Elena Muñóz Marte, middle-level party cadre; from the PSP: Félix Servio Ducoudray and Narciso Isa Conde, members of the National Secretariat, José Israel Cuello, member of the Central Committee, and Asdrúbal Domínguez, middle-level leader; from the MPD: Monchín Pinedo, Cayetano Rodríguez, Luis René Sánchez Cordova, all members of the Central Committee.

29. Rafael Francisco (Fafa) Taveras Rosario and Amín Abel Hasbún, "Se apróxima otro 24 de abril," *Claridad*, no. 28 (22 April 1969), p. 2. In fact, Peña Gómez's radio announcement took place a few minutes earlier, according to the chronology already given (see Chapter 5).

30. For reasons given above, a few members of the CC were absent from this meeting (interview with Narciso Isa Conde, one of the CC members taking part in the meeting). More important, from this point on the distinction between *jóvenes* and *viejos* will be disregarded. More dynamic and psychologically better prepared for an armed conflict, the *jóvenes* immediately took control of the party, leaving their old adversaries to play a secondary role.

NOTES TO PAGES 208-13

31. Interview with Narcisco Isa Conde.
32. Partido Comunista Dominicano (CC), "El Partido y la insurrección de abril: Documento autocrítico del Comité Central," in *El Popular*, no. 78 (16 Aug. 1965), pp. 8-9.
33. Interview with "Baby" Mejía.
34. Three CECP members failed to take part in this hastily called meeting: two— Norge Botello and Fafa Taveras—could not be reached in time. The third—Juan B. Mejía— was sick. The Military Bureau was represented by two or three of its leaders, notably "Baby" Mejía and Orlando Mazara (interviews with "Baby" Mejía, Norge Botello, Fafa Taveras, and María Elena Muñóz Marte. Muñóz Marte was not a member of the CECP and did not take part in the meeting. But she was in the house where the meeting was held, and several times she entered the room where the leaders were gathered. Hence our interest in her testimony).
35. Interview with "Baby" Mejía.
36. Interview with Norge Botello.
37. Interview with Norge Botello.
38. The MPD can be dealt with more quickly than the PSP and the 1J4, since much of what has been said about the two latter parties holds for the MPD as well.
39. Interview with Monchín Pinedo.
40. Interview with Monchín Pinedo.
41. Interview with Norge Botello.
42. Emilio Cordero Michel to Daniel Ozuna, letter of 22 Dec. 1964, Mexico City, D.F., among my personal papers.
43. The MPD leadership maintained this unity throughout the civil war. The 1J4, however—divided at the outbreak of the countercoup—saw its internal contradictions deepen throughout the crisis (see below, Chapter 10). The initial reactions of the PSP's Central Committee to the countercoup showed a unity that belied the existence of two antagonistic factions at its heart. This unity lasted throughout the civil war, fostered by the passive role played by the Ducoudray group. Thereafter the conflict between *viejos* and *jóvenes* erupted again, but it proved short-lived, since the *jóvenes* were now too strong. In 1966, Felíx Servio and Juan Ducoudray led a handful of other "historical leaders" out of the party. They founded a new PSP that exists today, ten years later, but has never been more than a small circle of "old-timers."
In August 1965 the old PSP became the Partido Comunista Dominicano (PCD). Led by the *jóvenes*, it abandoned its former pro-Soviet line and strengthened its ties with Cuba, while still maintaining its independence. Although it has not become a "giant of the far left," the PCD has grown over the last years. Among the leftists, many bitterly criticize the party for its "excessive prudence"; others see instead the manifestation of political maturity and skill.
44. One Dominican told me that the majority of the *gente* (people) in the capital opposed Bosch's return to power. His statement surprised me, since Santo Domingo was known to be the bastion of Boschism. But the misunderstanding was easily explained. For my interlocutor, a rich industrialist from Santiago, the Dominican population is divided into *gente* and *infelices*—the haves and the have-nots. Being a "reasonable" man, he readily acknowledged that the majority of Santo Domingans demanded Bosch's return to power. But only the opinion of the *gente* mattered to him.
45. *El Caribe*, 26 April 1965, p. 10.
46. *Listín Diario*, 26 April 1965, p. 9.
47. There is nothing more superficial than the "brilliant" studies published by many foreign (usually American) scholars after a brief stay in a Latin American country. The Latin American peasant's distrust of all efforts from the outside to uncover "his truth" is deep. The foreigner is a threat. And the foreigner is any person not part of the community. For the Dominican peasant in the Baní area, the "foreigner" is any peasant from the area of San Cristóbal, only twenty-five miles away. The "foreigner" is even that peasant who has not been a member of the community long enough.
Men who are complete strangers, whose physical appearance and language often betray a foreign origin, pretend, in the space of a few weeks, to master the secrets of this jealously guarded world. Carefully they transcribe the answers they have obtained, often through an interpreter. They forget that the peasant is giving all the "right" answers merely

to satisfy the curious strangers who could well be the agents of the local authorities the enemy. In the end, reports will be published, "scientific" data will be proclaimed—proving that the grants given the scholars were not wasted. Others will prepare to make other investigations, their enthusiasm stirred by the charm of the Latin American countries. A certain brand of "political science" will expand its fund of knowledge, which will increasingly border on the absurd.

48. Except in the very special case of *Prensa Libre* (see p. 214 below).

49. *El Caribe*, 26 April 1965, p. 10. Since Bosch had been overthrown on 25 September 1963, the PLE, which was founded on 21 November 1963, could not have been directly implicated in the coup. But its founder and "owner," Luis Amiama Tió, had signed the "Manifesto Addressed to the Dominican People by the Chiefs of the Armed Forces and the National Police, who have deposed the Ex-President of the Republic, Professor Juan Bosch" (see Chapter 3).

50. *El Caribe*, 26 April 1965, p. 10.

51. *Listín Diario*, 26 April 1965, p. 9.

52. This is the figure put forward by Lieutenant (Ret.) García Germán and is confirmed by other interviews I have held.

53. Interviews with Hernando Ramírez, Núñez Nogueras, García Germán, Sención Silverio, and Sergeant Polonio Pierret.

54. Two additional points limit the importance of the above-mentioned factor in both scope and time. First, this concern seems to have been shared by only a handful; in fact, with the occupation of the capital, most of the officers thought that the revolt would succeed. Second, the emissaries from San Isidro, not the tanks and planes of the *conjunto*, appeared in the city early in the morning. From that point on, the last doubts disappeared.

55. Interview with Hernando Ramírez.

56. Interview with Polonio Pierret.

57. The sources for this meeting are interviews with Guzmán, Lovatón Pittaluga, Martínez Francisco, and del Rosario Ceballos, whose recollections agree on all the important points. The few differences in details only confirm, to my mind, the authenticity of their accounts.

58. Interview with Lovatón Pittaluga.

59. Interview with Martínez Francisco.

60. Breisky, quoted by Lovatón Pittaluga, in an interview.

61. For a more precise account of the events, see Chapter 6.

62. After the outbreak of the countercoup, Rivera Caminero did not set foot in the Palace until around one in the morning of 26 April (see Chapter 8).

63. Connett, telegram to the State Department, Santo Domingo, 25 April 1965, 5:00 P.M., among my personal papers.

CHAPTER 8

1. Interview with Hernando Ramírez.

2. Could he have maintained anything else? On 27 April, less than thirty-six hours after his visit to the Palace, Rivera Caminero ordered the fleet to bombard the capital, where the constitutionalists were holding out (see Chapter 9). Eleven days later, on 8 May 1965, he became minister of the armed forces in the Government of National Reconstruction, which President Johnson's special envoy, former Ambassador Martin, had just created to thwart the constitutionalist government of Colonel Caamaño. On 3 September 1965, the Dominican crisis was "resolved" by the installation of Héctor García Godoy's government of "conciliation," imposed by the United States. In this new government, Rivera Caminero retained his post as armed forces minister and distinguished himself as one of the harshest persecutors of the vanquished constitutionalists. In particular, his responsibility in the bloody incident of the Hotel Matum in Santiago is clear. There, on 19 December 1965, in a

treacherous attack, army and air force units tried in vain to wipe out a large group of constitutionalist leaders (see Chapter 10). Given these facts, can anyone expect that Rivera Caminero will admit ever having pledged allegiance to the constitutionalist government of Molina Ureña, and so acknowledge his unbounded opportunism? Can anyone expect Rivera Caminero to do so, when he still occupies important positions in the Balaguer government, a government hardly known for its clemency toward military men who "betrayed" by choosing the side of the constitution?

In 1969, when interviewed by the author, Rivera Caminero was naval adviser to the president of the Republic and head of the Government's Flota Mercante Dominicana; in May 1975, Balaguer appointed him navy chief of staff.

3. The story is Rivera Caminero's own, as told to the author in an interview. The sentences in quotation marks are verbatim transcriptions of the admiral's words.

4. When Rivera Caminero arrived at the Palace, Molina Ureña was in the office that had belonged to the second Triumvir, Ramón Cáceres Troncoso. In that office, on the second floor, the talk between the admiral and the new president took place.

5. Interviews with Molina Ureña, Espaillat Nanita, Hernando Ramírez, Lovatón Pittaluga, Ledesma Pérez, and Moya Pons. Moya Pons was the only one of those present with "blue eyes" and "blond hair"—but no beard! He was from La Vega, however, a small town in the Cibao, where he had spent most of his life.

6. *El Caribe*, 26 April 1965, p. 8.

7. One of the constitutionalists in Molina Ureña's office, the young playwright Franklin Domínguez, jotted down the names of those navy officers who came to assure the new president of their support. The list, which is in my possession, includes (in addition to Admiral Rivera Caminero and Captains Amiama Castillo and Santana Carrasco) Commanders Arturo Bordas Betances and Guillermo Striddels; Lieutenant Commanders Emilio A. Guzmán Matos, Hugo Rodríguez Díaz, Oscar Miguel Jacobo, Plinio Caamaño Mota, and Augusto César Canó González; Lieutenant senior grade Rafael Peralta Céspedes; Lieutenants junior grade Rafael Santiago Díaz and Rubén Darío Jiménez Collado; and Ensign Augustín Aristy Santana.

8. *El Caribe*, 27 April 1965, p. 1.

9. Interviews with Lovatón Pittaluga and Ledesma Pérez.

10. "I believe that at the time Rivera Caminero was sincere. I think that at the meeting at the Palace in the afternoon [on the twenty-fifth] Guzmán [Matos] spoke without precise instructions from Rivera Caminero" (interview with Ledesma Pérez). (Lieutenant Commander Guzmán Matos was the navy's representative at the meeting in the Palace to which Ledesma Pérez refers; he had declared himself against a Boschist solution to the crisis.)

Of course, Ledesma Pérez may have been wrong about the "sincerity" of Rivera Caminero's rallying. What matters is that the constitutionalist leaders apparently believed in that sincerity (interviews with Molina Ureña, Hernando Ramírez, and others), which could only reinforce a dangerous optimism.

11. Interview with Hernando Ramírez.

12. *Listín Diario*, 27 April 1965, p. 2.

13. Interview with Hernando Ramírez.

14. Interview with Hernando Ramírez.

15. This was true notably of officers, at the Twenty-seventh of February in particular, who on the evening of the twenty-fourth had rallied to the revolt only after several hours of pressure, and of officers on duty in Santo Domingo who had waited until the twenty-fifth to join the revolt, after the rebel troops had entered the city—Lieutenant Colonel Vinicio Fernández Pérez and Colonel Milito Ludovino Fernández, for example. The last to join were the first to defect, with Ludovino Fernández—"the king of the opportunists"—sweeping the race. On the twenty-seventh he was at San Isidro, where he hastened to accuse the revolt of being under Communist influence. His statements were taped and used by Radio San Isidro for its anticonstitutionalist propaganda.

16. *El Caribe*, 27 April 1965, p. 8.

17. Antonio Llano Montes, *Santo Domingo: Barricadas de odio* (México, D.F.: Editores Mexicanos Unidos, 1966), p. 126. The book contains a highly interesting account of the creation of Dominican Armed Forces Radio, also known as "Radio San Isidro, The Voice of the Armed Forces."

18. The scurrility of Radio San Isidro's propaganda reappears in the works of certain stalwart anticonstitutionalists: in Antonia Llano Montes' *Santo Domingo: Barricadas de odio*, and in Danilo Brugal Alfau's *Tragedia en Santo Domingo: Documentos para la historia* (Santo Domingo: Editora del Caribe, 1966); and with slightly better style in Peter Nehemkis' *Latin America: Myth and Reality* (2d. ed. rev., New York: Mentor Books, 1966), pp. 258-300, and Jay Mallin's *Caribbean Crisis: Subversion Fails in the Dominican Republic* (Garden City, N.Y.: Doubleday, 1965).

19. On the twenty-sixth, the number of desertions was relatively limited, though not insignificant; on the twenty-seventh, however, they assumed dramatic proportions.

20. Interview with Oscar Hernández, constitutionalist leader from La Vega.

21. They could not use the other radio stations in the capital—Radio Cristal, Radio Comercial, Radio Guarachita, and so on; the antennas were in the eastern suburbs, east of the Ozama River, in San Isidro's territory.

22. "Radio San Isidro was situated at the end of the Ensanche Ozama, 5 miles from San Isidro, in a place of difficult access. Around it were few houses, all of them scattered widely and from which it was impossible to make out what was going on there . . . . Two tanks of the Armored Battalion and at least fifteen soldiers guarded the equipment. A dirt road which crossed the area was closed to traffic. Guards were set up in the area around the station." (Llano Montes, *Santo Domingo*, p. 127).

23. Georgetown University, Center for Strategic Studies, *Dominican Action—1965: Intervention or Cooperation?* Special Report Series # 2 (Washington, D.C.: Center for Strategic Studies, 1966), p. 23.

24. U.S., Congress, Senate, Committee on the Judiciary, Subcommittee to Investigate the Administration of the Internal Security Act and Other Internal Security Laws, *Communist Threat to the United States Through the Caribbean: Hearings: Testimony of Brigadier General Elías Wessin y Wessin*, 89 Cong., 1 sess., 1 October 1965 (Washington, D.C.: U.S. Government Printing Office, 1965), p. 259. Appendix IV of this document (pp. 252-62) contains the "transcript and translation of tapes of . . . [Radio Santo Domingo] broadcasts, or telegraphed reports about them."

25. Interview with Moya Pons.

26. *El Caribe*, 27 April 1965, p. 8.

27. Marcel Niedergang, *La Révolution de Saint-Domingue* ([Paris]: Plon, 1966), p. 52.

28. U.S., Congress, Senate, *Testimony of Brigadier General Elías Wessin y Wessin*, pp. 257, 259, 262, 256, 258.

29. A bridge on the northern border of Santo Domingo, at the junction of the Ozama and the Isabela rivers.

30. U.S., Congress, Senate, *Testimony of Brigadier General Elías Wessin y Wessin*, pp. 260, 257.

31. Niedergang, *La Révolution de Saint-Domingue*, p. 52.

32. U.S., Congress, Senate, *Testimony of Brigadier General Elías Wessin y Wessin*, p. 257.

33. *Listín Diario*, 27 April 1965, p. 4.

34. U.S., Congress, Senate, *Testimony of Brigadier General Elías Wessin y Wessin*, p. 260.

35. Tad Szulc, *Dominican Diary* (New York: Dell, 1966), p. 34.

36. "There was talk that the families of pilots in the Dominican Air Force would be taken as hostages to the Duarte Bridge, but that didn't happen" (*El Caribe*, 27 April 1965, p. 8).

37. Niedergang, *La Révolution de Saint-Domingue*, pp. 51-52.

38. Nehemkis, *Latin America*, p. 283.

39. Niedergang, *La Révolution de Saint-Domingue*, p. 52.

40. Contrary to Nehemkis' allegations *(Latin America*, p. 283).

41. Marcelino Zapico, *Revolución en Hispanoamérica: Lo que vi en Santo Domingo* (Madrid: Escalicer, 1966), p. 55. Father Zapico's testimony is particularly important since this Spanish priest can hardly be accused of a bias in favor of the revolt. Although he admits that "the people as a whole experienced enthusiasm for the revolution," that enthusiasm, while "undeniable," was "blind, mistaken." "Only the landing of the marines prevented the creation of another Cuba in the Caribbean" (ibid., pp. 111, 109).

42. Niedergang, *La Révolution de Saint-Domingue*, p. 51.

43. Statement by the committee of police officers, in *Listín Diario*, 27 April 1965, p. 1. The committee was undeniably representative. Among its members were Major Bolívar Belliard Sarubi, the police's press agent, and Colonel de los Santos Almarante, deputy police chief. They claimed to be speaking "in the name of the Chief of that institution, General Hernán Despradel Brache" (ibid.).

44. The growing sense of imminent peril—that San Isidro would attack—overcame many prejudices. Throughout the twenty-sixth, however, the Constitutionalist Military Command never issued orders to arm civilians. Yet neither did it try to use force to stop civilians from being armed. In truth, it is hard to see how it could have done so.

45. *Listín Diario*, 27 April 1965, p. 2. According to the testimony of a member of the 1J4 Military Bureau who took part in the operation, thirty-seven shotguns were distributed to the waiting civilians.

46. Interview with Evelio Hernández, a *catorcista* who took part in the operation. According to Hernández, credit for initiating the action is due to 1J4 members, who seized a few dozen shotguns.

47. Ramón A. Ferreras, *Guerra Patria* (Santo Domingo: n.p., 1966), p. 41. Neither the number of arms at the depot, nor therefore the number of civilians able to arm themselves, can be determined. The figure, however, no doubt stands between two and three thousand weapons. The arms were light and often of poor quality.

48. Here again no accurate figure can be cited. But on 25-26 April, the population in the capital had at their disposal the arms found at the Palace (two to three thousand); those handed out by the constitutionalist military even before the start of the civil war (a few hundred); and those distributed subsequently or abandoned by deserters (hardly more than a thousand). Another two or three hundred were "confiscated" either from armories or from the homes of certain "reactionaries" (see n. 51 below). To this tentative list must be added the arms (probably over a thousand) wrested from the police, especially by attacks on the various neighborhood police stations.

49. All the interviews I have held reveal one and the same phenomenon: the absence of contacts, let alone coordination, between the three far-leftist parties.

50. Aimé Césaire, "Et les chiens se taisaient" in *Les Armes Miraculeuses* (Paris: Editions Gallimard, 1970), p. 106.

51. Interview with "Baby" Mejía. After the failure of the meeting the night before (see Chapter 7), the Military Bureau "lost contact with the 1J4's Central Committee and worked out its activities independently." Early in the afternoon on the twenty-fifth, before the strafing of the Palace by de los Santos' planes, the leaders of the Military Bureau met with the organization's "zone chiefs" and decided to act. Their first concern was to seize arms, if possible striking at the enemy by disarming policemen in the streets and "breaking into the homes of reactionaries known to keep arms." These were modest actions, but so were the means at the disposal of the Military Bureau—the 1J4's armed branch (interview with "Baby" Mejía).

52. Although certain militants—of the 1J4, particularly—could boast of an excellent military training, they were nonetheless too few. Arms were distributed indiscriminately, and every far-leftist militant had to face competition from dozens of his fellow citizens.

53. Except for a few rare cases, the soldiers who joined in the attacks on the police stations were led by noncommissioned officers acting on their own initiative. Officers, apparently, took no part in these actions.

54. Interviews with Narciso Isa Conde and "Baby" Mejía.

55. A police captain at the Headquarters during the revolt's first days later told Major Núñez Nogueras: "If you had attacked the Police Headquarters, you would have taken it" (interview with Núñez Nogueras). When, in fact, on 30 April the Constitutionalist Military Command finally decided to attack the Fortaleza Ozama, it fell so easily that the time wasted in waiting was rued even more.

56. It should be recalled that the units rebelling against the Triumvirate were, for the most part, elite formations of a calibre far above the average Dominican army unit.

57. Although the Constitutionalist Military Command could have had only imperfect knowledge of the state of affairs at the Police Headquarters and at the Fortaleza Ozama, there was no lack of clues. Besides, a few probing attacks would have tested the two bases' vulnerability.

58. These officers were aware that the morale at San Isidro was extremely low, that disarray and fear were rampant. "One of the reasons for the panic that gripped San Isidro was indeed the fear of an attack by the [constitutionalist] rebels," later affirmed Colonel Benoit of the Nineteenth of November (interview). Even on the twenty-sixth, one of the few "constitutionalist" officers of the *conjunto* not yet arrested begged, in one last phone call: "Attack San Isidro, and you will take it" (interview with Núñez Nogueras).

59. There were significant differences in opinion among the various groups of "constitutionalist" officers as to which attitude the United States would adopt. No one conceived of the possibility of an American military intervention. Hernando Ramírez and the "optimists" expected nothing more than an "inevitable fit of temper," with no real consequences. The "pessimists," however, like the movement's "young Turks," believed that the American embassy would do all it could, short of military intervention, to help San Isidro crush the revolt.

60. What follows is based primarily on interviews with Hernando Ramírez, Núñez Nogueras, and Sención Silverio.

61. Had the disarray at San Isidro made it possible, the operation might have had a more ambitious target: arresting Wessin and a few other top officers and taking them as prisoners to Santo Domingo, or even, if necessary, shooting them on the spot (interview with Sención Silverio). But it should be stressed that such an action, however desirable, would not have been necessary to justify going ahead with the operation, whose raison d'être was already its minimum objective: destruction of some airplanes.

62. Interviews with Hernando Ramírez and Sención Silverio. Early in the afternoon on the twenty-fifth, General Montás Guerrero arrived in San Cristóbal from the capital after spending the morning at the Palace with Reid Cabral. From this point on, Montás Guerrero took over the real leadership of the Mella Battalion, with Pérez Aponte second in command. But one should not exaggerate the importance of this arrival, since the two officers belonged to the same clique: the San Cristóbal Group.

63. The Colonel Juan Antonio Minaya Fernández Air Base. Actually, the base had only a few aircraft: four P51s as against the thirty P51s and the dozen Vampires, among others, at the Nineteenth of November (see Chapter 4). Despite its inferior numbers, the base could have played an extremely significant role. Exploiting the element of surprise, the planes from Santiago could have attacked San Isidro, less than twenty minutes away, bombing the airstrips and the planes on the ground. The constitutionalist cause would have achieved a victory all the more decisive for its psychological impact.

64. Interviews with Sención Silverio and with Pedro Manuel Casals Victoria, a constitutionalist leader from Santiago.

65. "El aparente silencio del Cibao," *Ahora*, no. 107 (16 May 1965), p. 15.

66. Ibid.

67. Interviews with Casals Victoria and Renée Klang de Guzmán.

68. If the far left was weak in Santo Domingo, it was even weaker in the cities of the interior, with the possible exception of San Francisco de Macorís and La Romana. Beginning on the twenty-fourth, an added source of weakness undermined the far left in the interior, in Santiago as elsewhere, as its most dynamic leaders rushed off to Santo Domingo— where history was being made.

69. Even during normal times the Fortaleza was far from impressive. Theoretically it housed an infantry battalion (eight hundred men), but the battalion's various companies were scattered in tiny units throughout Santiago province, leaving little more than one company—perhaps two hundred men—inside the Fortaleza (interviews with Hernando Ramírez, Núñez Nogueras, and Sención Silverio).

70. Santo Domingo was only 110 miles from Santiago, and a highway linked the two cities. Couldn't it have been possible, in just a few hours, to reach the capital and to return with arms? But the road to Santo Domingo seemed to be a one-way street. That was where the decisive battle would be fought. Those who went there—be they militants of the far left or of the "bourgeois" parties (PRD, PRSC)—had no thought of returning.

71. Antonio Guzmán and Salvador Jorge Blanco, the most important PRDistas leaders of Santiago, had left the city on the twenty-fifth for Santo Domingo, as did the popular Aníbal Campagna, former UCN senator now close to the PRD (interviews with Guz-

mán, Jorge Blanco, and Campagna). But the significance of these absences should not be overemphasized. Like their friends remaining in Santiago, these men were not revolutionaries. It would be going too far to picture them inciting the people to seize arms and storm the Fortaleza. And yet, short of this, it is hard to see how their presence in Santiago could have changed anything.

72. Interview with Pedro Manuel Casals Victoria and Renée Klang de Guzmán. Both are among the constitutionalist leaders who remained in Santiago and participated in the conversations with de la Mota and Méndez Lara.

73. *El Caribe*, 27 April 1965, p. 1. For the first communiqué, see Chapter 7.

74. "El aparente silencio del Cibao," p. 15.

75. Interview with Hernando Ramírez.

76. Interviews with Núñez Nogueras and Sención Silverio. All the elements outlined above—in particular, the attitude of the Santiagans, the situation inside the Fortaleza San Luis and the air base, the opportunism of de la Mota and of Ramírez Gómez—seem to me to support Sención Silverio's and Núñez Nogueras' opinion, provided, of course, that the operation was carried out swiftly and decisively.

77. Not until the night of 26-27 April did the Constitutionalist Military Command decide to act. Yet the intervention, already too late, was badly prepared and even more badly executed. Former General Santiago Rodríguez Echavarría set out for Santiago with a dozen men at most. He failed to contact the constitutionalist leaders in Santiago, and he failed to seek the support of the population, which sincerely backed the constitutionalist cause. He did not even enter the city, but went directly to the air base, trusting, it appears, in the prestige he knew he enjoyed with many of the air force officers. He was practically alone as he went through the air base gate. On the twenty-fifth, such an action might have sufficed, since San Isidro seemed on the verge of surrender. But it was now the twenty-seventh, and San Isidro seemed on the verge of triumph. Santiago Rodríguez Echavarría was arrested quietly, without Ramírez Gómez's having to disavow publicly his declarations of support for the revolt. The air base then resumed its wait, with Ramírez Gómez still officially a constitutionalist. (Although the details of this episode vary from source to source, the version given here, which seems to me the most accurate, is based primarily on interviews with Sención Silverio and Casals Victoria.)

78. Report written after the civil war by an Academy officer for a senior constitutionalist officer (see Chapter 7, n. 6); hereafter cited as Officer's report.

79. Since the commander was a captain and the officer heading the cadets was a major, hierarchy offered an excellent excuse, on both sides, for the local commander's stepping aside.

80. Officer's report.

81. La Romana was the site of the La Romana Mill, the giant sugar complex owned by the South Puerto Rico Sugar Company, an American firm with control over approximately 30 percent of Dominican sugar production.

At La Romana there broke out and developed the only labor unrest to trouble the stifling calm of the Trujillo Era, the sugar workers' strike of January 1946 (see also Appendix II). It had a precedent—in the same city in 1942 another sugar workers' strike was attempted, but was swiftly crushed by the army. After Trujillo's death, labor unions sprung up at La Romana. Some of these were controlled by CONATRAL, the "reasonable," "democratic" labor federation that would distinguish itself by backing the *golpe* against Bosch and by its "understanding" attitude toward the Triumvirate. And yet, under Bosch and even under Reid Cabral, despite his repression and harassment, the Sindicado Unido de los Trabajadores de La Romana, controlled by the far left, maintained a preponderant influence. The PSP was to praise it as the labor union that "takes up and continues the great combative tradition of the sugar workers of La Romana, vanguard of the Dominican worker movement" (R. Salcedo, "La Agresión a los trabajadores del Central Romana," *El Popular*, no. 74 [5 March 1965], p. 5).

82. Officer's report.

83. Ibid.

84. Interview with Morilí Holguín.

CHAPTER 9

1. "Mop Up" was not the official name of the operation. It is used here for convenience.

2. The above statement is unequivocally confirmed by Abraham Lowenthal (*The Dominican Intervention* [Cambridge, Mass.: Harvard University Press, 1972], p. 84). Since Lowenthal, at best a mild critic of his government's Dominican policy, had access to classified material in Washington, his testimony on this point is of particular value.

3. Even Hernando Ramírez had come to recognize the increasingly equivocal stance of the navy. This led him to attempt a desperate move. In the early hours of the twenty-seventh, during a telephone conversation, he offered Rivera Caminero his own post as minister of the armed forces in the constitutionalist government. The gesture was futile. In the admiral's eyes, the constitutionalists were doomed, therefore the currency with which they hoped to buy his loyalty was worthless. Rivera Caminero answered Hernando Ramírez's offer by demanding that a military junta be installed, thus confirming suspicions about his betrayal. Once again, however, Hernando Ramírez refused to accept reality. The conversation ended, he persisted in believing that Rivera Caminero's refusal was not definitive, that the admiral's choice was still open (interview with Hernando Ramírez).

4. Georgetown University, Center for Strategic Studies, *Dominican Action–1965: Intervention or Cooperation?* Special Report Series 2 (Washington, D.C.: Center for Strategic Studies, 1966), p. 24. Because the authors of *Dominican Action–1965* had access to primary sources in Washington, their testimony is valuable in this instance.

5. Navy Captain Ramón Emilio ("Milo") Jiménez Reyes to Lieutenant Colonel Thomas Fishburn, in "Versión de la cinta magnetofónica grabada en la República Dominicana los días 26 y 27 de abril de 1965" ["Transcription of the Tape Recording Made in the Dominican Republic on 26 and 27 April 1965"], no. 3, p. 4. The recording was made by Bosch supporters who had been monitoring an open radio line over which the U.S. Air Force attaché, Lieutenant Colonel Fishburn, spoke with "loyalist" navy Captain Jiménez Reyes who was aboard a Dominican warship at Haina. The conversation was in English. I have heard and compared the tape to a transcript that is among my personal papers.

6. The talks, arranged at the initiative of the Americans, were held in the military attaché section of the embassy. Taking part for the constitutionalists were Hernando Ramírez, Captain Peña Taveras, and Captain Lachapelle Díaz; for the Americans, Lieutenant Colonel Fishburn and one or two other officers whom I have been unable to identify (interviews with Hernando Ramírez and Sención Silverio).

7. Interviews with Molina Ureña, Espaillat Nanita, Lovatón Pittaluga, and Ledesma Pérez. Rather than a possible meeting between "loyalists" and constitutionalists, Breisky's main concern was apparently the problems connected with the evacuation of American citizens. (See also below, n. 12.)

8. Now and then the voice of Jiménez Reyes, speaking in Spanish, can be heard only indistinctly. He is probably consulting with other "loyalist" officers, or asking for their instructions. After a gap of a few minutes, the conversation between Jiménez Reyes and Fishburn resumes.

9. Conversation between Fishburn and Jiménez Reyes, in "Versión de la cinta magnetofónica," pp. 3-4.

10. Ibid., p. 7.

11. Fishburn to Jiménez Reyes, in ibid., p. 20; also interviews with Molina Ureña and Espaillat Nanita.

12. "Versión de la cinta magnetofónica," p. 22. Lowenthal writes: "A political officer urged Connett to end the impasse by inviting both sides to send representatives to the Embassy's residence but Connett declined the suggestion. Once again, possible opportunities to resolve the crisis politically were missed" (*Dominican Intervention*, p. 91). But Lowenthal fails to understand that the United States was not searching for a negotiated settlement of the crisis, but rather wanted the constitutionalist revolt defeated, "even though it could mean more bloodshed." (see Chapter 7). Indeed, the real interest of the embassy in a truce on the morning of the twenty-seventh was to facilitate the evacuation of U.S. citizens.

13. Fishburn to Jiménez Reyes, "Versión de la cinta magnetofónica," p. 9. As already stated, on 26 April the U.S. embassy had advised American citizens in the capital to prepare for evacuation, to be conducted the next day by a naval task force (the Caribbean Ready Group). The six ships of this task force—including the aircraft carrier *Boxer*—had arrived at 2:00 A.M. on the twenty-sixth from Vieques Island (Puerto Rico) and were stationed at first about thirty miles off the Dominican coast. At 6:00 A.M., 27 April, the evacuees began to congregate on the grounds of the Hotel Embajador, in the western sector of Santo Domingo, away from the combat areas. In mid-morning, the much-touted incident of the Hotel Embajador took place, when twenty or thirty armed rebel civilians entered the hotel to search for some right-wing leaders who, they feared, might depart with the evacuees. They found no one, but harassed the Americans by firing a few shots at the ceilings in the saloons of the hotel. No American was harmed, and shortly thereafter the armed civilians departed. A little later, Breisky went to the Presidential Palace where he angrily complained about the episode. This was the only incident that marred the evacuation. In five hours, from 1:00 to 6:00 P.M., between 1,170 and 1,180 evacuees were taken aboard the ships of the task force; 684 evacuees followed the next day.

On the incident of the Hotel Embajador, Lowenthal aptly comments: "There is no doubt that American officials, especially in Washington, were genuinely frightened by the Hotel Embajador incident at first, but the incident soon became more significant as a means of discrediting the pro-Bosch movement than as a source of genuine concern. Secretary Rusk (in May) and President Johnson (in June) later spoke of the Hotel Embajador incident as if it had occurred on Wednesday 28 April, immediately before the decision to land the Marines" (*Dominican Intervention*, p. 204, n. 27). The reason that this incident, obviously of modest proportions, acquired a new importance a day later is obvious: on the twenty-eighth the constitutionalists were winning.

For details on the evacuation, see the article written by the commander of the naval task force, Captain James A. Dare, "Dominican Diary," *U.S. Naval Institute Proceedings* 91 (Dec. 1965), 37-45.

14. "Versión de la cinta magnetofónica," pp. 19, 20.

15. See *Listín Diario*, 28 April 1965, p. 1. The crew of the frigate *Gregorio Luperón* refused to join in the navy's betrayal and left Dominican territorial waters for Puerto Rico, where the ship's commander, Captain Augusto Lara Matos, asked for political asylum, as did a part of the crew (see *El Mundo* [San Juan], 29 April 1965, p. 38).

16. The Ozama River flows along the eastern flank of the capital. If they did not force their way across the Duarte Bridge—the only bridge linking directly the east bank and the capital—the troops of the *conjunto* would have had to make a long and arduous detour: crossing the Ozama northeast of the capital, then proceeding southwest over "unserviceable roads" toward the capital. Their advance would have been blocked by the Isabela River, which, before joining the Ozama, bordered Santo Domingo to the north. Again, there was a single bridge—the Cañita—"situated next to the cement factory, narrower [than the Duarte Bridge], easier for the rebels to defend, and which might collapse if crossed by armored vehicles" (Antonio Llano Montes, *Santo Domingo: Barricadas de odio* [México, D.F.: Editores Mexicanos Unidos, 1966], p. 131).

17. Senior constitutionalist officers gave this information to Benjamin Ruyle, first secretary at the American embassy, on the afternoon of 27 April. Ruyle's report, 27 April 1965, Santo Domingo, is among my personal papers.

18. At the outbreak of the countercoup, the Papal Nuncio, Monsignor Emanuele Clarizio, was in Puerto Rico. The International Airport at Punta Caucedo had been shut to civilian traffic on the afternoon of the twenty-fourth, and Bennett, still in the United States, advised Washington that no U.S. assistance should be offered to bring the Nuncio back from Puerto Rico (Lowenthal, *Dominican Intervention*, p. 97). The ambassador feared that the Nuncio would try to mediate to establish a cease-fire, whereas he wanted a crushing military defeat of the constitutionalists. Thus the Nuncio returned to the Dominican Republic only on 28 April. From the time he arrived he distinguished himself by his intensive efforts to bring about a negotiated settlement of the conflict, which won him the violent hostility of the Dominican right.

19. This was apparently the first—and last—contact between a member of the Molina Ureña government and an embassy other than that of the U.S. (interviews with Lovatón

Pittaluga, Ledesma Pérez, and Hernando Ramírez).
20. Details about this episode come from Lovatón Pittaluga. A good account is also given by the Dominican Julio César Estrella in his *La Revolución Dominicana y la crisis de la OEA* (Santo Domingo: ¡Ahora! 1965), pp. 13-14.
21. It is impossible to establish an accurate chronology of the battle at the bridge. The newspapers of the period, the interviews I have held, and the many works on the subject prove, by their very contradictions, that such an effort is futile. Approximate times can nevertheless be given. It was around one o'clock in the afternoon when Wessin's tanks and troops began their drive to cross the bridge. Around an hour later, they had succeeded.
22. Llano Montes, *Santo Domingo*, p. 130. Having come up the Ozama, a frigate of the Dominican navy bombarded the constitutionalist positions near the Duarte Bridge, "to protect the advancing tanks" (ibid., p. 129).
23. Ibid., p. 131.
24. Luis Lembert Peguero was apparently the only PRD leader to play a role of any importance during the critical period that began on 27 April and, because of the United States military intervention, continued into the first days of May. True, Jottin Cury played as important a role as Lembert Peguero during the same period. But Cury, a former UCN leader, had become a PRD member only a few weeks before the outbreak of the revolt; hence he did not yet hold the high positions within the party that would later be his because of the courage and the intelligence he showed during the civil war.
25. Marcel Niedergang, *La Révolution de Saint-Domingue* ([Paris]: Plon, 1966), pp. 57, 50.
26. Suffering from a severe attack of hepatitis, Hernando Ramírez was forced to give up his position as military chief of the revolt at about one o'clock that afternoon. In his place, Colonel Caamaño, minister of interior in the Molina Ureña government (see below n. 45), was given direction of all military operations—at Hernando Ramírez's own suggestion. Hernando Ramírez meant the abdication to be temporary—"until I have recovered" (interview with Hernando Ramírez). Judging by Ruyle's report ("the principal spokesman was Col. Hernando Ramírez"), Hernando Ramírez had already resumed his position as military commander by the time of the meeting at the American embassy. Of the two protagonists, Hernando Ramírez soon abandoned the struggle, and Caamaño became the revolt's real leader. On 4 May, at Ciudad Nueva, the Congress elevated Caamaño to the presidency of the Republic by an overwhelming majority.
27. Ruyle, Report to the State Department, 27 April 1965 [evening], Santo Domingo. Ruyle was the only American diplomat who, during the Triumvirate, maintained good relations with the leaders of the PRD's *duro* wing. He was also the only one who, because of his behavior during those days of crisis, was able to retain the respect of the PRD leaders.
28. Leopoldo A. Espaillat Nanita, "A Casals Pastoriza," *Listín Diario*, 18 Sept. 1969, p. 6. Espaillat Nanita was one of the "8 or 10 persons" (Ruyle, Report) who stayed with Molina Ureña at the Palace until the last minute.
29. Espaillat Nanita, "A Casals Pastoriza," p. 6.
30. Ruyle, Report.
31. Ibid.
32. Espaillat Nanita, "A Casals Pastoriza," p. 6.
33. After the outbreak of the countercoup, Bennett flew from Georgia to Washington, where he met on Monday the twenty-sixth with President Johnson. The next day a U.S. Air Force jet took him to the Punta Caucedo International Airport, in territory controlled by San Isidro. From there he was lifted by helicopter to the gardens of the United States embassy, where he arrived at 12:40 P.M. (Dare, "Dominican Diary," p. 41; John B. Martin, *Overtaken by Events: The Dominican Crisis from the Fall of Trujillo to the Civil War* [Garden City, N.Y.: Doubleday, 1966], p. 653; Tad Szulc, *Dominican Diary* [New York: Dell, 1966], p. 45).
34. Ruyle, Report.
35. Espaillat Nanita, "A Casals Pastoriza," p. 6.
36. Bennett, telegram, 27 April 1965, 9:30 P.M.
37. Ibid. Given his contempt for the constitutionalist leaders, Bennett must have been firmly convinced that they would rush, en masse, into the embassies. At the end of his report he adds: "Four actually requested asylum; denied in accordance standard US practice not to grant asylum" (ibid.).

38. Bennett employs the word "courteous" in his telegram of 27 April 1965, 9:30 P.M. The expression "gruff," used by Ledesma Pérez in a conversation with the author, aptly describes the reaction of the participants (see also Szulc, *Dominican Diary*, p. 48, and Dan Kurzman, *Santo Domingo: Revolt of the Damned* [New York: G. P. Putnam's Sons, 1965], pp. 151-53). Even more than his refusal to mediate, and more than his role in the American decision to intervene militarily in the Dominican Republic, Bennett's contemptuous way of humiliating the losers made him one "ugly American" the constitutionalists could never forgive.

39. A "legitimate movement," then, had "initiated this fratricide and called forth counter-reaction."

40. Bennett, telegram, 27 April 1965, 9:30 P.M. The errors of language have been left as they appear.

41. Many have accused Bosch of cowardice for his failure to return to the country during the civil war (see for instance Martin, *Overtaken by Events*, pp. 706-7). This accusation rests not on facts, but on hostility toward the man or the constitutionalist movement. The leaders of the conspiracy did not want Bosch to attempt a clandestine return before the outbreak of the countercoup, since such an attempt would have entailed unnecessary risks of arrest and would have provided the Triumvirate with a precious hostage (interviews with Hernando Ramírez, Molina Ureña, and Peña Gómez). Instead, according to the Enriquillo plan, a military plane would leave immediately after the success of the revolt to bring Bosch back from Puerto Rico. No plane arrived, of course. The civil war began, and the constitutionalists had no means to bring back their president, given the attitude of the Navy and the Air Force. Moreover, the International Airport at Punta Caucedo had been closed to the traffic since the afternoon of the twenty-fourth; besides, it lay in San Isidro's territory.

Bosch's return would have been no less impossible after the landing of the marines. In a matter of hours, all the "neutral" garrisons of the interior declared in favor of San Isidro, and the constitutionalists remained blockaded in a few square miles in the capital. Bosch has asserted, and U.S. officials have denied, that after 28 April he asked the Americans to bring him back to constitutionalist Santo Domingo (see for instance Juan Bosch, "A Tale of Two Nations," *New Leader*, 21 June 1965, pp. 4-7). Whether or not this accusation is true, it was certainly unreasonable to expect the United States to return to his followers the leader of a movement they opposed.

But then, what else could Bosch have done? Should he have tried to be smuggled into the constitutionalist redoubt? It is folly to expect that he would have succeeded, since he was under the constant surveillance of the FBI and American naval and air forces surrounded the Dominican Republic.

Thus, unable to rejoin his constitutionalist followers, Bosch remained in Puerto Rico until the conclusion of the civil war, when he was at last able to return to his country (see Chapter 10).

42. Molina Ureña did not take part in the first talks with Benoit (no civilian took part), but he was present at the afternoon meeting. His role, however, was minor (see Chapter 6).

43. Interview with Hernando Ramírez.

44. Interview with Hernando Ramírez.

45. Five decrees, all on 25 April, were issued during the brief life of the Molina Ureña regime. The first convened a special meeting of the legislative chambers in the National Congress Building on Monday, 26 April 1965, at 0800 hours. It was the only one to be carried out. On the morning of the twenty-sixth, the Congress met for the first time since Bosch's overthrow. The first order of business was to elect new officers: Aníbal Campagna, independent senator (formerly UCN) from Santiago province, replaced Casasnovas Garrido, deported on 3 November 1963 by the Triumvirate, as president of the Senate; César A. Canó Fortuna replaced Molina Ureña (now provisional president of the Republic) as president of the Chamber of Deputies. Then the only law was enacted: "the law of general amnesty for political prisoners and deportees" (*El Caribe*, 27 April 1965, p. 1).

On the twenty-seventh, around nine o'clock, the Congress reconvened as it had decided the day before. But the session was chaotic, and no concrete measures could be voted (interview with Aníbal Campagna). The collapse of the constitutionalist movement seemed imminent. The lawmakers quickly dispersed. They met again only a week later (3 May), this time to elect a new president of the Republic, Colonel Caamaño.

The second decree issued by the Molina Ureña government cashiered Wessin. The three remaining decrees named government officials for the province of Santiago.

No issue of the *Gaceta Oficial* covers the period of the Molina Ureña government. The five decrees, however, were read over Radio Santo Domingo TV, and the text can be found in U.S., Congress, Senate, Committee on the Judiciary, Subcommittee to Investigate the Administration of the Internal Security Act and Other Internal Security Laws, *Communist Threat to the United States Through the Caribbean: Hearings: Testimony of Brigadier General Elías Wessin y Wessin,* 89 Cong., 1 sess., 1 October 1965 (Washington, D.C.: U.S. Government Printing Office, 1965), pp. 257-59. The text of the first decree can also be found in *El Caribe,* 26 April 1965, p. 1.

Although there were no decrees announcing appointments to the cabinet, Molina Ureña named four ministers: Lieutenant Colonel Hernando Ramírez, minister of the armed forces; Colonel Caamaño, minister of the interior; Máximo Lovatón Pittaluga (PRD), minister of foreign affairs; Manuel R. Ledesma Pérez (PRD), minister without portfolio.

46. Ruyle, Report.

47. The other PRD leaders who had sought asylum—Peña Gómez, Lovatón Pittaluga, Manuel R. Ledesma Pérez, and so on—rejoined the constitutionalist ranks after only two or three days.

48. Some PRD leaders, particularly Lovatón Pittaluga and Ledesma Pérez, began to visit the Colombian embassy frequently, trying to persuade Molina Ureña to return to the constitutionalist zone (interviews with Lovatón Pittaluga and Ledesma Pérez).

49. This portrait of Molina Ureña rests on two long conversations with him and on interviews with persons who knew him well, including Máximo Lovatón Pittaluga, Manuel R. Ledesma Pérez, and Leopoldo Espaillat Nanita.

50. Molina Ureña served the Balaguer government as ambassador to France until May 1971.

51. Niedergang, *La Révolution de Saint-Domingue,* p. 70. It has been pointed out that Caamaño (like Fernández Domínguez) was the son of one of the worst of Trujillo's henchmen, General Fausto Caamaño, and that these two officers may have sought to atone for the sins of their fathers. At least in the case of Caamaño it is impossible to find any such desire before the outbreak of the revolt; as we have seen, he joined the conspiracy for quite different reasons. The transformation of Caamaño in fact began only after the outbreak of the revolt, and particularly in the afternoon of 27 April.

52. The following analysis is my own interpretation, based on three long conversations with Hernando Ramírez and interviews with many other actors of the period.

53. Nevertheless, contrary to the allegations of many U.S. newspapers, Hernando Ramírez has denied ever asserting that the constitutionalist movement was "heavily infiltrated" by the communists (*New York Times,* 30 July 1965, p. 7). "The democratic elements maintained control at all times over the non-democratic forces" (interview with Hernando Ramírez). But this fierce anti-Communist was opposed to the participation of the Communists in a struggle that, if only briefly, was a common one. As he explained, it was necesssary "to do without their services."

54. Hernando Ramírez did not return to the Dominican Republic until 20 September, seventeen days after the installation of the García Godoy government of "reconciliation." If his attitude during the civil war can be branded as desertion, one must still admit that never in the years that followed did he try to win pardon from the victors by betraying the cause he had championed. Although he deserted, he never declared that the revolt had been diverted toward "nondemocratic" ends. He remained in the armed forces, but his career was ruined, as were the careers of all the constitutionalist officers. A lieutenant colonel on 24 April 1965, today—twelve years later—Hernando Ramírez is still a Lieutenant colonel.

55. *New York Times,* 28 April 1965, p. 1, and *Washington Post,* 28 April 1965, p. A-1.

56. The description of the battle is based largely on interviews with participants. See also *Listín Diario* and *El Caribe* of 28 April 1965.

57. For some, all those who fought at the bridge to block Wessin's troops from entering the capital had to be criminals, murderers, thieves—especially if their skin was dark (interview with the late Carlos Sánchez y Sánchez, a Trujillista who died unreformed). I am far from sharing this view, though I must admit that it is widespread within certain Dominican circles—limited in numbers, but, alas, very powerful.

58. In particular, "an illogical use of cooperation and coordination between the armored vehicles and the infantry. On the twenty-seventh the infantry advance[d] on one side, the tanks on the other, uncoordinately. They [the "loyalists"] use[d] the tanks like guns, at a distance, while the infantry advance[d] out in the open" (interview with a senior constitutionalist officer).

59. Llano Montes, *Santo Domingo*, p. 129.

60. Marcelino Zapico, *Revolución en Hispanoamérica: Lo que vi en Santo Domingo* (Madrid: Escalicer, 1966), p. 53.

61. Llano Montes, *Santo Domingo*, p. 134.

62. It is hard to determine exactly how many "loyalist" troops were engaged in Operation Mop Up. Wessin later maintained that there were "approximately 600 men" (U.S., Congress, Senate, *Testimony of Brigadier General Elías Wessin y Wessin*, p. 159), as good a way as any to justify defeat. More objective—for a change—is Georgetown University, Center for Strategic Studies, *Dominican Action–1965*, which speaks of "a force of 1,500 men, with some artillery and thirty-one armored fighting vehicles of various types, including thirteen tanks" (p. 27). The actual figure stands most likely at around 2,000 men, the majority from the CEFA. Only some of de los Santos' men were engaged in the battle, perhaps because part of the personnel at the Nineteenth of November did not belong to combat units, but also probably because de los Santos, confident of success, was—like Montás Guerrero—already looking to the future. Several hundred men, moreover, were absent from the *conjunto*: the few on leave at the outbreak of the countercoup, and, particularly, those who deserted over the next few days (24-26 April)—a considerable number, it seems (interview with Colonel Benoit).

63. Georgetown University, Center for Strategic Studies, *Dominican Action–1965*, p. 31.

64. Interviews with Dean Rusk, Thomas Mann, and two CIA officials. See also Lowenthal, *Dominican Intervention*, pp. 95-96, and Charles Roberts, *LBJ's Inner Circle* (New York: Delacorte Press, 1965), p. 203.

It should again be stressed that after a brief moment of shock on the twenty-fifth—when they finally understood the real aim of the revolt—the feeling of crisis subsided both in the U.S. embassy in Santo Domingo and in Washington. The crucial decisions had been made immediately, with the approval of both the embassy and the State Department. These decisions seemed completely adequate: the revolt had to be crushed, and the San Isidro "loyalists" were strong enough to do it, with some discreet American help (such as pressure on Rivera Caminero by the U.S. navy attaché, or on Ramírez Gómez and de la Mota by the U.S. consul in Santiago [for the latter see Lowenthal, *Dominican Crisis*, p. 201, n. 9]). The events of 26 April strengthened the Americans' feeling of confidence. In the morning and the afternoon of the twenty-seventh, the embassy confidently expected Wessin's imminent triumph; in the evening it failed to realize the extent of the "loyalist" defeat in the battle at the bridge. Washington, which had been relying on the embassy's information, made the same mistake. Only on the twenty-eighth would the embassy and then Washington begin to awaken.

65. As Moreno pretends in *Barrios in Arms* (Pittsburgh: University of Pittsburgh Press, 1970), p. 39.

66. They could count on passivity not only from San Isidro but also from the anti-constitutionalist forces in the capital—the "refugees" in the Fortaleza Ozama and the Police Headquarters and in Intendencia and Transportación. They had missed their chance to strike at the constitutionalists when the latter were fully engaged at the bridge. Now it was too late. The failure of Operation Mop Up only heightened the panic and disorganization already rampant. Those frightened souls—whose only wish was to be forgotten—were hardly the ones to pose a threat to constitutionalist control of the capital.

True, a few dozen men of the Mella Battalion occupied the Presidential Palace during the night of 27-28 April, taking advantage of the fact that the Palace had been abandoned by the constitutionalists on the afternoon of the twenty-seventh. But that was the only "offensive" action by Montás Guerrero's forces, which showed a marked preference for inaction and wisely confined themselves to the city's western districts, where the chance of meeting any rebels was slim.

67. Kurzman, *Santo Domingo*, pp. 166-67.

68. Interviews with Hernando Ramírez, Sención Silverio, Núñez Nogueras, and García Germán.

69. Bennett, telegram, 28 April 1965, 3:00 P.M., Santo Domingo, among my personal papers.

70. Moreno, *Barrios in Arms*, p. 31.

71. Eight, at least: the two hosts—Wessin and de los Santos—and six "guests": General Hernán Despradel Brache, the chief of police; General (Ret.) Belisario Peguero Guerrero, the former chief of police; and four generals with no command—Renato Hungría Morel, Félix Hermida, Jr., and Manuel María García Urbáez, all of the army, and Miguel Atila Luna Pérez, of the air force.

72. Bennett, telegram, 28 April 1965, 3:00 P.M.

73. Quoted by Lowenthal, *Dominican Intervention*, p. 98.

74. Bennett, telegram, 28 April 1965, 1:43 P.M., Santo Domingo, among my personal papers.

75. Lowenthal, *Dominican Intervention*, p. 100, is my source for the telephone conversation between Bennett and Vaughn, and he is also the one who points out that Bundy probably made the final decision.

76. Georgetown University, Center for Stategic Studies, *Dominican Action—1965*, p. 32. Formation of a military junta held out a second advantage: it heightened the status of the "loyalist" generals, until then joined, at least on paper, in a Jefatura Mixta de Operaciones de las Fuerzas Armadas.

77. Szulc, *Dominican Diary*, p. 53. Colonel Benoit, however, is not unknown to the readers of this book. We have seen him, as de los Santos' representative, negotiate unsuccessfully with the constitutionalist leaders both on the morning and the afternoon of the twenty-fifth. We have seen him leave the Palace in haste following the air force attack. A little later, at the home of friends, he phoned de los Santos. He wanted to voice his indignation at the attack, which took place at the very moment he was conversing with the rebel leaders ("They could have killed me!"). Above all he wanted to be brought back to San Isidro. Shortly thereafter, one of de los Santos' helicopters landed in the La Feria district. Benoit could now go back to his "buddies" (interview with Benoit).

78. During the night of 25-26 April, Olgo Santana Carrasco had gone in person to the Palace to assure Molina Ureña of his adherence to the constitutionalist cause (see Chapter 8). This Junta Militar de Gobierno was only a facade. Benoit, Santana Carrasco, and Casado Saladin had no real power—probably the reason that they were chosen. They were mere figureheads, in place of the real "bosses," Wessin, de los Santos, and Rivera Caminero, whose names were too closely linked to the bombing of the capital. Their job was to take responsibility for odious acts decreed by others. Even today, Benoit still wonders "why, with so many generals at San Isidro, did they have to pick three colonels?" (interview). The answer is simple.

79. Bennett, telegram, 28 April 1965, 3:00 P.M.

80. Moreno, *Barrios in Arms*, pp. 31-32. My own sources for this episode are Martínez Francisco and Colonel Benoit. Moreno, however, had a source unavailable to me: a "loyalist" officer who took part in the abduction. All the versions coincide.

81. Interviews with Martínez Francisco and Benoit. The detail concerning Martínez Francisco's shaky hands was provided by Benoit.

82. Zapico, *Revolución en Hispanoamérica*, pp. 55-56.

83. Benoit admitted openly that "the morale at San Isidro was very low." The "loyalist" officers were convinced that only American military intervention could stop the rebels from capturing the *conjunto* (interview with Benoit).

84. "To Miami," no doubt. Indeed it is interesting to point out that Bennett himself put the word *retreat* in quotes.

85. Bennett, telegram, 28 April 1965, 5:16 P.M., Santo Domingo, among my personal papers. Italics added. "CRITIC" cables are those of the highest priority and usually reach Washington in a matter of minutes.

86. In fact, 536 marines landed. Marines had already come ashore on different occasions since the previous day to conduct the evacuation, but, to underline their peaceful intentions, they were unarmed. For details see Dare, "Dominican Diary," esp. p. 42, and Major General R. McC. Tompkins, "Ubique," *Marine Corps Gazette* 91 (Sept. 1965), esp. p. 35.

87. Benoit's original request for U.S. intervention centered on the danger of a "second Cuba," but failed to mention any need to protect American lives. The State Depart-

ment, however, felt the need to hide an intervention that was purely political in its aims under the cover of "humanitarianism." Undersecretary Mann telephoned Bennett between 6:00 and 6:30 P.M., instructing him to have Benoit put in writing a request for U.S. military intervention on the grounds that it was needed to protect American lives (see Martin, *Overtaken by Events*, p. 657). Benoit dutifully complied. Thus was born the myth of the humanitarian intervention—a splendid example of hypocrisy. For an excellent and penetrating satire of this "humanitarian intervention" see Art Buchwald, "Revolution and a Humanitarian Reason Named Sidney," *Washington Post*, 6 May 1965. The article is reproduced in Appendix III.

CHAPTER 10

1. This also marks the end of my detailed presentation of the Dominican crisis. An in-depth analysis of the events following 28 April and of the opposing forces would be fascinating. So far no one has done it. Since I already have the necessary material, I hope someday to devote myself to this task. For the present, however, I will offer only a sketch of the immediate consequences of the American intervention.

2. Speech, 28 April 1965, in *Department of State Bulletin* 52, no. 1531 (17 May 1965), p. 738.

3. "The viewpoint of Washington officials was that military action should be avoided as long as there was a chance the junta could prevail" (Georgetown University, Center for Strategic Studies, *Dominican Action—1965: Intervention or Cooperation?* Special Report Series #2 [Washington, D.C.: Center for Strategic Studies], p. 42). Martin uses almost the same words: "Washington leaders said that obviously the U.S. government wished to avoid military action 'as long as there is a reasonable chance orderly forces [the Benoit junta] can prevail' " (*Overtaken by Events: The Dominican Crisis from the Fall of Trujillo to the Civil War* [Garden City, N.Y.: Doubleday, 1966], p. 659). And Bennett stated: "I do not want to recommend actual intervention of U.S. troops in the fighting. This would take us down a torturous path. But I am quite prepared to recommend this action if canvass later this morning shows situation continuing to deteriorate" (telegram, 29 April 1965, 3:45 P.M., Santo Domingo, among my personal papers).

4. Tad Szulc, of the *New York Times*, was among the newsmen who, on the morning of 29 April, were on board the *Wood County* (one of the six ships of the navy's task force cruising off Santo Domingo), awaiting authorization from the American embassy to land. Szulc reported that "one of the newsmen standing on the flying bridge thought of turning on his transistor radio. To our utter amazement we found ourselves listening to official communications in open language concerning the activities in Santo Domingo. Then another reporter discovered that we could hear the ship's radio from another point on the flying bridge and thus monitor the fleet conversations. What we heard was most revealing as to the part the United States was playing in the Dominican civil war. In fact, this was our first direct exposure to what was really happening . . . . Then the embassy, the American dispatcher at San Isidro and the Boxer became engaged in lengthy exchanges about the needs of the junta and what was being done about this by United States authorities. Most of the discussion concerned the radio equipment about which Ambassador Bennett had been messaging Washington so earnestly the day before, about food for the loyalists and other items. The San Isidro dispatcher reported that 'rations were delivered to troops.' . . . He then went on to relay the message that 'de los Santos requests augmentation of supplies for the area' and apparently was requesting helicopters . . . . A few minutes later another message urged 'rations for additional men . . . .' San Isidro came back on the air to say that with the delivery of rations, 'expect good psychological effect.' And then a little later this: 'A significant morale boost is evident here since the arrival of rations.' . . . Shortly before 9 o'clock the Boxer requested details on 'the type of equipment needed' " (*Dominican Diary* [New York: Dell, 1966], pp. 66-68).

5. Interview with Narciso Isa Conde.

6. Interview with José Israel Cuello.
7. Interview with Jimmy Durán.
8. Interview with "Baby" Mejía. The "warriors" of the far left reacted like any ordinary PRDista, particularly since they realized that the American intervention was aimed primarily at them. Because of the importance of the 1J4, the reaction of that party will be examined in detail.

A large number of CECP members met late in the evening of the twenty-eighth. There was unanimous agreement that resistance was futile. They had to prepare for the future: "hide the arms, rescue the cadres, find safe places for the leaders" (interview with Jimmy Durán). In fact, "most of the leaders went into hiding" (interview with Norge Botello). So began Operation "Belleza" ("Beautification")—"washing off the smell of the trenches, taking a bath, having a shave" (interview with Fafa Taveras)—in short, getting rid of any outward signs that might betray them to the invader as "rebels." Only two CECP members—Norge Botello and Fafa Taveras—resisted the wave of panic. Botello was apparently one of those whose activity "stopped, as if something was imminent"; Taveras, however, strove more actively to restore a semblance of order to the *catorcista* ranks.

Leaders of the PSP and the MPD reacted similarly. Most of them went into hiding, leaving orders for their party's members to do the same. Those who remained played a passive role. Only a few tried to act.

9. Interview with Jimmy Durán.
10. Cited by Szulc, *Dominican Diary*, p. 68.
11. Martin, *Overtaken by Events*, p. 658.
12. Juan Miguel Román was the first of the 1J4 leaders to come back, probably as early as the afternoon of the twenty-ninth. "What we're witnessing is a rout. I feel ashamed of myself. I believe that in the next twenty-four hours we're going to go from heroes to shits" (Juan Miguel Román as quoted by Jimmy Durán , in an interview). Other members of the CECP followed his example, but not all; some preferred shame to danger and remained for several days in hiding: Luis Genao Espaillat, Roberto Duvergé, Pin Montás, and especially Fidelio Despradel, the real leader not of the *duros* but of the cowards. Later, Despradel amply demonstrated that his cowardice was more than just a momentary lapse; throughout the civil war he gave his comrades the benefit of his theoretical knowledge of imperialism, revolution, and armed struggle. Others, however, were left to risk their lives in the commando units—Fidelio always stayed away from the fighting.
13. Constitutionalist Military Command, "Al Pueblo dominicano," Santo Domingo, 29 April 1965, among my personal papers. Significantly, the tract makes no mention of the presence of American troops.
14. Speech, 30 April 1965, in *Department of State Bulletin* 52, no. 1351 (17 May 1965), p. 742.
15. Speech. 2 May 1965, in ibid., p. 745.
16. For the U.S. military operations between 30 April and 3 May see especially Major General R. McC. Tompkins, "Ubique," *Marine Corps Gazette* 49 (Sept. 1965): 36-39.
17. "The Junta is an unreal government, whose military forces have been badly mauled by the rampaging rebels" (*New York Times*, 2 May 1965).
18. "Tap Bennett and his fellow diplomats at the Embassy were so deeply committed to the notion that the rebel movement was Communist-controlled that they appeared unwilling to establish any contacts in the rebel area that might have contradicted their judgment" (Szulc, *Dominican Diary*, p. 94). Martin writes, "I had not known colonel Caamaño, . . . and I thought Imbert could tell me about him. . . . I asked him who was leading the rebels . . . . I asked Imbert how the whole thing started" (*Overtaken by Events*, pp. 666-67).
19. *New York Times*, 3 May 1965, p. 1. See also Martin, *Overtaken by Events*, p. 676.
20. Martin, *Overtaken by Events*, p. 681.
21. "I was the victim of a coup d'état" (interview with Benoit).
22. GRN, tract, Santo Domingo, [8 May 1965], among my personal papers.
23. Antonio Guzmán and Salvador Jorge Blanco.
24. Decree 2 of 27 September 1963, in *Gaceta Oficial* 8791, 30 Sept. 1963, and decree 1730 of 11 November 1964, in *Gaceta Oficial* 8905, 25 Nov. 1964, pp. 21-22.
25. *Overtaken by Events*, p. 684.

26. Postigo to Alfonso Rodríguez, letter [summer 1965], Santo Domingo, among my personal papers.

27. This paragraph is based on interviews with Postigo. Finding his participation in the GRN increasingly distasteful, Postigo resigned on 10 August 1965; he was replaced by Leonte Bernard Vásquez.

28. GRN, tract, Santo Domingo, [8 May 1965].

29. "Act of the Military Junta Government," 7 May 1965, in *Gaceta Oficial* 8943, 20 May 1965, p. 3.

30. Decree 7, in *Gaceta Oficial* 8943, 20 May 1965, p. 11. Arrested on 24 April by Peña Taveras and released immediately after the American military intervention, Rivera Cuesta was discharged from his position as army chief of staff by the GRN (decree 6 of 8 May 1965, in *Gaceta Oficial* 8943, 20 May 1965, p. 10). He became a colonel again, since the rank of general had been conferred on him for only as long as he held the post of chief of staff.

31. Decrees 1, 4, and 6 of 8 May 1965, in *Gaceta Oficial* 8943, 20 May 1965, pp. 6, 8, 10.

32. *New York Times*, 10 May 1965, p. 7.

33. Article 15: "No State or group of States has the right to intervene, directly or indirectly, for any reasons whatever, in the internal or external affairs of any other State. The foregoing principle prohibits not only armed forces but also any other form of interference or attempted threat against the personality of the State or against its political, economic and cultural elements."

Article 17: "The territory of a State is inviolable; it may not be the object, even temporarily, of military occupation or of other measures of force taken by another State, directly or indirectly, on any grounds whatever. No territorial acquisition or special advantages obtained either by force or by means of coercion shall be recognized."

34. Organization of American States, Secretary-General, *Informe del Secretario General de la Organización de los Estados Americanos en relación con la situación dominicana. Desde el 29 de abril de 1965 hasta la instalación del Gobierno Provisional*, DRCMRE, Official Documents, Ser. F/II.10 (Washington, D.C.: Pan American Union, 1965), p. 2.

35. *Washington Post*, 7 May 1965, p. A-19, and 4 May 1965, p. A-1.

36. *New York Times*, 7 May 1965, p. 14, and 4 May 1965, p. 1.

37. *Washington Post*, 8 May 1965, p. A-8.

38. This was acknowledged, a few days later, by the OAS's Credentials Committee, which recommended to the DRCMRE that "the Dominican Republic's seat at the Tenth Consultative Meeting be declared vacant" (Organization of American States, Credentials Committee, *Segundo informe de la Comisión de Credenciales*, 8 May 1965, Ser. F/II.10, [Washington, D.C.: Pan American Union, 1965], p. 3).

39. Votes against the resolution were cast by Chile, Ecuador, Mexico, Peru, and Uruguay, with Venezuela abstaining. These six states constituted, with varying degrees of fervor, the dissident minority.

40. *New York Times*, 13 May 1965, p. 20.

41. Of particular interest is the case of Argentina, whose military chiefs strongly favored participation in the IAPF. President Illía was not in the habit of opposing them, but the reaction of Congress—and of the population—was so violent that for once Illía chose to disobey his military "advisers."

42. The United States forces stationed in the Dominican Republic were in turn incorporated into the IAPF. On 1 June there were 13,284 American soldiers in the country, in addition to the thousands of sailors aboard ships patrolling the coasts and who were not part of the IAPF.

43. Santiago Estrella Veloz, "La Fuerza Interamericana de los dictadores," *Ahora*, no. 110 (3 Oct. 1965), p. 23.

44. *New York Times*, 29 May 1965, p. 2.

45. Organization of American States, Secretary-General, *Informe*, p. 4.

46. On 5 May a cease-fire known as the Act of Santo Domingo was signed by the constitutionalist government of Colonel Caamaño and the military junta of Colonel Benoit.

47. Jerome Slater, *Intervention and Negotiation* (New York: Harper and Row, 1970), pp. 82-83.

48. For an excellent analysis, see Tom Wicker, "Johnson Policies: A survey of Support," *New York Times*, 14 June 1965, p. 1.

49. For an analysis of the relations between the UN and the OAS prior to 1965, see Inis Claude, "The OAS, the UN and the United States," *International Conciliation*, no. 547 (March 1964), pp. 3-67.

The Security Council's role in the Dominican crisis was highly modest: some speeches, a few resolutions in favor of a cease-fire, and a request to U Thant, the UN secretary-general (14 May) to send a representative to the Dominican Republic. U Thant chose the Venezuelan José Antonio Mayobre for the mission. With no power—his task was simply to inform the Security Council of the Dominican situation—Mayobre had no influence on the course of events.

50. Szulc, *Dominican Diary*, p. 217.

51. Throughout its existence, the GRN had a dismal record regarding human rights and treatment of prisoners. A striking example is the conquest of the *barrios altos*, which ushered in a wave of atrocities; scores of prisoners were tortured and murdered. After the discovery of several corpses at the estate *Haras*, in "loyalist" territory, the Inter-American Commission on Human Rights (the only OAS body that performed creditably during the crisis) investigated. The commission concluded that the corpses were those of political prisoners executed by military and police elements of the GRN under a "policy of seeking to eliminate adversaries." Indeed, it was not uncommon for people arrested by the GRN to disappear mysteriously. The record of the GRN contrasted starkly with that of the Caamaño government, which carried out no political executions and was much more humane in the treatment of its prisoners.

See especially the various reports of the Inter-American Commission on Human Rights to the Tenth Meeting of Consultation and Anna P. Schreiber and Philippe S. E. Schreiber, "The Inter-American Commission on Human Rights in the Dominican Crisis," *International Organization* 22, no. 2 (Spring 1968), pp. 508-28.

52. *Washington Post*, 8 May 1965, p. A-15, and *New York Times*, 17 May 1965, p. 15.

53. *Washington Post*, 20 May 1965, p. A-1.

54. Interview with Morilí Holguín.

55. Foremost among my sources for the Guzmán negotiations are documents (notes, reports, memoranda, minutes, and others) provided by Antonio Guzmán. In addition, I have conducted a series of interviews, the most useful being those with Antonio Guzmán, Jottin Cury (foreign minister in the Caamaño government), Hugo Tolentino Dipp (member of President Caamaño's Advisory Committee), Juan Bosch, Thomas Mann, Major Núñez Nogueras (of the constitutionalist military staff), and José Francisco Peña Gómez. For the interested reader, American newspapers (particularly the *New York Times*, the *Washington Post*, and the *Wall Street Journal*) and Szulc's *Dominican Diary* (pp. 207-302) are readily available sources.

56. Martin, *Overtaken by Events*, p. 367. Like Bosch, Guzmán was a native of La Vega.

57. Several months later, Guzmán learned the identity of "Mr. Jackson": he was Abe Fortas, "the President's *homme de confiance*" (Theodore Draper, *The Dominican Revolt: A Case Study in American Policy* [New York: Commentary, 1968], p. 178).

58. Antonio Guzmán, "Informe al Gabinete y al Comando Militar Constitucionalista," Santo Domingo, 24 May 1965, among my personal papers. According to Guzmán, the Americans refused to give him a list with the names of these "Communists," explaining that they would provide the names once a final agreement on the government had been reached. They said only that the list would include between eighty and one hundred persons (interview with Guzmán).

59. Interview with Guzmán. See also Antonio Guzmán, "Condiciones en que puedo aceptar," San Juan, Puerto Rico, 15 May 1965, among my personal papers.

60. "Mr. Jackson," as quoted by Guzmán, in an interview.

61. For an example, see pp. 266-67 below. The Guzmán solution had the support not only of the PRD but also of Caamaño and the other constitutionalist military leaders. The 1J4 had only a fragmentary knowledge of the negotiations; its leaders had never talked with Guzmán, but they were "resigned." They realized that, given the prevailing balance of

power, the anti-Communist Guzmán was the least evil solution (interviews with Jimmy Durán and Norge Botello).

62. "Declaración de posición del señor Antonio Guzmán referente a la formación de un gobierno constitucional en la República Dominicana," Santo Domingo, [21 or 22 May 1965], among my personal papers. The "Declaración" is a memorandum from McGeorge Bundy to Guzmán (interview with Guzmán).

63. Guzmán, "Condiciones en que puedo aceptar."

64. Guzmán to McGeorge Bundy, memorandum, Santo Domingo, 20 May 1965, among my personal papers.

65. Bundy to Guzmán, memorandum, Santo Domingo, [21 or 22 May 1965], among my personal papers. The memorandum was top secret, and Guzmán was to conceal it from the Caamaño government. Of the constitutionalists, only Salvador Jorge Blanco knew of its existence (interview with Guzmán).

66. Antonio Guzmán, "Promemoria," Santo Domingo, [16 or 17 May 1965], among my personal papers.

67. In the "neutral" category were officers who were abroad—nearly all of them as military attachés—and had not taken part in the conflict. From the outset of the Guzmán negotiations, Colonel Caamaño had asked certain senior constitutionalist officers to draw up lists of "neutrals" who could be recommended to the Americans for the key posts in the armed forces. Two lists were drawn up: the first included officers reputed to be relatively favorable to the constitutionalists; the second named officers believed to be only slightly hostile. The second list was kept in reserve should the Americans prove intransigent (interview with Núñez Nogueras).

68. Guzmán to Bundy, memorandum, [21 or 22 May 1965], Santo Domingo, among my personal papers.

69. Interview with Guzmán. Regarding the presence of foreign troops on Dominican soil, the Guzmán solution stated that "it is in the interest of the Government of National Reconciliation that the Inter-American Peace Force establish its presence in the Dominican Republic as soon as possible. It is impossible, at this time, to predict how long the presence of the Inter-American Peace Force will be needed in the Dominican Republic, but the withdrawal of the units of that Force will begin as soon as possible." In the economic sphere, substantial American aid was contemplated, though the amount had not yet been set: "Mr. Guzmán has also been assured that the United States Government will offer considerable emergency assistance to help restore an active economic life in the Dominican Republic" ("Declaración de posición").

70. *New York Times*, 18 May 1965, p. 38. "The prospects for an agreement creating a regime under Mr. Guzmán . . . were reported tonight to be promising," announced the *Times* (22 May 1965, p. 1) four days later.

71. Interview with Guzmán.

72. Interview with Thomas Mann.

73. Guzmán, "Informe al Gabinete y al Comando Militar Constitucionalista."

74. Szulc, *Dominican Diary*, p. 282.

75. A full listing of the sources for this section would be too long. Generally speaking, with a few exceptions, all the Dominicans I have interviewed were questioned on this period as well (see the Bibliographical Essay). In addition, I have used a large number of documents: the *Gacetas Oficiales* of the two rival governments, tracts, internal documents of the political parties, and others. Also useful were newspapers of the period, especially Dominican newspapers.

76. The total figure for the commando units as well as their real figure as a fighting force has been reached through a series of interviews with constitutionalist officers, civilian leaders of commando units, and other constitutionalist personnel, in particular Major Núñez Nogueras, Lieutenant Sención Silverio, the *catorcista* commando leaders Norge Botello, Fafa Taveras, "Baby" Mejía, and the PRD leaders Peña Gomez and Bonaparte Gautreaux Piñeiro (vice-minister of the presidency in the Caamaño government). Additionally, I have in my possession the Constitutionalist Government's "Relación de los Comandos Beneficiados con la Ayuda Recibida del Gobierno Constitucional de la República Dominicana." José A. Moreno, *Barrios in Arms: Revolution in Santo Domingo* (Pittsburgh: University of

Pittsburgh Press, 1970), has on pp. 213-16 reproduced this list, adding the number of men in each unit as of July. His figures are, for the most part, correct.

77. In May 1965, about a dozen *catorcistas* led by Jimmy Durán left Ciudad Nueva to rouse the "guerrilla centers" in the southwest. They counted on contacts the 1J4 was supposed to have in the region, but these proved virtually nonexistent. Instead of enthusiasm for guerrilla action, the *catorcistas* found an atmosphere of terror. Arsenio Ortiz, second in command, was denounced, arrested, and executed. The others scattered and attempted to get back to Ciudad Nueva, each on his own.

78. The following year, after the electoral debacle of June 1966, even the shadow vanished, leaving only the memory of a glorious name and transitory splinter groups. Soon began the exodus of the 1J4 leaders. Some, like Norge Botello and Evelio Hernández, joined the PRD; others, like Fafa Taveras and Juan B. Mejía, the MPD. Fidelio Despradel, having failed in his bid for senator in the June election and deserted by his last supporters, began to write mediocre pamphlets in which he tried to prove himself a theoretician. For many *catorcistas*, the year 1966 marked the end of active political participation. Nursing an idealized memory of the 1J4, they could not bring themselves to join some other party. Bitter, unable to break with the dreams of the past, these *catorcistas* claim to be "available," ready to rush into the streets when the proper day arrives. . . . But they forget that only constant struggle makes a man into a revolutionary.

79. *El Mundo*, 29 May 1965, pp. 1, 20.

80. "El drama dominicano," tract, Santo Domingo, 30 July 1965.

81. The chief sources for this section are: (1) Interviews with Jottin Cury, Héctor Aristy, Antonio Guzmán, Aníbal Campagna, and Salvador Jorge Blanco (all members of the constitutionalist Negotiating Committee); with Hugo Tolentino Dipp (member of President Caamaño's Advisory Committee) and Emilio Rodríguez Demorizi (an adviser to President Caamaño); with the political leaders Juan Bosch (PRD), José Francisco Peña Gómez (PRD), Jimmy Durán (1J4), and Norge Botello (1J4); with the constitutionalist officers Núñez Nogueras, Sención Silverio, and García Germán; and a great many others. (2) A series of documents: (a) the minutes of all the meetings between the constitutionalist Negotiating Committee and the second ad hoc committee of the OAS (see below, n. 84); (b) the minutes of the meetings of President Caamaño's Advisory Committee; (c) the letters exchanged between the constitutionalist government and Héctor García Godoy; (d) the notes exchanged between the Caamaño government and the OAS second ad hoc committee; (e) the minutes of the meeting held at the Copello Building on 8 July 1965 (see n. 88 below); (f) the texts of the proposals made both by the constitutionalist Negotiating Committee and by the ad hoc committee of the OAS aimed at resolving the crisis, especially the various drafts of the Institutional Act and the Act of Dominican Reconciliation.

82. Antonio Guzmán and Salvador Jorge Blanco, "Informe al Gobierno Constitucionalista," Santo Domingo, 7 June 1965, among my personal papers.

83. For the constitutionalists the negotiations were conducted by a Negotiating Committee of six: Francisco Caamaño, president of the Republic; Jottin Cury, foreign minister; Héctor Aristy, minister of the presidency; Aníbal Campagna, president of the Senate; Salvador Jorge Blanco, attorney general; and Antonio Guzmán.

84. [Constitutionalist Government], "Notas taquigráficas tomadas de la reunión celebrada en el salón de conferencias de la presidencia, ubicado en el tercer piso del Edificio Copello, apartamento no. 301," Santo Domingo, 10 June 1965, pp. 1-12 bis, among my personal papers. This document is part of a series covering the meetings between the Negotiating Committee of the Constitutionalist Government and the Second Ad-Hoc Committee of the OAS during 10 June-29 August 1965 (hereafter referred to as "Notas taquigráficas").

85. The Caamaño government had promoted a certain number of constitutionalist officers, including Major Lora Fernández, Major Núñez Nogueras, and Captain Lachapelle Díaz who were made lieutenant colonels. Throughout this chapter, however, the ranks of constitutionalist officers are those they held on 24 April.

86. [Constitutionalist Government], "Propuesta del Gobierno Constitucional de la República Dominicana a la Comisión Ad-Hoc de la Organización de Estados Americanos en respuesta a su proposición para la solución del actual problema nacional," Santo Domingo, 23 June 1965, p. 3.

87. "Notas taquigráficas," 1 July 1965, pp. 2, 4. Italics added. "We don't need an ambassador," Aníbal Campagna retorted sharply (ibid., p. 9).

88. Statement by Salvador Jorge Blanco, in [Constitutionalist Government], "Reunión celebrada el 8 de julio del año 1965 en la tercera planta del edificio 'Copello,' sito en la casa no. 79 de la calle El Conde esquina a Sánchez, de Santo Domingo, Distrito Nacional, sede del Gobierno Constitucional de la República Dominicana, a la cual asistieron el ciudadano Presidente Constitucional de la República, Señor Francisco Alberto Caamaño Deñó, y representantes de diversas comisiones gubernamentales y políticas señaladas en la primera página," Santo Domingo, 8 July 1965, p. 3 (A copy of the minutes of this meeting is among my personal papers. This document is reproduced in Franklin J. Franco Pichardo, *República Dominicana: Clases, Crisis y Comandos* [Havana: Ediciones Casa de las Americas, 1966], pp. 207-39).

89. "Notas taquigráficas," 7 July 1965, p. 4.

90. Statement by Jottin Cury, in [Constitutionalist Government], "Reunión celebranda el 8 de julio," p. 8.

91. The PSP and the MPD did not take part in the meeting. In Ciudad Nueva the two parties were legal, but they did not participate in any decision-making body within the constitutionalist government, nor were they ever invited to take part in a vote. One explanation for this discriminatory treatment is that they were miniparties. But most important, they were Communist parties and thus a liability in the diplomatic and propagandistic battle being waged by the constitutionalist government. In that same battle the "democratic" PRSC was an asset; therefore, despite the party's extreme weakness, it had the right to vote alongside the PRD and the 1J4.

92. Organization of American States, "Propuesta de la Comisión ad-hoc para la solución de la crisis dominicana," Santo Domingo, 17 June 1965.

93. Statement by Juan B. Mejía, in [Constitutionalist Government], "Reunión celebrada el 8 de julio, p. 16.

94. Statement by José Francisco Peña Gómez, in ibid., p. 31.

95. Statement by Salvador Jorge Blanco, in ibid., p. 3.

96. Statement by Pablo R. Casimiro Castro, in ibid., p. 19.

97. Statement by Ramón Ledesma Pérez, in ibid., p. 14.

98. Statement by Casimiro Castro, in ibid., p. 21.

99. Statement by Peña Gómez, in ibid., p. 27.

100. The PRD, the cabinet, the Senate, and the Chamber of Deputies all voted in favor of the candidate. The representative of the constitutionalist military staff abstained, declaring that the armed forces should not intervene in political decisions, but would obey orders (ibid., p. 17). The PRSC and the 1J4 voted against Godoy, not because of a different assessment of the situation, but out of "principle": the refusal to yield to the invader and, especially, the desire of both parties to emphasize their "revolutionary intransigence" in the face of the PRD's "shaky compromises." This attitude was irresponsible and in the case of the PRSC even ridiculous since the latter was incapable of the slightest military contribution to the common struggle. The refusal of both parties was gratuitous since their votes were not necessary for Godoy to be accepted. Throughout the negotiations with the ad hoc committee, the PRSC and the 1J4 were harshly critical of the concessions made by the constitutionalist Negotiating Committee, but they were never able to offer an alternative solution. Nonetheless, they took care not to endanger the talks.

101. Statement by Francisco Caamaño, in "Notas taquigráficas," 27 July 1965, p. 4.

102. Statement by Hugo Tolentino Dipp, in notes taken during the meeting of 20 July 1965 of President Caamaño's Advisory Committee, Santo Domingo, among my personal papers.

The constitutionalists would have been greatly shocked had they been present at a 12 July meeting of Godoy, members of the GRN, and the Bunker Commission. Referring to the constitutionalist military, particularly regarding Imbert Barrera's demand for "the transfer of the officers abroad for five years," Godoy declared, "I am in complete agreement with this" (transcript of a meeting on 12 July 1965 of Imbert Barrera, Postigo and Rivera Caminero of the GRN, the Bunker Commission, and Godoy, in the author's possession).

103. Organization of American States, Tenth Consultative Meeting of Foreign Ministers, Second Ad Hoc Committee, note to the constitutional government's Negotiating Committee, Santo Domingo, 5 August 1965.

104.   "Reserva del 'Gobierno Constitucional' " to the Institutional Act, in *Gaceta Oficial* 8944, 4 Sept. 1965, pp. 6-7.

105.   Interview with Benoit. Benoit had already been the victim of a coup d'état in early May (see note 21 above).

106.   Much more than any other "loyalist," Wessin had become the symbol of evil for the Dominican urban masses; they saw him as the man who had unleashed planes and tanks against the nation's capital. He had also lost the sympathy and respect of the Americans, since, at the moment of truth, he had cowed before the constitutionalist revolt. At the same time, the new rising star among the "loyalist" military, Admiral Rivera Caminero, saw in Wessin not a comrade-in-arms, but a rival. And many other "loyalist" senior officers remembered his arrogance during the Triumvirate. Nor did Joaquín Balaguer, the Americans' candidate for the forthcoming presidential elections, forget that Wessin had been his bitter enemy. Thus Wessin's demise in September 1965 should come as no surprise. His disgrace pleased constitutionalists and "loyalists" alike. It was a token gesture toward the constitutionalists that in no way weakened the "loyalist" cause. On 4 September Godoy revoked the autonomy of the CEFA—a direct affront to Wessin. When the general tried to react with a show of force, moving his tanks on "maneuvers" toward the capital, the IAPF intervened with lightning speed to block the CEFA forces. The Americans put Wessin on a plane bound for the Canal Zone, not even allowing him time to pack a suitcase. From Panama the hapless general was taken to the United States, while Godoy retired him from the armed forces and named him consul general in Miami (decrees 55 and 57 of 9 and 10 September 1965).

Wessin gave a highly colorful and not always untrue history of his misadventures to a U.S. Senate subcommittee (U.S. Congress, Senate, Committee on the Judiciary, Subcommittee to Investigate the Administration of the Internal Security Act and Other Internal Security Laws, *Communist Threat to the United States Through the Caribbean: Hearings: Testimony of Brigadier General Elías Wessin y Wessin,* 89th Cong., 1st sess., 1 October 1965 [Washington, D.C.: U.S. Government Printing Office, 1965], pp. 162-76). See also his letter to Godoy, "Bitter Salt of a Stranger's Bread," *National Review* 17 (19 Oct. 1965), p. 911.

107.   For more information on the Matúm incident see the coverage by the Dominican press, especially *Ahora,* no. 114 (3 Jan. 1966), pp. 6-22 and 37. In English the best source is Theodore Draper, "The New Dominican Crisis," *New Leader,* 31 Jan. 1966, pp. 3-8. I have held numerous interviews on this episode, not only with constitutionalists who were at the Matúm, but also with Godoy, Rivera Caminero, and a "loyalist" officer who took part in the attack.

In his conversations with the author in 1968 and 1969, Godoy emphatically stressed that he immediately asked the IAPF to intervene and impose a cease-fire. He refused, however, to discuss the role of the Americans or the delayed intervention of the IAPF. In particular, he refused to state whether he thought the IAPF had acted as an accomplice of the "loyalist" attackers.

Ahora pointed to the extremely long delay before the IAPF enforced the cease-fire, but this fact escaped American journalists and is not raised in Draper's otherwise excellent article. General Palmer, in a 1977 interview with me, could not account for the delay.

In his book on the Dominican crisis, Jerome Slater deals with the Matúm incident, but in a very superficial and biased way, In a footnote he acknowledges that "a number of constitutionalists believe that the IAPF deliberately dragged its feet in getting to the battle, hoping that the beleaguered Caamaño forces would be killed before they arrived." Then he immediately concludes that "this is highly improbable, however, particularly as a number of civilians, including sixteen Americans and the U.S. Consul General in Santiago, were trapped in the besieged Hotel" (*Intervention and Negotiation,* p. 145). But the presence of Americans is hardly conclusive proof of the IAPF's innocence. Might not the American military have seen danger to a few civilians as but a small price to pay for the annihilation of the constitutionalist leadership? There was abundant reason, moreover, to hope that no American (or at most only a few) would be seriously hurt in a successful "loyalist" attack—and on 19 December, none was. And even if General Palmer was indeed a "loyalist" accomplice, he could hardly have asked U.S. citizens to avoid the Matúm on 19 December because an attack on the hotel was scheduled for that day. Above all, Slater fails to explain, or even to consider, the reason for the delay. He merely states that "within a few hours an IAPF unit, sent by helicopter at . . . [Godoy's] urgent request, had arrived at the hotel, obtained a cease-fire and transported the constitutionalists back to their base outside Santo Domingo" (ibid.).

108.   *New York Times*, 4 Jan. 1966, p. 5

109.   Interviews wtih Núñez Nogueras, Sención Silverio, García Germán, and "El Gato."

110.   Judging from the results, it would seem that the military studies of the cadets were not very successful: not one of them ever became an officer. In 1972 six remained in the armed forces, still as cadets! This was the punishment they endured for having chosen the side of the constitution on 25 April 1965.

111.   Godoy quoted by Sención Silverio, in an interview with the author. The final "solution" to the problem of the constitutionalist military active on 24 April 1965 came with Balaguer. He closed their separate camp and "reintegrated" them into the armed forces. But the meaning of this reintegration soon became obvious. Rather than endure constant provocations and unjust treatment, many constitutionalist officers and enlisted men left the armed forces. The few who remained have not had dazzling careers. Only one constitutionalist officer, Captain Lachapelle Díaz, has been promoted in the eleven years of the Balaguer government: he is now a major. The others have not been as fortunate: Hernando Ramírez, a lieutenant colonel in 1965, is still a lieutenant colonel in 1977; Peña Taveras was and remains a captain; Núñez Nogueras is still a major. The list could go on. But perhaps these men are lucky compared to their many comrades who paid for their constitutionalist crime with their lives, assassinated after September 1965.

Of course, the lot of the valiant warriors who held the "loyalist" flag in 1965 has been different. Poor Wessin is currently in exile, but many of his younger comrades-in-arms have enjoyed brilliant careers: "Chinino" Lluberes Montás, Francisco Amiama Castillo, "Milito" Jiménez Reyes, Rafael Guzmán Acosta, Enrique Pérez y Pérez, and Juan René Beauchamps Javier are all generals and admirals; they are rich and powerful. It is a well-deserved reward, for they are the "loyalists," the heroes of 1965, the defenders of the Western world and civilization and, above all, the devoted friends of their American masters.

112.   A cursory reading of the very moderate *Ahora* for this period proves these obvious truths.

113.   Interviews with Juan Bosch, Antonio Guzmán (the PRD's vice-presidential candidate), Antonio Abreu Flores, Ivelisse Prats-Ramírez de Pérez, and other PRD leaders of the period (or persons otherwise close to Bosch).

114.   For a discussion, see Chapter 2.

115.   There was a third candidate, the former president of the Council of State, Rafael Bonnelly. An obvious representative of the *gente de primera*, Bonnelly was so clearly identified as an enemy of the constitutionalists and a defender of the status quo that soon even many *de primera* realized that his candidacy was hopeless. They therefore chose to support Balaguer, a man whom they disliked, but who at least would oppose social reforms. At the polls, Bonnelly received less than 4 percent of the vote.

116.   See also Chapter 11.

CHAPTER 11

1.   Of course, not all the members of the *gente de primera* were vain, arrogant, corrupt, and eager to overthrow Bosch. I refer to them as a group, rather than considering the few individual exceptions.

2.   For the different attitudes of the Council of State (that is, the *gente de primera*) and the United States toward the military, see Chapter 3.

3.   Dean Rusk, speech, 25 January 1962, to the Eighth Meeting of Consultation of Ministers of Foreign Affairs of the OAS, Punta del Este, 22-31 January 1962, in *Department of State Bulletin* 46 (Jan.-June 1962), p. 275. For a more general discussion, see also Chapter 2.

4. The Peruvian military overthrew President Manuel Prado to prevent the election of Haya de la Torre, a man they hated. For more information on the Argentinian and Peruvian cases and the position of the United States, see Jerome Levinson and Juan de Onís, *The Alliance That Lost Its Way: A Critical Report on the Alliance for Progress* (Chicago: Quadrangle Books, 1972), pp. 77-82, and Edwin Lieuwen, *Generals Vs. Presidents: Neomilitarism in Latin America* (New York: Praeger, 1964), pp. 10-36 and 115-17. For their impact on the Dominican military see John B. Martin, *Overtaken by Events: The Dominican Crisis from the Fall of Trujillo to the Civil War* (Garden City, N.Y.: Doubleday, 1966), esp. p. 161.

5. By far the best sources for United States-Cuban relations in the nineteenth century are Philip S. Foner's *A History of Cuba and Its Relations with the United States* (New York: International Publishers, 1962 [vol. 1] and 1963 [vol. 2]) and *The Spanish-American-Cuban War and the Birth of American Imperialism*, 2 vols. (New York/London: Monthly Review Press, 1972). For U.S.-Cuban relations in 1933-34, the best sources are Luis E. Aguilar, *Cuba, 1933* (Ithaca/London: Cornell University Press, 1972), and Hugh Thomas, *Cuba, the Pursuit of Freedom* (New York: Harper & Row, 1971). Oddly enough, Foner's excellent books are very seldom cited in the literature. For an example of such strange disregard, see Gordon Connell-Smith, *The United States and Latin America* (New York: John Wiley and Sons, 1974). Connell-Smith offers an outstanding overview of U.S. relations with Latin America, but seems completely unaware of the existence of Foner's books.

6. See especially Jefferson's letter to James Madison (Monticello, 27 April 1809) in *The Writings of Thomas Jefferson*, Andrew A. Lipscomb and Albert E. Bergh, eds., 20 vols. (Washington, D.C.: The Thomas Jefferson Memorial Association, 1903), 12:275-77.

7. Even the very moderate Edwin Lieuwen acknowledges that the Kennedy administration welcomed the military *golpe* in Guatemala in March 1963, since it prevented the danger of free elections that former president Juan José Arévalo would certainly have won (*Generals Vs. Presidents*, esp. pp. 117-18). That the Kennedy administration could consider a "spiritual socialist" like Arévalo dangerous sheds additional light on the phobias of the administration and on its extremely narrow definition of a "democratic left."

8. At the time, the Americans remembered Balaguer as Trujillo's puppet and erroneously concluded that he was a weak personality who lacked the dynamism of a Reid Cabral.

9. In an early April 1965 telegram to the State Department asking for a further loan of $25 million to the Dominican Republic, Bennett wrote: "Little foxes, some of them Red, are chewing at the grapes. It is impossible to guarantee a good harvest in view of the many unfavorable aspects of the local scene. It is, however, fair to say that a diminution of our effort or failure to act will result in a bitter wine" (quoted by Rowland Evans and Robert Novak, *Lyndon B. Johnson: The Exercise of Power* [New York: Signet Books, 1968], p. 537). But Bennett did not consider the Reid Cabral government in danger—he only wanted to worry the State Department in order to obtain the money for his protégé. In this context, the allusion to the "red foxes" was a required feature of the scenario. Indeed, it must be stressed that throughout the period of the Triumvirate, Washington paid very little attention to the Dominican Republic because the situation in that country seemed stable (interview with two CIA officials). This view was shared in Cuba. The Havana Conference of November-December 1964 singled out six countries in the Western Hemisphere for the guerrilla effort. The Dominican Republic was not among them, since the left there was considered too weak.

10. For a most pathetic example, see Martin, *Overtaken by Events*, esp. pp. 672-76.

11. See Chapter 6.

12. For the position of Martin and the Kennedy administration toward Bosch, see Chapter 3.

13. Because of the "Castro-Communist threat," the U.S. government paid an inordinate amount of attention to the Dominican Republic in 1961 and, to a lesser degree, in 1962-63. Under the Triumvirate, the situation in the country at last seemed stabilized and the "Castro-Communist" danger appeared checked, particularly since the defeat of the *catorcista* guerrillas of November-December 1963. Thus Washington once more paid very little attention to the Dominican Republic. As stated in Chapter 9, n. 64, the success of the countercoup on 25 April 1965 produced a rude shock. But by that evening the Johnson

administration had already made its basic decisions. The constitutionalists seemed headed toward inevitable defeat, and the atmosphere of crisis in Washington began to subside. Throughout the twenty-sixth and twenty-seventh, the "loyalists" seemed increasingly close to victory, and therefore top government officials paid only modest attention to Dominican events. Then, on 28 April, came the stunning realization that San Isidro had been defeated and was on the verge of collapse. The Dominican Republic suddenly acquired more importance than Vietnam–a development for which the U.S. government was ill-prepared, after well over a year of neglect. CIA officials have pointed out in interviews with the author that reports on the Dominican Republic during the Triumvirate received scant attention from higher-ups in the bureaucracy. They have rightly stressed that this exemplifies a more general weakness of American bureaucracy that tends to ignore a small country once the situation there seems "stabilized"–to be caught by surprise if a sudden development occurs.

14. The first Americans (all military) were wounded and killed on 30 April, during their unprovoked attack on the constitutionalists. By the end of the civil war, at least forty-four American soldiers had been killed and more than three hundred wounded. This was typical of American "humanitarian" interventions. In the civil wars that preceded the U.S. interventions in Haiti (1915) and in the Dominican Republic (1916), no American had been hurt in any way. U.S. casualties began only once the occupation had started. It was the same in Nicaragua in 1927.

15. See Chapter 9, pp. 253-54.

16. See Chapter 10.

17. See Chapter 9, p. 253.

18. Johnson was aware that the intervention would provoke a storm in Latin America ("I told my [National] Security Council that it would be hard for me to live in the Hemisphere if I sent in the marines.") But he was also aware that he would incur the wrath of the American people if he allowed a "second Cuba" ("and I couldn't live in this country if I didn't [send in the marines]"). These quotes are from an off-the-record conversation of Johnson with U.S. journalists, courtesy of Philip Geyelin, at the time Washington correspondent of the *Wall Street Journal*.

19. Philip Geyelin summed it up very well: "When Bennett's 'critic' cable was brought into the President's office, a call had been made to Tom Mann, who was meeting with his staff at State. Meanwhile at the White House there was a brisk, brief discussion. One man who was there reported later that nobody felt much need to say anything. 'One or two spoke up, and the general conclusion was that there was no real choice. The president asked if there was any other view. By the time Mann called back with his recommendation, the decision had really been made to send in the Marines' " (*Lyndon B. Johnson and the World* [New York: Praeger, 1966], pp. 251-52).

There is no definitive list of all those who were with Johnson at that time. In his memoirs, Johnson mentions only Rusk, McNamara, Ball, McGeorge Bundy, and Bill Moyers (*The Vantage Point. Perspectives of the Presidency, 1963-1969* [New York/Chicago/San Francisco: Holt, Rinehart and Winston, 1971], p. 195). Others add Richard Goodwin; Theodore Draper includes in the group also Vice-president Humphrey and Adlai Stevenson (*The Dominican Revolt* [New York: Commentary, 1968], p. 83).

20. *New York Times*, 8 May 1965, p. 1.

21. In his apologetic *A Thousand Days*, Kennedy's court historian Arthur Schlesinger, Jr., quotes the complaint of a "good boy," Pepe Figueres, prominent member of the "democratic left made in USA." Figueres was not criticizing the Bay of Pigs per se, nor the violation of the OAS charter and of international law, but the fact that the administration had failed to inform him and Betancourt: " 'How can we have an alliance', he said, almost bitterly, 'if even our friends will not believe that we can be trusted with secrets? I may disagree with something, but I still can be trusted to keep quiet about it' " (*A Thousand Days: John F. Kennedy in the White House* [Boston: Houghton, Mifflin, 1965], p. 275). This is not only an excellent example of Kennedy's treatment of the OAS and even of his "democratic left," but also an excellent explanation of why Juan Bosch could not belong to that "democratic left."

22. For the U.S. handling of the OAS and the UN in the Guatemalan crisis, see especially Jerome Slater, *The OAS and United States Foreign Policy* (Columbus: Ohio State

University Press, 1967), pp. 115-29 and Gordon Connell-Smith, *The Inter-American System* (London: Oxford University Press, 1966), pp. 161-65 and 229-37. Oddly enough, Robert Kennedy mentioned the missile crisis as an example of U.S. respect for the OAS (*New York Times*, 8 May 1965, p. 8). He forgot that the United States had consulted the OAS only pro forma, once it had decided how it would act. In fact, the OAS met to give its approval only after President Kennedy had announced on television that the United States would begin the quarantine in a few hours.

23. By "correct" decision I obviously mean one that conformed to the well-understood interests of the Johnson and preceding administrations.

24. Georgetown University, Center for Strategic Studies, *Dominican Action–1965: Intervention or Cooperation?* Special Report Series #2 (Washington, D.C.: Center for Strategic Studies, 1966), p. ix.

25. "Kennedy commented wryly on the discrepancy between the European and American reactions. If he had been a British prime minister, he remarked, he would have been thrown out of office; but in the United States failure had increased his charm: 'If I had gone farther, they would have liked me even more'. At this point, Evelyn Lincoln brought in an advance on the new Gallup poll, showing an unprecedented 82 percent behind the administration. Kennedy tossed it aside and said, 'It's just like Eisenhower. The worse I do, the more popular I get' " (Schlesinger, *Thousand Days*, p. 292).

For the skillful public relations gimmicks that Kennedy used to achieve such results, see Richard J. Walton, *Cold War and Counter-Revolution: The Foreign Policy of John F. Kennedy* (Baltimore: Penguin Books, 1973), Chapter 3.

26. Speech, 2 May 1965, in *Department of State Bulletin* 52, no. 1351 (17 May 1965), p. 745, quoted in Chapter 10.

27. Geyelin, *Johnson*, p. 255.

28. The two best examples are Tad Szulc of the *New York Times* and Dan Kurzman of the *Washington Post* who have both written books on the Dominican crisis (Szulc, *Dominican Diary* [New York: Dell, 1966] and Kurzman, *Santo Domingo, Revolt of the Damned* [New York: G. P. Putnam's Sons, 1965]).

29. Interview with Seth Tillman, at the time chief of staff of the Senate Foreign Relations Committee.

30. See Chapter 10.

31. Abraham Lowenthal, "The Dominican Intervention in Retrospect," in Yale H. Ferguson, ed., *Contemporary Inter-American Relations* (Englewood Cliffs, N.J.: Prentice-Hall, 1972), p. 287.

32. Another accusation has often been leveled against Johnson: that the United States overreacted by sending too many troops to the Dominican Republic. It is hard to see the relevance of such criticism. A smaller number of American soldiers would still have represented a flagrant violation of international law, both in the letter of the law and in the eyes of world opinion. What the Johnson administration feared, not without reason, was that the revolt might spread from Santo Domingo to the rest of the country, either in the form of urban uprisings or guerrilla operations in the countryside, at least until the "loyalist" forces had been reorganized. Thus a large number of troops were sent to the Dominican Republic and were stationed not only in the capital, but throughout the country. This tactic was effective, as confirmed by the numerous interviews I had with constitutionalist leaders.

33. Jerome Slater, *Intervention and Negotiation: The United States and the Dominican Revolution* (New York: Harper & Row, 1970), p. 134.

34. In October 1967, Francisco Caamaño, still a military attaché in London, went to Holland and subsequently disappeared on the twenty-third.

The civil war initiated Caamaño's radicalization. The farce of Godoy's "conciliation" and the awareness of the true nature of the Balaguer regime accelerated this process. Caamaño could hardly have remained in London as Balaguer's military attaché. Rather than resign and return to the Dominican Republic, where the regime would have been able to control his moves, he accepted an invitation from Cuba, where he went clandestinely, hoping soon to return to his country to lead the *guerra de guerrillas*.

The years went by, and Caamaño remained in Cuba. The mystery of his disappearance increased his charisma in the Dominican Republic, as I witnessed in 1969, 1970, and 1971. In Santo Domingo and in the towns of the interior the people believed that the hero of 1965 was alive and that someday he would return to lead the armed fight against

Balaguer. His name was often acclaimed as loudly as that of Bosch. Many considered them twin leaders–military and political–of the same struggle.

Finally, on 3 February 1973, Caamaño landed with nine *guerrilleros* on the southern coast of the Dominican Republic. Apparently only the Comandos Clandestinos de la Revolución had been informed of his arrival. They were only a *grupito*, a handful of men, further weakened when their leader, Amaury Germán, was killed by the army on 12 January 1972.

The outcome was inevitable. On 16 February 1973, Francisco Alberto Caamaño Deñó was killed by the army at Nizaito, in the mountains between San José de Ocoa and Constanza. During the last days of his life, while he was once again fighting on Dominican soil, the Dominican press kept wondering whether he had really returned on what seemed an absurd enterprise. Meanwhile the PRD, the parties of the far left, and the university students all watched passively; government troops patrolled the capital and the other towns, arresting opposition leaders and spreading fear among the population.

Why did Caamaño remain in Cuba so long? Why did he return in February 1973, with only nine men and practically no contacts in the country? Was this a "Cuban-supported invasion," at a time when Cuba had replaced the "guerrilla offensive" with a successful diplomatic one in Latin America? We know too little to give a definitive answer, but several observations can be made.

There is a bitter irony in the story of Francisco Caamaño. On 8 October 1967, a few days before Caamaño disappeared from The Hague, the Bolivian high command had Che Guevara assassinated at La Higuera. Guevara's death symbolically marks the beginning of the decline of the Castroite guerrilla offensive in Latin America; its end would be consummated over the next two years.

There is little doubt that soon after Caamaño's arrival, the Cubans advised him to wait for the right moment and eventually tried to dissuade him from engaging in an adventure they now believed doomed to failure, one which for them could entail a heavy political cost.

Dominicans who visited Caamaño during his Cuban stay agree that he was growing increasingly frustrated, eager to return to his country, and convinced that the *focos guerrilleros* could succeed in the Dominican Republic.

Many of these visitors tried to discourage him, aware that the enterprise could end only in disaster. A few, however, told him what he wanted to hear because they shared his illusion. Eventually they became the only ones whose advice he would trust.

By 1973, the Cubans could have restrained Caamaño only by arresting him. Thus, they let him seek his destiny. He and his companions "invaded" the Dominican Republic from Guadeloupe, in order not to engage Cuba's responsibility. Cuba's restraint was so obvious that neither the Dominican government nor the United States accused Castro of complicity. Throughout the two weeks of Caamaño's final struggle in the Dominican Republic, the Cuban press refrained from attacks on the Balaguer regime and reported the events factually by using international news agencies' wires. Since then, *Granma* and *Bohemia* have referred to Caamaño on several occasions, Fidel Castro evoked his memory in a speech on 26 July 1973, and a Cuban school has been named for the dead leader. But these articles and elegies refer only to the Caamaño of 1965–ignoring his guerrilla struggle of 1973. The latter was an episode belonging to the 1960s, glorious but full of frustration, a past which Cuba has left behind.

Published documentation on Caamaño's guerrilla struggle and its background is sparse and mediocre. An interested reader should look at the Dominican press of the period and at the diverse articles on the subject that have been published in *Ahora* since then (such as José Monleón, "La Compañera de Caamaño habla sobre su muerte," *Ahora*, no. 691 [7 Feb. 1977], pp. 6-9). The Dominican Alejandro Ovalles has published a short book, *Caamaño, el Gobierno y las Guerrillas* (Santo Domingo: n.p., 1973), but its only value is that it reproduces some articles published in the Dominican press at the time. My major sources for Caamaño's stay in Cuba have been interviews in the Dominican Republic, both before and after 1973, with members of the Dominican far left, some of whom had spoken with Caamaño in Cuba. For obvious reasons, I am withholding their names. For a brief overview of Cuba's foreign policy in the early 1970s, the best source is Carmelo Mesa Lago, *Cuba in the 1970s* (Albuquerque: University of New Mexico Press, 1974), esp. Chap. 4.

35. In April 1965, Juan Bosch was still a devout believer in Western-style political democracy. Then in rapid succession came the shocks of the U.S. military intervention and the farce of Godoy's "conciliation." Bosch's hope that Joaquín Balaguer would foster some

degree of social progress and uphold political democracy was soon shattered. As a result, Bosch underwent a marked evolution, finally concluding that a Western-style democracy is incompatible with the historical and contemporary reality of his country.

After four years of self-imposed exile in Europe, Bosch returned to the Dominican Republic in 1971 to lead the opposition against the regime. His firm stance soon disturbed a number of leaders in his party who, perceiving the strength of the regime, preferred a more accommodating attitude; his personalism estranged others who accepted his outlook. For his part Bosch soon felt that the PRD had outlived its role: it was a party created to win elections in a situation where honest elections were impossible. A new party, with or without the same name, was necessary. It would first concentrate not on increasing its following, but on forming a smaller core. Before becoming a mass party, the new organization should first be one of cadres—unlike the old PRD, which was rich in numbers and poor in cadres.

By 1973 the Executive Committee of the PRD was split into two groups, one led by Peña Gómez, the other by Bosch. Rather than fight to retain control of the old party, Bosch chose to withdraw and founded the PLD. As a rule, the more "revolutionary" members of the Executive Committee followed, while a few, who resented Bosch's personalism, remained with Peña Gómez (a striking example is Ivelisse Pratts-Ramírez de Pérez, one of the most brilliant members of the PRD's Executive Committee).

This writer feels that the break with the "moderate" element in the PRD was a positive step and that the exigencies of the moment require cadres rather than a mass party. The presence of Antonio Abreu Flores, secretary-general of the PLD (Bosch is the party's president) gives hope for the immediate and the post-Bosch future, since Bosch is aging and is possibly near the end of his historical role. Abreu Flores is one of the most impressive members of the new Dominican political generation. A young man when a new political period began for the country in 1961, he has grown to be one of the most honest, able, and best-prepared Dominican political leaders.

Since 1965 Bosch has been a prolific author. In addition to numerous articles, he has written the following books: *El Pentagonismo, Sustituto del Imperialismo* (México, D.F.: Siglo XXI, 1968), a rambling diatribe against the United States written under the shock of the 1965 invasion and its aftermath; *El Próximo Paso: Dictadura con Respaldo Popular* (Santo Domingo: Editora Arte y Cine, 1970), an ill-fated effort to develop an original political model for the Dominican Republic; *Composición Social Dominicana, Historia e Interpretación*, 2d ed. (Santo Domingo: Editora Arte y Cine, 1970), an incisive but not always reliable sociological analysis of the Dominican past; and *De Cristóbal Colón a Fidel Castro: El Caribe, frontera imperial* (Madrid: Alfaguara, 1970), a penetrating history of the region. The PLD has published a biweekly since August 1974, *Vanguardia del Pueblo*, which includes in every issue an article written by Bosch.

36. Even a cursory reading of the few articles published on the Dominican Republic in the excellent British weeklies *Latin America* (since 7 Jan. 1977, *Latin American Political Report*) and *Latin American Economic Report* (5 Oct. 1973-) gives an idea of the character of the regime. I would refer those who might desire more information to the Dominican press, in particular the weekly *Ahora* and the dailies *El Nacional, Listín Diario, El Caribe,* and *Ultima Hora.* Some echoes appear on rare occasions in the U.S. press. The best source for economic information on the Dominican Republic is the World Bank, whose reports unfortunately cannot be quoted. For a useful survey of the Dominican economy, see the "Quarterly Economic Review: Cuba, Dominican Republic, Haiti, Puerto Rico," in *The Economist Intelligence Unit* (London, March 1953-). There is as yet no good book on the Balaguer regime.

37. Of the many elements that have characterized this formula, two deserve mention here: the relatively high degree of cohesion of the Dominican upper class throughout the period and Balaguer's control over the armed forces. The shock of the 1965 constitutionalist revolt led the *gente de primera* to realize the need for an alliance with the *nouveaux riches* of the Era, and thus with Balaguer. They accept this alliance grudgingly, able to control but not to forget completely their feelings of contempt and resentment for these parvenus. But if one day the upper class forgets the bitter lesson of 1965 and this informal alliance breaks down, a new danger will threaten their entrenched interests.

Since 1961, Balaguer is the president who has achieved the highest degree of control over the Dominican armed forces. The open support of the United States and the innumerable perquisites and flagrant corruption of the military provide only a partial explanation for this success. The same conditions prevailed under Donald Reid Cabral, yet he never obtained any personal influence over his officers and depended entirely on Wessin's support. By playing skillfully on the rivalries among his senior officers, by manipulating the different factions, and by preventing any one faction from dominating the others, Balaguer has avoided dependence on a single military leader. The "military crisis" of May 1975–when he imposed General Neit Nivar Seijas as police chief against the open opposition of the armed forces minister and the three joint chiefs of staff–was a clear manifestation of this control; in other times such a confrontation would have led either to a military coup or to a humiliating surrender of the president (on the episode see especially *Ahora*, no. 601 [19 May 1975], pp. 4-11. The British weekly *Latin America* also published two good articles on the subject, in its issues of 16 and 30 May 1975 [vol. 9, no. 19, p. 149, and no. 21, pp. 166-67, respectively]).

Obviously, since September 1965, one group of officers has had no place in the Dominican armed forces: those troublemakers who believe that their duty is to serve rather than to oppress the people and who desire social reforms and honesty in government in place of corruption and an unjust status quo. There are certainly at this time very few "constitutionalists" or *peruanistas* in the Dominican armed forces–a sad reality that any political opposition in the country has to take into account.

APPENDIX I

1. A good account of the conspiracy has yet to be published. My major source is the minutes of the interrogations of those conspirators arrested after the death of Trujillo (República Dominicana, Servicio Judicial, "Proceso Instruido con motivo de la muerte del Generalísimo Trujillo" [Ciudad Trujillo, 8 August 1961]. The minutes were never published, but I was able to read them in 1969). An additional source is my interview with Marcelino Vélez Santana, a member of the outer fringe of the conspiracy.

Of the many articles published on the subject in the Dominican and foreign press, the most useful are Miguel San José, "Siguen sin esclarecer muchos detalles en relación con la muerte de Trujillo" (*Ahora*, no. 60 [10 May 1964], p. 14), and Félix Servio Ducoudray Mansfield, "La Historia Secreta del 30 de Mayo" (*Ahora*, no. 603 [2 June 1975], pp. 80-83]). Valuable information can also be found in Robert D. Crassweller, *Trujillo: The Life and Times of a Caribbean Dictator* (New York: Macmillan, 1966), pp. 435-39; Howard J. Wiarda, *Dictatorship and Development: The Methods of Control in Trujillo's Dominican Republic* (Gainesville: University of Florida Press, 1968), pp. 170-73; Teodoro Tejeda Díaz, *Yo investigué la muerte de Trujillo* (Barcelona: Plaza and Janes, 1963); and Elena de la Souchère, *Crime à Saint-Domingue: L'affaire Trujillo-Galíndez* (Paris: Editions Albin Michel, 1972), Chap. 7. Finally, Arturo R. Espaillat offers some valuable data mixed with flagrant lies *(The Last Caesar* [Chicago: Henry Regnery, 1963], Chap. 2. Víctor Peña Rivera, a former chief of the Servicio de Inteligencia Militar for the Northern Region, is also of interest but suffers from the same faults as Espaillat in *Historia oculta de un Dictador, Trujillo* (New York: Plus Ultra, 1977), pp. 331-77.

For sources on the role of the United States in the conspiracy, see below, p. 304.

2. Even the die-hard *Trujillista* Arturo Espaillat acknowledged, in describing the motives of the conspirators, that "young, good-natured Lt. Amado García Guerrero . . . wanted only to free his republic from tyranny" (*The Last Caesar*, p. 13).

3. This was certainly true of Antonio de la Maza, a businessman and lumber magnate, whose brother Octavio had been killed by the regime in 1956. But in a more general sense, all these men had reason to seek revenge, for all had been humiliated by Trujillo on different occasions. For a detailed portrait of Antonio Imbert Barrera and Luis Amiama Tió, the only two members of the inner core to survive the end of the regime, see Chapter 2, n. 216.

4. Interview with Marcelino Vélez Santana. According to Howard Wiarda, who does not quote his source, the conspirators intended to form a provisional government after Trujillo's elimination and to hold elections that they "would win because of their exploitation of the roles they played in ridding the country of the hated tyrant" (*Dictatorship and Development*, p. 172). Even if Wiarda were correct, which I doubt, the difference would be only formal, for in any case, with or without elections, the conspirators did not intend to relinquish power, once they had seized it.

5. Espaillat, *The Last Caesar*, pp. 19-20. For another, less reliable version, see Wiarda, *Dictatorship and Development*, p. 172. In the end General Román Fernández paid a heavy price for his complicity and cowardice. His participation in the plot was discovered, he was arrested, tortured for several days, and finally murdered.

6. Personal interviews.

7. U.S. Congress, Senate, Select Committee to Study Governmental Operations with Respect to Intelligence Activities, *Alleged Assassination Plots Involving Foreign Leaders: An Interim Report*, 94 Cong., 1 sess. (Washington, D.C.: U.S. Government Printing Office, 1975). The account that follows is based largely on the report. For the best source before 1975 on the U.S. role in the assassination of Trujillo, see Norman Gall, "How Trujillo Died," *New Republic* 143, no. 15 (13 April 1963), pp. 19-20.

8. U.S. Congress, Senate, *Alleged Assassination Plots*, p. 191.

9. Ibid., p. 192.

10. "On March 20, 1961, the Station cabled a dissident request for five M3 or comparable machine guns specifying their wish that the arms be sent via the diplomatic pouch or similar means. The dissidents were said to feel that delivery by air drop or transfer at sea would overly-tax their resources. . . . The machine guns sought by the dissidents were clearly identified, in the State cable, as being sought for use in connection with an attempt to assassinate Trujillo" (ibid., p. 201).

11. Testimony of Richard Bissell, then deputy director for plans, of the CIA, in ibid., p. 205.

12. Cable, Headquarters to Station, 20 April 1961, in ibid., p. 206.

13. Record of Actions by National Security Council, 5 May 1961 (Approved by the president, 16 May 1961) in ibid., p. 209.

14. Throughout the period under consideration, the conspirators received from the United States only three pistols and three carbines that were delivered to them, at their request, in March and early April 1961, that is, before the change in U.S. policy regarding the assassination of Trujillo. There is no doubt that for Juan Tomás Díaz the value of these weapons was mostly psychological; they were proof to his co-conspirators of U.S. support. He believed that once they were ready to act, he and his friends would receive the necessary weapons from the Americans, such as the machine guns he requested in April. But by then, of course, it was too late.

15. U.S. Congress, Senate, *Alleged Assassination Plots*, p. 261.

16. Ibid., p. 213.

17. Ibid., p. 215. And Bissell, who testified before the committee, should know about it, since he was at the time the highest CIA official involved.

18. "Additional Views of Senator Howard H. Baker, Jr., " in ibid., p. 303.

APPENDIX II

1. The Popular Socialist Party

1. The literature on the PSP is extremely poor, both for the years after 1961 and for the period considered here (from the party's origins until the death of Trujillo). In his highly touted study on Communism in Latin America, Robert J. Alexander devotes a few pages to the PSP, but they are even more superficial and full of errors than the rest of the book

(*Communism in Latin America* [New Brunswick, N.J.: Rutgers University Press, 1963], pp. 298-303). Boris Goldenberg is immensely superior to Alexander in his analysis of Communism in Latin America (he provides the only serious study on the subject), but unluckily he has very little to say on the PSP, and what he says is wrong (*Kommunismus in Lateinamerika* [Stuttgart: Kohlhammer, 1971], esp. p. 102). Useful information can be found only in Jesús de Galíndez, *La Era de Trujillo: Un estudio casuistico de dictadura hispanoamericana* (Buenos Aires: Editorial Americana, 1962).

My major sources are: (1) Interviews with leaders of the PSP of the period, and in particular with Félix Servio Ducoudray Mansfield, Tulio Hostilio Arvelo Delgado, Justino José del Orbe, and Ramón Grullón Martínez; (2) *El Popular* (the party organ). I have examined the issues published from 1962, but many contain useful information for the period under examination here; (3) Internal documents of the PSP and of the 1J4; again, these documents belong to the period after 1961, but contain valuable data for the early period of the PSP; (4) A series of articles published by Francisco Alberto ("Chito") Henríquez Vásquez ("Siempre los hechos valdran más que las palabras," *Listín Diario*, 24 April, 1, 7, and 14 May 1971). Henríquez Vásquez was one of the founders and major leaders of the PSP until his expulsion from the party in 1947; (5) Also useful, in spite of its crass lies and low slanders, is Domincan Republic, Ministry for Home Affairs, *White Book of Communism in Dominican Republic* (Madrid: Gráficas Rey, 1958).

2. Galíndez, *La Era de Trujillo*, p. 213. For Trujillo's offer to take in the Dominican Republic up to one hundred thousand European refugees, see Chapter 1. In reality, only some five thousand Spaniards and about eight hundred Jews were admitted to the country. Both immigrations were, in fact, failures, especially the Spanish one. By the end of 1945, the bulk of the Spanish immigrants had left the Dominican Republic.

3. The ideology was still unknown, but not the terminology. A law of 20 October 1936 forbade all "Communist" activity. "Communist" was used as synonym for "criminal," "asocial"—that is, anti-Trujilloist.

4. Interview with Félix Servio Ducoudray.

5. *El Popular*, no. 22 (31 Jan. 1963), p. 1.

6. 1J4, Grupo Anti-Transformista, "La Revolución Dominicana, el partido proletario y el 14 de Junio. Tesis revolucionaria en defensa de la clase obrera y contra el Transformismo" (Santo Domingo, 6 July 1966), p. 27, among my personal papers.

7. Henríquez Vásquez, "Siempre los hechos" (IV), *Listín Diario*, 7 May 1970.

8. Robert D. Crassweller, *Trujillo: The Life and Times of a Caribbean Dictator* (New York: Macmillan, 1966), p. 218.

9. A "scandalous" event occurred in February 1946, when José Antonio Bonilla Atiles, dean of the Law School, published a letter in which he announced his refusal to sign a manifesto of intellectuals advocating Trujillo's reelection. According to Bonilla, there were other worthy candidates in the country. In an open letter, some forty students immediately supported his stance. These acts of revolt were the manifestation of an undercurrent of tension that had existed for many months. The Communist-led Dominican Revolutionary Youth was already active in the university. It was now joined by a non-Communist group, the Democratic Youth, led by Virgilio Díaz Grullón, son of a prominent *Trujillista*.

10. This was the period of the "Braden policy." Appointed assistant secretary for inter-American affairs in October 1945, Spruille Braden believed that the United States should maintain no more than "correct" relations with dictatorial regimes and reserve "a warmer feeling of friendship and a greater desire to cooperate" for "those governments which rest upon periodically and freely expressed consent of the governed" (quoted in Crassweller, *Trujillo*, p. 216). Thus, in the case of the Dominican Republic, the Braden policy, while not aiming at the overthrow of Trujillo, wished to make clear the U.S. disapproval of his regime—in stark contrast with past years of unabashed praise. The personality of Braden's "right-hand man," Ellis Briggs, whose dislike of Trujillo was well known, added to the worries of the Dominican regime and stirred among the anti-Trujillistas hopes that far exceeded the scope of the Braden policy.

11. Dominican Republic, Ministry for Home Affairs, *White Book of Communism*, p. 55. Mauricio Báez was the secretary-general of the Federation of Sugar Workers of San Pedro de Macorís, one of the trade unions whose organization Trujillo had recently allowed

as a part of his "parody of liberal indulgence." Báez had been active among the workers of the San Pedro de Macorís-La Romana region since the early 1930s. He had become the head of a small group of clandestine labor leaders who risked their lives, day after day, trying to organize the workers of the area, both those in the towns and in the sugar estates. Many labor leaders had already been killed. Of those who remained in 1944-46, the great majority were Communists.

12. Galíndez adds that the regime had also two other aims: to pretend that it tolerated full freedom even for extremist ideas and to confront the Dominican people—and above all the leisure classes—with a dilemma: Trujillo or Communism (*La Era de Trujillo*, p. 219).

13. Ibid., p. 220.

14. Interview with Justino José del Orbe.

15. Interview with Félix Servio Ducoudray.

16. *El Popular*, no. 29 (25 May 1963), p. 5.

17. *El 1J4*, no. 34 (31 Jan. 1962), p. 8.

18. Dominican Republic, Ministry for Home Affairs, *White Book on Communism*, pp. 90-92.

19. It would thus avoid "provoking public opinion," since any "rash" act would only exacerbate the repression. After the painful experience of 26 October, it did not try to organize any new public meetings.

20. Interview with Félix Servio Ducoudray, who quoted from his conversation with Ramón Marrero Aristy, vice-minister of labor and economy in 1946 and an intimate friend of the dictator. The regime's fear was reflected in the very generous concessions it granted to the strikers. Some salaries were increased by 100 percent—for the regime, this was unheard-of and humiliating (see also Galíndez, *La Era de Trujillo*, pp. 160-61; Galíndez, who at the time was working in the Dominican government, participated in the negotiations to settle the strike).

21. The convocation of a workers' congress had been a part of the agreement between Trujillo's representatives and the Dominican Communist leaders in Havana in the spring of 1946. But Trujillo was wrong if he hoped that fear of his wrath would eventually cow the Communists and transform the congress into another installment of his "parody of liberal indulgence." Because of the insistent demands of the delegates sent by the Confederación de Trabajadores Cubanos and by the Confederación de Trabajadores de América Latina, Trujillo agreed to an "explanatory campaign" to precede the congress. Twenty-four public meetings were held throughout the country in the summer of 1946, and for the first time in their lives many Dominicans heard the message of the Dominican Communist leaders. When the congress began on 24 September 1946, the regime was subjected to one more indignity. Instead of exalting the "democratic" and "proworker" nature of the Trujilloist dictatorship, some delegates dared to criticize it. In a dramatic show of independence, the congress elected two Communists, Mauricio Báez and Ramón Grullón Martínez, to the Executive Committee of the Dominican Confederation of Labor (Confederación Domincana del Trabajo).

22. See Galíndez, *La Era de Trujillo*, p. 219.

23. Dominican Republic, Ministry for Home Affairs, *White Book on Communism*, p. 94. On 14 June, Congress passed the law unanimously.

24. The university students of the non-Communist Democratic Youth met the same fate. Besides the PSP, they were the only group in the country that dared to express opposition to the dictatorship during the period of the "parody of liberal indulgence."

25. Interview with Félix Servio Ducoudray.

26. 1J4, Grupo Transformista, "Desarrollemos el aspecto más progresivo del contenido del partido, el aspecto proletario" (Santo Domingo, [1966]), Tema II, unpaginated, among my personal papers.

27. Some members of the PSP, led by Rafael ("Cocuyo") Peguero Mieses, managed to publish two or three mimeographed issues of an underground newspaper, *El Grito*, but the police cracked down swiftly. "Cocuyo" Mieses was murdered, others were arrested, and those few PSPistas still free abandoned all political activity.

28. The members of the Central Committee were scattered throughout the hemisphere, so that, whenever the CC was convened, "it was necessary to travel" (interview with Félix Servio Ducoudray). This entailed a good many difficulties, including financial ones.

The meetings of the CC, therefore, were rare. Between meetings, the party was run by CC members based in Mexico.

29. Interview with Tulio Arvelo.

30. Interview with Félix Servio Ducoudray.

31. The Movement of Dominican Liberation (Movimiento de Liberación Dominicana or MLD) was not a political party, but a nonpartisan movement with leftist leanings created by Dominican exiles in March 1959. Relying on the support of Castro and, to a lesser degree, on that of Betancourt, the MLD planned to launch an invasion of the Dominican homeland in the near future. Throughout the spring of 1959, at least six hundred volunteers trained in Cuba in camps set up in the province of Pinar del Rio. On 14 June, a C-46 transport plane provided by Venezuela carried 56 "invaders" to Constanza, in the Cordillera Central of the Dominican Republic. Six days later, two assault launches reached the northern coast of the Dominican Republic, near Maimón and Estero Hondo. Aboard were 129 men. Other groups should have followed. In an obvious imitation of the "Cuban model," and following the suggestions of its Cuban advisers, the MLD had planned to spread throughout the Dominican Republic a series of guerrilla *focos*. But the swift destruction of these first groups and the international complications that immediately arose (the Cuban complicity was too flagrant) put an end to a plan that was doomed from the outset since it completely neglected the Dominican reality. Of the 185 men who reached the Dominican Republic on 14 and 20 June 1959, only six were spared by the regime (Mayobanex Vargas, Poncio Pou Saleta, Almonte Pacheco, Medardo Germán, Delio Gómez Ochoa, and Pablito Mirabal). Those waiting in Cuba to join the invasion scattered.

For an account by one who survived, see Poncio Pou Saleta, "La Epopeya de junio de 1959: No nos rendimos al ejercito, nos rendimos al hambre," *El 1J4*, no. 60 (14 June 1962), p. 8. See also "Diario de campaña de Johnny Puigsubirá Miniño," *Ahora*, no. 606 (23 June 1975), pp. 12-19, and "Constanza, Maimón y Estero Hondo: Todavia sobreviven sus banderas," *Ahora*, no. 605 (16 June 1975), pp. 23-26. Official (Trujillista) versions are "Invasión Criminal: Castigo Ejemplar," *Revista de las Fuerzas Armadas* X, no. 99 (July 1959) pp. 4-22, and Gimbernard, "El Machete, arma gloriosa de ayer y de hoy," ibid., pp. 46-48. For an account by a former chief of Trujillo's Intelligence Service, see Arturo R. Espaillat, *Trujillo: The Last Caesar* (Chicago: Henry Regnery Co., 1963), pp. 152-56. As already stated, throughout his book Espaillat mixes interesting information with blatant lies.

32. The expression comes from *El Popular*, no. 32 (14 June 1963), pp. 6-7. The same issue contains the names of the nineteen PSPistas who died in June 1959.

33. Interview with José Israel Cuello Hernández, one of the two "infiltrators" (the other was Fidelio Despradel Roque). The activities of Cuello and Despradel will be discussed in the section devoted to the AP1J4.

2. The Fourteenth of June Movement

1. My major sources for the MR1J4 are: (1) interviews with some leaders and members of the movement, in particular Luis Rafael Gómez Pérez (member of the CC of the MR1J4), Rafael Francisco (Fafa) Taveras Rosario and Jaime (Jimmy) Durán Hernando; and with Emma Tavárez Justo, sister of Manuel Aurelio (Manolo) Tavárez Justo, the supreme leader of the movement who was killed by the armed forces in December 1963. (2) Two books written to give the official position of the Trujillo regime: Luis Henríquez Castillo, *Crimenes contra la Seguridad interior y exterior del Estado Dominicano* (Ciudad Trujillo: Editorial La Nación, 1960), and Rafael Valera Benitez, *Complot Develado. Genesis y Evolución del Movimiento Conspirativo Celular "14 de Junio" contra el Gobierno Dominicano, descubierto por el'SIM'en enero de 1960* (Ciudad Trujillo: Editora Handicap, 1960). Henríquez Castillo, who was at the time the presiding judge of the Appellate Court of Ciudad Trujillo, reproduces in his book the depositions of more than one hundred members of the MR1J4. Rafael Valera Benitez was a member of the MR1J4. In exchange for his freedom he was forced to write a book on the movement. Obviously both works contain falsifications and distortions of the truth; however, they also abound in very useful information, particularly valuable for persons already familiar with the history of the MR1J4. I

have checked the information contained in these two books with survivors of the MR1J4. (3) Issues of *El 1J4*, the party organ of the AP1J4, which began publication in August 1961. Additional information has appeared from time to time in the press of the post-Trujillo period.

For the AP1J4 during the period from July 1961 to January 1962, my major sources are: (1) the party organ, *EL 1J4*; (2) interviews with some leaders and members of the AP1J4, in particular Emma Tavárez, Jimmy Durán, Marco Rodríguez Sánchez, and Norge William Botello Fernández; (3) interviews with the future PSP leaders José Israel Cuello and Asdrúbal Domínguez Guerra, especially regarding the PSP infiltration of the AP1J4 in that period.

As pointed out in Chapter 2, throughout the book I refer to the AP1J4 by the shorter acronym of 1J4, as is common in the Dominican Republic.

2. Interview with Jimmy Durán. Many other former members of the MR1J4 have stressed to me the influence of Castro's struggle against Batista. Manolo Tavárez, the leader of the MR1J4, declared to the police after his arrest that the Cuban insurrection had "aroused unusual sympathies in some sectors of the Dominican society" (Manuel Aurelio [Manolo] Tavárez Justo, "Deposición", in Henríquez Castillo, *Crimenes*, p. 414).

3. Interview with Fafa Taveras.

4. Interview with Jimmy Durán.

5. "Junio del 59: Renacimiento de la dignidad," in *El 1J4*, no. 60 (14 June 1962), p. 2.

6. Interview with Jimmy Durán. The best summary of the causes behind this political awakening of many Dominicans, and especially of the youth, is probably the one given by a member of the MR1J4 to his torturers: "I was in the habit of listening to the radio broadcasts from Cuba, especially since Fidel Castro's victory; in particular, my anti-government stance grew stronger after the attempted invasion of June 1959" (Rafael González Mera, "Deposición," in Henríquez Castillo, *Crimenes*, p. 212).

7. Manolo and Minerva are two of the most fascinating figures in Dominican history. A portrait of Minerva Mirabal de Tavárez appears in note 26. Manolo is a recurring figure throughout the first chapters of this book. This young couple of the upper middle class had never joined the cohorts of sycophants surrounding the tyrant.

8. In 1959 the Church was still a faithful servant and an accomplice of the regime. As far as I could determine, only three priests took part in the underground movement against Trujillo: the Reverend Father Daniel Cruz Inoa of the High Church of Santiago, Father Ercilio de Jesús Moya, curate of Tenares, and Father Antonio Fabré, professor at the Seminary of La Romana. Their role, of some importance at the outset (in particular that of Father Cruz Inoa), had become minimal by the end of 1959.

9. These thirteen leaders were: Manuel Aurelio (Manolo) Tavárez Justo, twenty-nine years old, lawyer, delegate from Monte Cristi and the entire Cibao region; Minerva Mirabal de Tavárez, thirty-two, delegate from Monte Cristi and the entire Cibao region, the only woman to participate in the meeting (after the collapse of the movement, her presence at Mao was kept secret from the police and therefore is mentioned neither by Henríquez Castillo in *Crimenes* nor by Valera Benitez in *Complot Develado)*; Rafael Antonio (Pipe) Faxas Canto, twenty-three, painter, delegate from Ciudad Trujillo; José Ramón Leandro Guzmán Rodríguez, twenty-seven, engineer, delegate from Salcedo; Luis Antonio ("Nino") Alvarez Pereyra, thirty-five, landowner, delegate from San Francisco de Macorís; Carlos Conrado ("Charles") Bogaert Domínguez, thirty-six, landowner, delegate from Mao and Santiago; Efraín ("Gurúm") Dotel Recio, twenty-five, university student, delegate from Barahona; Julio Miguel Escoto Santana, thirty, lawyer, delegate from San Pedro de Macorís and the entire eastern region; Luis Rafael Gómez Pérez, twenty-six, university student, delegate from the southern region; Carlos Aurelio ("Cayeyo") Grisanty García, thirty-six, merchant, delegate from Santiago; Ramón Antonio ("Rodrigote") Rodríguez Cruz, fifty-three, landowner, delegate from La Vega; Germán Antonio ("El Guardia") Silverio Messon, twenty-four, university student, delegate from Puerto Plata; Miguel Antonio ("Güey") Teyeda Yanguela, twenty-four, landowner, delegate from San Francisco de Macorís.

10. Movimiento de Liberación Dominicana, "Programa minimo del Movimiento de Liberación Dominicana," March 1959, in my personal archives.

11. "Among other things that Mr. Manolo Lamarche had brought to my house were a pamphlet containing the manifesto and the "Programa minimo" of the Dominican Liberation Movement, [Castro's] *History will Absolve me*, and a newspaper, *Revolución de Cuba*" (José Ramón Leandro Guzmán Rodríguez, "Deposición," in Henríquez Castillo, *Crimenes*, p. 51).

12. Interview with Fafa Taveras.

13. Of the delegates gathered at Mao, only four seem to have shared Manolo's social sensitivity: Minerva Mirabal de Tavárez, Leandro Guzmán, Luis Gómez, and Pipe Faxas.

14. Interview with Jimmy Durán.

15. Fafa Taveras, the son of a small country shopkeeper, was the one exception among the leaders of the MR1J4.

16. Interview with Emma Tavárez.

17. Rafael Antonio (Pipe) Faxas Canto, "Deposición," in Henríquez Castillo, *Crimenes*, p. 138. Irlander Selig spoke in the same vein to other members of the underground. Indeed, it is difficult to fathom the reasons that drove him to make pledges he could not keep. The Dominican exiles were as weak and divided as ever. And even if he really met with the Venezuelan consul in San Juan, Puerto Rico, it is highly improbable, to say the least, that the talks were as successful as he claimed.

18. Tavárez Justo, "Deposición," in Henríquez Castillo, *Crimenes*, p. 415.

19. By 10 January 1960, at least five localities had been pinpointed. For details, see the depositions of Juan Moliné Pichardo, Pipe Faxas, and Charles Bogaert Domínguez, in ibid., pp. 40-41, 138, 141, 159.

20. Carlos Aurelio ("Cayeyo") Grisanty García, "Deposición," in ibid., p. 207.

21. Some leaders of the MR1J4 thought that the uprising should take place two or three days before the invaders of the MLD reached Dominican soil; others preferred that the uprising and the invasion take place simultaneously. At Mao, the conspirators decided to postpone a final decision on this question until Lama Mitre returned from New York. On one point, they all agreed: the help of the exiles was indispensable, but it was up to "those on the home front" to deal the fatal blow to the regime. See the depositions of Germán A. Silverio Messon, Efrain Dotel Recio, and Charles Bogaert Domínguez, in ibid., pp. 47, 159, 168.

22. At the time of the meeting at Mao, the MR1J4 allegedly had some one thousand members. This tentative figure fails to take into account the difference between "active" and "passive" members. The latter "did not participate actively in the conspiracy, but would join in the uprising" (Ramón Cáceres Troncoso, himself a "passive" member of the 1J4, "Deposición," in ibid., p. 94).

23. Robert D. Crassweller, *Trujillo: The Life and Times of a Caribbean Dictator* (New York: Macmillan, 1966), p. 372. Only a few members of the MR1J4 were able to escape the regime's vengeance. Among them was Guido ("Yuyo") d'Alessandro Tavárez, a cousin of Manolo Tavárez. D'Alessandro hid in the Papal Nunciatura, "and for two months the police and the intelligence agencies searched for him in vain. He was smuggled out of the Nunciatura in March, dressed as a priest, and was put aboard a United States Navy ship" (ibid., p. 373.).

24. *El Caribe*, 9 July 1961, p. 1.

25. Those members of the MR1J4 who had not been imprisoned by the regime were excluded from the assembly. This measure, which touched only a tiny minority of the former conspirators, is highly indicative of the spirit of the times.

26. Minerva was one of the four Mirabal sisters, "an authentic native beauty, svelte, her complexion of cinnamon color, jet black hair, lively dark eyes that shone, with a constant smile on her lips." Minerva was the beautiful wife of a young and brilliant lawyer, the mother of two children, and a member of the upper middle class. But she was much more than an "angelic homemaker" of the *Kinder, Küche, Kirche* variety—the distorted image of a woman that Dominican society held at the time. She was the rare exception.

How many Dominicans who grew up under the Trujillo regime can boast of having been imprisoned, before 1960, for their opposition to the dictatorship? Minerva had been imprisoned twice: in 1949, when she was twenty-two, and again in 1951. In 1957, she needed no prodding to join in a conspiracy against Trujillo. She was not following the lead of her husband. Together they were the founders of the Monte Cristi group. Along with

Asela Morel and Tomasina Cabral Mejía, Minerva was one of the few women to play a role in the underground movement. And she was, no less than Manolo Tavárez, Pipe Faxas, Luis Gómez, or Fafa Taveras, a driving force of that "hard-line" sector of the MR1J4 that dreamed of reforms and social justice.

In January 1960, the regime destroyed the MR1J4. On 22 January, Minerva was arrested, joining her sister María Teresa Mirabal de Guzmán, who had been imprisoned two days earlier. Together they endured the indignities and tortures of *La 40*. Then came Trujillo's "parody of liberal indulgence," and the two sisters were released on 8 and 9 August 1960. They were free, but doomed. Minerva and María Teresa Mirabal made no secret of their opposition to the regime. They were already becoming symbols. Incensed by their defiance, Trujillo decided that they should die.

In the evening of 25 November, a jeep drove along the road from Puerto Plata to Salcedo, through mountains and steep cliffs. Minerva and María Teresa were returning home, after visiting their husbands imprisoned in the Fortaleza de San Felipe, in Puerto Plata. Their sister, Patria Mirabal de González, accompanied them. Her husband was also in a prison, in La Victoria, near the capital.

The three women never reached Salcedo. Five agents of the Servicio de Inteligencia Militar in a truck arrested them on a mountain road, took them and their driver away, probably to a nearby finca belonging to Trujillo, where they were tortured and beaten to death. Then their bodies were placed in their own jeep, and the vehicle was pushed over a high cliff, in a clumsy effort to simulate an automobile accident. The ravaged corpses of Patria, thirty-five, María Teresa, twenty-five and Minerva, thirty-two, lay at the bottom of a ravine, but their names were becoming legends.

The quotations in this note are from Francisco N. Rodríguez V., "Minerva Mirabal de Tavárez"; Antonio J. Mejía Tatem, "Patria Mirabal de González"; Angel S. Forastieri, "María Teresa Mirabal de Guzmán"; and A. M. V., "Las Heroinas," *El 1J4*, no. 15 (25 Nov. 1961), pp. 9-14, 22-26. For details on the role of Trujillo in the murder of the Mirabals, see Crassweller, *Trujillo*, pp. 401-3. Víctor Peña Rivera, in 1960 the chief of the Servicio de Inteligencia Militar for the Northern Region, includes revealing but at times unreliable disclosures in *Historia oculta de un Dictador, Trujillo* (New York: Plus Ultra, 1977), pp. 277-84, 289-94.

27. The general assembly of 30 July had elected a CEC of fourteen members. But the government deported one of those, Tomás Josué Erickson Alvarez, on 27 October 1961; another, Ramón Isidro ("Moncho") Imbert Rainieri, resigned. A third, Luis Antonio Alvarez Pereyra, left for Puerto Rico on 31 July, the day after the general assembly. Therefore, the CEC consisted of only eleven members, five of whom also belonged to the UCN: José Antonio Fernández Caminero (vice-president of the UCN), Rafael Albuquerque Zayas-Bazán, Ramón Manuel Baquero Ricart, Miguel Angel Lama Mitre, and Asela Morel.

28. Interviews with José Israel Cuello, Emma Tavárez, Marco Rodríguez (of the AP1J4), and Asdrúbal Domínguez (for the latter, see also n. 29). José Israel Cuello had been an "active" member of the MR1J4 and the cofounder of an anti-Trujilloist cell at the University of Santo Domingo. He was arrested in January 1960. Fidelio Despradel had belonged to the "Tony Barreiro's group"—a handful of young university students who, during the summer of 1959, had detonated several bombs in the capital. He and his friends were arrested in September 1959. Thanks to their fathers' intervention, both Cuello and Despradel were released from jail after only a few months and permitted to leave the country "in order to study."

29. Interviews with José Israel Cuello and Asdrúbal Domínguez. The "apostolate" of Cuello and Despradel was not limited to the 1J4. They also tried to win converts for the PSP within the university, where from their arrival they had been nominated advisers to the Provisional Executive Committee (CEP) of the Federation of Dominican Students (FED). One student singled out for conversion by Fidelio Despradel was his old friend Asdrúbal Domínguez who, as president of the CEP of the FED, represented a particularly valuable conquest. Despradel was successful. Asdrúbal Domínguez became a sincere and brilliant member of the PSP.

30. Interview with Jimmy Durán.

31. Editorial, "La Misión de la OEA en Santo Domingo," *El 1J4*, no. 5 (17 Sept. 1961), p. 2, and "El 14 de Junio reafirma su postura social-cristiana y nacionalista," *El 1J4*, no. 15 (25 Nov. 1961), p. 5.

32. They belonged to a group of seventy-one Dominicans who were to take a "two month course on the application and function of democracy" (*Hispanic American Report*, Jan. 1962, p. 994). Among them was Norge Botello, future member of the Central Executive Committee of the 1J4 (see also Editorial, "El 1J4 los saluda," *El 1J4*, no. 14 (18 Nov. 1961], p. 2).

33. Juan Bosch, *Crisis de la democracia de América en la República Dominicana*, 3d ed. (México, D.F.: Centro de Estudios y Documentación Social, 1965), p. 74.

34. Editorial, "El pueblo dominicano se basta a sí mismo," *El 1J4*, no. 7 (30 Sept. 1961), p. 2.

35. Bosch, *Crisis*, p. 30.

36. These quotes are taken from a speech given by José Francisco Peña Gómez, in his capacity as PRD delegate, in "Reunión celebrada el 8 de julio del año 1965 en la tercera planta del edificio 'Copello,' . . . " p. 28 of the minutes, among my personal papers. Peña Gómez was referring to a specific situation that existed in July 1965 in the Dominican Republic, but his words retain their full value for the period under discussion here, that is, the months that followed the death of Trujillo.

37. Interview with Jimmy Durán.

38. In its 24 January 1962 issue, *El 1J4* attempted for the first time to explain "our conception of a Government of National Unity." The article stated that "in essence . . . the legislative power is the only one of the three classic powers of government that would cease its functions." It would be replaced by "representatives of the most important sectors of the populace: . . . workers, peasants, students, professionals, merchants, employees and manufacturers. . . . The workers would be represented by workers, . . . the students . . . by students . . . and so on." Harmony would prevail: "If the majority forces, the forces representative of the country, were incorporated into the government, they would in no way whatsoever antagonize or reject that government which represented them." The members of the Government of National Unity would be selected through elections "first on a local, and then on a national level . . . . This could be carried out in each sector: that is, the professionals would elect their own representatives, the workers would elect theirs, and so on. Perhaps the most difficult election would be that of the peasants, but for them a special formula could be worked out" (no information is provided on this formula).

This, then, was the solution proposed by the 1J4 to replace the Council of State immediately. This solution would be both immediate and provisional, since the Government of National Unity would subsequently be replaced by another, even more ill-defined, government ("En torno a Gobierno Unidad Nacional," *El 1J4*, no. 32 [24 Jan. 1962], p. 8).

39. The PRD was a political party, and therefore a competitor. In fact, the very personality of Bosch, the "professor," aroused the antipathy of the "young middle-class revolutionaries" of the 1J4.

40. Interview with Jimmy Durán.

41. *El 1J4*, no. 34 (31 Jan. 1962), p. 11.

3. The Dominican People's Movement

1. My major sources for this section are: (1) interviews with the MPD leaders Cayetano Rodríguez del Prado, Ramón A. ("Monchín") Pinedo Mejía, Luis René Sánchez Cordova, and with the PSP leaders Justino José del Orbe, Félix Servio Ducoudray, Tulio Arvelo, and Asdrúbal Domínguez; (2) the official history of the party, Movimiento Popular Dominicano (Comisión Política), *Documentos del Primer Pre-Congreso del Partido de la Clase Obrera* (Santo Domingo, 30 Sept. 1965), pp. 8-35; (3) articles that have appeared in the Dominican press since 1960 and some internal documents of the far left. The only book that contains some valuable information on the MPD for the period discussed here is Robert D. Crassweller's *Trujillo: The Life and Times of a Caribbean Dictator* (New York: Macmillan, 1966), pp. 378-79.

2. MPD, *Documentos*, p. 8.

3. Interview with Cayetano Rodríguez.

4. This is the one "serious case of insubordination" mentioned in speaking of the PSP exile during the 1950s (see Appendix–PSP).

5. MPD, *Documentos*, p. 9.

6. The PSP, however, viewed the 26 of July Movement with the same reserve as its "guide," the Cuban PSP.

7. MPD, *Documentos*, p. 12.

8. "The return of the MPD comrades to our country was the result of the tyrant's need to feign a climate of public liberties while facing powerful international pressure. The latter was caused above all by the conflict between Trujillo and Rómulo Betancourt. The puppet Betancourt better served the interests of the Yankee imperialists. Moreover, the Trujillo dictatorship showed signs of internal collapse. We successfully exploited the contradiction between American imperialism and one of its chief lackeys: Trujillo" (ibid., p. 13).

9. This is the title of a lengthy article written, most likely in 1956, by Pablo Antonio Martínez, one of the founders of the MPD (among my personal papers).

10. Crassweller, *Trujillo*, pp. 378-79. The exact address was 12 Avenida José Trujillo Valdez (today Avenida Duarte).

11. 1J4, Grupo Transformista, "Desarrollemos el aspecto más progresivo del contenido del Partido, el aspecto proletario" (Santo Domingo [1966]), Tema I, unpaginated, among my personal papers.

12. The Political Committee of the MPD was alluding to them in particular when it stated that "the founding fathers upheld the Marxist-Leninist doctrine in all its purity."

13. MPD, *Documentos*, pp. 15-16.

14. Crassweller, *Trujillo*, p. 379.

15. MPD, *Documentos*, p. 18.

16. Ibid., p. 14.

17. Ibid.

18. Interview with Asdrúbal Domínguez. The MPDists are particularly proud of two events of that period: (1) "An action without precedent in the thirty years of the dictatorship . . . : the protest march and the pickets demanding the liberation of comrade Ramón Emilio Feliu. The march began at our headquarters . . . and ended in front of the headquarters of the Military Intelligence Service—SIM—where the pickets were stationed. Comrade Feliu was murdered, but our pickets served as an example for a people yearning for freedom"; (2) the party's first "sally" outside the capital: the trip that July by an MPD committee to Santiago. "On that occasion a mass demonstration took place, culminating in clashes with the police . . . this being the first violent incident on native soil since the arrival of the MPD." The trip also saw "the formation of the first MPD committee in the interior of the country" (MPD, *Documentos*, pp. 16-17).

19. Crassweller, *Trujillo*, p. 379.

20. Florangel Cárdenas, "La Universidad de Santo Domingo. Un trayecto difícil: De la tiranía a la libertad," II, *Renovación*, no. 141 (14-20 Oct. 1969), p. 8.

21. MPD, *Documentos*, p. 21.

22. Interview with Luis René Sánchez Cordova.

23. Ibid.

24. "López Molina was able to win a certain measure of trust from Ramfis" (ibid.). But one wonders whether the price of that "trust" was not the abandonment by the MPD of all anti-Trujilloist activity in order to concentrate its efforts on anti-American propaganda.

25. *El Caribe*, 23 Oct. 1961, p. 1.

26. *Renovación*, no. 11 (10-16 June 1967), p. 2.

Bibliographical Essay

This essay does not claim to be exhaustive. I intend only to indicate the most significant sources for the subjects covered in this book. I refer those who desire additional information to four bibliographies: Deborah S. Hitt and Larman C. Wilson, *A Selected Bibliography of the Dominican Republic: A Century after the Restoration of Independence* (Washington, D.C.: American University, 1968); Howard J. Wiarda *Política y Gobierno en la República Dominicana, 1930-1960* (Santiago, D.R.: Universidad Católica Madre y Maestra, 1968); Wolf Grabendorff, *Bibliographie zu Politik und Gesellschaft der Dominikanischen Republik, Neuere Studien 1961-1971* (Munich: Weltforum Verlag, 1973); and Bernardo Vega, *Bibliografía de asuntos económicos dominicanos* (Santiago, D.R.: Asociación para el Desarrollo, 1965).

As the title indicates, Vega deals only with economic subjects, while the other three bibliographies are more comprehensive. Particularly valuable is the volume by Hitt and Wilson, which is competently annotated. Wiarda offers a good introduction on research facilities in the Dominican Republic and is particularly useful for the period between the death of Trujillo (30 May 1961) and the outbreak of the constitutionalist revolt (24 April 1965). Grabendorff includes sources that have appeared since the completion of the other bibliographies; he is also the most extensive for European sources.

While I will only discuss the most relevant works for the 1965 crisis, an almost complete list may be obtained by consulting the bibliographies by Hitt and Wilson, Wiarda, and Grabendorff. To my knowledge these authors overlook only Marcelino Zapico, *Revolución en Hispanoamérica. Lo que ví en Santo Domingo* (Madrid: Escalicer, 1966). *Revolución en Hispanoamérica* has some merit and will be discussed later, as will the only book on the crisis to have appeared since the completion of Grabendorff's bibliography, *La Revolución Dominicana de Abril vista por Cuba* by Antonio Ricardi, et al (Santo Domingo: Editora de la Universidad Autónoma de Santo Domingo, 1974).

While they cover at length the years after 1930, and especially after 1961, neither Hitt and Wilson, Wiarda, nor Grabendorff treat the pre-Trujillo period. This is why that period will receive special attention here.

On several occasions in the footnotes of the book I have discussed the literature on specific subjects that are outside the scope of this essay (for instance, sources on the far left during the Era of Trujillo and on the Galíndez affair). The literature on more general topics will be examined below.

427

INTRODUCTORY WORKS

The best general introduction to the Dominican Republic is Howard J. Wiarda, *The Dominican Republic. Nation in Transition* (New York-Washington-London: Praeger, 1969). Thomas Weil et al., *Area Handbook for the Dominican Republic* (Washington, D.C.: U. S. Government Printing Office, 1973), contains a good deal of information but is analytically poor and frequently biased. Two often mentioned books are *Haiti and the Dominican Republic* (New York-London: Oxford University Press, 1968) by Rayford W. Logan and *Quisqueya. A History of the Dominican Republic* (Seattle: University of Washington Press, 1964) by Selden Rodman. Both rely heavily on unsophisticated secondary sources (Rodman's presentation is particularly shallow). The best source of this kind in Spanish, Ricardo Pattee, *La República Dominicana* (Madrid: Ediciones Cultura Hispanica, 1967), is equally mediocre.

There are a few stimulating efforts at social analysis of Dominican reality. Juan Bosch, *Trujillo: Causas de una tiranía sin ejemplo* (Caracas: Grabados Nacionales, 1959), may be considered the first serious attempt toward a sociological interpretation of Dominican history. Bosch extends his research in *Composición Social Dominicana. Historia e Interpretación*, 2d ed. rev. (Santo Domingo: Editora Arte y Cine, 1970). A Marxist perspective is offered by Juan Isidro Jimenes Grullón, *La República Dominicana: una ficción* (Merida: Talleres Gráficos Universitarios, 1965). Still worth reading is an older work, Marcio A. Mejía Ricart, *Las Clases sociales en Santo Domingo* (Ciudad Trujillo: Libreria Dominicana, 1953). Pedro A. Pérez Cabral, *La Comunidad Mulata. El Caso Socio-Político de la República Dominicana* (Caracas: Gráfica Americana, 1967), is a sometimes incisive study of the impact of race on Dominican society. Howard J. Wiarda, *Dictatorship, Development and Disintegration: Politics and Social Change in the Dominican Republic*, 3 vols. (Ann Arbor, Mich.: Xerox University Microfilms, 1975), presents a helpful overview of social classes in the Dominican Republic (see esp. Vol. I, Chap. 5, pp. 349-432, and Vol. II, Chap. 10, pp. 753-806); his analysis rests, however, on secondary sources, particularly on the writings of Bosch.

While all the above works have merits, none can be considered a definitive study. Bosch and Jimenes Grullón in particular offer brilliant insights, but their arguments are often marred by inadequate historical knowledge.

Frank Moya Pons, *Manual de Historia Dominicana* (Santiago, D. R.: Universidad Católica Madre y Maestra, 1977), provides the only satisfactory coverage of both the colonial and national periods (general histories for the different periods will be discussed later). Two books by César Herrera, *Las Finanzas de la República Dominicana* (Ciudad Trujillo: Impresora Dominicana, 1955), and *De Hartmont a Trujillo* (Ciudad Trujillo: Impresora Dominicana, 1953), are the closest to an economic history of the Dominican Republic. Julio César Estrella, *La Moneda, La Banca y Las Finanzas en la República Dominicana*, 2 vols. (Santiago, D. R.: Universidad Católica Madre y Maestra, 1971), is a study of the country's financial institutions.

Wiarda's massive *Dictatorship, Development and Disintegration* warrants special comment. Wiarda, the foremost U. S. specialist on the Dominican Republic, deals in 1,921 pages with all aspects of Dominican reality, emphasizing this century but including ample reference to the past. Despite the obvious limits imposed by the enormous breadth of the subject, this work remains an extremely instructive one. Unfortunately, however, Wiarda adds little to his several published books and articles, with the result that in these three volumes some superb chapters alternate with others that are much less penetrating.

PART I: THE PRE-1965 PERIOD

1. The Dominican Republic until the End of the Haitian Occupation (1844). Serious historical research began in the Dominican Republic only after the death of Trujillo. Although the political convulsions of the country and poor state of the archives have slowed progress, some good works have appeared, predominantly by Dominican authors.

The most perceptive general account for the colonial period is Frank Moya Pons, *Historia Colonial de Santo Domingo* (Santiago, D. R.: Universidad Católica Madre y Maestra, 1974). Another recent contribution is Oscar Gil Díaz, *Apuntes para la Historia* (Santo Domingo: Impresora Arte y Cine, 1969). Now largely outdated, José Gabriel García, *Compendio de la Historia de Santo Domingo*, 4 vols. (Santo Domingo: Publicaciones ¡Ahora!, 1968), was long the foremost source for the colonial period. (García's work was first published in 1867 in a single volume and covered the country's history from the discovery of the island to 1821. It was later expanded to include the period to 1876, and this expanded version is the one published by ¡Ahora! in the edition cited above; Vols. I and II deal with the colonial period.) Antonio del Monte y Tejada, *Historia de Santo Domingo*, 3 vols. (Ciudad Trujillo: Impresora Dominicana, 1952-53; first complete edition published in 1892) is of some value for the eighteenth century.

Good monographs are rare. Roberto Cassá, *Los Tainos de la Española* (Santo Domingo: Editora de la Universidad Autónoma de Santo Domingo, 1974), is a thorough analysis of pre-Spanish society by a Soviet-trained historian. Again Moya Pons offers the best treatment of the early conquest period with *La Española en el Siglo XVI, 1493-1520* (Santiago, D. R.: Universidad Católica Madre y Maestra, 1971). A sound study is Troy S. Floyd, *The Columbus Dynasty in the Caribbean, 1492-1526* (Albuquerque: University of New Mexico Press, 1973). The literature for later periods of the colonial era is poor. Emilio Rodríguez Demorizi, ed., *Relaciones Históricas de Santo Domingo*, 3 vols. (Ciudad Trujillo: Archivo General de la Nación, 1942, 1945, 1947), is essentially a collection of documents important for an understanding of the end of the sixteenth and the seventeenth centuries. Manuel Arturo Peña Battle, *La Isla de la Tortuga* (Madrid: Ediciones Cultura Hispanica, 1951), analyzes with some skill the effects on seventeenth-century Dominican society of foreign penetration in the western regions of the island, but the account suffers from a violent pro-Spanish bias. For the eighteenth century, two old sources are still essential: Antonio Sánchez Valverde, *Idea del Valor de la Isla Española* (Ciudad Trujillo: Impresora Dominicana, 1957; first published in 1785); and Médéric L. E. Moreau de Saint-Méry, *Descripción de la parte Española de Santo Domingo* (Ciudad Trujillo: Editora Montalvo, 1944; first published in 1796).

Emilio Cordero Michel, *La Revolución Haitiana y Santo Domingo* (Santo Domingo: Editora Nacional, 1968), is a refreshing contrast to the anti-Haitian approach of traditional Dominican historiography, although some of his conclusions are debatable. For a brief discussion of the literature on the Haitian occupation (1822-44), see Chapter 1, notes 17 and 19.

Two recent volumes on race relations in the colonial period are Hugo Tolentino Dipp, *Raza e Historia en Santo Domingo*, Vol. I: *Los Origenes del Prejuicio Racial en América* (Santo Domingo: Editora de la Universidad Autónoma de Santo Domingo, 1974), and Franklin J. Franco Pichardo, *Los Negros, Los Mulatos y La Nación Dominicana* (Santo Domingo: Editora Nacional, 1970). Tolentino Dipp ably examines the sixteenth century; Franco Pichardo covers the whole period until 1844 but with many factual errors. An informative study is Carlos Larrazabal Blanco, *Los Negros y la Esclavitud en Santo Domingo* (Santo Domingo: Postigo, 1967).

2. The Period of Independence from 1844 to 1916. Satisfying general histories for this period are, again, sadly lacking, but Moya Pons, *Manual de Historia Dominicana*, pp. 267-473, is a substantial improvement on the existing literature. The standard works are: Ramón Marrero Aristy, *La República Dominicana. Origenes del pueblo cristiano más antiguo de América*, 3 vols. (Ciudad Trujillo: Editora del Caribe, 1957-58); Bernardo Pichardo, *Resumen de Historia Patria*, 5th ed. (Santo Domingo: Postigo, 1969); Jacinto Gimbernard, *Historia de Santo Domingo* (Santo Domingo: Editora Cultural Dominicana, 1972); Sumner Welles, *Naboth's Vineyard: The Dominican Republic, 1844-1924*, 2 vols. (Washington, D.C.: Savile Books, 1966; Welles' book has been discussed at some length in Chapter I, n. 17).

The few good monographs include Juan Isidro Jimenes Grullón, *El Mito de los Padres de la Patria* (Santo Domingo: Editora Cultural Dominicana, 1971), a provocative challenge to the traditional presentation of the Dominican "founding fathers"; Hugo Tolentino Dipp, *La Traición de Pedro Santana* (Santo Domingo: Impresos Brenty, 1968), a vivid essay on a key Dominican *caudillo*; and José Gabriel García, *Historia Moderna de la República Dominicana* (Santo Domingo: Publicaciones ¡Ahora!, 1968), an adequate treatment of the 1865-76 period. Helen Tilles Ortiz, "The Era de Lilís: Economic Development in the

Dominican Republic, 1880 to 1899" (Ph. D. dissertation, Georgetown University, 1975), provides the most thorough exposition of the Heureaux dictatorship. Luis Felipe Mejía, *De Lilís a Trujillo: historia contemporánea de la República Dominicana* (Caracas: Editorial Elite, 1944), offers a valuable political history of the Dominican Republic from 1900 to 1940.

The best social analysis of the period is Harry Hoetink, *El Pueblo Dominicano: 1850-1900. Apuntes para su Sociología Histórica* (Santiago, D. R.: Universidad Católica Madre y Maestra, 1971), which centers on the last twenty years of the century. Juan Isidro Jimenes Grullón, *Sociología Política Dominicana, 1844-1966,* Vol. I: *1844-1898* (Santo Domingo: Editora Taller, 1974), is interesting but not always reliable. Sociological studies mentioned among the introductory works naturally cover in varying degrees this as well as later periods.

3. U.S.-Dominican Relations until 1930. Welles' mediocre *Naboth's Vineyard* has already been discussed. Comprehensive in Charles Tansill, *The United States and Santo Domingo, 1798-1873. A Chapter in Caribbean Diplomacy* (Baltimore: Johns Hopkins Press, 1938). Antonio de la Rosa, *Las Finanzas de Santo Domingo y el Control Americano* (Santo Domingo: Editora Nacional, 1969), is excellent on American political and economic penetration during the administrations of Roosevelt and Taft (the real name of the author, a Haitian, is Alexandre Poujols; the book was first published in Paris in 1915). Dana Munro combines considerable information with an often superficial analysis in *Intervention and Dollar Diplomacy in the Caribbean, 1900-1921* (Princeton: Princeton University Press, 1964).

Also noteworthy for the pre-1916 period are: William R. Tansill, "Diplomatic Relations between the United State and the Dominican Republic, 1874-1899" (Ph. D. dissertation, Georgetown University, 1952); Edgard Duin, "Dominican-American Diplomatic Relations, 1895-1907" (Ph. D. dissertation, Georgetown University, 1955); Fred J. Rippy, "The Initiation of the Customs Receivership in the Dominican Republic" *(Hispanic American Historical Review 17* [November 1937]: 419-57); Jocasta Valenzuela Arias, "Les aspects politico-juridiques de l'intervention américaine à Saint-Domingue—1916" (Mémoire, University of Paris, Institut des Hautes Etudes Internationales, 1965); and, above all, David G. MacMichael, *The United States and the Dominican Republic, 1871-1940: A Cycle in Caribbean Diplomacy* (Ann Arbor, Michigan: Xerox University Microfilms, 1975, esp. Chaps. 1-15).

As already mentioned (Chapter 1, n. 60), there is as yet no thorough study of the Wilson administration's decision to invade the Dominican Republic in 1916. Nor is there a definitive work on the U. S. occupation (1916-24). The two most important studies are Melvin M. Knight, *The Americans in Santo Domingo* (New York: Vanguard Press, 1928), especially for the economic side, and Bruce J. Calder, *Some Aspects of the United States Occupation of the Dominican Republic* (Ph. D. dissertation, Ann Arbor, Mich.: Xerox University Microfilms,

1974), who deftly examines the guerrilla struggle in the eastern area of the country. Significant data can be found in U.S., Congress, Senate, *Inquiry into Occupation and Administration of Haiti and Santo Domingo. Hearings before a Select Committee on Haiti and Santo Domingo*, 67 Cong., 1st and 2d sess., 2 vols. (Washington, D.C.: U.S. Government Printing Office, 1922).

Other sources include Marvin Goldwert's *The Constabulary in the Dominican Republic and Nicaragua. Progeny and Legacy of United States Intervention*, Latin American Monographs, no. 1 (Gainesville: University of Florida Press, 1962); Max Henrique Ureña, *Los Yanquis en Santo Domingo: La verdad de los hechos comprobada por datos y documentos oficiales* (Madrid: M. Aguilar, 1929); Antonio Hoepelman and Juan A. Senior, eds., *Documentos históricos que se refieren a la intervención armada de los Estados Unidos de Norte-América y la implantación de un gobierno militar en la República Dominicana* (Santo Domingo: Imprenta de J. R. Viuda García, 1922); Carl Kelsey, "The American Intervention in Haiti and the Dominican Republic" (*Annals of the American Academy of Political and Social Sciences* 100, no. 189 [March 1922], pp. 113-202); Military Government of the Dominican Republic, *Santo Domingo—Its Past and Its Present Condition* (Santo Domingo: n.p., 1920); and MacMichael, *The United States and the Dominican Republic* (esp. pp. 420-504). Stephen M. Fuller and Graham A. Cosmas, *Marines in the Dominican Republic, 1916-1924* (Washington, D.C.: History and Museum Division Headquarters, U. S. Marine Corps, 1974), provide an amusing and not too clumsy apology for the Marine Corps during the occupation. Welles' biased *Naboth's Vineyard* is helpful, particularly for the background of the U. S. evacuation (chaps. 13-15). (For other sources on the evacuation, see above, Chapter 1, n. 78).

4. The Trujillo Era. While no definitive work has yet been published on the Era of Trujillo, three good studies are Robert D. Crassweller, *Trujillo: The Life and Times of a Caribbean Dictator* (New York: Macmillan, 1966); Howard J. Wiarda, *Dictatorship and Development: The Methods of Control in Trujillo's Dominican Republic*, Latin American Monographs, 2d Ser. no. 5 (Gainesville: University of Florida Press, 1968); Jesús de Galíndez, *La Era de Trujillo: Un estudio casuistico de dictadura latinoamericana* (Santiago, Chile: Editorial del Pacifico, 1956). The most vivid feeling of the Era is rendered by Juan Bosch in the last chapters of his *Trujillo* (pp. 121-99).

Of the many accounts written during the Era by Dominican exiles, the most valuable are *Trujillo: Little Caesar of the Caribbean* (Edinburgh-New York-Toronto: Thomas Nelson and Sons, 1958) by Germán E. Ornes Coiscou, a former servant of the regime; José Cordero Michel, *Análisis de la Era de Trujillo (Informe sobre la República Dominicana, 1959)*, 4th ed., (Santo Domingo: Editora de la Universidad Autónoma de Santo Domingo, 1975; first published in 1959); and Juan Isidro Jimenes Grullón, *Una Gestapo en América: Vida, tortura, agonía y muerte de presos políticos bajo la tiranía de Trujillo* (Santo Domingo: Editora Montalvo, 1962; first published in 1946). Abelardo R. Nanita, *Trujillo*, 5th ed., (Ciudad Trujillo: Impresora Dominicana, 1951), is probably the best of the numerous Dominican and foreign panegyrics of the dictator. In spite of its gross bias, the twenty-volume set *La Era de Trujillo: 25 Años de Historia Dominicana* (Ciudad Trujillo: Impresora Dominicana, 1955), published to celebrate the twenty-fifth anniversary of the regime, contains a wealth of information.

Of particular interest are two books written by former Trujillista officials after the collapse of the dictatorship: Arturo R. Espaillat, *The Last Caesar* (Chicago: Henry Regnery, 1963), and Víctor A. Peña Rivera, *Historia Oculta de un Dictador, Trujillo* (New York: Plus Ultra, 1977). Both must naturally be read with the awareness that they freely mix interesting information with outright lies.

Dominican-American relations during the Era are adeptly observed in Pope G. Atkins and Larman C. Wilson, *The United States and the Trujillo Regime* (New Brunswick, N.J.: Rutgers University Press, 1972). For relations in the early years of the Era, see also Dana G. Munro, *The United States and the Caribbean Republics, 1921-1933* (Princeton: Princeton University Press, 1974), pp. 294-308; MacMichael, *The United States and the Dominican Republic*, esp. pp. 640-89; and Earl R. Curry, "Dilemma in the Caribbean" (Ph.D. dissertation, University of Minnesota, 1965).

Not to be overlooked is a Dominican historical journal, *Eme Eme, Estudios Dominicanos* (Santiago, D. R.: Departamento de Publicaciones y Centro de Estudios Dominicanos of the Universidad Católica Madre y Maestra, June-July 1972-) that occasionally publishes articles on the Era but usually concentrates on earlier periods. Other articles on Dominican history (including the Era) sometimes appear in the Dominican press, especially in the weekly *Ahora* (15 January 1962-). Articles on more contemporary issues of an economic and sociological character appear in *Estudios Sociales* (Santiago, D. R.: Centro de Investigación y Acción Social, Jan. 1968-). *(Estudios Sociales* and *Eme Eme* are the country's only scholarly journals).

5. From the Death of Trujillo (30 May 1961) to the Outbreak of the Constitutionalist Revolt (24 April 1965). There are three important works on this period: Howard J. Wiarda, "The Aftermath of the Trujillo Dictatorship: The Emergence of a Pluralist Political System in the Dominican Republic" (Ph. D. dissertation, University of Florida, 1965); John B. Martin, *Overtaken by Events: The Dominican Crisis from the Death of Trujillo to the Civil War* (Garden City, N.Y.: Doubleday, 1966; see Parts I, II, and III); and Juan Bosch, *Crisis de la Democracia de América en la República Dominicana* (México, D. F.: Centro de Estudios y Documentación Sociales, 1964). All, however, have little or nothing to say on the Triumvirate. To these can be added various sections of Wiarda's *Dictatorship, Development and Disintegration* (where the Triumvirate is dealt with but superficially).

Wiarda's "Aftermath" and Martin's *Overtaken by Events* have already been discussed (Chapter 3, n. 7 and 14, respectively). Bosch's fascinating *Crisis de la Democracia*, which includes an incisive analysis of Dominican social classes in the early 1960s, can be misleading. One must constantly keep in mind that Bosch wrote this book in 1964, while he was organizing the constitutionalist conspiracy from his Puerto Rican exile. Thus parts of his exposition are colored by obvious considerations of political expediency.

Only a few other works are worth mentioning. André and Andrée Corten, *Cambio Social en Santo Domingo* (Rio Piedras, P. R.: Instituto de Estudios del Caribe, 1968), adequately examine the coexistence of Santo Domingo's modern and traditional sectors in this period. Wolfgang Schreyer, "Dominikanische Tragödie" (in Schreyer and Jürgen Hell, *Aufstand des Sisyphos* [Berlin: Deutscher Militärverlag, 1969], pp. 22-222) offers a perceptive and well-documented overview of the years between the death of Trujillo and the outbreak of the 1965 constitutionalist revolt (pp. 118-62). Paradoxically, the major weakness of this East German author is his too uncritical evaluation of the role of Ambassador Martin and in general of the Kennedy administration.

DeLesseps S. Morrison, *Latin American Mission: An Adventure in Hemispheric Diplomacy* (New York: Simon and Schuster, 1965; esp. pp. 112-43), helps illumine Kennedy's Dominican policy in the summer of 1961; a few insights can also be found in Arthur M. Schlesinger, Jr., *A Thousand Days: John F. Kennedy in the White House* (Boston: Houghton Mifflin, 1965). José Manuel Sánchez provides a fair account of the months following the death of Trujillo in *U. S. Intervention in the Caribbean, 1954-65. Decision-making and the Information Input* (Ann Arbor, Mich.: University Xerox Microfilms, 1972), pp. 166-217. Jerome Slater, *The OAS and United States Foreign Policy* (Ohio State University Press, 1967), pp. 183-216 and also 217-37, has an outstanding chapter on U. S. manipulation of the OAS to further its Dominican policy. Howard J. Wiarda, ed., *Dominican Republic. Election Factbook, June 1, 1966* (Washington, D. C.: Institute for the Comparative Study of Political Systems, 1966), contains some useful references for the 1962 elections; on the same subject see also Julio C. Campillo Pérez, *El Grillo y el Ruiseñor. Elecciones Presidenciales Dominicanas, Contribución a su Estudio* (Santo Domingo: Editora del Caribe, 1966, esp. pp. 191-205 and 339-47), a handy reference for the whole period since the independence of the country in 1844. Peter Nehemkis, *Latin America: Myth and Reality*, 2d ed. rev. (New York: Mentor Books, 1966), pp. 114-34, covers with a modicum of knowledge and a distracting anti-Bosch slant the 1962-63 period. Mok Chung Hoon discusses the overthrow of Bosch in "The 1963 Coup d'Etat in the Dominican Republic," *Caribbean Development and American Security: Case Study II* (Philadelphia: Foreign Policy Research Institute, University of Pennsylvania, 1966), pp. B 10-B 153, while the *golpistas* present their case none too skillfully in Centro de Enseñanza de las Fuerzas Armadas, *Libro Blanco de las Fuerzas Armadas y de la Policía Nacional de la República Dominicana: Estudios y pruebas documentales de las causas del movimiento reivindicador del 25 de Septiembre de 1963* (Santo Domingo: Editora del Caribe, 1964). Pericles B. Franco Ornes, a Dominican intellectual, voices his indignation in *Mi protesta contra el golpe militar* (Santo Domingo: Editora del Caribe, 1964).

Most of the books on the 1965 crisis cover at some length the period from May 1961 until the eve of the revolt, but their treatment is hardly adequate. Scholarly articles that deal with the period are also uncommon. The best are Howard J. Wiarda, "The Development of the Labor Movement in the Dominican Republic" (*Inter-American Economic Affairs* 20, no. 1, [Summer 1966]: 41-63), and "The Changing Political Orientation of the Catholic Church in the Dominican Republic" (*A Journal of Church and State* 7, no. 2 [Spring 1965]: 238-54); and Abraham Lowenthal, "Foreign Aid as a Political Instrument: The Case of the Dominican Republic" (*Public Policy* 14, [1965]: 141-60).

Economic sources for the period have been indicated in the relevant notes to Chapters 3 and 4. For a more extensive listing, see the bibliographies cited at the beginning of this essay.

For the Dominican press, the two leading dailies of the period are *Listín Diario* and *El Caribe*, both published in Santo Domingo. *El Caribe*, the daily with the largest circulation, has appeared without interruption since 1948; *Listín Diario*, closed by Trujillo in 1942, resumed publication on 1 August 1963. Both newspapers belonged to the "moderate right," but toward the end of the Bosch government *El Caribe's* owner-director, Germán Ornes, imposed on his newspaper a line that bordered on support for a coup d'etat. During the Triumvirate, *Listín Diario* again maintained a more responsible stance than *El Caribe*.

La Información of Santiago, the country's chief regional daily, was very spotty and weak in its coverage of political events. *La Nación*, the government's daily, ceased publication on 27 July 1963; a few weeks earlier, on 10 June, another daily, *Prensa Libre*, appeared in the capital. It was created to support a *golpista* line against Bosch and continued as an extreme right-wing newspaper throughout the Triumvirate (its printing presses were destroyed by a mob on 25 April 1965).

Very useful is *Ahora* (15 January 1962-). First published biweekly, then thrice monthly, it finally became, in 1964, a weekly. Rather unpromising at the outset, the quality of its reporting improved over time, particularly during 1964. It followed, by Dominican standards, a "liberal" line; although by no means *boschista*, it opposed the *golpe* and later was critical of the Triumvirate.

The most important party newspaper was *Unión Cívica*, the organ of the UCN, which appeared on 16 August 1961 and was first published twice a week, and then as a daily; it discontinued publication with the electoral debacle of 20 December 1962, its role being soon assumed by *Prensa Libre*.

Of the organs of the far left parties, *El 1J4* was banned in November 1963;

El Popular (PSP) and *Libertad* (MPD) were legal only during the Bosch government. When outlawed, these three newspapers nonetheless appeared intermittently throughout the 1961-65 period, *El Popular* being the most and *Libertad* the least regular.

For a more comprehensive list of newspapers of the period, see Wiarda, *Política y Gobierno*, pp. 133-42, and *Dictatorship, Development and Disintegration*, esp. pp. 1100-1123.

The issues of *El Caribe, Listín Diario, La Información,* and *Ahora* are in the archives of the respective newspapers. The Archivo General de la Nación houses an incomplete collection of *Prensa Libre, Unión Cívica,* and *La Nación*, but not a single issue of the "Castro-Communist" press. However, private archives exist and are fairly complete, particularly for the newspapers of the far left. For the latter, the Library of the Universidad Autónoma de Santo Domingo is of some use.

For the non-Dominican press, the best sources include a scholarly journal, *Hispanic American Report* (Oct. 1948-Nov. 1964), which contained a monthly review of events in the Dominican Republic; the dailies *New York Times, Miami Herald,* and *Christian Science Monitor*; and the magazines *New Leader, New Republic,* and *The Nation*. Wiarda, *Política y Gobierno* (pp. 71-115), provides an extensive list of major newspaper articles for this period. Valuable articles have also appeared since 1965, particularly in the Dominican press. Florangel Cardenas' study of the Dominican University student movement, the best to date, was printed in *Renovación* no. s 140-51 (7-13 Oct. 1969 through 3-9 Feb. 1970) as "La Universidad de Santo Domingo. Un trayecto difícil: De la tiranía a la libertad." A good account of the guerrilla struggle of November-December 1963, with supporting documents, was published in *Ahora* no. 524 (26 Nov. 1973): 2-72 ("10° Aniversario de la Liquidación de las Guerrillas de Tavárez Justo").

PART II: THE 1965 CRISIS

The literature on the 1965 crisis is customarily divided into three groups: "conservative" or "official," "liberal," and "radical" (see especially Abraham Lowenthal, *The Dominican Intervention* [Cambridge, Mass.: Harvard University Press, 1972], pp. 132-36). While convenient, these distinctions must be employed prudently, as they depend in part on the personal or ideological bias of the individual drawing them. Thus Lowenthal, after having divided the literature into the three above-mentioned groups, places himself in a fourth category, the "bureaucratic approach," of which he claims to be the sole representative on the subject (ibid., pp. 142-62). But for this writer Lowenthal fits neatly into the "liberal" family.

I define the three groups as follows: the "conservative" approach combines an apology of Johnson's Dominican policy with a violent anticonstitutionalist bias. Although of a disconcerting number of varieties, the "liberals" share at least two common traits. First, they avoid in varying ways a comprehensive critique of the foreign policy of the United States. Thus Theodore Draper, *The Dominican Revolt: A Case Study in American Policy* (New York: Commentary, 1968), is very harsh in his condemnation of Johnson's Dominican and Latin American policies, while making clear his approval of Kennedy's policies. On the other hand, Jerome Slater, *Intervention and Negotiation: The United States and the Dominican Republic* (New York: Harper and Row, 1970), not only criticizes the intervention, but also sees elements of continuity in the Dominican policies of the Kennedy and Johnson administrations. Having reached the edge of the precipice, he then hastily retreats, concluding that after the intervention Johnson tried to achieve a democratic solution in the Dominican Republic.

Second, members of the "liberal" group go from open sympathy toward the constitutionalists (Draper) to more ambivalent feelings (Lowenthal and Slater). While differing in their views of Donald Reid Cabral and the Triumvirate—from the frank condemnation by Draper to the more sympathetic position of Lowenthal—all are critical of the Gobierno de Reconstrucción Nacional (but with varying degrees of vehemence). Above all, the "liberals" concur in the violence of their anti-Communist feelings. Thus Draper emphatically supports the constitutionalists because he identifies them with the *Boschistas*, and he is at great pains to absolve the latter of the crime of contacts with the 1J4 during the conspiracy. If the "liberals" disapprove of the intervention, it is because they claim that there was no Communist "threat." But in no way do they state that the United States should have refrained from intervening had the alternative been a second Cuba.

The "radical" group unequivocally condemns the Latin American policy of the United States. In particular, it sees Johnson's Dominican policy not as an aberration, but as a logical outcome of long-standing policies that antedate Johnson; no real break, but rather continuity, is seen between the Kennedy and Johnson administrations. The "radical's" sympathy for the constitutionalists is complete, while their hostility toward the Dominican "Castro-Communists," if extant, is muted and in no way compares with that felt by the "liberals." For them Bosch's alleged collaboration with the 1J4 during the conspiracy would in no way have "tainted" the constitutionalist movement; and the "danger" of a second Cuba would not have diminished their condemnation of the U.S. intervention. Some "radicals" might even have welcomed it as a positive development. Finally, in discussing the motivations for the Dominican politics of the United States, the "radicals" tend to emphasize economic considerations.

In the following examination of the literature on the Dominican crisis, "conservative" and "radical" authors will be so designated—the others obviously fall in between. It should again be emphasized that the borders between the groups are amorphous. Thus Zapico, *Revolución en Hispanoamérica*, while supporting Johnson's Dominican policy, shares none of the anticonstitutionalist bias common to the "conservative" group. In three excellent articles ("Our Dominican Intervention," "The Solidarity of the Americas," and "Reconstruction in the Hemisphere," in the *Washington Post* of 4, 6, and 20 May 1965, respectively), Walter Lippmann openly supports Johnson's Dominican policy because the Dominican Republic "lies squarely within the sphere of influence of the United States," but, contrary to "conservative" authors, he admits that the intervention was "procedurally and legally" in contravention of the OAS Charter. Nor does Lippmann feel any need to unleash an anticonstitutionalist diatribe or to extoll the virtues of their enemies.

A major flaw undermines the extensive literature on the Domincan crisis: without exception the different authors share a lack of knowledge of the "Dominican" side of the events. One can only venture a few tentative explanations for this weakness. The speed and suddenness with which events unfolded, particularly in the first days of the revolt, made comprehension difficult, a problem naturally aggravated by poor knowledge of the preceding period. Major Dominican newspapers stopped publishing after the first days of the conflict. Those that did appear beginning in mid-May were all identified with either one or the other contending sides. Foreign newspapers kept no permanent correspondents in the Dominican Republic, and their journalists were unable to enter the country until 29 April, after the conclusion of the first part of the crisis.

Such factors tell only a part of the story. But further probing would require a series of unpleasant *ad hominem* arguments. More useful is an example of the erroneous conclusions to which lack of adequate knowledge has led. All who have written on the Dominican crisis have devoted many pages to the "Communist problem," a pervasive and poorly understood issue. Each of the three parties of the far left had published with varying regularity a newspaper since 1961-62. As noted previously, they are not easily accessible. Even if one is able to find these newspapers, the problem has just begun. *El 1J4* and *El Popular* (and to a much lesser degree *Libertad*) often gave not the true position of their respective parties, but rather the image they wanted to project to the public. The two could very well be opposites, as was the case for the 1J4 during the Bosch government and again during the Triumvirate. A certain number of communiqués of the far left have, of course, been published in the nonparty press, but here again this problem persists. To develop an accurate picture of the Dominican far left, it is necessary to gain access to internal party documents as well as to conduct searching interviews with party members. Letters exchanged among party leaders are also helpful. The internal documents and correspondence exist, as does the possibility of having fruitful interviews. Judging from the results, those who have written on the Dominican crisis have not been successful on any of these points. Instead they waste pages on speculations buttressed by the same few often quoted documents of common knowledge such as the issue of *El 1J4* of 14 March 1965 concerning the party's relations with the

PRD, the "Manifiesto" of the Central Committee of the PSP of 16 March 1965, or José Israel Cuello and Narciso Isa Conde's "Revolutionary Struggle in the Dominican Republic and its Lessons" (*World Marxist Review* 8:12 [Dec. 1965]: 92-103, and 9:1 [Jan. 1966]: 53-56). On this slim evidence they usually reach opposite conclusions often undauntedly presented as the product of serious research.

On the American side the three basic sources are the *Department of State Bulletin* (which contains the official defense of the administration's policy), the *Public Papers of the Presidents of the United States: Lyndon B. Johnson* (which includes all of Johnson's public statements on the Dominican crisis), and the *Congressional Record*. The most lucid attack by a member of Congress on Johnson's Dominican policy was delivered by J. William Fulbright—then chairman of the Senate Foreign Relations Committee that had a few weeks earlier conducted closed hearings on the Dominican crisis—in a speech on the floor of the Senate on 15 September 1965 ("The Situation in the Dominican Republic," *Congressional Record: Proceedings and Debates of the 89th Congress, First Session*, III, Part 18 [September 14-23, 1965], pp. 23855-61). The administration's policy was most forcefully defended by Undersecretary Thomas Mann before the annual convention of the Inter-American Press Association at San Diego, California, on 12 October 1965 ("The Dominican Crisis: Correcting some Misconceptions," *Department of State Bulletin* 53, no. 1376 [8 November 1965]: 730-38). Speeches and remarks by administration and other important political figures which are not recorded in the sources mentioned above can be found in the press of the period.

The hearings conducted by the Senate Foreign Relations Committee in July 1965 are still classified. The *Background Information Relating to the Dominican Republic* (Washington, D.C.: U. S. Government Printing Office, 1965), released by the Senate Foreign Relations Committee, provides a chronology of important events that covers in some detail the period from January 1960 to 28 June 1965 and a long appendix noting relevant public documents. The most valuable Senate document for the 1965 crisis is U. S., Congress, Senate, Committee on the Judiciary, Subcommittee to Investigate the Administration of the Internal Security Act and other Internal Security Laws, *Communist Threat to the United States through the Caribbean: Hearings: Testimony of Brigadier General Elías Wessin y Wessin*, 89th Cong., 1st sess., 1 October 1965 (Washington, D. C.: U. S. Government Printing Office, 1965). Less important are the hearings conducted by the same Senate Subcommittee, *Communist Threat to the United States through the Caribbean: Hearings. Testimony of Juan Isidro Tapia Adames and Alfonso L. Tarabochia*, 89 Cong., 1st sess., 9 and 16 December 1965 (Washington, D. C.: U. S. Government Printing Office, 1965).

During and after the crisis some privileged journalists and scholars were allowed access to a certain number of classified U.S. government documents;

the information they gathered has been reproduced in books, articles, and essays with inconsistent thoroughness. Two particularly valuable articles are by Max Frankel (*New York Times*, 14 November 1965) and David Kraslow (*Los Angeles Times*, 20 November 1965). The most useful books are Lowenthal, *The Dominican Intervention*, and Tad Szulc, *Dominican Diary* (New York: Dell Publishing Co., 1966); a chapter devoted to the crisis by Philip Geyelin is also revealing (*Lyndon B. Johnson and the World* [New York: Praeger, 1966], chap. 10, "The Dominican Republic—'Just like Alamo,' " pp. 236-57).

Some American protagonists in the 1965 Dominican crisis have written books or articles that contain significant information. The most informative is John B. Martin, who describes at length his activities in the Dominican Republic as Johnson's special envoy from 30 April to 17 May in chapter 27 of his *Overtaken by Events* ("Presidential Mission: 1965," pp. 637-703). In his memoirs, *The Vantage Point: Perspectives of the Presidency, 1963-1969* (New York-Chicago-San Francisco: Holt, Rinehart and Winston, 1971), Lyndon Johnson devotes most of a chapter to the Dominican Crisis ("A Time of Testing: Crises in the Caribbean," esp. pp. 187-205), barely supplementing what he had already argued publicly on many occasions throughout 1965. Senator Fulbright's thoughtful book, *The Arrogance of Power* (New York: Vintage Books, 1966), includes an excellent section on the Dominican crisis but he, too, expands little on his previous statements (see esp. pp. 82-97). Some U.S. military officers connected with the Dominican crisis have submitted articles. The most interesting is "Dominican Diary" by Captain James A. Dare (*U. S. Naval Institute Proceedings* 91 [December 1965]: 37-45). Also noteworthy are "The Army in the Dominican Republic" and "XVII Airborne Corps—All the Way", both by Lieutenant General Bruce Palmer, Jr., (in *Army* 15, [November 1965]: 43-44, 136, 138, and in *Army Digest* 22, no. 1 [January 1967]: 12-18, respectively); Major General R. McC. Tompkins, "Ubique" (*Marine Corps Gazette* 49 [September 1965]: 32-39); Major William E. Klein, "Stability Operations in Santo Domingo" (*Infantry Magazine* 56 [May-June 1966]: 35-39). The Brazilian contingent of the Inter-American Peace Force has published its official history, Colonel Carlos de Meira Mattos et al., *A Experiência do FAIBRÁS na República Dominicana* (Rio de Janeiro: Serviços Graficos do Fondação IBGE, n.d.).

The Organization of American States has published several sets of documents pertaining to its activities in the Dominican crisis (*Documents of the OAS Tenth Meeting of Consultation of Ministers of Foreign Affairs*). While lacking in great revelations, many of these documents are useful. The different issues of the *OAS Chronicle* from August 1965 to October 1966 summarize OAS activities in the period. More revealing are the classified minutes of the closed sessions of the Tenth Meeting of Consultation of Ministers of Foreign Affairs. These documents are obtainable with modest effort.

The debates in the United Nations Security Council and the organization's role in the crisis are recorded in the *Official Records of the United Nations Security Council* and are summarized in the *Annual Report of the Secretary*

General on the Work of the Organization: 16 June 1965-15 June 1966 and in the *United Nations Monthly Chronicle*.

Critical unpublished documents on U.S. policy as well as invaluable materials on the "Dominican" side of the crisis are privately held in the Dominican Republic. I possess orginals or photocopies of many of these. I have taken notes on others, according to their value and my requirements (footnotes to the relevant chapters provide a reference).

A body of material, voluminous but of limited value, is available to the public. However, because of the poor state of the Archivo General de la Nación and the country's public libraries, it is not always easy to locate. Each of the two contending governments published a *Gaceta Oficial* and issued numerous communiqués and official notes. Speeches by political leaders and statements by parties, professional organizations, church officials, and others appeared in large number in the press or as leaflets or pamphlets.

The two leading Dominican dailies, *Listín Diario* and *El Caribe*, temporarily ceased publication after 28 April. They appeared again in November 1965, well after the installation of the Godoy government. Their issues from 25 to 28 April are very helpful and can be consulted in the newspapers' respective archives. As noted previously, the presses of *Prensa Libre*, then Santo Domingo's only other daily, were wrecked on 25 April.

La Información of Santiago did not appear between 25 and 27 April. Issues were published on 28 and 29 April, and on 3, 4, and 5 May; beginning on 7 May, it appeared every other day for the next two weeks. Thereafter publication stopped until 10 September. The issues published during the civil war can be found in the archives of the newspaper, but are disappointing for the researcher. Always mediocre, *La Información* fell to even lower standards during the crisis, and its coverage of the events was practically worthless.

Ahora was published only twice during the crisis (no. 106 of 1 May 1965 and no. 107 of 16 May 1965). When it resumed publication on 18 September, it devoted the entire issue to the civil war (no. 108, "Gráficas y Documentos de la Revolución"). These three poignant issues are kept in the archives of *Ahora*.

In mid-May four new newspapers began to appear in Santo Domingo. Every two or three days the Gobierno de Reconstrucción Nacional printed a four-page bulletin, *Reconstrucción*, while a semiofficial daily, *La Hoja*, also espoused the government's viewpoint. In Ciudad Nueva two dailies were published: *La Nación*, the semiofficial organ of the constitutionalist government, and *Patria*, which expressed the most extreme views within the constitutionalist camp. Violent and often irresponsible, *Patria* hurt more than helped the constitutionalist cause by providing welcome ammunition to those claiming that the revolt was in the hands of extremists.

Throughout the crisis, the three parties of the far left continued issuing their organs in Ciudad Nueva. The Social Christians of the *duro* faction published some issues of *Diálogo*, as did the Confederación Autónoma de Sindicatos Cristianos (CASC) with its organ, *Pueblo*.

In the International Security Zone, American officials published *La Voz de la Zona de Seguridad,* later called *La Voz de la OEA,* to defend U. S. policy to the Dominicans.

American newspapers provided the most extensive foreign coverage of the crisis, chief among them the *New York Times,* the *Washington Post,* and the *Wall Street Journal. Le Monde,* although devoting less space to the crisis, provided a highly perceptive analysis.

Since September 1965 many articles, some documents, and interviews on the events of the civil war have been published in the Dominican press. Some have appeared in short-lived magazines, like *Unidad* (1966), *Claridad* (1969), and *Qué?* (1971), but more often in the established Dominican press, particularly in the dailies *Listín Diario* and *El Nacional* and the weeklies *Ahora* and *Renovación.*

Several Dominicans have written books on the 1965 crisis. *Tragedia en Santo Domingo. Documentos para la Historia* by Danilo Brugal Alfau (Santo Domingo: Editora del Caribe, 1966) and *Santo Domingo: Barricadas de Odio* by Antonio Llano Montes (México, D. F.: Editores Mexicanos Unidos, 1966) contain valuable information as well as slander and lies. Brugal Alfau, who was the director of the Department of Public Relations of the Gobierno de Reconstrucción Nacional, renders faithfully the official position of General Antonio Imbert Barrera and deals at length with the latter's conflict with the Americans. A Cuban exile, Llano Montes participated in the events as a close friend and adviser of General Elías Wessin y Wessin. His book views the crisis from Wessin's standpoint (by no means identical with that of Imbert Barrera) and offers important data.

Less informative are the books written by constitutionalists. *Guerra Patria* (Santo Domingo, 1966), a long, rambling account by Ramón A. ("Chino") Ferreras, the editor of *Patria,* includes vivid photographs. *Paso a la Libertad* (Santo Domingo: La Nación, 1965) by Darío Melendez, a constitutionalist officer captured early in the conflict, is also disappointing, but is much better written. Franklin J. Franco Pichardo, a PSP sympathizer, has received the Cuban Casa de las Américas prize for his *República Dominicana, Clases, Crisis y Comandos* (Havana: Ediciones Casa de Las Américas, 1966). This book is an ambitious effort to place the 1965 crisis in a larger historical context with particular emphasis on economic and social determinants. The final result, however, is a failure. The only value of this disjointed essay, abounding in factual errors, is that it reproduces the minutes of the key constitutionalist meeting of 8 July 1965. Two other proconstitutionalist authors, Rafael Emilio Sanabia, *Esta otra invasión* (Santo Domingo: Editora Arte y Cine, 1966), and Ubi Rivas, *Agresión* (Santo Domingo: n.p., 1965), disclose no new material. Fidelio Despradel, *Historia Gráfica de la Guerra de Abril* (Santo Domingo: Editora Cosmos, 1975), provides a very good collection of photographs.

Finally, there is *La Revolución Dominicana y la Crisis de la OEA* (Santo Domingo: ¡Ahora!, 1965) by Julio César Estrella, at the time executive director of *El Caribe*. This short book is a good survey of the crisis and carefully avoids choosing sides.

To a special category belong the books by one Spanish and two American priests who were in the Dominican Republic in April 1965 and remained there throughout the civil war: Zapico, *Revolución en Hispanoamérica*; James A. Clark, *The Church and the Crisis in the Dominican Republic* (Westminster, Md: Newman Press, 1966); and José A. Moreno, *Barrios in Arms: Revolution in Santo Domingo* (Pittsburgh: University of Pittsburgh Press, 1970). The paramount interest of Clark is the role of the Catholic Church in the Dominican Republic from the Era of Trujillo up to and including the 1965 crisis. This specialized focus could have been a welcome contribution, but the book is marred by the author's obsessive concern with presenting an apology for the Church. Zapico devotes only the first ninety-one pages of his book to the Dominican Republic. While neither profound nor particularly knowledgeable, he makes a sincere attempt to relate what he saw. Convinced that the revolt was Communist-dominated, he approves the American intervention, yet he is preoccupied with describing the rebels' behavior even when this means presenting them in a favorable light. Herein lies the value of the book. Moreno's study is the most revealing of the three. Active on the constitutionalist side in food distribution and medical care, the author enjoyed a unique position as a "participant-observer." He is also more insightful than Zapico and more objective than Clark. The chief merit of his book lies in its graphic account of aspects of daily life in some constitutionalist commando units.

Several journalists who covered the crisis in Santo Domingo have written books on the subject. The best are *La Révolution de Saint-Domingue* ([Paris] : Plon, 1966) by Marcel Niedergang of *Le Monde* and *Dominican Diary* by Tad Szulc of the *New York Times*. Of the two, Niedergang's style is more compelling and he succeeds in giving a "feeling" of the Dominican reality; Szulc, however, provides significant information on the American side. Also useful are *Santo Domingo: Revolt of the Damned* (New York: G. P. Putnam's Sons, 1965) by Dan Kurzman of the *Washington Post*, and the "radical" *Aquí Santo Domingo: La Tercera Guerra Sucia* edited by Uruguayan journalist Gregorio Selser (Buenos Aires: Editorial Palestra, 1966). In *Caribbean Crisis: Subversion Fails in the Dominican Republic* (Garden City, N. Y.: Doubleday, 1965), Jay Mallin unleashes an anticonstitutionalist diatribe that rests on a generous portion of fabrications. The book, commissioned in May 1965 by the U. S. Information Agency, is nevertheless worth reading because of its semiofficial character. A viewpoint from the opposite end of the political spectrum is presented with considerably greater elegance and skill by Gregorio Ortega, *Santo Domingo, 1965* (La Habana: Editorial Venceremos, 1965).

Besides the many journalistic accounts, several other books have been written on the Dominican crisis. The most important are Theodore Draper,

The Dominican Revolt, and Abraham F. Lowenthal, *The Dominican Intervention*. Lowenthal, who had access to U. S. government classified sources, is of special interest for the information he provides on American policy between 24 and 30 April. The major weakness of the book is its inadequate treatment of the Dominican side of the events (both before and during the days of crisis he focuses on), a flaw particularly regrettable since the author lived in the Dominican Republic from 1964 to 1966. Draper's book relies less on classified sources than Lowenthal's, but is more percepitve. Superbly written, sparkling with irony, it is the most brilliant "liberal" critique of Johnson's Dominican policy.

Some other books deserve comment. The authors of *Dominican Action— 1965. Intervention or Cooperation?* (Georgetown University, Center for Strategic Studies, Washington, D. C.: Georgetown University, 1966) have had access to classified documents, but they are sorrowfully lacking in both accuracy and intellectual honesty. The book is relevant, however, as an apology—official in fact if not in name—of Johnson's Dominican policy (and as such it has been distributed in several languages by the U. S. Information Agency). Jerome Slater, *Intervention and Negotiation*, covers in some detail the whole period from April 1965 through the 1966 elections. At times Slater is excellent (for instance in his devastating and accurate portrait of Ambassador Martin); too often, however, his analysis is weak and tainted by an inadequate knowledge of the facts (Slater's constant and rather petty criticisms of Draper's book have prompted the latter to an eloquent rejoinder, "The Dominican Intervention Reconsidered," *Political Science Quarterly* 86 [March 1971]: 1-36).

The Dominican Republic Crisis, 1965, edited by John Carey (Dobbs Ferry, N. Y.: Oceana Publications, 1967), includes a debate between Adolf Berle and Wolfgang Friedman on the legality of the U. S. military intervention. Leonard Meeker, at the time legal adviser to the State Department, had already put forth the official position of the American government on this subject in "The Dominican Situation in the Perspective of International Law" (*Department of State Bulletin* 53, no. 1359 [July 12, 1965]: 60-65).

The Lingering Crisis: A Case Study of the Dominican Republic, edited by Eugenio Chang-Rodríguez (New York: Las Américas, 1969), contains some good essays. *Dominican Republic: A Case Study in the New Imperialism* by the Institute for International Labor Research (New York: Institute for International Labor Research, [1966]) is a convenient compilation of statements and articles by such figures as Juan Bosch, José Figueres, and Teodoro Moscoso. *Marines in Santo Domingo* by Victor Perlo (New York: New Outlook Publishers, 1965) is an example of a "radical" approach that argues that the reason for the U. S. intervention was the protection of American economic interests. In the case of the Dominican crisis this thesis rests not on facts, but on ideological bias.

Those who read Russian will find the official Soviet viewpoint in *"Big Stick" over Santo Domingo* by Vladimir Georgievic Zukov and Vadim Listov

(Moscow: Mezdunarodnye otnosenija, 1969), and *The Dominican Republic and American Imperialism* by Jurij Petrovic Gorochov (Moscow: Akademija Nauk SSSR. Institut Latinskoj Ameriki, 1970). The view from Cuba is given in *La Revolución Dominicana de Abril vista por Cuba* by Antonio Ricardi, et al. (Santo Domingo: Editora de la Universidad Autónoma de Santo Domingo, 1974). The core of this book consists of five articles written in 1965 by Cuban scholars; an appendix contains four May 1965 speeches before the Security Council by Luis Gómez-Vanguemert, then Cuba's alternate delegate to the United Nations, and two speeches by Fidel Castro in the same month. Both the articles and the speeches were originally published in *Política Internacional* (Havana, no. 10 [April-May-June 1965]).

A large number of books of a more general character devote some space to the Dominican crisis. The two best contributions express different viewpoints. Fred Goff and Michael Locker, "The Violence of Domination: U. S. Power and the Dominican Republic" (in Irving L. Horowitz et al., eds., *Latin American Radicalism: A Documentary Report on Left and Nationalist Movements* [New York: Random House, 1969], pp. 249-81) place the 1965 crisis in historical perspective ad offer a well-researched and cogent overview of the whole period from Trujillo's rise to power. The major flaw of this "radical" essay is its exaggerated emphasis on the economic motivations of the Dominican policy of the United States. From a "liberal" perspective Philip Geyelin presents an incisive account and includes important information on the American side of the crisis in his *Lyndon B. Johnson and the World*. Other contributions can be found in books written by Washington-based journalists: Charles Roberts, *LBJ's Inner Circle* (New York: Delacorte Press, 1965; chap. 13, "Anatomy of a Crisis," pp. 197-211); Rowland Evans and Robert Novak, *Lyndon B. Johnson: The Exercise of Power* (New York: Signet Books, 1968; chap. 23, "The Dominican Intervention," pp. 534-54).

A fair summary of the crisis and its background is given by Richard Barnet, *Intervention and Revolution. America's Confrontation with Insurgent Movements Around the World* (New York-Cleveland: World Publishing Co., 1968; chap. 8, "The Dominican Republic: To the Johnson Doctrine," pp. 153-80). Those looking for an example of the "conservative" approach will read with interest Peter Nehemkis' bitter anti-Bosch harangue in his *Latin America: Myth and Reality*, 2d ed. rev. (New York: Mentor Books, 1966; "The Dominican Revolution and Its Aftermath," pp. 258-300). Yale B. Ferguson, ed., *Contemporary Inter-American Relations* (Englewood Cliffs, N.J.: Prentice-Hall, 1972), has several essays on the Dominican crisis, including Abraham Lowenthal's "The Dominican Intervention in Retrospect" (pp. 279-89).

The number of newspaper articles on the Dominican crisis is endless. Some of the most important have been cited in this essay. For additional sources, see especially Hitt and Wilson, *A Selected Bibliography*, and Wiarda, *Política y Gobierno*.

PART III: INTERVIEWS

The hundreds of persons interviewed for this book related material varying greatly in content and value. Only those persons who offered the most substantive testimony are listed below. Most sessions took place between 1968 and 1972, although some further interviewing was done up to 1977.

A word on procedure is probably in order. While some interviews were short (the two shortest lasted about thirty minutes, a few others about an hour), the average for each meeting was two to three hours (the record length was an interview with "Baby" Mejía Lluberes that went on from seven o'clock one morning until late into the evening). All but twenty-two of the persons below were interviewed more than once. Thus Colonel Pedro Bartolomé Benoit, with whom I spent seven long and fascinating afternoons, if not typical of all the persons I interviewed, is nonetheless representative of a fairly large group who were quite informative and generous with their time. With such persons I first sought to verify what was told me through interviews with other actors and/or further research, and then to return and confront my subject with the new evidence I had acquired. Over time this system produced impressive results. Additionally, I tried to organize joint conversations on specific topics with more than one informant. Often participants were of similar political leanings, but occasionally the discussions brought together political enemies (thus it was with me that PRD leader and former foreign affairs minister of the Molina Ureña government, Máximo Lovatón Pittaluga, and Colonel Benoit, president of the "loyalist" Military Junta, met in the spring of 1969 for the first time since 1965).

In exceptional cases (as with two CIA officials and "Marcelo," a former member of the 1J4's November-December 1963 guerrilla struggle) I was asked and agreed to withhold the name of the informant. In equally exceptional cases the supplier of a certain piece of information must remain anonymous. As a rule, however, I have used only information for which a proper source can be identified in the relevant footnote, for too large a departure from such a rule would seriously undermine the historical quality of the research.

Unless otherwise noted, the position given for each informant is the one held on 24 April 1965.

Abreu Flores, Antonio (Tonito): PRD cadre.

Aristy Pereyra, Héctor: Minister of the presidency under the Caamaño government (4 May-3 September 1965) and member of the Caamaño government's Negotiating Committee (June-August 1965).

Arnaud, Winston: PRD cadre.

Arvelo Delgado, Tulio Hostilio: PSP Central Committee member.

Benoit, Pedro Bartolomé: Air Force colonel (Nineteenth of November base). President of the San Isidro-based Military Junta (28 April-7 May 1965). Member of the Gobierno de Reconstrucción Nacional (GRN) (7 May-30 August 1965)

Bosch, Juan: President of the Dominican Republic (27 February-25 September 1963). President of the PRD and the leader of the Enriquillo movement.

Botello Fernández, Norge William: Member of the 1J4 Provisional Central Executive Committee (CECP). Leader of the B-2 commando unit in the civil war.

Campagna, Aníbal: President of the Senate under the Caamaño government and member of the Caamaño government's Negotiating Committee.

Casals Victoria, Pedro Manuel: Minister of finance under the First Triumvirate (26 September-22 December 1963). A constitutionalist leader from Santiago (April-August 1965).

Cordero Michel, Emilio: A leader of the 1J4's guerrilla struggle (November-December 1963). 1J4 CECP member (in exile).

Cuello Hernández, José Israel: PSP Central Committee member.

Cury, Jottin: Minister of foreign affairs under the Caamaño government and member of the Caamaño government's Negotiating Committee.

Del Orbe, Justino José: An early leader of the PSP. PSP "middle-level leader."

De los Santos, Emilio: President of the First Triumvirate.

Del Rosario Ceballos, Enriquillo: Dominican ambassador to the United States under the Bosch government. A PRD leader.

Despradel Roque, Fidelio: A leader of the 1J4's 1963 guerrilla struggle. 1J4 CECP member.

Domínguez Guerra, Asdrúbal: PSP "middle-level leader."

Ducoudray Mansfield, Félix Servio: An early leader of the PSP. PSP National Secretariat member.

Durán Hernando, Jaime (Jimmy): 1J4 CECP member.

Espaillat Nanita, Leopoldo: A PRD leader and close adviser of José Rafael Molina Ureña.

Estrella, Julio César: Executive director of *El Caribe*.

Gamundi Cordero, Rafael (Rafa): PRD cadre.

García Germán, Manuel Ramón: Army lieutenant (ret.). Member of the military arm of the Enriquillo movement. Constitutionalist captain.

García Godoy, Héctor: Candidate for provisional president of the Dominican Republic (June-August 1965). Provisional president of the Republic (3 September 1965-1 July 1966).

Gautreaux Piñeiro, Bonaparte (K-Bito): PRD cadre. Vice-minister of the presidency under the Caamaño government.

Goico, Félix: Considered for provisional president of the republic (June-July 1965).

Gómez Pérez, Luis Rafael: One of the founders of the Movimiento Revolucionario 14 de Junio (MR1J4) in 1959-60. PSP "middle-level leader."

González y González, Ernesto: Lieutenant of the Batalla de Las Carreras Military Academy until cashiered in October 1963. A member of the military arm of the Enriquillo movement. Constitutionalist captain.

Gutiérrez Félix, Euclides: Vice-minister of interior and police under the Caamaño government.

Grullón Martínez, Ramón: An early PSP leader.

Guzmán Fernández, Silvestre Antonio: A PRD leader. Considered for provisional president of the Republic (May 1965). Member of the Negotiating Committee of the Caamaño government.

Guzmán Rodríguez, Alberto: A PRSC leader.

Hernández, Oscar: A constitutionalist leader from La Vega (24-29 April 1965).

Hernández Brito, Evelio Antonio: 1J4 cadre.

Hernando Ramírez, Miguel Angel: Army lieutenant colonel and the military leader of the Enriquillo movement. Armed Forces minister of the Molina Ureña government (25-27 April 1965).

Hill, John Calvin: Consul and later consul general of the United States in the Dominican Republic (1961-62).

Holguín, Morilí: Lieutenant at the Centro de Entrenamiento de las Fuerzas Armadas (CEFA); CEFA captain in the civil war.

Imbert Barrera, Antonio: One of the two survivors of the inner core of the conspiracy that killed Trujillo. Member of the first and the second Councils of State (1-16 January 1962 and 18 January 1962-27 February 1963). Army general. President of the GRN.

Isa Conde, Narciso: PSP National Secretariat member.

Jequier, Pierre: Delegate of the International Red Cross Committee in Santo Domingo during the civil war.

Jimenes Grullón, Juan Isidro: President of the Alianza Social Demócrata, one of the six political parties represented in the cabinet of the First Triumvirate.

Jorge Blanco, Salvador: Attorney general of the Republic under the Caamaño government; member of the Caamaño government's Negotiating Committee.

Klang de Guzmán, Renée: PRD cadre and wife of Antonio Guzmán.

Ledesma Pérez, Manuel Ramón: A PRD leader. Minister without portfolio in the Caamaño government.

Lora Iglesias, Carmen Josefina: Member of the 1J4's 1963 guerrilla struggle. 1J4 cadre.

Lora Mercado, Francisco Augusto: First vice-president of the Reformist Party.

Lovatón Pittaluga, Máximo: A PRD leader. Minister of foreign affairs of the Molina Ureña government.

Mann, Thomas: U. S. assistant secretary of state for inter-American affairs from December 1963 until his appointment as undersecretary of state for economic affairs in March 1965.

Martínez Francisco, Antonio: PRD secretary-general.

Mejía Lluberes, Rafael ("Baby"): Leader of the 1J4's Military Bureau. Head of the Unidades Mobiles del 14 de Junio during the civil war.

Molina Peña, Luis Henry: Secretary-general of the Confederación Autónoma de Sindicatos Cristianos.

Molina Ureña, José Rafael: President of the Chamber of Deputies during the Bosch government. A key civilian leader of the Enriquillo movement. Provisional president of the Republic (25-27 April 1965).

Morales-Carrión, Arturo: Kennedy's special envoy to the Dominican Republic (November-December 1961) and deputy assistant secretary of state for inter-American affairs (1961-64). Director, Department of Information and Public Affairs of the Pan-American Union.

Moya Pons, Frank: Dominican intellectual.

Muñóz Marte, María Elena: 1J4 cadre.

Núñez Nogueras, Manuel Augustín: Major at the Batalla de Las Carreras Military Academy until cashiered in September 1964. Member of the military arm of the Enriquillo movement. Constitutionalist lieutenant colonel.

Padilla Deschamps, Josefina: A PRSC leader.

Palmer, Bruce: Lieutenant general, U. S. army. Commander of the U. S. occupation forces in the Dominican Republic and vice-commander of the Inter-American Peace Force (May 1965-January 1966).

Pastoriza Espaillat, Tomás (Jimmy): Rich and influential *de primera* businessman from Santiago. Brother-in-law and close adviser of Héctor García Godoy.

Peña Gómez, José Francisco: A PRD leader and key civilian leader of the Enriquillo movement. Head of the PRD in Santo Domingo during the civil war.

Pierret, Polonio: Army sergeant and member of the military arm of the Enriquillo movement. Constitutionalist noncommissioned officer.

Pinedo, Rafael Augusto: Deputy minister of foreign affairs under the Caamaño government.

Pinedo de Taveras, Magaly: 1J4 cadre.

Pinedo Mejía, Ramón Augustín (Monchín): MPD Central Committee member.

Plank, John N.: Director, U.S. Office of Research and Analysis for American Republics.

Postigo, Julio D.: Member of the GRN until his resignation on 10 August 1965.

Pratts-Ramírez de Pérez, Ivelisse: PRD cadre.

Reid Cabral, Donald: Member of the second Council of State. President of the second Triumvirate (23 December 1963-25 April 1965).

Rivera Caminero, Francisco Javier: Admiral; navy chief of staff. Minister of armed forces of the GRN. Minister of armed forces of the Godoy government from 10 September 1965 until 6 January 1966.

Rodríguez del Prado, Cayetano: MPD Central Committee member.

Rodríguez Demorizi, Emilio: Minister of education under the Balaguer government in 1961. An adviser of President Caamaño.

Rodríguez Sánchez, Marco: 1J4 CECP member.

Rusk, Dean: U. S. secretary of state.

Sánchez Cordova, Luis René: MPD Central Committee member.

Sánchez y Sánchez, Carlos: Close adviser of GRN's President Imbert Barrera.

Sención Silverio, Lorenzo: Lieutenant at the Batalla de Las Carreras Military Academy until cashiered in October 1963 and member of the military arm of the Enriquillo movement. Constitutionalist captain.

Tavárez Justo, Emma: 1J4 "middle-level leader." Sister of Manuel Aurelio (Manolo) Tavárez Justo, the leader of the 1J4 until his death on 21 December 1963.

Taveras Rosario, Francisco Rafael (Fafa): One of the founders of the MR1J4. 1J4 CECP member. Leader of the Comando Central del 14 de Junio in the civil war.

Tillman, Seth: Chief of staff of the U. S. Senate Foreign Relations Committee.

Tolentino Dipp, Hugo. Dominican intellectual. Member of the Advisory Committee of President Caamaño.

Vélez Santana, Marcelino Bienvenido: Member of the outer fringe of the conspiracy that killed Trujillo.

Vicioso Soto, Horacio: Minister of foreign affairs under the GRN.

Wessin y Wessin, Elías: General and director of the CEFA.

Index of Names

This index includes only references to participants. Authors cited throughout the book or participants appearing as sources rather than actors are not included.

As is common throughout Latin America, Dominicans have two family names: those of both parents or, in the case of a married woman, those of the father and the husband (the latter preceded by a "de"). In everyday use, however, the practice becomes highly arbitrary: some persons are referred to by only one family name, others by both, and still others usually by one but occasionally by both family names. Throughout this book I have sought to follow the everyday usage: thus, Juan Bosch Gaviño, Angel Miolán Reynoso, and Fidel Castro Ruz always appear as Juan Bosch, Angel Miolán, and Fidel Castro, but Juan Isidro Jimenes Grullón is identified by his full name. In those cases where the common practice is not consistent, I have adopted the following system: if an individual is mentional only occasionally throughout the book, or if there is a risk of confusion, I always give both family names; if, however, the person is mentioned often, I give both family names the first time, whether in the text or in a note, and thereafter I refer to him or her by the more common form. The same system applies to first names and nicknames. In the index I give the full name, but place in italics those parts of the name that are dropped throughout the book after the first occasion.

451